The C++ Standard Template Library

P.J. Plauger
Dinkumware, Ltd.

Alexander A. Stepanov
AT&T Labs

Meng Lee
Hewlett-Packard Laboratories

David R. Musser
Rensselaer Polytechnic Institute

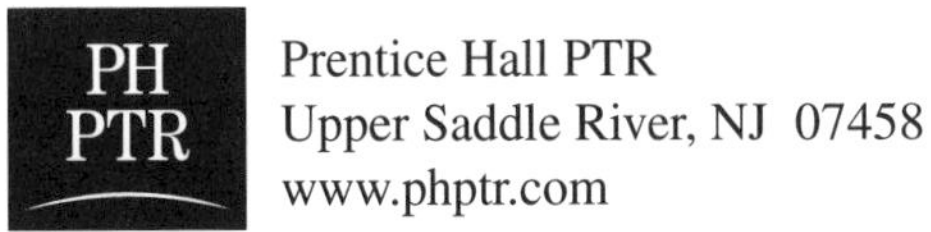

Prentice Hall PTR
Upper Saddle River, NJ 07458
www.phptr.com

ISBN 0-13-437633-1
90000
9 780134 376332

Library of Congress Cataloging-in-Publication Data

The C++ standard template library / P.J. Plauger ... [et al.].
p. cm.
Includes bibliographical references and index.
ISBN 0-13-437633-1
1. C++ (Computer program language) I. Plauger, P.J.

QA76.73.C153 C17 2000
005.13'3--dc21

00--065273

Editorial/Production Supervision: *Jan H. Schwartz*
Acquisitions Editor: *Paul Petralia*
Marketing Manager: *Bryan Gambrel*
Manufacturing Manager: *Alexis Heydt*
Editorial Assistant: *Justin Somma*
Cover Design Direction: *Jerry Votta*

Prentice-Hall, Inc.
Upper Saddle River, NJ 07458

Prentice Hall books are widely used by corporations and government agencies for training, marketing, and resale.

The publisher offers discounts on this book when ordered in bulk quantities.
For more information, contact Corporate Sales Department, phone: (800) 382-3419;
Fax: (201) 236-7141; e-mail: corpsales@prenhall.com
Or write: Prentice Hall PTR
Corporate Sales Department
One Lake Street
Upper Saddle River, NJ 07458

Printed in the United States of America
10 9 8 7 6 5 4 3 2 1

ISBN 0-13-437633-1

Prentice-Hall International (UK) Limited, **London**
Prentice-Hall of Australia Pty. Limited, **Sydney**
Prentice-Hall Canada Inc., **Toronto**
Prentice-Hall Hispanoamericana, S.A., **Mexico**
Prentice-Hall of India Private Limited, **New Delhi**
Prentice-Hall of Japan, Inc., **Tokyo**
Pearson Education Asia Pte. Ltd.
Editora Prentice-Hall do Brasil, Ltda., **Rio de Janeiro**

The authors are grateful to
Hewlett-Packard Laboratories
for making the
Standard Template Library
freely available to the public.

PERMISSIONS

The code in this book and its description are based on material that contains the following notice:

Excerpts from P.J. Plauger:

"Standard C/C++," monthly column in *The C/C++ Users Journal*
quarterly column in *The Journal of C Language Translation*
The Standard C Library, Prentice-Hall, 1992
The Draft Standard C++ Library, Prentice-Hall, 1995
The Dinkum C++ Library Reference, Dinkumware, Ltd., 1998
the Dinkum C++ Library

reprinted by permission of the author.

TRADEMARKS

TYPOGRAPHY

This book was typeset in Palatino, Avant Garde, and Courier bold by P.J. Plauger using Ventura Publisher 4.1.1.

Contents

Preface

The Standard Template Library (or STL for short) is a major component of the library portion of the ANSI/ISO Standard for the programming language C++. It was developed at Hewlett-Packard Labs by Alexander Stepanov and Meng Lee (**S&L95**), based heavily on earlier work by Stepanov and David R. Musser of Rensselaer Polytechnic Institute. (See **M&S87**, **M&S89**, and **M&S94**. All citations are listed in Appendix C: References.) You will find this software package to be a most ambitious, and coherent, use of templates in C++. Indeed, STL has already begun to alter significantly the way many programmers write C++ code.

This book shows you how to use the template classes and functions of STL as mandated by the C++ Standard (clauses 20 and 23-26). We focus here on STL as a fairly self-contained subset of a larger library defined for Standard C++. That library is designed to work, in turn, with the library defined for ANSI/ISO Standard C (**ANS89** and **ISO90**). Consequently, you can look on this book as a companion to two earlier works by P.J. Plauger, *The Standard C Library* (**Pla92**) and *The Draft Standard C++ Library* (**Pla95**). Taken together, these three books describe nearly all the library facilities of widespread interest to C++ programmers.

C++ Standard

The C++ Standard was formally approved in 1998 and should be stable for years to come. It is both an ANSI Standard (within the USA) and an ISO Standard (around the world). As part of the standardization process, the entire Standard C++ language and library were for the first time described completely and in one place. A relatively late event in that process was the incorporation of STL as part of the draft C++ Standard. More recent still is the wider dissemination of various implementations of Standard C++ compilers and libraries. Thus, much of what you will find in this book is news, even to experienced C++ programmers.

Similarly, the description of STL (precursors to **S&L95**) saw only limited circulation before its incorporation into the draft C++ Standard of July 1994. In the process of incorporation, it has been reorganized and changed in several significant ways. The STL in Standard C++ is *not* the package made widely available by Hewlett-Packard. It is *not* the version more recently enhanced by many different agencies. Thus, even programmers with early experience using STL can profit from this book. You will find here a complete presentation of STL as it is specified by the C++ Standard.

The book also shows you at least one way to *implement* STL. We present about 6,000 lines of tested, working code that is known to be portable across a number of C++ compilers. It is, in fact, essentially the same code that you will find distributed with Microsoft Visual C++, IBM Visual Age, as well as with C++ compilers offered by a number of other vendors. Minor changes have been made in formatting and notation, to make the book form of the code more readable and tutorial.

To a large extent, the code presented here works atop any C++ library. (See Appendix A: Interfaces.) It is designed to work particularly well, however, with a library that conforms closely to the C++ Standard. As much as possible, the code avoids forms that are non portable or not likely to be widely available. Code that relies on recent additions to the C++ language, such as template partial specialization, may still present problems with some compilers. You will find that commercial versions of this library indulge in various compromises to deal with such dialect issues.

One way or another, you can use the code presented here to gain valuable experience using a library of templates that is well on its way to becoming an important standard for the C++ world. Equally important, we believe that seeing a realistic implementation of STL can help you better understand how to use it.

And that introduces yet another goal. Besides presenting STL as standardized, and working code to implement it, this book also serves as a tutorial on how to use this library. You will find here useful background information on how the library came to take its present form, how it was *meant* to be used, and how it *should* be used. You don't have to read and understand all the code presented here to achieve that basic goal. Even a cursory study is beneficial. You certainly don't have to be a sophisticated user to profit from this book, but the programmer who is just an occasional sophisticate will find the information presented here invaluable.

Teaching you how to write C++ is *not* a goal of this book. We assume you know enough about C++ to read straightforward code. Where the code presented is not so straightforward, we explain the trickery involved.

extending STL

A final purpose of this book is to teach programmers how to design and implement extensions to the Standard Template Library. STL brings together numerous algorithms, data structures, and programming techniques. It is not, however, intended to supply a complete set of facilities that a programmer might need. Rather, it provides a core of the most widely used facilities. And it describes the rules by which this core code is written.

Once you learn to follow these rules, you can add your own algorithms that work with existing data structures. You can also add data structures that work with existing algorithms. Using the STL code presented here as an example, you will soon learn how to tackle new problems by writing a minimum of new code. And you will find that the new code is itself often reusable on future projects. That's what library design is all about, in the end.

structure of this book The book is structured much like the STL code itself. The C++ Standard specifies numerous headers, but only thirteen of these headers define all the templates in STL. A separate chapter covers each header. Additional chapters introduce STL as a whole and discuss three overarching topics — iterators, algorithms, and containers. Most of the headers have reasonably cohesive contents. That makes for reasonably cohesive discussions. One or two, however, are catchalls. Their corresponding chapters are perforce wider ranging.

Each chapter that describes a header follows the same pattern. It begins with a brief background section, followed by a functional description of the header contents, then by suggestions for how best to use the facilities defined in the header. We then present the C++ code that constitutes the header itself, accompanied by a commentary on how the code works. We also present a small test program for each header, to provide at least a cursory example of how each template definition might be used.

Each chapter ends with a set of exercises. In a university course based on this book, the exercises can serve as homework problems. Many of them are simple exercises in using the library, or in code rewriting. They drive home a point or illustrate reasonable variations in implementation. The more ambitious exercises are labeled as such. They can serve as a basis for more extended projects. The independent reader can use the exercises as stimulus for further thought.

The Code

The code presented in this book and its description are based on the version of STL made widely available by Hewlett-Packard Company. That version contains the following notice:

```
Copyright © 1994 by Hewlett-Packard Company

Permission to use, copy, modify, distribute, and sell this
software and its documentation for any purpose is hereby
granted without fee, provided that the above copyright
notice appear in all copies and that both that copyright
notice and this permission notice appear in supporting
documentation. Hewlett-Packard Company makes no
representations about the suitability of this software for
any purpose. It is provided "as is" without express or
implied warranty.
```

The code in this book has been tested, to various degrees, with C++ compilers from Microsoft, IBM, Edison Design Group, and Project GNU. It passes all the STL tests in the Dinkum C++ Proofer and the Dinkum Abridged Proofer, both quality-assurance tools for the corresponding libraries available commercially from Dinkumware, Ltd. It has also passed various versions of the commercial library validation suites available from Perennial Software and Plum Hall Inc. While we have taken pains to minimize errors, we cannot guarantee that none remain. Please note carefully the disclaimer on the copyright page.

Please note also that the code in this book is protected by copyright. It has *not* been placed in the public domain. Nor is it shareware. It is not protected by a "copy left" agreement, like code distributed by the Free Software Foundation (Project GNU). P.J. Plauger retains all rights. Dinkumware, Ltd. licenses it on a commercial basis.

The STL code that comes with a given C++ compiler may differ from the code presented here in various ways. This is true even of code based on that presented here. Dialects of C++ still abound, particularly in the complex area of template processing. Over time, all these dialects should converge, thanks to the completion of the C++ Standard. But for some time to come, you should consider the code presented here as reasonably representative of many implementations.

Acknowledgments

Hewlett-Packard supported much of the work that led to the development of STL in its current form. We gratefully acknowledge their significant contribution to this effort. We also thank them for making the original version of STL publicly available on a royalty-free basis. Their corporate generosity has materially aided the spread of STL throughout the C++ community.

Bjarne Stroustrup and Andy Koenig were both instrumental in convincing ANSI committee X3J16 (now J16) and ISO committee WG21 to add STL to the draft C++ Standard rather late in the process. This book would probably not have happened — certainly not in its current form — had they not provided such ardent support.

Matt Austern provided a number of useful comments on the final draft of this book. We appreciate his constructive criticism.

Some of the material presented here first appeared in monthly installments in *The C/C++ Users Journal*, in the "Standard C/C++" column by P.J. Plauger. We thank the publishers for the latitude granted in recycling this text.

Geoffrey Plauger assisted with the typographical design of this book.

P.J. Plauger
Concord, Massachusetts

Alexander Stepanov
Palo Alto, California

Meng Lee
Cupertino, California

David R. Musser
Loudonville, New York

Chapter 0: Introduction

Background

A *library* is a collection of program components that can be used in many programs. The programming language C++ has traditionally offered the usual library of assorted *functions* for performing input/output, computing math functions, and so on. Some of these functions come from the Standard C library (such as `printf`), others are peculiar to the Standard C++ library (such as `set_new_handler`). In all cases, however, a library function accepts argument expressions of some predetermined types and returns a value of some other predetermined type, or affects other stored values. Part of the design of a widely useful C or C++ library lies in guessing the most popular combinations of argument types to support in these various functions.

C++ improves on C in an important way. It extends the notion of a data structure in C to include member functions as well as member objects. Such *classes* in C++ can better encapsulate related data and the operations that can be performed on that data. Part of the design of a widely useful C++ class library lies in guessing the most popular combinations of member object types to support in these various classes.

More recently in its evolution, C++ has added *templates.* A template definition lets you defer the choice of certain types until you actually use the template, or *specialize* it. You can define both template classes and template functions. Within broad limits, a template class or function thus permits the programmer to tailor general code for specific actual types. As you might guess, a template library can offer considerably greater opportunities for code reuse than a conventional function or class library. Those opportunities were not lost on the committees that developed the standard for the C++ language.

ANSI X3J16
ISO WG21

The American National Standards Institute, or ANSI, standardizes computer programming languages in the United States. X3J16 was the name of the ANSI-authorized committee that began developing the standard for C++, starting in 1989. It is now called J16. The International Organisation for Standardisation, or ISO [sic], has a similar responsibility in the international arena. ISO formed the technical committee JTC1/SC22/WG21 in 1991 to work with X3J16 in forming a simultaneous ANSI/ISO Standard for C++. The term *Committee* serves in this book as shorthand for both

X3J16/J16 and WG21, which met together over a period of eight years — three times per year, each time for a week of intense effort — to develop the current C++ Standard.

Now officially known as IS 14882, the C++ Standard saw its last technical changes in November 1997. That means the document should be fairly stable from now on — an ISO standard is nominally frozen for at least five years. Before the draft began to stabilize, however, the Committee made some major changes and additions to the library. One widespread change was to introduce templates in place of most of the classes found in traditional C++ libraries. But probably the largest single change occurred in July 1994, when the Committee voted to add the Standard Template Library.

Standard Template Library

The Standard Template Library (or STL for short) is a large collection of software from Hewlett-Packard Labs (**S&L95** and **M&S96**). It was developed there by Alexander Stepanov (now at AT&T Labs), Meng Lee (still at Hewlett-Packard), and David R. Musser (at Rensselaer Polytechnic Institute). The current version is in C++, but the technology long predates the addition of templates to that language. In fact, Musser and Stepanov described an early implementation using Ada *generics*, a form of templates, over a decade ago (**M&S87** and **M&S89**). And that work was based on still earlier work by these two.

The result, as presented here, is upwards of 6,000 lines of highly refined code. Almost all of it takes the form of template classes and template functions. You can specialize these templates for a wide variety of types, either built-in or classes you define yourself. These specializations often come remarkably close to the best tailored code you can write by hand. And STL supplies algorithms and data structures that are devilishly hard to get right if you code them yourself. So you get the benefit of numerous well crafted solutions to common problems in a form that is efficient in code space and execution time as well.

You can categorize nearly all the STL code as falling into three broad areas: algorithms, containers, and iterators. Iterators are perhaps the most inventive and interesting of the three categories, but they are also the hardest to explain. Thus, we'll describe algorithms and containers first.

algorithms

Strictly speaking, an algorithm is a mathematical procedure for determining a result. It differs from a mathematical function in just a few ways. Probably the most important to us computer types is that an algorithm involves only a finite number of operations to complete. By contrast, a function can conceptually take an infinite number of operations, yet still yield a well defined result.

In programming, we use the term algorithm a bit more loosely. We take it to mean any function (in the C/C++ sense) that computes a useful result. A good algorithm does the job with an economy of operations and storage space, and with predictable time complexity. It is chary of special cases, like zero repetition counts, and it avoids gratuitous intermediate overflows and other computing anomalies. It is cohesive, presenting a narrow and sensible interface to the outside world.

Well coded algorithms are thus an important asset to the working programmer. We use them all the time, in the guise of the Standard C library, for example. All those math functions, string manipulators, and I/O facilities capture any number of algorithms in code that has proved to be remarkably reusable over the years.

In the case of a function library, the choice of data types is critical to reusability, as we mentioned at the outset. A square-root function is much more widely usable if it takes a **`double`** argument than if it takes an **`int`**. A sequence of **`char`** makes a more widely usable string or file than, say, a sequence of **`float`** elements. Imagine how much more useful all these functions could be, however, if you had some say in what data type should be used.

That's where templates come in. Within some limits, you can specialize a template function or class for one or more specific types, and the translator fills in the blanks for you. Those limits are dictated by any assumptions made, within the template, about what you can do with the parameter type. If the template wants to add one to an object of the parameter type, for example, then the type you choose had better define what it means to add one to an object of that type.

A significant achievement of STL is that it provides quite a number of useful algorithms. It does so in a helpful framework — the types you can substitute for its parameters fall into a handful of categories. Each of these categories is pretty clearly spelled out, and the template definitions are robustly written. Thus, there's a high probability you will guess right about what types you can use with a given algorithm, and there's an equally high probability that the code will do the right thing.

STL offers around 100 template functions that implement algorithms. On the simple end are templates like **`for_each`**, which calls the function you specify for each element of a sequence. On the complex end you will find things like **`stable_sort`**, which sorts in place a sequence using an ordering rule you specify, preserving the order of elements that compare equal under the ordering rule.

As you become familiar with STL, you find that more and more of the "interesting" code you used to write can now be written in just a few lines. Invoking an algorithm template or two does all the hard stuff. And it does the job better than you are likely to do.

containers Organizing data is as important as choosing the algorithms that manipulate it. How you structure a sequence of elements determines how messy or time consuming it is to add elements, remove them, visit them in various orders, or rearrange them. Indeed, the choice of data structures can make or break a program when it comes to implementing its most time-critical operations.

An interesting parallel exists in physics. Some computations are notoriously complex, particularly those that require matching up two solutions at a boundary. One approach to solving such problems is to change coordinate systems. Move to a system where the boundary looks simple and the equations are easy to solve. Of course, changing back and forth between coordinate systems may be messy in its own right. The advantage is that someone has probably solved that problem for you, so you can just recycle a known technique.

We in computing have repeatedly rediscovered a handful of useful ways to organize collections of data. Think of them as the moral equivalent of coordinate systems, for the analogy above. An array is good for quick random access, but it doesn't grow easily, and insertions are a real nuisance. A linked list makes light work of additions and insertions, at the cost of linear access to an arbitrary element, instead of random. And so on.

The sad thing is that we've all reimplemented vectors, lists, and other common data structures repeatedly over the years. The code in each case is highly similar, but it has to change in small ways to accommodate variations in the data being managed. Wouldn't it be nice if someone could implement a linked list once and for all in such a way that we'd all be happy to recycle that implementation?

That's where the STL containers come in. These are template classes that support the half dozen or so commonest ways to organize data. The template parameter lets you specify the type of data in each element. All that code for growing, shrinking, inserting, and visiting all the elements is provided once and for all by the containers themselves.

Once again, you slowly learn that much of the code you tend to write for a new program is just bookkeeping for a common data organization. An STL container or two can save some tedious effort.

iterators Iterators are the glue that pastes together algorithms and containers. They generalize the concept of a pointer in C by using the ability to overload operators for newly defined classes in C++. Consider, for example, the common pattern for summing the elements of a sequence bounded by the pointers `first` and `last`:

```
for (sum = 0; first != last; ++first)
    sum += *first;
```

Here, `first` sure looks like a pointer, but in C++ it need not be. It can, in fact, be any type that supports:

- comparison for (in)equality (`first != last`)
- dereferencing to access a value (`*first`)
- (pre)incrementing (`++first`)

Of course, you can also use a conventional object pointer in this code.

Add a few lines to the example above and you can make a template function that sums the values in a sequence of elements of arbitrary type `T`:

```
template<class T, class It> inline
   T sum_all( It first, It last)
   {T sum;
   for (sum = 0; first != last; ++first)
        sum += *first;
   return (sum); }
```

Add a few more requirements to those listed immediately above and you have the specifications for a typical iterator. In fact, this template function is very similar to the template function **accumulate**, described in Chapter 7: **<numeric>**.

Nearly all of the algorithms that STL provides work on sequences accessed via iterators. A handful of categories describes the various iterators around which the algorithm functions are defined. This is the organizing principle that gives STL much of its strength and flexibility.

Each STL container defines the iterators needed to access its elements. You can, of course, also supply your own iterators for your own data structures as well. Most important of all, ordinary pointers almost always work just fine as iterators. You don't have to define a bunch of fancy classes if you don't want to. And yet you can still easily extend the set of algorithms and containers that work within the STL framework.

Hewlett-Packard code

Hewlett-Packard Labs has kindly made their implementation of STL available to the public. You can use the code and the accompanying documentation freely, even redistribute it as part of commercial products. You pay no royalties. All they ask is that you reproduce their copyright and disclaimer notice, which is reasonably innocuous. (See page xi.)

Hewlett-Packard has also applied for several patents on some of the adaptive algorithms developed as part of STL. They have announced their intention to "let" these patents — allow them to be used without prior permission and with no royalties. You have to give the company top marks for good citizenship in this area.

Note, however, that the publicly available version of H-P STL, or a more recent repackaging thereof, is *not* what has been accepted as part of IS 14882, the C++ Standard. As with any proposal accepted by the Committee, the original STL specification has been reworked several times since it was first incorporated. Approved changes, large and small, affect nearly every corner of the STL code. As a result, programs you write using the existing packages may well have to change when you move to an implementation that conforms to the C++ Standard.

The very organization has changed, for example. As shipped by Hewlett-Packard, STL is organized into 48 headers:

```
algo.h       algobase.h  bool.h      bvector.h
defalloc.h   deque.h     faralloc.h  fdeque.h
flist.h      fmap.h      fmultmap.h  fmultset.h
fset.h       function.h  hdeque.h    heap.h
hlist.h      hmap.h      hmultmap.h  hmultset.h
hset.h       hugalloc.h  hvector.h   iterator.h
lbvector.h   ldeque.h    list.h      llist.h
lmap.h       lmultmap.h  lmultset.h  lngalloc.h
```

```
lset.h      map.h      multimap.h  multiset.h
neralloc.h  nmap.h     nmultmap.h  nmultset.h
nset.h      pair.h     projectn.h  set.h
stack.h     tempbuf.h  tree.h      vector.h
```

These are rearranged into thirteen headers in the C++ Standard:

```
algorithm  deque  functional  iterator  vector
list       map    memory      numeric
queue      set    stack       utility
```

The impact of this particular change is far reaching, but easily addressed. If you happen to have existing code that makes use of the Hewlett-Packard version of STL, it's not hard to change it for use with a standard-conforming implementation. Just alter your list of include files. Keep adding headers until the compiler stops complaining. (Note that this is not a *portable* solution to the porting problem. Different implementations may tolerate different sets of include directives. But this approach does get you on the air quickly.)

More fundamental changes occur in how containers allocate storage. In principle, they should affect only the more adventurous users of STL, such as those who endeavor to do their own storage allocation for a container. (See Chapter 4: **<memory>**.) Unfortunately, they can actually affect even the simplest uses of STL containers. You must be prepared to learn a number of new conventions as STL becomes more widely standardized.

commercial compilers

Commercial C++ compilers with properly updated versions of STL are now widely available on the market. The code presented in this book, for example, is a tutorial reformatting of the STL portion of the Dinkum C++ Library. That makes the code presented here a close cousin to the code shipped with Microsoft Visual C++, IBM Visual Age, as well as C++ compilers from several other vendors. (Any differences are due primarily to the need to accommodate compilers that may not yet support all the language features mandated by the C++ Standard.) Still other vendors may supply STL code with different etymology, but it too should conform to the C++ Standard. Commercial validation suites for the Standard C++ library are also now available from companies such as Dinkumware, Ltd. and Perennial Software. (What the validation suites do is keep the library vendors honest. Once the flurry of upgrading and debugging settles down, you can expect more uniformity among commercial offerings that include the new Standard C++ library with STL.) The code presented here passes all the relevant tests in the Dinkum C++ Proofer and the Dinkum Abridged Proofer, both from Dinkumware, Ltd.

This book focuses on STL as a fairly self-contained subset of the larger library defined for Standard C++. That library is designed to work, in turn, with the library defined for ANSI/ISO Standard C (**ANS89** and **ISO90**). Consequently, you can look on this book as a companion to two earlier works by P.J. Plauger, *The Standard C Library* (**Pla92**) and *The Draft Standard C++ Library* (**Pla95**). Taken together, these three books describe nearly all the library facilities of widespread interest to C++ programmers.

Each of the chapters of this book is organized much like this Introduction:

- It begins with a **Background** section, to put matters in perspective.
- The **Functional Description** that follows serves as a succinct reference. You will find this section much more valuable when you *reread* this book, because it is light on tutorial material and often contains unexplained forward references.
- The **Using** section tells you how you are likely to want to use the specific features described in the chapter.
- The **Implementing** section discusses issues that arise in making the features work in a typical implementation of STL. It presents actual code for each of the headers.
- **Testing** discusses issues that arise in testing an implementation of STL for basic functionality. It presents actual test code for each of the headers. Thus, it supplies simple but illustrative examples.
- **Exercises** at the end of each chapter are designed to make you think about what you have just read. If you are reading this book as part of a course, they may very well constitute part of your homework.

In keeping with the introductory nature of this chapter, the remaining sections discuss STL as a whole, rather than specific components. The remaining chapters describe those components in detail.

Functional Description

standard headers

All Standard C++ library entities are declared or defined in one or more standard headers. These include the preexisting Standard C headers, plus many new Standard C++ headers. The thirteen Standard C++ headers that constitute the Standard Template Library are listed on page 6. You include the contents of a standard header by naming it in an *include* directive, as in:

```
#include <algorithm>  // include all algorithms
```

You can include the standard headers in any order, a standard header more than once, or two or more standard headers that define the same macro or the same type. Do not include a standard header within a declaration. Do not define macros that have the same names as keywords before you include a standard header.

A Standard C++ header includes any other Standard C++ headers it needs to define needed types. A Standard C header never includes another standard header, by the way. A standard header declares or defines only the entities described for it in the C++ Standard.

Every function in the library is declared in a standard header. Unlike in Standard C, the standard header never provides a *masking macro,* with the same name as the function, that masks the function declaration and achieves the same effect.

namespace std All names in the Standard C++ headers, other than `operator new` and `operator delete`, are defined in a *namespace* called `std`, or in a namespace nested within `std`. Including a Standard C++ header does *not* generally introduce any library names into the current namespace.

Unless specifically indicated otherwise, you may not define names in the `std` namespace, or in a namespace nested within the `std` namespace. It is reserved for components of the Standard C++ library, current and future.

latitude An implementation has certain latitude in how it declares types and functions in the C++ library:

- Names of functions in the Standard C library may have either `extern "C++"` or `extern "C"` linkage. Thus, you should include the appropriate Standard C header rather than declare a library entity inline.
- A member function name in a library class may have additional function signatures over those listed in this document. You can be sure that a function call described here behaves as expected, but you cannot reliably take the address of a library member function. (The type may not be what you expect.)
- A library class may have undocumented (non-virtual) base classes. A class documented as derived from another class may, in fact, be derived from that class through other undocumented classes.
- A type defined as a synonym for some integer type may be the same as one of several different integer types.
- A library function that has no exception specification can throw an arbitrary exception, unless its definition clearly restricts such a possibility.

guarantees On the other hand, there are some restrictions you can count on:

- The Standard C library uses no *masking macros*. Only specific function signatures are reserved, not the names of the functions themselves.
- A library function name outside a class will *not* have additional, undocumented, function signatures. You can reliably take its address.
- Base classes and member functions described as virtual are assuredly virtual, while those described as non-virtual are assuredly non-virtual.
- Two types defined by the Standard C++ library are always different unless explicitly stated otherwise.
- Functions supplied by the library, including the default versions of replaceable functions, can throw *at most* those exceptions listed in any exception specification. No destructors supplied by the library throw exceptions. Functions in the Standard C library may propagate an exception, as when `qsort` calls a comparison function that throws an exception, but they do not otherwise throw exceptions.

Using STL

For maximum portability, you should always include explicitly any Standard C++ headers needed in a translation unit. What may work correctly with one implementation may not necessarily work correctly when moved to another. You can usually assume that one header must include another because of an obvious dependency, but you can still guess wrong about how a given implementation handles the actual dependencies.

namespaces Namespaces were added to C++ during standardization. You can think of a namespace as much like a class wrapper. It imposes a hierarchy on the names defined in a program much like directories organize the files on a disk.

You refer to the name `cin`, for example, as `std::cin`. Alternatively, you can write the omnibus declaration:

```
using namespace std;
```

which promotes all library names into the current namespace, so you need not write the `std::` prefix thereafter. To promote all library names into the global namespace, write this declaration at the top of each source file, immediately after all the library include directives. Also, if you include one of the C standard headers, such as `<stdio.h>`, the individual names declared or defined in that header are promoted into the global namespace for you. (Use the Standard C++ header `<cstdio>` if you just want the names declared in namespace `std`.)

Note that macro names are not subject to the rules for nesting namespaces.

Opinions vary about the tidiness of using this form of omnibus declaration. Some people feel that all new C++ code should religiously use the `std::` prefix in front of all library names. Others view this as clutter, which not so incidentally increases the cost of upgrading existing C++ code to conform to the C++ Standard. Our test code uses the omnibus, if only to simplify conversion for use with compilers that do not support namespaces, or don't support them well. We do not otherwise take a stand on this touchy issue of programming style.

dialects As a final caveat, we must emphasize once again that many dialects of C++ still exist. Features such as namespaces, member templates, and template partial specialization were added as the C++ Standard evolved. As of this writing, not all commercially available compilers implement all the language features required to fully support STL. Where we think it appropriate, we point out features of STL that might not be present if an implementation is lacking a specific language feature.

But don't let our conservatism dissuade you from using STL. Compilers are converging steadily to the C++ Standard. And even with the current state of affairs, the subset of STL you can rely upon across multiple implementations is large and powerful indeed.

Implementing STL

The code in this book is presented as a set of standard header files that accompanies a C++ compiler. Locate the directory that contains the standard headers and you will probably find files with similar names, such as `deque` or `iterator`. A word of warning, however. You cannot necessarily replace a standard header file with code from this book. The Standard Template Library is largely self contained, but it does interface with the rest of the Standard C++ library. How it does so can legitimately vary among implementations. We will discuss interface issues from time to time, but all we can do here is present one possible solution. It may not be the right one for a given compiler.

coding style The code in this book obeys a number of style rules. Most of the rules make sense for any project. A few are peculiar.

- Each *secret* macro or global name — a name private to this implementation of STL — begins with an uppercase letter, as in `Getint`. (We omit the leading underscore that should be present in a library name, for the sake of tutorial readability.)
- Code layout is reasonably uniform. Objects are usually declared within functions at the innermost possible nesting level. The indentation religiously shows the nesting of control structures.
- All functions are defined inline, within the header files, to keep them self contained. There are no separate source code files for the library.
- To keep the presentation from sprawling excessively, inline functions are written more compactly than is traditional for function definitions in C++ source files. (Even with this small sacrifice in readability, some of the header files are still quite large.)
- The code contains no `register` declarations. They are hard to place wisely and they clutter the code. Besides, modern compilers often ignore this advice and allocate registers much better than a programmer can.
- This book displays each C++ source file as one or more figures, each with a box around it. Each figure caption gives the name of the file. Larger files appear in successive installments — the figure caption for each installment warns you that the code in that figure represents only part of a source file.
- Each figure displays C++ source code with horizontal tab stops set every four columns. Displayed code differs from the actual C++ source file in two ways — comments to the right of code are right justified on the line, again to improve readability, and a box character (□) marks the end of the last line of code in each C++ source file.

The resulting code is quite dense at times. A typical coding project would add white space, and comments, to make it at least 30 per cent larger. (Some programmers would make it larger still, but we have the benefit of adjacent descriptive text in this book.)

The code also contains a few headers that are split into smaller pieces. The usual reason for such partitioning, in an actual implementation, is to disentangle circular references among the headers. Compilation time is a minor consideration, given today's high-speed computers. We explain the need for any added headers as we present them.

implementing headers As an example, Figure 0.1 shows the file `utility`, which implements the header `<utility>`. We'll discuss the details of this small header in Chapter 2: Utility. For now, we focus on the overall structure of the header.

First the obvious. Bracketing the header is the usual explanatory comment and *macro guard:*

```
// utility standard header
#ifndef _UTILITY_
#define _UTILITY_
.....
#endif /* _UTILITY_ */
```

Many C and C++ programmers will recognize this as a common idiom for protecting an include file against multiple inclusions. A typedef or a macro definition can be seen multiple times in a translation unit, so long as the resultant definition is the same each time. (This is called *benign redefinition.*) But essentially all other entities must be defined at most once. Here, defining the macro `_UTILITY_` serves as a first-time switch to ensure that the body of the header is considered just once, even if it is mentioned in multiple *include* directives within a translation unit. That protects against troublesome multiple definitions, while encouraging liberal use of *include* directives in user code.

The macro name `_UTILITY_` is chosen with similar care. Both the C and C++ Standards reserve certain sets of names for use by the implementor. In particular, names that begin with an underscore followed by an uppercase letter are strictly off limits to all but implementors. Thus, an implementation that uses names just from this set can be certain not to interfere with the proper translation of any conforming program. (Implementors of different parts of a library must still take care not to tread on each others' toes, however.)

includes The next line of interest is the *include* directive:

```
#include <iosfwd>
```

The header `<iosfwd>` is an invention of the Committee. It supplies several forward references (declarations of incomplete types) for templates and classes defined as part of other headers. Civilians seldom have occasion to include this header, but to implementors it is often a godsend. It helps break up any number of circular dependencies among the components of the Standard C++ library.

Strictly speaking, the header `<utility>` in this implementation has no use for any of the declarations in `<iosfwd>`. In practice, however, it simplifies the structure of how the standard headers include each other as needed. In this particular implementation, other headers that include `<utility>`

Figure 0.1: `utility`, **Part 1 of 2**

```
// utility standard header
#ifndef UTILITY_
#define UTILITY_
#include <iosfwd>
namespace std {
        // TEMPLATE STRUCT pair
template<class T1, class T2> struct pair {
    typedef T1 first_type;
    typedef T2 second_type;
    pair()
        : first(T1()), second(T2()) {}
    pair(const T1& V1, const T2& V2)
        : first(V1), second(V2) {}
    template<class U1, class U2>
        pair(const pair<U1, U2>& X)
        : first(X.first), second(X.second) {}
    T1 first;
    T2 second;
    };

        // pair TEMPLATE OPERATORS
template<class T1, class T2> inline
    bool operator==(const pair<T1, T2>& X,
        const pair<T1, T2>& Y)
    {return (X.first == Y.first && X.second == Y.second); }
template<class T1, class T2> inline
    bool operator!=(const pair<T1, T2>& X,
        const pair<T1, T2>& Y)
    {return (!(X == Y)); }
template<class T1, class T2> inline
    bool operator<(const pair<T1, T2>& X,
        const pair<T1, T2>& Y)
    {return (X.first < Y.first ||
        !(Y.first < X.first) && X.second < Y.second); }
template<class T1, class T2> inline
    bool operator>(const pair<T1, T2>& X,
        const pair<T1, T2>& Y)
    {return (Y < X); }
template<class T1, class T2> inline
    bool operator<=(const pair<T1, T2>& X,
        const pair<T1, T2>& Y)
    {return (!(Y < X)); }
template<class T1, class T2> inline
    bool operator>=(const pair<T1, T2>& X,
        const pair<T1, T2>& Y)
    {return (!(X < Y)); }
template<class T1, class T2> inline
    pair<T1, T2> make_pair(const T1& X, const T2& Y)
    {return (pair<T1, T2>(X, Y)); }

        // TEMPLATE OPERATORS
    namespace rel_ops {
template<class T> inline
    bool operator!=(const T& X, const T& Y)
    {return (!(X == Y)); }
```

Figure 0.2: `utility`, **Part 2 of 2**

```
template<class T> inline
     bool operator>(const T& X, const T& Y)
     {return (Y < X); }
template<class T> inline
     bool operator<=(const T& X, const T& Y)
     {return (!(Y < X)); }
template<class T> inline
     bool operator>=(const T& X, const T& Y)
     {return (!(X < Y)); }
     }
} /* namespace std */
#endif /* UTILITY_ */
```

need **<iosfwd>** in turn. It is thus a convenience to lob in this apparently gratuitous *include* directive here. See Appendix A: Interfaces for an overview of how the STL headers interact with each other, and with the other headers in the Standard C++ library.

We could have glossed over this implementation detail, dismissing it as an unwelcome distraction. We prefer, however, to underscore how difficult it is to get large quantities of software to cooperate successfully. This particular example also emphasizes that STL does not exist in a vacuum. Self contained as it is in many ways, it is still part of a (much) larger library.

namespaces Proceeding from the outside in, the next bit of structure in the header **<utility>** is the namespace declaration:

```
namespace std {
.....
}; /* namespace std */
```

This particular declaration ensures that all (non-macro) names defined inside the braces occupy the **std** namespace. We said earlier that a namespace behaves much like a class wrapper, but that is only approximately true. Unlike a class wrapper, a namespace declaration can occur repeatedly, within a given translation unit, naming the same namespace. All the contributions with the same name are effectively concatenated.

production code Real production code is not quite so tidy. Quite often, library code intended to be portable across multiple implementations is chock full of conditional directives. A given implementation turns on whatever features it can, given the multiplicity of C++ dialects that still exist. It disables, or supplies a simpler alternate form, for those it cannot. You get a Chinese menu of possibilities — at the cost of headers that border on the illegible. The code in this book is indeed based on a production version of STL that is complete. Showing that code here in its most general form would be a real education in the nitty gritty details of writing portable commercial code. But our primary goal in this book is to describe the intricacies of STL. That's quite a heavy enough undertaking without adding further distractions. Hence, we've chosen to derive from the production code a *tutorial* version that does essentially the same thing. The major difference is that it is designed to be significantly more readable.

We've made one additional concession to readability, as we mentioned earlier. Figure 0.1 makes liberal use of traditional names for types, such as **T1** and **T2**, and for objects, such as **X** and **Y**. These fairly arbitrary names often, if not always, agree with those used in the C++ Standard itself. They certainly follow widespread conventions for naming things in C++ (though perhaps object names might not be capitalized). Thus, names "internal" to the headers are chosen as much as possible to maximize understanding.

The only problem is, they don't conform to the requirements of the C++ Standard. No, there's no problem with "breaking" user code. Parameter names, and names nested inside classes and functions, don't leak out to pollute the containing environment. Rather, the problem is the other way around. Under a variety of circumstances, names chosen by the user can percolate into library declarations and definitions, altering their meanings in pernicious ways. The net effect is often a mysterious diagnostic. On occasion, you can even get a program that compiles but quietly misbehaves.

The easiest way to cause trouble is to define a macro with a common name like **T1** or **X**. If you do so before the first inclusion of a library header, the effect is to rewrite any declarations that make use of these names. Whether you cleverly subvert the library or inadvertently clobber it, serious programming is seldom well served by a library vulnerable to such attacks.

Yes, we know that **T1** and **X** are lousy names for macros. A serious programmer wouldn't dream of indulging in such antics. Most programmers soon learn to stylize names for defined types, macros, etc. to minimize the problems with later maintenance. But the C++ Standard nevertheless *permits* a program to define macros with these names — they are part of the name space reserved for use by the user. (A "name space," or set of names, should not be confused with the C++ *namespace* declaration, despite their similarities.)

You can, in fact, often cause trouble just by declaring types with these common names. We won't contrive an example here, but it is a well known problem in both C and C++. In too many contexts, a type in a containing environment alters the interpretation of a declaration, or even some expressions, in a nested environment.

reserved names Production library code should treat *all* names with the same caution it extends to macro names it contrives for its own purposes. That means writing stuff like:

```
template<class _T1, class _T2> inline
   bool operator==(const pair<_T1, _T2>& _X,
        const pair<_T1, _T2>& _Y)
   {return (_X.first == _Y.first
        && _X.second == _Y.second); }

template<class _T1, class _T2> inline
   bool operator<(const pair<_T1, _T2>& _X,
        const pair<_T1, _T2>& _Y)
   {return (_X.first < _Y.first ||
        !(_Y.first < _X.first) && _X.second < _Y.second); }
```

instead of the somewhat more readable equivalent in Figure 0.1. The example above is an actual excerpt from the production code. You can understand, perhaps, why we chose not to inflict yards of such code on people presumably more interested in learning STL.

Testing STL

Testing is a serious topic in its own right. (See **Pla95** for a more extensive discussion, which is nevertheless still superficial.) It is widely understood that a typical library function can never be exhaustively tested. The combinations of input values are often astronomical, particularly for floating-point arguments. Imagine how much worse the problem is for templates, which can be specialized for an open-ended set of parameter types.

We won't even try. Instead, we present a set of simple test programs. Each test exercises part or all of the facilities provided by one of the STL headers. You will find that these test programs focus primarily on external behavior. That means, essentially, that they comprise a very simple validation suite. Occasionally, however, they stray into the realm of testing internal structure. Some implementation errors are so common, and so pernicious, that we can't resist testing for them. Rarely do the programs stray into the realm of performance testing.

Most of all, you will find these tests to be remarkably superficial and simplistic. Nevertheless, even simple tests serve a useful purpose. You can see a basic working example of each feature, a real benefit with some of the more intricate constructs of STL. You can verify that a template satisfies its basic design goals with just a few lines of code. That reassures you that an implementation is sane. When changes occur (as they inevitably will), repeating the tests renews that assurance. Simple tests are well worth writing, and keeping around.

simple tests We have found that the best simple confidence tests, when successful, just print a standard reassuring message and exit with successful status to report correct execution. If at all possible, they say nothing else.

We construct test file names by preceding each header name with a `t`, then chopping, as necessary, to eight letters before the `.c` file extension. While the resulting name is sometimes mildly barbaric, it has the virtue of causing the least amount of distress to file managers on the largest number of operating environments. Thus, `tutility.c` tests the header `<utility>`. It verifies that the header defines what it is supposed to. And it ends by displaying the reassuring message:

```
SUCCESS testing <utility>
```

then takes a normal exit. That way, you can run this and other tests from a command script and simply test the exit status, if you choose.

Note that each of these files defines its own `main`. You link each with the Standard C++ library to produce a separate test program. You would *not* add any of these files to your Standard C++ object-module library. Each is designed to be run as a separate program.

Exercises

Exercise 0.1 In the example template shown earlier:

```
template<class T> inline
    T sum_all(T *first, T *last)
    {T sum;
    for (sum = 0; first != last; ++first)
         sum += *first;
    return (sum); }
```

determine whether the template can be successfully specialized for:

- type `int`
- type `float`
- a *void* type
- a pointer type

If you believe a type is unsuitable, explain why.

Exercise 0.2 For the template `sum_all` above, list all the operations must be supported on the parameter type `T` for this template to be successfully specialized.

Exercise 0.3 Define a class `X` for which the call `sum_all(x)` is well defined when `x` is an object of class `X`.

Exercise 0.4 What is the result of `sum_all(&x, &x)`? Do you think it would be better to have such a call return the value of `x` instead? Explain the reason for your preference.

Exercise 0.5 List the tests you would perform to establish a reasonable level of confidence that `sum_all` works as expected when specialized for type `float`.

Exercise 0.6 [Harder] List the tests you would perform to establish a reasonable level of confidence that `sum_all` works as expected when specialized for an arbitrary type `T`.

Exercise 0.7 [Very hard] How can you alter the definition of `sum_all` so that the template specializes "sensibly" even for a parameter type `T` with bizarre definitions for `operator=(const T&)` and `operator+=(const T&)`.

Chapter 1: Iterators

Background

Iterators are the glue that ties together all of the Standard Template Library. Essentially all of the algorithms supplied by STL are templates that you specialize for particular iterators that you specify. You are encouraged to write your own algorithm templates in the same style. Similarly, all the containers in the library supply iterators that let you access the sequences they control. You are encouraged to supply suitable iterators for any containers you define. Since an object pointer can serve as any category of iterator, this is not an onerous constraint.

`<utility>` `<iterator>` `<memory>`

We count three headers as glue: `<utility>`, `<iterator>`, and `<memory>`. Of these, the first is arguably more glue than iterator technology. But all three supply machinery used throughout STL. The next three chapters discuss these headers in detail. Be warned that the detail can be tedious at times, with few obvious payoffs until we discuss algorithms and containers later in this book. For now, we focus on the properties shared by all iterators — how to categorize them and how each category behaves.

Functional Description

An iterator in C++ is a generalization of an object pointer in C. Pointers themselves make perfectly fine iterators. The generalization comes from the ability to declare new classes in C++, and to overload many of the operators with new meanings for these classes. You can even talk about a *singular value* for an iterator, which (mis)behaves like an ill-defined pointer.

output iterators

You use an iterator to access the elements of an ordered sequence. *Access* is a general term that can mean either storing into an object or obtaining the stored value from an object. If all you want to do is create a new sequence by generating its values in order, you can write a loop like:

```
for (; <not done>; ++next)
    *next = <whatever>;
```

Here, `next` is an object of some iterator type `X`, `<not done>` is the predicate that determines when the loop terminates, and `<whatever>` is an expression of the element type `T`, or at least one convertible by assignment to type `T`.

Table 1.1: Properties of Output Iterators

Expression	Result Type	Meaning	Notes
X(a)	X	constructs a copy of a	destructor is visible, *X(a) = t has same effect as *a = t
X u(a) X u = a	X&	u is a copy of a	
r = a	X&	assigns a to r	result: *r = t has same effect as *a = t
*a = t	void	store new element in sequence	
++r	X&	point to next element	&r == &++r
r++	convertible to const X&	{X tmp = r; ++r; return tmp; }	
*r++ = t	void		

NOTES: X is iterator type; a has type X&; T is element type; t has type T

An iterator of type X that can be used this way is called an *output iterator.* From the above, it is easy to see that an output iterator must define at least the following operations:

- ***next = <whatever>** assigns **<whatever>** to the next element to generate in the sequence.
- **++next** alters **next** to designate the next element in the sequence.

A popular variant of this idiom in C uses slightly different notation:

```
while (<not done>)
    *next++ = <whatever>;
```

To support this idiom, the expression ***next++ = <whatever>** must combine the two operations described immediately above, just as for pointers in C.

An output iterator promises little more than these properties. (You can't even tell if an output iterator has gone too far.) Rounding out the set of operations is a copy constructor, a destructor, and an assignment operator, all with the usual sensible properties. In trade for these weak properties, an output iterator permits a wide variation of implementations. You can even write output to a file in the guise of storing output records one at a time on a suitable output iterator.

Table 1.1 shows the semimathematical notation conventionally used to describe the properties of output iterators. Similar tables appear later for the other categories of iterators. We find this notation helpful as a *supplement* to the example code and commentary above, but not necessarily as a complete replacement. The table doesn't make clear, for example, several important constraints on output iterators:

- You really must increment an output iterator after each store.
- You really shouldn't increment an output iterator more than once between stores.

If the output iterator is actually a pointer, these constraints aren't so obvious. But once you see the kind of clever tricks that STL plays with special-purpose output iterators, you will understand their need. You may also better appreciate some of the more esoteric entries in Table 1.1, such as the return type of `r++`. For now, just remember that an output iterator is intended to be used only in one of the stylized loops showed above.

input iterators Output iterators are for generating new sequences. To access stored values in order and in just one pass from an existing sequence, you need a slightly different idiom:

```
for (p = first; p != last; ++p)
    <process>(*p);
```

Here, `p`, `first`, and `last` are objects of some iterator type `X`, and `<process>` is a function that accepts an argument of the element type `T`. The sequence consist of the elements denoted by iterators in the half-open interval `[first, last)`.

Note that `last` does *not* denote an element of the sequence. Rather, it denotes some "end-of-sequence" marker, such as the first element beyond the end of the actual sequence. An empty sequence is one for which `first == last`. The C Standard blessed this idiom for walking arrays in C — you can store the address of the first element beyond an array in a pointer, but you can't dereference it. Iterators generalize this concept to a fare-the-well.

An iterator of type `X` that can be used this way is called an *input iterator.* From the above, it is easy to see that an input iterator must define at least the following operations:

- `p != q` is true if the iterators `p` and `q` of type `X` do not denote the same element. (For convenience, `p == q` is also always defined, as the logical inverse of `p != q`.)
- `*p` is an *rvalue* of type `T`. (An rvalue is an expression such as `-37` that has a value, but can't necessarily be used to reference an object.) The expression is not defined for `p == last`.
- `++p` alters `p` to designate the next element in a sequence after the one it originally designated. The expression is not defined for `p == last`.

A popular variant of this idiom in C uses slightly different notation:

```
while (first != last)
    <process>(*first++);
```

Table 1.2: Properties of Input Iterators

Expression	Result Type	Meaning	Notes
`X(a)`	`X`	constructs a copy of `a`	destructor is visible, `*X(a)` has same effect as `*a`
`X u(a)` `X u = a`	`X&`	`u` is a copy of `a`	once constructed `u == a`
`r = a`	`X&`	assigns `a` to `r`	result: `r == t`
`a == b`	convertible to `bool`	compare for equivalence	`a` and `b` in same domain of values
`a != b`	convertible to `bool`	`!(a == b)`	
`*a`	`T`	access element from sequence	`a` is not end-of-sequence
`a->m`	type of `m`	`(*a).m`	`T` has member `m`
`++r`	`X&`	point to next element	`&r == &++r`, `r` was not end-of-sequence, invalidates copies of `r`
`(void)r++`	`void`	`(void)++r`	
`*r++`	`T`	`{T tmp = *r; ++r; return tmp; }`	
NOTES: `X` is iterator type; `a` and `b` have type `X&`; `r` has type `X&`; `T` is element type; `t` has type `T`			

To support this idiom, the expression `*first++` must combine the two operations described immediately above, just as for pointers in C.

From these properties, it is safe to conclude that `[first, last)` is a finite sequence only if `last` is *reachable* from `first`. Put another way, incrementing `first` a finite number of times must eventually yield a value that compares equal to `last`.

Like its cousin the output iterator, an input iterator promises little more than these properties. Again rounding out the set of operations is a copy constructor, a destructor, and an assignment operator, with the usual sensible properties. The only other addition is the *points at* operator `p->m`, which is defined only when type `T` is a structured type. An input iterator also permits a wide variety of implementations.

end-of-sequence value You can even read input from a file in the guise of accessing input records one at a time using a suitable input iterator. For this trick to work, the input iterator defines an *end-of-sequence value* — a sort of all-purpose end-of-file marker. You store this end-of-sequence value in `last`. An iterator `first` that designates a real record does not compare equal to `last`. Incrementing `first` when it designates the last real record, however, alters it so that it subsequently compares equal to `last`. Thus, the same control structure that walks an array by incrementing a pointer can walk a file by incrementing an input iterator.

Table 1.2 shows the semimathematical notation conventionally used to describe the properties of input iterators. Once again, the table doesn't make clear all the important constraints on input iterators. It doesn't say, for example, that comparisons are guaranteed to make sense only when at least one of the two iterators has an end-of-sequence value. (You can't talk sensibly about two distinct places in the sequence, with an arbitrary input iterator type, just whether the sequence has been exhausted.) We encourage you to treat input iterators with the same caution we advised for output iterators. Use them only in one of the stylized loops showed above.

forward iterators Output and input iterators are particularly tricky, for the reasons we cited in passing. They can serve as interfaces to files of arbitrary length. A more conventional use of iterators, however, is to access sequences that are truly stored completely in memory. In such cases, you can use iterators that have rather less surprising properties.

Say, for example, that you are still content to access the elements of a sequence strictly from beginning to end. But you might want to both read and write the elements of the sequence. Or you might want to keep an occasional "bookmark" at some point you've visited earlier in the sequence. In such cases, you still use much the same control loops as we showed earlier for output and input iterators. You simply ask for iterators that behave a bit more like conventional pointers.

A *forward iterator* meets these requirements. As with input iterators, you can compare two forward iterators for equality or inequality, but now either or neither can be end-of-sequence. The two iterator values must, of course, inhabit the same domain of values, as before. A forward iterator can still have an end-of-sequence value, just like an input iterator, that behaves for all the world like the address of an array element just "off the end," or some other end-of-sequence marker. But a forward iterator can support either read-only or read/write access to the sequence. And you can have multiple active copies of a forward iterator pointing various places within the sequence.

You might think of a forward iterator as a pointer to an element of a singly linked list. You can tell when you're pointing off the end of a list. The null link serves as an end-of-sequence marker. If not, you can access the list element, or advance the pointer to the next element in the sequence. But you can't back up, and you can't access an arbitrary element of the list.

Table 1.3: Properties of Forward Iterators

Expression	Result Type	Meaning	Notes
`X()`	`X`	constructs a default value	destructor is visible, value may be end-of-sequence
`X u` `X u = a`	`X&`	`u` has default value	
`X(a)`	`X`	constructs a copy of `a`	destructor is visible, `*X(a)` has same effect as `*a`
`X u(a)` `X u = a`	`X&`	`u` is a copy of `a`	once constructed `u == a`
`r = a`	`X&`	assigns `a` to `r`	result: `r == a`
`a == b`	convertible to `bool`	compare for equivalence	`a` and `b` in same domain of values
`a != b`	convertible to `bool`	`!(a == b)`	
`*a`	`T&`	access element from sequence	`a` is not end-of-sequence, `a == b` implies `*a == *b`
`*a == t`	`T&`	store in element	`a` is not end-of-sequence, `X` is mutable
`a->m`	type of `m`	`(*a).m`	`T` has member `m`
`++r`	`X&`	point to next element	`&r == &++r`, `r` was not end-of-sequence, `r == s` implies `++r == ++s`
`r++`	convertible to `const X&`	`{X tmp = r; ++r; return tmp; }`	
`*r++`	`T&`	`{T tmp = *r; ++r; return tmp; }`	

NOTES: `X` is iterator type; `a` and `b` have type `X`; `r` and `s` have type `X&`; `T` is element type; `t` has type `T`

Table 1.4: Additional Properties of Bidirectional Iterators

Expression	Result Type	Meaning	Notes
`--r`	`X&`	point to previous element	`++s = r` for some `s`, `&r == &--r`, `r` was not end-of-sequence, `r == s` implies `--r == --s`
`r--`	convertible to `const X&`	`{X tmp = r; --r; return tmp; }`	
`*r--`	`T&`	`{T tmp = *r; --r; return tmp; }`	
NOTES: `X` is iterator type; `r` and `s` have type `X&`; `T` is element type; all other properties same as for forward iterator			

Strictly speaking, you *can* perform some of these operations with a forward iterator. But it takes some finagling, and you can't perform these operations in constant time, regardless of the length of the list. An implicit requirement for all iterators is that operations on them have no surprising overheads. An operation must certainly not take time that increases with the size of the sequence accessed by the iterator.

Table 1.3 shows the semimathematical notation conventionally used to describe the properties of forward iterators.

bidirectional iterators The next useful generalization of iterators, beyond forward iterators, is to permit both incrementing and decrementing. Quite a number of algorithms are much more efficiently implemented with just this extra bit of latitude. So STL defined a *bidirectional iterator* as a forward iterator that you can also run backwards through a sequence.

You might think of a bidirectional iterator as a pointer to an element of a doubly linked list. You can tell when you're pointing off the end of a list. The null link at the end serves as an end-of-sequence marker. If you're not pointing off the end, you can access the list element, or advance the pointer to the next element in the sequence. If you're not pointing at the first element, you can back up the pointer to the previous element in the sequence. But you can't access an arbitrary element of the list, at least not with a constant-time operation.

Table 1.4 shows the semimathematical notation conventionally used to describe the *additional* properties of bidirectional iterators. All the properties of forward iterators apply as well.

random-access iterators The final step in generalizing iterators takes us to the full power of object pointers in C. A *random-access* iterator supports the addition and subtraction of integer values, pointer subtraction, ordering comparison, and subscript-

Table 1.5: Additional Properties of Random-Access Iterators

Expression	Result Type	Meaning	Notes
`a < b`	convertible to `bool`	`b` is reachable from `a`	`a` and `b` in same domain of values
`a > b`	convertible to `bool`	`b < a`	
`a <= b`	convertible to `bool`	`!(b < a)`	
`a >= b`	convertible to `bool`	`!(a < b)`	

`r += n`	`X&`	`{Dist m = n;`
		`while (0 < m)`
		`--m, ++r;`
		`while (m < 0)`
		`++m, --r;`
		`return r; }`	

`a + n`
`n + a`
	`X`	`{X tmp = a;`
		`tmp += n;`
		`return tmp; }`	

`r -= n`	`X&`	`r += -n`	
`a - n`	`X`	`a + -n`	

`b - a`	`Dist`	`{Dist m = 0;`
		`while (a < b)`
		`++a, ++m;`
		`while (b < a)`
		`++b, --m;`
		`return m; }`
			`a` and `b` in same domain of values

`a[n]`	convertible to `T`	`*(a + n)`	

NOTES: `X` is iterator type; `a` and `b` have type `X`; `r` and `s` have type `X&`; `T` is element type; `Dist` is distance type for `X`; all other properties same as for bidirectional iterators

ing — as well as all the operations permitted for bidirectional iterators, of course. Some algorithms simply require this degree of flexibility to perform at all well. (Sorting and fast searching by binary chop are two obvious examples.)

Remember, however, that a random-access iterator is still *not* necessarily a C-style pointer. The difference of two such iterators, for example, is some type `Dist`, which may or may not be one of the basic integer types. You should be able to perform integer arithmetic with `Dist` objects, of course, but nothing prevents these creatures from being classes in their own right.

Table 1.5 shows the semimathematical notation conventionally used to describe the *additional* properties of random-access iterators. All the properties of bidirectional iterators apply as well.

Using Iterators

The STL facilities make widespread use of iterators, to mediate between the various algorithms and the sequences upon which they act. For brevity in the remainder of this book, the name of an iterator type (or its prefix) indicates the category of iterators required for that type. In order of increasing power, the categories are summarized here as:

- `OutIt` — An *output iterator* `X` can only have a value `V` stored indirectly through it, after which it *must* be incremented before the next store, as in `(*X++ = V)`, `(*X = V, ++X)`, or `(*X = V, X++)`.
- `InIt` — An *input iterator* `X` can represent an end-of-sequence value. If such an iterator does not compare equal to its end-of-sequence value, it can have a value `V` accessed indirect on it any number of times, as in `(V = *X)`. To progress to the next value, or end-of-sequence, you increment it, as in `++X`, `X++`, or `(V = *X++)`. Once you increment *any* copy of an input iterator, none of the other copies can safely be compared, dereferenced, or incremented thereafter.
- `FwdIt` — A *forward iterator* `X` can take the place of an output iterator if `*X` is mutable (in which case it *is* an output iterator). It can also take the place of (or *be*) an input iterator. You can, however, also read (via `V = *X`) what you just wrote (via `*X = V`) through a forward iterator. And you can make multiple copies of a forward iterator, each of which can be dereferenced and incremented independently.
- `BidIt` — A *bidirectional iterator* `X` can take the place of (or *be*) a forward iterator. You can, however, also decrement a bidirectional iterator, as in `--X`, `X--`, or `(V = *X--)`.
- `RanIt` — A *random-access iterator* `X` or `Y` can take the place of (or *be*) a bidirectional iterator. You can also perform much the same integer arithmetic on a random-access iterator that you can on an object pointer. For `N` an integer object, you can write `X[N]`, `X < Y`, `X - N`, and `N + X`.

Note that an object pointer can take the place of (or *be*) a random-access iterator, or any other for that matter.

iterator categories The hierarchy of iterator categories can be summarize by showing three sequences. For write-only access to a sequence, you can use any of:

```
output iterator
   -> forward iterator
   -> bidirectional iterator
   -> random-access iterator
```

The right arrow means "can be replaced by." So any algorithm that calls for an output iterator should work nicely with a forward iterator, for example, but *not* the other way around.

For read-only access to a sequence, you can use any of:

```
input iterator
   -> forward iterator
   -> bidirectional iterator
   -> random-access iterator
```

An input iterator is the weakest of all categories, in this case.

Finally, for read/write access to a sequence, you can use any of:

```
forward iterator
   -> bidirectional iterator
   -> random-access iterator
```

Remember that an object pointer can always serve as a random-access iterator. Hence, it can serve as any category of iterator, so long as it supports the proper read/write access to the sequence it designates.

This "algebra" of iterators is fundamental to practically everything else in the Standard Template Library. It is important to understand the promises, and limitations, of each iterator category to see how iterators are used by containers and algorithms in STL.

Exercises

Exercise 1.1 Describe the weakest category of iterator required:

- to supply an infinite number of zeros
- to write a sequence of values to a file
- to implement a stack (last-in first-out queue)

Exercise 1.2 What categories of iterators can you use in place of:

- an output iterator
- a read-only forward iterator
- a random-access iterator

Exercise 1.3 Iterators could also be based on the Fortran-style `DO` loop:

```
for (p = first; p <= last; ++p)
    <process>(*p);
```

Explain the relative merits of this style and the one chosen by STL, as described on page 19.

Exercise 1.4 Why would you want to write an algorithm to use other than random-access iterators?

Exercise 1.5 Why would you want to define a data structure that supports access only by iterators other than random access?

Exercise 1.6 **[Harder]** Write the template class `bidir<FwdIt>` that behaves like a bidirectional iterator when specialized for `FwdIt` a forward-iterator type. In what ways do you have to compromise the expected behavior of a bidirectional iterator?

Exercise 1.7 **[Very hard]** Write the template class `ran_read<InIt>` that behaves like a read-only random-access iterator when specialized for `InIt` an input-iterator type.

Chapter 2: `<utility>`

Background

The header `<utility>` is rather small. It contains a handful of templates used throughout STL. As originally specified, the handful was somewhat bigger, though still small. The need for two of its inhabitants was eliminated, however. The classes **`empty`** and **`restrictor`**, in the Hewlett-Packard implementation, were artifacts designed to avoid early problems in translating some template definitions. With improvements in available translator technology, the need for these classes has disappeared.

What's left is template class **`pair`**, some associated template functions and operators, and four other template operators. The template class is used for representing a pair of objects as a single object — a convenience when you want a function to return a pair of values, or when you want a container to store elements that are pairs of values. The four template operators flesh out **`operator== and operator<`**, defined for two operands of the same type, by defining the remaining relational operators in a consistent fashion.

`pair` You can construct an object of template class **`pair<T, U>`** with explicit initial values, or let the default constructor supply default initial values. There's no fancy information hiding here — you can access the first member object of the pair **`x`** (with type **`T`**) as **`x.first`**, and the second (with type **`U`**) as **`x.second`**.

Using a member template constructor, you can also construct an object of template class **`pair<T, U>`** from an object of template class **`pair<V, W>`**. The corresponding members supply the initial values.

`make_pair` The template function **`make_pair`** is a handy companion. With it, you can often contrive the **`pair`** object you need on the fly. Sadly, however, you can't always do what you want. Template functions ignore any **`const`** attributes when determining template parameters. (At least they're supposed to — some current compilers are erratic in this area.) So you can't reliably contrive with **`make_pair`** a **`pair`** object that has one or more const member objects. And that's just what the containers **`map`** and **`multimap`** sometimesneed. (See Chapter 14: **`<map>`**.) Still, the template function has its uses.

operator==
operator<

Sometimes it makes sense to compare two **pair** objects **x** and **y**. Two template operators perform the essential comparison operations. Equality is the easier of the two to justify. **x** and **y** are arguably equal if their corresponding member objects are equal. But what does it mean to say that one pair is "less than" another?

You can begin by assuming that the first of the two member objects carries more weight than the second. In that case, **x** is less than **y** for sure if **x.first < y.first**. You can then go on to add the case where **x.first == x.second && x.second < y.second**. Curiously, however, the operator function isn't defined exactly that way. Rather, it is expressed purely in terms of **operator<**, as defined for each of the member object types:

```
template<class T, class U> inline
    bool operator<(const pair<T, U>& x,
        const pair<T, U>& y)
    {return (x.first < y.first ||
        !(y.first < x.first) && x.second < y.second); }
```

With a bit of head scratching, you can convince yourself that the form actually used is equivalent to the logic outlined above — at least if the comparison operators have their usual intuitive definition for the member object types.

One reason for this peculiar form is simple elegance. Much better to define a template in terms of just one operator function per parameter type instead of two. Another reason is even subtler, however. Defining ordering relationships in terms of just a single **operator<** function is a bit more robust, and more powerful, than requiring a whole family of interrelated comparison operators. We'll explain why in more detail in conjunction with some of the algorithms that impose order on sequences. (See Chapter 5: Algorithms.) All we'll say for now is that STL worries considerably about seemingly small details like this. That's one of its strengths.

operator!=

Perhaps now you can guess why the four remaining templates are present in the header **<utility>**. The first supplies a sensible definition of **operator!=** for any type **T** that defines **operator==(const T&, const T&)**. STL code freely intermixes the use of these two operators, for example, in comparing iterators to control loops over sequences. In the presence of this template, all you have to do is define **operator==** for a class and the library fills in the obvious blanks.

operator>
operator<=
operator>=

The other three template functions flesh out **operator<** in a similar way, to provide compatible definitions of the other three relational operators: **operator>**, **operator<=**, and **operator>=**. Here, however, the result is somewhat more controversial. The definitions provided enforce what is called a *total ordering* on objects of type **T**. In many cases, that's exactly what the programmer expects, but not always.

Some classes may define only a *partial ordering*. A classic example of a partial ordering is a dependency tree. Other classes may choose to define these operators in ways that have little or nothing to do with conventional ordering rules. In those cases, the presence of these template functions is a downright nuisance. They cause ambiguities, or generate surprising code, or support notation that the class designer might find actively distasteful.

These template functions are defined in the namespace `rel_ops`, nested within namespace `std`. They do not participate in overload resolution within the program unless you explicitly request them, as described below.

Functional Description

```
namespace std {
template<class T, class U>
    struct pair;

        // TEMPLATE FUNCTIONS
template<class T, class U>
    pair<T, U> make_pair(const T& x, const U& y);
template<class T, class U>
    bool operator==(const pair<T, U>& x,
        const pair<T, U>& y);
template<class T, class U>
    bool operator!=(const pair<T, U>& x,
        const pair<T, U>& y);
template<class T, class U>
    bool operator<(const pair<T, U>& x,
        const pair<T, U>& y);
template<class T, class U>
    bool operator>(const pair<T, U>& x,
        const pair<T, U>& y);
template<class T, class U>
    bool operator<=(const pair<T, U>& x,
        const pair<T, U>& y);
template<class T, class U>
    bool operator>=(const pair<T, U>& x,
        const pair<T, U>& y);

namespace rel_ops {
    template<class T>
        bool operator!=(const T& x, const T& y);
    template<class T>
        bool operator<=(const T& x, const T& y);
    template<class T>
        bool operator>(const T& x, const T& y);
    template<class T>
        bool operator>=(const T& x, const T& y);
        };
    };
```

Include the STL standard header `<utility>` to define several templates of general use throughout the Standard Template Library.

Four template operators — `operator!=`, `operator<=`, `operator>`, and `operator>=` — define a *total ordering* on pairs of operands of the same type, given definitions of `operator==` and `operator<`.

If an implementation supports namespaces, these template operators are defined in the `rel_ops` namespace, nested within the `std` namespace. If you wish to make use of these template operators, write the declaration:

```
using namespace std::rel_ops;
```

which promotes the template operators into the current namespace.

- **make_pair**

```
template<class T, class U>
    pair<T, U> make_pair(const T& x, const U& y);
```

The template function returns `pair<T, U>(x, y)`.

- **operator!=**

```
template<class T>
    bool operator!=(const T& x, const T& y);
template<class T, class U>
    bool operator!=(const pair<T, U>& x,
        const pair<T, U>& y);
```

The template function returns `!(x == y)`.

- **operator==**

```
template<class T, class U>
    bool operator==(const pair<T, U>& x,
        const pair<T, U>& y);
```

The template function returns `x.first == y.first && x.second == y.second`.

- **operator<**

```
template<class T, class U>
    bool operator<(const pair<T, U>& x,
        const pair<T, U>& y);
```

The template function returns `x.first < y.first || !(y.first < x.first && x.second < y.second)`.

- **operator<=**

```
template<class T>
    bool operator<=(const T& x, const T& y);
template<class T, class U>
    bool operator<=(const pair<T, U>& x,
        const pair<T, U>& y);
```

The template function returns `!(y < x)`.

- **operator>**

```
template<class T>
    bool operator>(const T& x, const T& y);
template<class T, class U>
    bool operator>(const pair<T, U>& x,
        const pair<T, U>& y);
```

The template function returns `y < x`.

- **operator>=**

```
template<class T>
    bool operator>=(const T& x, const T& y);
template<class T, class U>
    bool operator>=(const pair<T, U>& x,
        const pair<T, U>& y);
```

The template function returns `!(x < y)`.

▫ **pair**

```
template<class T, class U>
    struct pair {
    typedef T first_type;
    typedef U second_type
    T first;
    U second;
    pair();
    pair(const T& x, const U& y);
    template<class V, class W>
        pair(const pair<V, W>& pr);
    };
```

The template class stores a pair of objects, `first`, of type `T`, and `second`, of type `U`. The type definition `first_type`, is the same as the template parameter `T`, while `second_type`, is the same as the template parameter `U`.

The first (default) constructor initializes `first` to `T()` and `second` to `U()`. The second constructor initializes `first` to `x` and `second` to `y`. The third (template) constructor initializes `first` to `pr.first` and `second` to `pr.second`. `T` and `U` each need supply only a default constructor, single-argument constructor, and a destructor.

Using `<utility>`

Chances are good that, if you include *any* STL header in a translation unit, `<utility>` will be included as well. You include it explicitly only if you need one or more of the definitions it provides and you can't count on another STL header to drag it in. But chances are also good that you *will* need one or more of the entities defined in this header. If you get a translator diagnostic that, say, `pair` is undefined, remember that you can satisfy the need cheaply by including this header.

pair **make_pair** To summarize very briefly, the template class `pair` is a convenient vehicle for returning a pair of related values on a function call. If neither of the two types is a const type, you can generate a `pair` object, storing the values `x` and `y`, on the fly by calling `make_pair(x, y)`. Otherwise, you should favor the explicit constructor call `pair<T, U>(x, y)`.

As we mentioned earlier in passing, the definition of template class `pair` includes a member template constructor:

```
template<class U1, class U2>
    pair(const pair<U1, U2>& x)
    : first(x.first), second(x.second) {}
```

This constructor can pave over some of the problems with `make_pair`. It lets you assign the result of the call `make_pair(x, y)` to an object of class `pair<T, U>` so long as the respective component types are assignment compatible. The function doesn't have to get the types exactly right. But handy as it is, this constructor is not always available with current compilers. For maximum portability, you should favor the less graceful constructor `pair<T, U>(x, y)`.

Figure 2.1: `utility`

```
// utility standard header
#ifndef UTILITY_
#define UTILITY_
#include <iosfwd>
namespace std {
          // TEMPLATE STRUCT pair
template<class T1, class T2> struct pair {
     typedef T1 first_type;
     typedef T2 second_type;
     pair()
          : first(T1()), second(T2()) {}
     pair(const T1& V1, const T2& V2)
          : first(V1), second(V2) {}
     template<class U1, class U2>
          pair(const pair<U1, U2>& X)
          : first(X.first), second(X.second) {}
     T1 first;
     T2 second;
     };

          // pair TEMPLATE OPERATORS
template<class T1, class T2> inline
     bool operator==(const pair<T1, T2>& X,
          const pair<T1, T2>& Y)
     {return (X.first == Y.first && X.second == Y.second); }
template<class T1, class T2> inline
     bool operator!=(const pair<T1, T2>& X,
          const pair<T1, T2>& Y)
     {return (!(X == Y)); }
template<class T1, class T2> inline
     bool operator<(const pair<T1, T2>& X,
          const pair<T1, T2>& Y)
     {return (X.first < Y.first ||
          !(Y.first < X.first) && X.second < Y.second); }
template<class T1, class T2> inline
     bool operator>(const pair<T1, T2>& X,
          const pair<T1, T2>& Y)
     {return (Y < X); }
template<class T1, class T2> inline
     bool operator<=(const pair<T1, T2>& X,
          const pair<T1, T2>& Y)
     {return (!(Y < X)); }
template<class T1, class T2> inline
     bool operator>=(const pair<T1, T2>& X,
          const pair<T1, T2>& Y)
     {return (!(X < Y)); }
template<class T1, class T2> inline
     pair<T1, T2> make_pair(const T1& X, const T2& Y)
     {return (pair<T1, T2>(X, Y)); }

          // TEMPLATE OPERATORS
     namespace rel_ops {
template<class T> inline
     bool operator!=(const T& X, const T& Y)
     {return (!(X == Y)); }
```

Figure 2.2: `utility`

```
template<class T> inline
     bool operator>(const T& X, const T& Y)
     {return (Y < X); }
template<class T> inline
     bool operator<=(const T& X, const T& Y)
     {return (!(Y < X)); }
template<class T> inline
     bool operator>=(const T& X, const T& Y)
     {return (!(X < Y)); }
     }
} /* namespace std */
#endif /* UTILITY_ */
```

□

`operator!=` `operator>` `operator<=` `operator>=`

If you define equality comparisons (`operator==(const T&)`) between two objects of a class `T` that you define, then add to your code the using directive described on page 29 earlier in this chapter, you get the obvious definition of inequality comparisons (`operator!=(const T&)`) for free. To define a total ordering (see page 28) on objects of class `T`, you need define only the comparison for less than (`operator<(const T&)`).

It is not clear how useful these four template operators are in real life, however. The lookup rules for overloaded operators have become quite convoluted with the introduction of namespaces. Not all compilers seem to get them exactly right. Those that do may well not do what you want. We suggest that you not rely on the definitions in namespace `std::relops` in code that you write. You are probably better off replicating these templates in the namespace you use for the rest of your code.

Implementing <utility>

`utility`

Figure 2.1 shows the file `utility`, which implements the header `<utility>`. We've discussed its few small peculiarities earlier in this chapter. Otherwise, there's not much to it.

Testing <utility>

`tdefines.c`

Figure 2.3 shows the file `tutility.c`. It is fairly simple, since the header it tests is rather small and has little to test in the bargain. Mostly, it checks for the overt presence of all the definitions. If all goes well, the program prints:

```
SUCCESS testing <utility>
```

and takes a normal exit.

Figure 2.3: `tutility.c`

```
// test <utility>
#include <assert.h>
#include <iostream>
#include <utility>
using namespace std;

typedef pair<int, char> Pair_ic;
Pair_ic p0;

class Int {
public:
     Int(int v)
          : val(v) {}
     bool operator==(Int x) const
          {return (val == x.val); }
     bool operator<(Int x) const
          {return (val < x.val); }
private:
     int val;
     };

     // TEST <utility>
int main()
     {Pair_ic p1 = p0, p2(3, 'a');

     // TEST pair
     assert(p1.first == 0);
     assert(p1.second == 0);
     assert(p2.first == 3);
     assert(p2.second == 'a');
     assert(p2 == make_pair((Pair_ic::first_type)3,
          (Pair_ic::second_type)'a'));
     assert(p2 < make_pair((Pair_ic::first_type)4,
          (Pair_ic::second_type)'a'));
     assert(p2 < make_pair((Pair_ic::first_type)3,
          (Pair_ic::second_type)'b'));
     assert(p1 != p2);
     assert(p2 > p1);
     assert(p2 <= p2);
     assert(p2 >= p2);

     // TEST rel_ops
     using namespace std::rel_ops;
     Int a(2), b(3);
     assert(a == a);
     assert(a < b);
     assert(a != b);
     assert(b > a);
     assert(a <= b);
     assert(b >= a);
     cout << "SUCCESS testing <utility>" << endl;
     return (0); }
```
□

Exercises

Exercise 2.1 Write the template class `trio<class T, class U, class V>`, modeled after template class `pair`, that stores three objects of arbitrary types.

Exercise 2.2 How can you achieve the same effect as template class `trio`, from the previous exercise, using just template class `pair`?

Exercise 2.3 It is often desirable to construct a `pair<T, U>` object where either `T` or `U` is a const type. Does the following definition let you do so? If not, why not?

```
template<class T, class U> inline
    pair<T, U> make_pair(T& x, U& y)
    {return (pair<T, U>(x, y)); }
```

Exercise 2.4 [Harder] Describe a reasonable coding situation where the expression `x.first < y.first || !(y.first < x.first) && x.second < y.second` is not the same as `x.first < y.first || x.first == y.first && x.second < y.second`.

Exercise 2.5 [Very hard] How can you use template function `operator<=(const T& x, const T& y)` throughout the Standard Template Library without having it affect classes defined outside the library?

Chapter 3: `<iterator>`

Background

As the name implies, the header `<iterator>` provides lots of machinery used by iterators. Nothing in this header is very complicated, but it contains lots of details that need explaining. Moreover, iterators come in five basic flavors, or categories, not counting object pointers, which can serve as any category of iterator. So you will find that many of the things presented here also come in as many as half a dozen different versions.

Because the header is so large, we present it in pieces. Many of the pieces serve disjoint needs, anyway.

iterator properties The first order of business is to impose some order on all these categories of iterators. In writing algorithms, it is often useful to know several properties of a given iterator `X`. The most widely asked questions are:

- What *category* (output, input, forward, etc.) does `X` occupy?
- What *element type* (usually written `T`) does `*X` designate?
- What *distance type* (usually written `Dist`) does `N` have to be to count all the elements that can be designated by incrementing `X` repeatedly?

Remember that STL consists almost exclusively of templates. All a template can know is the type or types for which it is specialized — and a few types derived therefrom. If you want to convey this sort of extra information, you have two basic choices. You can add template parameters to smuggle in the information, or you can package the extra information as part of the type of the iterator itself.

`iterator` Clearly, the second approach is more elegant, if you can pull it off. It turns out that you can, mostly. The easy way is to derive any iterator classes you define from a base class with the necessary properties. Template class `iterator` defines the prototypical base class:

```
template<class C, class T, class Dist = ptrdiff_t
    class Pt = T *, class Rt = T&>
    struct iterator {
    typedef C iterator_category;
    typedef T value_type;
    typedef Dist difference_type;
    typedef Pt pointer;
    typedef Rt reference;
    };
```

The only thing special about this template class is the names of the member types it defines. You don't need it in an iterator class that defines the member types another way. We will describe the uses of these five member types throughout this chapter.

iterator tags For the first template parameter, which defines the iterator category, you must use one of the defined *iterator tags:*

```
struct output_iterator_tag {};
struct input_iterator_tag {};
struct forward_iterator_tag
    : public input_iterator_tag {};
struct bidirectional_iterator_tag
    : public forward_iterator_tag {};
struct random_access_iterator_tag
    : public bidirectional_iterator_tag {};
```

These are simply empty structures used to convey unique types, with no accompanying values to construct or destroy. The inheritance hierarchy replicates the hierarchy of read-only iterators shown on page 25. That proves to be handy when you overload a function on different iterator categories, as we discuss later in this chapter, on page 82.

Thus, for example, you build a forward iterator on the basic structure:

```
class My_it
    : public iterator<forward_iterator_tag, char, long>
    {..... }
```

An algorithm can determine the iterator category from the type `My_it::iterator_category`, the type of an element from `My_it::value_type`, and the distance type from `My_it::distance_type`. This particular form of iterator `My_it` can march through a binary file with elements of type `char`. Arithmetic on `My_it` iterators, being of type `long` in this particular example, can follow much the same rules as for the ancient C library functions `fseek` and `ftell`, which work with `long` offsets into a file.

Note, by the way, that an output iterator conventionally has the base class `iterator<output_iterator, void, void, void, void>`. It has no need to deliver up the parameter types `T` or `Dist`. You can only store an element through an output iterator — you can't read it back. And you can't do arithmetic on such iterators. So all that matters is the type of the iterator category.

iterator categories Now we can explore how to answer the first of the three questions posed above, given just this small hook. Determining the iterator category typically matters when you have more than one way to implement an algorithm. Here's a simple example from the STL header `<algorithm>`. The template function `reverse` reverses the elements in a sequence by swapping pairs of elements from the outside in. It can do so with two bidirectional iterators, using the template function `iter_swap` to do the actual swaps:

```
template<class BidIt> inline
    void reverse(BidIt first, BidIt last)
    {for (; first != last && first != --last; ++first)
        iter_swap(first, last); }
```

But you can implement the code a tad faster if you know the iterators are actually random access:

```
template<class RanIt> inline
    void reverse(RanIt first, RanIt last)
    {for (; first < last; ++first)
         iter_swap(first, --last); }
```

If all iterators are based on the classes shown above, you can indulge in a small bit of trickery to choose wisely between these two alternatives. Just use the iterator category to select among overloaded definitions of the template function **Reverse**:

```
template<class BidIt> inline
    void reverse(BidIt first, BidIt last)
    {Reverse(first, last,
         typename BidIt::iterator_category()); }

template<class BidIt> inline
    void Reverse(BidIt first, BidIt last,
         bidirectional_iterator_tag)
    {for (; first != last && first != --last; ++first)
         iter_swap(first, last); }

template<class RanIt> inline
    void Reverse(RanIt first, RanIt last,
         random_access_iterator_tag)
    {for (; first < last; ++first)
         iter_swap(first, --last); }
```

The specialization of **reverse** now translates to a call to some flavor of **Reverse**. The flavor chosen depends on the definition of the member type **iterator_category** for the iterator, which supplies the type of the template parameter. In the function call, the constructor **BidIt::iterator_category()** returns a nebbish object of one of the iterator tag types.

The net result is that the template specialization machinery is commandeered to act as a kind of translation-time *switch* statement. A moderately smart translator should even be able to optimize away the extra function call and dummy argument setup. Neat, huh?

Well, it's not quite neat enough. STL prides itself on blending well with existing coding practice. In particular, it permits the use of object pointers practically anywhere an iterator is permitted. The scheme shown above doesn't accommodate iterators that are simply pointers. Moreover, there's no simple way to extend the definition of **Reverse** to handle an open-ended set of object-pointer types. A bit more machinery is called for.

We will, in fact, describe *two* distinct sets of machinery to solve this problem. The first set represents the ideal — it is now called for by the C++ Standard. It has the unfortunate drawback that it requires a language feature that is not universally available at this writing. The second set is pragmatic — it has been used to make STL work since its earliest days.

iterator_traits The official solution is to introduce yet another template class, called **iterator_traits**. Its sole template parameter is the iterator type whose properties you wish to inquire about.

```
template<class It>
    struct iterator_traits {
    typedef typename It::iterator_category iterator_category;
    typedef typename It::value_type value_type;
    typedef typename It::distance_type distance_type;
    typedef typename It::pointer pointer;
    typedef typename It::reference reference;
    };
```

On the face of it, this doesn't add much. All the new class seems to do is echo the type definitions of its template parameter, which is presumably based on template class **iterator**. But the new template class offers an important opportunity, to introduce a *partial specialization* that handles all pointer types:

```
template<class T>
    struct iterator_traits<T *> {
    typedef random_access_iterator_tag iterator_category;
    typedef T value_type;
    typedef ptrdiff_t distance_type;
    typedef T *pointer;
    typedef T& reference;
    };
```

(The library also contains a slightly different partial specialization for const pointers.) This definition decrees that all pointers are random-access iterators, with distance type **ptrdiff_t**. You may recall that the C Standard established **ptrdiff_t** as the integer type that represents the difference between any two object pointers pointing into the same array. It is a typedef defined in the Standard C header **<stddef.h>**.

Now we can rewrite template function **reverse** as:

```
template<class BidIt> inline
    void reverse(BidIt first, BidIt last)
    {Reverse(first, last, typename iterator_traits<BidIt>::
        iterator_category()); }
```

If **BidIt** is a class based on template class **iterator**, the generic form of the template class **iterator_traits** is specialized. The member type **iterator_category** is then defined in terms of **BidIt::iterator_category**. But if **BidIt** is a pointer type, the partial specialization is specialized instead. The member type **iterator_category** is then decreed to be **random_access_iterator_tag**.

Iter_cat Partial template specialization is not universally supported at present, however. We need machinery that does the job reliably today. Fortunately, function overloading supplies the necessary magic. We define the template function **Iter_cat** in two forms:

```
template<class C, class T, class Dist> inline
    C Iter_cat(const iterator<C, T, Dist>&)
    {C x;
    return (x); }

template<class T> inline
    random_access_iterator_tag Iter_cat(const T *)
    {random_access_iterator_tag x;
    return (x); }
```

As an aside, in the original implementation of STL this template function is called `iterator_category`. That name is no longer reserved in the C++ Standard, so we use instead a name reserved to implementors (at least when the leading underscore is present). Also, the two functions can, in principle, simply return the result of a constructor call, as in `C()`. The more long-winded form used here sidesteps some soft spots in existing compilers. The code in this book, like most working C++ code, has occasional curiosities like this as a practical necessity.

Now we can rewrite template function `reverse` as:

```
template<class BidIt> inline
    void reverse(BidIt first, BidIt last)
    {Reverse(first, last, Iter_cat(first)); }
```

If `BidIt` is a class based on template class `iterator`, the first form of the template function `Iter_cat` is called. The function returns an object of the same type as the first template parameter for `iterator`, which is the same as the member type `BidIt::iterator_category`. But if `BidIt` is a pointer type, the second form is called instead. The function unequivocally returns an object of type `random_access_iterator_tag`.

The code in this book uses template function `Iter_cat`, rather than the template class `iterator_traits`, so that it is more easily adapted to compilers still in transition.

Val_type Now to answer the remaining two questions posed much earlier. If you want to determine the element type `T` associated with an iterator of type `It`, you can in principle write the type name `iterator_traits<It>::value_type`. But this once again relies on the presence of partial specialization to work properly when `It` is an object pointer type. So in practice, the code in this book uses another template function. This one is called `Val_type`. If a compiler supports partial specialization, you can write this template function simply as:

```
template<class It> inline
    typename iterator_traits<It>::value_type *Val_type(It)
    {return (0); }
```

If a compiler does not support partial specialization, however, you can get the same effect with a pair of overloads:

```
template<class C, class T, class D,
    class Pt, class Rt> inline
    T *Val_type(iterator, T, D, Pt, Rt)
    {return (0); }

template<class T> inline
    T *Val_type(const T *)
    {return (0); }
```

(The older name, no longer permitted by the C++ Standard, is `value_type`. A commercial implementation replaces this with something like `_Val_type`.)

None of the versions of this function returns an object of type `T`, which is the actual type of interest. Doing so could cause all sorts of problems with types that describe very large objects, or that have "interesting" side effects during construction and destruction, or that just plain take a long time to manipulate and copy about. So instead, the functions each return a *pointer* to the desired type. That's enough of a hook for the templates to work their magic.

Here, for example, is how the template function **iter_swap**, used by **reverse** in earlier examples, is implemented:

```
template<class FwdIt1, class FwdIt2> inline
    void iter_swap(FwdIt1 x, FwdIt2 y)
    {Iter_swap(x, y, Val_type(x)); }

template<class FwdIt1, class FwdIt2, class T> inline
    void Iter_swap(FwdIt1 x, FwdIt2 y, T *)
    {T Tmp = *x;
    *x = *y, *y = Tmp; }
```

To swap two values, you need a temporary object to hold one value for a time. So **iter_swap** calls a secret template function **Iter_swap**, adding an extra argument. The **T *** return type of **value_type** matches the **T *** parameter type of **Iter_swap**. Thus, the element type **T** is smuggled from the iterator base (or extracted from the object pointer used as an iterator) and delivered to where it is needed in the working function.

Dist_type Similarly, if you want to determine the type used to measure the distance between two iterators of type **It**, you can in principle simply write the type name **iterator_traits<It>::distance_type**. In practice, the code in this book uses the template function **Dist_type**. The version that uses partial specialization looks like:

```
template<class It> inline
    typename iterator_traits::difference_type
        *Dist_type(It)
    {return (0); }
```

while the alternative that does not use partial specialization looks like:

```
template<class C, class T, class D,
    class Pt, class Rt> inline
    D *Dist_type(iterator<C, T, D, Pt, Rt>)
    {return (0); }
template<class T> inline
    ptrdiff_t *Dist_type(const T *)
    {return (0); }
```

(The older name is **distance_type**.)

advance **distance** Two other operations are often useful, if not always expressed in operator notation, across nearly all categories of iterators:

- **X += N** adds the **Dist** object **N** to the iterator **X**. **N** can be negative only for a bidirectional or random-access iterator.
- **N = X2 - X1** assigns to **N** the difference between the two iterators **X2** and **X1**. **N** can be negative only for random-access iterators.

These operations make no sense for arbitrary output iterators, of course. For input iterators they *barely* make sense — doing either computation leaves an input iterator useless for anything else. STL includes them more for completeness than for general utility.

Operator notation like this is convenient, but historically STL has made little use of it. The forms `X += N` and `X2 - X1` are required only for random-access iterators. They cannot be fully supported by the weaker iterator categories. The basic operations on iterators must take amortized constant time — not time proportional to the distance between two iterators, for example. So it is arguably misleading even to define operations that take linear time. Instead, the algorithms in STL make use of two template functions:

```
template<class InIt, class Dist> inline
    void advance(InIt& p, Dist n);

template<class InIt> inline
    typename iterator_traits<InIt>::distance_type
    distance(InIt first, InIt last);
```

The first essentially computes `p += n`, the second returns `n = last - first`, but only for iterator categories for which it makes sense to do so. And if one of these functions takes more than constant time for a given iterator category, that extra time complexity is taken into account in determining the time complexity of the algorithm in which the function is called.

Template class **distance** also illustrates one of those situations where the introduction of **iterator_traits** pays off. The template function **Dist_type** can't deliver up its answer in time to define the return value of a template function, as is required by the definition of **distance** given above. So in this implementation, we define **distance** as returning type **ptrdiff_t**. But just to play safe, we consistently use in its place the template function **Distance**, declared as:

```
template<class InIt, class D> inline
    void Distance(InIt first, InIt last, D n0);
```

It computes `n0 += last - first`, in an object of the desired distance type **D**. (**Distance** is a renaming of the older version of template function **distance**.)

Thus, in this implementation we can avoid the need for a translator that supports partial template specialization, except for the template classes that specifically make use of this language feature.

specialized iterators The remainder of header **<iterator>** defines an assortment of specialized iterators:

- reverse iterators
- insertion iterators
- stream iterators
- stream buffer iterators

reverse iterators A reverse iterator, as its name implies, steps backward through a sequence when you step the iterator forward. Equally, it steps forward through a sequence when you step the iterator backward. It is a handy tool when you find it useful to sometimes operate on a sequence in reverse order — no need to actually reverse the sequence, then reverse it again later, just to perform the backward operation.

reverse_ iterator Template class reverse_iterator is a random-access iterator declared as:

```
template<class RanIt>
    class reverse_iterator;
```

Here RanIt is the underlying random-access iterator type that you want to run backwards. So you might define:

```
typedef reverse_iterator<char *> Revptr;
```

to define an iterator type Revptr that walks backward through an array of char.

The template class stores just one object, the underlying iterator of class RanIt. Anyone can obtain the value of this object by calling the member function base(). A class derived from reverse_iterator can access it as the protected object current.

The template class reverse_iterator is an excellent prototype for any random-access iterator class you choose to develop, by the way. It supplies all the needed member functions. It is also accompanied, in header <iterator>, by all the template operators you need to define for it as well. We will make use of this particular iterator within the container template classes vector (Chapter 10: <vector>) and deque (Chapter 12: <deque>).

reverse bidirectional iterators Once upon a time, there was also a template class reverse_bidirectional_iterator. Its obvious function was to turn a bidirectional iterator into a reverse iterator. Late in the standardization process, however, this template class was eliminated. The Committee decided that template class reverse_iterator could do the same job.

It took a language change to make this substitution possible. A random-access iterator defines member functions, such as operator+= for adding an integer offset to the iterator, that a bidirectional iterator cannot support. Many older compilers would check all template member functions for valid expressions even if the member functions were never actually called. The Committee eventually made clear that such member functions should be checked only if called. The change solves a similar problem with iterator template classes that define operator->, which makes sense only for an iterator that designates a class, struct, or union type.

As with any change, however, it takes a while for compilers to catch up. Some compilers still complain, making reverse_iterator unsuitable for use with bidirectional iterators. So the implementation presented here retains template class reverse_bidirectional_iterator under a new name, as Revbidit. You will not see this template class again, in this presentation. But some compilers make use of it in the container template classes list (Chapter 11: <list>), set and multiset (Chapter 13: <set>) and map and multimap (Chapter 14: <map>).

We retain template class `Revbidit` here for yet another reason. It is an excellent prototype for any bidirectional iterator class you choose to develop. It supplies all the needed member functions, including all the template operators required for a bidirectional iterator.

insertion iterators You often have occasion to generate a sequence of elements in one pass from beginning to end. An output iterator is the ideal agent for disposing of the generated elements. It has the weakest semantic requirements of any of the iterator categories that let you write a sequence. Those weak requirements permit considerable latitude in writing output iterators.

Say, for example, you want to insert the generated sequence in some container object `c` of type `Cont`. The container template classes defined in STL have a number of uniform properties you can exploit. In particular:

- Every container defines its element type as `Cont::value_type` and the type of an iterator over the controlled sequence as `Cont::iterator`.
- Any container that supports constant-time insertions at the end of its controlled sequence defines the member function:

  `C.push_back(Cont::value_type&)`
- Any container that supports constant-time insertions at the beginning of its controlled sequence defines the member function:

  `C.push_front(Cont::value_type&)`
- Any container that supports constant-time insertions before an arbitrary element designated by an iterator defines the member function:

  `C.insert(Cont::value_type&, Cont::iterator)`

The last function returns an iterator that designates the inserted element.

Of course, nothing prevents you from defining your own containers that follow these rules. On the contrary — STL encourages you to follow its models so that your additions integrate well with the rest of STL.

The header `<iterator>` defines several template classes that use these member functions:

- `back_insert_iterator` — `back_insert_iterator<Cont>` is an output iterator that appends generated elements to a container object of type `Cont`.
- `front_insert_iterator` — `front_insert_iterator<Cont>` is an output iterator that prepends generated elements. (Yes, the generated elements end up in reverse order at the beginning of the controlled sequence.)
- `insert_iterator` — `insert_iterator<Cont, Iter>` is an output iterator that inserts generated elements before an element that you specify with an iterator.

Each of these template classes stores a reference to the container object, with the protected name `container`. The last one also stores the insertion point in an object with the protected name `iter`.

The header `<iterator>` also defines three related template functions:

- `back_inserter` — `back_inserter(Cont&)` returns a `back_insert_iterator` for the container argument.

front_inserter
- **front_inserter(Cont&)** returns a **front_insert_iterator** for the container argument.

inserter
- **inserter(Cont&, Iter)** returns an **insert_iterator** for the container and iterator arguments.

These provide a handy way to concoct insertion iterators on the fly.

stream iterators If you can deliver a generated sequence to a container, using some clever form of output iterator, you should certainly be able to insert the sequence into an output stream, using some other clever form. Equally, you should be able to obtain a sequence of elements from an input stream, using some clever form of input iterator. Indeed, that is the case.

Say you have elements of type **T** for which are defined a stream *extractor:*

```
istream& operator>>(istream&, T&);
```

That's all you need to read characters from an input stream such as **cin**, convert them to a value of type **T**, and store the value in an object **X**, just by writing:

```
cin >> X;
```

istream_iterator The template class **istream_iterator<T>** does this for you, in the guise of obtaining an element from a sequence using an input iterator. (The template class has additional parameters, for dealing with fancier input streams, but the defaults work fine with the widely used **istream**.) If you write:

```
typedef istream_iterator<int, ptrdiff_t> Int_init;
Int_init int_in(cin);
```

then the expression ***int_in++** extracts an **int** from **cin** and delivers it as the value of the expression.

You should, of course, first test that such a value is available in the input stream. The proper way to do so is to compare **int_it** for equality with the *end-of-sequence* value that signals end of file. (See page 21.) The default constructor always yields an object with this end-of-sequence value. Thus, you can write:

```
Int_init first(cin), last;
```

and proceed to extract elements from a stream until you reach end of file, by writing either the stylized loop:

```
for (p = first; p != last; ++p)
    <process>(*p);
```

or its variant:

```
while (first != last)
    <process>(*first++);
```

ostream_iterator The header **<iterator>** also defines the template class **ostream_iterator**. It defines an output iterator for inserting elements into an output stream. Say you have elements of type **T** for which are defined a stream *inserter:*

```
ostream& operator<<(ostream&, T);
```

That's all you need to convert a value of type `T` to a character sequence and write the sequence to an output stream such as `cout`, just by writing:

```
cout << X;
```

The template class `ostream_iterator` does this for you, in the guise of storing a generated element into a sequence using an output iterator. (Once again, the template class has additional parameters, for dealing with fancier output streams, but the defaults work fine with the widely used `ostream`.) If you write:

```
typedef ostream_iterator<int> Int_outit;
Int_outit int_out(cout);
```

then the expression `*int_out++ = X` inserts the `int` value `X` into `cout`. Even better, the declaration:

```
Int_outit int_out(cout, " ");
```

appends a space to each inserted value, so the fields generated from the inserted values don't all run together.

stream buffer iterators A late addition to STL is a pair of iterators for inserting and extracting elements of type `E` (typically of type `char`) directly to and from a *stream buffer.* The template class `basic_streambuf<E, T>` defines the stream-buffer objects that mediate transfers between an actual stream, such as a file, and program storage. It is a templatized version of the older iostreams class `streambuf`, which performs a function analogous to the Standard C library type `FILE`. Here, `T` stands for a "traits" class, which supplies assorted information about the element type `E`.

We won't delve into all the intricacies of iostreams as it has been standardized. That is a large topic unto itself. Suffice it to say that the template class `istreambuf_iterator<E, T>` plays a crucial role in this new machinery. *Every* character read from an input stream is obtained through the intermediary of an input iterator of this type. Similarly, every character written to an output stream is delivered through an output iterator of type `ostreambuf_iterator<E, T>`.

The machinery defined in the header `<iterator>` is used throughout STL. You should cultivate enough familiarity with it to use it comfortably. It is hard to write good algorithms without making heavy use of the iterator properties outlined at the beginning of this chapter. It is amazing how often the insertion iterators come in handy when you muck about with containers. And if you perform truly serious work with iostreams, you can't avoid working with the stream-buffer iterators at the very least.

But this header has an equally important use, as we emphasize one last time. Of the five categories of iterators, only forward iterators have no prototype defined within this header. All the others have excellent models for you to imitate and elaborate upon. Use them.

Functional Description

```
namespace std {
struct input_iterator_tag;
struct output_iterator_tag;
struct forward_iterator_tag;
struct bidirectional_iterator_tag;
struct random_access_iterator_tag;

        // TEMPLATE CLASSES
template<class C, class T, class Dist,
    class Pt, class Rt>
    struct iterator;
template<class It>
    struct iterator_traits;
template<class T>
    struct iterator_traits<T *>
template<class RanIt>
    class reverse_iterator;
template<class Cont>
    class back_insert_iterator;
template<class Cont>
    class front_insert_iterator;
template<class Cont>
    class insert_iterator;
template<class U, class E, class T, class Dist>
    class istream_iterator;
template<class U, class E, class T>
    class ostream_iterator;
template<class E, class T>
    class istreambuf_iterator;
template<class E, class T>
    class ostreambuf_iterator;

        // TEMPLATE FUNCTIONS
template<class RanIt>
    bool operator==(
        const reverse_iterator<RanIt>& lhs,
        const reverse_iterator<RanIt>& rhs);
template<class U, class E, class T, class Dist>
    bool operator==(
        const istream_iterator<U, E, T, Dist>& lhs,
        const istream_iterator<U, E, T, Dist>& rhs);
template<class E, class T>
    bool operator==(
        const istreambuf_iterator<E, T>& lhs,
        const istreambuf_iterator<E, T>& rhs);
template<class RanIt>
    bool operator!=(
        const reverse_iterator<RanIt>& lhs,
        const reverse_iterator<RanIt>& rhs);
template<class U, class E, class T, class Dist>
    bool operator!=(
        const istream_iterator<U, E, T, Dist>& lhs,
        const istream_iterator<U, E, T, Dist>& rhs);
template<class E, class T>
    bool operator!=(
        const istreambuf_iterator<E, T>& lhs,
        const istreambuf_iterator<E, T>& rhs);
template<class RanIt>
    bool operator<(
```

```
            const reverse_iterator<RanIt>& lhs,
            const reverse_iterator<RanIt>& rhs);
template<class RanIt>
    bool operator>(
        const reverse_iterator<RanIt>& lhs,
        const reverse_iterator<RanIt>& rhs);
template<class RanIt>
    bool operator<=(
        const reverse_iterator<RanIt>& lhs,
        const reverse_iterator<RanIt>& rhs);
template<class RanIt>
    bool operator>=(
        const reverse_iterator<RanIt>& lhs,
        const reverse_iterator<RanIt>& rhs);
template<class RanIt>
    Dist operator-(
        const reverse_iterator<RanIt>& lhs,
        const reverse_iterator<RanIt>& rhs);
template<class RanIt>
    reverse_iterator<RanIt> operator+(
        Dist n,
        const reverse_iterator<RanIt>& rhs);
template<class Cont>
    back_insert_iterator<Cont> back_inserter(Cont& x);
template<class Cont>
    front_insert_iterator<Cont> front_inserter(Cont& x);
template<class Cont, class Iter>
    insert_iterator<Cont> inserter(Cont& x, Iter it);
template<class InIt, class Dist>
    void advance(InIt& it, Dist n);
template<class Init>
    iterator_traits<InIt>::difference_type
        distance(InIt first, InIt last);
    };
```

Include the STL standard header `<iterator>` to define a number of classes, template classes, and template functions that aid in the declaration and manipulation of iterators.

▫ advance

```
template<class InIt, class Dist>
    void advance(InIt& it, Dist n);
```

The template function effectively advances `it` by incrementing it `n` times. If `InIt` is a random-access iterator type, the function evaluates the expression `it += n`. Otherwise, it performs each increment by evaluating `++it`. If `InIt` is an input or forward iterator type, `n` must not be negative.

▫ back_insert_iterator

```
template<class Cont>
    class back_insert_iterator
        : public iterator<output_iterator_tag,
            void, void, void, void> {
public:
    typedef Cont container_type;
    typedef typename Cont::reference reference;
    typedef typename Cont::value_type value_type;
    explicit back_insert_iterator(Cont& x);
    back_insert_iterator&
        operator=(typename Cont::const_reference val);
```

```
    back_insert_iterator& operator*();
    back_insert_iterator& operator++();
    back_insert_iterator operator++(int);
protected:
    Cont *container;
    };
```

The template class describes an output iterator object. It inserts elements into a container of type `Cont`, which it accesses via the protected pointer object it stores called `container`. The container must define:

- the member type `const_reference`, which is the type of a constant reference to an element of the sequence controlled by the container
- the member type `reference`, which is the type of a reference to an element of the sequence controlled by the container
- the member type `value_type`, which is the type of an element of the sequence controlled by the container
- the member function `push_back(value_type c)`, which appends a new element with value `c` to the end of the sequence

back_insert_iterator::back_insert_iterator

```
explicit back_insert_iterator(Cont& x);
```

The constructor initializes `container` with `&x`.

back_insert_iterator::container_type

```
typedef Cont container_type;
```

The type is a synonym for the template parameter `Cont`.

back_insert_iterator::operator*

```
back_insert_iterator& operator*();
```

The member function returns `*this`.

back_insert_iterator::operator++

```
back_insert_iterator& operator++();
back_insert_iterator operator++(int);
```

The member functions both return `*this`.

back_insert_iterator::operator=

```
back_insert_iterator&
    operator=(typename Cont::const_reference val);
```

The member function evaluates `container. push_back(val)`, then returns `*this`.

back_insert_iterator::reference

```
typedef typename Cont::reference reference;
```

The type describes a reference to an element of the sequence controlled by the associated container.

back_insert_iterator::value_type

```
typedef typename Cont::value_type value_type;
```

The type describes the elements of the sequence controlled by the associated container.

▫ **back_inserter**

```
template<class Cont>
    back_insert_iterator<Cont> back_inserter(Cont& x);
```

The template function returns `back_insert_iterator<Cont>(x)`.

▫ **bidirectional_iterator_tag**

```
struct bidirectional_iterator_tag
    : public forward_iterator_tag {
    };
```

The type is the same as `iterator<It>::iterator_category` when `It` describes an object that can serve as a bidirectional iterator.

▫ **distance**

```
template<class Init>
    typename iterator_traits<InIt>::difference_type
        distance(InIt first, InIt last);
```

The template function sets a count `n` to zero. It then effectively advances `first` and increments `n` until `first == last`. If `InIt` is a random-access iterator type, the function evaluates the expression `n += last - first`. Otherwise, it performs each iterator increment by evaluating `++first`.

▫ **forward_iterator_tag**

```
struct forward_iterator_tag
    : public input_iterator_tag {
    };
```

The type is the same as `iterator<It>::iterator_category` when `It` describes an object that can serve as a forward iterator.

▫ **front_insert_iterator**

```
template<class Cont>
    class front_insert_iterator
        : public iterator<output_iterator_tag,
            void, void, void, void> {
public:
    typedef Cont container_type;
    typedef typename Cont::reference reference;
    typedef typename Cont::value_type value_type;
    explicit front_insert_iterator(Cont& x);
    front_insert_iterator&
        operator=(typename Cont::const_reference val);
    front_insert_iterator& operator*();
    front_insert_iterator& operator++();
    front_insert_iterator operator++(int);
protected:
    Cont *container;
    };
```

The template class describes an output iterator object. It inserts elements into a container of type `Cont`, which it accesses via the protected pointer object it stores called `container`. The container must define:

- the member type **`const_reference`**, which is the type of a constant reference to an element of the sequence controlled by the container
- the member type **`reference`**, which is the type of a reference to an element of the sequence controlled by the container
- the member type **`value_type`**, which is the type of an element of the sequence controlled by the container
- the member function **`push_front(value_type c)`**, which prepends a new element with value **`c`** to the beginning of the sequence

▫ **`front_insert_iterator::container_type`**

```
typedef Cont container_type;
```

The type is a synonym for the template parameter **`Cont`**.

▫ **`front_insert_iterator::front_insert_iterator`**

```
explicit front_insert_iterator(Cont& x);
```

The constructor initializes **`container`** with **`&x`**.

▫ **`front_insert_iterator::operator*`**

```
front_insert_iterator& operator*();
```

The member function returns **`*this`**.

▫ **`front_insert_iterator::operator++`**

```
front_insert_iterator& operator++();
front_insert_iterator operator++(int);
```

The member functions both return **`*this`**.

▫ **`front_insert_iterator::operator=`**

```
front_insert_iterator&
    operator=(typename Cont::const_reference val);
```

The member function evaluates **`container. push_front(val)`**, then returns **`*this`**.

▫ **`front_insert_iterator::reference`**

```
typedef typename Cont::reference reference;
```

The type describes a reference to an element of the sequence controlled by the associated container.

▫ **`front_insert_iterator::value_type`**

```
typedef typename Cont::value_type value_type;
```

The type describes the elements of the sequence controlled by the associated container.

▫ **`front_inserter`**

```
template<class Cont>
    front_insert_iterator<Cont> front_inserter(Cont& x);
```

The template function returns **`front_insert_iterator<Cont>(x)`**.

input_iterator_tag

```
struct input_iterator_tag {
    };
```

The type is the same as `iterator<It>::iterator_category` when `It` describes an object that can serve as an input iterator.

insert_iterator

```
template<class Cont>
    class insert_iterator
        : public iterator<output_iterator_tag,
            void, void, void, void> {
public:
    typedef Cont container_type;
    typedef typename Cont::reference reference;
    typedef typename Cont::value_type value_type;
    insert_iterator(Cont& x,
        typename Cont::iterator it);
    insert_iterator&
        operator=(typename Cont::const_reference val);
    insert_iterator& operator*();
    insert_iterator& operator++();
    insert_iterator& operator++(int);
protected:
    Cont *container;
    typename Cont::iterator iter;
    };
```

The template class describes an output iterator object. It inserts elements into a container of type `Cont`, which it accesses via the protected pointer object it stores called `container`. It also stores the protected iterator object, of class `Cont::iterator`, called `iter`. The container must define:

- the member type `const_reference`, which is the type of a constant reference to an element of the sequence controlled by the container
- the member type `iterator`, which is the type of an iterator for the container
- the member type `reference`, which is the type of a reference to an element of the sequence controlled by the container
- the member type `value_type`, which is the type of an element of the sequence controlled by the container
- the member function `insert(iterator it, value_type c)`, which inserts a new element with value `c` immediately before the element designated by `it` in the controlled sequence, then returns an iterator that designates the inserted element

insert_iterator::container_type

```
typedef Cont container_type;
```

The type is a synonym for the template parameter `Cont`.

insert_iterator::insert_iterator

```
insert_iterator(Cont& x,
    typename Cont::iterator it);
```

The constructor initializes `container` with `&x`, and `iter` with `it`.

- **insert_iterator::operator***

```
insert_iterator& operator*();
```

The member function returns `*this`.

- **insert_iterator::operator++**

```
insert_iterator& operator++();
insert_iterator& operator++(int);
```

The member functions both return `*this`.

- **insert_iterator::operator=**

```
insert_iterator&
    operator=(typename Cont::const_reference val);
```

The member function evaluates `iter = container. insert(iter, val)`, then returns `*this`.

- **insert_iterator::reference**

```
typedef typename Cont::reference reference;
```

The type describes a reference to an element of the sequence controlled by the associated container.

- **insert_iterator::value_type**

```
typedef typename Cont::value_type value_type;
```

The type describes the elements of the sequence controlled by the associated container.

- **inserter**

```
template<class Cont, class Iter>
    insert_iterator<Cont> inserter(Cont& x, Iter it);
```

The template function returns `insert_iterator<Cont>(x, it)`.

- **istream_iterator**

```
template<class U, class E = char,
    class T = char_traits>
    class Dist = ptrdiff_t>
    class istream_iterator
        : public iterator<input_iterator_tag,
            U, Dist, U *, U&> {
public:
    typedef E char_type;
    typedef T traits_type;
    typedef basic_istream<E, T> istream_type;
    istream_iterator();
    istream_iterator(istream_type& is);
    const U& operator*() const;
    const U *operator->() const;
    istream_iterator<U, E, T, Dist>& operator++();
    istream_iterator<U, E, T, Dist> operator++(int);
    };
```

The template class describes an input iterator object. It extracts objects of class `U` from an *input stream*, which it accesses via an object it stores, of type pointer to `basic_istream<E, T>`. After constructing or incrementing an object of class `istream_iterator` with a non-null stored pointer, the object attempts to extract and store an object of type `U` from the associated input stream. If the extraction fails, the object effectively replaces the stored pointer with a null pointer (thus making an end-of-sequence indicator).

▫ **istream_iterator::char_type**

```
typedef E char_type;
```

The type is a synonym for the template parameter `E`.

▫ **istream_iterator::istream_iterator**

```
istream_iterator();
istream_iterator(istream_type& is);
```

The first constructor initializes the input stream pointer with a null pointer. The second constructor initializes the input stream pointer with `&is`, then attempts to extract and store an object of type `U`.

▫ **istream_iterator::istream_type**

```
typedef basic_istream<E, T> istream_type;
```

The type is a synonym for `basic_istream<E, T>`.

▫ **istream_iterator::operator***

```
const U& operator*() const;
```

The operator returns the stored object of type `U`.

▫ **istream_iterator::operator->**

```
const U *operator->() const;
```

The operator returns `&**this`.

▫ **istream_iterator::operator++**

```
istream_iterator<U, E, T, Dist>& operator++();
istream_iterator<U, E, T, Dist> operator++(int);
```

The first operator attempts to extract and store an object of type `U` from the associated input stream. The second operator makes a copy of the object, increments the object, then returns the copy.

▫ **istream_iterator::traits_type**

```
typedef T traits_type;
```

The type is a synonym for the template parameter `T`.

▫ **istreambuf_iterator**

```
template<class E, class T = char_traits<E> >
    class istreambuf_iterator
        : public iterator<input_iterator_tag,
            E, typename T::off_type, E *, E&> {
public:
    typedef E char_type;
    typedef T traits_type;
    typedef typename T::int_type int_type;
    typedef basic_streambuf<E, T> streambuf_type;
    typedef basic_istream<E, T> istream_type;
```

```
istreambuf_iterator(streambuf_type *sb = 0) throw();
istreambuf_iterator(istream_type& is) throw();
const E& operator*() const;
const E *operator->() const;
istreambuf_iterator& operator++();
istreambuf_iterator operator++(int);
bool equal(const istreambuf_iterator& rhs) const;
};
```

The template class describes an input iterator object. It extracts elements of class **E** from an *input stream buffer*, which it accesses via an object it stores, of type pointer to **basic_streambuf<E, T>**. After constructing or incrementing an object of class **istreambuf_iterator** with a non-null stored pointer, the object effectively attempts to extract and store an object of type **E** from the associated itput stream. (The extraction may be delayed, however, until the object is actually dereferenced or copied.) If the extraction fails, the object effectively replaces the stored pointer with a null pointer (thus making an end-of-sequence indicator).

- **istreambuf_iterator::char_type**

```
typedef E char_type;
```

The type is a synonym for the template parameter **E**.

- **istreambuf_iterator::equal**

```
bool equal(const istreambuf_iterator& rhs) const;
```

The member function returns true only if the stored stream buffer pointers for the object and **rhs** are both null pointers or are both non-null pointers.

- **istreambuf_iterator::int_type**

```
typedef typename T::int_type int_type;
```

The type is a synonym for **T::int_type**.

- **istreambuf_iterator::istream_type**

```
typedef basic_istream<E, T> istream_type;
```

The type is a synonym for **basic_istream<E, T>**.

- **istreambuf_iterator::istreambuf_iterator**

```
istreambuf_iterator(streambuf_type *sb = 0) throw();
istreambuf_iterator(istream_type& is) throw();
```

The first constructor initializes the input stream-buffer pointer with **sb**. The second constructor initializes the input stream-buffer pointer with **is.rdbuf()**, then (eventually) attempts to extract and store an object of type **E**.

- **istreambuf_iterator::operator***

```
const E& operator*() const;
```

The operator returns the stored object of type **E**.

istreambuf_iterator::operator++

```
istreambuf_iterator& operator++();
istreambuf_iterator operator++(int);
```

The first operator (eventually) attempts to extract and store an object of type **E** from the associated input stream. The second operator makes a copy of the object, increments the object, then returns the copy.

istreambuf_iterator::operator->

```
const E *operator->() const;
```

The operator returns **&**this**.

istreambuf_iterator::streambuf_type

```
typedef basic_streambuf<E, T> streambuf_type;
```

The type is a synonym for **basic_streambuf<E, T>**.

istreambuf_iterator::traits_type

```
typedef T traits_type;
```

The type is a synonym for the template parameter **T**.

iterator

```
template<class C, class T, class Dist = ptrdiff_t
    class Pt = T *, class Rt = T&>
    struct iterator {
    typedef C iterator_category;
    typedef T value_type;
    typedef Dist difference_type;
    typedef Pt pointer;
    typedef Rt reference;
    };
```

The template class can serve as a convenient base class for an iterator class that you define. It defines the member types **iterator_category** (a synonym for the template parameter **C**), **value_type** (a synonym for the template parameter **T**), **difference_type** (a synonym for the template parameter **Dist**), **pointer** (a synonym for the template parameter **Pt**), and **reference** (a synonym for the template parameter **T**).

Note that **value_type** should *not* be a constant type even if **pointer** points at an object of const type and **reference** designates an object of const type.

iterator_traits

```
template<class It>
    struct iterator_traits {
    typedef typename It::iterator_category
iterator_category;
    typedef typename It::value_type value_type;
    typedef typename It::difference_type difference_type;
    typedef typename It::pointer pointer;
    typedef typename It::reference reference;
    };
template<class T>
    struct iterator_traits<T *> {
    typedef random_access_iterator_tag iterator_category;
```

```
        typedef T value_type;
        typedef ptrdiff_t difference_type;
        typedef T *pointer;
        typedef T& reference;
        };
    template<class T>
        struct iterator_traits<const T *> {
        typedef random_access_iterator_tag iterator_category;
        typedef T value_type;
        typedef ptrdiff_t difference_type;
        typedef const T *pointer;
        typedef const T& reference;
        };
```

The template class determines several critical types associated with the iterator type `It`. It defines the member types `iterator_category` (a synonym for `It::iterator_category`), `value_type` (a synonym for `It::value_type`), `difference_type` (a synonym for `It::difference_type`), `pointer` (a synonym for `It::pointer`), and `reference` (a synonym for `It::reference`).

The partial specializations determine the critical types associated with an object pointer type `T *`. In this implementation, you can also use several template functions that do not make use of partial specialization:

```
template<class C, class T, class Dist>
    C Iter_cat(const iterator<C, T, Dist>&);
template<class T>
    random_access_iterator_tag Iter_cat(const T *);

template<class C, class T, class Dist>
    T *Val_type(const iterator<C, T, Dist>&);
template<class T>
    T *Val_type(const T *);

template<class C, class T, class Dist>
    Dist *Dist_type(const iterator<C, T, Dist>&);
template<class T>
    ptrdiff_t *Dist_type(const T *);
```

which determine several of the same types a bit more indirectly. You use these functions as arguments on a function call. Their sole purpose is to supply a useful template class parameter to the called function.

▫ **operator!=**

```
template<class RanIt>
    bool operator!=(
        const reverse_iterator<RanIt>& lhs,
        const reverse_iterator<RanIt>& rhs);
template<class U, class E, class T, class Dist>
    bool operator!=(
        const istream_iterator<U, E, T, Dist>& lhs,
        const istream_iterator<U, E, T, Dist>& rhs);
template<class E, class T>
    bool operator!=(
        const istreambuf_iterator<E, T>& lhs,
        const istreambuf_iterator<E, T>& rhs);
```

The template operator returns `!(lhs == rhs)`.

▫ **operator==**

```
template<class RanIt>
    bool operator==(
        const reverse_iterator<RanIt>& lhs,
        const reverse_iterator<RanIt>& rhs);
template<class U, class E, class T, class Dist>
    bool operator==(
        const istream_iterator<U, E, T, Dist>& lhs,
        const istream_iterator<U, E, T, Dist>& rhs);
template<class E, class T>
    bool operator==(
        const istreambuf_iterator<E, T>& lhs,
        const istreambuf_iterator<E, T>& rhs);
```

The first template operator returns true only if `lhs.current == rhs.current`. The second template operator returns true only if both `lhs` and `rhs` store the same stream pointer. The third template operator returns `lhs.equal(rhs)`.

▫ **operator<**

```
template<class RanIt>
    bool operator<(
        const reverse_iterator<RanIt>& lhs,
        const reverse_iterator<RanIt>& rhs);
```

The template operator returns `rhs.current < lhs.current` [sic].

▫ **operator<=**

```
template<class RanIt>
    bool operator<=(
        const reverse_iterator<RanIt>& lhs,
        const reverse_iterator<RanIt>& rhs);
```

The template operator returns `!(rhs < lhs)`.

▫ **operator>**

```
template<class RanIt>
    bool operator>(
        const reverse_iterator<RanIt>& lhs,
        const reverse_iterator<RanIt>& rhs);
```

The template operator returns `rhs < lhs`.

▫ **operator>=**

```
template<class RanIt>
    bool operator>=(
        const reverse_iterator<RanIt>& lhs,
        const reverse_iterator<RanIt>& rhs);
```

The template operator returns `!(lhs < rhs)`.

▫ **operator+**

```
template<class RanIt>
    reverse_iterator<RanIt> operator+(Dist n,
        const reverse_iterator<RanIt>& rhs);
```

The template operator returns `rhs + n`.

▫ **operator-**

```
template<class RanIt>
    Dist operator-(
        const reverse_iterator<RanIt>& lhs,
        const reverse_iterator<RanIt>& rhs);
```

The template operator returns `rhs.current - lhs.current` [sic].

▫ **ostream_iterator**

```
template<class U, class E = char,
    class T = char_traits<E>  >
    class ostream_iterator
        : public iterator<output_iterator_tag,
            void, void, void, void> {
public:
    typedef U value_type;
    typedef E char_type;
    typedef T traits_type;
    typedef basic_ostream<E, T> ostream_type;
    ostream_iterator(ostream_type& os);
    ostream_iterator(ostream_type& os, const E *delim);
    ostream_iterator<U, E, T>& operator=(const U& val);
    ostream_iterator<U, E, T>& operator*();
    ostream_iterator<U, E, T>& operator++();
    ostream_iterator<U, E, T> operator++(int);
    };
```

The template class describes an output iterator object. It inserts objects of class `U` into an *output stream,* which it accesses via an object it stores, of type pointer to `basic_ostream<E, T>`. It also stores a pointer to a *delimiter string,* a null-terminated string of elements of type `E`, which is appended after each insertion. (Note that the string itself is *not* copied by the constructor.

▫ **ostream_iterator::char_type**

```
typedef E char_type;
```

The type is a synonym for the template parameter `E`.

▫ **ostream_iterator::operator***

```
ostream_iterator<U, E, T>& operator*();
```

The operator returns `*this`.

▫ **ostream_iterator::operator++**

```
ostream_iterator<U, E, T>& operator++();
ostream_iterator<U, E, T> operator++(int);
```

The operators both return `*this`.

▫ **ostream_iterator::operator=**

```
ostream_iterator<U, E, T>& operator=(const U& val);
```

The operator inserts `val` into the output stream associated with the object, then returns `*this`.

▫ **ostream_iterator::ostream_iterator**

```
ostream_iterator(ostream_type& os);
ostream_iterator(ostream_type& os, const E *delim);
```

The first constructor initializes the output stream pointer with **&os**. The delimiter string pointer designates an empty string. The second constructor initializes the output stream pointer with **&os** and the delimiter string pointer with **delim**.

ostream_iterator::ostream_type

```
typedef basic_ostream<E, T> ostream_type;
```

The type is a synonym for **basic_ostream<E, T>**.

ostream_iterator::traits_type

```
typedef T traits_type;
```

The type is a synonym for the template parameter **T**.

ostream_iterator::value_type

```
typedef U value_type;
```

The type is a synonym for the template parameter **U**.

ostreambuf_iterator

```
template<class E, class T = char_traits<E> >
    class ostreambuf_iterator
        : public iterator<output_iterator_tag,
            void, void, void, void> {
public:
    typedef E char_type;
    typedef T traits_type;
    typedef basic_streambuf<E, T> streambuf_type;
    typedef basic_ostream<E, T> ostream_type;
    ostreambuf_iterator(streambuf_type *sb) throw();
    ostreambuf_iterator(ostream_type& os) throw();
    ostreambuf_iterator& operator=(E x);
    ostreambuf_iterator& operator*();
    ostreambuf_iterator& operator++();
    T1 operator++(int);
    bool failed() const throw();
    };
```

The template class describes an output iterator object. It inserts elements of class **E** into an *output stream buffer*, which it accesses via an object it stores, of type pointer to **basic_streambuf<E, T>**.

ostreambuf_iterator::char_type

```
typedef E char_type;
```

The type is a synonym for the template parameter **E**.

ostreambuf_iterator::failed

```
bool failed() const throw();
```

The member function returns true only if no insertion into the output stream buffer has earlier failed.

ostreambuf_iterator::operator*

```
ostreambuf_iterator& operator*();
```

The operator returns ***this**.

▫ **ostreambuf_iterator::operator++**

```
ostreambuf_iterator& operator++();
T1 operator++(int);
```

The first operator returns `*this`. The second operator returns an object of some type `T1` that can be converted to `ostreambuf_iterator<E, T>`.

▫ **ostreambuf_iterator::operator=**

```
ostreambuf_iterator& operator=(E x);
```

The operator inserts `x` into the associated stream buffer, then returns `*this`.

▫ **ostreambuf_iterator::ostream_type**

```
typedef basic_ostream<E, T> ostream_type;
```

The type is a synonym for `basic_ostream<E, T>`.

▫ **ostreambuf_iterator::ostreambuf_iterator**

```
ostreambuf_iterator(streambuf_type *sb) throw();
ostreambuf_iterator(ostream_type& os) throw();
```

The first conttructor initializes the output stream-buffer pointer with `sb`. The second constructor initializes the output stream-buffer pointer with `os.rdbuf()`. (The stored pointer must not be a null pointer.)

▫ **ostreambuf_iterator::streambuf_type**

```
typedef basic_streambuf<E, T> streambuf_type;
```

The type is a synonym for `basic_streambuf<E, T>`.

▫ **ostreambuf_iterator::traits_type**

```
typedef T traits_type;
```

The type is a synonym for the template parameter `T`.

▫ **output_iterator_tag**

```
struct output_iterator_tag {
    };
```

The type is the same as `iterator<It>::iterator_category` when `It` describes an object that can serve as a output iterator.

▫ **random_access_iterator_tag**

```
struct random_access_iterator_tag
    : public bidirectional_iterator_tag {
    };
```

The type is the same as `iterator<It>::iterator_category` when `It` describes an object that can serve as a random-access iterator.

▫ **reverse_iterator**

```
template<class RanIt>
    class reverse_iterator : public iterator<
        typename iterator_traits<RanIt>::iterator_category,
        typename iterator_traits<RanIt>::value_type,
        typename iterator_traits<RanIt>::difference_type,
        typename iterator_traits<RanIt>::pointer,
        typename iterator_traits<RanIt>::reference> {
```

```
        typedef typename iterator_traits<RanIt>::difference_type
            Dist;
        typedef typename iterator_traits<RanIt>::pointer
            Ptr;
        typedef typename iterator_traits<RanIt>::reference
            Ref;
    public:
        typedef RanIt iterator_type;
        reverse_iterator();
        explicit reverse_iterator(RanIt x);
        template<class U>
            reverse_iterator(const reverse_iterator<U>& x);
        RanIt base() const;
        Ref operator*() const;
        Ptr operator->() const;
        reverse_iterator& operator++();
        reverse_iterator operator++(int);
        reverse_iterator& operator--();
        reverse_iterator operator--();
        reverse_iterator& operator+=(Dist n);
        reverse_iterator operator+(Dist n) const;
        reverse_iterator& operator-=(Dist n);
        reverse_iterator operator-(Dist n) const;
        Ref operator[](Dist n) const;
    protected:
        RanIt current;
        };
```

The template class describes an object that behaves like a random-access iterator, only in reverse. It stores a random-access iterator of type **RanIt** in the protected object **current**. Incrementing the object **x** of type **reverse_iterator** decrements **x.current**, and decrementing **x** increments **x.current**. Moreover, the expression ***x** evaluates to ***(current - 1)**, of type **Ref**. Typically, **Ref** is type **T&**.

Thus, you can use an object of class **reverse_iterator** to access in reverse order a sequence that is traversed in order by a random-access iterator.

Several STL containers specialize **reverse_iterator** for **RanIt** a bidirectional iterator. In these cases, you must not call any of the member functions **operator+=**, **operator+**, **operator-=**, **operator-**, or **operator[]**.

▫ **reverse_iterator::base**

```
RanIt base() const;
```

The member function returns **current**.

▫ **reverse_iterator::iterator_type**

```
typedef RanIt iterator_type;
```

The type is a synonym for the template parameter **RanIt**.

▫ **reverse_iterator::operator***

```
Ref operator*() const;
```

The operator returns ***(current - 1)**.

- **reverse_iterator::operator+**

```
reverse_iterator operator+(Dist n) const;
```

The operator returns `reverse_iterator(*this) += n`.

- **reverse_iterator::operator++**

```
reverse_iterator& operator++();
reverse_iterator operator++(int);
```

The first (preincrement) operator evaluates `--current`. then returns `*this`.

The second (postincrement) operator makes a copy of `*this`, evaluates `--current`, then returns the copy.

- **reverse_iterator::operator+=**

```
reverse_iterator& operator+=(Dist n);
```

The operator evaluates `current - n`. then returns `*this`.

- **reverse_iterator::operator-**

```
reverse_iterator operator-(Dist n) const;
```

The operator returns `reverse_iterator(*this) -= n`.

- **reverse_iterator::operator--**

```
reverse_iterator& operator--();
reverse_iterator operator--();
```

The first (predecrement) operator evaluates `++current`. then returns `*this`.

The second (postdecrement) operator makes a copy of `*this`, evaluates `++current`, then returns the copy.

- **reverse_iterator::operator-=**

```
reverse_iterator& operator-=(Dist n);
```

The operator evaluates `current + n`. then returns `*this`.

- **reverse_iterator::operator->**

```
Ptr operator->() const;
```

The operator returns `&**this`.

- **reverse_iterator::operator[]**

```
Ref operator[](Dist n) const;
```

The operator returns `*(*this + n)`.

- **reverse_iterator::pointer**

```
typedef Ptr pointer;
```

The type is a synonym for the template parameter `Ref`.

- **reverse_iterator::reference**

```
typedef Ref reference;
```

The type is a synonym for the template parameter `Ref`.

▫ **reverse_iterator::reverse_iterator**

```
reverse_iterator();
explicit reverse_iterator(RanIt x);
template<class U>
    reverse_iterator(const reverse_iterator<U>& x);
```

The first constructor initializes **current** with its default constructor. The second constructor initializes **current** with **x.current**.

The template constructor initializes **current** with **x.base()**.

Using <iterator>

Chances are good that, if you include *any* STL header in a translation unit, **<iterator>** will be included as well. You include it explicitly only if you need one or more of the definitions it provides and you can't count on another STL header to drag it in. But chances are also good that you *will* need one or more of the entities defined in this header. If you get a translator diagnostic that, say, **reverse_iterator** is undefined, remember that you can satisfy the need cheaply by including this header.

Here's a brief run-down of the definitions in **<iterator>**:

iterator An iterator can be an object pointer or a class that you define. If you define your own iterator class, you must define several member types. The easiest way to do so is to derive the iterator class publicly, wherever possible, from an existing iterator. Otherwise, follow one of these patterns:

```
class OutIt
    : public iterator<output_iterator_tag, void, void,
        void, void>
    {.....}  // for an output iterator
class InIt
    : public iterator<input_iterator_tag, T, Dist>
    {.....}  // for an input iterator
class FwdIt
    : public iterator<forward_iterator_tag, T, Dist>
    {.....}  // for a forward iterator
class BidIt
    : public iterator<bidirectional_iterator_tag, T, Dist>
    {.....}  // for a bidirectional iterator
class RanIt
    : public iterator<random_access_iterator_tag, T, Dist>
    {.....}  // for a random-access iterator
```

Here, **T** is the element type for the iterator and **Dist** is its distance type. For an object pointer of type **T ***, the category is **random_access_iterator_tag**, the element type is of course **T** and the distance type is **ptrdiff_t**.

You can manipulate iterators **first** and **last**, of type **Iter**, in one of two ways. On an implementation that supports partial specialization, you can write:

iterator_traits

advance

distance

```
iterator_traits<Iter>::iterator_category
    // the iterator category type
iterator_traits<Iter>::value_type
    // the element type
iterator_traits<Iter>::distance_type
    // the distance type
advance(first, N)
    // adds N to X
N = distance(first, last)
    // returns the distance from first to last
```

If partial specialization is not supported, or if you can't be certain that it is, the version of STL shown in this book lets you write instead:

Iter_cat

Val_type

Dist_type

advance

Distance

```
Iter_cat(first)
    // returns an object of the iterator category type
Val_type(first)
    // returns a null pointer to the element type
Dist_type(first)
    // returns a null pointer to the distance type
advance(first, N)
    // adds N to X
Distance(first, last, N)
    // adds to N the distance from first to last
```

In all cases, the iterator category is one of the empty structure types:

iterator tags

```
output_iterator_tag
input_iterator_tag
forward_iterator_tag
bidirectional_iterator_tag
random_access_iterator_tag
```

Each of the last three tags is publicly derived from the one right above it.

reverse_iterator

Given a random-access iterator of type `RanIt`, you can define a related reverse iterator `RevIt` that steps backward through a sequence:

```
typedef reverse_iterator<RanIt> RevIt;
```

To walk the sequence designated by `RanIt` iterators in the range `[first, last)` in reverse order, you can then write:

```
RevIt rfirst(last), rlast(first);
for (; rfirst != rlast; ++rfirst)
    <process>(rfirst);
```

For a bidirectional iterator of type `BidIt`, you can probably use `reverse_iterator` as above. Just be sure to treat the resultant reverse iterator as a bidirectional iterator — operations defined only for random-access iterators will probably produce mysterious compiler diagnostics. But if this usage is not supported by a given implementation, or if you can't be certain that it is, the version of STL shown in this book lets you write instead:

Revbidit

```
typedef Revbidit<BidIt> RevBidIt;
RevBidIt rfirst(last), rlast(first);
for (; rfirst != rlast; ++rfirst)
    <process>(rfirst);
```

insertion iterators

You use insertion iterators to insert elements into a container in the guise of storing a generated sequence through an output iterator.

back_insert_iterator

Given a container of type `Cont`, you can define an output iterator `OutIt` that inserts elements at the end of the controlled sequence:

```
typedef back_insert_iterator<Cont> Outit;
```

You can then, say, append the sequence designated by iterators in the range `[first, last)` to the container `c` using the template function `copy` (see Chapter 6: `<algorithm>`):

```
OutIt it(c);
copy(first, last, it);
```

back_ inserter Or you can generate the needed output iterator on the fly, to append the sequence to the container, by writing:

```
copy(first, last, back_inserter(c));
```

The iterator performs insertions by calling `Cont::push_back(const T&)`. An STL container defines this member function only if it can perform the operation efficiently.

front_insert_ iterator You can also define an output iterator `OutIt` that inserts elements *in reverse order* at the beginning of the controlled sequence:

```
typedef front_insert_iterator<Cont> Outit;
```

To prepend a sequence in reverse order, you can write:

```
OutIt it(c);
copy(first, last, it);
```

front_ inserter Or you can generate the needed output iterator on the fly, to prepend the reversed sequence to the container, by writing:

```
copy(first, last, front_inserter(c));
```

The iterator performs insertions by calling `Cont::push_front(const T&)`. An STL container defines this member function only if it can perform the operation efficiently.

insert_ iterator Finally, you can define an output iterator `OutIt` that inserts elements immediately before a place you designate in the controlled sequence:

```
typedef insert_iterator<Cont> Outit;
```

To insert a sequence, you designate the insertion point with an iterator. To prepend a sequence to a container *without reversing the sequence,* for example, you can write:

```
OutIt it(c, c.begin());
copy(first, last, it);
```

The member function `begin()`, for any STL container, returns an iterator that points to the first element of the controlled sequence, or just past the end of an empty controlled sequence. In either case, it defines the point before which you want to insert the copied sequence.

inserter To generate the needed output iterator on the fly, to insert the sequence at the beginning of the container, you can write:

```
copy(first, last, inserter(c, c.begin()));
```

The iterator performs insertions by calling `Cont::insert(Cont::iterator, const T&)`, which returns an iterator designating the newly inserted element. Every STL container defines this member function, whatever the cost.

stream iterators An input stream sometimes consists of a sequence of fields each of which you wish to extract as an object of some type `T`. The conventional way to process such a stream is to write, for example:

```
T x;
while (cin >> x)
    <process>(x);
```

The loop terminates when an extraction from the standard input fails, typically at end of file.

`istream_iterator` You can perform much the same logic, in the guise of walking a sequence with an input iterator, by introducing an object of class `istream_iterator`:

```
typedef istream_iterator<T,
    char, char_traits<char> > InIt;
```

This particular type definition makes `InIt` suitable for use with an object of class `istream`, such as `cin`. The template class `char_traits` is part of a much more general mechanism, introduced as part of the C++ Standard, for specifying input and output streams. Using default template arguments, you can omit all but the first type in the list, writing just `istream_iterator<T>`.

Given this type definition, you can then write:

```
InIt first(cin), last;
while (first != last)
    <process>(*first++);
```

The iterator performs the extractions for you, as needed. Do not attempt to access the input stream other than through `first`, however. Don't read the stream directly, and don't create another iterator to read from it. Each iterator must read ahead, from time to time, so the input stream is rarely left in a state that is easy to describe, even after `first` is destroyed.

Sometimes you wish to insert into an output stream a sequence of fields each of which is generated from an object of some type `T`. The conventional way to generate such a stream is to write, for example:

```
while (<not done>)
    {T x = <next value>;
    cout << x; }
```

`ostream_iterator` You can perform much the same logic, in the guise of storing a generated sequence through an output iterator, by introducing an object of class `ostream_iterator`:

```
typedef ostream_iterator<T,
    char, char_traits<char> > OutIt;
```

This particular type definition makes `OutIt` suitable for use with an object of class `ostream`, such as `cout`. Using default template arguments, you can omit all but the first type in the list, writing just `ostream_iterator<T>`.

Then you can write:

```
Outit next(cout);
while (<not done>)
    {T x = <next value>;
    *next++ = x; }
```

If you want to append a common text string to each such insertion, write instead something like:

```
OutIt next(cout, "\n");
while (<not done>)
    {T x = <next value>;
    *next++ = x; }
```

In this case, each inserted item is followed by a newline character. Note that the null-terminated string you specify in the constructor is *not* copied. You must ensure that the lifetime of the string exceeds that of the iterator.

It is safe to intersperse writes to the output stream through **next** and through other mechanisms, by the way. The iterator performs no buffering of the output field it generates.

stream buffer iterators

You can extract individual elements from an input stream in the guise of accessing the elements of a sequence with an input iterator. To do so for, say, the standard input stream, you write:

istreambuf_iterator

```
typedef istreambuf_iterator<char,
    char_traits<char> > InIt;
```

This particular type definition makes **InIt** suitable for use with an object of class **istream**, such as **cin**. Using default template arguments, you can omit all but the first type in the list, writing just **istreambuf_iterator<char>**.

You can then declare:

```
InIt first(cin), last;
```

If **first != last**, the expression ***first** yields the next character (element of type **char**) available to be read from the standard input stream. The iterator actually stores a pointer **p** to the underlying stream buffer, of class **streambuf** in this case. You could just as well have declared **first** as:

```
InIt first(cin->rdbuf());
```

The iterator performs the extractions for you, as needed, by calling either **p->sgetc()** or **p->sbumpc()**. Do not attempt to access the input stream other than through **first**. The iterator must read ahead, so the input stream is rarely left in a state that is easy to describe. Don't read the stream directly, and don't create another iterator to read from it. If **first** is destroyed, however, you can be certain that the first unread element is the next one available from the stream buffer. Put simply, an input stream should at any time have at most one object of class **istreambuf_iterator** associated with it. While that object exists, it should be the sole source of elements extracted from the input stream.

You can insert individual elements into an output stream in the guise of storing the elements of a generated sequence through an output iterator. To do so for, say, the standard output stream, you write:

ostreambuf_iterator

```
typedef ostreambuf_iterator<char,
    char_traits<char> > OutIt;
```

This particular type definition makes **OutIt** suitable for use with an object of class **ostream**, such as **cout**. Using default template arguments, you can omit all but the first type in the list, writing just `ostreambuf_iterator<char>`. You can then declare:

```
OutIt next(cout);
```

The expression `*next++ = c` inserts the character `c` (of type `char`) into the standard output stream. The iterator actually stores a pointer `p` to the underlying stream buffer, of class `streambuf` in this case. You could just as well have declared `next` as:

```
OutIt next(cout->rdbuf());
```

The iterator performs the insertions for you by calling `p->sputc(c)`.

It is safe to intersperse writes to the output stream through `next` and through other mechanisms, by the way. The iterator performs no buffering of the output field it generates.

Implementing `<iterator>`

This implementation moves some of the facilities nominally defined in the header `<iterator>` to another header. The added header `<xutility>` (not specified in the C++ Standard) holds a number of definitions used throughout a typical Standard C++ library, even in a program that does not explicitly include `<iterator>`. An implementation is at liberty to rearrange definitions this way so long as any program that includes `<iterator>` also assuredly includes `<xutility>`. And indeed that is the case here.

An implementation introduces extra "internal" headers such as `<xutility>` for a couple of different reasons. The Standard C++ library contains a number of circular dependencies — such as between objects of class `basic_string`, which can throw exceptions, and objects of class `exception`, which can be constructed from `basic_string` objects. The library also contains some rather large headers — such as `<algorithm>` and `<iterator>` — only part of which might be needed by other library headers. In either of these two cases, moving some definitions into an extra internal header makes the implementor's task more tractable.

`<xutility>` Figures 3.1 through 3.11 show the file `xutility`. It contains the most widely used definitions from both `<iterator>` and `<algorithm>`. We will discuss contributions from the latter header in Chapter 6: `<algorithm>`. `xutility` first defines the iterator tags, which are simply empty classes. Iterator tags store no values; they convey information as template parameters through their types, and their type hierarchy.

`Int_iterator_tag` Note the added tag, `Int_iterator_tag`, which we have not discussed so far. It signals the presence of a template parameter that has an integer type, much as `input_iterator_tag` signals a corresponding template parameter that can serve as an input iterator. `Int_iterator_tag` is used by various overloads of function `Iter_cat`, discussed below, just like the other iterator tags. It proves useful in implementing several of the template container classes, which must resolve certain ambiguities between overloads of some member template functions.

Figure 3.1: xutility part 1

```
// xutility internal header
#ifndef XUTILITY_
#define XUTILITY_
#include <utility>
namespace std {

//   ITERATOR STUFF (from <iterator>)

          // ITERATOR TAGS
struct input_iterator_tag {};
struct output_iterator_tag {};
struct forward_iterator_tag
     : public input_iterator_tag {};
struct bidirectional_iterator_tag
     : public forward_iterator_tag {};
struct random_access_iterator_tag
     : public bidirectional_iterator_tag  {};
struct Int_iterator_tag {};

          // TEMPLATE CLASS iterator
template<class C, class T, class D = ptrdiff_t,
     class Pt = T *, class Rt = T&>
     struct iterator {
     typedef C iterator_category;
     typedef T value_type;
     typedef D difference_type;
     typedef Pt pointer;
     typedef Rt reference;
     };

template<class T, class D, class Pt, class Rt>
     struct Bidit : public iterator<bidirectional_iterator_tag,
          T, D, Pt, Rt> {};
template<class T, class D, class Pt, class Rt>
     struct Ranit : public iterator<random_access_iterator_tag,
          T, D, Pt, Rt> {};
struct Outit : public iterator<output_iterator_tag,
     void, void, void, void> {};

          // TEMPLATE CLASS iterator_traits
template<class It>
     struct iterator_traits {
     typedef typename It::iterator_category iterator_category;
     typedef typename It::value_type value_type;
     typedef typename It::difference_type difference_type;
     typedef typename It::pointer pointer;
     typedef typename It::reference reference;
     };

template<class T>
     struct iterator_traits<T *> {
     typedef random_access_iterator_tag iterator_category;
     typedef T value_type;
     typedef ptrdiff_t difference_type;
```

Figure 3.2: xutility part 2

```
     typedef T *pointer;
     typedef T& reference;
     };
template<class T>
     struct iterator_traits<const T *> {
     typedef random_access_iterator_tag iterator_category;
     typedef T value_type;
     typedef ptrdiff_t difference_type;
     typedef const T *pointer;
     typedef const T& reference;
     };

          // TEMPLATE FUNCTION Iter_cat
template<class C, class T, class D,
     class Pt, class Rt> inline
     C Iter_cat(const iterator<C, T, D, Pt, Rt>&)
     {C X;
     return (X); }
template<class T> inline
     random_access_iterator_tag Iter_cat(const T *)
     {random_access_iterator_tag X;
     return (X); }

          // INTEGER FUNCTION Iter_cat
inline Int_iterator_tag Iter_cat(bool)
     {Int_iterator_tag X;
     return (X); }
inline Int_iterator_tag Iter_cat(char)
     {Int_iterator_tag X;
     return (X); }
inline Int_iterator_tag Iter_cat(signed char)
     {Int_iterator_tag X;
     return (X); }
inline Int_iterator_tag Iter_cat(unsigned char)
     {Int_iterator_tag X;
     return (X); }
inline Int_iterator_tag Iter_cat(wchar_t)
     {Int_iterator_tag X;
     return (X); }
inline Int_iterator_tag Iter_cat(short)
     {Int_iterator_tag X;
     return (X); }
inline Int_iterator_tag Iter_cat(unsigned short)
     {Int_iterator_tag X;
     return (X); }
inline Int_iterator_tag Iter_cat(int)
     {Int_iterator_tag X;
     return (X); }
inline Int_iterator_tag Iter_cat(unsigned int)
     {Int_iterator_tag X;
     return (X); }
inline Int_iterator_tag Iter_cat(long)
     {Int_iterator_tag X;
     return (X); }
```

Figure 3.3: xutility part 3

```
inline Int_iterator_tag Iter_cat(unsigned long)
     {Int_iterator_tag X;
     return (X); }

          // TEMPLATE FUNCTION Distance
template<class InIt> inline
     typename iterator_traits<InIt>::difference_type
          distance(InIt F, InIt L)
     {typename iterator_traits<InIt>::difference_type
          N = 0;
     Distance2(F, L, N, Iter_cat(F));
     return (N); }
template<class InIt, class D> inline
     void Distance(InIt F, InIt L, D& N)
     {Distance2(F, L, N, Iter_cat(F)); }
template<class InIt, class D> inline
     void Distance2(InIt F, InIt L, D& N,
          input_iterator_tag)
     {for (; F != L; ++F)
          ++N; }
template<class InIt, class D> inline
     void Distance2(InIt F, InIt L, D& N,
          forward_iterator_tag)
     {for (; F != L; ++F)
          ++N; }
template<class InIt, class D> inline
     void Distance2(InIt F, InIt L, D& N,
          bidirectional_iterator_tag)
     {for (; F != L; ++F)
          ++N; }
template<class RanIt, class D> inline
     void Distance2(RanIt F, RanIt L, D& N,
          random_access_iterator_tag)
     {N += L - F; }

          // TEMPLATE CLASS Ptrit
template<class T, class D, class Pt, class Rt,
     class Pt2, class Rt2>
     class Ptrit : public iterator<random_access_iterator_tag,
          T, D, Pt, Rt> {
public:
     typedef Ptrit<T, D, Pt, Rt, Pt2, Rt2> Myt;
     Ptrit()
          {}
     explicit Ptrit(Pt P)
          : current(P) {}
     Ptrit(const Ptrit<T, D, Pt2, Rt2, Pt2, Rt2>& X)
          : current(X.base()) {}
     Pt base() const
          {return (current); }
     Rt operator*() const
          {return (*current); }
     Pt operator->() const
          {return (&**this); }
```

Figure 3.4: `xutility` **part 4**

```
        Myt& operator++()
            {++current;
            return (*this); }
        Myt operator++(int)
            {Myt Tmp = *this;
            ++current;
            return (Tmp); }
        Myt& operator--()
            {--current;
            return (*this); }
        Myt operator--(int)
            {Myt Tmp = *this;
            --current;
            return (Tmp); }
        bool operator==(int Y) const
            {return (current == (Pt)Y); }
        bool operator==(const Myt& Y) const
            {return (current == Y.current); }
        bool operator!=(const Myt& Y) const
            {return (!(*this == Y)); }
        Myt& operator+=(D N)
            {current += N;
            return (*this); }
        Myt operator+(D N) const
            {return (Myt(current + N)); }
        Myt& operator-=(D N)
            {current -= N;
            return (*this); }
        Myt operator-(D N) const
            {return (Myt(current - N)); }
        Rt operator[](D N) const
            {return (*(*this + N)); }
        bool operator<(const Myt& Y) const
            {return (current < Y.current); }
        bool operator>(const Myt& Y) const
            {return (Y < *this); }
        bool operator<=(const Myt& Y) const
            {return (!(Y < *this)); }
        bool operator>=(const Myt& Y) const
            {return (!(*this < Y)); }
        D operator-(const Myt& Y) const
            {return (current - Y.current); }
protected:
        Pt current;
        };

template<class T, class D, class Pt, class Rt,
        class Pt2, class Rt2> inline
        Ptrit<T, D, Pt, Rt, Pt2, Rt2>
            operator+(D N,
                const Ptrit<T, D, Pt, Rt, Pt2, Rt2>& Y)
        {return (Y + N); }
```

Figure 3.5: xutility part 5

```
        // TEMPLATE CLASS reverse_iterator
template<class RanIt>
    class reverse_iterator : public iterator<
        typename iterator_traits<RanIt>::iterator_category,
        typename iterator_traits<RanIt>::value_type,
        typename iterator_traits<RanIt>::difference_type,
        typename iterator_traits<RanIt>::pointer,
        typename iterator_traits<RanIt>::reference> {
public:
    typedef reverse_iterator<RanIt> Myt;
    typedef typename iterator_traits<RanIt>::difference_type D;
    typedef typename iterator_traits<RanIt>::pointer Pt;
    typedef typename iterator_traits<RanIt>::reference Rt;
    typedef RanIt iterator_type;
    reverse_iterator()
        {}
    explicit reverse_iterator(RanIt X)
        : current(X) {}
    template<class U>
        reverse_iterator(const reverse_iterator<U>& X)
        : current(X.base()) {}
    RanIt base() const
        {return (current); }
    Rt operator*() const
        {RanIt Tmp = current;
        return (*--Tmp); }
    Pt operator->() const
        {return (&**this); }
    Myt& operator++()
        {--current;
        return (*this); }
    Myt operator++(int)
        {Myt Tmp = *this;
        --current;
        return (Tmp); }
    Myt& operator--()
        {++current;
        return (*this); }
    Myt operator--(int)
        {Myt Tmp = *this;
        ++current;
        return (Tmp); }
    bool Eq(const Myt& Y) const
        {return (current == Y.current); }
        // random-access only beyond this point
    Myt& operator+=(D N)
        {current -= N;
        return (*this); }
    Myt operator+(D N) const
        {return (Myt(current - N)); }
    Myt& operator-=(D N)
        {current += N;
        return (*this); }
    Myt operator-(D N) const
        {return (Myt(current + N)); }
```

Figure 3.6: `xutility` **part 6**

```
     Rt operator[](D N) const
          {return (*(*this + N)); }
     bool Lt(const Myt& Y) const
          {return (Y.current < current); }
     D Mi(const Myt& Y) const
          {return (Y.current - current); }
protected:
     RanIt current;
     };

          // reverse_iterator TEMPLATE OPERATORS
template<class RanIt, class D> inline
     reverse_iterator<RanIt> operator+(D N,
          const reverse_iterator<RanIt>& Y)
     {return (Y + N); }
template<class RanIt> inline
     typename reverse_iterator<RanIt>::D
          operator-(const reverse_iterator<RanIt>& X,
          const reverse_iterator<RanIt>& Y)
     {return (X.Mi(Y)); }
template<class RanIt> inline
     bool operator==(const reverse_iterator<RanIt>& X,
          const reverse_iterator<RanIt>& Y)
     {return (X.Eq(Y)); }
template<class RanIt> inline
     bool operator!=(const reverse_iterator<RanIt>& X,
          const reverse_iterator<RanIt>& Y)
     {return (!(X == Y)); }
template<class RanIt> inline
     bool operator<(const reverse_iterator<RanIt>& X,
          const reverse_iterator<RanIt>& Y)
     {return (X.Lt(Y)); }
template<class RanIt> inline
     bool operator>(const reverse_iterator<RanIt>& X,
          const reverse_iterator<RanIt>& Y)
     {return (Y < X); }
template<class RanIt> inline
     bool operator<=(const reverse_iterator<RanIt>& X,
          const reverse_iterator<RanIt>& Y)
     {return (!(Y < X)); }
template<class RanIt> inline
     bool operator>=(const reverse_iterator<RanIt>& X,
          const reverse_iterator<RanIt>& Y)
     {return (!(X < Y)); }

          // TEMPLATE CLASS Revbidit
template<class BidIt>
     class Revbidit : public iterator<
          typename iterator_traits<BidIt>::iterator_category,
          typename iterator_traits<BidIt>::value_type,
          typename iterator_traits<BidIt>::difference_type,
          typename iterator_traits<BidIt>::pointer,
          typename iterator_traits<BidIt>::reference> {
public:
     typedef Revbidit<BidIt> Myt;
```

Figure 3.7: `xutility` **part 7**

```
	typedef typename iterator_traits<BidIt>::difference_type D;
	typedef typename iterator_traits<BidIt>::pointer Pt;
	typedef typename iterator_traits<BidIt>::reference Rt;
	typedef BidIt iterator_type;
	Revbidit()
		{}
	explicit Revbidit(BidIt X)
		: current(X) {}
	BidIt base() const
		{return (current); }
	Rt operator*() const
		{BidIt Tmp = current;
		return (*--Tmp); }
	Pt operator->() const
		{Rt Tmp = **this;
		return (&Tmp); }
	Myt& operator++()
		{--current;
		return (*this); }
	Myt operator++(int)
		{Myt Tmp = *this;
		--current;
		return (Tmp); }
	Myt& operator--()
		{++current;
		return (*this); }
	Myt operator--(int)
		{Myt Tmp = *this;
		++current;
		return (Tmp); }
	bool operator==(const Myt& Y) const
		{return (current == Y.current); }
	bool operator!=(const Myt& Y) const
		{return (!(*this == Y)); }
protected:
	BidIt current;
	};

		// TEMPLATE CLASS istreambuf_iterator
template<class E, class Tr>
	class istreambuf_iterator
		: public iterator<input_iterator_tag,
			E, typename Tr::off_type, E *, E&> {
public:
	typedef istreambuf_iterator<E, Tr> Myt;
	typedef E char_type;
	typedef Tr traits_type;
	typedef basic_streambuf<E, Tr> streambuf_type;
	typedef basic_istream<E, Tr> istream_type;
	typedef typename traits_type::int_type int_type;

	istreambuf_iterator(streambuf_type *Sb = 0) throw ()
		: Sbuf(Sb), Got(Sb == 0) {}
	istreambuf_iterator(istream_type& I) throw ()
		: Sbuf(I.rdbuf()), Got(I.rdbuf() == 0) {}
```

Figure 3.8: `xutility` **part 8**

```
        const E& operator*() const
            {if (!Got)
                ((Myt *)this)->Peek();
            return (Val); }
        const E *operator->() const
            {return (&**this); }
        Myt& operator++()
            {Inc();
            return (*this); }
        Myt operator++(int)
            {if (!Got)
                Peek();
            Myt Tmp = *this;
            Inc();
            return (Tmp); }
        bool equal(const Myt& X) const
            {if (!Got)
                ((Myt *)this)->Peek();
            if (!X.Got)
                ((Myt *)&X)->Peek();
            return (Sbuf == 0 && X.Sbuf == 0
                || Sbuf != 0 && X.Sbuf != 0); }
private:
        void Inc()
            {if (Sbuf == 0
                || traits_type::eq_int_type(traits_type::eof(),
                    Sbuf->sbumpc()))
                Sbuf = 0, Got = true;
            else
                Got = false; }
        E Peek()
            {int_type C;
            if (Sbuf == 0
                || traits_type::eq_int_type(traits_type::eof(),
                    C = Sbuf->sgetc()))
                Sbuf = 0;
            else
                Val = traits_type::to_char_type(C);
            Got = true;
            return (Val); }
        streambuf_type *Sbuf;
        bool Got;
        E Val;
        };

            // istreambuf_iterator TEMPLATE OPERATORS
template<class E, class Tr> inline
        bool operator==(const istreambuf_iterator<E, Tr>& X,
            const istreambuf_iterator<E, Tr>& Y)
        {return (X.equal(Y)); }
template<class E, class Tr> inline
        bool operator!=(const istreambuf_iterator<E, Tr>& X,
            const istreambuf_iterator<E, Tr>& Y)
        {return (!(X == Y)); }
```

Figure 3.9: `xutility` **part 9**

```
          // TEMPLATE CLASS ostreambuf_iterator
template<class E, class Tr>
     class ostreambuf_iterator
          : public Outit {
     typedef ostreambuf_iterator<E, Tr> Myt;
public:
     typedef E char_type;
     typedef Tr traits_type;
     typedef basic_streambuf<E, Tr> streambuf_type;
     typedef basic_ostream<E, Tr> ostream_type;

     ostreambuf_iterator(streambuf_type *Sb) throw ()
          : Failed(false), Sbuf(Sb) {}
     ostreambuf_iterator(ostream_type& O) throw ()
          : Failed(false), Sbuf(O.rdbuf()) {}
     Myt& operator=(E X)
          {if (Sbuf == 0
               || traits_type::eq_int_type(Tr::eof(),
                    Sbuf->sputc(X)))
               Failed = true;
          return (*this); }
     Myt& operator*()
          {return (*this); }
     Myt& operator++()
          {return (*this); }
     Myt& operator++(int)
          {return (*this); }
     bool failed() const throw ()
          {return (Failed); }
private:
     bool Failed;
     streambuf_type *Sbuf;
     };

//   ALGORITHM STUFF (from <algorithm>)

          // TEMPLATE FUNCTION copy
template<class InIt, class OutIt> inline
     OutIt copy(InIt F, InIt L, OutIt X)
     {for (; F != L; ++X, ++F)
          *X = *F;
     return (X); }

          // TEMPLATE FUNCTION copy_backward
template<class BidIt1, class BidIt2> inline
     BidIt2 copy_backward(BidIt1 F, BidIt1 L, BidIt2 X)
     {while (F != L)
          *--X = *--L;
     return (X); }

          // TEMPLATE FUNCTION equal
template<class InIt1, class InIt2> inline
     bool equal(InIt1 F, InIt1 L, InIt2 X)
     {return (mismatch(F, L, X).first == L); }
```

Figure 3.10: `xutility` **part 10**

```
        // TEMPLATE FUNCTION equal WITH PRED
template<class InIt1, class InIt2, class Pr> inline
    bool equal(InIt1 F, InIt1 L, InIt2 X, Pr P)
    {return (mismatch(F, L, X, P).first == L); }

        // TEMPLATE FUNCTION fill
template<class FwdIt, class T> inline
    void fill(FwdIt F, FwdIt L, const T& X)
    {for (; F != L; ++F)
        *F = X; }

        // TEMPLATE FUNCTION fill_n
template<class OutIt, class Sz, class T> inline
    void fill_n(OutIt F, Sz N, const T& X)
    {for (; 0 < N; --N, ++F)
        *F = X; }

        // TEMPLATE FUNCTION lexicographical_compare
template<class InIt1, class InIt2> inline
    bool lexicographical_compare(InIt1 F1, InIt1 L1,
        InIt2 F2, InIt2 L2)
    {for (; F1 != L1 && F2 != L2; ++F1, ++F2)
        if (*F1 < *F2)
            return (true);
        else if (*F2 < *F1)
            return (false);
    return (F1 == L1 && F2 != L2); }

        // TEMPLATE FUNCTION lexicographical_compare WITH PRED
template<class InIt1, class InIt2, class Pr> inline
    bool lexicographical_compare(InIt1 F1, InIt1 L1,
        InIt2 F2, InIt2 L2, Pr P)
    {for (; F1 != L1 && F2 != L2; ++F1, ++F2)
        if (P(*F1, *F2))
            return (true);
        else if (P(*F2, *F1))
            return (false);
    return (F1 == L1 && F2 != L2); }

        // TEMPLATE FUNCTION max
template<class T> inline
    const T& max(const T& X, const T& Y)
    {return (X < Y ? Y : X); }

        // TEMPLATE FUNCTION max WITH PRED
template<class T, class Pr> inline
    const T& max(const T& X, const T& Y, Pr P)
    {return (P(X, Y) ? Y : X); }

        // TEMPLATE FUNCTION min
template<class T> inline
    const T& min(const T& X, const T& Y)
    {return (Y < X ? Y : X); }
```

Figure 3.11: xutility part 11

```
        // TEMPLATE FUNCTION min WITH PRED
template<class T, class Pr> inline
    const T& min(const T& X, const T& Y, Pr P)
    {return (P(Y, X) ? Y : X); }

        // TEMPLATE FUNCTION mismatch
template<class InIt1, class InIt2> inline
    pair<InIt1, InIt2> mismatch(InIt1 F, InIt1 L, InIt2 X)
    {for (; F != L && *F == *X; ++F, ++X)
        ;
    return (pair<InIt1, InIt2>(F, X)); }

        // TEMPLATE FUNCTION mismatch WITH PRED
template<class InIt1, class InIt2, class Pr> inline
    pair<InIt1, InIt2> mismatch(InIt1 F, InIt1 L, InIt2 X, Pr P)
    {for (; F != L && P(*F, *X); ++F, ++X)
        ;
    return (pair<InIt1, InIt2>(F, X)); }

        // TEMPLATE FUNCTION swap
template<class T> inline
    void swap(T& X, T& Y)
    {T Tmp = X;
    X = Y, Y = Tmp; }
} /* namespace std */
#endif /* XUTILITY_ */
```
□

iterator **Bidit** **Ranit** **Outit** The header then defines template class **iterator**. It also defines two template classes derived from **iterator** — **Bidit** for describing bidirectional iterators and **Ranit** for describing random-access iterators. These templates are helpful in avoiding naming problems within several of the container template classes, which both refer to **iterator** and redefine the name. Class **Outit**, by contrast, serves primarily as a convenient shorthand for defining output iterators throughout the STL headers.

iterator_traits **Iter_cat** **Val_type** **Dist_type** Template class **iterator_traits** is the more recently introduced mechanism for determining the properties of iterators. The two partial specializations, for pointers and for const pointers, are a necessary part of this mechanism. For implementations that do not support partial specialization, the template functions **Iter_cat**, **Val_type**, and **Dist_type** provide approximately the same information, as we discussed earlier in this chapter. Each of these three template function comes in at least two versions, one that accepts some form of **iterator** argument and one that accepts a pointer. **Iter_cat** is further overloaded on all the basic integer types; these overloads all return an object of class **Int_iterator_tag** to identify an "iterator" parameter that is actually an integer. With these three template functions, the function overload resolution machinery makes up for the possible absence of partial specialization.

distance **Distance** Template function **distance** is the standard mechanism for determining the difference between two iterators in a range. Once again, we also retain an older mechanism that does not depend on **iterator_traits** (and partial specialization) to work properly with object pointers. Template function **Distance** increments its third argument by the computed difference, rather than return the computed difference as the value of the function. Both template functions defer to template function **Distance2** to perform the common simple task of computing the actual difference. As simple as the task may be, it still varies among the different categories of iterators. Here is a classic example of the use of tag overloading to select among alternate implementations of an algorithm.

It is also an example of yet another practical limitation of some current C++ translators. The overloads for **forward_iterator_tag** and **bidirectional_iterator_tag** should not be necessary. The whole idea behind deriving these tags from **input_iterator_tag** is to avoid the need to overload on the former if the latter does the job, as is the case here. But we find that some translators fail to resolve overloads properly with the more Spartan list. Hence, we include redundant definitions, for purely pragmatic reasons, to make the code more portable.

Ptrit Template class **Ptrit** is yet another concession to compiler limitations. It wraps an object pointer with a class derived from **iterator** that has all the necessary attributes of a random-access iterator. You will see how it is used in Chapter 10: **<vector>**. In a full implementation of the Standard C++ library, it can also be used by template class **basic_string**. The class **vector<T>** *can* define an iterator that is just a synonym for the object pointer **T ***. Indeed, many implementations indulge this latitude. This implementation prefers to define such an iterator as **Ptrit<T, ptrdiff_t, T *, T&, T *, T&>**, for two reasons:

- It avoids the need for template partial specialization when declaring the reverse iterator for **vector<T>**, using template class **reverse_iterator**. (See below.)
- It guards against a variety of unsafe programming practices, where the programmer inadvertently confuses object pointers and iterators.

Ptrit has the added virtue that it serves as a good prototype for an random-access iterator class.

The last two template parameters may at first seem redundant. Closer inspection reveals, however, that they help specify some sort of converting constructor. For a const iterator, this constructor converts its non-const cousin to a const iterator. For a non-const iterator, this constructor simply becomes an explicitly specified default copy constructor. (You do not want to permit implicit conversion from a const iterator to a non-const iterator, but you do want implicit conversion the other way around.)

reverse_iterator Template class **reverse_iterator** creates a reverse iterator from a random-access iterator. None of the code for **reverse_iterator** is particularly tricky once you understand the essential design principle behind reverse iterators. It is captured in the member function **operator*()**:

```
Ref operator*() const
    {return (*(current - 1)); }
```

Put simply, a reverse iterator returns the element just *before* the one designated by **current**. The reason why is simple, once you think about it. You typically designate a sequence by the range of iterators **[first, last)**. The half-open interval notation means that **first** is part of a non-empty sequence but **last** is just past the end.

You designate a range of reverse iterators by the range of **current** values **[last, first)**. For **last** to work as the value stored in **current**, it has to designate the element at **current - 1** in a non-empty sequence. Once you make this shift, all the other properties of iterators follow pretty naturally.

Revbidit Template class **Revbidit** creates a reverse iterator from a bidirectional iterator. Most of the same comments apply as for template class **reverse_iterator**. The essential "trick" lies in the definition of member function **operator*()**, as before.

istreambuf_iterator Template class **istreambuf_iterator** creates an input iterator that extracts elements of type **E** (typically **char**) from a stream buffer. While perhaps not as strange as output iterators (see, for example, template class **ostreambuf_iterator** immediately below), input iterators are equally stylized. The delicate design issues for an input iterator are:

- reading ahead, to have an input value on hand when it's needed
- detecting and recording end of sequence (end of file)
- creating an end-of-sequence value
- comparing two iterators to determine whether both are at end of sequence

Template class **istreambuf_iterator** serves as a good prototype for input iterators, but you should compare it to others in this implementation to study the reasons for any differences. For example, this template class differs from the older template class **istream_iterator** (described later in this chapter) primarily in its read-ahead logic. The latter class is obliged to read an number of elements to determine the next value of type **U** to extract, so it makes little effort to minimize read ahead.

The Standard C++ library, on the other hand can create and destroy any number of objects of template class **istreambuf_iterator**, in the process of extracting values from an input stream. The destruction of each such object must leave the input stream in a known state, with no loss of unconsumed input. A stream buffer lets you "peek" at an element — obtain its value without pointing past it in the stream — with the member function **sgetc()**. But even that operation can cause the program to hang indefinitely if, for example, the stream buffer is associated with an interactive input stream such as a keyboard. Thus, the iterator defers any attempt to peek at the next element until it is obliged to deliver its value on a call to a member function. Note that a peek must occur before comparing an iterator with another, to determine whether the iterator has just reached the end of sequence.

ostreambuf_iterator Template class **ostreambuf_iterator** creates an output iterator that inserts elements of type **E** (typically **char**) into a stream buffer. It differs from the older template class **ostream_iterator** (described later in this chapter) primarily in its handling of output errors. Typically, an output iterator behaves as an infinite sink for generated elements. It has no way to report that it can store no more. But the Standard C++ library needs a way to pass up the line any failures reported by the underlying stream buffer. Thus, the added member function **failed** and its associated logic.

On the face of it, the member operator definitions in this template class are outrageous. They do not supply the semantics normally associated with their operators:

- **operator*()** returns a reference to the iterator, not the designated element.
- **operator++()** does not advance the iterator.
- **operator++(int)** does not advance the iterator.
- **operator=(E)** is a most unconventional overload of the assignment operator. It performs the actual output operation and effectively advances the iterator in the bargain.

Remember, however, that an output iterator **next** is meant to be used in just one or two stylized ways:

```
for (;<not done>; ++next)
    *next = <whatever>;
```

or

```
while (<not done>)
    *next++ = <whatever>
```

Walk through the member operator definitions for these two stylized loops. You will see that the operators supply the absolute minimum functionality needed to supply the semantics required for output iterators.

Thus, template class **ostreambuf_iterator** serves as a good prototype for any output iterator you might choose to write. STL defines several flavors of output iterators, in this and subsequent chapters. Study them carefully, for both their differences and their similarities. Output iterators are powerful tools, but they are peculiar enough to hide any number of pitfalls.

iterator The remainder of the file **xutility** consists of definitions associated with the header **<algorithm>**. See Chapter 6: **<algorithm>** for a discussion of such definitions. Figures 3.12 through 3.15 show the file **iterator**. It defines the remaining entities, not already defined in **xutility**, associated with the header **<iterator>**

back_insert_iterator Template class **back_insert_iterator** creates an output iterator that appends elements to a container. As with other output iterators, it does so through an unusual assignment operator, in this case **operator=(Cont::const_reference V)**. It performs the actual append by calling **container->push_back(V)** for the designated container.

Figure 3.12: `iterator` part 1

```
// iterator standard header
#ifndef ITERATOR_
#define ITERATOR_
#include <xutility>
namespace std {
          // TEMPLATE CLASS back_insert_iterator
template<class C>
     class back_insert_iterator
          : public Outit {
public:
     typedef C container_type;
     typedef typename C::reference reference;
     typedef typename C::value_type value_type;
     explicit back_insert_iterator(C& X)
          : container(&X) {}
     back_insert_iterator<C>& operator=(
          typename C::const_reference V)
          {container->push_back(V);
          return (*this); }
     back_insert_iterator<C>& operator*()
          {return (*this); }
     back_insert_iterator<C>& operator++()
          {return (*this); }
     back_insert_iterator<C> operator++(int)
          {return (*this); }
protected:
     C *container;
     };
template<class C> inline
     back_insert_iterator<C> back_inserter(C& X)
     {return (back_insert_iterator<C>(X)); }

          // TEMPLATE CLASS front_insert_iterator
template<class C>
     class front_insert_iterator
          : public Outit {
public:
     typedef C container_type;
     typedef typename C::reference reference;
     typedef typename C::value_type value_type;
     explicit front_insert_iterator(C& X)
          : container(&X) {}
     front_insert_iterator<C>& operator=(
          typename C::const_reference V)
          {container->push_front(V);
          return (*this); }
     front_insert_iterator<C>& operator*()
          {return (*this); }
     front_insert_iterator<C>& operator++()
          {return (*this); }
     front_insert_iterator<C> operator++(int)
          {return (*this); }
protected:
     C *container;
     };
```

Figure 3.13: `iterator` **part 2**

```
template<class C> inline
     front_insert_iterator<C> front_inserter(C& X)
     {return (front_insert_iterator<C>(X)); }

          // TEMPLATE CLASS insert_iterator
template<class C>
     class insert_iterator
          : public Outit {
public:
     typedef C container_type;
     typedef typename C::reference reference;
     typedef typename C::value_type value_type;
     insert_iterator(C& X, typename C::iterator I)
          : container(&X), iter(I) {}
     insert_iterator<C>& operator=(
          typename C::const_reference V)
          {iter = container->insert(iter, V);
          ++iter;
          return (*this); }
     insert_iterator<C>& operator*()
          {return (*this); }
     insert_iterator<C>& operator++()
          {return (*this); }
     insert_iterator<C>& operator++(int)
          {return (*this); }
protected:
     C *container;
     typename C::iterator iter;
     };
template<class C, class XI> inline
     insert_iterator<C> inserter(C& X, XI I)
     {return (insert_iterator<C>(X, C::iterator(I))); }

          // TEMPLATE CLASS istream_iterator
template<class T, class E = char,
     class Tr = char_traits<E>,
     class Dist = ptrdiff_t>
     class istream_iterator
          : public iterator<input_iterator_tag, T, Dist,
               T *, T&> {
public:
     typedef istream_iterator<T, E, Tr, Dist> Myt;
     typedef E char_type;
     typedef Tr traits_type;
     typedef basic_istream<E, Tr> istream_type;
     istream_iterator()
          : Istr(0) {}
     istream_iterator(istream_type& I)
          : Istr(&I) {Getval(); }
     const T& operator*() const
          {return (Val); }
     const T *operator->() const
          {return (&**this); }
```

Figure 3.14: `iterator` **part 3**

```
    Myt& operator++()
        {Getval();
        return (*this); }
    Myt operator++(int)
        {Myt Tmp = *this;
        Getval();
        return (Tmp); }
    bool Equal(const Myt& X) const
        {return (Istr == X.Istr); }
protected:
    void Getval()
        {if (Istr != 0 && !(*Istr >> Val))
            Istr = 0; }
    istream_type *Istr;
    T Val;
    };

        // istream_iterator TEMPLATE OPERATORS
template<class T, class E, class Tr, class Dist> inline
    bool operator==(
        const istream_iterator<T, E, Tr, Dist>& X,
        const istream_iterator<T, E, Tr, Dist>& Y)
    {return (X.Equal(Y)); }
template<class T, class E, class Tr, class Dist> inline
    bool operator!=(
        const istream_iterator<T, E, Tr, Dist>& X,
        const istream_iterator<T, E, Tr, Dist>& Y)
    {return (!(X == Y)); }

        // TEMPLATE CLASS ostream_iterator
template<class T, class E = char,
    class Tr = char_traits<E> >
    class ostream_iterator
        : public Outit {
public:
    typedef T value_type;
    typedef E char_type;
    typedef Tr traits_type;
    typedef basic_ostream<E, Tr> ostream_type;
    ostream_iterator(ostream_type& O,
        const E *D = 0)
        : Ostr(&O), Delim(D) {}
    ostream_iterator<T, E, Tr>& operator=(const T& X)
        {*Ostr << X;
        if (Delim != 0)
            *Ostr << Delim;
        return (*this); }
    ostream_iterator<T, E, Tr>& operator*()
        {return (*this); }
    ostream_iterator<T, E, Tr>& operator++()
        {return (*this); }
    ostream_iterator<T, E, Tr> operator++(int)
        {return (*this); }
```

Figure 3.15: `iterator` part 4

```
protected:
     const E *Delim;
     ostream_type *Ostr;
     };

          // TEMPLATE FUNCTION Val_type
template<class It> inline
     typename iterator_traits<It>::value_type *Val_type(It)
     {return (0); }

          // TEMPLATE FUNCTION advance
template<class InIt, class D> inline
     void advance(InIt& I, D N)
     {Advance(I, N, Iter_cat(I)); }
template<class InIt, class D> inline
     void Advance(InIt& I, D N, input_iterator_tag)
     {for (; 0 < N; --N)
          ++I; }
template<class FwdIt, class D> inline
     void Advance(FwdIt& I, D N, forward_iterator_tag)
     {for (; 0 < N; --N)
          ++I; }
template<class BidIt, class D> inline
     void Advance(BidIt& I, D N, bidirectional_iterator_tag)
     {for (; 0 < N; --N)
          ++I;
     for (; N < 0; ++N)
          --I; }
template<class RanIt, class D> inline
     void Advance(RanIt& I, D N, random_access_iterator_tag)
     {I += N; }

          // TEMPLATE FUNCTION Dist_type
template<class It> inline
     typename iterator_traits<It>::difference_type
          *Dist_type(It)
     {return (0); }
} /* namespace std */
#endif /* ITERATOR_ */
```
□

`back_ inserter` Template function **`back_inserter`** constructs an object of class **`back_insert_iterator<Cont>`** suitable for use with its container argument.

`front_ insert_ iterator` Template class **`front_insert_iterator`** creates an output iterator that prepends elements (in reverse order) to a container, by calling **`container->push_front(V)`**. It otherwise closely resembles template class **`back_insert_iterator`**.

`front_ inserter` Template function **`front_inserter`** constructs an object of class **`front_insert_iterator<Cont>`** suitable for use with its container argument.

`insert_ iterator` Template class **`insert_iterator`** creates an output iterator that inserts elements at a designated point within a container. Unlike template class

back_insert_iterator, such an iterator must also store the iterator **iter**, which designates the insertion point within the iterator. Note the difference in return values, between the two template classes, for the member function **operator++(int)**. An iterator that stores changing state information must return a reference to an up-to-date version of the iterator. The conventional practice of returning a new object just won't do.

inserter Template function **inserter** constructs an object of class **insert_iterator<Cont, Iter>** suitable for use with its container argument.

istream_iterator Template class **istream_iterator** creates an input iterator that extracts values of type **U** from an input stream, using a suitable overload of **operator>>**. Compare it to template class **istreambuf_iterator**, described earlier in this chapter.

ostream_iterator Template class **ostream_iterator** creates an output iterator that inserts values of type **U** into an output stream, using a suitable overload of **operator<<**. It follows the usual form for output iterators. Compare it to template class **ostreambuf_iterator**, described earlier in this chapter.

Val_type **Dist_type** Template function **Val_type** returns a null pointer whose type reveals the "value type" of its iterator argument (the member type **value_type**). Similarly, template function **Dist_type** returns the "distance type" (the member type **difference_type**, which was once called **distance_type**). We discussed the historical reasons for these apparently trivial functions earlier in this chapter.

advance Finally, template function **advance** performs the apparently simple task of advancing an iterator a specified number of times. But it is much like the template function **distance** described earlier. The best way to advance an iterator varies among the different categories. We once again make use of tag overloading to select among alternate implementations of an algorithm.

Testing <iterator>

titerato.c Figures 3.16 through 3.20 show the file **titerato.c**. Because the header **<iterator>** is so large, the program tests the various parts in groups:

- the templates that determine various properties of iterators, and perform simple manipulations of iterators
- template class **reverse_iterator**
- insertion iterators
- template class **istream_iterator**
- template class **ostream_iterator**
- template class **istreambuf_iterator**
- template class **ostreambuf_iterator**

If all goes well, the program prints:

```
SUCCESS testing <iterator>
```

and takes a normal exit.

Figure 3.16: `titerato.c` part 1

```
// test <iterator>
#include <assert.h>
#include <iostream>
#include <string.h>
#include <strstream>
#include <deque>
#include <iterator>
using namespace std;

typedef char *PtrIt;

     // TEST GENERAL PROPERTY TEMPLATES
void takes_ran_tag(random_access_iterator_tag)
     {}

void test_prop()
     {random_access_iterator_tag *ran_tag =
          (random_access_iterator_tag *)0;
     bidirectional_iterator_tag *bid_tag =
          (random_access_iterator_tag *)0;
     forward_iterator_tag *fwd_tag =
          (bidirectional_iterator_tag *)0;
     input_iterator_tag *in_tag =
          (forward_iterator_tag *)0;
     output_iterator_tag *p_out_tag = 0;

     typedef iterator<input_iterator_tag, float, short,
          float *, float&> Iter;
     float fl;
     Iter::iterator_category *it_tag =
          (input_iterator_tag *)0;
     Iter::value_type *it_val = (float *)0;
     Iter::difference_type *it_dist = (short *)0;
     Iter::pointer it_ptr = (float *)0;
     Iter::reference it_ref = fl;

     typedef iterator_traits<Iter> Traits;
     Traits::iterator_category *tr_tag =
          (input_iterator_tag *)0;
     Traits::value_type *tr_val = (float *)0;
     Traits::difference_type *tr_dist = (short *)0;
     Traits::pointer tr_ptr = (float *)0;
     Traits::reference tr_ref = fl;

     typedef iterator_traits<PtrIt> Ptraits;
     char ch;
     takes_ran_tag(Ptraits::iterator_category());
     Ptraits::value_type *ptr_val = (char *)0;
     Ptraits::difference_type *ptr_dist = (ptrdiff_t *)0;
     Ptraits::pointer ptr_ptr = (char *)0;
     Ptraits::reference ptr_ref = ch;

     const char *pc = "abcdefg";
     advance(pc, 4);
     assert(*pc == 'e');
```

Figure 3.17: `titerato.c` part 2

```
     advance(pc, -1);
     assert(*pc == 'd');
     assert(distance(pc, pc + 3) == 3); }

     // TEST reverse_iterator
typedef reverse_iterator<PtrIt> RevIt;
class MyrevIt : public RevIt {
public:
     MyrevIt(RevIt::iterator_type p)
          : RevIt(p) {}
     RevIt::iterator_type get_current() const
          {return (current); }
     };

void test_revit()
     {char *pc = (char *)"abcdefg" + 3;
     PtrIt pcit(pc);
     RevIt::iterator_type *p_iter = (PtrIt *)0;
     RevIt rit0, rit(pcit);

     assert(rit.base() == pcit);
     assert(*rit == 'c');
     assert(*++rit == 'b');
     assert(*rit++ == 'b' && *rit == 'a');
     assert(*--rit == 'b');
     assert(*rit-- == 'b' && *rit == 'c');
     assert(*(rit += 2) == 'a');
     assert(*(rit -= 2) == 'c');
     assert(*(rit + 2) == 'a' && *rit == 'c');
     assert(*(rit - 2) == 'e' && *rit == 'c');
     assert(rit[2] == 'a');
     assert(rit == rit);
     assert(!(rit < rit) && rit < rit + 1);
     assert((rit + 2) - rit == 2);

     MyrevIt myrit(pc);
     assert(myrit.get_current() == pcit); }

//   TEST INSERTION ITERATORS
typedef deque<char, allocator<char> > Cont;
typedef back_insert_iterator<Cont> BackIt;
class MybackIt : public BackIt {
public:
     MybackIt(BackIt::container_type& c)
          : BackIt(c) {}
     BackIt::container_type *get_container() const
          {return (container); }
     };

typedef front_insert_iterator<Cont> FrontIt;
class MyfrontIt : public FrontIt {
public:
     MyfrontIt(FrontIt::container_type& c)
          : FrontIt(c) {}
```

Figure 3.18: `titerato.c` **part 3**

```
    FrontIt::container_type *get_container() const
        {return (container); }
    };

typedef insert_iterator<Cont> InsIt;
class MyinsIt : public InsIt {
public:
    MyinsIt(InsIt::container_type& c, Cont::iterator it)
        : InsIt(c, it) {}
    InsIt::container_type *get_container() const
        {return (container); }
    Cont::iterator get_iterator() const
        {return (iter); }
    };

void test_inserts()
    {Cont c0;
    char ch;
    BackIt::container_type *pbi_cont = (Cont *)0;
    BackIt::reference pbi_ref = ch;
    BackIt::value_type *pbi_val = (char *)0;
    BackIt bit(c0);
    *bit = 'a', ++bit;
    *bit++ = 'b';
    assert(c0[0] == 'a' && c0[1] == 'b');
    MybackIt mybkit(c0);
    assert(mybkit.get_container() == &c0);
    *back_inserter(c0)++ = 'x';
    assert(c0[2] == 'x');

    FrontIt::container_type *pfi_cont = (Cont *)0;
    FrontIt::reference pfi_ref = ch;
    FrontIt::value_type *pfi_val = (char *)0;
    FrontIt fit(c0);
    *fit = 'c', ++fit;
    *fit++ = 'd';
    assert(c0[0] == 'd' && c0[1] == 'c');
    MyfrontIt myfrit(c0);
    assert(myfrit.get_container() == &c0);
    *front_inserter(c0)++ = 'y';
    assert(c0[0] == 'y');

    InsIt::container_type *pii_cont = (Cont *)0;
    InsIt::reference pii_ref = ch;
    InsIt::value_type *pii_val = (char *)0;
    InsIt iit(c0, c0.begin());
    *iit = 'e', ++iit;
    *iit++ = 'f';
    assert(c0[0] == 'e' && c0[1] == 'f');
    MyinsIt myinsit(c0, c0.begin());
    assert(myinsit.get_container() == &c0);
    assert(myinsit.get_iterator() == c0.begin());
    *inserter(c0, c0.begin())++ = 'z';
    assert(c0[0] == 'z'); }
```

Figure 3.19: `titerato.c` **part 4**

```
     // TEST istream_iterator
void test_istreamit()
     {istrstream istr("0 1 2 3");
     typedef istream_iterator<int, char,
          char_traits<char>, ptrdiff_t> IstrIt;
     IstrIt::char_type *p_char = (char *)0;
     IstrIt::traits_type *p_traits = (char_traits<char> *)0;
     IstrIt::istream_type *p_istream = (istream *)0;
     IstrIt iit0, iit(istr);
     int n;
     for (n = 0; n < 5 && iit != iit0; ++n)
          assert(*iit++ == n);
     assert(n == 4); }

     // TEST ostream_iterator
void test_ostreamit()
     {ostrstream ostr0, ostr;
     typedef ostream_iterator<int, char,
          char_traits<char> > OstrIt;
     OstrIt::value_type *p_val = (int *)0;
     OstrIt::char_type *p_char = (char *)0;
     OstrIt::traits_type *p_traits = (char_traits<char> *)0;
     OstrIt::ostream_type *p_ostream =
          (basic_ostream<char, char_traits<char> > *)0;
     OstrIt oit0(ostr0), oit(ostr, "||");
     *oit0 = 1, ++oit0;
     *oit0++ = 2;
     ostr0 << ends;
     assert(strcmp(ostr0.str(), "12") == 0);
     ostr.freeze(false);

     *oit = 1, ++oit;
     *oit++ = 2;
     ostr << ends;
     assert(strcmp(ostr.str(), "1||2||") == 0);
     ostr.freeze(false); }

     // TEST istreambuf_iterator
void test_istrbufit()
     {istrstream istr("0123"), istr1("");
     typedef istreambuf_iterator<char,
          char_traits<char> > IsbIt;
     IsbIt::char_type *p_char = (char *)0;
     IsbIt::traits_type *p_traits = (char_traits<char> *)0;
     IsbIt::int_type *p_int = (int *)0;
     IsbIt::streambuf_type *p_streambuf =
          (basic_streambuf<char, char_traits<char> > *)0;
     IsbIt::istream_type *p_istream =
          (basic_istream<char, char_traits<char> > *)0;
     IsbIt iit0, iit(istr), iit1(istr1.rdbuf());
     int n;
     for (n = 0; n < 5 && iit != iit0; ++n)
          assert(*iit++ == n + '0');
     assert(n == 4);
     assert(iit0.equal(iit1)); }
```

Figure 3.20: `titerato.c` **part 5**

```
     // TEST ostreambuf_iterator
void test_ostrbufit()
     {ostrstream ostr;
     typedef ostreambuf_iterator<char,
          char_traits<char> > OsbIt;
     OsbIt::char_type *p_char = (char *)0;
     OsbIt::traits_type *p_traits = (char_traits<char> *)0;
     OsbIt::streambuf_type *p_streambuf =
          (basic_streambuf<char, char_traits<char> > *)0;
     OsbIt::ostream_type *p_ostream =
          (basic_ostream<char, char_traits<char> > *)0;
     OsbIt oit0((OsbIt::streambuf_type *)0), oit(ostr);
     *oit0++ = 'x';
     assert(oit0.failed());

     *oit = '1', ++oit;
     *oit++ = '2';
     ostr << ends;
     assert(strcmp(ostr.str(), "12") == 0);
     assert(!oit.failed());
     ostr.freeze(false); }

     // TEST <iterator>
int main()
     {test_prop();
     test_revit();
     test_inserts();
     test_istreamit();
     test_ostreamit();
     test_istrbufit();
     test_ostrbufit();
     cout << "SUCCESS testing <iterator>" << endl;
     return (0); }
```

Exercises

Exercise 3.1 Why isn't `input_iterator_tag` derived from `output_iterator_tag`?

Exercise 3.2 Why doesn't STL define a template class `reverse_forward_iterator`?

Exercise 3.3 Define an iterator that inserts elements at the beginning of a container, without reversing them as does an object of template class `front_insert_iterator`.

Exercise 3.4 Define an iterator that inserts elements at the end of a container, reversing them as does an object of template class `front_insert_iterator`.

Exercise 3.5 For an iterator, the member function `operator++(int)` typically returns a copy of the iterator. Yet template class `insert_iterator` and template class `ostreambuf_iterator` each return a reference to the object itself. Explain why this is necessary.

Exercise 3.6 Define the template class `forward_iterator<FwdIt>` that simply "wraps" a forward iterator of class `FwdIt`. Be sure to include all operations required of forward iterators.

Exercise 3.7 [**Harder**] Define a set of "strict" iterators, to wrap iterators of each of the five categories. The strict iterators should report any violation of proper protocol when they are used in a program. They should also report any attempt to advance an iterator outside a range determined when the iterator is constructed.

Exercise 3.8 [**Very hard**] How can you verify that a given iterator always honors the protocol required by its category?

Chapter 4: `<memory>`

Background

Of the thirteen STL headers, the header `<memory>` is by far the hardest to describe. It deals primarily with unusual ways to allocate storage for the elements of a container. It also provides machinery for managing temporary storage during the execution of certain algorithms. Earlier STL code had roughly equivalent mechanisms that were less ambitious. On the popular PC architecture, for example, containers could allocate elements on either a "near" or a "far" heap —, by employing alternate pointer representations not contemplated in the C Standard. As adopted into the C++ Standard, however, this ad hoc machinery was replaced by *allocators* — objects that mediate the allocation and freeing of element storage.

`allocator` The flagship component of the header `<memory>` is thus the template class `allocator`, which is specialized to produce all default allocators for containers. The original version of this template class was soon replaced with a more ambitious version. The new version had one significant drawback — it was unimplementable at the time of its introduction, given then current C++ compiler technology. That version was subsequently twice replaced with still other ambitious versions — which, unfortunately, were equally unimplementable at the time. Only recently are the language features needed to support allocators becoming at all widespread. Hence, real-world experience with using allocators is perforce still limited.

The good news is that you seldom need to concern yourself directly with the workings of allocators. The ones you get by default do pretty much what you'd expect. The bad news is that allocators are nevertheless ubiquitous. One of the parameters of every STL container template class, defined in the Standard C++ library at least, is the type of its allocator. One of the objects stored in every container object is its allocator. Fortunately, a default template argument can specify the default allocator type for you, and a default function argument can whomp up a default allocator object for you. Allocators may be a headache for implementors, given their subtleties and the demands they make on C++ translators. But they need not be a comparable nuisance to programmers who simply want to use STL.

Our initial goal in this chapter is to justify the utility of template class `allocator` in writing STL code. We show how allocators work, along with their supporting template functions. We outline the circumstances that might lead you to define your own allocators. We show, as usual, how to implement template class **allocator** and the other facilities in the header **<memory>**. Along the way, we also describe some of the compromise allocators you are likely to encounter with compilers that lack all the required machinery.

why allocators One of the important services provided by the template container classes is storage management. A container object allocates and frees storage for the elements of the sequence it manages. Some containers must also allocate additional storage. A list, for example, needs to store the pointers that link elements together, as well as the elements themselves. A deque maintains a map — an array of pointers — separate from the blocks of memory that store elements. The container thus encapsulates two important services:

- It hides the details of how storage allocation and freeing actually occurs.
- It ensures that all allocated storage is eventually freed.

An allocator object handles the first job, on behalf of the container object. It has member functions that allocate and deallocate objects of a given type. It can also construct and destroy such objects in the storage provided. It can even give you some idea about how many objects of a given type can be simultaneously allocated.

You associate an allocator with a container in two stages. When you specialize the template container type, you specify the allocator *type* as well as the type of elements the container maintains. For example, to define a class **Mylist** that maintains a list of **float** elements with an allocator of class **Myalloc**, you might write:

```
#include <list>
.....
typedef list<float, Myalloc> Mylist;
```

Then when you construct an object of class **Mylist**, you specify the actual *allocator object*, as in:

```
Myalloc an_allocator;
Mylist a_list(an_allocator);
```

Using default template arguments, however, you can avoid these details and write simply:

```
typedef list<float> Mylist2;
```

The default allocator supplied in this case is **allocator<float>**. Similarly, you can omit the allocator argument from a constructor, as in:

```
Mylist a_list;
```

The default allocator object supplied in this case is **Myalloc()**.

custom allocators Why would you want to write a custom allocator? You might, for example, want to maintain a pool of freed list elements. The default allocator satisfies each request for a new element by calling **operator new**. It likewise calls **operator delete** for each element that is freed. But it is much faster, on average, to recycle list elements from such a pool. A custom allocator could add deallocated elements to a free list, and satisfy allocation requests from this free list whenever possible.

But allocators do more than support private storage pools. They also specify the various *types* connected with accessing the objects they allocate and free. Here is where things get abstruse. In a typical C++ program, you know several things about an object **x** of type **T**:

- The expression **&x** has type **T ***, or **const T ***.
- A reference to **x** has type **T&**, or **const T&**.
- For **p** a pointer to **x**, the expression ***p** has type **T**.
- The number of elements in the largest possible array of **T** can be represented as type **size_t**.
- The difference between two pointers to **T** has type **ptrdiff_t**.

All this is too obvious for words, if you understand the underpinnings of C and C++. It is just not necessarily true.

far pointers Consider, for example, a PC-based implementation that supports a *far heap*, as we mentioned earlier. The heap is implemented in storage addressed by special far pointers that may be larger than conventional pointers. This may not be standard C++, but it is certainly a widely supported dialect. It might make sense to allocate all your list elements on the far heap, even though the rest of the program is compiled using pointers of conventional size. In such a situation:

- The expression **&x** has type **T far ***, or **const T far ***.
- A reference to **x** has type **T far &**, or **const T far &**.
- For **p** a far pointer to **x**, the expression ***p** has type **T** (as before).
- The number of elements in the largest possible array of **T** can be represented as type **unsigned long**.
- The difference between two pointers to **T** has type **long**.

allocator limitations An allocator class contains type definitions for these basic properties. Each STL container is carefully written in terms of the types solicited from its allocator type parameter. You can thus perform some moderately daring feats of storage management, for elements of an STL container, with a skillfully crafted allocator template class. How daring? That is the subject of some debate. Opinions differ within the Committee about how much latitude the C++ Standard permits in redefining the basic operations on allocated objects. Near and far pointers are nonstandard extensions, so the C++ Standard is silent on this particular topic. Implementations exist that support far heaps, but they are nonportable.

smart pointers In a portable C++ program, you can certainly maintain a storage pool as we described above. But can you define an allocator that returns "smart" pointers for allocated objects? A smart pointer **p** is an object of some class that behaves much like a pointer. So ***p** yields a reference to an object, but it gives the member function **operator*()** a chance to perform some magic along the way. Perhaps the allocator maintains a storage pool outside the program, such as in a disk file. Then the smart pointer can read the appropriate object into an in-memory cache on demand. (Writing a caching allocator in all its glory is a nontrivial exercise which we will forego here. It is too much of a distraction from the main topic.)

We C++ programmers have grown skilled, over the years, at defining and manipulating various kinds of smart pointers. But we have had less success at playing games with references. Yes, you can define your own version of the unary address-of operator (`operator&()`) for a class you write, but you'd better be careful if you do. It's hard to write code that can tolerate exotic references. Put simply, the expression `&*p` had better yield a conventional pointer, to an object that resides in program storage, no matter how smart `p` tries to be. Otherwise, it is next to impossible to write container template classes that work properly in all cases.

Allocators may have provisions for all sorts of alternate addressing schemes, but the C++ Standard remains conservative. It says that programmers can rely on the conventional definitions of address arithmetic when they write code that uses allocators. More to the point, an *implementation* is free to code the STL containers on the assumption that programmer-supplied allocators are equally conventional. For example, the code can assume that `&x` yields a pointer to `T`, for `x` an lvalue of type `T`. It can also assume that pointers are really C-style pointers — that there are no smart pointers, proxies, or other bits of trickery.

equal allocators There is yet another limitation imposed on allocators by the C++ Standard. Since an allocator is an object, it can store data, at least in principle. You might want to use this capability to define an allocator class that maintains separate pools of storage in different groups of allocator objects. Each allocator object stores a pointer to the pool that it is prepared to use. The stored pointers can differ among allocator objects of the same type. Perhaps you know that one group of vector objects will be swapping sequences of elements repeatedly among the group. It makes sense to construct all vectors in that group with allocator objects from the same group.

If two allocator objects compare equal, you can allocate an element with one of the objects and free it with the other. They designate the same pool of storage. A conscientious container can use this information to advantage to optimize a swap with the contents of another container. The swap code knows it must resort to copying all those elements only if the two allocator objects do not compare equal. Otherwise, it can just rearrange a few pointers to perform the swap.

But once again, the C++ Standard chose to be more conservative in the end. It says that programmers can assume that all allocator objects of the same type will compare equal. More specifically, an implementation is free to code the STL containers on the assumption that this is true of programmer-supplied allocators. It can assume that there are no private storage pools maintained within a collection of allocator objects of the same type.

Thus, for example, all swaps can be fast; but you, the programmer cannot write a portable allocator that maintains multiple storage pools as described above.

The implementation presented here is a bit more gracious. The container template classes permit an allocator to define a pointer as some class type. They even go to the trouble of constructing and destroying any such pointers, just in case those operations are nontrivial. The containers permit two allocator objects to compare unequal — and assume that they manage distinct storage pools if so. The code nevertheless assumes that you can create a null pointer by assigning a constant integer expression with value zero to a pointer object. And it assumes that the expression **&x** yields a conventional pointer. Even with these constraints, you can still write some fairly ambitious allocators and the containers presented here will do right by them. Just don't assume that you can move such ambitious code to an arbitrary implementation of Standard C++. You can't.

allocator So much for the esoteric aspects of allocators. Here's the machinery you're likely to use in real life. Template class **allocator** is the default allocator used by all STL containers, as we mentioned earlier. It also serves as the prototype for any allocator you define yourself. It defines all the types needed to describe how to address and manipulate allocated objects. The member type definitions are:

```
typedef size_t size_type;
typedef ptrdiff_t difference_type;
typedef T *pointer;
typedef const T *const_pointer;
typedef T& reference;
typedef const T& const_reference;
typedef T value_type;
```

address The member function **address**, in both const and non-const versions, is essentially a smart version of the unary **operator&** operator (as in **&x**). It ensures that the address of an allocated object has the proper pointer representation. Template class **allocator** simply returns **&x** for the call **address(x)**.

Most of the remaining member functions behave as their names imply:

- **allocate** allocates an array of elements of type **T**.
- **deallocate** frees an array earlier allocated by the same allocator (or by an allocator that compares equal to it, as we describe later).
- **construct** constructs an object of type **T** in the "raw" (unconstructed) storage indicated.
- **destroy** destroys an object in place, without deallocating its storage.
- **max_size** tells how many elements you can address in an array of **T** elements.

rebind Where the real magic comes in is with the member template **rebind**:

```
template<class U>
   struct rebind {
        typedef allocator<U> other;
        };
```

What it does is let the program generate a name for the type **allocator<U>** given just the type **allocator<T>**. Here's how. Say we've specialized a **list** container, along the lines described earlier. Only this time, we'll write the type definition in terms of template class **allocator**:

```
typedef list<float, allocator<float> > Mylist;
```

So we've supplied template class **list** with a recipe for allocating **float** objects. Every **list** object comes complete with a private member object, call it **myal**, that is fully prepared to carry out this recipe on demand.

Only problem is, that's not what **list** cares about. It wants to allocate elements that contain forward and backward pointers that link the list together. In this particular case, the elements look something like:

```
struct Myelement {
    Myelement *next, *prev;
    float item;
    };
```

But an **allocator<float>** object knows how to allocate only arrays of one or more **float** objects. What the container really needs is an object of class **allocator<Myelement>**. To declare such an object, the container says something like:

```
allocator<float>::rebind<Myelement>::other
    Myalloc(myal);
```

The template member struct **rebind** supplies a way to name the needed allocator type. And the template constructor promises that **Myalloc** can be constructed from the object **myal**, even though the types of the two objects have only a family relationship. The net result is that the container can whomp up whatever flavor allocator it needs, given the one we're told to supply for it.

interim allocators What a clever trick. The only problem is that STL needs a compiler that supports member template *classes*, not just the more conventional member template *functions*, to pull off the trick. That particular feature seems to be one of the last ones added to commercial C++ compilers. Finding a suitable interim form that avoids member template classes has been a real challenge for implementors. Sadly, implementors have risen to the challenge by defining different, incompatible alternatives.

Here's one interim form, which is used by the commercial version of the implementation we show here. It doesn't try too hard. Where a container needs an allocator other than the one supplied, it cuts a few corners:

- The various member types are assumed to be the same as for template class **allocator**, following the conventional rules of C++.
- The supplied allocator object is assumed to have an added member function **Charalloc(size_type n)** that can allocate an arbitrary object whose size is **n** bytes.
- Any object allocated this way can be subsequently freed by calling the member function **deallocate** in the supplied member object.

In summary, allocators promise flexible programmer control over how a container allocates and frees storage for the elements of the sequence it manages. How much practical flexibility you get is still open to debate, in the absence of experience. For now, the conservative course is to stick with the default allocators. Leave it to the library implementors to supply something that works.

other mechanisms The common theme for all entities defined in the header `<allocator>` is storage management. Allocators do the job for STL containers, but there are still other mechanisms in this header. For example, some STL algorithms can benefit from the use of a temporary storage area, if it can be made available. So an obvious need exists for mechanisms that allocate such storage, free it, and ensure that chunks of it don't get mislaid. C programmers will recognize these services as just a somewhat more structured version of the old standbys `malloc` and `free`.

But C++ has an additional need. A typical object must be constructed, once allocated, then destroyed, before it is freed. By contrast, the basic object types inherited from C can be adequately initialized just by assignment, and they need no special preparation before they are freed. So an important concomitant to any machinery for storage allocation and freeing in C++ is comparable machinery for constructing and destroying the objects in question.

`uninitialized_copy` `uninitialized_fill` Template container `vector`, for example, represents its sequence of elements as a contiguous array. (See Chapter 10: `<vector>`.) You can initialize its elements from another sequence, or by replicating a value throughout the sequence. To alter the length of the sequence, the container must typically allocate raw storage as an array of the desired size, then copy over the existing storage. All these operations can be expressed in terms of a handful of simple algorithms:

`uninitialized_fill_n`

```
template<class InIt, class FwdIt> inline
   FwdIt uninitialized_copy(InIt first, InIt last,
         FwdIt x);
template<class FwdIt, class T> inline
   void uninitialized_fill(FwdIt first, FwdIt last,
         const T& x);
template<class FwdIt, class Size, class T> inline
   void uninitialized_fill_n(FwdIt first, Size n,
         const T& x);
```

The first algorithm copies the sequence designated by the range of iterators `[first, last)` to the sequence beginning at `x`. (Remember that `InIt` can be any kind of input iterator, and `FwdIt` can be any kind of forward iterator.) It does so by *constructing* each element of the destination sequence using its copy constructor.

The second algorithm operates treats the specified range as a destination instead of a source. It constructs each element of the sequence designated by `[first, last)` by copying the value `x`. The third does much the same, except that the destination sequence consists of `n` elements beginning at `first`.

exception safety These three template functions perform an additional service. A template specialization is a heady mix of implementor-supplied and programmer-supplied code. Neither party has complete control over the final product, but the library implementor nevertheless has certain obligations. If programmer-supplied code throws an exception, the vendor-supplied portion must behave sensibly. A late addition to the C++ Standard is a general requirement that operations on containers have predictable behavior even in the presence of thrown exceptions. You may not always like the result, but the container must at least be left in a state where it can be properly destroyed. Moreover, it must not lose track of allocated storage or fail to destroy any objects that it has constructed. And that's where these three template functions can help out.

All three make a simple promise. If an exception is thrown during their execution, they will catch the exception, destroy any objects they have constructed, and rethrow the exception. That can be a pretty handy service, for code that implements an STL container. As a matter of fact, the code presented here doesn't use these particular template functions. (But see Chapter 10: `<vector>` for similar private member functions.) A container that you write should obey the same constraints as the STL containers, however, so these template functions can prove handy to you.

temporary buffers We mentioned earlier that some algorithms can make use of temporary storage. Sorting, merging, and partitioning can often be performed faster by copying elements to and from a scratch area, instead of working in place with just one or two temporary objects. The header `<memory>` meets this need by defining a pair of template functions for allocating and freeing a *temporary buffer:*

```
template<class T> inline
   pair<T *, ptrdiff_t>
        get_temporary_buffer(ptrdiff_t n);
template<class T> inline
   void return_temporary_buffer(T *p);
```

`get_temporary_buffer` **`return_temporary_buffer`** The first template function lets you allocate storage for an array of up to `n` objects of type `T` by calling `get_temporary_buffer<T>(n)`. If the first member of the returned `pair` is not a null pointer, then it has the value `p`, a pointer to the beginning of the allocated storage. Its actual size is given by the second member, which may be less than `n`. You are obliged to return any storage successfully allocated this way by calling `return_temporary_buffer(p)`.

The algorithms in STL never request more than one such buffer at a time. They are also pretty tolerant of being short changed. If no buffer can be allocated, or if it is smaller than requested, the algorithm still works correctly, It merely slows down.

Algorithms that make use of temporary buffers face an administrative problem. The first time you store a value in an element of such a buffer you have to construct the element. The fill and copy algorithms shown above can sometimes do the job, but not always. In many cases, the algorithm is generating elements on the fly. It really wants to pretend that it's working with just another iterator.

raw_ storage_ iterator That's where template class **raw_storage_iterator** comes in. It is an output iterator, accepting a sequence of generated values in strictly increasing order with no backing up or multiple stores to the same object. Its peculiar claim to fame is that it stores a generated sequence in raw storage. Thus, it constructs elements as it goes.

Algorithms that use temporary buffers face additional administrative problems. Once an element of the temporary buffer is constructed, subsequent stores must *not* involve construction, lest they commit the sin of double construction. So an algorithm that makes multiple passes over a temporary buffer must keep careful track. Elements not yet constructed get constructed, while recycled elements get assigned. And before the temporary buffer can be freed, any constructed elements must be meticulously destroyed.

The original STL code from Hewlett-Packard endeavors to do all these things with inline logic. The result is added complexity, in algorithms that are complex to begin with. And the inevitable consequence is occasional bugs, when the bookkeeping goes awry. So we choose here a more structured approach that encapsulates most of the messy logic involved in using temporary buffers.

Temp_ iterator We introduce the template class **Temp_iterator**. It is an output iterator that manages a temporary buffer, but it is rather more thorough than template class **raw_storage_iterator**:

- The constructor **Temp_iterator<T>(n)** requests a temporary buffer that can hold up to **n** elements of type **T**.
- Its destructor automatically frees any temporary buffer so obtained.
- The iterator keeps track of the usage high-water mark within the buffer. It constructs stored elements or assigns them as needed.
- And, of course, it destroys elements as needed before freeing the buffer.

That's not the end of it. A copy of **Temp_iterator<T>** uses the same storage as the original, so the bookkeeping is correct even when such iterators are returned by value from functions. The template class also defines a handful of special member functions for controlling rescans of the buffer:

- **Init()** resumes storing at the beginning of the buffer.
- **First()** returns a pointer to the beginning of the buffer.
- **Last()** returns a pointer to the next place to store (just past the last element stored) in the buffer.
- **Maxlen()** returns the length of the buffer.

We describe the usage of **Temp_iterator** in more detail in conjunction with the algorithms that use it.

Suffice it to say that the implementation of STL presented here makes no direct use of get_temporary_buffer or return_temporary_buffer. It makes no use at all of raw_storage_iterator. We've found that Temp_iterator provides a much more structured solution.

auto_ptr Template class auto_ptr is not part of the original STL proposal. Rather, it is a later addition that was parked in the header <memory> as the most suitable resting place. It is designed to deal with the problem of storage leaks that can occur in the presence of exceptions.

Put simply, an auto_ptr<T> encapsulates a pointer to an allocated object of type T — one obtained by calling operator new:

- An auto_ptr<T> object "owns" the object it points at, assuming its stored pointer is not null.
- Ownership can be transferred by assignment or by copy construction, in which case the original owner replaces its stored object pointer with a null pointer.
- Ownership can be given away explicitly by calling the member function release.
- When the auto_ptr<T> object is destroyed, it deletes the object designated by a pointer that it still owns.

Why have all this machinery? A thrown exception is meticulous about destroying any dynamically allocated objects (storage class auto or register) that go out of scope as the exception is passed up the line. But it cannot know to destroy objects allocated by explicit calls to operator new, as in a new expression. They must be deallocated by explicit calls to operator delete, as in a delete expression. Template class auto_ptr provides a way to tie explicitly allocated storage to dynamically allocated storage. It ensures that the controlled object is deleted however the pointer that controls it goes out of scope.

Functional Description

```
namespace std {
template<class T>
    class allocator;
template<>
    class allocator<void>;
template<class FwdIt, class T>
    class raw_storage_iterator;
template<class T>
    class auto_ptr;

        // TEMPLATE OPERATORS
template<class T>
    bool operator==(allocator<T>& lhs,
        allocator<T>& rhs);
template<class T>
    bool operator!=(allocator<T>& lhs,
        allocator<T>& rhs);
```

```
        // TEMPLATE FUNCTIONS
template<class T>
    pair<T *, ptrdiff_t>
        get_temporary_buffer(ptrdiff_t n);
template<class T>
    void return_temporary_buffer(T *p);
template<class InIt, class FwdIt>
    FwdIt uninitialized_copy(InIt first, InIt last,
        FwdIt result);
template<class FwdIt, class T>
    void uninitialized_fill(FwdIt first, FwdIt last,
        const T& x);
template<class FwdIt, class Size, class T>
    void uninitialized_fill_n(FwdIt first, Size n,
        const T& x);
    };
```

Include the STL standard header **<memory>** to define a class, an operator, and several templates that help allocate and free objects.

allocator

```
template<class T>
    class allocator {
    typedef size_t size_type;
    typedef ptrdiff_t difference_type;
    typedef T *pointer;
    typedef const T *const_pointer;
    typedef T& reference;
    typedef const T& const_reference;
    typedef T value_type;
    pointer address(reference x) const;
    const_pointer address(const_reference x) const;
    template<class U>
        struct rebind;
    allocator();
    template<class U>
        allocator(const allocator<U>& x);
    template<class U>
        allocator& operator=(const allocator<U>& x);
    template<class U>
        pointer allocate(size_type n, const U *hint = 0);
    void deallocate(pointer p, size_type n);
    void construct(pointer p, const T& val);
    void destroy(pointer p);
    size_type max_size() const;
    };
```

The template class describes an object that manages storage allocation and freeing for arrays of objects of type **T**. An object of class **allocator** is the default *allocator object* specified in the constructors for several container template classes in the Standard C++ library.

Template class **allocator** supplies several type definitions that are rather pedestrian. They hardly seem worth defining. But another class with the same members might choose more interesting alternatives. Constructing a container with an allocator object of such a class gives individual control over allocation and freeing of elements controlled by that container.

For example, an allocator object might allocate storage on a *private heap*. Or it might allocate storage on a *far heap*, requiring nonstandard pointers to access the allocated objects. Or it might specify, through the type definitions it supplies, that elements be accessed through special *accessor objects* that manage *shared memory*, or perform automatic *garbage collection*. Hence, a class that allocates storage using an allocator object should use these types religiously for declaring pointer and reference objects (as do the containers in the Standard C++ library).

Thus, an allocator defines the types (among others):

- `pointer` — behaves like a pointer to `T`
- `const_pointer` — behaves like a const pointer to `T`
- `reference` — behaves like a reference to `T`
- `const_reference` — behaves like a const reference to `T`

These types specify the form that pointers and references must take for allocated elements. (`allocator::pointer` is not necessarily the same as `T *` for all allocator objects, even though it has this obvious definition for class `allocator`.)

▫ **`allocator::address`**

```
pointer address(reference x) const;
const_pointer address(const_reference x) const;
```

The member functions return the address of `x`, in the form that pointers must take for allocated elements.

▫ **`allocator::allocate`**

```
template<class U>
    pointer allocate(size_type n, const U *hint = 0);
```

The member function allocates storage for an array of `n` elements of type `T`, by calling `operator new(n)`. It returns a pointer to the allocated object. The `hint` argument helps some allocators in improving locality of reference — a valid choice is the address of an object earlier allocated by the same allocator object, and not yet deallocated. To supply no hint, use a null pointer argument instead.

▫ **`allocator::allocator`**

```
allocator();
template<class U>
    allocator(const allocator<U>& x);
```

The constructor does nothing. In general, however, an allocator object constructed from another allocator object should compare equal to it (and hence permit intermixing of object allocation and freeing between the two allocator objects).

▫ **`allocator::const_pointer`**

```
typedef const T *pointer;
```

The pointer type describes an object **p** that can designate, via the expression ***p**, any const object that an object of template class **allocator** can allocate.

▫ **allocator::const_reference**

```
typedef const T& const_reference;
```

The reference type describes an object **x** that can designate any const object that an object of template class **allocator** can allocate.

▫ **allocator::construct**

```
void construct(pointer p, const T& val);
```

The member function constructs an object of type **T** at **p** by evaluating the placement **new** expression **new ((void *)p) T(val)**.

▫ **allocator::deallocate**

```
void deallocate(pointer p, size_type n);
```

The member function frees storage for the array of **n** objects of type **T** beginning at **p**, by calling **operator delete(p)**. The pointer **p** must have been earlier returned by a call to **allocate** for an allocator object that compares equal to ***this**, allocating an array object of the same size and type. **deallocate** never throws an exception.

▫ **allocator::destroy**

```
void destroy(pointer p);
```

The member function destroys the object designated by **p**, by calling the destructor **p->T::~T()**.

▫ **allocator::difference_type**

```
typedef ptrdiff_t difference_type;
```

The signed integer type describes an object that can represent the difference between the addresses of any two elements in a sequence that an object of template class **allocator** can allocate.

▫ **allocator::max_size**

```
size_type max_size() const;
```

The member function returns the length of the longest sequence of elements of type **T** that an object of class **allocator** *might* be able to allocate.

▫ **allocator::operator=**

```
template<class U>
    allocator& operator=(const allocator<U>& x);
```

The template assignment operator does nothing. In general, however, an allocator object assigned to another allocator object should compare equal to it (and hence permit intermixing of object allocation and freeing between the two allocator objects).

▫ **allocator::pointer**

```
typedef T *pointer;
```

The pointer type describes an object `p` that can designate, via the expression `*p`, any object that an object of template class `allocator` can allocate.

- **`allocator::rebind`**

```
template<class U>
    struct rebind {
    typedef allocator<U> other;
    };
```

The member template class defines the type `other`. Its sole purpose is to provide the type name `allocator<U>` given the type name `allocator<T>`.

For example, given an allocator object `al` of type `A`, you can allocate an object of type `U` with the expression:

```
A::rebind<U>::other(al).allocate(1, (U *)0)
```

Or, you can simply name its pointer type by writing the type:

```
A::rebind<U>::other::pointer
```

- **`allocator::reference`**

```
typedef T& reference;
```

The reference type describes an object `x` that can designate any object that an object of template class `allocator` can allocate.

- **`allocator::size_type`**

```
typedef size_t size_type;
```

The unsigned integer type describes an object that can represent the length of any sequence that an object of template class `allocator` can allocate.

- **`allocator::value_type`**

```
typedef T value_type;
```

The type is a synonym for the template parameter `T`.

- **`allocator<void>`**

```
template<>
    class allocator<void> {
    typedef void *pointer;
    typedef const void *const_pointer;
    typedef void value_type;
    template<class U>
        struct rebind;
    allocator();
    template<class U>
        allocator(const allocator<U>);
    template<class U>
        allocator<void>& operator=(const allocator<U>);
    };
```

The class explicitly specializes template class allocator for type *void*. Its constructors and assignment operator behave the same as for the template class, but it defines only the types `const_pointer`, `pointer`, `value_type`, and the nested template class `rebind`.

auto_ptr

```
template<class T>
    class auto_ptr {
    template<U>
        struct auto_ptr_ref;
   T *q;
public:
    typedef T element_type;
    explicit auto_ptr(T *p = 0) throw();
    auto_ptr(auto_ptr<T>& rhs) throw();
    template<class U>
        auto_ptr(auto_ptr<U>& rhs) throw();
    auto_ptr(auto_ptr_ref<T> rhs) throw();
    ~auto_ptr();
    template<class U>
        operator auto_ptr<U>() throw();
    template<class U>
        operator auto_ptr_ref<U>() throw();
    template<class U>
        auto_ptr<T>& operator=(auto_ptr<U>& rhs) throw();
    auto_ptr<T>& operator=(auto_ptr<T>& rhs) throw();
    T& operator*() const throw();
    T *operator->() const throw();
    T *get() const throw();
    T *release() const throw();
    void reset(T *p = 0);
    };
```

The class describes an object that stores a pointer (call it **q**) to an allocated object of type **T**. The stored pointer must either be null or designate an object allocated by a **new** expression. An object constructed with a non-null pointer owns the pointer. It transfers ownership if its stored value is assigned to another object. (It replaces the stored value after a transfer with a null pointer.) The destructor for **auto_ptr<T>** deletes the allocated object if it owns it. Hence, an object of class **auto_ptr<T>** ensures that an allocated object is automatically deleted when control leaves a block, even via a thrown exception. You should not construct two **auto_ptr<T>** objects that own the same object.

You can pass an **auto_ptr<T>** object by value as an argument to a function call. You can return such an object by value as well. (Both operations depend on the implicit construction of intermediate objects of class **auto_ptr<T>::auto_ptr_ref<U>**, by various subtle conversion rules.) You cannot, however, reliably manage a sequence of **auto_ptr<T>** objects with an STL container.

auto_ptr::auto_ptr

```
explicit auto_ptr(T *p = 0) throw();
auto_ptr(auto_ptr<T>& rhs) throw();
auto_ptr(auto_ptr_ref<T> rhs) throw();
template<class U>
    auto_ptr(auto_ptr<U>& rhs) throw();
```

The first constructor stores **p** as the pointer to the allocated object. The second constructor transfers ownership of the pointer stored in **rhs**, by storing **rhs.release()** in the constructed object. The third constructor behaves the same as the second, except that it stores `rhs.ref.release()`, where `ref` is the reference stored in `rhs`.

The template constructor behaves the same as the second constructor, provided that a pointer to `U` can be implicitly converted to a pointer to `T`.

▫ **auto_ptr::auto_ptr_ref**

```
template<U>
    struct auto_ptr_ref {
    auto_ptr_ref(auto_ptr<U>& rhs);
    };
```

The member class describes an object that stores a reference to an object of class `auto_ptr<T>`.

▫ **auto_ptr::~auto_ptr**

```
~auto_ptr();
```

The destructor evaluates the expression `delete q`.

▫ **auto_ptr::element_type**

```
typedef T element_type;
```

The type is a synonym for the template parameter `T`.

▫ **auto_ptr::get**

```
T *get() const throw();
```

The member function returns the stored pointer.

▫ **auto_ptr::operator=**

```
template<class U>
    auto_ptr<T>& operator=(auto_ptr<U>& rhs) throw();
auto_ptr<T>& operator=(auto_ptr<>& rhs) throw();
```

The assignment evaluates the expression `delete q`, but only if the stored pointer value `q` changes as a result of the assignment. It then transfers ownership of the pointer stored in `rhs`, by storing `rhs.release()` in `*this`. The function returns `*this`.

▫ **auto_ptr::operator***

```
T& operator*() const throw();
```

The indirection operator returns `*get()`. Hence, the stored pointer must not be null.

▫ **auto_ptr::operator->**

```
T *operator->() const throw();
```

The selection operator returns `get()`, so that the expression `al->m` behaves the same as `(al.get())->m`, where `al` is an object of class `auto_ptr<T>`. Hence, the stored pointer must not be null, and `T` must be a class, structure, or union type with a member `m`.

▫ **auto_ptr::operator auto_ptr<U>**

```
template<class U>
    operator auto_ptr<U>() throw();
```

The type cast operator returns `auto_ptr<U>(*this)`.

- **`auto_ptr::operator auto_ptr_ref<U>`**

```
template<class U>
    operator auto_ptr_ref<U>() throw();
```

The type cast operator returns `auto_ptr_ref<U>(*this)`.

- **`auto_ptr::release`**

```
T *release() throw();
```

The member replaces the stored pointer with a null pointer and returns the previously stored pointer.

- **`auto_ptr::reset`**

```
void reset(T *p = 0);
```

The member function evaluates the expression `delete q`, but only if the stored pointer value `q` changes as a result of function call. It then replaces the stored pointer with `p`.

- **`get_temporary_buffer`**

```
template<class T>
    pair<T *, ptrdiff_t>
        get_temporary_buffer(ptrdiff_t n);
```

The template function allocates storage for a sequence of at most `n` elements of type `T`, from an unspecified source (which may well be the standard heap used by `operator new`). It returns a value `pr`, of type `pair<T *, ptrdiff_t>`. If the function allocates storage, `pr.first` designates the allocated storage and `pr.second` is the number of elements in the longest sequence the storage can hold. Otherwise, `pr.first` is a null pointer.

- **`operator!=`**

```
template<class T>
    bool operator!=(allocator<T>& lhs,
        allocator<T>& rhs);
```

The template operator returns false.

- **`operator==`**

```
template<class T>
    bool operator==(allocator<T>& lhs,
        allocator<T>& rhs);
```

The template operator returns true. (Two allocator objects should compare equal only if an object allocated through one can be deallocated through the other. If the value of one object is determined from another by assignment or by construction, the two object should compare equal.)

- **`raw_storage_iterator`**

```
template<class FwdIt, class T>
    class raw_storage_iterator
        : public iterator<output_iterator_tag,
            void, void, void, void> {
public:
    typedef FwdIt iter_type;
```

```
typedef T element_type;
explicit raw_storage_iterator(FwdIt it);
raw_storage_iterator<FwdIt, T>& operator*();
raw_storage_iterator<FwdIt, T>&
    operator=(const T& val);
raw_storage_iterator<FwdIt, T>& operator++();
raw_storage_iterator<FwdIt, T> operator++(int);
};
```

The class describes an output iterator that constructs objects of type `T` in the sequence it generates. An object of class `raw_storage_iterator<FwdIt, T>` accesses storage through a forward iterator object, of class `FwdIt`, that you specify when you construct the object. For an object `it` of class `FwdIt`, the expression `&*it` must designate unconstructed storage for the next object (of type `T`) in the generated sequence.

raw_storage_iterator::element_type

```
typedef T element_type;
```

The type is a synonym for the template parameter `T`.

raw_storage_iterator::iter_type

```
typedef FwdIt iter_type;
```

The type is a synonym for the template parameter `FwdIt`.

raw_storage_iterator::operator*

```
raw_storage_iterator<FwdIt, T>& operator*();
```

The indirection operator returns `*this` (so that `operator=(const T&)` can perform the actual store in an expression such as `*x = val`).

raw_storage_iterator::operator=

```
raw_storage_iterator<FwdIt, T>& operator=(const T& val);
```

The assignment operator constructs the next object in the output sequence using the stored iterator value `it`, by evaluating the placement `new` expression `new ((void *)&*it) T(val)`. The function returns `*this`.

raw_storage_iterator::operator++

```
raw_storage_iterator<FwdIt, T>& operator++();
raw_storage_iterator<FwdIt, T> operator++(int);
```

The first (preincrement) operator increments the stored output iterator object, then returns `*this`.

The second (postincrement) operator makes a copy of `*this`, increments the stored output iterator object, then returns the copy.

raw_storage_iterator::raw_storage_iterator

```
explicit raw_storage_iterator(FwdIt it);
```

The constructor stores `it` as the output iterator object.

return_temporary_buffer

```
template<class T>
    void return_temporary_buffer(T *p);
```

The template function frees the storage designated by `p`, which must be earlier allocated by a call to `get_temporary_buffer`.

▫ **uninitialized_copy**

```
template<class InIt, class FwdIt>
    FwdIt uninitialized_copy(InIt first, InIt last,
        FwdIt result);
```

The template function effectively executes:

```
while (first != last)
    new ((void *)&*result++) U(*first++);
return first;
```

where `U` is `iterator_traits<InIt>::value_type`, unless the code throws an exception. In that case, all constructed objects are destroyed and the exception is rethrown.

▫ **uninitialized_fill**

```
template<class FwdIt, class T>
    void uninitialized_fill(FwdIt first, FwdIt last,
        const T& x);
```

The template function effectively executes:

```
while (first != last)
    new ((void *)&*first++) U(x);
```

where `U` is `iterator_traits<FwdIt>::value_type`, unless the code throws an exception. In that case, all constructed objects are destroyed and the exception is rethrown.

▫ **uninitialized_fill_n**

```
template<class FwdIt, class Size, class T>
    void uninitialized_fill_n(FwdIt first, Size n,
        const T& x);
```

The template function effectively executes:

```
while (0 < n--)
    new ((void *)&*first++) U(x);
```

where `U` is `iterator_traits<FwdIt>::value_type`, unless the code throws an exception. In that case, all constructed objects are destroyed and the exception is rethrown.

Using <memory>

Chances are good that, if you include *any* STL header in a translation unit, `<memory>` will be included as well. You include it explicitly only if you need one or more of the definitions it provides and you can't count on another STL header to drag it in. But chances are also good that you *will* need one or more of the entities defined in this header. If you get a translator diagnostic that, say, `uninitialized_fill` is undefined, remember that you can satisfy the need cheaply by including this header.

Here's a brief run-down of the definitions in `<memory>`:

allocator You write template class **allocator** as the allocator type when you specialize a container template class, as in:

```
typedef list<char, allocator<char> > Mylist;
```

Using a default template argument, however, you can avoid at least this mention of allocators. All container constructors in STL will also supply a default allocator object, so you need not mention allocators at all.

If you want to use an **allocator** object directly, or write your own allocator, study carefully how the container template classes use allocators later in this book.

uninitialized_copy Template function **uninitialized_copy(first, last, x)** copies *from* the sequence designated by **[first, last)** *to* the unconstructed sequence beginning at **x**. Each element in the generated sequence is initialized with a copy constructor. If an exception is thrown during execution of this template function, all constructed objects are destroyed and the exception is rethrown.

uninitialized_fill **uninitialized_fill_n** Template function **uninitialized_fill(first, last, x)**, on the other hand, copies *to* the unconstructed sequence designated by **[first, last)** *from* the single element **x**. Each element in the generated sequence is once again initialized with a copy constructor. Template function **uninitialized_fill_n(first, n, x)** is much the same, except that the unconstructed sequence consists of **n** elements beginning at **first**. If an exception is thrown during execution of either of these template functions, all constructed objects are destroyed and the exception is rethrown.

get_temporary_buffer Template function **get_temporary_buffer<T>(n)** allocates raw storage for an array of up to **n** elements of type **T**. If, in the return value **x**, **x.first** is a null pointer, the function allocated no storage. Otherwise, **x.second** stores the actual number of elements allocated, which is never larger than **n**.

return_temporary_buffer You return any storage allocated with the expression **x = get_temporary_buffer** by calling **return_temporary_buffer(x.first)**. An implementation does not necessarily supply more than one such temporary buffer at a time.

raw_storage_iterator The template class **raw_storage_iterator<FwdIt, T>** defines an output iterator that constructs each element of type **T** that it stores through an iterator of type **FwdIt**. You construct such an output iterator with the declaration:

```
raw_storage_iterator<FwdIt, T> x(iter);
```

where **iter** is an object of type **FwdIt** that designates the first element of the unconstructed sequence to store.

auto_ptr The template class **auto_ptr<T>** defines a "smart pointer" to objects of type **T**. You construct such a pointer with the declaration:

```
auto_ptr<T> p(new T);
```

Subsequently, ***p** designates the newly allocated object, and **p->m** designates the member **m** of the object, if such a member exists. When **p** is destroyed, its associated object of type **T** is also destroyed.

You can transfer "ownership" of the object (the obligation to destroy it) by assigning or copying the smart pointer, as in:

```
auto_ptr<T> q = p;
```

In this case, `p` subsequently stores a null pointer. Or you can simply give up ownership by calling `p.release()`, in which case you assume responsibility for destroying the allocated object.

Be *very* careful in passing objects of class `auto_ptr<T>` as arguments on a function call, or in returning such objects. Keeping track of ownership can be tricky. Don't even try to store such objects in container elements. Containers do not guarantee to copy them in predictable ways that keep proper track of ownership.

Implementing `<memory>`

This implementation moves some of the facilities nominally defined in the header `<memory>` to another header. The added header `<xmemory>` (not specified in the C++ Standard) holds a number of definitions used throughout a typical Standard C++ library, even in a program that does not explicitly include `<memory>`. Recall that, in the previous chapter, we discussed why some of the facilities nominally defined in the header `<iterator>` actually appear in the added header `<xutility>`.

`xmemory` Figures 4.1 through 4.2 show the file `xmemory`. It begins with one bit of trickery. Near the top of the file is a small group of macro definitions:

`FARQ`

```
#ifndef FARQ
 #define FARQ
 #define PDFT    ptrdiff_t
 #define SIZT    size_t
#endif
```

These are designed to help produce a far heap allocator, if the mood strikes you. Simply change the usual header *include* directive from:

```
#include <memory>
```

to:

```
#define FARQ far
#define PDFT long
#define SIZT unsigned long
#include <memory>
```

and the resulting template class `allocator` manages a far heap for you. (You may have to tweak the code a bit for the peculiarities of a given implementation.) The need for such antics has declined in recent years with the widespread availability of PCs with comfortably large storage. But plenty of code is still in use that works with far pointers. A far heap allocator is a simple example of an alternate allocator that is even potentially useful.

`Allocate` **`Construct`** **`Destroy`** The template functions `Allocate`, `Construct`, and `Destroy` each performs the obvious function suggested by its name. The first two exist in this form because they're used in more than one place among the STL headers. The last one solves a nuisancy problem. Many compilers today issue warning messages when asked to generate a destructor for a scalar type, such as **char** or **wchar_t**. We supply explicit specializations for these two types because practically every program that uses the full Standard C++ library tries to destroy them, as a result of library template specializations. Earlier versions of STL provide dummy destructors for even more of the scalar types. But the list is endless, given all the pointer types you can write, so we decided to stop at two here.

allocator Template class **allocator** is the star of this show, however. It is a deceptively simple template class, particularly given our extensive discussion of the implementation problems it presents. What you cannot see, however, is that a significant part of this template class requires alternate implementation techniques, given currently available translators. What you see here is the asymptotic form, to which implementations are slowly converging.

allocator<void> Following the template definition is an explicit specialization for class **allocator<void>**. It actually makes sense sometimes to write this type, if only to declare generic pointers of the appropriate flavor. But many of the

Figure 4.1: xmemory part 1

```
// xmemory internal header (from <memory>)
#ifndef XMEMORY_
#define XMEMORY_
#include <new>
#include <xutility>

#ifndef FARQ                          /* specify standard memory model */
 #define FARQ
 #define PDFT   ptrdiff_t
 #define SIZT   size_t
#endif

namespace std {
          // TEMPLATE FUNCTION Allocate
template<class T> inline
     T FARQ *Allocate(SIZT N, T FARQ *)
     {return ((T FARQ *)operator new(N * sizeof (T))); }

          // TEMPLATE FUNCTION Construct
template<class T1, class T2> inline
     void Construct(T1 FARQ *P, const T2& V)
     {new ((void FARQ *)P) T1(V); }

          // TEMPLATE FUNCTION Destroy
template<class T> inline
     void Destroy(T FARQ *P)
     {P->~T(); }
template<> inline void Destroy(char FARQ *P)
     {}
template<> inline void Destroy(wchar_t FARQ *P)
     {}
```

Figure 4.2: xmemory part 2

```
        // TEMPLATE CLASS allocator
template<class T>
    class allocator {
public:
    typedef SIZT size_type;
    typedef PDFT difference_type;
    typedef T FARQ *pointer;
    typedef const T FARQ *const_pointer;
    typedef T FARQ& reference;
    typedef const T FARQ& const_reference;
    typedef T value_type;
    template<class U>
        struct rebind {
            typedef allocator<U> other;
        };
    pointer address(reference X) const
        {return (&X); }
    const_pointer address(const_reference X) const
        {return (&X); }
    allocator()
        {}
    allocator(const allocator<T>&)
        {}
    template<class U>
        allocator(const allocator<U>&)
        {}
    template<class U>
        allocator<T>& operator=(const allocator<U>&)
        {return (*this); }
    template<class U>
        pointer allocate(size_type N, const U *)
        {return (Allocate(N, (pointer)0)); }
    pointer allocate(size_type N)
        {return (Allocate(N, (pointer)0)); }
    void deallocate(pointer P, size_type)
        {operator delete(P); }
    void construct(pointer P, const T& V)
        {Construct(P, V); }
    void destroy(pointer P)
        {Destroy(P); }
    SIZT max_size() const
        {SIZT N = (SIZT)(-1) / sizeof (T);
        return (0 < N ? N : 1); }
    };

        // allocator TEMPLATE OPERATORS
template<class T, class U> inline
    bool operator==(const allocator<T>&, const allocator<U>&)
    {return (true); }
template<class T, class U> inline
    bool operator!=(const allocator<T>&, const allocator<U>&)
    {return (false); }
```

Figure 4.3: `xmemory` **part 3**

```
          // CLASS allocator<void>
template<> class allocator<void> {
public:
     typedef void T;
     typedef T FARQ *pointer;
     typedef const T FARQ *const_pointer;
     typedef T value_type;
     template<class U>
          struct rebind {
               typedef allocator<U> other;
          };

     allocator()
          {}
     allocator(const allocator<T>&)
          {}
     template<class U>
          allocator(const allocator<U>&)
          {}
     template<class U>
          allocator<T>& operator=(const allocator<U>&)
          {return (*this); }
     };
} /* namespace std */
#endif /* XMEMORY_ */
```

member types and functions are nonsensical for **void**. The explicit specialization supplies only the members that make sense.

Accompanying template class **allocator** are two template operators. The first lets you compare for equality any two **allocator<T>** objects, regardless of their template parameters. And they always compare equal. The second simply defines the inequality operator consistently. As we discussed earlier, equality among allocator objects has a special meaning. If two such objects compare equal, they presumably work from the same storage pool. An object you allocate with one such allocator object can be deallocated with the other. The template containers in this implementation perform a check for equality of allocator objects before shuttling allocated elements between different container objects.

We speak of allocators in the general sense for a good reason. Nothing prevents you from defining a whole new class and using it as an allocator. You don't even have to derive such a class from template class **allocator**. You must, however, provide all the functionality supplied by **allocator**. Otherwise, the translator will complain or the resulting code will misbehave.

Part of that functionality includes the member template class **rebind**. Given the way it works, you're pretty much constrained to write an allocator as a template class in its own right. Nevertheless, you still have considerable latitude in how you write such creatures.

memory Figures 4.4 through 4.5 show the file `memory`. It defines the remaining entities, not already defined in `xmemory`, associated with the header `<memory>`.

get_temporary_buffer The function call `get_temporary_buffer<T>(n)` endeavors to supply uninitialized storage for an array of `n` elements of type `T`. It keeps halving the requested size so long as the allocation request keeps failing. (The algorithms for which `get_temporary_buffer` was designed are grateful for whatever scratch storage they can get.) Template function `return_temporary_buffer` returns any storage so allocated. Note, by the way, that you cannot simply call `get_temporary_buffer(n)` since the argument does not supply sufficient information to determine the template parameter. Thus the explicit parameter list following the function name in the call above. This notation is a relatively recent addition to the C++ Standard, so not all compilers support it to date. For such compilers, you may have to change the call to `get_temporary_buffer(n, (T *)0)`. It doesn't conform to the C++ Standard, but it is at least usable.

return_temporary_buffer

nothrow This implementation uses a special form of `operator new` that was introduced as part of the C++ standardization effort. The call `operator new(N, nothrow)` returns a null pointer if it cannot allocate an object of `N` bytes. (`nothrow`, and this overload of `operator new`, are defined in the standard header `<new>`.) Since `get_temporary_buffer` is permitted to allocate less than the requested storage, or none at all, it would be bad manners to throw an exception while determining a workable temporary buffer size. `operator new(N)`, by contrast, is obliged to throw an exception if it cannot allocate the requested object.

uninitialized_copy The three template functions `uninitialized_copy`, `uninitialized_fill`, and `uninitialized_fill_n` are all apparently quite simple, at least when defined in terms of the template function `Construct` described above. Two considerations make them a bit messy to implement, however. First, all three template functions really want to know the value type corresponding to an iterator argument. This is a common need among template functions, and you can see here the common way that need is met (at least for an implementation that doesn't depend on template partial specialization to make `iterator_traits` work properly). Each of the three template functions calls a helper function with an added argument. Template function `Val_type` supplies a dummy argument to communicate the desired type information to the helper. A smart enough compiler should eliminate the actual passing of the dummy argument. An even smarter compiler should inline the helper function and eliminate the added call altogether. (Much of STL is written in the hope and expectation that such optimizations will become commonplace among C++ compilers.)

uninitialized_fill

uninitialized_fill_n

exception safety A second complicating factor is the need to behave predictably if an exeception is thrown. Each function does its work in a try block, keeping track of how much progress it has made. If a programmer-supplied constructor throws an exception, the function catches it, destroys any objects already constructed, and rethrows the exception.

Figure 4.4: memory part 1

```
// memory standard header
#ifndef MEMORY_
#define MEMORY_
#include <iterator>
#include <xmemory>
namespace std {
		// TEMPLATE FUNCTION get_temporary_buffer
template<class T> inline
	pair<T FARQ *, PDFT>
		get_temporary_buffer(PDFT N)
	{T FARQ *P;
	for (P = 0; 0 < N; N /= 2)
		if ((P = (T FARQ *)operator new(
			(SIZT)N * sizeof (T), nothrow)) != 0)
			break;
	return (pair<T FARQ *, PDFT>(P, N)); }

		// TEMPLATE FUNCTION return_temporary_buffer
template<class T> inline
	void return_temporary_buffer(T *P)
	{operator delete(P); }

		// TEMPLATE FUNCTION uninitialized_copy
template<class InIt, class FwdIt> inline
	FwdIt uninitialized_copy(InIt F, InIt L, FwdIt X)
	{return (Uninit_copy(F, L, X, Val_type(F))); }
template<class InIt, class FwdIt, class T> inline
	FwdIt Uninit_copy(InIt F, InIt L, FwdIt X, T *)
	{FwdIt Xs = X;
	try {
	for (; F != L; ++X, ++F)
		Construct(&*X, T(*F));
	} catch (...) {
	for (; Xs != X; ++Xs)
		Destroy(&*Xs);
	throw;
	}
	return (X); }

		// TEMPLATE FUNCTION uninitialized_fill
template<class FwdIt, class Tval> inline
	void uninitialized_fill(FwdIt F, FwdIt L, const Tval& V)
	{Uninit_fill(F, L, V, Val_type(F)); }
template<class FwdIt, class Tval, class T> inline
	void Uninit_fill(FwdIt F, FwdIt L, const Tval& V, T *)
	{FwdIt Fs = F;
	try {
	for (; F != L; ++F)
		Construct(&*F, T(V));
	} catch (...) {
	for (; Fs != F; ++Fs)
		Destroy(&*Fs);
	throw;
	}}
```

Figure 4.5: memory part 2

```
        // TEMPLATE FUNCTION uninitialized_fill_n
template<class FwdIt, class S, class Tval> inline
    void uninitialized_fill_n(FwdIt F, S N, const Tval& V)
    {Uninit_fill_n(F, N, V, Val_type(F)); }
template<class FwdIt, class S, class Tval, class T> inline
    void Uninit_fill_n(FwdIt F, S N, const Tval& V,
        T *)
    {FwdIt Fs = F;
    try {
    for (; 0 < N; --N, ++F)
        Construct(&*F, T(V));
    } catch (...) {
    for (; Fs != F; ++Fs)
        Destroy(&*Fs);
    throw;
    }}

        // TEMPLATE CLASS raw_storage_iterator
template<class OutIt, class T>
    class raw_storage_iterator
        : public Outit {
public:
    typedef OutIt iter_type;
    typedef T element_type;
    explicit raw_storage_iterator(OutIt X)
        : Next(X) {}
    raw_storage_iterator<OutIt, T>& operator*()
        {return (*this); }
    raw_storage_iterator<OutIt, T>& operator=(const T& X)
        {Construct(&*Next, X);
        return (*this); }
    raw_storage_iterator<OutIt, T>& operator++()
        {++Next;
        return (*this); }
    raw_storage_iterator<OutIt, T> operator++(int)
        {raw_storage_iterator<OutIt, T> Ans = *this;
        ++Next;
        return (Ans); }
private:
    OutIt Next;
    };

        // TEMPLATE CLASS Temp_iterator
template<class T>
    class Temp_iterator
        : public Outit {
public:
    typedef T FARQ *Pty;
    Temp_iterator(PDFT N = 0)
        {pair<Pty, PDFT> Pair =
            get_temporary_buffer<T>(N);
        Buf.Begin = Pair.first;
```

Figure 4.6: `memory` **part 3**

```
            Buf.Cur = Pair.first;
            Buf.Hiwater = Pair.first;
            Buf.Len = Pair.second;
            Pb = &Buf; }
        Temp_iterator(const Temp_iterator<T>& X)
            {Buf.Begin = 0;
            Buf.Cur = 0;
            Buf.Hiwater = 0;
            Buf.Len = 0;
            *this = X; }
        ~Temp_iterator()
            {if (Buf.Begin != 0)
                {for (Pty F = Buf.Begin;
                    F != Buf.Hiwater; ++F)
                    Destroy(&*F);
                return_temporary_buffer(Buf.Begin); }}
        Temp_iterator<T>& operator=(const Temp_iterator<T>& X)
            {Pb = X.Pb;
            return (*this); }
        Temp_iterator<T>& operator=(const T& V)
            {if (Pb->Cur < Pb->Hiwater)
                *Pb->Cur++ = V;
            else
                {Construct(&*Pb->Cur, V);
                Pb->Hiwater = ++Pb->Cur; }
            return (*this); }
        Temp_iterator<T>& operator*()
            {return (*this); }
        Temp_iterator<T>& operator++()
            {return (*this); }
        Temp_iterator<T>& operator++(int)
            {return (*this); }
        Temp_iterator<T>& Init()
            {Pb->Cur = Pb->Begin;
            return (*this); }
        Pty First() const
            {return (Pb->Begin); }
        Pty Last() const
            {return (Pb->Cur); }
        PDFT Maxlen() const
            {return (Pb->Len); }
private:
        struct Bufpar {
            Pty Begin;
            Pty Cur;
            Pty Hiwater;
            PDFT Len;
            } Buf, *Pb;
        };

            // TEMPLATE CLASS auto_ptr
template<class T>
        class auto_ptr {
```

Figure 4.7: memory part 4

```
                // TEMPLATE CLASS auto_ptr_ref
    template<class U>
        struct auto_ptr_ref {
        auto_ptr_ref(auto_ptr<U>& Y)
            : Ref(Y) {}
        auto_ptr<U>& Ref;
        };
public:
    typedef T element_type;
    explicit auto_ptr(T *P = 0) throw ()
        : Ptr(P) {}
    auto_ptr(auto_ptr<T>& Y) throw ()
        : Ptr(Y.release()) {}
    auto_ptr(auto_ptr_ref<T> Y) throw ()
        : Ptr(Y.Ref.release()) {}
    template<class U>
        operator auto_ptr<U>() throw ()
        {return (auto_ptr<U>(*this)); }
    template<class U>
        operator auto_ptr_ref<U>() throw ()
        {return (auto_ptr_ref<U>(*this)); }
    template<class U>
        auto_ptr<T>& operator=(auto_ptr<U>& Y) throw ()
        {reset(Y.release());
        return (*this); }
    template<class U>
        auto_ptr(auto_ptr<U>& Y) throw ()
        : Ptr(Y.release()) {}
    auto_ptr<T>& operator=(auto_ptr<T>& Y) throw ()
        {reset(Y.release());
        return (*this); }
    ~auto_ptr()
        {delete Ptr; }
    T& operator*() const throw ()
        {return (*get()); }
    T *operator->() const throw ()
        {return (get()); }
    T *get() const throw ()
        {return (Ptr); }
    T *release() throw ()
        {T *Tmp = Ptr;
        Ptr = 0;
        return (Tmp); }
    void reset(T* P = 0)
        {if (P != Ptr)
            delete Ptr;
        Ptr = P; }
private:
    T *Ptr;
    };
} /* namespace std */
#endif /* MEMORY_ */
```
□

raw_storage_iterator Template class **raw_storage_iterator** follows the usual pattern for output iterators. Its peculiar talent is that it constructs objects in raw storage as it "outputs" them. Template class **Temp_iterator** is a similar output iterator, but with rather more machinery. It allocates a temporary buffer on construction, if possible, then frees any such buffer obtained on destruction. It knows when to construct raw storage and when to assign to previously constructed storage. It also maintains a quick-and-dirty kind of an underlying "implementation" sub-object called **Bufpar**. A copy of an iterator shares the original subobject.

Temp_iterator

This is far from a complete or robust design. To do a thorough job, the sub-object should be a separate entity that is reference counted. It should encapsulate more of its own maintenance functions. Nevertheless, the simple design presented here economically meets the needs of the algorithms that use **Temp_iterator**. They are sufficiently stylized to avoid the need for more thorough semantics.

auto_ptr Finally, template class **auto_ptr** provides a form of smart pointer. An object of class **auto_ptr<T>** stores a pointer to an object of type **T** that has been allocated on the heap (with a **new** expression). Its straightforward task is to delete, in its destructor, the object it owns. Where things get messy, however, is with all those member template functions. They are intended to permit interconversion or assignment between objects whose stored pointers can be interconverted or assigned. (It should be possible, for example, to assign an object of class **auto_ptr<const int>** to an object of class **auto_ptr<int>**.) They are also intended to permit the passing of such objects as arguments on function calls and as return values on function returns. That is the reason for the addition of the (private!) nested class **auto_ptr_ref** and the interesting constructor and template type-cast operator that deal with objects of this nested class.

The theoretical underpinnings for this approach rest on a fairly esoteric loophole in the C++ Standard. We will not attempt to describe the language issues here. We simply observe that template class **auto_ptr** stresses practically every C++ compiler we know of. It *does* work in its current form with at least two reasonably complete compilers, but it has to be simplified to work with all others. Its precise specification is also likely to change in small ways, in response to Defect Reports submitted to the Committee. So as a practical matter, it is wise not to depend on the more ambitious features of **auto_ptr** in code that you write. Even if the code appears to work properly, it may not be very portable, and it may have to change over time.

Testing <memory>

tmemory.c Figures 4.8 and 4.9 show the file **tmemory.c**. The header **<memory>** is sufficiently large that it makes sense to have the program test the various parts of the header in groups:

- the templates that determine various properties of iterators, and perform simple manipulations of iterators
- template class **allocator**
- template function **uninitialized_copy** and friends
- temporary buffers and raw-storage iterators
- template class **auto_ptr**

None of the tests are particularly stringent — particularly for template class **allocator**. Most tests are for just the most basic functionality.

If all goes well, the program prints:

```
SUCCESS testing <memory>
```

and takes a normal exit.

Figure 4.8: tmemory.c Part 1

```
// test <memory>
#include <assert.h>
#include <iostream>
#include <memory>
#include <new>
using namespace std;

        // CLASS Myint
static size_t cnt;
class Myint {
public:
        Myint(int x)
                : val(x) {++cnt; }
        Myint(const Myint& x)
                : val(x.val) {++cnt; }
        ~Myint()
                {--cnt; }
        int get_val() const
                {return (val); }
private:
        int val;
        };

typedef allocator<float> Myal;
Myal get_al()
        {return (Myal()); }

        //      TEST allocator
void test_alloc()
        {float fl;
        Myal::size_type *p_size = (size_t *)0;
        Myal::difference_type *p_val = (ptrdiff_t *)0;
        Myal::pointer *p_ptr = (float **)0;
        Myal::const_pointer *p_cptr = (const float **)0;
        Myal::reference p_ref = fl;
        Myal::const_reference p_cref = (const float&)fl;
        Myal::value_type *p_dist = (float *)0;
```

Figure 4.9: `tmemory.c` **part 2**

```
     Myal::rebind<int>::pointer *p_iptr = (int **)0;
     Myal al0 = get_al(), al(al0);

     allocator<void>::pointer *pv_ptr = (void **)0;
     allocator<void>::const_pointer *pv_cptr = (const void **)0;
     allocator<void>::value_type *pv_dist = (void *)0;
     Myal::rebind<int>::pointer *pv_iptr = (int **)0;
     allocator<void> alv0, alv(alv0);
     alv = alv0;

     float *pfl = al0.address(fl);
     assert(pfl == &fl);
     pfl = al.allocate(3, 0);
     al.construct(&pfl[2], 2.0F);
     assert(pfl[2] == 2.0F);
     al.destroy(pfl);
     al.deallocate(pfl, 1);
     assert(0 < al0.max_size());
     assert(al0 == al);
     assert(!(al0 != al0));
     al.destroy(pfl);
     al.deallocate(pfl, 1); }

     //   TEST UNINITIALIZED COPY AND FILL
void test_uninit()
     {cnt = 0;
     Myint *p = (Myint *)operator new(6 * sizeof (Myint));
     uninitialized_fill(p, p + 2, 3);
     assert(p[1].get_val() == 3 && cnt == 2);
     uninitialized_fill_n(p + 2, 2, 5);
     assert(p[3].get_val() == 5 && cnt == 4);
     assert(uninitialized_copy(p + 1, p + 3, p + 4) == p + 6);
     assert(p[4].get_val() == 3 && cnt == 6);
     assert(p[5].get_val() == 5);
     operator delete(p); }

     // TEST TEMPORARY BUFFERS
void test_tempbuf()
     {pair<short *, ptrdiff_t> tbuf =
          get_temporary_buffer(5);
     assert(tbuf.first != 0 && tbuf.second == 5);
     typedef raw_storage_iterator<short *, short> Rit;
     Rit::iter_type *p_iter = (short **)0;
     Rit::element_type *p_elem = (short *)0;
     Rit it(tbuf.first);
     for (int i = 0; i < 5; ++i)
          {*it++ = i;
          assert(tbuf.first[i] == i); }
     return_temporary_buffer(tbuf.first); }

     // TEST auto_ptr
void test_autoptr()
     {cnt = 0;
     typedef auto_ptr<Myint> Myptr;
     Myptr::element_type *p_elem = (Myint *)0;
```

Figure 4.10: `tmemory.c` part 3

```
     Myptr p0;
     assert(p0.get() == 0);
          {Myptr p1(new Myint(3));
          Myint *p = p1.get();
          assert(cnt == 1);
          assert(p->get_val() == 3
               && (*p1).get_val() == 3
               && p1.release()->get_val() == 3
               && p1.get() == 0);
          delete(p);
          assert(cnt == 0); }
     assert(cnt == 0);
          {Myptr p2(new Myint(5));
          assert(cnt == 1); }
     assert(cnt == 0);
          {Myptr p3(new Myint(7)), p4(p3);
          assert(cnt == 1);
          assert(p3.get() == 0 && p4.get()->get_val() == 7);
          p3 = p4;
          assert(p4.get() == 0 && p3.get()->get_val() == 7);
          p3.reset();
          assert(p3.get() == 0 && cnt == 0);
          p4.reset();
          assert(p4.get() == 0); }
     assert(cnt == 0); }

     // TEST <memory>
int main()
     {test_alloc();
     test_uninit();
     test_tempbuf();
     test_autoptr();
     cout << "SUCCESS testing <memory>" << endl;
     return (0); }
```

Exercise

Exercise 4.1 Why doesn't the explicit specialization `allocator<void>` define the member types `reference` and `const_reference`?

Exercise 4.2 How would you use the allocator member function `max_size`?

Exercise 4.3 Write an allocator that maintains a list of previously allocated objects, which it reuses in preference to allocating a new object with `operator new`.

Exercise 4.4 Some operations on sequences — such as sorting, merging, and rotating — can be performed more easily by copying the result to a new location than by rearranging elements in place. How could you use a temporary buffer to gain some of the benefit of the copying approach in performing the operation in place? How is the benefit compromised (if at all) when the temporary buffer is not as large as you would like?

Exercise 4.5 Can template class `auto_ptr` "own" an array object? If so, describe how to declare and use such a smart pointer. If not, describe how to extend the syntax of `auto_ptr` to support array objects.

Exercise 4.6 **[Harder]** Write an allocator that stores objects in a disk file and maintains a small cache of active objects in program memory.

Exercise 4.7 **[Very hard]** Under what circumstances should an allocator define the member functions `construct` and `destroy` differently than for template class `allocator`?

Chapter 5: Algorithms

Background

Algorithms are the workhorses of the Standard Template Library. They take the form of numerous template functions. Thus, algorithms are the part of STL that most closely resembles a traditional function library. The major difference, as we keep emphasizing, is that these are *template* functions. They are not supplied as a linkable library of precompiled object modules. Rather, they are typically defined completely in the STL headers. You can specialize each template function numerous ways, greatly enhancing its usefulness as a generic program component.

iterators

With rare exceptions, these template functions use iterator arguments to manipulate sequences. That is why we have devoted the first part of this book to a detailed presentation of iterators, dry as that topic may be at times. You are now better prepared to appreciate the implications of all these algorithms, knowing as you do the broad potential of iterators.

The template functions are fairly self-contained. You can drop them into all sorts of places with remarkably little additional supporting code, particularly if the iterators you use are conventional object pointers. Thus, the machinery we present in the next few chapters should be more quickly and obviously useful in *any* C++ code that you write.

containers

These algorithms work well with the STL containers we describe later in this book. Indeed, many of the member functions in container template classes use them to advantage. But please note, *it is not necessary to understand containers to use these algorithms.* None of the algorithms use the STL containers directly. Rather, they manipulate the sequences controlled by container objects, using iterators supplied by the member functions associated with those objects. That is why we save containers for last in this book. You can understand algorithms without knowing about containers, but it is harder to describe containers without a knowledge of algorithms.

`<algorithm>`
`<numeric>`
`<functional>`

We have already presented a handful of algorithms in earlier headers. See, for example, **`uninitialized_copy`**, **`uninitialized_fill`**, and **`uninitialized_fill_n`** in Chapter 4: **`<memory>`**. Two headers define the remaining algorithms: **`<algorithm>`** and **`<numeric>`**. One additional header, **`<functional>`**, defines a number of template classes that describe *function objects,* which can be used to advantage with many algorithms.

A critical part of many an algorithm is a certain test that it must perform. For example, to find the smallest element of a sequence requires some definition of the predicate "smallest." More specifically, the algorithm must repeatedly determine the boolean result of an expression such as `smaller(x, y)`, where `x` and `y` are elements of the sequence. An obvious solution in this case is to use the expression `x < y` — and indeed many algorithms do so. You could, for example, declare the template function:

```
template<class FwdIt>
    FwdIt smallest(FwdIt first, FwdIt last);
```

which returns the iterator that designates the smallest element in the interval `[first, last)`, using `operator<` to compare elements.

function objects But it seems a pity to hardwire such a critical aspect of the algorithm, particularly when the template machinery allows so much latitude in accessing the sequence itself. That's where function objects come in. A function object doesn't necessarily store any data. Like the iterator tags described in Chapter 3: `<iterator>`, the type itself conveys much of the needed information. Here is one way to declare a function object `f`:

```
struct smaller_int {
    bool operator()(int x, int y) const
        {return (x < y); }
    } f;
```

You can treat `f` for all the world as the name of a function. If the signature is correct, for example, the expression `f(x, y)` calls the member function defined for `smaller_int`.

Thus, you can declare a version of the template function `smallest` that looks something like:

```
template<class FwdIt, class Pred>
    FwdIt smallest(FwdIt first, FwdIt last, Pred pr);
```

and supply what you mean by `smallest` when you actually call the function, as in:

```
int get_smallest(int *first, int *last)
    {return (*smallest(first, last, smaller_int())); }
```

The third argument generates a trivial object whose sole purpose is to determine the actual type of the parameter `Pred` when the template function is specialized.

Note, by the way, that this third argument can be a pointer to a function. You could rewrite the example as:

```
bool is_smaller_int(int x, int y)
    {return (x < y); }

int get_smallest(int *first, int *last)
    {return (smallest(first, last, &is_smaller_int)); }
```

(The ampersand is optional.) Both C and C++ allow the expression `pfn(x, y)` as an alternative to the sometimes more revealing form `(*pfn)(x, y)`, so the template specialization produces valid code.

Function objects have several advantages over pointers to functions:

- A function object can define multiple overloads.
- It can make use of its stored value when the function is called.
- It can be replaced by a function pointer as needed.
- It is more likely to result in inline code in place of a function call.

An algorithm characterized by some critical predicate typically occurs in two forms in the Standard Template Library, much like the template function `smallest` shown above. One form is hardwired with the most likely form of the predicate. A second form is parametrized on the type of an added function object argument.

The net effect of this approach is to nearly double the volume of code required to implement algorithms, at least in a typical implementation. But the payoff is that you get slightly more compact and efficient code for the most used predicates, without sacrificing the power that comes with using function objects when you need them.

You will find that function objects can be very powerful indeed. Chapter 8: `<functional>` supplies the gory details.

Functional Description

The descriptions of algorithms employ several shorthand phrases:

in the range ■ The phrase "in the range `[A, B)`" means the sequence of zero or more discrete values beginning with `A` up to but not including `B`. A range is valid only if `B` is *reachable* from `A` — you can store `A` in an object `N` (`N = A`), increment the object zero or more times (`++N`), and have the object compare equal to `B` after a finite number of increments (`N == B`).

each `N` in the range ■ The phrase "each `N` in the range `[A, B)`" means that `N` begins with the value `A` and is incremented zero or more times until it equals the value `B`. The case `N == B` is *not* in the range.

lowest value ■ The phrase "the lowest value of `N` in the range `[A, B)` such that X" means that the condition X is determined for each `N` in the range `[A, B)` until the condition X is met.

highest value ■ The phrase "the highest value of `N` in the range `[A, B)` such that X" usually means that X is determined for each `N` in the range `[A, B)`. The function stores in `K` a copy of `N` each time the condition X is met. If any such store occurs, the function replaces the final value of `N` (which equals `B`) with the value of `K`. For a bidirectional or random-access iterator, however, it can also mean that `N` begins with the highest value in the range and is decremented over the range until the condition X is met.

`X - Y` ■ Expressions such as `X - Y`, where `X` and `Y` can be iterators other than random-access iterators, are intended in the mathematical sense. The function does not necessarily evaluate `operator-` if it must determine such a value. The same is also true for expressions such as `X + N` and `X - N`, where `N` is an integer type.

strict weak ordering Several algorithms make use of a predicate that must impose a *strict weak ordering* on pairs of elements from a sequence. For the predicate `pr(X, Y)`:

- `pr(X, X)` is false (`X` can't be ordered before itself)
- **equivalent ordering** `X` and `Y` have an *equivalent ordering* if `!pr(X, Y) && !pr(Y, X)` (`X == Y` need not be defined)
- `pr(X, Y) && pr(Y, Z)` implies `pr(X, Z)` (ordering is transitive)

Some of these algorithms implicitly use the predicate `X < Y`, and some use a predicate `pr(X, Y)` passed as a function object. Predicates that satisfy the "strict weak ordering" requirement are `X < Y` and `X > Y` for the arithmetic types and for `string` objects Note, however, that predicates such as `X <= Y` and `X >= Y` for these same types do *not* satisfy this requirement.

ordered by A sequence of elements designated by iterators in the range `[first, last)` is "a sequence *ordered by* `operator<`" if, for each `N` in the range `[0, last - first)` and for each `M` in the range `(N, last - first)` the predicate `!(*(first + M) < *(first + N))` is true. (Note that the elements are sorted in *ascending* order.) The predicate function `operator<`, or any replacement for it, must not alter either of its operands. Moreover, it must impose a strict weak ordering on the operands it compares.

heap A sequence of elements designated by iterators in the range `[first, last)` is "a heap ordered by `operator<`" if:

- For each `N` in the range `[1, last - first)` the predicate `!(*first < *(first + N))` is true. (The first element is the largest.)
- It is possible to insert (`push_heap`) a new element or remove (`pop_heap`) the largest element in logarithmic time and preserve the heap discipline in the resulting sequence.

Its internal structure is otherwise known only to the template functions `make_heap`, `pop_heap`, and `push_heap`. (See Chapter 6: **<algorithm>**.) As with an ordered sequence, the predicate function `operator<`, or any replacement for it, must not alter either of its operands, and it must impose a strict weak ordering on the operands it compares.

Using Algorithms

You use the STL algorithms much like you use a conventional function library. Include the header that defines the template function you wish to use. Be warned, however, that the failure modes for an ill-formed program can be quite different. If you call a conventional function incorrectly, the translator either issues a diagnostic or quietly converts one or more arguments to the expected types. The latter case can lead to curious runtime behavior, but it is the sort of curiosity that modern debuggers are designed to help pinpoint.

If you specialize a template function incorrectly, the translator may do the same, or it may choose a wrong type for a template parameter. Such an incorrect type can generate truly mysterious diagnostics, particularly for a template that specializes other templates. With multiple specializations of a template, even runtime debugging can be a challenge.

To mitigate this problem, the single most important thing you can do is minimize the use of implicit type conversion in function argument expressions. This is generally a good idea anyway, particularly in the presence of multiple function overloads. The type of an argument expression can influence the choice of overloads, possibly incorrectly if no exact match exists for the argument type. You are fortunate if the translator reports an ambiguity, rather than guessing wrong.

A template function can use the argument type to determine a template parameter type, so the opportunities for going astray are all the more varied. The code in this book makes judicious use of type casts, in argument expressions, to minimize the likelihood that the type will prove incorrect. We encourage you to adopt a similar style.

Exercises

Exercise 5.1 Write both forms of the template function `smallest` described earlier in this chapter.

Exercise 5.2 Alter the template functions you wrote for the previous exercise to work properly with input iterators, rather than forward iterators.

Exercise 5.3 In the following sequence, does `dominates` constitute a strict weak ordering? If not, why not?

```
rock dominates scissors
scissors dominates paper
paper dominates rock
```

Exercise 5.4 Which of the following sequences are possible heaps?

```
{1}
{1, 1}
{1, 2}
{8, 7, 6, 5, 4, 3, 2, 1}
```

Exercise 5.5 Write the template class `less` such that `less<T>()(x, y)` returns true if `x` is less than `y`, where both arguments are of type `T`.

Exercise 5.6 Write the template class `less_by` such that `less_by<T>(d)(x, y)` returns true if `x + d` is less than `y`, where `d` and both arguments are of type `T`.

Exercise 5.7 [Harder] Write the template function `is_less_by` such that a pointer to a specialization of the template function can take the place of the function object `less_by<T>(d)` in the previous exercise.

Exercise 5.8 [Very hard] How do you order a sequence, such as a prioritized list of tasks, whose ordering rule varies during the ordering process?

Chapter 6: <algorithm>

Background

The header **<algorithm>** is far and away the largest in the Standard Template Library. The next largest header is only a third its size. Nevertheless, the header **<algorithm>** is in many ways the easiest to understand. That's because it consists of a large number of template functions, each of which can be considered largely in isolation.

Functional Description

```
namespace std {
template<class InIt, class Fun>
    Fun for_each(InIt first, InIt last, Fun f);
template<class InIt, class T>
    InIt find(InIt first, InIt last, const T& val);
template<class InIt, class Pred>
    InIt find_if(InIt first, InIt last, Pred pr);
template<class FwdIt1, class FwdIt2>
    FwdIt1 find_end(FwdIt1 first1, FwdIt1 last1,
        FwdIt2 first2, FwdIt2 last2);
template<class FwdIt1, class FwdIt2, class Pred>
    FwdIt1 find_end(FwdIt1 first1, FwdIt1 last1,
        FwdIt2 first2, FwdIt2 last2, Pred pr);
template<class FwdIt1, class FwdIt2>
    FwdIt1 find_first_of(FwdIt1 first1, FwdIt1 last1,
        FwdIt2 first2, FwdIt2 last2);
template<class FwdIt1, class FwdIt2, class Pred>
    FwdIt1 find_first_of(FwdIt1 first1, FwdIt1 last1,
        FwdIt2 first2, FwdIt2 last2, Pred pr);
template<class FwdIt>
    FwdIt adjacent_find(FwdIt first, FwdIt last);
template<class FwdIt, class Pred>
    FwdIt adjacent_find(FwdIt first, FwdIt last, Pred pr);
template<class InIt, class T, class Dist>
    typename iterator_traits<InIt>::difference_type
        count(InIt first, InIt last,
            const T& val);
template<class InIt, class Pred, class Dist>
    typename iterator_traits<InIt>::difference_type
        count_if(InIt first, InIt last,
            Pred pr);
template<class InIt1, class InIt2>
    pair<InIt1, InIt2> mismatch(InIt1 first, InIt1 last,
        InIt2 x);
```

```
template<class InIt1, class InIt2, class Pred>
    pair<InIt1, InIt2> mismatch(InIt1 first, InIt1 last,
        InIt2 x, Pred pr);
template<class InIt1, class InIt2>
    bool equal(InIt1 first, InIt1 last, InIt2 x);
template<class InIt1, class InIt2, class Pred>
    bool equal(InIt1 first, InIt1 last, InIt2 x, Pred pr);
template<class FwdIt1, class FwdIt2>
    FwdIt1 search(FwdIt1 first1, FwdIt1 last1,
        FwdIt2 first2, FwdIt2 last2);
template<class FwdIt1, class FwdIt2, class Pred>
    FwdIt1 search(FwdIt1 first1, FwdIt1 last1,
        FwdIt2 first2, FwdIt2 last2, Pred pr);
template<class FwdIt, class Dist, class T>
    FwdIt search_n(FwdIt first, FwdIt last,
        Dist n, const T& val);
template<class FwdIt, class Dist, class T, class Pred>
    FwdIt search_n(FwdIt first, FwdIt last,
        Dist n, const T& val, Pred pr);
template<class InIt, class OutIt>
    OutIt copy(InIt first, InIt last, OutIt x);
template<class BidIt1, class BidIt2>
    BidIt2 copy_backward(BidIt1 first, BidIt1 last,
        BidIt2 x);
template<class T>
    void swap(T& x, T& y);
template<class FwdIt1, class FwdIt2>
    FwdIt2 swap_ranges(FwdIt1 first, FwdIt1 last,
        FwdIt2 x);
template<class FwdIt1, class FwdIt2>
    void iter_swap(FwdIt1 x, FwdIt2 y);
template<class InIt, class OutIt, class Unop>
    OutIt transform(InIt first, InIt last, OutIt x,
        Unop uop);
template<class InIt1, class InIt2, class OutIt,
    class Binop>
    OutIt transform(InIt1 first1, InIt1 last1,
        InIt2 first2, OutIt x, Binop bop);
template<class FwdIt, class T>
    void replace(FwdIt first, FwdIt last,
        const T& vold, const T& vnew);
template<class FwdIt, class Pred, class T>
    void replace_if(FwdIt first, FwdIt last,
        Pred pr, const T& val);
template<class InIt, class OutIt, class T>
    OutIt replace_copy(InIt first, InIt last, OutIt x,
        const T& vold, const T& vnew);
template<class InIt, class OutIt, class Pred, class T>
    OutIt replace_copy_if(InIt first, InIt last, OutIt x,
        Pred pr, const T& val);
template<class FwdIt, class T>
    void fill(FwdIt first, FwdIt last, const T& x);
template<class OutIt, class Size, class T>
    void fill_n(OutIt first, Size n, const T& x);
template<class FwdIt, class Gen>
    void generate(FwdIt first, FwdIt last, Gen g);
template<class OutIt, class Pred, class Gen>
    void generate_n(OutIt first, Dist n, Gen g);
template<class FwdIt, class T>
    FwdIt remove(FwdIt first, FwdIt last, const T& val);
template<class FwdIt, class Pred>
```

```
    FwdIt remove_if(FwdIt first, FwdIt last, Pred pr);
template<class InIt, class OutIt, class T>
    OutIt remove_copy(InIt first, InIt last, OutIt x,
        const T& val);
template<class InIt, class OutIt, class Pred>
    OutIt remove_copy_if(InIt first, InIt last, OutIt x,
        Pred pr);
template<class FwdIt>
    FwdIt unique(FwdIt first, FwdIt last);
template<class FwdIt, class Pred>
    FwdIt unique(FwdIt first, FwdIt last, Pred pr);
template<class InIt, class OutIt>
    OutIt unique_copy(InIt first, InIt last, OutIt x);
template<class InIt, class OutIt, class Pred>
    OutIt unique_copy(InIt first, InIt last, OutIt x,
        Pred pr);
template<class BidIt>
    void reverse(BidIt first, BidIt last);
template<class BidIt, class OutIt>
    OutIt reverse_copy(BidIt first, BidIt last, OutIt x);
template<class FwdIt>
    void rotate(FwdIt first, FwdIt middle, FwdIt last);
template<class FwdIt, class OutIt>
    OutIt rotate_copy(FwdIt first, FwdIt middle,
        FwdIt last, OutIt x);
template<class RanIt>
    void random_shuffle(RanIt first, RanIt last);
template<class RanIt, class Fun>
    void random_shuffle(RanIt first, RanIt last, Fun& f);
template<class BidIt, class Pred>
    BidIt partition(BidIt first, BidIt last, Pred pr);
template<class BidIt, class Pred>
    BidIt stable_partition(BidIt first, BidIt last,
        Pred pr);
template<class RanIt>
    void sort(RanIt first, RanIt last);
template<class RanIt, class Pred>
    void sort(RanIt first, RanIt last, Pred pr);
template<class BidIt>
    void stable_sort(BidIt first, BidIt last);
template<class BidIt, class Pred>
    void stable_sort(BidIt first, BidIt last, Pred pr);
template<class RanIt>
    void partial_sort(RanIt first, RanIt middle,
        RanIt last);
template<class RanIt, class Pred>
    void partial_sort(RanIt first, RanIt middle,
        RanIt last, Pred pr);
template<class InIt, class RanIt>
    RanIt partial_sort_copy(InIt first1, InIt last1,
        RanIt first2, RanIt last2);
template<class InIt, class RanIt, class Pred>
    RanIt partial_sort_copy(InIt first1, InIt last1,
        RanIt first2, RanIt last2, Pred pr);
template<class RanIt>
    void nth_element(RanIt first, RanIt nth, RanIt last);
template<class RanIt, class Pred>
    void nth_element(RanIt first, RanIt nth, RanIt last,
        Pred pr);
template<class FwdIt, class T>
    FwdIt lower_bound(FwdIt first, FwdIt last,
```

```
        const T& val);
template<class FwdIt, class T, class Pred>
    FwdIt lower_bound(FwdIt first, FwdIt last,
        const T& val, Pred pr);
template<class FwdIt, class T>
    FwdIt upper_bound(FwdIt first, FwdIt last,
        const T& val);
template<class FwdIt, class T, class Pred>
    FwdIt upper_bound(FwdIt first, FwdIt last,
        const T& val, Pred pr);
template<class FwdIt, class T>
    pair<FwdIt, FwdIt> equal_range(FwdIt first,
        FwdIt last, const T& val);
template<class FwdIt, class T, class Pred>
    pair<FwdIt, FwdIt> equal_range(FwdIt first,
        FwdIt last, const T& val, Pred pr);
template<class FwdIt, class T>
    bool binary_search(FwdIt first, FwdIt last,
        const T& val);
template<class FwdIt, class T, class Pred>
    bool binary_search(FwdIt first, FwdIt last,
        const T& val, Pred pr);
template<class InIt1, class InIt2, class OutIt>
    OutIt merge(InIt1 first1, InIt1 last1,
        InIt2 first2, InIt2 last2, OutIt x);
template<class InIt1, class InIt2, class OutIt,
    class Pred>
    OutIt merge(InIt1 first1, InIt1 last1,
        InIt2 first2, InIt2 last2, OutIt x, Pred pr);
template<class BidIt>
    void inplace_merge(BidIt first, BidIt middle,
        BidIt last);
template<class BidIt, class Pred>
    void inplace_merge(BidIt first, BidIt middle,
        BidIt last, Pred pr);
template<class InIt1, class InIt2>
    bool includes(InIt1 first1, InIt1 last1,
        InIt2 first2, InIt2 last2);
template<class InIt1, class InIt2, class Pred>
    bool includes(InIt1 first1, InIt1 last1,
        InIt2 first2, InIt2 last2, Pred pr);
template<class InIt1, class InIt2, class OutIt>
    OutIt set_union(InIt1 first1, InIt1 last1,
        InIt2 first2, InIt2 last2, OutIt x);
template<class InIt1, class InIt2, class OutIt,
    class Pred>
    OutIt set_union(InIt1 first1, InIt1 last1,
        InIt2 first2, InIt2 last2, OutIt x, Pred pr);
template<class InIt1, class InIt2, class OutIt>
    OutIt set_intersection(InIt1 first1, InIt1 last1,
        InIt2 first2, InIt2 last2, OutIt x);
template<class InIt1, class InIt2, class OutIt,
    class Pred>
    OutIt set_intersection(InIt1 first1, InIt1 last1,
        InIt2 first2, InIt2 last2, OutIt x, Pred pr);
template<class InIt1, class InIt2, class OutIt>
    OutIt set_difference(InIt1 first1, InIt1 last1,
        InIt2 first2, InIt2 last2, OutIt x);
template<class InIt1, class InIt2, class OutIt,
    class Pred>
    OutIt set_difference(InIt1 first1, InIt1 last1,
```

```
        InIt2 first2, InIt2 last2, OutIt x, Pred pr);
template<class InIt1, class InIt2, class OutIt>
    OutIt set_symmetric_difference(InIt1 first1,
        InIt1 last1, InIt2 first2, InIt2 last2, OutIt x);
template<class InIt1, class InIt2, class OutIt,
    class Pred>
    OutIt set_symmetric_difference(InIt1 first1,
        InIt1 last1, InIt2 first2, InIt2 last2, OutIt x,
            Pred pr);
template<class RanIt>
    void push_heap(RanIt first, RanIt last);
template<class RanIt, class Pred>
    void push_heap(RanIt first, RanIt last, Pred pr);
template<class RanIt>
    void pop_heap(RanIt first, RanIt last);
template<class RanIt, class Pred>
    void pop_heap(RanIt first, RanIt last, Pred pr);
template<class RanIt>
    void make_heap(RanIt first, RanIt last);
template<class RanIt, class Pred>
    void make_heap(RanIt first, RanIt last, Pred pr);
template<class RanIt>
    void sort_heap(RanIt first, RanIt last);
template<class RanIt, class Pred>
    void sort_heap(RanIt first, RanIt last, Pred pr);
template<class T>
    const T& max(const T& x, const T& y);
template<class T, class Pred>
    const T& max(const T& x, const T& y, Pred pr);
template<class T>
    const T& min(const T& x, const T& y);
template<class T, class Pred>
    const T& min(const T& x, const T& y, Pred pr);
template<class FwdIt>
    FwdIt max_element(FwdIt first, FwdIt last);
template<class FwdIt, class Pred>
    FwdIt max_element(FwdIt first, FwdIt last, Pred pr);
template<class FwdIt>
    FwdIt min_element(FwdIt first, FwdIt last);
template<class FwdIt, class Pred>
    FwdIt min_element(FwdIt first, FwdIt last, Pred pr);
template<class InIt1, class InIt2>
    bool lexicographical_compare(InIt1 first1,
        InIt1 last1, InIt2 first2, InIt2 last2);
template<class InIt1, class InIt2, class Pred>
    bool lexicographical_compare(InIt1 first1,
        InIt1 last1, InIt2 first2, InIt2 last2, Pred pr);
template<class BidIt>
    bool next_permutation(BidIt first, BidIt last);
template<class BidIt, class Pred>
    bool next_permutation(BidIt first, BidIt last,
        Pred pr);
template<class BidIt>
    bool prev_permutation(BidIt first, BidIt last);
template<class BidIt, class Pred>
    bool prev_permutation(BidIt first, BidIt last,
        Pred pr);
    };
```

Include the STL standard header `<algorithm>` to define numerous template functions that perform useful algorithms. The descriptions that follow make extensive use of common template parameter names (or prefixes) to indicate the least powerful category of iterator permitted as an actual argument type:

- `OutIt` — to indicate an output iterator
- `InIt` — to indicate an input iterator
- `FwdIt` — to indicate a forward iterator
- `BidIt` — to indicate a bidirectional iterator
- `RanIt` — to indicate a random-access iterator

The descriptions of these templates employ a number of conventions common to all algorithms.

adjacent_find

```
template<class FwdIt>
    FwdIt adjacent_find(FwdIt first, FwdIt last);
template<class FwdIt, class Pred>
    FwdIt adjacent_find(FwdIt first, FwdIt last, Pred pr);
```

The first template function determines the lowest `N` in the range `[0, last - first)` for which `N + 1 != last - first` and the predicate `*(first + N) == *(first + N + 1)` is true. It then returns `first + N`. If no such value exists, the function returns `last`. It evaluates the predicate exactly `N + 1` times.

The second template function behaves the same, except that the predicate is `pr(*(first + N), *(first + N + 1))`.

binary_search

```
template<class FwdIt, class T>
    bool binary_search(FwdIt first, FwdIt last,
        const T& val);
template<class FwdIt, class T, class Pred>
    bool binary_search(FwdIt first, FwdIt last,
        const T& val, Pred pr);
```

The first template function determines whether a value of `N` exists in the range `[0, last - first)` for which `*(first + N)` has equivalent ordering to `val`, where the elements designated by iterators in the range `[first, last)` form a sequence ordered by `operator<`. If so, the function returns true. If no such value exists, it returns false.

The function evaluates the ordering predicate `X < Y` at most `ceil(log(last - first)) + 2` times.

The second template function behaves the same, except that it replaces `operator<(X, Y)` with `pr(X, Y)`.

copy

```
template<class InIt, class OutIt>
    OutIt copy(InIt first, InIt last, OutIt x);
```

The template function evaluates `*(x + N) = *(first + N))` once for each `N` in the range `[0, last - first)`, for strictly increasing values of `N` beginning with the lowest value. It then returns `x + N`. If `x` and `first` designate regions of storage, `x` must not be in the range `[first, last)`.

- **copy_backward**

```
template<class BidIt1, class BidIt2>
    BidIt2 copy_backward(BidIt1 first, BidIt1 last,
        BidIt2 x);
```

The template function evaluates `*(x - N - 1) = *(last - N - 1))` once for each `N` in the range `[0, last - first)`, for strictly increasing values of `N` beginning with the lowest value. It then returns `x - (last - first)`. If `x` and `first` designate regions of storage, `x` must not be in the range `[first, last)`.

- **count**

```
template<class InIt, class T>
    typename iterator_traits<InIt>::difference_type
        count(InIt first, InIt last, const T& val);
```

The template function sets a count `n` to zero. It then executes `++n` for each `N` in the range `[0, last - first)` for which the predicate `*(first + N) == val` is true. Here, `operator==` must impose an equivalence relationship between its operands. The function returns `n`. It evaluates the predicate exactly `last - first` times.

- **count_if**

```
template<class InIt, class Pred, class Dist>
    typename iterator_traits<InIt>::difference_type
        count_if(InIt first, InIt last,
            Pred pr);
```

The template function sets a count `n` to zero. It then executes `++n` for each `N` in the range `[0, last - first)` for which the predicate `pr(*(first + N))` is true. The function returns `n`. It evaluates the predicate exactly `last - first` times.

- **equal**

```
template<class InIt1, class InIt2>
    bool equal(InIt1 first, InIt1 last, InIt2 x);
template<class InIt1, class InIt2, class Pred>
    bool equal(InIt1 first, InIt1 last, InIt2 x, Pred pr);
```

The first template function returns true only if, for each `N` in the range `[0, last1 - first1)`, the predicate `*(first1 + N) == *(first2 + N)` is true. Here, `operator==` must impose an equivalence relationship between its operands. The function evaluates the predicate at most once for each `N`.

The second template function behaves the same, except that the predicate is `pr(*(first1 + N), *(first2 + N))`.

- **equal_range**

```
template<class FwdIt, class T>
    pair<FwdIt, FwdIt> equal_range(FwdIt first,
        FwdIt last, const T& val);
```

```
template<class FwdIt, class T, class Pred>
    pair<FwdIt, FwdIt> equal_range(FwdIt first,
        FwdIt last, const T& val, Pred pr);
```

The first template function effectively returns `pair(lower_bound(first, last, val), upper_bound(first, last, val))`, where the elements designated by iterators in the range `[first, last)` form a sequence ordered by `operator<`. Thus, the function determines the largest range of positions over which `val` can be inserted in the sequence and still preserve its ordering.

The function evaluates the ordering predicate `X < Y` at most `ceil(2 * log(last - first)) + 1`.

The second template function behaves the same, except that it replaces `operator<(X, Y)` with `pr(X, Y)`.

▫ **fill**

```
template<class FwdIt, class T>
    void fill(FwdIt first, FwdIt last, const T& x);
```

The template function evaluates `*(first + N) = x` once for each `N` in the range `[0, last - first)`.

▫ **fill_n**

```
template<class OutIt, class Size, class T>
    void fill_n(OutIt first, Size n, const T& x);
```

The template function evaluates `*(first + N) = x` once for each `N` in the range `[0, n)`.

▫ **find**

```
template<class InIt, class T>
    InIt find(InIt first, InIt last, const T& val);
```

The template function determines the lowest value of `N` in the range `[0, last - first)` for which the predicate `*(first + N) == val` is true. Here, `operator==` must impose an equivalence relationship between its operands. It then returns `first + N`. If no such value exists, the function returns `last`. It evaluates the predicate at most once for each `N`.

▫ **find_end**

```
template<class FwdIt1, class FwdIt2>
    FwdIt1 find_end(FwdIt1 first1, FwdIt1 last1,
        FwdIt2 first2, FwdIt2 last2);
template<class FwdIt1, class FwdIt2, class Pred>
    FwdIt1 find_end(FwdIt1 first1, FwdIt1 last1,
        FwdIt2 first2, FwdIt2 last2, Pred pr);
```

The first template function determines the highest value of `N` in the range `[0, last1 - first1 - (last2 - first2))` such that for each `M` in the range `[0, last2 - first2)`, the predicate `*(first1 + N + M) == *(first2 + N + M)` is true. Here, `operator==` must impose an equivalence relationship between its operands. It then returns `first1 + N`. If no such value exists, the function returns `last1`. It evaluates the predicate at most (last2 - first2) * (last1 - first1 - (last2 - first2) + 1) times.

The second template function behaves the same, except that the predicate is pr(*(first1 + N + M), *(first2 + N + M)).

▫ **find_first_of**

```
template<class FwdIt1, class FwdIt2>
    FwdIt1 find_first_of(FwdIt1 first1, FwdIt1 last1,
        FwdIt2 first2, FwdIt2 last2);
template<class FwdIt1, class FwdIt2, class Pred>
    FwdIt1 find_first_of(FwdIt1 first1, FwdIt1 last1,
        FwdIt2 first2, FwdIt2 last2, Pred pr);
```

The first template function determines the lowest value of N in the range [0, last1 - first1) such that for some M in the range [0, last2 - first2), the predicate *(first1 + N) == *(first2 + M) is true. Here, operator== must impose an equivalence relationship between its operands. It then returns first1 + N. If no such value exists, the function returns last1.

It evaluates the predicate at most (last1 - first1) * (last2 - first2) times.

The second template function behaves the same, except that the predicate is pr(*(first1 + N), *(first2 + M)).

▫ **find_if**

```
template<class InIt, class Pred>
    InIt find_if(InIt first, InIt last, Pred pr);
```

The template function determines the lowest value of N in the range [0, last - first) for which the predicate pred(*(first + N)) is true. It then returns first + N. If no such value exists, the function returns last. It evaluates the predicate at most once for each N.

▫ **for_each**

```
template<class InIt, class Fun>
    Fun for_each(InIt first, InIt last, Fun f);
```

The template function evaluates f(*(first + N)) once for each N in the range [0, last - first). It then returns f.

▫ **generate**

```
template<class FwdIt, class Gen>
    void generate(FwdIt first, FwdIt last, Gen g);
```

The template function evaluates *(first + N) = g() once for each N in the range [0, last - first).

▫ **generate_n**

```
template<class OutIt, class Pred, class Gen>
    void generate_n(OutIt first, Dist n, Gen g);
```

The template function evaluates *(first + N) = g() once for each N in the range [0, n).

▫ **includes**

```
template<class InIt1, class InIt2>
    bool includes(InIt1 first1, InIt1 last1,
        InIt2 first2, InIt2 last2);
template<class InIt1, class InIt2, class Pred>
    bool includes(InIt1 first1, InIt1 last1,
        InIt2 first2, InIt2 last2, Pred pr);
```

The first template function determines whether a value of `N` exists in the range `[0, last2 - first2)` such that, for each `M` in the range `[0, last1 - first1)`, `*(first1 + M)` and `*(first2 + N)` do not have equivalent ordering, where the elements designated by iterators in the ranges `[first1, last1)` and `[first2, last2)` each form a sequence ordered by `operator<`. If so, the function returns false. If no such value exists, it returns true. Thus, the function determines whether the ordered sequence designated by iterators in the range `[first2, last2)` all have equivalent ordering with some element designated by iterators in the range `[first1, last1)`.

The function evaluates the predicate at most `2 * ((last1 - first1) + (last2 - first2)) - 1` times.

The second template function behaves the same, except that it replaces `operator<(X, Y)` with `pr(X, Y)`.

▫ **inplace_merge**

```
template<class BidIt>
    void inplace_merge(BidIt first, BidIt middle,
        BidIt last);
template<class BidIt, class Pred>
    void inplace_merge(BidIt first, BidIt middle,
        BidIt last, Pred pr);
```

The first template function reorders the sequences designated by iterators in the ranges `[first, middle)` and `[middle, last)`, each ordered by `operator<`, to form a merged sequence of length `last - first` beginning at `first` also ordered by `operator<`. The merge occurs without altering the relative order of elements within either original sequence. Moreover, for any two elements from different original sequences that have equivalent ordering, the element from the ordered range `[first, middle)` precedes the other.

The function evaluates the ordering predicate `X < Y` at most `ceil((last - first) * log(last - first))` times. (Given enough temporary storage, it can evaluate the predicate at most `(last - first) - 1` times.)

The second template function behaves the same, except that it replaces `operator<(X, Y)` with `pr(X, Y)`.

▫ **iter_swap**

```
template<class FwdIt1, class FwdIt2>
    void iter_swap(FwdIt1 x, FwdIt2 y);
```

The template function leaves the value originally stored in `*y` subsequently stored in `*x`, and the value originally stored in `*x` subsequently stored in `*y`.

- **lexicographical_compare**

```
template<class InIt1, class InIt2>
    bool lexicographical_compare(InIt1 first1,
        InIt1 last1, InIt2 first2, InIt2 last2);
template<class InIt1, class InIt2, class Pred>
    bool lexicographical_compare(InIt1 first1,
        InIt1 last1, InIt2 first2, InIt2 last2, Pred pr);
```

The first template function determines `K`, the number of elements to compare as the smaller of `last1 - first1` and `last2 - first2`. It then determines the lowest value of `N` in the range `[0, K)` for which `*(first1 + N)` and `*(first2 + N)` do not have equivalent ordering. If no such value exists, the function returns true only if `K < (last2 - first2)`. Otherwise, it returns true only if `*(first1 + N) < *(first2 + N)`. Thus, the function returns true only if the sequence designated by iterators in the range `[first1, last1)` is lexicographically less than the other sequence.

The function evaluates the ordering predicate `X < Y` at most `2 * K` times.

The second template function behaves the same, except that it replaces `operator<(X, Y)` with `pr(X, Y)`.

- **lower_bound**

```
template<class FwdIt, class T>
    FwdIt lower_bound(FwdIt first, FwdIt last,
        const T& val);
template<class FwdIt, class T, class Pred>
    FwdIt lower_bound(FwdIt first, FwdIt last,
        const T& val, Pred pr);
```

The first template function determines the highest value of `N` in the range `(0, last - first]` such that, for each `M` in the range `[0, N)` the predicate `*(first + M) < val` is true, where the elements designated by iterators in the range `[first, last)` form a sequence ordered by `operator<`. It then returns `first + N`. Thus, the function determines the lowest position before which `val` can be inserted in the sequence and still preserve its ordering.

The function evaluates the ordering predicate `X < Y` at most `ceil(log(last - first)) + 1` times.

The second template function behaves the same, except that it replaces `operator<(X, Y)` with `pr(X, Y)`.

- **make_heap**

```
template<class RanIt>
    void make_heap(RanIt first, RanIt last);
template<class RanIt, class Pred>
    void make_heap(RanIt first, RanIt last, Pred pr);
```

The first template function reorders the sequence designated by iterators in the range `[first, last)` to form a heap ordered by `operator<`.

The function evaluates the ordering predicate `X < Y` at most `3 * (last - first)` times.

The second template function behaves the same, except that it replaces `operator<(X, Y)` with `pr(X, Y)`.

▫ **max**

```
template<class T>
    const T& max(const T& x, const T& y);
template<class T, class Pred>
    const T& max(const T& x, const T& y, Pred pr);
```

The first template function returns `y` if `x < y`. Otherwise it returns `x`. `T` need supply only a single-argument constructor and a destructor.

The second template function behaves the same, except that it replaces `operator<(X, Y)` with `pr(X, Y)`.

▫ **max_element**

```
template<class FwdIt>
    FwdIt max_element(FwdIt first, FwdIt last);
template<class FwdIt, class Pred>
    FwdIt max_element(FwdIt first, FwdIt last, Pred pr);
```

The first template function determines the lowest value of `N` in the range `[0, last - first)` such that, for each `M` in the range `[0, last - first)` the predicate `*(first + N) < *(first + M)` is false. It then returns `first + N`. Thus, the function determines the lowest position that contains the largest value in the sequence.

The function evaluates the ordering predicate `X < Y` exactly `max((last - first) - 1, 0)` times.

The second template function behaves the same, except that it replaces `operator<(X, Y)` with `pr(X, Y)`.

▫ **merge**

```
template<class InIt1, class InIt2, class OutIt>
    OutIt merge(InIt1 first1, InIt1 last1,
        InIt2 first2, InIt2 last2, OutIt x);
template<class InIt1, class InIt2, class OutIt,
    class Pred>
    OutIt merge(InIt1 first1, InIt1 last1,
        InIt2 first2, InIt2 last2, OutIt x, Pred pr);
```

The first template function determines `K`, the number of elements to copy as `(last1 - first1) + (last2 - first2)`. It then alternately copies two sequences, designated by iterators in the ranges `[first1, last1)` and `[first2, last2)` and each ordered by `operator<`, to form a merged sequence of length `K` beginning at `x`, also ordered by `operator<`. The function then returns `x + K`.

The merge occurs without altering the relative order of elements within either sequence. Moreover, for any two elements from different sequences that have equivalent ordering, the element from the ordered range [first1, last1) precedes the other. Thus, the function merges two ordered sequences to form another ordered sequence.

If x and first1 designate regions of storage, the range [x, x + K) must not overlap the range [first1, last1). If x and first2 designate regions of storage, the range [x, x + K) must not overlap the range [first2, last2). The function evaluates the ordering predicate X < Y at most K - 1 times.

The second template function behaves the same, except that it replaces operator<(X, Y) with pr(X, Y).

▫ **min**

```
template<class T>
    const T& min(const T& x, const T& y);
template<class T, class Pred>
    const T& min(const T& x, const T& y, Pred pr);
```

The first template function returns y if y < x. Otherwise it returns x. T need supply only a single-argument constructor and a destructor.

The second template function behaves the same, except that it replaces operator<(X, Y) with pr(X, Y).

▫ **min_element**

```
template<class FwdIt>
    FwdIt min_element(FwdIt first, FwdIt last);
template<class FwdIt, class Pred>
    FwdIt min_element(FwdIt first, FwdIt last, Pred pr);
```

The first template function determines the lowest value of N in the range [0, last - first) such that, for each M in the range [0, last - first) the predicate *(first + M) < *(first + N) is false. It then returns first + N. Thus, the function determines the lowest position that contains the smallest value in the sequence.

The function evaluates the ordering predicate X < Y exactly max((last - first) - 1, 0) times.

The second template function behaves the same, except that it replaces operator<(X, Y) with pr(X, Y).

▫ **mismatch**

```
template<class InIt1, class InIt2>
    pair<InIt1, InIt2> mismatch(InIt1 first, InIt1 last,
        InIt2 x);
template<class InIt1, class InIt2, class Pred>
    pair<InIt1, InIt2> mismatch(InIt1 first, InIt1 last,
        InIt2 x, Pred pr);
```

The first template function determines the lowest value of N in the range [0, last1 - first1) for which the predicate !(*(first1 + N) == *(first2 + N)) is true. Here, operator== must impose an equivalence relationship between its operands. It then returns pair(first1 + N, first2 + N). If no such value exists, N has the value last1 - first1. The function evaluates the predicate at most once for each N.

The second template function behaves the same, except that the predicate is `pr(*(first1 + N), *(first2 + N))`.

▫ **`next_permutation`**

```
template<class BidIt>
    bool next_permutation(BidIt first, BidIt last);
template<class BidIt, class Pred>
    bool next_permutation(BidIt first, BidIt last,
        Pred pr);
```

The first template function determines a repeating sequence of permutations, whose initial permutation occurs when the sequence designated by iterators in the range `[first, last)` is ordered by `operator<`. (The elements are sorted in *ascending* order.) It then reorders the elements in the sequence, by evaluating `swap(X, Y)` for the elements `X` and `Y` zero or more times, to form the next permutation. The function returns true only if the resulting sequence is not the initial permutation. Otherwise, the resultant sequence is the one next larger lexicographically than the original sequence. No two elements may have equivalent ordering.

The function evaluates `swap(X, Y)` at most `(last - first) / 2`.

The second template function behaves the same, except that it replaces `operator<(X, Y)` with `pr(X, Y)`.

▫ **`nth_element`**

```
template<class RanIt>
    void nth_element(RanIt first, RanIt nth, RanIt last);
template<class RanIt, class Pred>
    void nth_element(RanIt first, RanIt nth, RanIt last,
        Pred pr);
```

The first template function reorders the sequence designated by iterators in the range `[first, last)` such that for each `N` in the range `[0, nth - first)` and for each `M` in the range `[nth - first, last - first)` the predicate `!(*(first + M) < *(first + N))` is true. Moreover, for `N` equal to `nth - first` and for each `M` in the range `(nth - first, last - first)` the predicate `!(*(first + M) < *(first + N))` is true. Thus, if `nth != last` the element `*nth` is in its proper position if elements of the entire sequence were sorted in *ascending* order, ordered by `operator<`. Any elements before this one belong before it in the sort sequence, and any elements after it belong after it.

The function evaluates the ordering predicate `X < Y` a number of times proportional to `last - first`, on average.

The second template function behaves the same, except that it replaces `operator<(X, Y)` with `pr(X, Y)`.

▫ **`partial_sort`**

```
template<class RanIt>
    void partial_sort(RanIt first, RanIt middle,
        RanIt last);
template<class RanIt, class Pred>
```

```
        void partial_sort(RanIt first, RanIt middle,
            RanIt last, Pred pr);
```

The first template function reorders the sequence designated by iterators in the range `[first, last)` such that for each `N` in the range `[0, middle - first)` and for each `M` in the range `(N, last - first)` the predicate `!(*(first + M) < *(first + N))` is true. Thus, the smallest `middle - first` elements of the entire sequence are sorted in *ascending* order, ordered by `operator<`. The order of the remaining elements is otherwise unspecified.

The function evaluates the ordering predicate `X < Y` a number of times proportional at most to `(last - first) * log(middle - first)`.

The second template function behaves the same, except that it replaces `operator<(X, Y)` with `pr(X, Y)`.

▫ **partial_sort_copy**

```
template<class InIt, class RanIt>
    RanIt partial_sort_copy(InIt first1, InIt last1,
        RanIt first2, RanIt last2);
template<class InIt, class RanIt, class Pred>
    RanIt partial_sort_copy(InIt first1, InIt last1,
        RanIt first2, RanIt last2, Pred pr);
```

The first template function determines `K`, the number of elements to copy as the smaller of `last1 - first1` and `last2 - first2`. It then copies and reorders `K` elements of the sequence designated by iterators in the range `[first1, last1)` such that the `K` elements copied to `first2` are ordered by `operator<`. Moreover, for each `N` in the range `[0, K)` and for each `M` in the range `(0, last1 - first1)` corresponding to an uncopied element, the predicate `!(*(first2 + M) < *(first1 + N))` is true. Thus, the smallest `K` elements of the entire sequence designated by iterators in the range `[first1, last1)` are copied and sorted in *ascending* order to the range `[first2, first2 + K)`.

The function evaluates the ordering predicate a number of times `X < Y` proportional at most to `(last - first) * log(K)`.

The second template function behaves the same, except that it replaces `operator<(X, Y)` with `pr(X, Y)`.

▫ **partition**

```
template<class BidIt, class Pred>
    BidIt partition(BidIt first, BidIt last, Pred pr);
```

The template function reorders the sequence designated by iterators in the range `[first, last)` and determines the value `K` such that for each `N` in the range `[0, K)` the predicate `pr(*(first + N))` is true, and for each `N` in the range `[K, last - first)` the predicate `pr(*(first + N))` is false. The function then returns `first + K`.

The predicate must not alter its operand. The function evaluates `pr(*(first + N))` exactly `last - first` times, and swaps at most `(last - first) / 2` pairs of elements.

▫ **pop_heap**

```
template<class RanIt>
    void pop_heap(RanIt first, RanIt last);
template<class RanIt, class Pred>
    void pop_heap(RanIt first, RanIt last, Pred pr);
```

The first template function reorders the sequence designated by iterators in the range `[first, last)` to form a new heap, ordered by `operator<` and designated by iterators in the range `[first, last - 1)`, leaving the original element at `*first` subsequently at `*(last - 1)`. The original sequence must designate an existing heap, also ordered by `operator<`. Thus, `first != last` must be true and `*(last - 1)` is the element to remove from (pop off) the heap.

The function evaluates the ordering predicate `X < Y` at most `ceil(2 * log(last - first))` times.

The second template function behaves the same, except that it replaces `operator<(X, Y)` with `pr(X, Y)`.

▫ **prev_permutation**

```
template<class BidIt>
    bool prev_permutation(BidIt first, BidIt last);
template<class BidIt, class Pred>
    bool prev_permutation(BidIt first, BidIt last,
        Pred pr);
```

The first template function determines a repeating sequence of permutations, whose initial permutation occurs when the sequence designated by iterators in the range `[first, last)` is the *reverse* of one ordered by `operator<`. (The elements are sorted in *descending* order.) It then reorders the elements in the sequence, by evaluating `swap(X, Y)` for the elements `X` and `Y` zero or more times, to form theprevious permutation. The function returns true only if the resulting sequence is not the initial permutation. Otherwise, the resultant sequence is the one next smaller lexicographically than the original sequence. No two elements may have equivalent ordering.

The function evaluates `swap(X, Y)` at most `(last - first) / 2`.

The second template function behaves the same, except that it replaces `operator<(X, Y)` with `pr(X, Y)`.

▫ **push_heap**

```
template<class RanIt>
    void push_heap(RanIt first, RanIt last);
template<class RanIt, class Pred>
    void push_heap(RanIt first, RanIt last, Pred pr);
```

The first template function reorders the sequence designated by iterators in the range `[first, last)` to form a new heap ordered by `operator<`. Iterators in the range `[first, last - 1)` must designate an existing heap, also ordered by `operator<`. Thus, `first != last` must be true and `*(last - 1)` is the element to add to (push on) the heap.

The function evaluates the ordering predicate `X < Y` at most `ceil(log(last - first))` times.

The second template function behaves the same, except that it replaces `operator<(X, Y)` with `pr(X, Y)`.

▫ **random_shuffle**

```
template<class RanIt>
    void random_shuffle(RanIt first, RanIt last);
template<class RanIt, class Fun>
    void random_shuffle(RanIt first, RanIt last, Fun& f);
```

The first template function evaluates `swap(*(first + N), *(first + M))` once for each `N` in the range `[1, last - first)`, where `M` is a value from some uniform random distribution over the range `[0, N]`. Thus, the function randomly shuffles the order of elements in the sequence.

The function evaluates `M` and calls `swap` exactly `last - first - 1` times.

The second template function behaves the same, except that `M` is `(Dist)f((Dist)N)`, where `Dist` is a type convertible to `iterator_traits:: difference_type`, and `f` is a function that you specify.

▫ **remove**

```
template<class FwdIt, class T>
    FwdIt remove(FwdIt first, FwdIt last, const T& val);
```

The template function effectively assigns `first` to `X`, then executes the statement:

```
if (!(*(first + N) == val))
    *X++ = *(first + N);
```

once for each `N` in the range `[0, last - first)`. Here, `operator==` must impose an equivalence relationship between its operands. It then returns `X`. Thus, the function removes from the resulting sequence all elements for which the predicate `*(first + N) == val` is true, without altering the relative order of remaining elements, and returns the iterator value that designates the end of the resulting sequence.

▫ **remove_copy**

```
template<class InIt, class OutIt, class T>
    OutIt remove_copy(InIt first, InIt last, OutIt x,
        const T& val);
```

The template function effectively executes the statement:

```
if (!(*(first + N) == val))
    *x++ = *(first + N);
```

once for each `N` in the range `[0, last - first)`. Here, `operator==` must impose an equivalence relationship between its operands. It then returns `x`. Thus, the function removes from the resulting sequence all elements for which the predicate `*(first + N) == val` is true, without altering the relative order of remaining elements, and returns the iterator value that designates the end of the resulting sequence.

If `x` and `first` designate regions of storage, the range `[x, x + (last - first))` must not overlap the range `[first, last)`.

▫ **`remove_copy_if`**

```
template<class InIt, class OutIt, class Pred>
    OutIt remove_copy_if(InIt first, InIt last, OutIt x,
        Pred pr);
```

The template function effectively executes the statement:

```
if (!pr(*(first + N)))
    *x++ = *(first + N);
```

once for each `N` in the range `[0, last - first)`. It then returns `x`. Thus, the function removes from the resulting sequence all elements for which the predicate `pr(*(first + N))` is true, without altering the relative order of remaining elements, and returns the iterator value that designates the end of the resulting sequence.

If `x` and `first` designate regions of storage, the range `[x, x + (last - first))` must not overlap the range `[first, last)`.

▫ **`remove_if`**

```
template<class FwdIt, class Pred>
    FwdIt remove_if(FwdIt first, FwdIt last, Pred pr);
```

The template function effectively assigns `first` to `X`, then executes the statement:

```
if (!pr(*(first + N)))
    *X++ = *(first + N);
```

once for each `N` in the range `[0, last - first)`. It then returns `X`. Thus, the function removes from the resulting sequence all elements for which the predicate `pr(*(first + N))` is true, without altering the relative order of remaining elements, and returns the iterator value that designates the end of the resulting sequence.

▫ **`replace`**

```
template<caass FwdIt, class T>
    void replace(FwdIt first, FwdIt last,
        const T& vold, const T& vnew);
```

The template function executes the statement:

```
if (*(first + N) == vold)
    *(first + N) = vnew;
```

once for each `N` in the range `[0, last - first)`. Here, `operator==` must impose an equivalence relationship between its operands.

▫ **`replace_copy`**

```
template<class InIt, class OutIt, class T>
    OutIt replace_copy(InIt first, InIt last, OutIt x,
        const T& vold, const T& vnew);
```

The template function executes the statement:

```
if (*(first + N) == vold)
    *(x + N) = vnew;
```

```
else
    *(x + N) = *(first + N)
```

once for each `N` in the range `[0, last - first)`. Here, `operator==` must impose an equivalence relationship between its operands.

The function returns the iterator value that designates the end of the resulting sequence.

If `x` and `first` designate regions of storage, the range `[x, x + (last - first))` must not overlap the range `[first, last)`.

▫ **replace_copy_if**

```
template<class InIt, class OutIt, class Pred, class T>
    OutIt replace_copy_if(InIt first, InIt last, OutIt x,
        Pred pr, const T& val);
```

The template function executes the statement:

```
if (pr(*(first + N)))
    *(x + N) = val;
else
    *(x + N) = *(first + N)
```

once for each `N` in the range `[0, last - first)`.

If `x` and `first` designate regions of storage, the range `[x, x + (last - first))` must not overlap the range `[first, last)`.

The function returns the iterator value that designates the end of the resulting sequence.

▫ **replace_if**

```
template<class FwdIt, class Pred, class T>
    void replace_if(FwdIt first, FwdIt last,
        Pred pr, const T& val);
```

The template function executes the statement:

```
if (pr(*(first + N)))
    *(first + N) = val;
```

once for each `N` in the range `[0, last - first)`.

▫ **reverse**

```
template<class BidIt>
    void reverse(BidIt first, BidIt last);
```

The template function evaluates `swap(*(first + N), *(last - 1 - N)` once for each `N` in the range `[0, (last - first) / 2)`. Thus, the function reverses the order of elements in the sequence.

▫ **reverse_copy**

```
template<class BidIt, class OutIt>
    OutIt reverse_copy(BidIt first, BidIt last, OutIt x);
```

The template function evaluates `*(x + N) = *(last - 1 - N)` once for each `N` in the range `[0, last - first)`. It then returns `x + (last - first)`. Thus, the function reverses the order of elements in the sequence that it copies.

If `x` and `first` designate regions of storage, the range `[x, x + (last - first))` must not overlap the range `[first, last)`.

- **rotate**

```
template<class FwdIt>
    void rotate(FwdIt first, FwdIt middle, FwdIt last);
```

The template function leaves the value originally stored in `*(first + (N + (middle - last)) % (last - first))` subsequently stored in `*(first + N)` for each `N` in the range `[0, last - first)`. Thus, if a "left" shift by one element leaves the element originally stored in `*(first + (N + 1) % (last - first))` subsequently stored in `*(first + N)`, then the function can be said to rotate the sequence either left by `middle - first` elements or right by `last - middle` elements. Both `[first, middle)` and `[middle, last)` must be valid ranges. The function swaps at most `last - first` pairs of elements.

- **rotate_copy**

```
template<class FwdIt, class OutIt>
    OutIt rotate_copy(FwdIt first, FwdIt middle,
        FwdIt last, OutIt x);
```

The template function evaluates `*(x + N) = *(first + (N + (middle - first)) % (last - first))` once for each `N` in the range `[0, last - first)`. Thus, if a "left" shift by one element leaves the element originally stored in `*(first + (N + 1) % (last - first))` subsequently stored in `*(first + N)`, then the function can be said to rotate the sequence either left by `middle - first` elements or right by `last - middle` elements as it copies. Both `[first, middle)` and `[middle, last)` must be valid ranges.

The function returns the iterator value that designates the end of the resulting sequence.

If `x` and `first` designate regions of storage, the range `[x, x + (last - first))` must not overlap the range `[first, last)`.

- **search**

```
template<class FwdIt1, class FwdIt2>
    FwdIt1 search(FwdIt1 first1, FwdIt1 last1,
        FwdIt2 first2, FwdIt2 last2);
template<class FwdIt1, class FwdIt2, class Pred>
    FwdIt1 search(FwdIt1 first1, FwdIt1 last1,
        FwdIt2 first2, FwdIt2 last2, Pred pr);
```

The first template function determines the lowest value of `N` in the range `[0, (last1 - first1) - (last2 - first2))` such that for each `M` in the range `[0, last2 - first2)`, the predicate `*(first1 + N + M) == *(first2 + M)` is true. Here, `operator==` must impose an equivalence relationship between its operands. It then returns `first1 + N`. If no such value exists, the function returns `last1`. It evaluates the predicate at most `(last2 - first2) * (last1 - first1)` times.

The second template function behaves the same, except that the predicate is `pr(*(first1 + N + M), *(first2 + M))`.

▫ **search_n**

```
template<class FwdIt, class Dist, class T>
    FwdIt search_n(FwdIt first, FwdIt last,
        Dist n, const T& val);
template<class FwdIt, class Dist, class T, class Pred>
    FwdIt search_n(FwdIt first, FwdIt last,
        Dist n, const T& val, Pred pr);
```

The first template function determines the lowest value of `N` in the range `[0, (last - first) - n)` such that for each `M` in the range `[0, n)`, the predicate `*(first + N + M) == val` is true. Here, `operator==` must impose an equivalence relationship between its operands. It then returns `first + N`. If no such value exists, the function returns `last`. It evaluates the predicate at most `n * (last - first)` times.

The second template function behaves the same, except that the predicate is `pr(*(first + N + M), val)`.

▫ **set_difference**

```
template<class InIt1, class InIt2, class OutIt>
    OutIt set_difference(InIt1 first1, InIt1 last1,
        InIt2 first2, InIt2 last2, OutIt x);
template<class InIt1, class InIt2, class OutIt,
    class Pred>
    OutIt set_difference(InIt1 first1, InIt1 last1,
        InIt2 first2, InIt2 last2, OutIt x, Pred pr);
```

The first template function alternately copies values from two sequences designated by iterators in the ranges `[first1, last1)` and `[first2, last2)`, both ordered by `operator<`, to form a merged sequence of length `K` beginning at `x`, also ordered by `operator<`. The function then returns `x + K`.

The merge occurs without altering the relative order of elements within either sequence. Moreover, for two elements from different sequences that have equivalent ordering that would otherwise be copied to adjacent elements, the function copies only the element from the ordered range `[first1, last1)` and skips the other. An element from one sequence that has equivalent ordering with no element from the other sequence is copied from the ordered range `[first1, last1)` and skipped from the other. Thus, the function merges two ordered sequences to form another ordered sequence that is effectively the difference of two sets.

If `x` and `first1` designate regions of storage, the range `[x, x + K)` must not overlap the range `[first1, last1)`. If `x` and `first2` designate regions of storage, the range `[x, x + K)` must not overlap the range `[first2, last2)`. The function evaluates the ordering predicate `X < Y` at most `2 * ((last1 - first1) + (last2 - first2)) - 1` times.

The second template function behaves the same, except that it replaces `operator<(X, Y)` with `pr(X, Y)`.

- **set_intersection**

```
template<class InIt1, class InIt2, class OutIt>
    OutIt set_intersection(InIt1 first1, InIt1 last1,
        InIt2 first2, InIt2 last2, OutIt x);
template<class InIt1, class InIt2, class OutIt,
    class Pred>
    OutIt set_intersection(InIt1 first1, InIt1 last1,
        InIt2 first2, InIt2 last2, OutIt x, Pred pr);
```

The first template function alternately copies values from two sequences designated by iterators in the ranges `[first1, last1)` and `[first2, last2)`, both ordered by `operator<`, to form a merged sequence of length `K` beginning at `x`, also ordered by `operator<`. The function then returns `x + K`.

The merge occurs without altering the relative order of elements within either sequence. Moreover, for two elements from different sequences that have equivalent ordering that would otherwise be copied to adjacent elements, the function copies only the element from the ordered range `[first1, last1)` and skips the other. An element from one sequence that has equivalent ordering with no element from the other sequence is also skipped. Thus, the function merges two ordered sequences to form another ordered sequence that is effectively the intersection of two sets.

If `x` and `first1` designate regions of storage, the range `[x, x + K)` must not overlap the range `[first1, last1)`. If `x` and `first2` designate regions of storage, the range `[x, x + K)` must not overlap the range `[first2, last2)`. The function evaluates the ordering predicate `X < Y` at most `2 * ((last1 - first1) + (last2 - first2)) - 1` times.

The second template function behaves the same, except that it replaces `operator<(X, Y)` with `pr(X, Y)`.

- **set_symmetric_difference**

```
template<class InIt1, class InIt2, class OutIt>
    OutIt set_symmetric_difference(InIt1 first1,
        InIt1 last1, InIt2 first2, InIt2 last2, OutIt x);
template<class InIt1, class InIt2, class OutIt,
    class Pred>
    OutIt set_symmetric_difference(InIt1 first1,
        InIt1 last1, InIt2 first2, InIt2 last2, OutIt x,
            Pred pr);
```

The first template function alternately copies values from two sequences designated by iterators in the ranges `[first1, last1)` and `[first2, last2)`, both ordered by `operator<`, to form a merged sequence of length `K` beginning at `x`, also ordered by `operator<`. The function then returns `x + K`.

The merge occurs without altering the relative order of elements within either sequence. Moreover, for two elements from different sequences that have equivalent ordering that would otherwise be copied to adjacent elements, the function copies neither element. An element from one sequence that has equivalent ordering with no element from the other sequence is copied. Thus, the function merges two ordered sequences to form another ordered sequence that is effectively the symmetric difference of two sets.

If `x` and `first1` designate regions of storage, the range `[x, x + K)` must not overlap the range `[first1, last1)`. If `x` and `first2` designate regions of storage, the range `[x, x + K)` must not overlap the range `[first2, last2)`. The function evaluates the ordering predicate `X < Y` at most `2 * ((last1 - first1) + (last2 - first2)) - 1` times.

The second template function behaves the same, except that it replaces `operator<(X, Y)` with `pr(X, Y)`.

▫ `set_union`

```
template<class InIt1, class InIt2, class OutIt>
    OutIt set_union(InIt1 first1, InIt1 last1,
        InIt2 first2, InIt2 last2, OutIt x);
template<class InIt1, class InIt2, class OutIt,
    class Pred>
    OutIt set_union(InIt1 first1, InIt1 last1,
        InIt2 first2, InIt2 last2, OutIt x, Pred pr);
```

The first template function alternately copies values from two sequences designated by iterators in the ranges `[first1, last1)` and `[first2, last2)`, both ordered by `operator<`, to form a merged sequence of length `K` beginning at `x`, also ordered by `operator<`. The function then returns `x + K`.

The merge occurs without altering the relative order of elements within either sequence. Moreover, for two elements from different sequences that have equivalent ordering that would otherwise be copied to adjacent elements, the function copies only the element from the ordered range `[first1, last1)` and skips the other. Thus, the function merges two ordered sequences to form another ordered sequence that is effectively the union of two sets.

If `x` and `first1` designate regions of storage, the range `[x, x + K)` must not overlap the range `[first1, last1)`. If `x` and `first2` designate regions of storage, the range `[x, x + K)` must not overlap the range `[first2, last2)`. The function evaluates the ordering predicate `X < Y` at most `2 * ((last1 - first1) + (last2 - first2)) - 1` times.

The second template function behaves the same, except that it replaces `operator<(X, Y)` with `pr(X, Y)`.

▫ `sort`

```
template<class RanIt>
    void sort(RanIt first, RanIt last);
template<class RanIt, class Pred>
    void sort(RanIt first, RanIt last, Pred pr);
```

The first template function reorders the sequence designated by iterators in the range `[first, last)` to form a sequence ordered by `operator<`. Thus, the elements are sorted in *ascending* order.

The function evaluates the ordering predicate `X < Y` a number of times proportional at most to `(last - first) * log(last - first)`.

The second template function behaves the same, except that it replaces `operator<(X, Y)` with `pr(X, Y)`.

▫ **sort_heap**

```
template<class RanIt>
    void sort_heap(RanIt first, RanIt last);
template<class RanIt, class Pred>
    void sort_heap(RanIt first, RanIt last, Pred pr);
```

The first template function reorders the sequence designated by iterators in the range `[first, last)` to form a sequence that is ordered by `operator<`. The original sequence must designate a heap, also ordered by `operator<`. Thus, the elements are sorted in *ascending* order.

The function evaluates the ordering predicate `X < Y` at most `ceil((last - first) * log(last - first))` times.

The second template function behaves the same, except that it replaces `operator<(X, Y)` with `pr(X, Y)`.

▫ **stable_partition**

```
template<class BidIt, class Pred>
    BidIt stable_partition(BidIt first, BidIt last,
        Pred pr);
```

The template function reorders the sequence designated by iterators in the range `[first, last)` and determines the value `K` such that for each `N` in the range `[0, K)` the predicate `pr(*(first + N))` is true, and for each `N` in the range `[K, last - first)` the predicate `pr(*(first + N))` is false. It does so without altering the relative order of either the elements designated by indexes in the range `[0, K)` or the elements designated by indexes in the range `[K, last - first)`. The function then returns `first + K`.

The predicate must not alter its operand. The function evaluates `pr(*(first + N))` exactly `last - first` times, and swaps at most `ceil((last - first) * log(last - first))` pairs of elements. (Given enough temporary storage, it can replace the swaps with at most `2 * (last - first)` assignments.)

▫ **stable_sort**

```
template<class BidIt>
    void stable_sort(BidIt first, BidIt last);
template<class BidIt, class Pred>
    void stable_sort(BidIt first, BidIt last, Pred pr);
```

The first template function reorders the sequence designated by iterators in the range `[first, last)` to form a sequence ordered by `operator<`. It does so without altering the relative order of elements that have equivalent ordering. Thus, the elements are sorted in *ascending* order.

The function evaluates the ordering predicate `X < Y` a number of times proportional at most to `(last - first) * (log(last - first))^2`. (Given enough temporary storage, it can evaluate the predicate a number of times proportional to at most `(last - first) * log(last - first)`.)

The second template function behaves the same, except that it replaces `operator<(X, Y)` with `pr(X, Y)`.

▫ **swap**

```
template<class T>
    void swap(T& x, T& y);
```

The template function leaves the value originally stored in `y` subsequently stored in `x`, and the value originally stored in `x` subsequently stored in `y`.

▫ **swap_ranges**

```
template<class FwdIt1, class FwdIt2>
    FwdIt2 swap_ranges(FwdIt1 first, FwdIt1 last,
        FwdIt2 x);
```

The template function evaluates `swap(*(first + N), *(x + N))` once for each `N` in the range `[0, last - first)`. It then returns `x + (last - first)`. If `x` and `first` designate regions of storage, the range `[x, x + (last - first))` must not overlap the range `[first, last)`.

▫ **transform**

```
template<class InIt, class OutIt, class Unop>
    OutIt transform(InIt first, InIt last, OutIt x,
        Unop uop);
template<class InIt1, class InIt2, class OutIt,
    class Binop>
    OutIt transform(InIt1 first1, InIt1 last1,
        InIt2 first2, OutIt x, Binop bop);
```

The first template function evaluates `*(x + N) = uop(*(first + N))` once for each `N` in the range `[0, last - first)`. It then returns `x + (last - first)`. The call `uop(*(first + N))` must not alter `*(first + N)`.

The second template function evaluates `*(x + N) = bop(*(first1 + N), *(first2 + N))` once for each `N` in the range `[0, last1 - first1)`. It then returns `x + (last1 - first1)`. The call `bop(*(first1 + N), *(first2 + N))` must not alter either `*(first1 + N)` or `*(first2 + N)`.

▫ **unique**

```
template<class FwdIt>
    FwdIt unique(FwdIt first, FwdIt last);
template<class FwdIt, class Pred>
    FwdIt unique(FwdIt first, FwdIt last, Pred pr);
```

The first template function effectively assigns `first` to `X`, then executes the statement:

```
if (N == 0 || !(*(first + N) == V))
    V = *(first + N), *X++ = V;
```

once for each `N` in the range `[0, last - first)`. It then returns `X`. Thus, the function repeatedly removes from the resulting sequence the second of a pair of elements for which the predicate `*(first + N) == *(first + N - 1)` is true, until only the first of a sequence of equal elements survives. Here, `operator==` must impose an equivalence relationship between its operands. It does so without altering the relative order of remaining elements, and returns the iterator value that designates the end of the resulting sequence. The function evaluates the predicate at most `last - first` times.

The second template function behaves the same, except that it executes the statement:

```
if (N == 0 || !pr(*(first + N), V))
    V = *(first + N), *X++ = V;
```

▫ **unique_copy**

```
template<class InIt, class OutIt>
    OutIt unique_copy(InIt first, InIt last, OutIt x);
template<class InIt, class OutIt, class Pred>
    OutIt unique_copy(InIt first, InIt last, OutIt x,
        Pred pr);
```

The first template function effectively executes the statement:

```
if (N == 0 || !(*(first + N) == V))
    V = *(first + N), *x++ = V;
```

once for each `N` in the range `[0, last - first)`. It then returns `x`. Thus, the function repeatedly removes from the resulting sequence it copies the second of a pair of elements for which the predicate `*(first + N) == *(first + N - 1)` is true, until only the first of a sequence of equal elements survives. Here, `operator==` must impose an equivalence relationship between its operands. It does so without altering the relative order of remaining elements, and returns the iterator value that designates the end of the copied sequence.

If `x` and `first` designate regions of storage, the range `[x, x + (last - first))` must not overlap the range `[first, last)`.

The second template function behaves the same, except that it executes the statement:

```
if (N == 0 || !pr(*(first + N), V))
    V = *(first + N), *x++ = V;
```

▫ **upper_bound**

```
template<class FwdIt, class T>
    FwdIt upper_bound(FwdIt first, FwdIt last,
        const T& val);
template<class FwdIt, class T, class Pred>
    FwdIt upper_bound(FwdIt first, FwdIt last,
        const T& val, Pred pr);
```

The first template function determines the highest value of `N` in the range `(0, last - first]` such that, for each `M` in the range `[0, N)` the predicate `!(val < *(first + M))` is true, where the elements designated by iterators in the range `[first, last)` form a sequence ordered by `operator<`. It then returns `first + N`. Thus, the function determines the highest position before which `val` can be inserted in the sequence and still preserve its ordering.

The function evaluates the ordering predicate `X < Y` at most `ceil(log(last - first)) + 1` times.

The second template function behaves the same, except that it replaces `operator<(X, Y)` with `pr(X, Y)`.

Using <algorithm>

Include the header `<algorithm>` to make use of any of the numerous template functions it defines. The summary that follows makes only the briefest mention of each algorithm, to supply an overview of what's available. Note, by the way, that references to a count `n` may indicate either a specific integer argument value or the difference between two iterator arguments. See the alphabetical listing in the previous section for details.

A handful of the template functions defined in `<algorithm>` manipulates pairs of elements only — the remainder manipulate sequences. The handful consists of:

- `max` To determine the larger of two elements, using `operator<` or a function object, call `max`.
- `min` To determine the smaller of two elements, using `operator<` or a function object, call `min`.
- `swap` To exchange two stored values, call `swap`.
- `iter_swap` To exchange two stored values designated by iterators, call `iter_swap`.

A number of template functions scan sequences in various ways without altering them:

- `max_element` To find the largest element in a sequence, using `operator<` or a function object, call `max_element`.
- `min_element` To find the smallest element in a sequence, using `operator<` or a function object, call `min_element`.
- `equal` To compare two sequences element by element for equality, using `operator==` or a function object, call `equal`.
- `lexicographical_compare` To compare two sequences element by element to see whether one sequence is ordered "before" the other, using `operator<` or a function object, call `lexicographical_compare`.
- `mismatch` To determine where two sequences first differ, using `operator==` or a function object, call `mismatch`.
- `find` To determine the first element in a sequence that equals a specified value, call `find`.
- `find_if` To determine the first element `x` in a sequence that causes `pr(x)` to return true for the function object `pr`, call `find_if`.

adjacent_find ■ To determine the first pair of adjacent elements that compare equal, using **operator==** or a function object, call **adjacent_find**.

count ■ To count the number of elements in a sequence that equal a specified value, call **count**.

count_if ■ To count the number of elements **x** in a sequence that cause **pr(x)** to return true for the function object **pr**, call **count_if**.

search ■ To determine the earliest appearance of one sequence in another, comparing elements for equality using **operator==** or a function object, call **search**.

search_n ■ To determine the earliest appearance in a sequence of a repetition of a specified value **n** times, comparing elements for equality using **operator==** or a function object, call **search_n**.

find_end ■ To determine the latest appearance of one sequence in another, comparing elements for equality using **operator==** or a function object, call **find_end**.

find_first_of ■ To determine the earliest appearance in one sequence of any member of another sequence, comparing elements for equality using **operator==** or a function object, call **find_first_of**.

Several template functions perform an operation on each member of a sequence:

for_each ■ To call **op(x)**, using the function object **op**, for each element **x** in a sequence, call **for_each**.

generate ■ To assign **fun()**, using the function object **fun**, to each element in a sequence, call **generate**.

generate_n ■ To assign **fun()**, using the function object **fun**, to the first **n** elements in a sequence, call **generate_n**.

transform ■ To assign to a sequence the values **op(x)**, using the function object **op**, from the corresponding elements **x** in an existing sequence, call **transform**. You can also call **transform** to assign to a sequence the values **op(x, y)** from the corresponding elements **x** and **y** in two existing sequences.

Several template functions assign an existing sequence, or a repetition of values, to a sequence:

copy ■ To copy one sequence to another, from beginning to end, call **copy**.

copy_backward ■ To copy one sequence to another, in reverse order, call **copy_backward**.

fill ■ To assign a specified value to each element of a sequence, call **fill**.

fill_n ■ To assign a specified value to the first **n** elements of a sequence, call **fill_n**.

swap_ranges ■ To exchange the values stored in two sequences, call **swap_ranges**.

Several template functions replace elements of one specified value in a sequence with another specified value:

replace ■ To replace each element of one specified value with another specified value, call **replace**.

- **replace_if** To replace with a specified value each element **x** for which **pr(x)** is true, using the function object **pr**, call **replace_if**.
- **replace_copy** To copy a sequence, replacing each element of one specified value with another specified value, call **replace_copy**.
- **replace_copy_if** To copy a sequence, replacing with a specified value each element **x** for which **pr(x)** is true, using the function object **pr**, call **replace_copy_if**.

Several template functions remove zero or more elements from a sequence:

- **remove** To remove all elements of a specified value, call **remove**.
- **remove_if** To remove each element **x** for which **pr(x)** is true, using the function object **pr**, call **remove_if**.
- **remove_copy** To copy a sequence, removing all elements of a specified value, call **remove_copy**.
- **remove_copy_if** To copy a sequence, removing each element **x** for which **pr(x)** is true, using the function object **pr**, call **remove_copy_if**.
- **unique** To remove all but the first of a subsequence of elements that compare equal, using **operator==** or a function object, call **unique**.
- **unique_copy** To copy a sequence, removing all but the first of a subsequence of elements that compare equal, using **operator==** or a function object, call **unique_copy**.

Several template functions alter the order of the elements in a sequence:

- **reverse** To reverse the elements in a sequence, call **reverse**.
- **reverse_copy** To copy a sequence, reversing its elements, call **reverse_copy**.
- **rotate** To rotate by **n** positions the elements in a sequence, call **rotate**.
- **rotate_copy** To copy a sequence, rotating by **n** positions its elements, call **rotate_copy**.
- **random_shuffle** To shuffle (randomly reorder) the elements in a sequence, call **random_shuffle**.

A special form of reordering is to impose on a sequence some degree of order that was not initially present:

- **partition** To move to the beginning of a sequence those elements **x** for which **pr(x)** is true, using the function object **pr**, call **partition**.
- **stable_partition** To partition a sequence as above, but without reordering any pairs of elements within each subpartition, call **stable_partition**.
- **sort** To put the elements of a sequence in ascending order, using **operator<** or a function object, call **sort**.
- **stable_sort** To sort a sequence as above, but without reordering any pairs of elements that are unordered, call **stable_sort**.
- **partial_sort** To sort just the smallest **n** elements in ascending order, using **operator<** or a function object, and move them to the beginning of a sequence, call **partial_sort**.
- **partial_sort_copy** To copy a sequence, sorting just the largest **n** elements as above, call **partial_sort_copy**.

nth_element ■ To place element `n` in ascending order, using `operator<` or a function object, call `nth_element`. Elements before element `n` in the resulting sequence should indeed sort before it, and elements after element `n` should sort after it, but these remaining elements are otherwise not completely sorted.

Two template functions merge two ordered sequences to form a similarly ordered sequence:

merge ■ To merge two ordered sequences to generate a new sequence, using `operator<` or a function object, call `merge`.

inplace_merge ■ To merge two contiguous ordered subsequences in place, using `operator<` or a function object, call `inplace_merge`.

Several template functions scan a sequence of increasing values ordered by `operator<` or a function object:

lower_bound ■ To determine the first element in an ordered sequence not less than a specified value, using `operator<` or a function object, call `lower_bound`.

upper_bound ■ To determine the last element in an ordered sequence not less than a specified value, using `operator<` or a function object, call `upper_bound`.

equal_range ■ To determine both the lower and upper bounds for a specified value in an ordered sequence as above, call `equal_range`.

binary_search ■ To determine whether an ordered sequence contains a member with ordering equivalent to a specified value, using `operator<` or a function object, call `binary_search`. Note that "equivalent ordering" is not necessarily equality.

Several template functions take as input two sequences of increasing values, both ordered by `operator<` or a function object:

includes ■ To determine whether one ordered sequence includes elements equivalent to each of the elements in a second sequence, call `includes`.

set_union ■ To merge two ordered sequences to generate a new sequence, preserving no elements from the second sequence with ordering equivalent to the first, call `set_union`. This operation is roughly equivalent to forming the union (logical OR) of two sets of values.

set_intersection ■ To merge two ordered sequences to generate a new sequence, preserving only elements from the first sequence with ordering equivalent to the second, call `set_intersection`. This operation is roughly equivalent to forming the intersection (logical AND) of two sets of values.

set_difference ■ To merge two ordered sequences to generate a new sequence, preserving only elements from the first sequence with ordering *not* equivalent to the second, call `set_difference`. This operation is roughly equivalent to forming the difference of two sets of values.

set_symmetric_difference ■ To merge two ordered sequences to generate a new sequence, preserving only elements from either sequence with ordering not equivalent to the other, call `set_symmetric_difference`. This operation is roughly equivalent to forming the symmetric difference of two sets of values.

- Several template functions administer a sequence as a *heap* (see page 134) whose values are ordered by `operator<` or a function object:
- `make_heap` To reorder a sequence as a heap, using `operator<` or a function object, call `make_heap`.
- `push_heap` To add an element to a heap, using `operator<` or a function object, call `push_heap`.
- `pop_heap` To remove the largest element from a heap, using `operator<` or a function object, call `pop_heap`.
- `sort_heap` To sort a heap (in *ascending* order) using `operator<` or a function object, call `sort_heap`.

Finally, two template functions generate all the permutations of a sequence ordered by `operator<` or a function object:

- `next_permutation` To permute the elements in a sequence, call `next_permutation`. The template function returns false when it leaves the elements all in *ascending* order.
- `prev_permutation` To permute the elements in a sequence, you can also call `prev_permutation`. The template function returns false when it leaves the elements all in *descending* order. Note that this template function generates permutations in exactly the reverse order of `next_permutation`.

Implementing `<algorithm>`

`algorithm` Some of the algorithms normally associated with the header `<algorithm>` we already showed in Chapter 3: `<iterator>`. This implementation places a number of template functions in the internal header `<xutility>`. There you will find the template functions `copy`, `copy_backward`, `equal`, `fill`, `fill_n`, `lexicographical_compare`, `mismatch`, `max`, `min`, and `swap`. The last three of these each operate on just a pair of elements; the remainder operate on sequences of elements. None of the template functions are at all complex. Just one is worthy of some remark.

`lexicographical_compare` Template function `lexicographical_compare` illustrates the difference between equality and "equivalent ordering." (See page 134.) Values `x` and `y` are equal if `x == y` is true. They have equivalent ordering if `!(x < y) && !(y < x)`. Note that the latter is defined purely in terms of `operator<`. For the integer types, equality and equivalent ordering are the same, but that is not necessarily the case for any other types.

Figures 6.1 through 6.29 show the file `algorithm`, which implements the remainder of the header `<algorithm>`. Because this header is so large, we confine our customary running commentary to highlights only. Like the template functions in `xutility`, much of the code in `algorithm` warrants little remark.

`CHUNK_SIZE` `SORT_MAX` The header begins with two constants. The template function `Buffered_merge_sort` sorts a sequence in chunks of `CHUNK_SIZE` elements, then merges the chunks. Various template functions that sort perform an insertion sort on any subsequence not larger than `SORT_MAX` elements.

Figure 6.1: `algorithm` **part 1**

```
// algorithm standard header
#ifndef ALGORITHM_
#define ALGORITHM_
#include <memory>
namespace std {
          // COMMON SORT PARAMETERS
const int CHUNK_SIZE = 7;
const int SORT_MAX = 16;

          // TEMPLATE FUNCTION for_each
template<class InIt, class Fn> inline
     Fn for_each(InIt F, InIt L, Fn Op)
     {for (; F != L; ++F)
          Op(*F);
     return (Op); }

          // TEMPLATE FUNCTION find
template<class InIt, class T> inline
     InIt find(InIt F, InIt L, const T& V)
     {for (; F != L; ++F)
          if (*F == V)
               break;
     return (F); }

          // TEMPLATE FUNCTION find_if
template<class InIt, class Pr> inline
     InIt find_if(InIt F, InIt L, Pr P)
     {for (; F != L; ++F)
          if (P(*F))
               break;
     return (F); }

          // TEMPLATE FUNCTION adjacent_find
template<class FwdIt> inline
     FwdIt adjacent_find(FwdIt F, FwdIt L)
     {for (FwdIt Fb; (Fb = F) != L && ++F != L; )
          if (*Fb == *F)
               return (Fb);
     return (L); }

          // TEMPLATE FUNCTION adjacent_find WITH PRED
template<class FwdIt, class Pr> inline
     FwdIt adjacent_find(FwdIt F, FwdIt L, Pr P)
     {for (FwdIt Fb; (Fb = F) != L && ++F != L; )
          if (P(*Fb, *F))
               return (Fb);
     return (L); }

          // TEMPLATE FUNCTION count
template<class InIt, class T> inline
     typename iterator_traits<InIt>::difference_type
          count(InIt F, InIt L, const T& V)
     {typename iterator_traits<InIt>::difference_type
          N = 0;
```

Figure 6.2: algorithm part 2

```
    for (; F != L; ++F)
        if (*F == V)
            ++N;
    return (N); }

        // TEMPLATE FUNCTION count_if
template<class InIt, class Pr> inline
    typename iterator_traits<InIt>::difference_type
        count_if(InIt F, InIt L, Pr P)
    {typename iterator_traits<InIt>::difference_type
        N = 0;
    for (; F != L; ++F)
        if (P(*F))
            ++N;
    return (N); }

        // TEMPLATE FUNCTION search
template<class FwdIt1, class FwdIt2> inline
    FwdIt1 search(FwdIt1 F1, FwdIt1 L1,
        FwdIt2 F2, FwdIt2 L2)
    {return (Search(F1, L1, F2, L2,
        Dist_type(F1), Dist_type(F2))); }
template<class FwdIt1, class FwdIt2, class Pd1, class Pd2> inline
    FwdIt1 Search(FwdIt1 F1, FwdIt1 L1, FwdIt2 F2, FwdIt2 L2,
        Pd1 *, Pd2 *)
    {Pd1 D1 = 0;
    Distance(F1, L1, D1);
    Pd2 D2 = 0;
    Distance(F2, L2, D2);
    for (; D2 <= D1; ++F1, --D1)
        {FwdIt1 X1 = F1;
        for (FwdIt2 X2 = F2; ; ++X1, ++X2)
            if (X2 == L2)
                return (F1);
            else if (!(*X1 == *X2))
                break; }
    return (L1); }

        // TEMPLATE FUNCTION search WITH PRED
template<class FwdIt1, class FwdIt2, class Pr> inline
    FwdIt1 search(FwdIt1 F1, FwdIt1 L1,
        FwdIt2 F2, FwdIt2 L2, Pr P)
    {return (Search(F1, L1, F2, L2, P,
        Dist_type(F1), Dist_type(F2))); }
template<class FwdIt1, class FwdIt2, class Pd1, class Pd2,
    class Pr> inline
    FwdIt1 Search(FwdIt1 F1, FwdIt1 L1, FwdIt2 F2, FwdIt2 L2,
        Pr P, Pd1 *, Pd2 *)
    {Pd1 D1 = 0;
    Distance(F1, L1, D1);
    Pd2 D2 = 0;
    Distance(F2, L2, D2);
    for (; D2 <= D1; ++F1, --D1)
        {FwdIt1 X1 = F1;
        for (FwdIt2 X2 = F2; ; ++X1, ++X2)
```

Figure 6.3: `algorithm` **part 3**

```
                if (X2 == L2)
                     return (F1);
                else if (!P(*X1, *X2))
                     break; }
     return (L1); }

          // TEMPLATE FUNCTION search_n
template<class FwdIt1, class Pd2, class T> inline
     FwdIt1 search_n(FwdIt1 F1, FwdIt1 L1, Pd2 N, const T& V)
     {return (Search_n(F1, L1, N, V, Dist_type(F1))); }
template<class FwdIt1, class Pd2, class T, class Pd1> inline
     FwdIt1 Search_n(FwdIt1 F1, FwdIt1 L1,
          Pd2 N, const T& V, Pd1 *)
     {Pd1 D1 = 0;
     Distance(F1, L1, D1);
     for (; N <= D1; ++F1, --D1)
          {FwdIt1 X1 = F1;
          for (Pd2 D2 = N; ; ++X1, --D2)
               if (D2 == 0)
                    return (F1);
               else if (!(*X1 == V))
                    break; }
     return (L1); }

          // TEMPLATE FUNCTION search_n WITH PRED
template<class FwdIt1, class Pd2, class T, class Pr> inline
     FwdIt1 search_n(FwdIt1 F1, FwdIt1 L1,
          Pd2 N, const T& V, Pr P)
     {return (Search_n(F1, L1,
          N, V, P, Dist_type(F1))); }
template<class FwdIt1, class Pd2,
     class T, class Pd1, class Pr> inline
     FwdIt1 Search_n(FwdIt1 F1, FwdIt1 L1,
          Pd2 N, const T& V, Pr P, Pd1 *)
     {Pd1 D1 = 0;
     Distance(F1, L1, D1);
     for (; N <= D1; ++F1, --D1)
          {FwdIt1 X1 = F1;
          for (Pd2 D2 = N; ; ++X1, --D2)
               if (D2 == 0)
                    return (F1);
               else if (!P(*X1, V))
                    break; }
     return (L1); }

          // TEMPLATE FUNCTION find_end
template<class FwdIt1, class FwdIt2> inline
     FwdIt1 find_end(FwdIt1 F1, FwdIt1 L1,
          FwdIt2 F2, FwdIt2 L2)
     {return (Find_end(F1, L1, F2, L2,
          Dist_type(F1), Dist_type(F2))); }
template<class FwdIt1, class FwdIt2, class Pd1, class Pd2> inline
     FwdIt1 Find_end(FwdIt1 F1, FwdIt1 L1,
          FwdIt2 F2, FwdIt2 L2, Pd1 *, Pd2 *)
     {Pd1 D1 = 0;
```

Figure 6.4: algorithm part 4

```
     Distance(F1, L1, D1);
     Pd2 D2 = 0;
     Distance(F2, L2, D2);
     FwdIt1 Ans = L1;
     if (0 < D2)
          for (; D2 <= D1; ++F1, --D1)
               {FwdIt1 X1 = F1;
               for (FwdIt2 X2 = F2; ; ++X1)
                    if (!(*X1 == *X2))
                         break;
                    else if (++X2 == L2)
                         {Ans = F1;
                         break; }}
     return (Ans); }

          // TEMPLATE FUNCTION find_end WITH PRED
template<class FwdIt1, class FwdIt2, class Pr> inline
     FwdIt1 find_end(FwdIt1 F1, FwdIt1 L1,
          FwdIt2 F2, FwdIt2 L2, Pr P)
     {return (Find_end(F1, L1, F2, L2, P,
          Dist_type(F1), Dist_type(F2))); }
template<class FwdIt1, class FwdIt2, class Pd1, class Pd2,
     class Pr> inline
     FwdIt1 Find_end(FwdIt1 F1, FwdIt1 L1,
          FwdIt2 F2, FwdIt2 L2, Pr P, Pd1 *, Pd2 *)
     {Pd1 D1 = 0;
     Distance(F1, L1, D1);
     Pd2 D2 = 0;
     Distance(F2, L2, D2);
     FwdIt1 Ans = L1;
     if (0 < D2)
          for (; D2 <= D1; ++F1, --D1)
               {FwdIt1 X1 = F1;
               for (FwdIt2 X2 = F2; ; ++X1)
                    if (!P(*X1, *X2))
                         break;
                    else if (++X2 == L2)
                         {Ans = F1;
                         break; }}
     return (Ans); }

          // TEMPLATE FUNCTION find_first_of
template<class FwdIt1, class FwdIt2> inline
     FwdIt1 find_first_of(FwdIt1 F1, FwdIt1 L1,
          FwdIt2 F2, FwdIt2 L2)
     {for (; F1 != L1; ++F1)
          for (FwdIt2 X2 = F2; X2 != L2; ++X2)
               if (*F1 == *X2)
                    return (F1);
     return (F1); }

          // TEMPLATE FUNCTION find_first_of WITH PRED
template<class FwdIt1, class FwdIt2, class Pr> inline
     FwdIt1 find_first_of(FwdIt1 F1, FwdIt1 L1,
          FwdIt2 F2, FwdIt2 L2, Pr P)
```

Figure 6.5: `algorithm` **part 5**

```
     {for (; F1 != L1; ++F1)
          for (FwdIt2 X2 = F2; X2 != L2; ++X2)
               if (P(*F1, *X2))
                    return (F1);
     return (F1); }

          // TEMPLATE FUNCTION iter_swap
template<class FwdIt1, class FwdIt2> inline
     void iter_swap(FwdIt1 X, FwdIt2 Y)
     {Iter_swap(X, Y, Val_type(X)); }
template<class FwdIt1, class FwdIt2, class T> inline
     void Iter_swap(FwdIt1 X, FwdIt2 Y, T *)
     {T Tmp = *X;
     *X = *Y, *Y = Tmp; }

          // TEMPLATE FUNCTION swap_ranges
template<class FwdIt1, class FwdIt2> inline
     FwdIt2 swap_ranges(FwdIt1 F, FwdIt1 L, FwdIt2 X)
     {for (; F != L; ++F, ++X)
          iter_swap(F, X);
     return (X); }

          // TEMPLATE FUNCTION transform WITH UNARY OP
template<class InIt, class OutIt, class Uop> inline
     OutIt transform(InIt F, InIt L, OutIt X, Uop U)
     {for (; F != L; ++F, ++X)
          *X = U(*F);
     return (X); }

          // TEMPLATE FUNCTION transform WITH BINARY OP
template<class InIt1, class InIt2, class OutIt, class Bop> inline
     OutIt transform(InIt1 F1, InIt1 L1, InIt2 F2, OutIt X, Bop B)
     {for (; F1 != L1; ++F1, ++F2, ++X)
          *X = B(*F1, *F2);
     return (X); }

          // TEMPLATE FUNCTION replace
template<class FwdIt, class T> inline
     void replace(FwdIt F, FwdIt L, const T& Vo, const T& Vn)
     {for (; F != L; ++F)
          if (*F == Vo)
               *F = Vn; }

          // TEMPLATE FUNCTION replace_if
template<class FwdIt, class Pr, class T> inline
     void replace_if(FwdIt F, FwdIt L, Pr P, const T& V)
     {for (; F != L; ++F)
          if (P(*F))
               *F = V; }

          // TEMPLATE FUNCTION replace_copy
template<class InIt, class OutIt, class T> inline
     OutIt replace_copy(InIt F, InIt L, OutIt X,
          const T& Vo, const T& Vn)
```

Figure 6.6: `algorithm` part 6

```
     {for (; F != L; ++F, ++X)
          *X = *F == Vo ? Vn : *F;
     return (X); }

          // TEMPLATE FUNCTION replace_copy_if
template<class InIt, class OutIt, class Pr, class T> inline
     OutIt replace_copy_if(InIt F, InIt L, OutIt X,
          Pr P, const T& V)
     {for (; F != L; ++F, ++X)
          *X = P(*F) ? V : *F;
     return (X); }

          // TEMPLATE FUNCTION generate
template<class FwdIt, class Gen> inline
     void generate(FwdIt F, FwdIt L, Gen G)
     {for (; F != L; ++F)
          *F = G(); }

          // TEMPLATE FUNCTION generate_n
template<class OutIt, class Pd, class Gen> inline
     void generate_n(OutIt F, Pd N, Gen G)
     {for (; 0 < N; --N, ++F)
          *F = G(); }

          // TEMPLATE FUNCTION remove
template<class FwdIt, class T> inline
     FwdIt remove(FwdIt F, FwdIt L, const T& V)
     {F = find(F, L, V);
     if (F == L)
          return (F);
     else
          {FwdIt Fb = F;
          return (remove_copy(++F, L, Fb, V)); }}

          // TEMPLATE FUNCTION remove_if
template<class FwdIt, class Pr> inline
     FwdIt remove_if(FwdIt F, FwdIt L, Pr P)
     {F = find_if(F, L, P);
     if (F == L)
          return (F);
     else
          {FwdIt Fb = F;
          return (remove_copy_if(++F, L, Fb, P)); }}

          // TEMPLATE FUNCTION remove_copy
template<class InIt, class OutIt, class T> inline
     OutIt remove_copy(InIt F, InIt L, OutIt X, const T& V)
     {for (; F != L; ++F)
          if (!(*F == V))
               *X++ = *F;
     return (X); }

          // TEMPLATE FUNCTION remove_copy_if
template<class InIt, class OutIt, class Pr> inline
     OutIt remove_copy_if(InIt F, InIt L, OutIt X, Pr P)
```

Figure 6.7: `algorithm` **part 7**

```
    {for (; F != L; ++F)
        if (!P(*F))
            *X++ = *F;
    return (X); }

        // TEMPLATE FUNCTION unique
template<class FwdIt> inline
    FwdIt unique(FwdIt F, FwdIt L)
    {F = adjacent_find(F, L);
    return (unique_copy(F, L, F)); }

        // TEMPLATE FUNCTION unique WITH PRED
template<class FwdIt, class Pr> inline
    FwdIt unique(FwdIt F, FwdIt L, Pr P)
    {F = adjacent_find(F, L, P);
    return (unique_copy(F, L, F, P)); }

        // TEMPLATE FUNCTION unique_copy
template<class InIt, class OutIt> inline
    OutIt unique_copy(InIt F, InIt L, OutIt X)
    {return (F == L ? X :
        Unique_copy(F, L, X, Iter_cat(F))); }
template<class InIt, class OutIt> inline
    OutIt Unique_copy(InIt F, InIt L, OutIt X,
        input_iterator_tag)
    {return (Unique_copy(F, L, X, Val_type(F))); }
template<class InIt, class OutIt, class T> inline
    OutIt Unique_copy(InIt F, InIt L, OutIt X, T *)
    {T V = *F;
    for (*X++ = V; ++F != L; )
        if (!(V == *F))
            V = *F, *X++ = V;
    return (X); }
template<class FwdIt, class OutIt> inline
    OutIt Unique_copy(FwdIt F, FwdIt L, OutIt X,
        forward_iterator_tag)
    {FwdIt Fb = F;
    for (*X++ = *Fb; ++F != L; )
        if (!(*Fb == *F))
            Fb = F, *X++ = *Fb;
    return (X); }
template<class BidIt, class OutIt> inline
    OutIt Unique_copy(BidIt F, BidIt L, OutIt X,
        bidirectional_iterator_tag)
    {return (Unique_copy(F, L, X, forward_iterator_tag())); }
template<class RanIt, class OutIt> inline
    OutIt Unique_copy(RanIt F, RanIt L, OutIt X,
        random_access_iterator_tag)
    {return (Unique_copy(F, L, X, forward_iterator_tag())); }

        // TEMPLATE FUNCTION unique_copy WITH PRED
template<class InIt, class OutIt, class Pr> inline
    OutIt unique_copy(InIt F, InIt L, OutIt X, Pr P)
    {return (F == L ? X :
        Unique_copy(F, L, X, P, Iter_cat(F))); }
```

Figure 6.8: `algorithm` part 8

```
template<class InIt, class OutIt, class Pr> inline
     OutIt Unique_copy(InIt F, InIt L, OutIt X, Pr P,
          input_iterator_tag)
     {return (Unique_copy(F, L, X, P, Val_type(F))); }
template<class InIt, class OutIt, class T, class Pr> inline
     OutIt Unique_copy(InIt F, InIt L, OutIt X, Pr P, T *)
     {T V = *F;
     for (*X++ = V; ++F != L; )
          if (!P(V, *F))
               V = *F, *X++ = V;
     return (X); }
template<class FwdIt, class OutIt, class Pr> inline
     OutIt Unique_copy(FwdIt F, FwdIt L, OutIt X, Pr P,
          forward_iterator_tag)
     {FwdIt Fb = F;
     for (*X++ = *Fb; ++F != L; )
          if (!P(*Fb, *F))
               Fb = F, *X++ = *Fb;
     return (X); }
template<class BidIt, class OutIt, class Pr> inline
     OutIt Unique_copy(BidIt F, BidIt L, OutIt X, Pr P,
          bidirectional_iterator_tag)
     {return (Unique_copy(F, L, X, P,
          forward_iterator_tag())); }
template<class RanIt, class OutIt, class Pr> inline
     OutIt Unique_copy(RanIt F, RanIt L, OutIt X, Pr P,
          random_access_iterator_tag)
     {return (Unique_copy(F, L, X, P,
          forward_iterator_tag())); }

          // TEMPLATE FUNCTION reverse
template<class BidIt> inline
     void reverse(BidIt F, BidIt L)
     {Reverse(F, L, Iter_cat(F)); }
template<class BidIt> inline
     void Reverse(BidIt F, BidIt L, bidirectional_iterator_tag)
     {for (; F != L && F != --L; ++F)
          iter_swap(F, L); }
template<class RanIt> inline
     void Reverse(RanIt F, RanIt L, random_access_iterator_tag)
     {for (; F < L; ++F)
          iter_swap(F, --L); }

          // TEMPLATE FUNCTION reverse_copy
template<class BidIt, class OutIt> inline
     OutIt reverse_copy(BidIt F, BidIt L, OutIt X)
     {for (; F != L; ++X)
          *X = *--L;
     return (X); }

          // TEMPLATE FUNCTION rotate
template<class FwdIt> inline
     void rotate(FwdIt F, FwdIt M, FwdIt L)
     {if (F != M && M != L)
          Rotate(F, M, L, Iter_cat(F)); }
```

Figure 6.9: `algorithm` **part 9**

```
template<class FwdIt> inline
     void Rotate(FwdIt F, FwdIt M, FwdIt L,
          forward_iterator_tag)
     {for (FwdIt X = M; ; )
          {iter_swap(F, X);
          if (++F == M)
               if (++X == L)
                    break;
               else
                    M = X;
          else if (++X == L)
               X = M; }}
template<class BidIt> inline
     void Rotate(BidIt F, BidIt M, BidIt L,
          bidirectional_iterator_tag)
     {reverse(F, M);
     reverse(M, L);
     reverse(F, L); }
template<class RanIt> inline
     void Rotate(RanIt F, RanIt M, RanIt L,
               random_access_iterator_tag)
     {Rotate(F, M, L, Dist_type(F), Val_type(F)); }
template<class RanIt, class Pd, class T> inline
     void Rotate(RanIt F, RanIt M, RanIt L, Pd *, T *)
     {Pd D = M - F;
     Pd N = L - F;
     for (Pd I = D; I != 0; )
          {Pd J = N % I;
          N = I, I = J; }
     if (N < L - F)
          for (; 0 < N; --N)
               {RanIt X = F + N;
               RanIt Y = X;
               T V = *X;
               RanIt Z = Y + D == L ? F : Y + D;
               while (Z != X)
                    {*Y = *Z;
                    Y = Z;
                    Z = D < L - Z ? Z + D
                         : F + (D - (L - Z)); }
               *Y = V; }}

          // TEMPLATE FUNCTION rotate_copy
template<class FwdIt, class OutIt> inline
     OutIt rotate_copy(FwdIt F, FwdIt M, FwdIt L, OutIt X)
     {X = copy(M, L, X);
     return (copy(F, M, X)); }

          // TEMPLATE FUNCTION random_shuffle
template<class RanIt> inline
     void random_shuffle(RanIt F, RanIt L)
     {if (F != L)
          Random_shuffle(F, L, Dist_type(F)); }
template<class RanIt, class Pd> inline
     void Random_shuffle(RanIt F, RanIt L, Pd *)
```

Figure 6.10: algorithm part 10

```
    {const int RBITS = 15;
    const int RMAX = (1U << RBITS) - 1;
    RanIt X = F;
    for (unsigned long D = 2; ++X != L; ++D)
        {unsigned long Rm = RMAX;
        unsigned long Rn = rand() & RMAX;
        for (; Rm < D && Rm != ~0UL;
            Rm = Rm << RBITS | RMAX)
            Rn = Rn << RBITS | RMAX;
        iter_swap(X, F + Pd(Rn % D)); }}

        // TEMPLATE FUNCTION random_shuffle WITH RANDOM FN
template<class RanIt, class Pf> inline
    void random_shuffle(RanIt F, RanIt L, Pf& R)
    {if (F != L)
        Random_shuffle(F, L, R, Dist_type(F)); }
template<class RanIt, class Pf, class Pd> inline
    void Random_shuffle(RanIt F, RanIt L, Pf& R, Pd *)
    {RanIt X = F;
    for (unsigned long D = 2; ++X != L; ++D)
        iter_swap(X, F + Pd(R(D))); }

        // TEMPLATE FUNCTION partition
template<class BidIt, class Pr> inline
    BidIt partition(BidIt F, BidIt L, Pr P)
    {for (; ; ++F)
        {for (; F != L && P(*F); ++F)
            ;
        if (F == L)
            break;
        for (; F != --L && !P(*L); )
            ;
        if (F == L)
            break;
        iter_swap(F, L); }
    return (F); }

        // TEMPLATE FUNCTION stable_partition
template<class BidIt, class Pr> inline
    BidIt stable_partition(BidIt F, BidIt L, Pr P)
    {return (F == L ? F : Stable_partition(F, L, P,
        Dist_type(F), Val_type(F))); }
template<class BidIt, class Pr, class Pd, class T> inline
    BidIt Stable_partition(BidIt F, BidIt L, Pr P, Pd *, T *)
    {Pd N = 0;
    Distance(F, L, N);
    Temp_iterator<T> Xb(N);
    return (Stable_partition(F, L, P, N, Xb)); }
template<class BidIt, class Pr, class Pd, class T> inline
    BidIt Stable_partition(BidIt F, BidIt L, Pr P, Pd N,
        Temp_iterator<T>& Xb)
    {if (N == 1)
        return (P(*F) ? L : F);
    else if (N <= Xb.Maxlen())
        {BidIt X = F;
```

Figure 6.11: `algorithm` **part 11**

```
          for (Xb.Init(); F != L; ++F)
               if (P(*F))
                    *X++ = *F;
               else
                    *Xb++ = *F;
          copy(Xb.First(), Xb.Last(), X);
          return (X); }
     else
          {BidIt M = F;
          advance(M, N / 2);
          BidIt Lp = Stable_partition(F, M, P, N / 2, Xb);
          BidIt Rp = Stable_partition(M, L, P, N - N / 2, Xb);
          Pd D1 = 0;
          Distance(Lp, M, D1);
          Pd D2 = 0;
          Distance(M, Rp, D2);
          return (Buffered_rotate(Lp, M, Rp, D1, D2, Xb)); }}

          // TEMPLATE FUNCTION sort
template<class RanIt> inline
     void sort(RanIt F, RanIt L)
     {if (L - F <= SORT_MAX)
          Insertion_sort(F, L);
     else
          {Sort(F, L, L - F);
          Insertion_sort(F, F + SORT_MAX);
          Sort_end(F + SORT_MAX, L, Val_type(F)); }}
template<class RanIt, class T>
     void Sort_end(RanIt F, RanIt L, T *)
     {for (; F != L; ++F)
          Unguarded_insert(F, T(*F)); }
template<class RanIt, class Pd> inline
     void Sort(RanIt F, RanIt L, Pd Ideal)
     {for (; SORT_MAX < L - F; )
          if (Ideal == 0)
               {make_heap(F, L);
               sort_heap(F, L);
               break; }
          else
               {RanIt M = Unguarded_partition(F, L,
                    Val_type(F));
               Sort(F, M, Ideal /= 2);
               F = M; }}
template<class RanIt, class T> inline
     RanIt Unguarded_partition(RanIt F, RanIt L, T *)
     {RanIt M = F + (L - F) / 2;
     if (*M < *F)
          iter_swap(F, M);
     if (*(L - 1) < *M)
          iter_swap(M, L - 1);
     if (*M < *F)
          iter_swap(F, M);
     for (T Piv = *M; ; ++F)
          {for (; *F < Piv; ++F)
               ;
```

Figure 6.12: `algorithm` part 12

```
          for (; Piv < *--L; )
               ;
          if (L <= F)
               return (F);
          iter_swap(F, L); }}
template<class BidIt> inline
     void Insertion_sort(BidIt F, BidIt L)
     {Insertion_sort_1(F, L, Val_type(F)); }
template<class BidIt, class T> inline
     void Insertion_sort_1(BidIt F, BidIt L, T *)
     {if (F != L)
          for (BidIt M = F; ++M != L; )
               {T V = *M;
               if (!(V < *F))
                    Unguarded_insert(M, V);
               else
                    {BidIt Mp1 = M;
                    copy_backward(F, M, ++Mp1);
                    *F = V; }}}
template<class BidIt, class T> inline
     void Unguarded_insert(BidIt L, T V)
     {for (BidIt M = L; V < *--M; L = M)
          *L = *M;
     *L = V; }

          // TEMPLATE FUNCTION sort WITH PRED
template<class RanIt, class Pr> inline
     void sort(RanIt F, RanIt L, Pr P)
     {if (L - F <= SORT_MAX)
          Insertion_sort(F, L, P);
     else
          {Sort(F, L, L - F, P);
          Insertion_sort(F, F + SORT_MAX, P);
          Sort_end(F + SORT_MAX, L, P, Val_type(F)); }}
template<class RanIt, class Pr, class T>
     void Sort_end(RanIt F, RanIt L, Pr P, T *)
     {for (; F != L; ++F)
          Unguarded_insert(F, T(*F), P); }
template<class RanIt, class Pd, class Pr> inline
     void Sort(RanIt F, RanIt L, Pd Ideal, Pr P)
     {for (; SORT_MAX < L - F; )
          if (Ideal == 0)
               {make_heap(F, L, P);
               sort_heap(F, L, P);
               break; }
          else
               {RanIt M = Unguarded_partition(F, L, P,
                    Val_type(F));
               Sort(F, M, Ideal /= 2, P);
               F = M; }}
template<class RanIt, class Pr, class T> inline
     RanIt Unguarded_partition(RanIt F, RanIt L, Pr P, T *)
     {RanIt M = F + (L - F) / 2;
     if (P(*M, *F))
          iter_swap(F, M);
```

Figure 6.13: algorithm part 13

```
        if (P(*(L - 1), *M))
            iter_swap(M, L - 1);
        if (P(*M, *F))
            iter_swap(F, M);
        for (T Piv = *M; ; ++F)
            {for (; P(*F, Piv); ++F)
                ;
            for (; P(Piv, *--L); )
                ;
            if (L <= F)
                return (F);
            iter_swap(F, L); }}
template<class BidIt, class Pr> inline
    void Insertion_sort(BidIt F, BidIt L, Pr P)
    {Insertion_sort_1(F, L, P, Val_type(F)); }
template<class BidIt, class T, class Pr> inline
    void Insertion_sort_1(BidIt F, BidIt L, Pr P, T *)
    {if (F != L)
        for (BidIt M = F; ++M != L; )
            {T V = *M;
            if (!P(V, *F))
                Unguarded_insert(M, V, P);
            else
                {BidIt Mp1 = M;
                copy_backward(F, M, ++Mp1);
                *F = V; }}}
template<class BidIt, class T, class Pr> inline
    void Unguarded_insert(BidIt L, T V, Pr P)
    {for (BidIt M = L; P(V, *--M); L = M)
        *L = *M;
    *L = V; }

        // TEMPLATE FUNCTION stable_sort
template<class BidIt> inline
    void stable_sort(BidIt F, BidIt L)
    {if (F != L)
        Stable_sort(F, L, Dist_type(F), Val_type(F)); }
template<class BidIt, class Pd, class T> inline
    void Stable_sort(BidIt F, BidIt L, Pd *, T *)
    {Pd N = 0;
    Distance(F, L, N);
    Temp_iterator<T> Xb(N);
    Stable_sort(F, L, N, Xb); }
template<class BidIt, class Pd, class T> inline
    void Stable_sort(BidIt F, BidIt L, Pd N,
        Temp_iterator<T>& Xb)
    {if (N <= SORT_MAX)
        Insertion_sort(F, L);
    else
        {Pd N2 = (N + 1) / 2;
        BidIt M = F;
        advance(M, N2);
        if (N2 <= Xb.Maxlen())
            {Buffered_merge_sort(F, M, N2, Xb);
            Buffered_merge_sort(M, L, N - N2, Xb); }
```

Figure 6.14: algorithm part 14

```
          else
               {Stable_sort(F, M, N2, Xb);
               Stable_sort(M, L, N - N2, Xb); }
          Buffered_merge(F, M, L, N2, N - N2, Xb); }}
template<class BidIt, class Pd, class T> inline
     void Buffered_merge_sort(BidIt F, BidIt L, Pd N,
          Temp_iterator<T>& Xb)
     {BidIt M = F;
     for (Pd I = N; CHUNK_SIZE <= I; I -= CHUNK_SIZE)
          {BidIt Mn = M;
          advance(Mn, (int)CHUNK_SIZE);
          Insertion_sort(M, Mn);
          M = Mn; }
     Insertion_sort(M, L);
     for (Pd D = CHUNK_SIZE; D < N; D *= 2)
          {Chunked_merge(F, L, Xb.Init(), D, N);
          Chunked_merge(Xb.First(), Xb.Last(), F,
               D *= 2, N); }}
template<class BidIt, class OutIt, class Pd> inline
     void Chunked_merge(BidIt F, BidIt L, OutIt X, Pd D, Pd N)
     {Pd D2 = D * 2;
     for (; D2 <= N; N -= D2)
          {BidIt F1 = F;
          advance(F1, D);
          BidIt F2 = F1;
          advance(F2, D);
          X = merge(F, F1, F1, F2, X);
          F = F2; }
     if (N <= D)
          copy(F, L, X);
     else
          {BidIt F1 = F;
          advance(F1, D);
          merge(F, F1, F1, L, X); }}

          // TEMPLATE FUNCTION stable_sort WITH PRED
template<class BidIt, class Pr> inline
     void stable_sort(BidIt F, BidIt L, Pr P)
     {if (F != L)
          Stable_sort(F, L,
               Dist_type(F), Val_type(F), P); }
template<class BidIt, class Pd, class T, class Pr> inline
     void Stable_sort(BidIt F, BidIt L, Pd *, T *, Pr P)
     {Pd N = 0;
     Distance(F, L, N);
     Temp_iterator<T> Xb(N);
     Stable_sort(F, L, N, Xb, P); }
template<class BidIt, class Pd, class T, class Pr> inline
     void Stable_sort(BidIt F, BidIt L, Pd N,
          Temp_iterator<T>& Xb, Pr P)
     {if (N <= SORT_MAX)
          Insertion_sort(F, L, P);
     else
          {Pd N2 = (N + 1) / 2;
          BidIt M = F;
```

Figure 6.15: `algorithm` **part 15**

```
          advance(M, N2);
          if (N2 <= Xb.Maxlen())
               {Buffered_merge_sort(F, M, N2, Xb, P);
               Buffered_merge_sort(M, L, N - N2, Xb, P); }
          else
               {Stable_sort(F, M, N2, Xb, P);
               Stable_sort(M, L, N - N2, Xb, P); }
          Buffered_merge(F, M, L, N2, N - N2, Xb, P); }}
template<class BidIt, class Pd, class T, class Pr> inline
     void Buffered_merge_sort(BidIt F, BidIt L, Pd N,
          Temp_iterator<T>& Xb, Pr P)
     {BidIt M = F;
     for (Pd I = N; CHUNK_SIZE <= I; I -= CHUNK_SIZE)
          {BidIt Mn = M;
          advance(Mn, (int)CHUNK_SIZE);
          Insertion_sort(M, Mn, P);
          M = Mn; }
     Insertion_sort(M, L, P);
     for (Pd D = CHUNK_SIZE; D < N; D *= 2)
          {Chunked_merge(F, L, Xb.Init(), D, N, P);
          Chunked_merge(Xb.First(), Xb.Last(), F,
               D *= 2, N, P); }}
template<class BidIt, class OutIt, class Pd, class Pr> inline
     void Chunked_merge(BidIt F, BidIt L, OutIt X,
          Pd D, Pd N, Pr P)
     {Pd D2 = D * 2;
     for (; D2 <= N; N -= D2)
          {BidIt F1 = F;
          advance(F1, D);
          BidIt F2 = F1;
          advance(F2, D);
          X = merge(F, F1, F1, F2, X, P);
          F = F2; }
     if (N <= D)
          copy(F, L, X);
     else
          {BidIt F1 = F;
          advance(F1, D);
          merge(F, F1, F1, L, X, P); }}

          // TEMPLATE FUNCTION partial_sort
template<class RanIt> inline
     void partial_sort(RanIt F, RanIt M, RanIt L)
     {Partial_sort(F, M, L, Val_type(F)); }
template<class RanIt, class T> inline
     void Partial_sort(RanIt F, RanIt M, RanIt L, T *)
     {make_heap(F, M);
     for (RanIt I = M; I < L; ++I)
          if (*I < *F)
               Pop_heap(F, M, I, T(*I), Dist_type(F));
     sort_heap(F, M); }

          // TEMPLATE FUNCTION partial_sort WITH PRED
template<class RanIt, class Pr> inline
     void partial_sort(RanIt F, RanIt M, RanIt L, Pr P)
```

Figure 6.16: algorithm part 16

```
     {Partial_sort(F, M, L, P, Val_type(F)); }
template<class RanIt, class T, class Pr> inline
     void Partial_sort(RanIt F, RanIt M, RanIt L, Pr P, T *)
     {make_heap(F, M, P);
     for (RanIt I = M; I < L; ++I)
          if (P(*I, *F))
               Pop_heap(F, M, I, T(*I), P, Dist_type(F));
     sort_heap(F, M, P); }

          // TEMPLATE FUNCTION partial_sort_copy
template<class InIt, class RanIt> inline
     RanIt partial_sort_copy(InIt F1, InIt L1, RanIt F2, RanIt L2)
     {return (Partial_sort_copy(F1, L1, F2, L2,
          Dist_type(F2), Val_type(F1))); }
template<class InIt, class RanIt, class Pd, class T> inline
     RanIt Partial_sort_copy(InIt F1, InIt L1, RanIt F2, RanIt L2,
          Pd *, T *)
     {RanIt X = F2;
     if (X != L2)
          {for (; F1 != L1 && X != L2; ++F1, ++X)
               *X = *F1;
          make_heap(F2, X);
          for (; F1 != L1; ++F1)
               if (*F1 < *F2)
                    Adjust_heap(F2, Pd(0), Pd(X - F2),
                         T(*F1));
          sort_heap(F2, X); }
     return (X); }

          // TEMPLATE FUNCTION partial_sort_copy WITH PRED
template<class InIt, class RanIt, class Pr> inline
     RanIt partial_sort_copy(InIt F1, InIt L1, RanIt F2, RanIt L2,
          Pr P)
     {return (Partial_sort_copy(F1, L1, F2, L2, P,
          Dist_type(F2), Val_type(F1))); }
template<class InIt, class RanIt, class Pd,
     class T, class Pr> inline
     RanIt Partial_sort_copy(InIt F1, InIt L1, RanIt F2, RanIt L2,
          Pr P, Pd *, T *)
     {RanIt X = F2;
     if (X != L2)
          {for (; F1 != L1 && X != L2; ++F1, ++X)
               *X = *F1;
          make_heap(F2, X, P);
          for (; F1 != L1; ++F1)
               if (P(*F1, *F2))
                    Adjust_heap(F2, Pd(0), Pd(X - F2),
                         T(*F1), P);
          sort_heap(F2, X, P); }
     return (X); }

          // TEMPLATE FUNCTION nth_element
template<class RanIt> inline
     void nth_element(RanIt F, RanIt Nth, RanIt L)
     {for (; SORT_MAX < L - F; )
```

Figure 6.17: `algorithm` **part 17**

```
          {RanIt M = Unguarded_partition(F, L,
               Val_type(F));
          if (M <= Nth)
               F = M;
          else
               L = M; }
     Insertion_sort(F, L); }

          // TEMPLATE FUNCTION nth_element WITH PRED
template<class RanIt, class Pr> inline
     void nth_element(RanIt F, RanIt Nth, RanIt L, Pr P)
     {for (; SORT_MAX < L - F; )
          {RanIt M = Unguarded_partition(F, L, P,
               Val_type(F));
          if (M <= Nth)
               F = M;
          else
               L = M; }
     Insertion_sort(F, L, P); }

          // TEMPLATE FUNCTION lower_bound
template<class FwdIt, class T> inline
     FwdIt lower_bound(FwdIt F, FwdIt L, const T& V)
     {return (Lower_bound(F, L, V, Dist_type(F))); }
template<class FwdIt, class T, class Pd> inline
     FwdIt Lower_bound(FwdIt F, FwdIt L, const T& V, Pd *)
     {Pd N = 0;
     Distance(F, L, N);
     for (; 0 < N; )
          {Pd N2 = N / 2;
          FwdIt M = F;
          advance(M, N2);
          if (*M < V)
               F = ++M, N -= N2 + 1;
          else
               N = N2; }
     return (F); }

          // TEMPLATE FUNCTION lower_bound WITH PRED
template<class FwdIt, class T, class Pr> inline
     FwdIt lower_bound(FwdIt F, FwdIt L, const T& V, Pr P)
     {return (Lower_bound(F, L, V, P, Dist_type(F))); }
template<class FwdIt, class T, class Pd, class Pr> inline
     FwdIt Lower_bound(FwdIt F, FwdIt L, const T& V, Pr P, Pd *)
     {Pd N = 0;
     Distance(F, L, N);
     for (; 0 < N; )
          {Pd N2 = N / 2;
          FwdIt M = F;
          advance(M, N2);
          if (P(*M, V))
               F = ++M, N -= N2 + 1;
          else
               N = N2; }
     return (F); }
```

Figure 6.18: algorithm part 18

```
        // TEMPLATE FUNCTION upper_bound
template<class FwdIt, class T> inline
    FwdIt upper_bound(FwdIt F, FwdIt L, const T& V)
    {return (Upper_bound(F, L, V, Dist_type(F))); }
template<class FwdIt, class T, class Pd> inline
    FwdIt Upper_bound(FwdIt F, FwdIt L, const T& V, Pd *)
    {Pd N = 0;
    Distance(F, L, N);
    for (; 0 < N; )
        {Pd N2 = N / 2;
        FwdIt M = F;
        advance(M, N2);
        if (!(V < *M))
            F = ++M, N -= N2 + 1;
        else
            N = N2; }
    return (F); }

        // TEMPLATE FUNCTION upper_bound WITH PRED
template<class FwdIt, class T, class Pr> inline
    FwdIt upper_bound(FwdIt F, FwdIt L, const T& V, Pr P)
    {return (Upper_bound(F, L, V, P, Dist_type(F))); }
template<class FwdIt, class T, class Pd, class Pr> inline
    FwdIt Upper_bound(FwdIt F, FwdIt L, const T& V, Pr P, Pd *)
    {Pd N = 0;
    Distance(F, L, N);
    for (; 0 < N; )
        {Pd N2 = N / 2;
        FwdIt M = F;
        advance(M, N2);
        if (!P(V, *M))
            F = ++M, N -= N2 + 1;
        else
            N = N2; }
    return (F); }

        // TEMPLATE FUNCTION equal_range
template<class FwdIt, class T> inline
    pair<FwdIt, FwdIt> equal_range(FwdIt F, FwdIt L, const T& V)
    {return (Equal_range(F, L, V, Dist_type(F))); }
template<class FwdIt, class T, class Pd> inline
    pair<FwdIt, FwdIt> Equal_range(FwdIt F, FwdIt L,
        const T& V, Pd *)
    {Pd N = 0;
    Distance(F, L, N);
    for (; 0 < N; )
        {Pd N2 = N / 2;
        FwdIt M = F;
        advance(M, N2);
        if (*M < V)
            F = ++M, N -= N2 + 1;
        else if (V < *M)
            N = N2;
```

Figure 6.19: `algorithm` **part 19**

```
            else
                {FwdIt F2 = lower_bound(F, M, V);
                advance(F, N);
                FwdIt L2 = upper_bound(++M, F, V);
                return (pair<FwdIt, FwdIt>(F2, L2)); }}
        return (pair<FwdIt, FwdIt>(F, F)); }

            // TEMPLATE FUNCTION equal_range WITH PRED
template<class FwdIt, class T, class Pr> inline
    pair<FwdIt, FwdIt> equal_range(FwdIt F, FwdIt L, const T& V,
        Pr P)
    {return (Equal_range(F, L, V, P, Dist_type(F))); }
template<class FwdIt, class T, class Pd, class Pr> inline
    pair<FwdIt, FwdIt> Equal_range(FwdIt F, FwdIt L, const T& V,
        Pr P, Pd *)
    {Pd N = 0;
    Distance(F, L, N);
    for (; 0 < N; )
        {Pd N2 = N / 2;
        FwdIt M = F;
        advance(M, N2);
        if (P(*M, V))
            F = ++M, N -= N2 + 1;
        else if (P(V, *M))
            N = N2;
        else
            {FwdIt F2 = lower_bound(F, M, V, P);
            advance(F, N);
            FwdIt L2 = upper_bound(++M, F, V, P);
            return (pair<FwdIt, FwdIt>(F2, L2)); }}
    return (pair<FwdIt, FwdIt>(F, F)); }

        // TEMPLATE FUNCTION binary_search
template<class FwdIt, class T> inline
    bool binary_search(FwdIt F, FwdIt L, const T& V)
    {FwdIt I = lower_bound(F, L, V);
    return (I != L && !(V < *I)); }

        // TEMPLATE FUNCTION binary_search WITH PRED
template<class FwdIt, class T, class Pr> inline
    bool binary_search(FwdIt F, FwdIt L, const T& V, Pr P)
    {FwdIt I = lower_bound(F, L, V, P);
    return (I != L && !P(V, *I)); }

        // TEMPLATE FUNCTION merge
template<class InIt1, class InIt2, class OutIt> inline
    OutIt merge(InIt1 F1, InIt1 L1, InIt2 F2, InIt2 L2, OutIt X)
    {for (; F1 != L1 && F2 != L2; ++X)
        if (*F2 < *F1)
            *X = *F2, ++F2;
        else
            *X = *F1, ++F1;
    X = copy(F1, L1, X);
    return (copy(F2, L2, X)); }
```

Figure 6.20: `algorithm` **part 20**

```
          // TEMPLATE FUNCTION merge WITH PRED
template<class InIt1, class InIt2, class OutIt, class Pr> inline
     OutIt merge(InIt1 F1, InIt1 L1, InIt2 F2, InIt2 L2, OutIt X,
          Pr P)
     {for (; F1 != L1 && F2 != L2; ++X)
          if (P(*F2, *F1))
               *X = *F2, ++F2;
          else
               *X = *F1, ++F1;
     X = copy(F1, L1, X);
     return (copy(F2, L2, X)); }

          // TEMPLATE FUNCTION inplace_merge
template<class BidIt> inline
     void inplace_merge(BidIt F, BidIt M, BidIt L)
     {if (F != L)
          Inplace_merge(F, M, L,
               Dist_type(F), Val_type(F)); }
template<class BidIt, class Pd, class T> inline
     void Inplace_merge(BidIt F, BidIt M, BidIt L, Pd *, T *)
     {Pd D1 = 0;
     Distance(F, M, D1);
     Pd D2 = 0;
     Distance(M, L, D2);
     Temp_iterator<T> Xb(D1 < D2 ? D1 : D2);
     Buffered_merge(F, M, L, D1, D2, Xb); }
template<class BidIt, class Pd, class T> inline
     void Buffered_merge(BidIt F, BidIt M, BidIt L,
          Pd D1, Pd D2, Temp_iterator<T>& Xb)
     {if (D1 == 0 || D2 == 0)
          ;
     else if (D1 + D2 == 2)
          {if (*M < *F)
               iter_swap(F, M); }
     else if (D1 <= D2 && D1 <= Xb.Maxlen())
          {copy(F, M, Xb.Init());
          merge(Xb.First(), Xb.Last(), M, L, F); }
     else if (D2 <= Xb.Maxlen())
          {copy(M, L, Xb.Init());
          Merge_backward(F, M, Xb.First(), Xb.Last(), L); }
     else
          {BidIt Fn, Ln;
          Pd D1n, D2n;
          if (D2 < D1)
               {D1n = D1 / 2, D2n = 0;
               Fn = F;
               advance(Fn, D1n);
               Ln = lower_bound(M, L, *Fn);
               Distance(M, Ln, D2n); }
          else
               {D1n = 0, D2n = D2 / 2;
               Ln = M;
               advance(Ln, D2n);
               Fn = upper_bound(F, M, *Ln);
               Distance(F, Fn, D1n); }
```

Figure 6.21: `algorithm` **part 21**

```
          BidIt Mn = Buffered_rotate(Fn, M, Ln,
               D1 - D1n, D2n, Xb);
          Buffered_merge(F, Fn, Mn, D1n, D2n, Xb);
          Buffered_merge(Mn, Ln, L,
               D1 - D1n, D2 - D2n, Xb); }}
template<class BidIt1, class BidIt2, class BidIt3> inline
     BidIt3 Merge_backward(BidIt1 F1, BidIt1 L1,
          BidIt2 F2, BidIt2 L2, BidIt3 X)
     {for (; ; )
          if (F1 == L1)
               return (copy_backward(F2, L2, X));
          else if (F2 == L2)
               return (copy_backward(F1, L1, X));
          else if (*--L2 < *--L1)
               *--X = *L1, ++L2;
          else
               *--X = *L2, ++L1; }
template<class BidIt, class Pd, class T> inline
     BidIt Buffered_rotate(BidIt F, BidIt M, BidIt L,
          Pd D1, Pd D2, Temp_iterator<T>& Xb)
     {if (D1 <= D2 && D1 <= Xb.Maxlen())
          {copy(F, M, Xb.Init());
          copy(M, L, F);
          return (copy_backward(Xb.First(), Xb.Last(), L)); }
     else if (D2 <= Xb.Maxlen())
          {copy(M, L, Xb.Init());
          copy_backward(F, M, L);
          return (copy(Xb.First(), Xb.Last(), F)); }
     else
          {rotate(F, M, L);
          advance(F, D2);
          return (F); }}

          // TEMPLATE FUNCTION inplace_merge WITH PRED
template<class BidIt, class Pr> inline
     void inplace_merge(BidIt F, BidIt M, BidIt L, Pr P)
     {if (F != L)
          Inplace_merge(F, M, L, P,
               Dist_type(F), Val_type(F)); }
template<class BidIt, class Pd, class T, class Pr> inline
     void Inplace_merge(BidIt F, BidIt M, BidIt L, Pr P,
          Pd *, T *)
     {Pd D1 = 0;
     Distance(F, M, D1);
     Pd D2 = 0;
     Distance(M, L, D2);
     Temp_iterator<T> Xb(D1 < D2 ? D1 : D2);
     Buffered_merge(F, M, L, D1, D2, Xb, P); }
template<class BidIt, class Pd, class T, class Pr> inline
     void Buffered_merge(BidIt F, BidIt M, BidIt L,
          Pd D1, Pd D2, Temp_iterator<T>& Xb, Pr P)
     {if (D1 == 0 || D2 == 0)
          ;
```

Figure 6.22: algorithm part 22

```
    else if (D1 + D2 == 2)
        {if (P(*M, *F))
            iter_swap(F, M); }
    else if (D1 <= D2 && D1 <= Xb.Maxlen())
        {copy(F, M, Xb.Init());
        merge(Xb.First(), Xb.Last(), M, L, F, P); }
    else if (D2 <= Xb.Maxlen())
        {copy(M, L, Xb.Init());
        Merge_backward(F, M, Xb.First(), Xb.Last(),
            L, P); }
    else
        {BidIt Fn, Ln;
        Pd D1n, D2n;
        if (D2 < D1)
            {D1n = D1 / 2, D2n = 0;
            Fn = F;
            advance(Fn, D1n);
            Ln = lower_bound(M, L, *Fn, P);
            Distance(M, Ln, D2n); }
        else
            {D1n = 0, D2n = D2 / 2;
            Ln = M;
            advance(Ln, D2n);
            Fn = upper_bound(F, M, *Ln, P);
            Distance(F, Fn, D1n); }
        BidIt Mn = Buffered_rotate(Fn, M, Ln,
            D1 - D1n, D2n, Xb);
        Buffered_merge(F, Fn, Mn, D1n, D2n, Xb, P);
        Buffered_merge(Mn, Ln, L,
            D1 - D1n, D2 - D2n, Xb, P); }}
template<class BidIt1, class BidIt2, class BidIt3, class Pr> inline
    BidIt3 Merge_backward(BidIt1 F1, BidIt1 L1,
        BidIt2 F2, BidIt2 L2, BidIt3 X, Pr P)
    {for (; ; )
        if (F1 == L1)
            return (copy_backward(F2, L2, X));
        else if (F2 == L2)
            return (copy_backward(F1, L1, X));
        else if (P(*--L2, *--L1))
            *--X = *L1, ++L2;
        else
            *--X = *L2, ++L1; }

        // TEMPLATE FUNCTION includes
template<class InIt1, class InIt2> inline
    bool includes(InIt1 F1, InIt1 L1, InIt2 F2, InIt2 L2)
    {for (; F1 != L1 && F2 != L2; )
        if (*F2 < *F1)
            return (false);
        else if (*F1 < *F2)
            ++F1;
        else
            ++F1, ++F2;
    return (F2 == L2); }
```

Figure 6.23: `algorithm` **part 23**

```
        // TEMPLATE FUNCTION includes WITH PRED
template<class InIt1, class InIt2, class Pr> inline
    bool includes(InIt1 F1, InIt1 L1, InIt2 F2, InIt2 L2, Pr P)
    {for (; F1 != L1 && F2 != L2; )
        if (P(*F2, *F1))
            return (false);
        else if (P(*F1, *F2))
            ++F1;
        else
            ++F1, ++F2;
    return (F2 == L2); }

        // TEMPLATE FUNCTION set_union
template<class InIt1, class InIt2, class OutIt> inline
    OutIt set_union(InIt1 F1, InIt1 L1,
        InIt2 F2, InIt2 L2, OutIt X)
    {for (; F1 != L1 && F2 != L2; )
        if (*F1 < *F2)
            *X++ = *F1, ++F1;
        else if (*F2 < *F1)
            *X++ = *F2, ++F2;
        else
            *X++ = *F1, ++F1, ++F2;
    X = copy(F1, L1, X);
    return (copy(F2, L2, X)); }

        // TEMPLATE FUNCTION set_union WITH PRED
template<class InIt1, class InIt2, class OutIt, class Pr> inline
    OutIt set_union(InIt1 F1, InIt1 L1,
        InIt2 F2, InIt2 L2, OutIt X, Pr P)
    {for (; F1 != L1 && F2 != L2; )
        if (P(*F1, *F2))
            *X++ = *F1, ++F1;
        else if (P(*F2, *F1))
            *X++ = *F2, ++F2;
        else
            *X++ = *F1, ++F1, ++F2;
    X = copy(F1, L1, X);
    return (copy(F2, L2, X)); }

        // TEMPLATE FUNCTION set_intersection
template<class InIt1, class InIt2, class OutIt> inline
    OutIt set_intersection(InIt1 F1, InIt1 L1,
        InIt2 F2, InIt2 L2, OutIt X)
    {for (; F1 != L1 && F2 != L2; )
        if (*F1 < *F2)
            ++F1;
        else if (*F2 < *F1)
            ++F2;
        else
            *X++ = *F1++, ++F2;
    return (X); }
```

Figure 6.24: algorithm part 24

```
        // TEMPLATE FUNCTION set_intersection WITH PRED
template<class InIt1, class InIt2, class OutIt, class Pr> inline
    OutIt set_intersection(InIt1 F1, InIt1 L1,
        InIt2 F2, InIt2 L2, OutIt X, Pr P)
    {for (; F1 != L1 && F2 != L2; )
        if (P(*F1, *F2))
            ++F1;
        else if (P(*F2, *F1))
            ++F2;
        else
            *X++ = *F1++, ++F2;
    return (X); }

        // TEMPLATE FUNCTION set_difference
template<class InIt1, class InIt2, class OutIt> inline
    OutIt set_difference(InIt1 F1, InIt1 L1,
        InIt2 F2, InIt2 L2, OutIt X)
    {for (; F1 != L1 && F2 != L2; )
        if (*F1 < *F2)
            *X++ = *F1, ++F1;
        else if (*F2 < *F1)
            ++F2;
        else
            ++F1, ++F2;
    return (copy(F1, L1, X)); }

        // TEMPLATE FUNCTION set_difference WITH PRED
template<class InIt1, class InIt2, class OutIt, class Pr> inline
    OutIt set_difference(InIt1 F1, InIt1 L1,
        InIt2 F2, InIt2 L2, OutIt X, Pr P)
    {for (; F1 != L1 && F2 != L2; )
        if (P(*F1, *F2))
            *X++ = *F1, ++F1;
        else if (P(*F2, *F1))
            ++F2;
        else
            ++F1, ++F2;
    return (copy(F1, L1, X)); }

        // TEMPLATE FUNCTION set_symmetric_difference
template<class InIt1, class InIt2, class OutIt> inline
    OutIt set_symmetric_difference(InIt1 F1, InIt1 L1,
        InIt2 F2, InIt2 L2, OutIt X)
    {for (; F1 != L1 && F2 != L2; )
        if (*F1 < *F2)
            *X++ = *F1, ++F1;
        else if (*F2 < *F1)
            *X++ = *F2, ++F2;
        else
            ++F1, ++F2;
    X = copy(F1, L1, X);
    return (copy(F2, L2, X)); }
```

Figure 6.25: `algorithm` part 25

```
        // TEMPLATE FUNCTION set_symmetric_difference WITH PRED
template<class InIt1, class InIt2, class OutIt, class Pr> inline
    OutIt set_symmetric_difference(InIt1 F1, InIt1 L1,
        InIt2 F2, InIt2 L2, OutIt X, Pr P)
    {for (; F1 != L1 && F2 != L2; )
        if (P(*F1, *F2))
            *X++ = *F1, ++F1;
        else if (P(*F2, *F1))
            *X++ = *F2, ++F2;
        else
            ++F1, ++F2;
    X = copy(F1, L1, X);
    return (copy(F2, L2, X)); }

        // TEMPLATE FUNCTION push_heap
template<class RanIt> inline
    void push_heap(RanIt F, RanIt L)
    {Push_heap_0(F, L, Dist_type(F), Val_type(F)); }
template<class RanIt, class Pd, class T> inline
    void Push_heap_0(RanIt F, RanIt L, Pd *, T *)
    {Push_heap(F, Pd(L - F - 1), Pd(0), T(*(L - 1))); }
template<class RanIt, class Pd, class T> inline
    void Push_heap(RanIt F, Pd H, Pd J, T V)
    {for (Pd I = (H - 1) / 2; J < H && *(F + I) < V;
        I = (H - 1) / 2)
        *(F + H) = *(F + I), H = I;
    *(F + H) = V; }

        // TEMPLATE FUNCTION push_heap WITH PRED
template<class RanIt, class Pr> inline
    void push_heap(RanIt F, RanIt L, Pr P)
    {Push_heap_0(F, L, P,
        Dist_type(F), Val_type(F)); }
template<class RanIt, class Pd, class T, class Pr> inline
    void Push_heap_0(RanIt F, RanIt L, Pr P, Pd *, T *)
    {Push_heap(F, Pd(L - F - 1), Pd(0),
        T(*(L - 1)), P); }
template<class RanIt, class Pd, class T, class Pr> inline
    void Push_heap(RanIt F, Pd H, Pd J, T V, Pr P)
    {for (Pd I = (H - 1) / 2; J < H && P(*(F + I), V);
        I = (H - 1) / 2)
        *(F + H) = *(F + I), H = I;
    *(F + H) = V; }

        // TEMPLATE FUNCTION pop_heap
template<class RanIt> inline
    void pop_heap(RanIt F, RanIt L)
    {Pop_heap_0(F, L, Val_type(F)); }
template<class RanIt, class T> inline
    void Pop_heap_0(RanIt F, RanIt L, T *)
    {Pop_heap(F, L - 1, L - 1, T(*(L - 1)),
        Dist_type(F)); }
template<class RanIt, class Pd, class T> inline
    void Pop_heap(RanIt F, RanIt L, RanIt X, T V, Pd *)
```

Figure 6.26: `algorithm` part 26

```
    {*X = *F;
    Adjust_heap(F, Pd(0), Pd(L - F), V); }
template<class RanIt, class Pd, class T> inline
    void Adjust_heap(RanIt F, Pd H, Pd N, T V)
    {Pd J = H;
    Pd K = 2 * H + 2;
    for (; K < N; K = 2 * K + 2)
        {if (*(F + K) < *(F + (K - 1)))
            --K;
        *(F + H) = *(F + K), H = K; }
    if (K == N)
        *(F + H) = *(F + (K - 1)), H = K - 1;
    Push_heap(F, H, J, V); }

        // TEMPLATE FUNCTION pop_heap WITH PRED
template<class RanIt, class Pr> inline
    void pop_heap(RanIt F, RanIt L, Pr P)
    {Pop_heap_0(F, L, P, Val_type(F)); }
template<class RanIt, class T, class Pr> inline
    void Pop_heap_0(RanIt F, RanIt L, Pr P, T *)
    {Pop_heap(F, L - 1, L - 1, T(*(L - 1)), P,
        Dist_type(F)); }
template<class RanIt, class Pd, class T, class Pr> inline
    void Pop_heap(RanIt F, RanIt L, RanIt X, T V, Pr P, Pd *)
    {*X = *F;
    Adjust_heap(F, Pd(0), Pd(L - F), V, P); }
template<class RanIt, class Pd, class T, class Pr> inline
    void Adjust_heap(RanIt F, Pd H, Pd N, T V, Pr P)
    {Pd J = H;
    Pd K = 2 * H + 2;
    for (; K < N; K = 2 * K + 2)
        {if (P(*(F + K), *(F + (K - 1))))
            --K;
        *(F + H) = *(F + K), H = K; }
    if (K == N)
        *(F + H) = *(F + (K - 1)), H = K - 1;
    Push_heap(F, H, J, V, P); }

        // TEMPLATE FUNCTION make_heap
template<class RanIt> inline
    void make_heap(RanIt F, RanIt L)
    {if (2 <= L - F)
        Make_heap(F, L, Dist_type(F), Val_type(F)); }
template<class RanIt, class Pd, class T> inline
    void Make_heap(RanIt F, RanIt L, Pd *, T *)
    {Pd N = L - F;
    for (Pd H = N / 2; 0 < H; )
        --H, Adjust_heap(F, H, N, T(*(F + H))); }

        // TEMPLATE FUNCTION make_heap WITH PRED
template<class RanIt, class Pr> inline
    void make_heap(RanIt F, RanIt L, Pr P)
    {if (2 <= L - F)
        Make_heap(F, L, P,
            Dist_type(F), Val_type(F)); }
```

Figure 6.27: algorithm part 27

```
template<class RanIt, class Pd, class T, class Pr> inline
      void Make_heap(RanIt F, RanIt L, Pr P, Pd *, T *)
      {Pd N = L - F;
      for (Pd H = N / 2; 0 < H; )
            --H, Adjust_heap(F, H, N, T(*(F + H)), P); }

            // TEMPLATE FUNCTION sort_heap
template<class RanIt> inline
      void sort_heap(RanIt F, RanIt L)
      {for (; 1 < L - F; --L)
            pop_heap(F, L); }

            // TEMPLATE FUNCTION sort_heap WITH PRED
template<class RanIt, class Pr> inline
      void sort_heap(RanIt F, RanIt L, Pr P)
      {for (; 1 < L - F; --L)
            pop_heap(F, L, P); }

            // TEMPLATE FUNCTION max_element
template<class FwdIt> inline
      FwdIt max_element(FwdIt F, FwdIt L)
      {FwdIt X = F;
      if (F != L)
            for (; ++F != L; )
                  if (*X < *F)
                        X = F;
      return (X); }

            // TEMPLATE FUNCTION max_element WITH PRED
template<class FwdIt, class Pr> inline
      FwdIt max_element(FwdIt F, FwdIt L, Pr P)
      {FwdIt X = F;
      if (F != L)
            for (; ++F != L; )
                  if (P(*X, *F))
                        X = F;
      return (X); }

            // TEMPLATE FUNCTION min_element
template<class FwdIt> inline
      FwdIt min_element(FwdIt F, FwdIt L)
      {FwdIt X = F;
      if (F != L)
            for (; ++F != L; )
                  if (*F < *X)
                        X = F;
      return (X); }

            // TEMPLATE FUNCTION min_element WITH PRED
template<class FwdIt, class Pr> inline
      FwdIt min_element(FwdIt F, FwdIt L, Pr P)
      {FwdIt X = F;
      if (F != L)
            for (; ++F != L; )
```

Figure 6.28: `algorithm` **part 28**

```
                if (P(*F, *X))
                    X = F;
    return (X); }

        // TEMPLATE FUNCTION next_permutation
template<class BidIt> inline
    bool next_permutation(BidIt F, BidIt L)
    {BidIt I = L;
    if (F == L || F == --I)
        return (false);
    for (; ; )
        {BidIt Ip = I;
        if (*--I < *Ip)
            {BidIt J = L;
            for (; !(*I < *--J); )
                ;
            iter_swap(I, J);
            reverse(Ip, L);
            return (true); }
        if (I == F)
            {reverse(F, L);
            return (false); }}}

        // TEMPLATE FUNCTION next_permutation WITH PRED
template<class BidIt, class Pr> inline
    bool next_permutation(BidIt F, BidIt L, Pr P)
    {BidIt I = L;
    if (F == L || F == --I)
        return (false);
    for (; ; )
        {BidIt Ip = I;
        if (P(*--I, *Ip))
            {BidIt J = L;
            for (; !P(*I, *--J); )
                ;
            iter_swap(I, J);
            reverse(Ip, L);
            return (true); }
        if (I == F)
            {reverse(F, L);
            return (false); }}}

        // TEMPLATE FUNCTION prev_permutation
template<class BidIt> inline
    bool prev_permutation(BidIt F, BidIt L)
    {BidIt I = L;
    if (F == L || F == --I)
        return (false);
    for (; ; )
        {BidIt Ip = I;
        if (!(*--I < *Ip))
            {BidIt J = L;
            for (; *I < *--J; )
                ;
            iter_swap(I, J);
```

Figure 6.29: `algorithm` part 29

```
                reverse(Ip, L);
                return (true); }
            if (I == F)
                {reverse(F, L);
                return (false); }}}

            // TEMPLATE FUNCTION prev_permutation WITH PRED
template<class BidIt, class Pr> inline
        bool prev_permutation(BidIt F, BidIt L, Pr P)
        {BidIt I = L;
        if (F == L || F == --I)
            return (false);
        for (; ; )
            {BidIt Ip = I;
            if (!P(*--I, *Ip))
                {BidIt J = L;
                for (; P(*I, *--J); )
                    ;
                iter_swap(I, J);
                reverse(Ip, L);
                return (true); }
            if (I == F)
                {reverse(F, L);
                return (false); }}}
} /* namespace std */
#endif /* ALGORITHM_ */
```

Thus, both constants represent approximate crossover points in choosing between complementary algorithms. They are not likely to need further tuning — they are presented here more for visibility than to ease of change.

count **count_if** The template functions **count** and **count_if** both have return types that can be expressed only if an implementation supports partial specialization. You can't even use the usual trick of invoking another template function to determine the problematic type. Some implementations may replace the type that cannot be named with **ptrdiff_t**. For all but the most exotic iterators, **difference_type** is a synonym for **ptrdiff_t** anyway.

search But just in case an iterator does indeed have an exotic difference type (and an implementation can't rely on the use of **iterator_traits**), template function **search** illustrates how to deal with it. It calls another template function **Search**. with two added arguments. Each of the added arguments uses the template function **Dist_type** to present a **difference_type** as a template function type. Thus, **Search** can declare counters appropriate for each of the pairs of iterators originally presented to **search**.

You've now seen the use of helper template functions to determine iterator categories with **Iter_cat**, such as template function **distance** in Chapter 3: **<iterator>**. You've seen the use of helper template functions to determine value types with **Val_type**, such as template function **uninitialized_copy** in Chapter 4: **<memory>**. And here you see how

`Dist_type` determines difference types for `search`. We will not call specific attention to this machinery again.

`unique_copy` Still worthy of brief remark, however, is template function `unique_copy`. It uses `Iter_cat` to select different algorithms for different iterator categories. In this case, the difference is relatively small, but notable. Input iterators do not support "bookmarks" earlier in a sequence. They thus require that the earlier element used for comparisons be stored in a temporary object, however large that may prove to be. Forward (and stronger) iterators need store only a temporary iterator object, which is more likely to be of a reasonable size.

As we've observed before, the overloads for bidirectional and random-access iterators are supposedly not necessary, but we still encounter C++ compilers that need them. Thus, they are included for robustness, as a matter of current practical necessity.

`reverse` Template function `reverse` illustrates a similar, small optimization. Random-access iterators support comparisons with `operator<`, which is slightly more efficient than the two-step test required for bidirectional iterators.

`rotate` Template function `rotate` is probably the most adaptive of all the algorithms in STL:

- For forward iterators, it performs `n` swaps to rotate `n` elements.
- For bidirectional iterators, it reverses two subsequences, then the entire sequence, to effect the rotation.
- For random-access iterators, it rotates a minimum number of subcycles within the sequence.

The last two versions are well worth careful study, particularly if you are not familiar with these particular algorithms.

`random_shuffle` Template function `random_shuffle` needs a good source of random numbers, naturally enough. The numbers must be (more or less) uniformly distributed over the range `[0, n)`, where `n` is the length of the sequence. Unfortunately, the *type* of `n` depends on the template parameter — it could in principle be a type whose objects maintain arbitrary precision.

This implementation doesn't try to solve such an open-ended problem. It accumulates random bits, as needed, in an `unsigned long` object by repeated calls to the Standard C library function `rand`, declared in `<stdlib.h>`. Since `rand` is not required to generate more than 15 random bits, it may be necessary to call it more than once. If you indeed try to shuffle the bytes on a 10 GB disk, this algorithm will fail. Moreover, common implementations of `rand` have known deficiencies that can affect demanding applications of random numbers. (The random-number generator supplied with the Hewlett-Packard version of STL is rather more ambitious, but it suffers the same problem with limited range.) Chances are, however, that `random_shuffle` is adequately random for typical applications.

stable_partition Template function **stable_partition** makes effective use of a temporary buffer, if one is available. The first overload of the template function **Stable_partition** requests a buffer possibly large enough to hold the entire sequence. (Template class **Temp_iterator** is described on page 105.) Whatever length buffer it gets, the second overload uses to advantage. If the sequence is larger than the buffer, the second function falls back on a classic divide-and-conquer strategy to reduce the problem to one of manageable size. In the absence of any temporary buffer at all, that means repeatedly halving intervals until each is of length one.

Template function **Buffered_rotate**, described below in conjunction with **inplace_merge**, also makes use of any temporary buffer. Its job here is to rearrange the adjacent, but out of order, subpartitions obtained by recursive calls to **Stable_partition**.

stable_partition is one of several template functions defined in the header **<algorithm>** that profits from the use of temporary storage when it is available. Note that all such algorithms run faster given a temporary buffer, but they always work, one way or another, even without such a buffer.

sort Template function **sort** makes use of a number of additional functions to do its job as quickly as possible. For any subsequence not longer than **SORT_MAX** elements, it relies on the template function **Insertion_sort** to perform the actual ordering. It, in turn, calls on **Insertion_sort_1** to perform an insertion sort, which makes up in simplicity (on a short enough sequence) what it lacks in sophistication. The template function **Unguarded_insert** gets its name from the trust it puts in its arguments — it assumes that it will terminate before it runs past the beginning of the (sub)sequence.

Template function **Sort** thus performs only a coarse sort. By divide and conquer, it ensures that a long sequence is sorted into chunks, each having at most **SORT_MAX** elements. The chunks are in proper order but the elements within each chunk are not. It ends by calling template function **Sort_end** to perform the final ordering. **Sort_end** can be naive yet still fast because each call it makes to **Unguarded_insert** will perform only a local rearrangement of elements.

Template function **Sort** also makes use of an interesting strategy developed by one of us (Dave Musser) called *intro sort*. It behaves much like a traditional *quick sort,* but with a small amount of added bookkeeping. Each recursive call to **Sort** includes an estimate, called **Ideal**, of how many elements need to be sorted in this subinterval. In the ideal case, each partitioning splits an interval into two subintervals of equal length. For that ideal case, **Sort** recurses exactly $log_2(N)$ times to sort a sequence with N elements. Quick sort is notoriously fast when sorting sequences with near-ideal partitioning, and notoriously slow when sorting sequences with pathological partitioning. Thus the need to keep an eye on how the quick sort is progressing.

Sort sticks with the quick sort approach, on each recursive call, until it is asked to sort a sequence of no more than **SORT_MAX** elements (which is not worth the bother) or it has exceeded its "ideal" quota of recursive calls. Strictly speaking, it allows up to four extra recursive calls, since **SORT_MAX** is 16. But in any event, when **Sort** eventually despairs of performing a quick sort in good time, it changes strategies. It sorts the subinterval by calling **make_heap** and **sort_heap**, also defined in the header **<algorithm>**. These two functions conspire to perform a *heap sort,* which tends to be slower than a quick sort but which has *much* better time complexity in the worst case. In fact, this combined strategy can guarantee a worst-case time complexity of *N*log(N).* The cost in extra code is amply repaid with better bounds on performance.

For the traditional quick sort, **Sort** calls **Unguarded_partition**. That template function first determines a pivot value that is assuredly within the range of values in the subsequence. It does so by sorting the first, middle, and last elements of the subsequence in place, then using the resulting middle element as the pivot value. Rearranging these three elements has the added benefit of dislodging annoying values from the favored positions at the beginning and end. This minimizes a number of potential pathologies, such as a sequence initially in reverse order, or an ordered sequence with a new smallest element added at the end. Once the pivot is determined, elements to the left of the pivot that belong to its right are swapped with elements similarly out of place to the right of the pivot. This process repeats until the subinterval is suitably partitioned.

stable_sort Template function **stable_sort** is similar to **sort**, but it has a slightly more difficult job. The second overload of template function **Stable_sort** performs a divide and conquer as needed, until it makes subsequences short enough to order by some other scheme. If the algorithm can acquire a temporary buffer of sufficient size, it uses that buffer in calls to **Buffered_merge_sort**. Otherwise, it relies on **Insertion_sort**, which fortunately performs a stable sort, to order short subsequences.

Template function **Buffered_merge_sort** does almost the exact opposite of **sort**. First it sorts subsequences of length **CHUNK_SIZE** within the sequence, by calling **Insertion_sort**, then it merges these chunks into ever larger ordered subsequences until the entire sequence is stably ordered. Each call to **Chunked_merge** merges chunks twice as big as the previous call. Merging occurs first to the temporary buffer, then back to the original sequence.

partial_sort Template function **partial_sort** calls **Partial_sort**, which begins by making a heap out of the first **n** elements of the sequence — the number of elements to eventually leave ordered. The function then repeatedly compares the top of the heap ***first**, which is the largest element in the heap, with each element later in the sequence. A call to **Pop_heap** (described later in this chapter) exchanges the smaller element with the top of the heap, then restores the heap discipline. Sorting the resultant heap yields the desired partial ordering of the sequence.

partial_ sort_copy Template function **partial_sort_copy** behaves much the same as **partial_sort**, but with a few significant differences. It calls the template function **Partial_sort_copy**, which copies to the destination sequence enough elements to fill that sequence, if possible, then makes the destination sequence into a heap. Any elements remaining in the source sequence are compared against the top of the heap ***F2**. A call to **Adjust_heap** (also described later in this chapter) replaces the top of the heap with the smaller element, then restores the heap discipline. Sorting the resultant heap once again yields the desired partial ordering of the sequence.

nth_element Template function **nth_element** performs the usual divide and conquer sort. We described earlier the use of **Unguarded_partition**. In this case, however, the algorithm ignores any partition that doesn't contain element number **n**. Once it creates a small enough partition containing that element, it calls **Insertion_sort** to finish the (partial) job.

inplace_ merge Template function **inplace_merge** incorporates a number of different strategies. The basic approach is divide and conquer, as carried out by **Buffered_merge**. That function uses a temporary buffer, for small enough subintervals, to perform a more conventional merge while copying. Note the special template function **Merge_backward** for the case where the destination subsequence begins with one of the two source subsequences.

When the temporary buffer is not large enough, **Buffered_merge** partitions the larger of the two sequences into two subsequences roughly equal in length. It then determines how much of the other subsequence needs to be swapped with one of these halves. The iterator **Fn** marks the partition point in the subsequence to the left of **M**, while **Ln** marks the partition point in the right subsequence. Template function **Buffered_rotate** performs the exchange by rotating the subsequence **[Fn, Fn)** about **M**. The inplace merge then reduces to two similar but smaller problems.

Buffered_rotate is used by both **stable_partition**, described above, and **inplace_merge**. If it can copy to a temporary buffer the smaller of the two subsequences it wants to exchange, it does so. Otherwise, it falls back on the more general template function **rotate** to do the job.

push_heap The heap template functions maintain a heap discipline in a sequence:

- Element zero is the top of the heap, and stores the largest element.
- The child elements at **2 * k + 1** and **2 * k + 2**, if present, are smaller than the parent element at **k**.

Template function **push_heap** assumes that the heap sequence has been extended with a new element at the end. It copies this value, creating a "hole" at the end of the heap. Template function **Push_heap** percolates the hole toward the top of the heap until it is high enough or until the new value is not greater than the parent of the hole. The parameter **j** determines how high is "high enough." It is always zero in this case.

pop_heap Template function `pop_heap` calls `Pop_heap` to swap the top of the heap with the element at the end, then restore the heap discipline. That function, in turn, tells `Adjust_heap` that a hole now exists at element zero, and that the value originally stored at the end of the sequence must now be properly inserted in the heap.

Template function `Adjust_heap` percolates a hole down the heap until it has no children. It then calls `Push_heap` to percolate the hole back up the heap to the proper place to store the specified value. `Adjust_heap` is called from template function `Partial_sort_copy` and from several places among the heap template functions.

make_heap Template function `make_heap` simply creates a hole at each element in the first half of the heap sequence, then calls `Adjust_heap` to establish the heap discipline among the children of that element.

prev_permutation Template function `prev_permutation` looks for the rightmost pair of adjacent elements that are in sort order. If no such pair exists, the function restores the initial permutation, by reversing the entire sequence, and returns true. Otherwise, it rearranges the remainder of the sequence, beginning with that pair, so as to generate the next permutation, and returns true. (Walk through all the permutations of three or four elements to see how the permutations are generated in lexicographically decreasing order.)

next_permutation Template function `next_permutation` behaves the same as `prev_permutation`, except that it inverts the predicates that test the order of pairs of elements.

Figure 6.30: talgorit.c

```
// test <algorithm>
#include <assert.h>
#include <ctype.h>
#include <iostream>
#include <string.h>
#include <algorithm>
#include <functional>
using namespace std;

     // FUNCTION OBJECTS
equal_to<char> equf;
less<char> lessf;

     // TEST SINGLE-ELEMENT TEMPLATE FUNCTIONS
void test_single(char *first, char *last)
     {assert(max('0', '2') == '2');
     assert(max('0', '2', lessf) == '2');
     assert(min('0', '2') == '0');
     assert(min('0', '2', lessf) == '0');
     strcpy(first, "abcdefg");
     swap(first[0], first[1]);
     assert(strcmp(first, "bacdefg") == 0);
     iter_swap(&first[0], &first[1]);
     assert(strcmp(first, "abcdefg") == 0); }
```

Figure 6.31: `talgorit.c` **part 2**

```
     // TEST SEARCHING TEMPLATE FUNCTIONS
void test_find(char *first, char *last)
     {strcpy(first, "abccefg");
     assert(*max_element(first, last) == 'g');
     assert(*max_element(first, last, lessf) == 'g');
     assert(*min_element(first, last) == 'a');
     assert(*min_element(first, last, lessf) == 'a');
     assert(equal(first, last, first));
     assert(equal(first, last, first, equf));
     assert(lexicographical_compare(first, last - 1,
          first, last));
     assert(lexicographical_compare(first, last - 1,
          first, last, lessf));
     assert(mismatch(first, last, first).second == last);
     assert(mismatch(first, last, first, equf).second == last);

     assert(find(first, last, 'c') == first + 2);
     assert(find_if(first, last, bind2nd(equf, 'c'))
          == first + 2);
     assert(adjacent_find(first, last) == first + 2);
     assert(adjacent_find(first, last, equf) == first + 2);
     assert(count(first, last, 'c') == 2);
     assert(count_if(first, last, bind2nd(equf, 'c')) == 2);
     assert(search(first, last, first + 2, last) == first + 2);
     assert(search(first, last, first + 2, last, equf)
          == first + 2);
     assert(search_n(first, last, 2, 'c') == first + 2);
     assert(search_n(first, last, 2, 'c', equf) == first + 2);
     assert(find_end(first, last, first + 2, last) == first + 2);
     assert(find_end(first, last, first + 2, last, equf)
          == first + 2);
     assert(find_first_of(first, last, first + 2, last)
          == first + 2);
     assert(find_first_of(first, last, first + 2, last, equf)
          == first + 2); }

     // TEST GENERATING TEMPLATE FUNCTIONS
size_t gen_count = 0;
void count_c(char ch)
     {if (ch == 'c')
          ++gen_count; }
char gen_x()
     {return ('x'); }

void test_generate(char *first, char *last, char *dest)
     {plus<char> plusf;
     strcpy(first, "abccefg");
     for_each(first, last, &count_c);
     assert(gen_count == 2);
     generate(first, first + 2, &gen_x);
     assert(strcmp(first, "xxccefg") == 0);
     generate_n(first + 3, last - first - 3, &gen_x);
     assert(strcmp(first, "xxcxxxx") == 0);
     assert(transform(first, last, dest,
```

Figure 6.32: `talgorit.c` part 3

```
        bind2nd(plusf, '\1')) == dest + 7);
    assert(strcmp(dest, "yydyyyy") == 0);
    assert(transform(first, last, "\1\1\1\2\1\1\1", dest,
        plusf) == dest + 7);
    assert(strcmp(dest, "yydzyyy") == 0); }

    // TEST COPYING TEMPLATE FUNCTIONS
void test_copy(char *first, char *last, char *dest)
    {strcpy(first, "abcdefg");
    copy(first, first + 3, first + 1);
    assert(strcmp(first, "aaaaefg") == 0);
    copy_backward(first + 2, first + 5, first + 3);
    assert(strcmp(first, "eaeaefg") == 0);
    fill(first, first + 3, 'x');
    assert(strcmp(first, "xxxaefg") == 0);
    fill_n(first, 2, 'y');
    assert(strcmp(first, "yyxaefg") == 0);

    swap_ranges(first, first + 3, first + 4);
    assert(strcmp(first, "efgayyx") == 0);
    replace(first, last, 'y', 'c');
    assert(strcmp(first, "efgaccx") == 0);
    replace_if(first, last, bind2nd(equf, 'c'), 'z');
    assert(strcmp(first, "efgazzx") == 0);
    replace_copy(first, last, dest, 'z', 'c');
    assert(strcmp(dest, "efgaccx") == 0);
    replace_copy_if(first, last, dest, bind2nd(equf, 'z'), 'y');
    assert(strcmp(dest, "efgayyx") == 0); }

    // TEST MUTATING TEMPLATE FUNCTIONS
void test_mutate(char *first, char *last, char *dest)
    {strcpy(first, "abcdefg"), strcpy(dest, first);
    remove(first, last, 'c');
    assert(strcmp(first, "abdefgg") == 0);
    remove_if(first, last, bind2nd(equf, 'd'));
    assert(strcmp(first, "abefggg") == 0);
    remove_copy(first, last, dest, 'e');
    assert(strcmp(dest, "abfgggg") == 0);
    remove_copy_if(first, last, dest, bind2nd(equf, 'e'));
    assert(strcmp(dest, "abfgggg") == 0);

    unique(dest, dest + 8);
    assert(strcmp(dest, "abfg") == 0);
    unique(dest, dest + 5, lessf);
    assert(strcmp(dest, "a") == 0);
    unique_copy(first, last + 1, dest);
    assert(strcmp(dest, "abefg") == 0);
    unique_copy(first, last + 1, dest, equf);
    assert(strcmp(dest, "abefg") == 0);

    reverse(first, last);
    assert(strcmp(first, "gggfeba") == 0);
    reverse_copy(first, last, dest);
    assert(strcmp(dest, "abefggg") == 0);
    rotate(first, first + 2, last);
```

Figure 6.33: `talgorit.c` **part 4**

```
     assert(strcmp(first, "gfebagg") == 0);
     rotate_copy(first, first + 2, last, dest);
     assert(strcmp(dest, "ebagggf") == 0);
     random_shuffle(first, last); }

     // TEST ORDERING TEMPLATE FUNCTIONS
bool cmp_caseless(char c1, char c2)
     {return (tolower(c1) < tolower(c2)); }

void test_order(char *first, char *last, char *dest)
     {greater<char> greatf;
     strcpy(first, "gfedcba");
     stable_partition(first, last, bind2nd(lessf, 'd'));
     assert(strcmp(first, "cbagfed") == 0);
     assert(partition(first, last, bind2nd(equf, 'd'))
          == first + 1);
     sort(first, last);
     assert(strcmp(first, "abcdefg") == 0);
     sort(first, last, greatf);
     assert(strcmp(first, "gfedcba") == 0);
     partial_sort(first, first + 2, last);
     assert(first[0] == 'a' && first[1] == 'b');
     partial_sort(first, first + 2, last, greatf);
     assert(first[0] == 'g' && first[1] == 'f');
     stable_sort(first, last);
     assert(strcmp(first, "abcdefg") == 0);
     rotate(first, first + 2, last);
     inplace_merge(first, last - 2, last);
     assert(strcmp(first, "abcdefg") == 0);
     rotate(first, first + 2, last);
     inplace_merge(first, last - 2, last, lessf);
     assert(strcmp(first, "abcdefg") == 0);

     strcpy(dest, "tuvwxyz");
     partial_sort_copy(first, last, dest, dest + 1);
     assert(strcmp(dest, "auvwxyz") == 0);
     partial_sort_copy(first, last, dest, dest + 1, greatf);
     assert(strcmp(dest, "guvwxyz") == 0);
     nth_element(first, first + 2, last, greatf);
     assert(first[2] == 'e');
     nth_element(first, first + 2, last);
     assert(first[2] == 'c');

     strcpy(first, "dCcbBba");
     stable_sort(first, last, &cmp_caseless);
     assert(strcmp(first, "abBbCcd") == 0);
     merge(first + 5, last, first, first + 5, dest);
     assert(strcmp(dest, "abBbCcd") == 0);
     merge(first + 5, last, first, first + 5, dest, lessf);
     assert(strcmp(dest, "abBbCcd") == 0); }

     // TEST SEARCHING TEMPLATE FUNCTIONS
void test_search(char *first, char *last)
     {char val = 'c';
     strcpy(first, "abcccfg");
```

Figure 6.34: `talgorit.c` **part 5**

```
     assert(lower_bound(first, last, val) == first + 2);
     assert(lower_bound(first, last, val, lessf) == first + 2);
     assert(upper_bound(first, last, val) == first + 5);
     assert(upper_bound(first, last, val, lessf) == first + 5);
     assert(equal_range(first, last, val).first == first + 2);
     assert(equal_range(first, last, val, lessf).second
          == first + 5);
     assert(binary_search(first, last, val));
     assert(binary_search(first, last, val, lessf));
     assert(includes(first, last, first + 3, last));
     assert(includes(first, last, first + 3, last, lessf)); }

     // TEST SET TEMPLATE FUNCTIONS
void test_set(char *first, char *last, char *dest)
     {strcpy(first, "abccefg"), strcpy(dest, first);
     set_union(first, first + 3, first + 3, last, dest);
     assert(strcmp(dest, "abcefgg") == 0);
     set_union(first, first + 3, first + 3, last, dest, lessf);
     assert(strcmp(dest, "abcefgg") == 0);
     set_intersection(first, first + 3, first + 3, last, dest);
     assert(strcmp(dest, "cbcefgg") == 0);
     set_intersection(first, first + 3, first + 3, last,
          dest, lessf);
     assert(strcmp(dest, "cbcefgg") == 0);
     set_difference(first, first + 3, first + 3, last, dest);
     assert(strcmp(dest, "abcefgg") == 0);
     set_difference(first, first + 3, first + 3, last,
          dest, lessf);
     assert(strcmp(dest, "abcefgg") == 0);
     set_symmetric_difference(first, first + 3, first + 3, last,
          dest);
     assert(strcmp(dest, "abefggg") == 0);
     set_symmetric_difference(first, first + 3, first + 3, last,
          dest, lessf);
     assert(strcmp(dest, "abefggg") == 0); }

     // TEST HEAP TEMPLATE FUNCTIONS
void test_heap(char *first, char *last)
     {strcpy(first, "abccefg");
     make_heap(first, last);
     assert(first[0] == 'g');
     make_heap(first, last, lessf);
     assert(first[0] == 'g');
     pop_heap(first, last);
     assert(last[-1] == 'g' && first[0] == 'f');
     pop_heap(first, last - 1, lessf);
     assert(last[-2] == 'f' && first[0] == 'e');
     push_heap(first, last - 1);
     assert(first[0] == 'f');
     push_heap(first, last, lessf);
     assert(first[0] == 'g');
     sort_heap(first, last);
     assert(strcmp(first, "abccefg") == 0);
     make_heap(first, last, lessf);
     sort_heap(first, last, lessf);
```

Figure 6.35: `talgorit.c` part 6

```
        assert(strcmp(first, "abccefg") == 0); }

        // TEST PERMUTING TEMPLATE FUNCTIONS
void test_permute(char *first, char *last)
        {strcpy(first, "abcdefg");
        next_permutation(first, last);
        assert(strcmp(first, "abcdegf") == 0);
        next_permutation(first, last, lessf);
        assert(strcmp(first, "abcdfeg") == 0);
        prev_permutation(first, last);
        assert(strcmp(first, "abcdegf") == 0);
        prev_permutation(first, last, lessf);
        assert(strcmp(first, "abcdefg") == 0); }

        // TEST <algorithm>
int main()
        {char buf[] = "abccefg";
        char dest[] = "1234567";
        char *first = buf, *last = buf + 7;
        test_single(first, last);
        test_find(first, last);
        test_generate(first, last, dest);
        test_copy(first, last, dest);
        test_mutate(first, last, dest);
        test_order(first, last, dest);
        test_search(first, last);
        test_set(first, last, dest);
        test_heap(first, last);
        test_permute(first, last);

        cout << "SUCCESS testing <algorithm>" << endl;
        return (0); }
```
□

Testing `<algorithm>`

`talgorit.c` Figures 6.30 through 6.35 show the file `talgorit.c`. It makes only a cursory test of each of the template functions defined in the header `<algorithm>`, testing groups of related functions, as usual. The tests make extensive use of function objects declared in the header `<functional>`. (See Chapter 8: `<functional>`.) For example, the specialization `equal_to<char>` behaves much the same as `operator==(char, char)`. A more elaborate usage is `bind2nd(equf, 'c')`, which returns a function object `f` such that `f(ch)` is equivalent to `ch == 'c'` for the `char` object `ch`.

If all goes well, the program prints:

```
SUCCESS testing <algorithm>
```

and takes a normal exit.

Exercises

Exercise 6.1 An early version of template function `adjacent_find` supposedly called for input iterators. Why was the specification changed to forward iterators?

Exercise 6.2 The template function object `less`, defined in the header `<functional>`, defines `less(x, y)` as `x < y`. Describe the relative merits of the existing definition of template function `max` with the functional equivalent:

```
template<class T> inline
    const T& max(const T& x, const T& y)
    {return (max(x, y, less)); }
```

Exercise 6.3 The template function `count` has a companion template function called `count_if` that takes a predicate. Why is the name `count` not simply overloaded? List all the pairs of template functions that follow this pattern.

Exercise 6.4 Some forms of floating-point arithmetic have at least one representation that is "not a number" (NaN). If `x` is a NaN and `y` is any floating-point value, including another NaN, then all comparisons such as `x < y`, `x != y`, `y >= x`, etc. are false. Show the effect of these rules on tests for equivalent ordering.

Exercise 6.5 Under what circumstances would you want to use the template function `nth_element` instead of `sort`? When would you do the reverse?

Exercise 6.6 What is the behavior of template functions `next_permutation` and `prev_permutation` given a sequence where two or more elements have equivalent ordering?

Exercise 6.7 **[Harder]** Alter the template functions `next_permutation` and `prev_permutation` so that they cycle through all distinguishable permutations, in the required order, even when two or more elements have equivalent ordering.

Exercise 6.8 **[Very hard]** Alter template function `sort` so that it works properly with forward iterators instead of random-access iterators.

Chapter 7: <numeric>

Background

The header <numeric> is small. It contains a handful of template functions that perform simple arithmetic operations on the elements of a sequence. It could arguably have been subsumed as part of the header <algorithm>, described in the previous chapter. Indeed, the original version of STL mostly lumped all such algorithms in one header.

Note that these algorithms need not be confined to operations on the arithmetic types. Given suitable overloads for the operators used by the template functions, you can perform very general operations, in the guise of simple arithmetic. You can, for example, use template function **accumulate** to concatenate **string** objects. By defining your own classes, and/or function objects, you can stretch the definition of arithmetic to the limit.

Functional Description

```
namespace std {
template<class InIt, class T>
    T accumulate(InIt first, InIt last, T val);
template<class InIt, class T, class Pred>
    T accumulate(InIt first, InIt last, T val, Pred pr);
template<class InIt1, class InIt2, class T>
    T inner_product(InIt1 first1, InIt1 last1,
        Init2 first2, T val);
template<class InIt1, class InIt2, class T,
    class Pred1, class Pred2>
    T inner_product(InIt1 first1, InIt1 last1,
        Init2 first2, T val, Pred1 pr1, Pred2 pr2);
template<class InIt, class OutIt>
    OutIt partial_sum(InIt first, InIt last,
        OutIt result);
template<class InIt, class OutIt, class Pred>
    OutIt partial_sum(InIt first, InIt last,
        OutIt result, Pred pr);
template<class InIt, class OutIt>
    OutIt adjacent_difference(InIt first, InIt last,
        OutIt result);
template<class InIt, class OutIt, class Pred>
    OutIt adjacent_difference(InIt first, InIt last,
        OutIt result, Pred pr);
    };
```

Include the STL standard header `<numeric>` to define several template functions useful for computing numeric values. The descriptions of these templates employ a number of conventions common to all algorithms.

▫ **accumulate**

```
template<class InIt, class T>
    T accumulate(InIt first, InIt last, T val);
template<class InIt, class T, class Pred>
    T accumulate(InIt first, InIt last, T val, Pred pr);
```

The first template function repeatedly replaces `val` with `val + *I`, for each value of the `InIt` iterator `I` in the interval `[first, last)`. It then returns `val`.

The second template function repeatedly replaces `val` with `pr(val, *I)`, for each value of the `InIt` iterator `I` in the interval `[first, last)`. It then returns `val`.

▫ **adjacent_difference**

```
template<class InIt, class OutIt>
    OutIt adjacent_difference(InIt first, InIt last,
        OutIt result);
template<class InIt, class OutIt, class Pred>
    OutIt adjacent_difference(InIt first, InIt last,
        OutIt result, Pred pr);
```

The first template function stores successive values beginning at `result`, for each value of the `InIt` iterator `I` in the interval `[first, last)`. The first value `val` stored (if any) is `*I`. Each subsequent value stored is `*I - val`, and `val` is replaced by `*I`. The function returns `result` incremented `last - first` times.

The second template function stores successive values beginning at `result`, for each value of the `InIt` iterator `I` in the interval `[first, last)`. The first value `val` stored (if any) is `*I`. Each subsequent value stored is `pr(*I, val)`, and `val` is replaced by `*I`. The function returns `result` incremented `last - first` times.

▫ **inner_product**

```
template<class InIt1, class InIt2, class T>
    T inner_product(InIt1 first1, InIt1 last1,
        Init2 first2, T val);
template<class InIt1, class InIt2, class T,
    class Pred1, class Pred2>
    T inner_product(InIt1 first1, InIt1 last1,
        Init2 first2, T val, Pred1 pr1, Pred2 pr2);
```

The first template function repeatedly replaces `val` with `val + (*I1 * *I2)`, for each value of the `InIt1` iterator `I1` in the interval `[first1, last2)`. In each case, the `InIt2` iterator `I2` equals `first2 + (I1 - first1)`. The function returns `val`.

The second template function repeatedly replaces `val` with `pr1(val, pr2(*I1, *I2))`, for each value of the `InIt1` iterator `I1` in the interval [first1, last2). In each case, the InIt2 iterator I2 equals first2 + (I1 - first1). The function returns val.

▫ partial_sum

```
template<class InIt, class OutIt>
    OutIt partial_sum(InIt first, InIt last,
        OutIt result);
template<class InIt, class OutIt, class Pred>
    OutIt partial_sum(InIt first, InIt last,
        OutIt result, Pred pr);
```

The first template function stores successive values beginning at result, for each value of the InIt iterator I in the interval [first, last). The first value val stored (if any) is *I. Each subsequent value val stored is val + *I. The function returns result incremented last - first times.

The second template function stores successive values beginning at result, for each value of the InIt iterator I in the interval [first, last). The first value val stored (if any) is *I. Each subsequent value val stored is pr(val, *I). The function returns result incremented last - first times.

Using <numeric>

Include the header <numeric> to make use of any of the template functions it defines. The summary that follows makes only the briefest mention of each algorithm, to supply an overview of what's available.

accumulate
- To sum all the elements of a sequence, using operator+ or a specified binary operator, call accumulate.

inner_product
- To sum the products of corresponding elements of two sequences, using operator+ and operator* or two specified binary operators, call inner_product.

partial_sum
- To generate a sequence of sums, each adding one more element from a sequence, using operator+ or a specified binary operator, call partial_sum.

adjacent_difference
- To generate a sequence of differences between adjacent pairs of elements from a sequence, using operator- or a specified binary operator, call adjacent_difference.

Implementing <numeric>

numeric

Figures 7.1 and 7.2 show the file numeric. The template functions are all simple, with no surprises.

Testing <numeric>

tnumeric.c

Figure 7.3 shows the file tnumeric.c. It too is fairly simple, since the header is rather small. The only unusual practice is the use of the function object addf in place of the conventional operator- in the second version

Figure 7.1: `numeric` **part 1**

```
// numeric standard header
#ifndef NUMERIC_
#define NUMERIC_
#include <iterator>
namespace std {
          // TEMPLATE FUNCTION accumulate
template<class InIt, class T> inline
     T accumulate(InIt F, InIt L, T V)
     {for (; F != L; ++F)
          V = V + *F;
     return (V); }
          // TEMPLATE FUNCTION accumulate WITH BINOP
template<class InIt, class T, class Bop> inline
     T accumulate(InIt F, InIt L, T V, Bop B)
     {for (; F != L; ++F)
          V = B(V, *F);
     return (V); }
          // TEMPLATE FUNCTION inner_product
template<class InIt1, class InIt2, class T> inline
     T inner_product(InIt1 F, InIt1 L, InIt2 X, T V)
     {for (; F != L; ++F, ++X)
          V = V + *F * *X;
     return (V); }
          // TEMPLATE FUNCTION inner_product WITH BINOPS
template<class InIt1, class InIt2, class T,
     class Bop1, class Bop2> inline
     T inner_product(InIt1 F, InIt1 L, InIt2 X, T V,
          Bop1 B1, Bop2 B2)
     {for (; F != L; ++F, ++X)
          V = B1(V, B2(*F, *X));
     return (V); }
          // TEMPLATE FUNCTION partial_sum
template<class InIt, class OutIt> inline
     OutIt partial_sum(InIt F, InIt L, OutIt X)
     {return (F == L ? X
          : Partial_sum(F, L, X, Val_type(F))); }
template<class InIt, class OutIt, class T> inline
     OutIt Partial_sum(InIt F, InIt L, OutIt X, T *)
     {T V = *F;
     for (*X = V; ++F != L; *++X = V)
          V = V + *F;
     return (++X); }
          // TEMPLATE FUNCTION partial_sum WITH BINOP
template<class InIt, class OutIt, class Bop> inline
     OutIt partial_sum(InIt F, InIt L, OutIt X, Bop B)
     {return (F == L ? X
          : Partial_sum(F, L, X, B, Val_type(F))); }
template<class InIt, class OutIt, class Bop, class T> inline
     OutIt Partial_sum(InIt F, InIt L, OutIt X, Bop B, T *)
     {T V = *F;
     for (*X = V; ++F != L; *++X = V)
          V = B(V, *F);
     return (++X); }
          // TEMPLATE FUNCTION adjacent_difference
template<class InIt, class OutIt> inline
```

Figure 7.2: numeric part 2

```
     OutIt adjacent_difference(InIt F, InIt L, OutIt X)
     {return (F == L ? X
          : Adjacent_difference(F, L, X, Val_type(F))); }
template<class InIt, class OutIt, class T> inline
     OutIt Adjacent_difference(InIt F, InIt L, OutIt X, T *)
     {T V = *F;
     for (*X = V; ++F != L; )
          {T Tmp = *F;
          *++X = Tmp - V;
          V = Tmp; }
     return (++X); }
          // TEMPLATE FUNCTION adjacent_difference WITH BINOP
template<class InIt, class OutIt, class Bop> inline
     OutIt adjacent_difference(InIt F, InIt L, OutIt X, Bop B)
     {return (F == L ? X
          : Adjacent_difference(F, L, X, B, Val_type(F))); }
template<class InIt, class OutIt, class Bop, class T> inline
     OutIt Adjacent_difference(InIt F, InIt L, OutIt X,
          Bop B, T *)
     {T V = *F;
     for (*X = V; ++F != L; )
          {T Tmp = *F;
          *++X = B(Tmp, V);
          V = Tmp; }
     return (++X); }
} /* namespace std */
#endif /* NUMERIC_ */
```
□

of **adjacent_difference**. We chose this form to illustrate that a template function need not perform the operation suggested by its name, given a function-object argument. (It also produces a more interesting result.)

If all goes well, the program prints:

```
SUCCESS testing <numeric>
```

and takes a normal exit.

Exercises

Exercise 7.1 Rewrite both versions of template function **adjacent_difference** to eliminate the temporary object **tmp**. Can you also eliminate the temporary object **val**? If not, why not?

Exercise 7.2 Show how to use template function **accumulate** to concatenate a sequence of **string** objects.

Exercise 7.3 Show how to use template function **accumulate** to test whether a sequence consists solely of positive elements that never decrease in value.

Exercise 7.4 Write a template function that generates the next row of Pascal's triangle from a given row. What template function defined in **<numeric>** can you use to advantage?

Figure 7.3: `tnumeric.c`

```
// test <numeric>
#include <assert.h>
#include <iostream>
#include <string.h>
#include <functional>
#include <numeric>
using namespace std;

     // FUNCTION OBJECTS
multiplies<char> multipliesf;
plus<char> plusf;

     // TEST <numeric>
int main()
     {char buf[] = "\1\2\3\4\5\6";
     char dest[] = "123456";
     char *first = buf, *last = buf + 6;
     char val = 0;
     assert(accumulate(first, last, val) == 21);
     assert(accumulate(first, last, val, plusf) == 21);
     assert(inner_product(first, last, first, val) == 91);
     assert(inner_product(first, last, first, val,
          plusf, multipliesf) == 91);
     partial_sum(first, last, dest);
     assert(strcmp(dest, "\1\3\6\12\17\25") == 0);
     adjacent_difference(first, last, dest);
     assert(strcmp(dest, "\1\1\1\1\1\1") == 0);
     partial_sum(first, last, dest, plusf);
     assert(strcmp(dest, "\1\3\6\12\17\25") == 0);
     adjacent_difference(first, last, dest, plusf);
     assert(strcmp(dest, "\1\3\5\7\11\13") == 0);

     cout << "SUCCESS testing <numeric>" << endl;
     return (0); }
```

Exercise 7.5 [**Harder**] Specify a template function that multiplies two matrices, each stored as a sequence of rows, and stores the result in a third sequence. What category of iterators must the template function require?

Exercise 7.6 [**Very hard**] Implement the template function from the previous exercise.

Chapter 8: <functional>

Background

Function objects greatly enhance the power of algorithms in the Standard Template Library. Each one encapsulates a critical predicate or other calculation, keeping it separate from the more pedestrian bookkeeping of the template function that implements an algorithm. You can, of course, write your own function objects. Sometimes you can use a pointer to an existing function as a function object. But in many cases, you just need a function object that computes a common, simple expression.

That's where the header `<functional>` comes in. It defines a number of template classes suitable for declaring function objects. We have already made use of some of these, in the testing of the algorithm template functions described in earlier chapters. (See Chapter 6: `<algorithm>` and Chapter 7: `<numeric>`.)

unary_function The simplest of these template classes produce function objects designed to be called with a single argument. Thus, they behave like unary functions. These particular classes are based on the template class `unary_function`:

```
template<class A, class R>
    struct unary_function {
    typedef A argument_type;
    typedef R result_type;
    };
```

The idea is that any unary function object defined in the header `<functional>` reveals its argument type as the member type `argument_type`, inherited from the base `unary_function`. It similarly reveals its return type as the member type `result_type`.

negate An object `X` of the template class `negate<T>`, for example, ensures that the call `X(a)` returns `-a`, where `a` has type `T`. The template class is defined simply as:

```
template<class T>
    struct negate : unary_function<T, T> {
    T operator()(const T& x) const
        {return (-x); }
    };
```

Note that both the argument and return types are the same, as is often the case.

binary_function Next simplest are the template classes that produce function objects designed to be called with two arguments of the same type. Thus, they behave like binary functions. These particular classes are based on the template class `binary_function`:

```
template<class A1, class A2, class R>
    struct binary_function {
    typedef A1 first_argument_type;
    typedef A2 second_argument_type;
    typedef R result_type;
    };
```

As before, the idea is that any binary function object defined in the header `<functional>` reveals its first argument type as the member type `first_argument_type`, inherited from the base `binary_function`. It similarly reveals its second argument type as the member type `second_argument_type` and its return type as the member type `result_type`.

plus An object `X` of the template class `plus<T>`, for example, ensures that the call `X(a, b)` returns `a + b`, where `a` and `b` have type `T`. The template class is defined simply as:

```
template<class T>
    struct plus : binary_function<T, T, T> {
    T operator()(const T& x, const T& y) const
        {return (x + y); }
    };
```

We summarize all of these simple unary and binary function objects later in this chapter. (See Using `<functional>`, beginning on page 226.)

compound function objects Several template classes defined in the header `<functional>` describe function objects that store other function objects. Thus, we call them *compound function objects.* Calling the compound function object results in a call to the stored object.

binder1st bind1st A particularly interesting example is the template class `binder1st`, which stores both a binary function object `f` and the first argument `a` to supply on each call to that object. The resulting unary function object `X` ensures that the call `X(b)` returns `f(a, b)`. You might use such a creature with template function `transform`, defined in `<algorithm>`, to add a constant term to each element of a sequence. As a convenience, template function `bind1st` will generate an object of class `binder1st<T>` for you, as with the call `bind1st(plus<double>(), 3.0)`. Calling the returned object with a `double` argument returns that argument incremented by 3.

pointer function objects Finally, the header `<functional>` defines several template classes that store pointers or references to functions. We call them *pointer function objects.* Calling such an object results in a call using the stored pointer or reference. Unfortunately, the set of required template classes is open ended. You need different template class for pointers versus references, for global versus member functions versus const member functions, for a function with no arguments versus one, two, and so on. All that STL can do is supply the simpler cases, which are more likely to be used in practice. If you need a version that is not supplied, model it after a similar one presented here.

Functional Description

```
namespace std {
template<class Arg, class Result>
    struct unary_function;
template<class Arg1, class Arg2, class Result>
    struct binary_function;
template<class T>
    struct plus;
template<class T>
    struct minus;
template<class T>
    struct multiplies;
template<class T>
    struct divides;
template<class T>
    struct modulus;
template<class T>
    struct negate;
template<class T>
    struct equal_to;
template<class T>
    struct not_equal_to;
template<class T>
    struct greater;
template<class T>
    struct less;
template<class T>
    struct greater_equal;
template<class T>
    struct less_equal;
template<class T>
    struct logical_and;
template<class T>
    struct logical_or;
template<class T>
    struct logical_not;
template<class Pred>
    struct unary_negate;
template<class Pred>
    struct binary_negate;
template<class Pred>
    class binder1st;
template<class Pred>
    class binder2nd;
template<class Arg, class Result>
    class pointer_to_unary_function;
template<class Arg1, class Arg2, class Result>
    class pointer_to_binary_function;
template<class R, class T>
    struct mem_fun_t;
template<class R, class T, class A>
    struct mem_fun1_t;
template<class R, class T>
    struct const_mem_fun_t;
template<class R, class T, class A>
    struct const_mem_fun1_t;
template<class R, class T>
    struct mem_fun_ref_t;
template<class R, class T, class A>
    struct mem_fun1_ref_t;
```

```
template<class R, class T>
    struct const_mem_fun_ref_t;
template<class R, class T, class A>
    struct const_mem_fun1_ref_t;

        // TEMPLATE FUNCTIONS
template<class Pred>
    unary_negate<Pred> not1(const Pred& pr);
template<class Pred>
    binary_negate<Pred> not2(const Pred& pr);
template<class Pred, class T>
    binder1st<Pred> bind1st(const Pred& pr, const T& x);
template<class Pred, class T>
    binder2nd<Pred> bind2nd(const Pred& pr, const T& x);
template<class Arg, class Result>
    pointer_to_unary_function<Arg, Result>
        ptr_fun(Result (*)(Arg));
template<class Arg1, class Arg2, class Result>
    pointer_to_binary_function<Arg1, Arg2, Result>
        ptr_fun(Result (*)(Arg1, Arg2));
template<class R, class T>
    mem_fun_t<R, T> mem_fun(R (T::*pm)());
template<class R, class T, class A>
    mem_fun1_t<R, T, A> mem_fun(R (T::*pm)(A arg));
template<class R, class T>
    const_mem_fun_t<R, T> mem_fun(R (T::*pm)() const);
template<class R, class T, class A>
    const_mem_fun1_t<R, T, A> mem_fun(R (T::*pm)(A arg)
const);
template<class R, class T>
    mem_fun_ref_t<R, T> mem_fun_ref(R (T::*pm)());
template<class R, class T, class A>
    mem_fun1_ref_t<R, T, A>
        mem_fun_ref(R (T::*pm)(A arg));
template<class R, class T>
    const_mem_fun_ref_t<R, T> mem_fun_ref(R (T::*pm)()
const);
template<class R, class T, class A>
    const_mem_fun1_ref_t<R, T, A>
        mem_fun_ref(R (T::*pm)(A arg) const);
    };
```

Include the STL standard header `<functional>` to define several templates that help construct *function objects,* objects of a type that defines `operator()`. A function object can thus be a function pointer, but in the more general case the object can store additional information that can be used during a function call.

▫ **binary_function**

```
template<class Arg1, class Arg2, class Result>
    struct binary_function {
    typedef Arg1 first_argument_type;
    typedef Arg2 second_argument_type;
    typedef Result result_type;
    };
```

The template class can serve as a convenient base for classes that define a member function of the form:

```
result_type operator()(const first_argument_type&,
    const second_argument_type&) const
```

Hence, all such *binary functions* can refer to their first argument type as `first_argument_type`, their second argument type as `second_argument_type`, and their return type as `result_type`.

▫ **binary_negate**

```
template<class Pred>
    class binary_negate
        : public binary_function<
            typename Pred::first_argument_type,
            typename Pred::second_argument_type, bool> {
public:
    explicit binary_negate(const Pred& pr);
    bool operator()(
        const typename Pred::first_argument_type& x,
        const typename Pred::second_argument_type& y) const;
    };
```

The template class stores a copy of `pr`, which must be a binary function object. It defines its member function `operator()` as returning `!pr(x, y)`.

▫ **bind1st**

```
template<class Pred, class T>
    binder1st<Pred> bind1st(const Pred& pr, const T& x);
```

The function returns `binder1st<Pred>(pr, typename Pred::first_argument_type(x))`.

▫ **bind2nd**

```
template<class Pred, class T>
    binder2nd<Pred> bind2nd(const Pred& pr, const T& y);
```

The function returns `binder2nd<Pred>(pr, typename Pred::second_argument_type(y))`.

▫ **binder1st**

```
template<class Pred>
    class binder1st
        : public unary_function<
            typename Pred::second_argument_type,
            typename Pred::result_type> {
public:
    typedef typename Pred::second_argument_type
argument_type;
    typedef typename Pred::result_type result_type;
    binder1st(const Pred& pr,
        const typename Pred::first_argument_type& x);
    result_type operator()(const argument_type& y) const;
protected:
    Pred op;
    typename Pred::first_argument_type value;
    };
```

The template class stores a copy of `pr`, which must be a binary function object, in `op`, and a copy of `x` in `value`. It defines its member function `operator()` as returning `op(value, y)`.

- **binder2nd**

```
template<class Pred>
    class binder2nd
        : public unary_function<
            typename Pred::first_argument_type,
            typename Pred::result_type> {
public:
    typedef typename Pred::first_argument_type
argument_type;
    typedef typename Pred::result_type result_type;
    binder2nd(const Pred& pr,
        const typename Pred::second_argument_type& y);
    result_type operator()(const argument_type& x) const;
protected:
    Pred op;
    typename Pred::second_argument_type value;
    };
```

The template class stores a copy of **pr**, which must be a binary function object, in **op**, and a copy of **y** in **value**. It defines its member function **operator()** as returning **op(x, value)**.

- **const_mem_fun_t**

```
template<class R, class T>
    struct const_mem_fun_t
        : public unary_function<T *, R> {
    explicit const_mem_fun_t(R (T::*pm)() const);
    R operator()(const T *p) const;
    };
```

The template class stores a copy of **pm**, which must be a pointer to a member function of class **T**, in a private member object. It defines its member function **operator()** as returning **(p->*pm)() const**.

- **const_mem_fun_ref_t**

```
template<class R, class T>
    struct const_mem_fun_ref_t
        : public unary_function<T, R> {
    explicit const_mem_fun_t(R (T::*pm)() const);
    R operator()(const T& x) const;
    };
```

The template class stores a copy of **pm**, which must be a pointer to a member function of class **T**, in a private member object. It defines its member function **operator()** as returning **(x.*pm)() const**.

- **const_mem_fun1_t**

```
template<class R, class T, class A>
    struct const_mem_fun1_t
        : public binary_function<T *, A, R> {
    explicit const_mem_fun1_t(R (T::*pm)(A) const);
    R operator()(const T *p, A arg) const;
    };
```

The template class stores a copy of **pm**, which must be a pointer to a member function of class **T**, in a private member object. It defines its member function **operator()** as returning **(p->*pm)(arg) const**.

- `const_mem_fun1_ref_t`

```
template<class R, class T, class A>
    struct const_mem_fun1_ref_t
        : public binary_function<T, A, R> {
    explicit const_mem_fun1_ref_t(R (T::*pm)(A) const);
    R operator()(const T& x, A arg) const;
    };
```

The template class stores a copy of `pm`, which must be a pointer to a member function of class `T`, in a private member object. It defines its member function `operator()` as returning `(x.*pm)(arg) const`.

- `divides`

```
template<class T>
    struct divides : public binary_function<T, T, T> {
    T operator()(const T& x, const T& y) const;
    };
```

The template class defines its member function as returning `x / y`.

- `equal_to`

```
template<class T>
    struct equal_to
        : public binary_function<T, T, bool> {
    bool operator()(const T& x, const T& y) const;
    };
```

The template class defines its member function as returning `x == y`.

- `greater`

```
template<class T>
    struct greater : public binary_function<T, T, bool> {
    bool operator()(const T& x, const T& y) const;
    };
```

The template class defines its member function as returning `x > y`. The member function defines a total ordering if `T` is an object pointer type.

- `greater_equal`

```
template<class T>
    struct greater_equal
        : public binary_function<T, T, bool> {
    bool operator()(const T& x, const T& y) const;
    };
```

The template class defines its member function as returning `x >= y`. The member function defines a total ordering if `T` is an object pointer type.

- `less`

```
template<class T>
    struct less : public binary_function<T, T, bool> {
    bool operator()(const T& x, const T& y) const;
    };
```

The template class defines its member function as returning `x < y`. The member function defines a total ordering if `T` is an object pointer type.

- **less_equal**

```
template<class T>
    struct less_equal
        : public binary_function<T, T, bool> {
    bool operator()(const T& x, const T& y) const;
    };
```

The template class defines its member function as returning `x <= y`. The member function defines a total ordering if `T` is an object pointer type.

- **logical_and**

```
template<class T>
    struct logical_and
        : public binary_function<T, T, bool> {
    bool operator()(const T& x, const T& y) const;
    };
```

The template class defines its member function as returning `x && y`.

- **logical_not**

```
template<class T>
    struct logical_not : public unary_function<T, bool> {
    bool operator()(const T& x) const;
    };
```

The template class defines its member function as returning `!x`.

- **logical_or**

```
template<class T>
    struct logical_or
        : public binary_function<T, T, bool> {
    bool operator()(const T& x, const T& y) const;
    };
```

The template class defines its member function as returning `x || y`.

- **mem_fun**

```
template<class R, class T>
    mem_fun_t<R, T> mem_fun(R (T::*pm)());
template<class R, class T, class A>
    mem_fun1_t<R, T, A> mem_fun(R (T::*pm)(A));
template<class R, class T>
    const_mem_fun_t<R, T> mem_fun(R (T::*pm)() const);
template<class R, class T, class A>
    const_mem_fun1_t<R, T, A> mem_fun(R (T::*pm)(A) const);
```

The template function returns `pm` cast to the return type.

- **mem_fun_ref**

```
template<class R, class T>
    mem_fun_ref_t<R, T> mem_fun_ref(R (T::*pm)());
template<class R, class T, class A>
    mem_fun1_ref_t<R, T, A> mem_fun_ref(R (T::*pm)(A));
template<class R, class T>
    const_mem_fun_ref_t<R, T>
        mem_fun_ref(R (T::*pm)() const);
template<class R, class T, class A>
    const_mem_fun1_ref_t<R, T, A>
        mem_fun_ref(R (T::*pm)(A) const);
```

The template function returns `pm` cast to the return type.

▫ **mem_fun_t**

```
template<class R, class T>
    struct mem_fun_t : public unary_function<T *, R> {
    explicit mem_fun_t(R (T::*pm)());
    R operator()(T *p) const;
    };
```

The template class stores a copy of `pm`, which must be a pointer to a member function of class `T`, in a private member object. It defines its member function `operator()` as returning `(p->*pm)()`.

▫ **mem_fun_ref_t**

```
template<class R, class T>
    struct mem_fun_ref_t
        : public unary_function<T, R> {
    explicit mem_fun_t(R (T::*pm)());
    R operator()(T& x) const;
    };
```

The template class stores a copy of `pm`, which must be a pointer to a member function of class `T`, in a private member object. It defines its member function `operator()` as returning `(x.*pm)()`.

▫ **mem_fun1_t**

```
template<class R, class T, class A>
    struct mem_fun1_t
        : public binary_function<T *, A, R> {
    explicit mem_fun1_t(R (T::*pm)(A));
    R operator()(T *p, A arg) const;
    };
```

The template class stores a copy of `pm`, which must be a pointer to a member function of class `T`, in a private member object. It defines its member function `operator()` as returning `(p->*pm)(arg)`.

▫ **mem_fun1_ref_t**

```
template<class R, class T, class A>
    struct mem_fun1_ref_t
        : public binary_function<T, A, R> {
    explicit mem_fun1_ref_t(R (T::*pm)(A));
    R operator()(T& x, A arg) const;
    };
```

The template class stores a copy of `pm`, which must be a pointer to a member function of class `T`, in a private member object. It defines its member function `operator()` as returning `(x.*pm)(arg)`.

▫ **minus**

```
template<class T>
    struct minus : public binary_function<T, T, T> {
    T operator()(const T& x, const T& y) const;
    };
```

The template class defines its member function as returning `x - y`.

▫ **modulus**

```
template<class T>
    struct modulus : public binary_function<T, T, T> {
```

```
    T operator()(const T& x, const T& y) const;
    };
```

The template class defines its member function as returning `x % y`.

- `multiplies`

```
template<class T>
    struct multiplies : public binary_function<T, T, T> {
    T operator()(const T& x, const T& y) const;
    };
```

The template class defines its member function as returning `x * y`.

- `negate`

```
template<class T>
    struct negate : public unary_function<T, T> {
    T operator()(const T& x) const;
    };
```

The template class defines its member function as returning `-x`.

- `not1`

```
template<class Pred>
    unary_negate<Pred> not1(const Pred& pr);
```

The template function returns `unary_negate<Pred>(pr)`.

- `not2`

```
template<class Pred>
    binary_negate<Pred> not2(const Pred& pr);
```

The template function returns `binary_negate<Pred>(pr)`.

- `not_equal_to`

```
template<class T>
    struct not_equal_to
        : public binary_function<T, T, bool> {
    bool operator()(const T& x, const T& y) const;
    };
```

The template class defines its member function as returning `x != y`.

- `plus`

```
template<class T>
    struct plus : public binary_function<T, T, T> {
    T operator()(const T& x, const T& y) const;
    };
```

The template class defines its member function as returning `x + y`.

- `pointer_to_binary_function`

```
template<class Arg1, class Arg2, class Result>
    class pointer_to_binary_function
        : public binary_function<Arg1, Arg2, Result> {
public:
    explicit pointer_to_binary_function(
        Result (*pf)(Arg1, Arg2));
    Result operator()(const Arg1 x, const Arg2 y) const;
    };
```

The template class stores a copy of `pf`. It defines its member function `operator()` as returning `(*pf)(x, y)`.

- **pointer_to_unary_function**

```
template<class Arg, class Result>
    class pointer_to_unary_function
        : public unary_function<Arg, Result> {
public:
    explicit pointer_to_unary_function(
        Result (*pf)(Arg));
    Result operator()(const Arg x) const;
    };
```

The template class stores a copy of `pf`. It defines its member function `operator()` as returning `(*pf)(x)`.

- **ptr_fun**

```
template<class Arg, class Result>
    pointer_to_unary_function<Arg, Result>
        ptr_fun(Result (*pf)(Arg));
template<class Arg1, class Arg2, class Result>
    pointer_to_binary_function<Arg1, Arg2, Result>
        ptr_fun(Result (*pf)(Arg1, Arg2));
```

The first template function returns `pointer_to_unary_function<Arg, Result>(pf)`.

The second template function returns `pointer_to_binary_function<Arg1, Arg2, Result>(pf)`.

- **unary_function**

```
template<class Arg, class Result>
    struct unary_function {
    typedef Arg argument_type;
    typedef Result result_type;
    };
```

The template class can serve as a convenient base for classes that define a member function of the form:

```
result_type operator()(const argument_type&) const
```

Hence, all such *unary functions* can refer to their sole argument type as `argument_type` and their return type as `result_type`.

- **unary_negate**

```
template<class Pred>
    class unary_negate
        : public unary_function<
            typename Pred::argument_type,
            bool> {
public:
    explicit unary_negate(const Pred& pr);
    bool operator()(
        const typename Pred::argument_type& x) const;
    };
```

The template class stores a copy of `pr`, which must be a unary function object. It defines its member function `operator()` as returning `!pr(x)`.

Using <functional>

unary_function Include the header <numeric> to make use of any of the template classes or functions it defines. We summarize most of these in three tables. Table 8.1, for example, shows all the simple function objects defined in this header. If you want to add to this set, be sure to base all unary function objects on the template class `unary_function`, as in:

```
template<class T>
    struct logical_not : unary_function<T, bool> {
    bool operator()(const T& x) const
        {return (!x); }
    };
```

binary_function Similarly, you should base all binary function objects on the template class `binary_function`, as in

```
template<class T>
    struct plus : binary_function<T, T, T> {
    T operator()(const T& x, const T& y) const
        {return (x + y); }
    };
```

compound function objects Table 8.2 shows all the compound function objects defined in this header. Note that these template classes make use of the member types defined in the base classes `unary_function` and `binary_function`. Thus the above caveats. Note also that each template class has a corresponding template function, also shown in the table, to generate a suitable compound function object on the fly.

Table 8.1: Function Objects

Declare	So That	Returns
`plus<T> X;`	`X(a, b)`	`a + b`
`minus<T> X;`	`X(a, b)`	`a - b`
`multiplies<T> X;`	`X(a, b)`	`a * b`
`divides<T> X;`	`X(a, b)`	`a / b`
`modulus<T> X;`	`X(a, b)`	`a % b`
`equal_to<T> X;`	`X(a, b)`	`a == b`
`not_equal_to<T> X;`	`X(a, b)`	`a != b`
`greater<T> X;`	`X(a, b)`	`a > b`
`less<T> X;`	`X(a, b)`	`a < b`
`greater_equal<T> X;`	`X(a, b)`	`a >= b`
`less_equal<T> X;`	`X(a, b)`	`a <= b`
`logical_and<T> X;`	`X(a, b)`	`a && b`
`logical_or<T> X;`	`X(a, b)`	`a || b`
`logical_not<T> X;`	`X(a)`	`!a`
`negate<T> X;`	`X(a)`	`-a`

NOTES: `a` and `b` have type `T`

pointer function objects Finally, Table 8.3 shows all the pointer function objects defined in this header. Each of these template classes also has a corresponding template function to generate the pointer function object on the fly.

Table 8.2: Compound Function Objects

Declare/Call	So That	Returns
binary_negate<F> X(f); X = not2(f);	X(a, b)	!f(a, b)
unary_negate<G> X(g); X = not1(g);	X(a)	!g(a)
binder1st<F> X(f, a); X = bind1st(f, a);	X(b)	f(a, b)
binder2nd<F> X(f, b); X = bind2nd(f, b);	X(a)	f(a, b)
NOTES: f has type F based on binary_function, g has type G based on unary_function		

Table 8.3: Pointer Function Objects

Declare/Call	So That	Returns
pointer_to_binary_function<T1, T2, R> X(pf); X = ptr_fun(pf);	X(a, b)	(*pf)(a, b)
pointer_to_unary_function<T1, R> X(pf); X = ptr_fun(pf);	X(a)	(*pf)(a)
mem_fun1_t<R, T, T1> X(pm); X = mem_fun(pm);	X(p, a)	(p->*pm)(a)
mem_fun1_ref_t<R, T, T1> X(pm); X = mem_fun_ref(pm);	X(t, a)	(t.*pm)(a)
mem_fun_t<R, T> X(pm); X = mem_fun(pm);	X(p)	(p->*pm)()
mem_fun_ref_t<R, T> X(pm); X = mem_fun_ref(pm);	X(t)	(t.*pm)()
const_mem_fun1_t<R, T, T1> X(pcm); X = mem_fun(pcm);	X(p, a)	(p->*pcm)(a)
const_mem_fun1_ref_t<R, T, T1> X(pcm); X = mem_fun_ref(pcm);	X(t, a)	(t.*pcm)(a)
const_mem_fun_t<R, T> X(pcm); X = mem_fun(pcm);	X(p)	(p->*pcm)()
const_mem_fun_ref_t<R, T> X(pcm); X = mem_fun_ref(pcm);	X(t)	(t.*pcm)()
NOTES: a has type T1, b has type T2, *pf is a function, *pm is a member function, *pcm is a const member function p has type T *, t has type T&, return type is R		

Figure 8.1: functional part 1

```
// functional standard header
#ifndef FUNCTIONAL_
#define FUNCTIONAL_
namespace std {
        // TEMPLATE STRUCT unary_function
template<class A, class R>
    struct unary_function {
    typedef A argument_type;
    typedef R result_type;
    };

        // TEMPLATE STRUCT binary_function
template<class A1, class A2, class R>
    struct binary_function {
    typedef A1 first_argument_type;
    typedef A2 second_argument_type;
    typedef R result_type;
    };

        // TEMPLATE STRUCT plus
template<class T>
    struct plus : binary_function<T, T, T> {
    T operator()(const T& X, const T& Y) const
        {return (X + Y); }
    };

        // TEMPLATE STRUCT minus
template<class T>
    struct minus : binary_function<T, T, T> {
    T operator()(const T& X, const T& Y) const
        {return (X - Y); }
    };

        // TEMPLATE STRUCT multiplies
template<class T>
    struct multiplies : binary_function<T, T, T> {
    T operator()(const T& X, const T& Y) const
        {return (X * Y); }
    };

        // TEMPLATE STRUCT divides
template<class T>
    struct divides : binary_function<T, T, T> {
    T operator()(const T& X, const T& Y) const
        {return (X / Y); }
    };

        // TEMPLATE STRUCT modulus
template<class T>
    struct modulus : binary_function<T, T, T> {
    T operator()(const T& X, const T& Y) const
        {return (X % Y); }
    };
```

Figure 8.2: `functional` part 2

```
        // TEMPLATE STRUCT negate
template<class T>
    struct negate : unary_function<T, T> {
    T operator()(const T& X) const
        {return (-X); }
    };

        // TEMPLATE STRUCT equal_to
template<class T>
    struct equal_to : binary_function<T, T, bool> {
    bool operator()(const T& X, const T& Y) const
        {return (X == Y); }
    };

        // TEMPLATE STRUCT not_equal_to
template<class T>
    struct not_equal_to : binary_function<T, T, bool> {
    bool operator()(const T& X, const T& Y) const
        {return (X != Y); }
    };

        // TEMPLATE STRUCT greater
template<class T>
    struct greater : binary_function<T, T, bool> {
    bool operator()(const T& X, const T& Y) const
        {return (X > Y); }
    };

        // TEMPLATE STRUCT less
template<class T>
    struct less : binary_function<T, T, bool> {
    bool operator()(const T& X, const T& Y) const
        {return (X < Y); }
    };

        // TEMPLATE STRUCT greater_equal
template<class T>
    struct greater_equal : binary_function<T, T, bool> {
    bool operator()(const T& X, const T& Y) const
        {return (X >= Y); }
    };

        // TEMPLATE STRUCT less_equal
template<class T>
    struct less_equal : binary_function<T, T, bool> {
    bool operator()(const T& X, const T& Y) const
        {return (X <= Y); }
    };

        // TEMPLATE STRUCT logical_and
template<class T>
    struct logical_and : binary_function<T, T, bool> {
    bool operator()(const T& X, const T& Y) const
        {return (X && Y); }
    };
```

Figure 8.3: `functional` **part 3**

```
        // TEMPLATE STRUCT logical_or
template<class T>
    struct logical_or : binary_function<T, T, bool> {
    bool operator()(const T& X, const T& Y) const
        {return (X || Y); }
    };

        // TEMPLATE STRUCT logical_not
template<class T>
    struct logical_not : unary_function<T, bool> {
    bool operator()(const T& X) const
        {return (!X); }
    };

        // TEMPLATE CLASS unary_negate
template<class Ufn>
    class unary_negate
    : public unary_function<typename Ufn::argument_type, bool> {
public:
    explicit unary_negate(const Ufn& X)
        : Fn(X) {}
    bool operator()(const typename Ufn::argument_type& X) const
        {return (!Fn(X)); }
protected:
    Ufn Fn;
    };

        // TEMPLATE FUNCTION not1
template<class Ufn> inline
    unary_negate<Ufn> not1(const Ufn& X)
        {return (unary_negate<Ufn>(X)); }

        // TEMPLATE CLASS binary_negate
template<class Bfn>
    class binary_negate
    : public binary_function<typename Bfn::first_argument_type,
        typename Bfn::second_argument_type, bool> {
public:
    explicit binary_negate(const Bfn& X)
        : Fn(X) {}
    bool operator()(const typename Bfn::first_argument_type& X,
        const typename Bfn::second_argument_type& Y) const
        {return (!Fn(X, Y)); }
protected:
    Bfn Fn;
    };

        // TEMPLATE FUNCTION not2
template<class Bfn> inline
    binary_negate<Bfn> not2(const Bfn& X)
        {return (binary_negate<Bfn>(X)); }
        // TEMPLATE CLASS binder1st
template<class Bfn>
    class binder1st
```

Figure 8.4: functional part 4

```
    : public unary_function<typename Bfn::second_argument_type,
         typename Bfn::result_type> {
public:
    typedef unary_function<typename Bfn::second_argument_type,
         typename Bfn::result_type> Base;
    typedef typename Base::argument_type argument_type;
    typedef typename Base::result_type result_type;
    binder1st(const Bfn& X,
         const typename Bfn::first_argument_type& Y)
         : op(X), value(Y) {}
    result_type operator()(const argument_type& X) const
         {return (op(value, X)); }
protected:
    Bfn op;
    typename Bfn::first_argument_type value;
    };

         // TEMPLATE FUNCTION bind1st
template<class Bfn, class T> inline
    binder1st<Bfn> bind1st(const Bfn& X, const T& Y)
         {typename Bfn::first_argument_type Arg(Y);
         return (binder1st<Bfn>(X, Arg)); }

         // TEMPLATE CLASS binder2nd
template<class Bfn>
    class binder2nd
    : public unary_function<typename Bfn::first_argument_type,
         typename Bfn::result_type> {
public:
    typedef unary_function<typename Bfn::first_argument_type,
         typename Bfn::result_type> Base;
    typedef typename Base::argument_type argument_type;
    typedef typename Base::result_type result_type;
    binder2nd(const Bfn& X,
         const typename Bfn::second_argument_type& Y)
         : op(X), value(Y) {}
    result_type operator()(const argument_type& X) const
         {return (op(X, value)); }
protected:
    Bfn op;
    typename Bfn::second_argument_type value;
    };

         // TEMPLATE FUNCTION bind2nd
template<class Bfn, class T> inline
    binder2nd<Bfn> bind2nd(const Bfn& X, const T& Y)
         {typename Bfn::second_argument_type Arg(Y);
         return (binder2nd<Bfn>(X, Arg)); }
         // TEMPLATE CLASS pointer_to_unary_function
template<class A, class R>
    class pointer_to_unary_function
         : public unary_function<A, R> {
public:
    explicit pointer_to_unary_function(R (*X)(A))
         : Fn(X) {}
```

Figure 8.5: `functional` **part 5**

```
      R operator()(A X) const
            {return (Fn(X)); }
protected:
      R (*Fn)(A);
      };

            // TEMPLATE CLASS pointer_to_binary_function
template<class A1, class A2, class R>
      class pointer_to_binary_function
            : public binary_function<A1, A2, R> {
public:
      explicit pointer_to_binary_function(
            R (*X)(A1, A2))
            : Fn(X) {}
      R operator()(A1 X, A2 Y) const
            {return (Fn(X, Y)); }
protected:
      R (*Fn)(A1, A2);
      };

            // TEMPLATE FUNCTION ptr_fun
template<class A, class R> inline
      pointer_to_unary_function<A, R>
            ptr_fun(R (*X)(A))
            {return (pointer_to_unary_function<A, R>(X)); }
template<class A1, class A2, class R> inline
      pointer_to_binary_function<A1, A2, R>
            ptr_fun(R (*X)(A1, A2))
            {return (pointer_to_binary_function<A1, A2, R>(X)); }
            // TEMPLATE CLASS mem_fun_t
template<class R, class T>
      class mem_fun_t : public unary_function<T *, R> {
public:
      explicit mem_fun_t(R (T::*Pm)())
            : Ptr(Pm) {}
      R operator()(T *P) const
            {return ((P->*Ptr)()); }
private:
      R (T::*Ptr)();
      };

            // TEMPLATE CLASS mem_fun1_t
template<class R, class T, class A>
      class mem_fun1_t : public binary_function<T *, A, R> {
public:
      explicit mem_fun1_t(R (T::*Pm)(A))
            : Ptr(Pm) {}
      R operator()(T *P, A Arg) const
            {return ((P->*Ptr)(Arg)); }
private:
      R (T::*Ptr)(A);
      };

            // TEMPLATE CLASS const_mem_fun_t
template<class R, class T>
```

Figure 8.6: functional part 6

```
     class const_mem_fun_t
          : public unary_function<const T *, R> {
public:
     explicit const_mem_fun_t(R (T::*Pm)() const)
          : Ptr(Pm) {}
     R operator()(const T *P) const
          {return ((P->*Ptr)()); }
private:
     R (T::*Ptr)() const;
     };

          // TEMPLATE CLASS const_mem_fun1_t
template<class R, class T, class A>
     class const_mem_fun1_t
          : public binary_function<T *, A, R> {
public:
     explicit const_mem_fun1_t(R (T::*Pm)(A) const)
          : Ptr(Pm) {}
     R operator()(const T *P, A Arg) const
          {return ((P->*Ptr)(Arg)); }
private:
     R (T::*Ptr)(A) const;
     };

          // TEMPLATE FUNCTION mem_fun
template<class R, class T> inline
     mem_fun_t<R, T> mem_fun(R (T::*Pm)())
     {return (mem_fun_t<R, T>(Pm)); }
template<class R, class T, class A> inline
     mem_fun1_t<R, T, A> mem_fun(R (T::*Pm)(A))
     {return (mem_fun1_t<R, T, A>(Pm)); }
template<class R, class T> inline
     const_mem_fun_t<R, T>
          mem_fun(R (T::*Pm)() const)
     {return (const_mem_fun_t<R, T>(Pm)); }
template<class R, class T, class A> inline
     const_mem_fun1_t<R, T, A>
          mem_fun(R (T::*Pm)(A) const)
     {return (const_mem_fun1_t<R, T, A>(Pm)); }

          // TEMPLATE CLASS mem_fun_ref_t
template<class R, class T>
     class mem_fun_ref_t : public unary_function<T, R> {
public:
     explicit mem_fun_ref_t(R (T::*Pm)())
          : Ptr(Pm) {}
     R operator()(T& X) const
          {return ((X.*Ptr)()); }
private:
     R (T::*Ptr)();
     };

          // TEMPLATE CLASS mem_fun1_ref_t
template<class R, class T, class A>
     class mem_fun1_ref_t : public binary_function<T, A, R> {
```

Figure 8.7: `functional` **part 7**

```
public:
     explicit mem_fun1_ref_t(R (T::*Pm)(A))
          : Ptr(Pm) {}
     R operator()(T& X, A Arg) const
          {return ((X.*Ptr)(Arg)); }
private:
     R (T::*Ptr)(A);
     };

          // TEMPLATE CLASS const_mem_fun_ref_t
template<class R, class T>
     class const_mem_fun_ref_t
          : public unary_function<T, R> {
public:
     explicit const_mem_fun_ref_t(R (T::*Pm)() const)
          : Ptr(Pm) {}
     R operator()(const T& X) const
          {return ((X.*Ptr)()); }
private:
     R (T::*Ptr)() const;
     };

          // TEMPLATE CLASS const_mem_fun1_ref_t
template<class R, class T, class A>
     class const_mem_fun1_ref_t
          : public binary_function<T, A, R> {
public:
     explicit const_mem_fun1_ref_t(R (T::*Pm)(A) const)
          : Ptr(Pm) {}
     R operator()(const T& X, A Arg) const
          {return ((X.*Ptr)(Arg)); }
private:
     R (T::*Ptr)(A) const;
     };

          // TEMPLATE FUNCTION mem_fun_ref
template<class R, class T> inline
     mem_fun_ref_t<R, T> mem_fun_ref(R (T::*Pm)())
     {return (mem_fun_ref_t<R, T>(Pm)); }
template<class R, class T, class A> inline
     mem_fun1_ref_t<R, T, A>
          mem_fun_ref(R (T::*Pm)(A))
     {return (mem_fun1_ref_t<R, T, A>(Pm)); }
template<class R, class T> inline
     const_mem_fun_ref_t<R, T>
          mem_fun_ref(R (T::*Pm)() const)
     {return (const_mem_fun_ref_t<R, T>(Pm)); }
template<class R, class T, class A> inline
     const_mem_fun1_ref_t<R, T, A>
          mem_fun_ref(R (T::*Pm)(A) const)
     {return (const_mem_fun1_ref_t<R, T, A>(Pm)); }
} /* namespace std */
#endif /* FUNCTIONAL_ */
```
□

Implementing `<functional>`

functional Figures 8.1 through 8.6 show the file **functional**. While there is a lot of niggling detail, none of the template classes or functions are at all surprising. We simply present the code without further comment.

Testing `<functional>`

tfunctio.c Figures 8.8 through 8.10 show the file **tfunctio.c**. Like the implementation itself, the tests are simple and repetitious. Mostly, they check for the overt presence of all the definitions. If all goes well, the program prints:

```
SUCCESS testing <functional>
```

and takes a normal exit.

Figure 8.8: tfunctio.c part 1

```
// test <functional>
#include <assert.h>
#include <iostream>
#include <string.h>
#include <algorithm>
#include <functional>
using namespace std;

     // TEST SIMPLE FUNCTION OBJECTS
void test_simple(char *first, char *last, char *dest)
     {typedef unary_function<char, int> Uf;
     Uf::argument_type *pa0 = (char *)0;
     Uf::result_type *pr0 = (int *)0;
     typedef binary_function<char, int, float> Bf;
     Bf::first_argument_type *pa1 = (char *)0;
     Bf::second_argument_type *pa2 = (int *)0;
     Bf::result_type *pr1 = (float *)0;

     char *mid = first + 2;
     strcpy(first, "\4\3\2\1"), strcpy(dest, "abcd");
     transform(first, mid, mid, dest, plus<char>());
     assert(strcmp(dest, "\6\4cd") == 0);
     transform(first, mid, mid, dest, minus<char>());
     assert(strcmp(dest, "\2\2cd") == 0);
     transform(first, mid, mid, dest, multiplies<char>());
     assert(strcmp(dest, "\10\3cd") == 0);
     transform(first, mid, mid, dest, divides<char>());
     assert(strcmp(dest, "\2\3cd") == 0);
     transform(first, mid, first + 1, dest, modulus<char>());
     assert(strcmp(dest, "\1\1cd") == 0);
     transform(first, mid, dest, negate<char>());
     assert(((signed char *)dest)[0] == -4
          && ((signed char *)dest)[1] == -3);

     transform(first, mid, "\4\4", dest, equal_to<char>());
     assert(memcmp(dest, "\1\0cd", 4) == 0);
     transform(first, mid, "\4\4", dest, not_equal_to<char>());
     assert(memcmp(dest, "\0\1cd", 4) == 0);
```

Figure 8.9: `tfunctio.c` **part 2**

```
        transform(first, mid, "\3\3", dest, greater<char>());
        assert(memcmp(dest, "\1\0cd", 4) == 0);
        transform(first, mid, "\4\4", dest, less<char>());
        assert(memcmp(dest, "\0\1cd", 4) == 0);
        transform(first, mid, "\4\4", dest, greater_equal<char>());
        assert(memcmp(dest, "\1\0cd", 4) == 0);
        transform(first, mid, "\3\3", dest, less_equal<char>());
        assert(memcmp(dest, "\0\1cd", 4) == 0);

        transform(last - 1, last + 1, "\1\0",
            dest, logical_and<char>());
        assert(memcmp(dest, "\1\0cd", 4) == 0);
        transform(last - 1, last + 1, dest, logical_not<char>());
        assert(memcmp(dest, "\0\1cd", 4) == 0);
        transform(last - 1, last + 1, "\0\0",
            dest, logical_or<char>());
        assert(strcmp(dest, "\1\0cd") == 0); }

        // TEST COMPOUND FUNCTION OBJECTS
void test_compound(char *first, char *last, char *dest)
        {char *mid = first + 2;
        strcpy(first, "\4\3\2\1"), strcpy(dest, "abcd");
        unary_negate<logical_not<char> > unop(logical_not<char>());
        transform(last - 1, last + 1, dest, unop);
        transform(last - 1, last + 1, dest + 2,
            not1(logical_not<char>()));
        assert(memcmp(dest, "\1\0\1\0", 4) == 0);
        binary_negate<less<char> > binop(less<char>());
        transform(first, mid, "\5\2", dest, binop);
        transform(first, mid, "\5\2", dest + 2, not2(less<char>()));
        assert(memcmp(dest, "\0\1\0\1", 4) == 0);

        binder1st<plus<char> > add1(plus<char>(), '\1');
        transform(first, mid, dest, add1);
        transform(mid, last, dest + 2, bind1st(plus<char>(), '\1'));
        assert(strcmp(dest, "\5\4\3\2") == 0);
        binder2nd<minus<char> > sub1(minus<char>(), '\1');
        transform(first, mid, dest, sub1);
        transform(mid, last, dest + 2, bind2nd(minus<char>(), '\1'));
        assert(memcmp(dest, "\3\2\1\0", 4) == 0); }

        // TEST POINTER FUNCTION OBJECTS
char ufn(char ch)
        {return (ch + 1); }
char bfn(char ch1, char ch2)
        {return (ch1 + ch2); }
struct Myclass {
        char fn0()
            {return ('\7'); }
        char fn1(char ch)
            {return (ch + 1); }
        } mycl;
struct Mycclass {
        char fn0() const
            {return ('\7'); }
```

Figure 8.10: `tfunctio.c` **part 3**

```
     char fn1(char ch) const
          {return (ch + 1); }
     } myccl;

void test_pointer(char *first, char *last, char *dest)
     {char *mid = first + 2;
     strcpy(first, "\4\3\2\1"), strcpy(dest, "abcd");
     pointer_to_unary_function<char, char> uf(ufn);
     transform(first, mid, dest, uf);
     transform(mid, last, dest + 2, ptr_fun(ufn));
     assert(strcmp(dest, "\5\4\3\2") == 0);
     pointer_to_binary_function<char, char, char> bf(bfn);
     transform(first, mid, "\2\2", dest, bf);
     transform(mid, last, "\2\2", dest + 2, ptr_fun(bfn));
     assert(strcmp(dest, "\6\5\4\3") == 0);

     mem_fun_t<char, Myclass> mf(Myclass::fn0);
     assert(mf(&mycl) == '\7');
     assert(mem_fun(Myclass::fn0)(&mycl) == '\7');
     mem_fun1_t<char, Myclass, char> mf1(Myclass::fn1);
     assert(mf1(&mycl, '\3') == '\4');
     assert(mem_fun1(Myclass::fn1)(&mycl, '\3') == '\4');
     mem_fun_ref_t<char, Myclass> mfr(Myclass::fn0);
     assert(mfr(mycl) == '\7');
     assert(mem_fun_ref(Myclass::fn0)(mycl) == '\7');
     mem_fun1_ref_t<char, Myclass, char> mf1r(Myclass::fn1);
     assert(mf1r(mycl, '\3') == '\4');
     assert(mem_fun1_ref(Myclass::fn1)(mycl, '\3') == '\4');

     const_mem_fun_t<char, Mycclass> cmf(Mycclass::fn0);
     assert(cmf(&myccl) == '\7');
     const_mem_fun1_t<char, Mycclass, char> cmf1(Mycclass::fn1);
     assert(cmf1(&myccl, '\3') == '\4');
     const_mem_fun_ref_t<char, Mycclass> cmfr(Mycclass::fn0);
     assert(cmfr(myccl) == '\7');
     const_mem_fun1_ref_t<char, Mycclass, char>
          cmf1r(Mycclass::fn1);
     assert(cmf1r(myccl, '\3') == '\4'); }

     // TEST <functional>
int main()
     {char buf[] = "\4\3\2\1";
     char dest[] = "abcd";
     char *first = buf, *last = buf + 4;
     test_simple(first, last, dest);
     test_compound(first, last, dest);
     test_pointer(first, last, dest);

     cout << "SUCCESS testing <functional>" << endl;
     return (0); }
```
□

Exercises

Exercise 8.1 Write the template classes that implement the function objects for the binary operators `&`, `|`, and `*`, and for the unary operators `~` and `+`. Why would you want the last of these classes (which does almost nothing)?

Exercise 8.2 Write template class `binderfgh` such that the declarator `X(f, g, h)` causes `X(a)` to return `f(g(a), h(a))`. Why would you want such a template class?

Exercise 8.3 Write the template function `bindfgh` that returns an object of template class `binderfgh`. Why would you want such a template function?

Exercise 8.4 [**Harder**] Use the results of the previous exercises to write an expression that returns the function object `X` such that `X(a)` returns the value of the function `c2 * x * x + c1 * x + c0` at `a`.

Exercise 8.5 [**Very hard**] Write a program that translates an arbitrary function of `x`, involving only C++ operators, into code that generates a function object `X` such that `X(a)` returns the value of the arbitrary function at `a`.

Chapter 9: Containers

Background

A container is a class that manages a sequence. Member functions let you insert new elements in the sequence, erase (delete) existing elements, and locate them. The functions return iterators to designate elements in the sequence, so you can apply the various algorithms described in earlier chapters to part or all of the controlled sequence.

time complexity Managing a sequence involves tradeoffs. If you plan to make frequent insertions and/or erasures throughout a sequence, for example, you might prefer a container that performs such actions in *constant time* — the time to perform an insertion or erasure does not increase with *N*, the number of elements in the sequence. Such a container is not likely to help you locate a given element in constant time as well, however. You have to decide which operations have more influence on overall program performance, then choose a suitable container type.

For this particular tradeoff, you can also compromise. It is possible for a container to support insertions, erasures, and locates all in time proportional to the logarithm of *N* (written *log N*). The logarithm increases with *N*, but much more slowly than *N*, so such time complexity may be quite satisfactory all the way around. But you then pay the price in a different dimension.

storage overhead To support logarithmic behavior such as this, a container must represent its controlled sequence as some sort of ordered tree data structure. A tree stores three pointers along with the value of each element, to designate the parent element and two children. And the storage allocator may quietly add even more overhead. If the element value itself requires a large amount of storage, the additional overhead may be unimportant. But if the element value requires little storage, and the program allocates numerous elements, the extra overhead for a tree may prove to be prohibitive. In that case, one of the simpler container types will supply a better tradeoff. It will require fewer pointers per element, perhaps even none, at the cost of worse time complexity for certain operations on the controlled sequence.

STL thus provides an assortment of different container template classes for you to choose among. In all cases, one of the template parameters is the type of elements you wish to store in the controlled sequence. You can

Table 9.1: Container Time and Space Complexity

	`vector`	`deque`	`list`	`set/map`
insert/erase	*N*	*N*	constant	*log N*
prepend	*(N)*	constant	constant	*(log N)*
find(val)	*(N)*	*(N)*	*(N)*	*log N*
X[*N*]	constant	constant	*(N)*	*(N)*
pointers	0	1	2	3

NOTES: *(N)* or *(log N)* — time complexity for operations not directly supported by member functions

specialize these classes for elements of any object type that meets just a few minimum requirements:

- The object type **`T`** must have an accessible default constructor.
- It must have an accessible destructor.
- It must have an accessible assignment operator with sensible semantics and the signature **`operator=(const T&)`**.

The STL container template classes are typically implemented as:

- `vector` **`vector`** — an array of *N* or more contiguous elements
- `list` **`list`** — a bidirectional linked list of nodes, each containing an element
- `deque` **`deque`** — an array of *N* or more contiguous pointers to separately allocated elements
- `set` **`set`** — a red/black tree of nodes, each containing an element, ordered by some predicate applied to pairs of elements and with no two elements having equivalent ordering
- `multiset` **`multiset`** — a set that also permits pairs of elements having equivalent ordering
- `map` **`map`** — a set of {key, value} pairs, ordered by some predicate applied to pairs of keys
- `multimap` **`multimap`** — a map that also permits pairs of keys having equivalent ordering

Table 9.1 summarizes the time complexity of operations on each of these template container classes. It also shows the number of additional pointers required for each element of the controlled sequence, again neglecting any overhead added by the storage allocator.

container adapters The Standard Template Library also defines several *container adapters.* These are "almost" containers that are implemented in terms of other containers. They intentionally restrict how you can access elements:

- `stack` **`stack`** — a last-in/first-out (LIFO) queue of values
- `queue` **`queue`** — a first-in/first-out (FIFO) queue of values
- `priority_queue` **`priority_queue`** — a queue ordered by some predicate on pairs of stored values so that it delivers the highest-priority element first

We save these container adapters for last, in subsequent chapters.

Functional Description

```
namespace std {
template<class T>
    class Cont;

        // TEMPLATE FUNCTIONS
template<class T>
    bool operator==(
        const Cont<T>& lhs,
        const Cont<T>& rhs);
template<class T>
    bool operator!=(
        const Cont<T>& lhs,
        const Cont<T>& rhs);
template<class T>
    bool operator<(
        const Cont<T>& lhs,
        const Cont<T>& rhs);
template<class T>
    bool operator>(
        const Cont<T>& lhs,
        const Cont<T>& rhs);
template<class T>
    bool operator<=(
        const Cont<T>& lhs,
        const Cont<T>& rhs);
template<class T>
    bool operator>=(
        const Cont<T>& lhs,
        const Cont<T>& rhs);
template<class T>
    void swap(
        Cont<T>& lhs,
        Cont<T>& rhs);
    };
```

A *container* is an STL template class that manages a sequence of elements. Such elements can be of any object type that supplies a copy constructor, a destructor, and an assignment operator (all with sensible behavior, of course). The destructor may not throw an exception. This document describes the properties required of all such containers, in terms of a generic template class **Cont** whose parameter type **T** is the element type. An actual container template class may have additional template parameters. It will certainly have additional member functions.

The STL template container classes are:

```
deque
list
map
multimap
multiset
set
vector
```

basic_string The Standard C++ library template class **basic_string** also meets the requirements for a template container class.

▫ **Cont**

```
template<class T>
    class Cont {
public:
    typedef T0 size_type;
    typedef T1 difference_type;
    typedef T2 reference;
    typedef T3 const_reference;
    typedef T4 value_type;
    typedef T5 iterator;
    typedef T6 const_iterator;
    typedef T7 reverse_iterator;
    typedef T8 const_reverse_iterator;
    iterator begin();
    const_iterator begin() const;
    iterator end();
    const_iterator end() const;
    reverse_iterator rbegin();
    const_reverse_iterator rbegin() const;
    reverse_iterator rend();
    const_reverse_iterator rend() const;
    size_type size() const;
    size_type max_size() const;
    bool empty() const;
    iterator erase(iterator it);
    iterator erase(iterator first, iterator last);
    void clear();
    void swap(Cont& x);
    };
```

The template class describes an object that controls a varying-length sequence of elements, typically of type `T`. The sequence is stored in different ways, depending on the actual container.

exception safety A container constructor or member function may find occasion to call the constructor `T(const T&)` or the function `T::operator=(const T&)`. If such a call throws an exception, the container object is obliged to maintain its integrity, and to rethrow any exception it catches. That is, you can safely swap, assign to, erase, or destroy a container object after it throws one of these exceptions. In general, however, you cannot otherwise predict the state of the sequence controlled by the container object.

A few additional caveats:

- If the expression `~T()` throws an exception, the resulting state of the container object is undefined.
- If the container stores an allocator object `al`, and `al` throws an exception other than as a result of a call to `al.allocate`, the resulting state of the container object is undefined.
- If the container stores a function object `comp`, to determine how to order the controlled sequence, and `comp` throws an exception of any kind, the resulting state of the container object is undefined.

The container classes defined by STL satisfy several additional requirements, as described in the following paragraphs.

Container template class **list** provides deterministic, and useful, behavior even in the presence of the exceptions described above. For example, if an exception is thrown during the insertion of one or more elements, the container is left unaltered and the exception is rethrown.

For *all* the container classes defined by STL, if an exception is thrown during calls to the following member functions:

```
insert // single element inserted
push_back
push_front
```

the container is left unaltered and the exception is rethrown.

For *all* the container classes defined by STL, no exception is thrown during calls to the following member functions:

```
erase // single element erased
pop_back
pop_front
```

Moreover, no exception is thrown while copying an iterator returned by a member function.

The member function **swap** makes additional promises for *all* container classes defined by STL:

- The member function throws an exception only if the container stores an allocator object **al**, and **al** throws an exception when copied.
- References, pointers, and iterators that designate elements of the controlled sequences being swapped remain valid.

allocators An object of a container class defined by STL allocates and frees storage for the sequence it controls through a stored object of type **A**, which is typically a template parameter. Such an allocator object must have the same external interface as an object of class **allocator**<T>. In particular, **A** must be the same type as **A::rebind<value_type>::other**

For *all* container classes defined by STL, the member function:

```
A get_allocator() const;
```

returns a copy of the stored allocator object. Note that the stored allocator object is *not* copied when the container object is assigned. All constructors initialize the value stored in **allocator**, to **A()** if the constructor contains no allocator parameter.

According to the C++ Standard a container class defined by STL can assume that:

- All objects of class **A** compare equal.
- Type **A::const_pointer** is the same as **const T ***.
- Type **A::const_reference** is the same as **const T&**.
- Type **A::pointer** is the same as **T ***.
- Type **A::reference** is the same as **T&**.

In this implementation, however, containers do *not* make such simplifying assumptions. Thus, they work properly with allocator objects that are more ambitious:

- All objects of class **A** need not compare equal. (You can maintain multiple pools of storage.)
- Type **A::const_pointer** need not be the same as **const T ***. (A const pointer can be a class.)
- Type **A::pointer** need not be the same as **T ***. (A pointer can be a class.)

Cont::begin

```
const_iterator begin() const;
iterator begin();
```

The member function returns an iterator that points at the first element of the sequence (or just beyond the end of an empty sequence).

Cont::clear

```
void clear();
```

The member function calls **erase(begin(), end())**.

Cont::const_iterator

```
typedef T6 const_iterator;
```

The type describes an object that can serve as a constant iterator for the controlled sequence. It is described here as a synonym for the unspecified type **T6**.

Cont::const_reference

```
typedef T3 const_reference;
```

The type describes an object that can serve as a constant reference to an element of the controlled sequence. It is described here as a synonym for the unspecified type **T3** (typically **A::const_reference**).

Cont::const_reverse_iterator

```
typedef T8 const_reverse_iterator;
```

The type describes an object that can serve as a constant reverse iterator for the controlled sequence. It is described here as a synonym for the unspecified type **T8** (typically **reverse_iterator <const_iterator>**).

Cont::difference_type

```
typedef T1 difference_type;
```

The signed integer type describes an object that can represent the difference between the addresses of any two elements in the controlled sequence. It is described here as a synonym for the unspecified type **T1** (typically **A::difference_type**).

Cont::empty

```
bool empty() const;
```

The member function returns true for an empty controlled sequence.

- **`Cont::end`**

```
const_iterator end() const;
iterator end();
```

The member function returns an iterator that points just beyond the end of the sequence.

- **`Cont::erase`**

```
iterator erase(iterator it);
iterator erase(iterator first, iterator last);
```

The first member function removes the element of the controlled sequence pointed to by `it`. The second member function removes the elements of the controlled sequence in the range `[first, last)`. Both return an iterator that designates the first element remaining beyond any elements removed, or `end()` if no such element exists.

The member functions never throw an exception.

- **`Cont::iterator`**

```
typedef T5 iterator;
```

The type describes an object that can serve as an iterator for the controlled sequence. It is described here as a synonym for the unspecified type `T5`. An object of type `iterator` can be cast to an object of type `const_iterator`.

- **`Cont::max_size`**

```
size_type max_size() const;
```

The member function returns the length of the longest sequence that the object can control, in constant time regardless of the length of the controlled sequence.

- **`Cont::rbegin`**

```
const_reverse_iterator rbegin() const;
reverse_iterator rbegin();
```

The member function returns a reverse iterator that points just beyond the end of the controlled sequence. Hence, it designates the beginning of the reverse sequence.

- **`Cont::reference`**

```
typedef T2 reference;
```

The type describes an object that can serve as a reference to an element of the controlled sequence. It is described here as a synonym for the unspecified type `T2` (typically `A::reference`). An object of type `reference` can be cast to an object of type `const_reference`.

- **`Cont::rend`**

```
const_reverse_iterator rend() const;
reverse_iterator rend();
```

The member function returns a reverse iterator that points at the first element of the sequence (or just beyond the end of an empty sequence). Hence, it designates the end of the reverse sequence.

- **`Cont::reverse_iterator`**

```
typedef T7 reverse_iterator;
```

The type describes an object that can serve as a reverse iterator for the controlled sequence. It is described here as a synonym for the unspecified type `T7` (typically `reverse_iterator <iterator>`).

- **`Cont::size`**

```
size_type size() const;
```

The member function returns the length of the controlled sequence, in constant time regardless of the length of the controlled sequence.

- **`Cont::size_type`**

```
typedef T0 size_type;
```

The unsigned integer type describes an object that can represent the length of any controlled sequence. It is described here as a synonym for the unspecified type `T0` (typically `A::size_type`).

- **`Cont::swap`**

```
void swap(Cont& x);
```

The member function swaps the controlled sequences between `*this` and `x`. If `get_allocator() == x.get_allocator()`, it does so in constant time. Otherwise, it performs a number of element assignments and constructor calls proportional to the number of elements in the two controlled sequences.

- **`Cont::value_type`**

```
typedef T4 value_type;
```

The type is a synonym for the template parameter `T`. It is described here as a synonym for the unspecified type `T4` (typically `A::value_type`).

- **`operator!=`**

```
template<class T>
    bool operator!=(
        const Cont <T>& lhs,
        const Cont <T>& rhs);
```

The template function returns `!(lhs == rhs)`.

- **`operator==`**

```
template<class T>
    bool operator==(
        const Cont <T>& lhs,
        const Cont <T>& rhs);
```

The template function overloads `operator==` to compare two objects of template class `Cont`. The function returns `lhs.size() == rhs.size() && equal(lhs. begin(), lhs. end(), rhs.begin())`.

- `operator<`

```
template<class T>
    bool operator<(
        const Cont <T>& lhs,
        const Cont <T>& rhs);
```

The template function overloads `operator<` to compare two objects of template class `Cont`. The function returns `lexicographical_compare(lhs. begin(), lhs. end(), rhs.begin(), rhs.end())`.

- `operator<=`

```
template<class T>
    bool operator<=(
        const Cont <T>& lhs,
        const Cont <T>& rhs);
```

The template function returns `!(rhs < lhs)`.

- `operator>`

```
template<class T>
    bool operator>(
        const Cont <T>& lhs,
        const Cont <T>& rhs);
```

The template function returns `rhs < lhs`.

- `operator>=`

```
template<class T>
    bool operator>=(
        const Cont <T>& lhs,
        const Cont <T>& rhs);
```

The template function returns `!(lhs < rhs)`.

- `swap`

```
template<class T>
    void swap(
        Cont <T>& lhs,
        Cont <T>& rhs);
```

The template function executes `lhs.swap(rhs)`.

Using Containers

To make use of any of the STL containers or container adapters, include the header that defines its template class:

- `<deque>` `deque` is defined in `<deque>`.
- `<list>` `list` is defined in `<list>`.
- `<map>` `map` and `multimap` are defined in `<map>`.
- `<set>` `set` and `multiset` are defined in `<set>`.
- `<queue>` `priority_queue` and `queue` are defined in `<queue>`.
- `<stack>` `stack` is defined in `<stack>`.
- `<vector>` `vector` is defined in `<vector>`.

Subsequent chapters describe each of these headers in detail.

common properties Each of the STL containers has a number of unique properties, as you might expect. How you construct a container object, how you insert elements into it, and how you subsequently locate those elements varies considerably among containers. But the container template classes also have a number of common properties, which we describe here. For example, each defines a number of member types that supply useful information about the container:

value_type
- **value_type** is the type of an element of the controlled sequence.

size_type
- **size_type** is the type that can represent the length of any controlled sequence.

difference_type
- **difference_type** is the type that can represent algebraic differences between objects of type **iterator**.

allocator_type
allocator_type is the type of the allocator object that supplies all storage for the controlled sequence.

iterator
- **iterator** is the type of any iterator, returned by a *non-const* container member function, that lets you access the controlled sequence.

const_iterator
- **const_iterator** is the type of any iterator, returned by a *const* container member function, that lets you access the controlled sequence.

reverse_iterator
- **reverse_iterator** is the type of any *reverse* iterator, returned by a *non-const* container member function, that lets you access the controlled sequence.

const_reverse_iterator
- **const_reverse_iterator** is the type of any *reverse* iterator, returned by a *const* container member function, that lets you access the controlled sequence

reference
- **reference** is the type of any reference, returned by a non-const container member function, that lets you access an element of the controlled sequence.

const_reference
- **const_reference** is the type of any reference, returned by a const container member function, that lets you access an element of the controlled sequence.

Several member functions return iterators. The member function **erase(iterator)**, for example, returns an iterator that designates the (remaining) element just beyond the one removed by the function. If you want to access the entire controlled sequence directly, however, you typically call:

begin
- **begin** to obtain an iterator that designates the beginning of the controlled sequence

end
- **end** to obtain an iterator that designates the end of the controlled sequence

rbegin
- **rbegin** to obtain a reverse iterator that designates the end of the controlled sequence

rend
- **rend** to obtain a reverse iterator that designates the beginning of the controlled sequence

erase clear Given an iterator, or a range of iterators, you can erase one or more elements of the controlled sequence by calling **erase**. Or you can remove all elements by calling **clear**.

size **empty** **max_size** You can determine the number of elements in the controlled sequence by calling the member function **size**. If you merely want to determine whether any elements are present, call **empty**. The member function **max_size** provides a hint as to how long a sequence the container can control. Note, however, that available memory might impose much more severe limits than the size reported by this function.

get_ allocator It is not likely that you will have occasion to work directly with the allocator object stored in a container object. But if you do, you can obtain a copy of the allocator object by calling the member function **get_allocator**.

swap Finally, each container template class supplies an override for the template function **swap**. (See Chapter 6: **<algorithm>**.) If the two container objects to be swapped store allocator objects that compare equal, the overriding function swaps the two controlled sequences just by manipulating the stored control information. That approach can be dramatically faster than the brute-force approach that must otherwise be employed.

Exercises

Exercise 9.1 Fill in the table below. The left column gives a formula for the time in microseconds to locate an element in a sequence containing *N* elements. Atop each of the remaining columns is a value for *N*. Express each time in a form that maximizes understanding (microseconds, seconds, years, or whatever):

Time Complexity	$N = 10^1$	$N = 10^5$	$N = 10^9$
N^2 µsec			
10 * N			
5 * log N			
300			

Exercise 9.2 For each of the container template classes defined in STL, describe a practical situation where using that class naturally models the existing data structure. (The operations you need to perform on the data structure are typically efficient for the container template class you choose.)

Exercise 9.3 Which of the container template classes defined in STL make sense as the underlying implementation of a stack?

Exercise 9.4 [**Harder**] How would you implement a template container class that can locate elements that match some predicate in essentially constant time, regardless of the length of the controlled sequence? What tradeoffs must you make to achieve such a goal?

Exercise 9.5 [**Very hard**] How would you implement a template container class that can both locate elements that match some predicate and insert new elements adjacent to them in essentially constant time?

Chapter 10: <vector>

Background

<vector>

vector

The header <vector> defines just the template class **vector**, which is a container that stores its controlled sequence as an array of contiguous elements. Thus, this particular container stores no additional pointers per element. You can access element number **i** in container **v**, by writing **v[i]**, in constant time. On the other hand, the container imposes no order on the controlled sequence. You can locate an element with a given value only by scanning the controlled sequence from beginning to end. Such an operation requires *linear time* — time proportional to *N*, the number of elements in the sequence. Prepending or inserting an element typically requires that the container copy down all the elements, or even allocate a whole new array and then copy over existing elements to their new positions in the array. Such reallocations can be performed in linear time, at least with a bit of cleverness that we will describe later on in this chapter.

Template class **vector** does provide for an important ad hoc optimization, however. It lets you *reserve* storage for an array larger than necessary for the current sequence length. Given reserve storage, the container can avoid the need to reallocate storage when inserting new elements. It simply rearranges the elements within the existing array. Similarly, the container can erase elements by rearrangement, making the reserve storage larger. All these operations still take time proportional to *N*, but they are nevertheless faster.

Even more important, reserve storage lets the container *append* a new element, or erase the last element, in constant time. That means that template class **vector** can serve as an acceptable way to implement a stack. You have the added burden of guessing how much additional storage to reserve. If you guess wrong, the cost of extending the controlled sequence rises dramatically. Nevertheless, a vector can sometimes make a reasonable stack.

basic_string

Template class **vector** warrants comparison with one other creature. The Standard C++ library also defines template class **basic_string**, as a generalization of numerous string classes from past practice. Template class **basic_string** was not part of STL as originally defined by Hewlett-Packard. It has nevertheless accreted, during the standardization process, all the properties required of an STL container. (We do not describe `basic_string` in this book.)

One template parameter of class `basic_string` is the element type — it need not always be type `char`. And a `basic_string` object is pretty much obliged to store its controlled sequence as an array. So the question arises, when does it make sense to use `basic_string` and when `vector`? Here are a few guidelines:

- **PODS** A `basic_string` element cannot have a nontrivial constructor or destructor. It must, in fact, be the kind of type you can declare in a C program. You can assign an object of such a type by performing a bitwise copy. (The formal name for this category of type is POD, for "plain old data structure.") A `vector` element, by contrast, is any type that has some kind of constructor, a fairly conventional assignment operator, and a destructor.
- **char_traits** Template class `basic_string` requires a "traits" class as another of its template parameters. Traits specify critical aspects of how to move and compare sequences of elements, and how to read and write files of elements. The Standard C++ library supplies template class `char_traits`, with specializations for the element types `char` and `wchar_t`. If none of these meet your needs, you can and must define your own. A `vector` element, by contrast, makes no use of such traits.
- **null termination** A `basic_string` object can deliver up a null-terminated sequence. A `vector` object just deals with the sequence of elements you store in it.
- **copy on write** A `basic_string` object can use copy-on-write semantics, which can improve performance considerably for certain patterns of usage. Template class `vector` cannot, in general, perform such an optimization.

Template class `basic_string` also defines oodles of additional member functions that do string-ish things to the controlled sequence. You could, of course, avoid using these additional member functions and just do vector-ish things. Usually, one of the considerations listed above dictates which of the two containers makes more sense in a given application.

`string` `wstring` So in summary, you use template class `vector` when you need fast random access to elements of the controlled sequence. Growing a `vector` object is relatively expensive, unless you can anticipate growth well enough to reserve spare capacity in advance. For elements of type `char` or `wchar_t`, it might make more sense to use template class `basic_string` instead. For your convenience, the Standard C++ library defines `string` as a synonym for `basic_string<char, char_traits<char> >`, and `wstring` as a synonym for `basic_string<wchar_t, char_traits<wchar_t> >`.

`vector<bool>` **`flip`** **`swap`** The header `<vector>` also supplies a partial specialization of template class `vector`, to control a sequence of elements of type `bool`. It does so partly in the interest of storage economy. The specialization stores eight (or more) elements per byte of array storage, instead of requiring one (or more) bytes per element. It also defines the member function `flip`, for inverting an element, and **swap**, for swapping two elements. Thus, you can declare and manipulate large boolean vectors with reasonable storage efficiency.

Functional Description

```
namespace std {
template<class T, class A>
    class vector;
template<class A>
    class vector<bool>;

        // TEMPLATE FUNCTIONS
template<class T, class A>
    bool operator==(
        const vector<T, A>& lhs,
        const vector<T, A>& rhs);
template<class T, class A>
    bool operator!=(
        const vector<T, A>& lhs,
        const vector<T, A>& rhs);
template<class T, class A>
    bool operator<(
        const vector<T, A>& lhs,
        const vector<T, A>& rhs);
template<class T, class A>
    bool operator>(
        const vector<T, A>& lhs,
        const vector<T, A>& rhs);
template<class T, class A>
    bool operator<=(
        const vector<T, A>& lhs,
        const vector<T, A>& rhs);
template<class T, class A>
    bool operator>=(
        const vector<T, A>& lhs,
        const vector<T, A>& rhs);
template<class T, class A>
    void swap(
        vector<T, A>& lhs,
        vector<T, A>& rhs);
    };
```

Include the STL standard header `<vector>` to define the container template class `vector` and several supporting templates.

▫ **operator!=**

```
template<class T, class A>
    bool operator!=(
        const vector <T, A>& lhs,
        const vector <T, A>& rhs);
```

The template function returns `!(lhs == rhs)`.

▫ **operator==**

```
template<class T, class A>
    bool operator==(
        const vector <T, A>& lhs,
        const vector <T, A>& rhs);
```

The template function overloads `operator==` to compare two objects of template class `vector`. The function returns `lhs.size() == rhs.size() && equal(lhs. begin(), lhs. end(), rhs.begin())`.

- **operator<**

```
template<class T, class A>
    bool operator<(
        const vector <T, A>& lhs,
        const vector <T, A>& rhs);
```

The template function overloads `operator<` to compare two objects of template class `vector`. The function returns `lexicographical_compare(lhs. begin(), lhs. end(), rhs.begin(), rhs.end())`.

- **operator<=**

```
template<class T, class A>
    bool operator<=(
        const vector <T, A>& lhs,
        const vector <T, A>& rhs);
```

The template function returns `!(rhs < lhs)`.

- **operator>**

```
template<class T, class A>
    bool operator>(
        const vector <T, A>& lhs,
        const vector <T, A>& rhs);
```

The template function returns `rhs < lhs`.

- **operator>=**

```
template<class T, class A>
    bool operator>=(
        const vector <T, A>& lhs,
        const vector <T, A>& rhs);
```

The template function returns `!(lhs < rhs)`.

- **swap**

```
template<class T, class A>
    void swap(
        vector <T, A>& lhs,
        vector <T, A>& rhs);
```

The template function executes `lhs.swap(rhs)`.

- **vector**

```
template<class T, class A = allocator<T> >
    class vector {
public:
    typedef A allocator_type;
    typedef typename A::pointer pointer;
    typedef typename A::const_pointer
        const_pointer;
    typedef typename A::reference reference;
    typedef typename A::const_reference
        const_reference;
    typedef typename A::value_type value_type;
    typedef T0 iterator;
```

```
typedef T1 const_iterator;
typedef T2 size_type;
typedef T3 difference_type;
typedef reverse_iterator<const_iterator>
    const_reverse_iterator;
typedef reverse_iterator<iterator>
    reverse_iterator;
vector();
explicit vector(const A& al);
explicit vector(size_type n);
vector(size_type n, const T& x);
vector(size_type n, const T& x,
    const A& al);
vector(const vector& x);
template<class InIt>
    vector(InIt first, InIt last);
template<class InIt>
    vector(InIt first, InIt last,
        const A& al);
void reserve(size_type n);
size_type capacity() const;
iterator begin();
const_iterator begin() const;
iterator end();
const_iterator end() const;
reverse_iterator rbegin();
const_reverse_iterator rbegin() const;
reverse_iterator rend();
const_reverse_iterator rend() const;
void resize(size_type n);
void resize(size_type n, T x);
size_type size() const;
size_type max_size() const;
bool empty() const;
A get_allocator() const;
reference at(size_type pos);
const_reference at(size_type pos) const;
reference operator[](size_type pos);
const_reference operator[](size_type pos);
reference front();
const_reference front() const;
reference back();
const_reference back() const;
void push_back(const T& x);
void pop_back();
template<class InIt>
    void assign(InIt first, InIt last);
void assign(size_type n, const T& x);
iterator insert(iterator it, const T& x);
void insert(iterator it, size_type n, const T& x);
template<class InIt>
    void insert(iterator it, InIt first, InIt last);
iterator erase(iterator it);
iterator erase(iterator first, iterator last);
void clear();
void swap(vector& x);
};
```

The template class describes an object that controls a varying-length sequence of elements of type **T**. The sequence is stored as an array of **T**.

The object allocates and frees storage for the sequence it controls through a stored allocator object of class **A**. Such an allocator object must have the same external interface as an object of template class **allocator**. Note that the stored allocator object is *not* copied when the container object is assigned.

Vector reallocation occurs when a member function must grow the controlled sequence beyond its current storage capacity. Other insertions and erasures may alter various storage addresses within the sequence. In all such cases, iterators or references that point at altered portions of the controlled sequence become *invalid*.

- **vector::allocator_type**

```
typedef A allocator_type;
```

The type is a synonym for the template parameter **A**.

- **vector::assign**

```
template<class InIt>
    void assign(InIt first, InIt last);
void assign(size_type n, const T& x);
```

If **InIt** is an integer type, the first member function behaves the same as **assign((size_type)first, (T)last)**. Otherwise, the first member function replaces the sequence controlled by ***this** with the sequence **[first, last)**, which must *not* overlap the initial controlled sequence. The second member function replaces the sequence controlled by ***this** with a repetition of **n** elements of value **x**.

- **vector::at**

```
const_reference at(size_type pos) const;
reference at(size_type pos);
```

The member function returns a reference to the element of the controlled sequence at position **pos**. If that position is invalid, the function throws an object of class **out_of_range**.

- **vector::back**

```
reference back();
const_reference back() const;
```

The member function returns a reference to the last element of the controlled sequence, which must be non-empty.

- **vector::begin**

```
const_iterator begin() const;
iterator begin();
```

The member function returns a random-access iterator that points at the first element of the sequence (or just beyond the end of an empty sequence).

- **vector::capacity**

```
size_type capacity() const;
```

The member function returns the storage currently allocated to hold the controlled sequence, a value at least as large as `size()`.

vector::clear

```
void clear();
```

The member function calls `erase( begin(), end())`.

vector::const_iterator

```
typedef T1 const_iterator;
```

The type describes an object that can serve as a constant random-access iterator for the controlled sequence. It is described here as a synonym for the implementation-defined type `T1`.

vector::const_pointer

```
typedef typename A::const_pointer
    const_pointer;
```

The type describes an object that can serve as a constant pointer to an element of the controlled sequence.

vector::const_reference

```
typedef typename A::const_reference
    const_reference;
```

The type describes an object that can serve as a constant reference to an element of the controlled sequence.

vector::const_reverse_iterator

```
typedef reverse_iterator<const_iterator>
    const_reverse_iterator;
```

The type describes an object that can serve as a constant reverse iterator for the controlled sequence.

vector::difference_type

```
typedef T3 difference_type;
```

The signed integer type describes an object that can represent the difference between the addresses of any two elements in the controlled sequence. It is described here as a synonym for the implementation-defined type `T3`.

vector::empty

```
bool empty() const;
```

The member function returns true for an empty controlled sequence.

vector::end

```
const_iterator end() const;
iterator end();
```

The member function returns a random-access iterator that points just beyond the end of the sequence.

▫ **vector::erase**

```
iterator erase(iterator it);
iterator erase(iterator first, iterator last);
```

The first member function removes the element of the controlled sequence pointed to by `it`. The second member function removes the elements of the controlled sequence in the range `[first, last)`. Both return an iterator that designates the first element remaining beyond any elements removed, or `end()` if no such element exists.

Erasing `N` elements causes `N` destructor calls and an assignment for each of the elements between the insertion point and the end of the sequence. No reallocation occurs, so iterators and references become invalid only from the first element erased through the end of the sequence.

The member functions never throw an exception.

▫ **vector::front**

```
reference front();
const_reference front() const;
```

The member function returns a reference to the first element of the controlled sequence, which must be non-empty.

▫ **vector::get_allocator**

```
A get_allocator() const;
```

The member function returns the stored allocator object.

▫ **vector::insert**

```
iterator insert(iterator it, const T& x);
void insert(iterator it, size_type n, const T& x);
template<class InIt>
    void insert(iterator it, InIt first, InIt last);
```

Each of the member functions inserts, before the element pointed to by `it` in the controlled sequence, a sequence specified by the remaining operands. The first member function inserts a single element with value `x` and returns an iterator that points to the newly inserted element. The second member function inserts a repetition of `n` elements of value `x`.

If `InIt` is an integer type, the last member function behaves the same as `insert(it, (size_type)first, (T)last)`. Otherwise, the last member function inserts the sequence `[first, last)`, which must *not* overlap the initial controlled sequence.

When inserting a single element, the number of element copies is linear in the number of elements between the insertion point and the end of the sequence. When inserting a single element at the end of the sequence, the amortized number of element copies is constant. When inserting `N` elements, the number of element copies is linear in `N` plus the number of elements between the insertion point and the end of the sequence — except when the template member is specialized for `InIt` an input iterator, which behaves like `N` single insertions.

If reallocation occurs, the capacity increases by some fixed factor (at least), and all iterators and references become invalid. If no reallocation occurs, iterators become invalid only from the point of insertion through the end of the sequence.

If an exception is thrown during the insertion of a single element, the container is left unaltered and the exception is rethrown. If an exception is thrown during the insertion of multiple elements, and the exception is not thrown while copying an element, the container is left unaltered and the exception is rethrown.

▫ **`vector::iterator`**

```
typedef T0 iterator;
```

The type describes an object that can serve as a random-access iterator for the controlled sequence. It is described here as a synonym for the implementation-defined type `T0`.

▫ **`vector::max_size`**

```
size_type max_size() const;
```

The member function returns the length of the longest sequence that the object can control.

▫ **`vector::operator[]`**

```
const_reference operator[](size_type pos) const;
reference operator[](size_type pos);
```

The member function returns a reference to the element of the controlled sequence at position `pos`. If that position is invalid, the behavior is undefined.

▫ **`vector::pointer`**

```
typedef typename A::pointer pointer;
```

The type describes an object that can serve as a pointer to an element of the controlled sequence.

▫ **`vector::pop_back`**

```
void pop_back();
```

The member function removes the last element of the controlled sequence, which must be non-empty.

The member function never throws an exception.

▫ **`vector::push_back`**

```
void push_back(const T& x);
```

The member function inserts an element with value `x` at the end of the controlled sequence.

If an exception is thrown, the container is left unaltered and the exception is rethrown.

vector::rbegin

```
const_reverse_iterator rbegin() const;
reverse_iterator rbegin();
```

The member function returns a reverse iterator that points just beyond the end of the controlled sequence. Hence, it designates the beginning of the reverse sequence.

vector::reference

```
typedef typename A::reference reference;
```

The type describes an object that can serve as a reference to an element of the controlled sequence.

vector::rend

```
const_reverse_iterator rend() const;
reverse_iterator rend();
```

The member function returns a reverse iterator that points at the first element of the sequence (or just beyond the end of an empty sequence). Hence, it designates the end of the reverse sequence.

vector::reserve

```
void reserve(size_type n);
```

If `n` is greater than `max_size()`, the member function reports a *length error* by throwing an object of class `length_error`. Otherwise, it ensures that `capacity()` henceforth returns at least `n`.

vector::resize

```
void resize(size_type n);
void resize(size_type n, T x);
```

The member functions both ensure that `size()` henceforth returns `n`. If it must make the controlled sequence longer, the first member function appends elements with value `T()`, while the second member function appends elements with value `x`. To make the controlled sequence shorter, both member functions call `erase(begin() + n, end())`.

vector::reverse_iterator

```
typedef reverse_iterator<iterator>
    reverse_iterator;
```

The type describes an object that can serve as a reverse iterator for the controlled sequence.

vector::size

```
size_type size() const;
```

The member function returns the length of the controlled sequence.

vector::size_type

```
typedef T2 size_type;
```

The unsigned integer type describes an object that can represent the length of any controlled sequence. It is described here as a synonym for the implementation-defined type `T2`.

vector::swap

```
void swap(vector& x);
```

The member function swaps the controlled sequences between `*this` and `x`. If `get_allocator() == x.get_allocator()`, it does so in constant time, it throws no exceptions, and it invalidates no references, pointers, or iterators that designate elements in the two controlled sequences. Otherwise, it performs a number of element assignments and constructor calls proportional to the number of elements in the two controlled sequences.

vector::value_type

```
typedef typename A::value_type value_type;
```

The type is a synonym for the template parameter `T`.

vector::vector

```
vector();
explicit vector(const A& al);
explicit vector(size_type n);
vector(size_type n, const T& x);
vector(size_type n, const T& x, const A& al);
vector(const vector& x);
template<class InIt>
    vector(InIt first, InIt last);
template<class InIt>
    vector(InIt first, InIt last, const A& al);
```

All constructors store an allocator object and initialize the controlled sequence. The allocator object is the argument `al`, if present. For the copy constructor, it is `x.get_allocator()`. Otherwise, it is `A()`.

The first two constructors specify an empty initial controlled sequence. The third constructor specifies a repetition of `n` elements of value `T()`. The fourth and fifth constructors specify a repetition of `n` elements of value `x`. The sixth constructor specifies a copy of the sequence controlled by `x`. If `InIt` is an integer type, the last two constructors specify a repetition of `(size_type)first` elements of value `(T)last`. Otherwise, the last two constructors specify the sequence `[first, last)`.

vector<bool, A>

```
template<class A>
    class vector<bool, A> {
public:
    class reference;
    typedef bool const_reference;
    typedef T0 iterator;
    typedef T1 const_iterator;
    typedef T4 pointer;
    typedef T5 const_pointer;
    void flip();
    static void swap(reference x, reference y);
```

```
// rest same as template class vector
    };
```

The class is a partial specialization of template class **vector** for elements of type **bool**. It alters the definition of four member types (to optimize the packing and unpacking of elements) and adds two member functions. Its behavior is otherwise the same as for template class **vector**.

▫ **vector<bool, A>::const_iterator**

```
typedef T1 const_iterator;
```

The type describes an object that can serve as a constant random-access iterator for the controlled sequence. It is described here as a synonym for the unspecified type **T1**.

▫ **vector<bool, A>::const_pointer**

```
typedef T5 const_pointer;
```

The type describes an object that can serve as a pointer to a constant element of the controlled sequence. It is described here as a synonym for the unspecified type **T5**.

▫ **vector<bool, A>::const_reference**

```
typedef bool const_reference;
```

The type describes an object that can serve as a constant reference to an element of the controlled sequence, in this case **bool**.

▫ **vector<bool, A>::flip**

```
void flip();
```

The member function inverts the values of all the members of the controlled sequence.

▫ **vector<bool, A>::iterator**

```
typedef T0 iterator;
```

The type describes an object that can serve as a random-access iterator for the controlled sequence. It is described here as a synonym for the unspecified type **T0**.

▫ **vector<bool, A>::pointer**

```
typedef T4 pointer;
```

The type describes an object that can serve as a pointer to an element of the controlled sequence. It is described here as a synonym for the unspecified type **T4**.

▫ **vector<bool, A>::reference**

```
class reference {
public:
    reference& operator=(const reference& x);
    reference& operator=(bool x);
    void flip();
    bool operator~() const;
    operator bool() const;
    };
```

The type describes an object that can serve as a reference to an element of the controlled sequence. Specifically, for two objects **x** and **y** of class **reference**:

- **bool(x)** yields the value of the element designated by **x**
- **~x** yields the inverted value of the element designated by **x**
- **x.flip()** inverts the value stored in **x**
- **y = bool(x)** and **y = x** both assign the value of the element designated by **x** to the element designated by **y**

It is unspecified how member functions of class **vector<bool>** construct objects of class **reference** that designate elements of a controlled sequence. The default constructor for class **reference** generates an object that refers to no such element.

▫ **vector<bool, A>::swap**

```
void swap(reference x, reference y);
```

The static member function swaps the members of the controlled sequences designated by **x** and **y**.

Using <vector>

vector Include the header **<vector>** to make use of template class **vector**. You can specialize **vector** to store elements of type **T** by writing a type definition such as:

```
typedef vector<T, allocator<T> > Mycont;
```

Using a default template argument, you can omit the second argument.

Template class **vector** supports all the common operations on containers, as we described in Chapter 9: Containers. (See the discussion beginning on page 248.) We summarize here only those properties peculiar to template class **vector**.

constructors To construct an object of class **vector<T, A>**, you can write any of:

- **vector()** to declare an empty vector.
- **vector(al)** as above, also storing the allocator object **al**.
- **vector(n)** to declare a vector with **n** elements, each constructed with the default constructor **T()**.
- **vector(n, val)** to declare a vector with **n** elements, each constructed with the copy constructor **T(val)**.
- **vector(n, val, al)** as above, also storing the allocator object **al**.
- **vector(first, last)** to declare a vector with initial elements copied from the sequence designated by **[first, last)**
- **vector(first, last, al)** as above, also storing the allocator object **al**.

If you have specialized the template class for an allocator of type allocator<T>, which is the customary (and default) thing to do, there is nothing to be gained by specifying an explicit allocator argument al. Such an argument matters only for some allocators that the program defines explicitly. (See the discussion of allocators in Chapter 4: <memory>.)

The following descriptions all assume that cont is an object of class vector<T, A>.

An object of class vector<T, A> can reserve storage for an array larger than is actually required at a given moment. The excess storage remains unconstructed until it becomes part of the active array:

- **reserve** To ensure that cont allocates storage for at least n elements, call cont.reserve(n)
- **capacity** To determine the maximum array size, measured in elements, that can be currently accommodated by cont, without the need to reallocate storage, call cont.capacity().

As we mentioned earlier in this chapter, having spare capacity is important if you want to use a vector<T, A> object as an efficient stack.

resize To change the length of the controlled sequence to n elements, call cont.resize(n). Excess elements are erased. If the sequence must be extended, elements with the value T() are inserted as needed at the end. You can also call cont.resize(n, val) to extend the sequence with elements that store the value val.

clear To remove all elements, call cont.clear(). Note, however, that neither clear nor resize promises to reduce the amount of reserved storage. (The result of calling cont.capacity() will not necessarily be smaller, as a result of calling cont.clear() or cont.resize(n), even if it could be.) This implementation does indeed release all reserved storage if you call cont.clear() or if you assign to it a vector with zero size, but that behavior is not required by the C++ Standard. The one sure way to release all reserved storage is with the peculiar idiom:

```
cont.swap(vector<T, A>());
```

This expression statement constructs a temporary empty vector and swaps its contents with cont. The temporary is destroyed at the end of the statement, taking any allocated storage obtained from cont along with it.

front To access the first element of the controlled sequence, call cont.front().
back To access the last element, call cont.back(). If cont is not a const object, the expression is an lvalue, so you can alter the value stored in the element by writing an expression such as cont.front() = T(). If the sequence is empty, however, these expressions have undefined behavior.

operator[] To access element i (counting from zero), write the expression cont[i].
at If cont is not a const object, the expression is an lvalue. cont[i] has undefined behavior if i is not in the half-open interval [0, cont.size()). You can also write cont.at(i) in place of cont[i]. For this call, however, if i is not a valid element number, member function at throws an object of class out_of_range.

push_back **pop_back** To append an object with stored value `x`, call `cont.push_back(x)`. To remove the last element, call `cont.pop_back()`. The sequence must be non-empty or the call has undefined bahavior. Template class `vector` does not define the member functions `push_front` and `pop_front`. They would require time proportional to the number of elements in the controlled sequence, given the constraints on how a vector can be implemented.

assign To replace the controlled sequence with the elements from a sequence designated by `[first, last)`, call `cont.assign(first, last)`. The sequence must not be part of the initial controlled sequence. To replace the controlled sequence with `n` copies of the value `x`, call `cont.assign(n, x)`.

insert To insert an element storing the value `x` before the element designated by the iterator `it`, call `cont.insert(it, x)`. The return value is an iterator designating the inserted element. To insert the elements of a sequence designated by `[first, last)` before the element designated by the iterator `it`, call `cont.insert(it, first, last)`. The sequence must not be any part of the initial controlled sequence. To insert `n` copies of the value `x`, call `cont.insert(it, n, x)`.

erase To erase the element designated by the iterator `it`, call `cont.erase(it)`. The return value is an iterator designating the element just beyond the erased element. To erase a range of elements designated by `[first, last)`, call `cont.erase(first, last)`.

vector <bool> The template `vector<bool, A>` is a partial specialization of template class `vector`. It ensures that any specialization you write for `vector` whose first parameter is `bool` invokes an alternate definition. You can write the specialization `vector<bool>`, which uses the default allocator. But the partial specialization also lets you specify an explicit allocator parameter `A`, if you can contrive a reason for doing so.

Bvector An implementation that does not support partial specialization faces several difficulties with `vector<bool>`, notational and otherwise. It is generally wise to avoid writing this form explicitly throughout a program — some implementations may supply an alternate name for `vector<bool>`. This implementation supplies the alias `Bvector`, for example, as an accommodation to older compilers. A robust practice is to introduce a single type definition such as:

```
typedef Bvector vector_bool;
```

and use `vector_bool` throughout the program instead of `vector<bool>` or any implementation-specific alias.

`vector<bool>` behaves much like any other specialization of `vector<T, A>`. It does not quite meet all the requirements of an STL container, but it comes close enough for most needs. It also has a couple of added features:

flip
- To flip (invert the value of) element `i`, write the expression `cont[i].flip()` or `cont.at(i).flip()`.
- To flip all the elements in the controlled sequence, write `cont.flip()`.

swap
- To swap the values stored in elements `i` and `j`, write `cont.swap(cont[i], cont[j])`.

vector<bool> also carries the implicit promise that it will store its controlled sequence with reasonable efficiency. A common implementation uses one bit per element instead of a separate byte (or even a 32-bit integer) per element.

Implementing <vector>

vector Figures 10.1 through 10.16 show the file vector. It defines template class vector, along with a few template functions that take vector operands. It also defines a partial specialization of vector for elements of type bool.

Vector_val The file begins by defining template class Vector_val. The specialization Vector_val<T, A> serves as a public base class for vector<T, A>. Its sole purpose in life is to store the allocator object Alval. As you may recall from earlier discussions, all controlled storage for *any* STL container is managed through an allocator object specified when you construct the container object. (See Chapter 4: <memory> for a discussion of allocators, and Chapter 9: Containers for a generic discussion of containers.) Allocators were originally invented to allocate and free arrays of objects of some element type T. They have since been made far more ambitious, and complex. But template class vector is content with the most direct use of allocator functionality:

- It allocates arrays by calling Alval.allocate and frees them by calling Alval.deallocate.
- It constructs elements by calling Alval.construct and destroys elements by calling Alval.destroy.
- It estimates the maximum permissible sequence length by calling Alval.max_size.

As you will see in subsequent chapters, it doesn't get any simpler than this.

zero-size allocators But even this simple usage presents an annoying implementation issue. Alval is typically an object with no member objects. (The C++ Standard doesn't promise any benefit to an allocator that stores member objects.) Unfortunately, such an object can seldom occupy zero space, despite its nonexistent contents. A vector<T, A> object can easily grow from 12 to 16 bytes, in a typical implementation, just because it is obliged to store an allocator object that itself requires no storage. For other STL containers, the percentage increase in size can be even greater.

Fortunately, the C++ Standard provides a way to avoid this regrettable overhead. It permits an implementation to reserve zero space in an object of a derived class if an object of the base class has no member objects. All you have to do is put the allocator object all by itself in a base object and a smart compiler is free to economize space. This implementation does so with all allocator objects, in the hope and expectation that such space optimizations will become commonplace. The resulting code is somewhat less readable, but the payoff is worth the extra complexity.

rebind Template class `Vector_val` has an added bit of complexity that is not strictly necessary. It defines the allocator type `Alty` by using the allocator template member class `rebind` to map the allocator template parameter `A`. Strictly speaking, `A` must already be an allocator for objects of type `T`, so the mapping should do nothing. For the containers presented in subsequent chapters, however, this is often *not* the case. They need allocators for types other than the element type presented as a template parameter. This implementation chooses to map *all* allocator template parameters in the interest of robustness. Even if you specialize a container with an allocator for objects of the improper type, all the containers will generate the appropriate allocator objects anyway.

The heart of a `vector` object is the data it stores to represent the controlled sequence. Besides the allocator object, a `vector` stores three pointers:

First
- `First` is a pointer to the first element of the allocated array that stores the controlled sequence. It is a null pointer if no array has been allocated.

Last
- `Last` is a pointer just past the last active element, if `First` is not null.

End
- `End` is a pointer just past the last element of the array, if `First` is not null.

An obvious invariant, then, is:

```
First == 0 || First <= Last && Last <= End
```

Buy **Clear** **Destroy** A handful of protected member functions perform a number of common operations. The call `Buy(N)` allocates an array of `N` elements and initializes the three pointer member objects appropriately. `Destroy(F, L)` destroys array elements in the range designated by `[F, L)`. (Note that the arguments are pointers, not iterators.) And `Clear()` destroys any allocated array and clears the three pointer member objects.

Ucopy **Ufill** An STL container is obliged to recover from an exception thrown by a programmer-supplied constructor. To this end, the Standard C++ library supplies three template functions that are prepared to deal with exceptions while initializing a sequence. They are `uninitialized_copy`, `uninitialized_fill`, and `uninitialized_fill_n`. (See Chapter 6: `<algorithm>`.) But none of these template functions quite meet the needs of template class `vector`, which is obliged to have an allocator object perform all object construction. It defines the protected template member function `Ucopy` and the protected member function `Ufill` to perform similar, but better tailored, services.

The call `Ucopy(F, L, Q)`, for example, initializes array elements beginning at `Q` (a pointer) with values from the sequence designated by `[F, L)` (arbitrary iterator types). And the call `Ufill(Q, N, X)` initializes `N` array elements beginning at `Q` (also a pointer) with the value `X`. In either case, the function catches a thrown exception, destroys any objects it has constructed, and rethrows the exception.

Xlen **Xran** Finally, the protected member function `Xlen` is the agent called upon to throw an object of class `length_error`, and `Xran` is the agent called upon to throw an object of class `out_of_range`. Each constructs an exception object with a message peculiar to template class `vector`.

Figure 10.1: `vector` **Part 1**

```
// vector standard header
#ifndef VECTOR_
#define VECTOR_
#include <memory>
#include <stdexcept>
namespace std {

          // TEMPLATE CLASS Vector_val
template<class T, class A>
     class Vector_val {
protected:
     Vector_val(A Al = A())
          : Alval(Al) {}
     typedef typename A::template
          rebind<T>::other Alty;
     Alty Alval;
     };

          // TEMPLATE CLASS vector
template<class T, class Ax = allocator<T> >
     class vector : public Vector_val<T, Ax> {
public:
     typedef vector<T, Ax> Myt;
     typedef Vector_val<T, Ax> Mybase;
     typedef typename Mybase::Alty A;
     typedef A allocator_type;
     typedef typename A::size_type size_type;
     typedef typename A::difference_type difference_type;
     typedef typename A::pointer Tptr;
     typedef typename A::const_pointer Ctptr;
     typedef Tptr pointer;
     typedef Ctptr const_pointer;
     typedef typename A::reference reference;
     typedef typename A::const_reference const_reference;
     typedef typename A::value_type value_type;
     typedef Ptrit<value_type, difference_type, Tptr,
          reference, Tptr, reference> iterator;
     typedef Ptrit<value_type, difference_type, Ctptr,
          const_reference, Tptr, reference> const_iterator;
     typedef std::reverse_iterator<iterator>
          reverse_iterator;
     typedef std::reverse_iterator<const_iterator>
          const_reverse_iterator;
     vector()
          : Mybase()
          {Buy(0); }
     explicit vector(const A& Al)
          : Mybase(Al)
          {Buy(0); }
     explicit vector(size_type N)
          : Mybase()
          {if (Buy(N))
               Last = Ufill(First, N, T()); }
     vector(size_type N, const T& V)
          : Mybase()
```

Figure 10.2: `vector` Part 2

```
        {if (Buy(N))
            Last = Ufill(First, N, V); }
    vector(size_type N, const T& V, const A& Al)
        : Mybase(Al)
        {if (Buy(N))
            Last = Ufill(First, N, V); }
    vector(const Myt& X)
        : Mybase(X.Alval)
        {if (Buy(X.size()))
            Last = Ucopy(X.begin(), X.end(), First); }
    template<class It>
        vector(It F, It L)
        : Mybase()
        {Construct(F, L, Iter_cat(F)); }
    template<class It>
        vector(It F, It L, const A& Al)
        : Mybase(Al)
        {Construct(F, L, Iter_cat(F)); }
    template<class It>
        void Construct(It F, It L, Int_iterator_tag)
        {size_type N = (size_type)F;
        if (Buy(N))
            Last = Ufill(First, N, (T)L); }
    template<class It>
        void Construct(It F, It L, input_iterator_tag)
        {Buy(0);
        insert(begin(), F, L); }
    ~vector()
        {Clear(); }
    Myt& operator=(const Myt& X)
        {if (this == &X)
            ;
        else if (X.size() == 0)
            {Clear(); }
        else if (X.size() <= size())
            {pointer Q = copy(X.begin(), X.end(), First);
            Destroy(Q, Last);
            Last = First + X.size(); }
        else if (X.size() <= capacity())
            {const_iterator S = X.begin() + size();
            copy(X.begin(), S, First);
            Last = Ucopy(S, X.end(), Last); }
        else
            {Destroy(First, Last);
            Mybase::Alval.deallocate(First,
                End - First);
            if (Buy(X.size()))
                Last = Ucopy(X.begin(), X.end(), First); }
        return (*this); }
    void reserve(size_type N)
        {if (max_size() < N)
            Xlen();
        else if (capacity() < N)
            {pointer Q = Mybase::Alval.allocate(N,
                (void *)0);
```

Figure 10.3: `vector` **Part 3**

```
            try {
            Ucopy(begin(), end(), Q);
            } catch (...) {
            Mybase::Alval.deallocate(Q, N);
            throw;
            }
            if (First != 0)
                {Destroy(First, Last);
                Mybase::Alval.deallocate(First,
                    End - First); }
            End = Q + N;
            Last = Q + size();
            First = Q; }}
    size_type capacity() const
        {return (First == 0 ? 0 : End - First); }
    iterator begin()
        {return (iterator(First)); }
    const_iterator begin() const
        {return (const_iterator(First)); }
    iterator end()
        {return (iterator(Last)); }
    const_iterator end() const
        {return (const_iterator(Last)); }
    reverse_iterator rbegin()
        {return (reverse_iterator(end())); }
    const_reverse_iterator rbegin() const
        {return (const_reverse_iterator(end())); }
    reverse_iterator rend()
        {return (reverse_iterator(begin())); }
    const_reverse_iterator rend() const
        {return (const_reverse_iterator(begin())); }
    void resize(size_type N)
        {resize(N, T()); }
    void resize(size_type N, T X)
        {if (size() < N)
            insert(end(), N - size(), X);
        else if (N < size())
            erase(begin() + N, end()); }
    size_type size() const
        {return (First == 0 ? 0 : Last - First); }
    size_type max_size() const
        {return (Mybase::Alval.max_size()); }
    bool empty() const
        {return (size() == 0); }
    A get_allocator() const
        {return (Mybase::Alval); }
    const_reference at(size_type P) const
        {if (size() <= P)
            Xran();
        return (*(begin() + P)); }
    reference at(size_type P)
        {if (size() <= P)
            Xran();
        return (*(begin() + P)); }
```

Figure 10.4: `vector` **Part 4**

```
const_reference operator[](size_type P) const
     {return (*(begin() + P)); }
reference operator[](size_type P)
     {return (*(begin() + P)); }
reference front()
     {return (*begin()); }
const_reference front() const
     {return (*begin()); }
reference back()
     {return (*(end() - 1)); }
const_reference back() const
     {return (*(end() - 1)); }
void push_back(const T& X)
     {insert(end(), X); }
void pop_back()
     {erase(end() - 1); }
template<class It>
     void assign(It F, It L)
     {Assign(F, L, Iter_cat(F)); }
template<class It>
     void Assign(It F, It L, Int_iterator_tag)
     {assign((size_type)F, (T)L); }
template<class It>
     void Assign(It F, It L, input_iterator_tag)
     {erase(begin(), end());
     insert(begin(), F, L); }
void assign(size_type N, const T& X)
     {T Tx = X;
     erase(begin(), end());
     insert(begin(), N, Tx); }
iterator insert(iterator P, const T& X)
     {size_type Off = size() == 0 ? 0 : P - begin();
     insert(P, (size_type)1, X);
     return (begin() + Off); }
void insert(iterator P, size_type M, const T& X)
     {T Tx = X;
     size_type N = capacity();
     if (M == 0)
          ;
     else if (max_size() - size() < M)
          Xlen();
     else if (N < size() + M)
          {N = max_size() - N / 2 < N
               ? 0 : N + N / 2;
          if (N < size() + M)
               N = size() + M;
          pointer S = Mybase::Alval.allocate(N,
               (void *)0);
          pointer Q;
          try {
          Q = Ucopy(begin(), P, S);
          Q = Ufill(Q, M, Tx);
          Ucopy(P, end(), Q);
          } catch (...) {
```

Figure 10.5: `vector` **Part 5**

```
                Destroy(S, Q);
                Mybase::Alval.deallocate(S, N);
                throw;
                }
                if (First != 0)
                     {Destroy(First, Last);
                     Mybase::Alval.deallocate(First,
                          End - First); }
                End = S + N;
                Last = S + size() + M;
                First = S; }
           else if ((size_type)(end() - P) < M)
                {Ucopy(P, end(), P.base() + M);
                try {
                Ufill(Last, M - (end() - P), Tx);
                } catch (...) {
                Destroy(P.base() + M, Last + M);
                throw;
                }
                Last += M;
                fill(P, end() - M, Tx); }
           else
                {iterator Oend = end();
                Last = Ucopy(Oend - M, Oend, Last);
                copy_backward(P, Oend - M, Oend);
                fill(P, P + M, Tx); }}
     template<class It>
          void insert(iterator P, It F, It L)
          {Insert(P, F, L, Iter_cat(F)); }
     template<class It>
          void Insert(iterator P, It F, It L,
               Int_iterator_tag)
          {insert(P, (size_type)F, (T)L); }
     template<class It>
          void Insert(iterator P, It F, It L,
               input_iterator_tag)
          {for (; F != L; ++F, ++P)
               P = insert(P, *F); }
     template<class It>
          void Insert(iterator P, It F, It L,
               forward_iterator_tag)
          {size_type M = 0;
          Distance(F, L, M);
          size_type N = capacity();
          if (M == 0)
               ;
          else if (max_size() - size() < M)
               Xlen();
          else if (N < size() + M)
               {N = max_size() - N / 2 < N
                    ? 0 : N + N / 2;
               if (N < size() + M)
                    N = size() + M;
               pointer S = Mybase::Alval.allocate(N,
                    (void *)0);
```

Figure 10.6: `vector` **Part 6**

```
                pointer Q;
                try {
                Q = Ucopy(begin(), P, S);
                Q = Ucopy(F, L, Q);
                Ucopy(P, end(), Q);
                } catch (...) {
                Destroy(S, Q);
                Mybase::Alval.deallocate(S, N);
                throw;
                }
                if (First != 0)
                     {Destroy(First, Last);
                     Mybase::Alval.deallocate(First,
                          End - First); }
                End = S + N;
                Last = S + size() + M;
                First = S; }
           else if ((size_type)(end() - P) < M)
                {Ucopy(P, end(), P.base() + M);
                It Mid = F;
                advance(Mid, end() - P);
                try {
                Ucopy(Mid, L, Last);
                } catch (...) {
                Destroy(P.base() + M, Last + M);
                throw;
                }
                Last += M;
                copy(F, Mid, P); }
           else if (0 < M)
                {iterator Oend = end();
                Last = Ucopy(Oend - M, Oend, Last);
                copy_backward(P, Oend - M, Oend);
                copy(F, L, P); }}
      iterator erase(iterator P)
           {copy(P + 1, end(), P);
           Destroy(Last - 1, Last);
           --Last;
           return (P); }
      iterator erase(iterator F, iterator L)
           {if (F != L)
                {pointer S = copy(L, end(), F.base());
                Destroy(S, Last);
                Last = S; }
           return (F); }
      void clear()
           {erase(begin(), end()); }
      bool Eq(const Myt& X) const
           {return (size() == X.size()
                && equal(begin(), end(), X.begin())); }
      bool Lt(const Myt& X) const
           {return (lexicographical_compare(begin(), end(),
                X.begin(), X.end())); }
```

Figure 10.7: `vector` **Part 7**

```
     void swap(Myt& X)
          {if (Mybase::Alval == X.Alval)
               {std::swap(First, X.First);
               std::swap(Last, X.Last);
               std::swap(End, X.End); }
          else
               {Myt Ts = *this; *this = X, X = Ts; }}
protected:
     bool Buy(size_type N)
          {First = 0, Last = 0, End = 0;
          if (N == 0)
               return (false);
          else
               {First = Mybase::Alval.allocate(N,
                    (void *)0);
               Last = First;
               End = First + N;
               return (true); }}
     void Clear()
          {if (First != 0)
               {Destroy(First, Last);
               Mybase::Alval.deallocate(First,
                    End - First); }
          First = 0, Last = 0, End = 0; }
     void Destroy(pointer F, pointer L)
          {for (; F != L; ++F)
               Mybase::Alval.destroy(F); }
     template<class It>
          pointer Ucopy(It F, It L, pointer Q)
          {pointer Qs = Q;
          try {
          for (; F != L; ++Q, ++F)
               Mybase::Alval.construct(Q, *F);
          } catch (...) {
          Destroy(Qs, Q);
          throw;
          }
          return (Q); }
     pointer Ufill(pointer Q, size_type N, const T &X)
          {pointer Qs = Q;
          try {
          for (; 0 < N; --N, ++Q)
               Mybase::Alval.construct(Q, X);
          } catch (...) {
          Destroy(Qs, Q);
          throw;
          }
          return (Q); }
     void Xlen() const
          {throw length_error("vector<T> too long"); }
     void Xran() const
          {throw out_of_range("vector<T> subscript"); }
     pointer First, Last, End;
     };
```

Figure 10.8: `vector` **Part 8**

```
          // vector TEMPLATE FUNCTIONS
template<class T, class A> inline
     bool operator==(const vector<T, A>& X,
          const vector<T, A>& Y)
     {return (X.Eq(Y)); }
template<class T, class A> inline
     bool operator!=(const vector<T, A>& X,
          const vector<T, A>& Y)
     {return (!(X == Y)); }
template<class T, class A> inline
     bool operator<(const vector<T, A>& X,
          const vector<T, A>& Y)
     {return (X.Lt(Y)); }
template<class T, class A> inline
     bool operator>(const vector<T, A>& X,
          const vector<T, A>& Y)
     {return (Y < X); }
template<class T, class A> inline
     bool operator<=(const vector<T, A>& X,
          const vector<T, A>& Y)
     {return (!(Y < X)); }
template<class T, class A> inline
     bool operator>=(const vector<T, A>& X,
          const vector<T, A>& Y)
     {return (!(X < Y)); }
template<class T, class A> inline
     void swap(vector<T, A>& X, vector<T, A>& Y)
     {X.swap(Y); }

          // CLASS vector<bool, allocator>
typedef unsigned int Vbase;
const int VBITS = 8 * sizeof (Vbase);             // min CHAR_BITS

template<class A>
     class vector<bool, A> {
public:
     typedef typename A::size_type size_type;
     typedef typename A::difference_type Dift;
     typedef std::vector<Vbase,
          typename A::template rebind<Vbase>::other>
               Vbtype;
     typedef std::vector<bool, A> Myt;
     typedef Dift difference_type;
     typedef bool T;
     typedef A allocator_type;
          // CLASS reference
     class reference {
     public:
          reference()
               : Mask(0), Ptr(0) {}
          reference(size_t Off, Vbase *P)
               : Mask((Vbase)1 << Off), Ptr(P) {}
          reference& operator=(const reference& X)
               {return (*this = bool(X)); }
          reference& operator=(bool V)
```

Figure 10.9: `vector` **Part 9**

```
            {if (V)
                *Ptr |= Mask;
            else
                *Ptr &= ~Mask;
            return (*this); }
        void flip()
            {*Ptr ^= Mask; }
        bool operator~() const
            {return (!bool(*this)); }
        operator bool() const
            {return ((*Ptr & Mask) != 0); }
    protected:
        Vbase Mask, *Ptr;
        };
    typedef reference Reft;
    typedef bool const_reference;
    typedef bool value_type;

        // CLASS iterator
    class const_iterator;
    class iterator
        : public Ranit<bool, Dift, Reft *, Reft> {
    public:
        typedef Ranit<bool, Dift, Reft *, Reft> Mybase;
        typedef typename Mybase::iterator_category
            iterator_category;
        typedef typename Mybase::value_type value_type;
        typedef typename Mybase::difference_type
            difference_type;
        typedef typename Mybase::pointer pointer;
        typedef typename Mybase::reference reference;
        friend class const_iterator;
        iterator()
            : Off(0), Ptr(0) {}
        iterator(size_t O, typename Vbtype::iterator P)
            : Off(O), Ptr(P.base()) {}
        reference operator*() const
            {return (Reft(Off, Ptr)); }
        iterator& operator++()
            {Inc();
            return (*this); }
        iterator operator++(int)
            {iterator Tmp = *this;
            Inc();
            return (Tmp); }
        iterator& operator--()
            {Dec();
            return (*this); }
        iterator operator--(int)
            {iterator Tmp = *this;
            Dec();
            return (Tmp); }
        iterator& operator+=(difference_type N)
            {Off += N;
            Ptr += Off / VBITS;
```

Figure 10.10: `vector` **Part 10**

```
            Off %= VBITS;
            return (*this); }
        iterator& operator-=(difference_type N)
            {return (*this += -N); }
        iterator operator+(difference_type N) const
            {iterator Tmp = *this;
            return (Tmp += N); }
        iterator operator-(difference_type N) const
            {iterator Tmp = *this;
            return (Tmp -= N); }
        difference_type operator-(const iterator X) const
            {return (VBITS * (Ptr - X.Ptr)
                + (difference_type)Off
                - (difference_type)X.Off); }
        reference operator[](difference_type N) const
            {return (*(*this + N)); }
        bool operator==(const iterator& X) const
            {return (Ptr == X.Ptr && Off == X.Off); }
        bool operator!=(const iterator& X) const
            {return (!(*this == X)); }
        bool operator<(const iterator& X) const
            {return (Ptr < X.Ptr
                || Ptr == X.Ptr && Off < X.Off); }
        bool operator>(const iterator& X) const
            {return (X < *this); }
        bool operator<=(const iterator& X) const
            {return (!(X < *this)); }
        bool operator>=(const iterator& X) const
            {return (!(*this < X)); }
    protected:
        void Dec()
            {if (Off != 0)
                --Off;
            else
                Off = VBITS - 1, --Ptr; }
        void Inc()
            {if (Off < VBITS - 1)
                ++Off;
            else
                Off = 0, ++Ptr; }
        size_t Off;
        Vbase *Ptr;
        };
    typedef iterator Myit;

        // CLASS const_iterator
    class const_iterator : public Ranit<bool, Dift,
        const_reference *, const_reference> {
    public:
        typedef Ranit<bool, Dift,
            const_reference *, const_reference> Mybase;
        typedef typename Mybase::iterator_category
            iterator_category;
        typedef typename Mybase::value_type value_type;
```

Figure 10.11: `vector` **Part 11**

```
typedef typename Mybase::difference_type
     difference_type;
typedef typename Mybase::pointer pointer;
typedef typename Mybase::reference reference;
const_iterator()
     : Off(0), Ptr(0) {}
const_iterator(size_t O,
     typename Vbtype::const_iterator P)
     : Off(O), Ptr(P.base()) {}
const_iterator(const Myit& X)
     : Off(X.Off), Ptr(X.Ptr) {}
const_reference operator*() const
     {return (Reft(Off, (Vbase *)Ptr)); }
const_iterator& operator++()
     {Inc();
     return (*this); }
const_iterator operator++(int)
     {const_iterator Tmp = *this;
     Inc();
     return (Tmp); }
const_iterator& operator--()
     {Dec();
     return (*this); }
const_iterator operator--(int)
     {const_iterator Tmp = *this;
     Dec();
     return (Tmp); }
const_iterator& operator+=(difference_type N)
     {Off += N;
     Ptr += Off / VBITS;
     Off %= VBITS;
     return (*this); }
const_iterator& operator-=(difference_type N)
     {return (*this += -N); }
const_iterator operator+(difference_type N) const
     {const_iterator Tmp = *this;
     return (Tmp += N); }
const_iterator operator-(difference_type N) const
     {const_iterator Tmp = *this;
     return (Tmp -= N); }
difference_type operator-(const const_iterator X) const
     {return (VBITS * (Ptr - X.Ptr)
          + (difference_type)Off
          - (difference_type)X.Off); }
const_reference operator[](difference_type N) const
     {return (*(*this + N)); }
bool operator==(const const_iterator& X) const
     {return (Ptr == X.Ptr && Off == X.Off); }
bool operator!=(const const_iterator& X) const
     {return (!(*this == X)); }
bool operator<(const const_iterator& X) const
     {return (Ptr < X.Ptr
          || Ptr == X.Ptr && Off < X.Off); }
bool operator>(const const_iterator& X) const
     {return (X < *this); }
```

Figure 10.12: `vector` Part 12

```
        bool operator<=(const const_iterator& X) const
            {return (!(X < *this)); }
        bool operator>=(const const_iterator& X) const
            {return (!(*this < X)); }
    protected:
        void Dec()
            {if (Off != 0)
                --Off;
            else
                Off = VBITS - 1, --Ptr; }
        void Inc()
            {if (Off < VBITS - 1)
                ++Off;
            else
                Off = 0, ++Ptr; }
        size_t Off;
        const Vbase *Ptr;
        };

    typedef iterator pointer;
    typedef const_iterator const_pointer;
    typedef std::reverse_iterator<iterator>
        reverse_iterator;
    typedef std::reverse_iterator<const_iterator>
        const_reverse_iterator;

    vector()
        : Size(0), Vec() {}
    explicit vector(const A& Al)
        : Size(0), Vec(Al) {}
    explicit vector(size_type N, const bool V = false)
        : Size(0), Vec(Nw(N), V ? -1 : 0)
        {Trim(N); }
    vector(size_type N, const bool V, const A& Al)
        : Size(0), Vec(Nw(N), V ? -1 : 0, Al)
        {Trim(N); }
    template<class It>
        vector(It F, It L)
        : Size(0), Vec()
        {BConstruct(F, L, Iter_cat(F)); }
    template<class It>
        vector(It F, It L, const A& Al)
        : Size(0), Vec(Al)
        {BConstruct(F, L, Iter_cat(F)); }
    template<class It>
        void BConstruct(It F, It L, Int_iterator_tag)
        {size_type N = (size_type)F;
        Vec.assign(N, (T)L ? -1 : 0);
        Trim(N); }
    template<class It>
        void BConstruct(It F, It L, input_iterator_tag)
        {insert(begin(), F, L); }
    ~vector()
        {Size = 0; }
```

Figure 10.13: `vector` **Part 13**

```
void reserve(size_type N)
     {Vec.reserve(Nw(N)); }
size_type capacity() const
     {return (Vec.capacity() * VBITS); }
iterator begin()
     {return (iterator(0, Vec.begin())); }
const_iterator begin() const
     {return (const_iterator(0, Vec.begin())); }
iterator end()
     {iterator Tmp = begin();
     if (0 < Size)
          Tmp += Size;
     return (Tmp); }
const_iterator end() const
     {const_iterator Tmp = begin();
     if (0 < Size)
          Tmp += Size;
     return (Tmp); }
reverse_iterator rbegin()
     {return (reverse_iterator(end())); }
const_reverse_iterator rbegin() const
     {return (const_reverse_iterator(end())); }
reverse_iterator rend()
     {return (reverse_iterator(begin())); }
const_reverse_iterator rend() const
     {return (const_reverse_iterator(begin())); }
void resize(size_type N, bool X = false)
     {if (size() < N)
          insert(end(), N - size(), X);
     else if (N < size())
          erase(begin() + N, end()); }
size_type size() const
     {return (Size); }
size_type max_size() const
     {return (Vec.max_size() * VBITS); }
bool empty() const
     {return (size() == 0); }
A get_allocator() const
     {return (Vec.get_allocator()); }
const_reference at(size_type P) const
     {if (size() <= P)
          Xran();
     return (*(begin() + P)); }
reference at(size_type P)
     {if (size() <= P)
          Xran();
     return (*(begin() + P)); }
const_reference operator[](size_type P) const
     {return (*(begin() + P)); }
reference operator[](size_type P)
     {return (*(begin() + P)); }
reference front()
     {return (*begin()); }
const_reference front() const
     {return (*begin()); }
```

Figure 10.14: vector Part 14

```
reference back()
     {return (*(end() - 1)); }
const_reference back() const
     {return (*(end() - 1)); }
void push_back(const bool X)
     {insert(end(), X); }
void pop_back()
     {erase(end() - 1); }
template<class It>
     void assign(It F, It L)
     {Assign(F, L, Iter_cat(F)); }
template<class It>
     void Assign(It F, It L, Int_iterator_tag)
     {assign((size_type)F, (T)L); }
template<class It>
     void Assign(It F, It L, input_iterator_tag)
     {erase(begin(), end());
     insert(begin(), F, L); }
void assign(size_type N, const T& X)
     {T Tx = X;
     erase(begin(), end());
     insert(begin(), N, Tx); }
iterator insert(iterator P, const bool X)
     {size_type Off = P - begin();
     insert(P, (size_type)1, X);
     return (begin() + Off); }
void insert(iterator P, size_type M, const bool X)
     {if (M == 0)
          ;
     else if (max_size() - size() < M)
          Xlen();
     else
          {if (size() + M <= capacity())
               ;
          else if (size() == 0)
               {Vec.resize(Nw(size() + M), 0);
               P = begin(); }
          else
               {size_type Off = P - begin();
               Vec.resize(Nw(size() + M), 0);
               P = begin() + Off;
               copy_backward(P, end(), end() + M); }
          fill(P, P + M, X);
          Size += M; }}
template<class It>
     void insert(iterator P, It F, It L)
     {Insert(P, F, L, Iter_cat(F)); }
template<class It>
     void Insert(iterator P, It F, It L,
          Int_iterator_tag)
     {insert(P, (size_type)F, (T)L); }
template<class It>
     void Insert(iterator P, It F, It L,
          input_iterator_tag)
     {size_type Off = P - begin();
```

Figure 10.15: `vector` **Part 15**

```
        for (; F != L; ++F, ++Off)
            insert(begin() + Off, *F); }
    template<class It>
        void Insert(iterator P, It F, It L,
            forward_iterator_tag)
        {size_type M = 0;
        Distance(F, L, M);
        if (M == 0)
            ;
        else if (max_size() - size() < M)
            Xlen();
        else
            {if (size() + M <= capacity())
                ;
            else if (size() == 0)
                {Vec.resize(Nw(size() + M), 0);
                P = begin(); }
            else
                {size_type Off = P - begin();
                Vec.resize(Nw(size() + M), 0);
                P = begin() + Off;
                copy_backward(P, end(), end() + M); }
            copy(F, L, P);
            Size += M; }}
    iterator erase(iterator P)
        {copy(P + 1, end(), P);
        Trim(Size - 1);
        return (P); }
    iterator erase(iterator F, iterator L)
        {iterator S = copy(L, end(), F);
        Trim(S - begin());
        return (F); }
    void clear()
        {erase(begin(), end()); }
    void flip()
        {for (typename Vbtype::iterator S = Vec.begin();
            S != Vec.end(); ++S)
            *S = ~*S;
        Trim(Size); }
    bool Eq(const Myt& X) const
        {return (Size == X.Size && Vec == X.Vec); }
    bool Lt(const Myt& X) const
        {return (lexicographical_compare(begin(), end(),
            X.begin(), X.end())); }
    void swap(Myt& X)
        {std::swap(Size, X.Size);
        Vec.swap(X.Vec); }
    static void swap(reference X, reference Y)
        {bool V = X;
        X = Y;
        Y = V; }
protected:
    static size_type Nw(size_type N)
        {return ((N + VBITS - 1) / VBITS); }
```

Figure 10.16: vector Part 16

```
    void Trim(size_type N)
        {if (size() < N && max_size() <= N)
            Xlen();
        size_type M = Nw(N);
        if (M < Vec.size())
            Vec.erase(Vec.begin() + M, Vec.end());
        Size = N;
        N %= VBITS;
        if (0 < N)
            Vec[M - 1] &= ((Vbase)1 << N) - 1; }
    void Xlen() const
        {throw out_of_range("vector<bool> too long"); }
    void Xran() const
        {throw out_of_range("vector<bool> subscript"); }
    size_type Size;
    Vbtype Vec;
    };

typedef vector<bool, allocator<bool> > Bvector;
} /* namespace std */
#endif /* VECTOR_ */
```

The template member function:

```
template<class It>
    void insert(iterator P, It F, It L);
```

Int_ iterator_ tag

makes use of an interesting device. (So do two template constructors and another template member function, but **insert** is most illustrative.) It employs different strategies depending on whether **It** is an input iterator or a forward iterator (or even stronger). The technique for choosing the most appropriate strategy is one we've seen several times in earlier chapters. The basic trick is to choose among overloads of the template member function **Insert** based on the return type of the template function **Iter_cat(F)**. But here is a new wrinkle. One of the overloads is selected when **Iter_cat(F)** returns an object of type **Int_iterator_tag**:

```
template<class It>
    void Insert(iterator P, It F, It L,
        Int_iterator_tag)
    {insert(P, (size_type)F, (T)L); }
```

This template member function puts quite a different spin on the interpretation of the two "iterators," **F** and **L**. It treats the first as a repetition count and the second as the value to store in an element, using the template member function:

```
iterator insert(iterator P, const T& X);
```

Why all this rewriting? The C++ Standard recognizes that the template version of **insert** can be mistakenly selected at times. Consider an object **cont** of type **vector<size_t>**. The call **cont.insert(begin(), 3, 0)** is clearly intended to insert three elements with value zero at the beginning of the controlled sequence. Nevertheless, it looks for all the world like a call with two iterators of type **int**. All the C++ Standard says is that an implementation must "do the right thing." It does not specify how.

This implementation introduces a bogus iterator category that subsumes all integers (which can never be true iterators). It defines the corresponding iterator tag **Int_iterator_tag**, and overloads **Iter_cat** to return an object of this type for all of the integer types. (See Chapter 3: **<iterator>**.) It then relies on the usual tag overloading (see page 82) to discriminate the case of integer arguments from true iterators.

insert Two versions of member function **insert** (one is a template) allocate a new array if the existing array lacks the capacity to store the resulting controlled sequence. The standard technique is to double the array size each time it must grow. The total number of constructor calls — for initial element creation plus subsequent copying between arrays — remains linear in the total length of the controlled sequence. Allocations presumably have a fixed cost independent of the size of the storage requested; and they increase logarithmically with the total length. Thus, the amortized cost of adding each element can be kept essentially constant, as required by the C++ Standard. The price you pay is less efficient utilization of storage. Spare capacity fluctuates between zero and 50 per cent of the total array size. So on average, a growing controlled sequence has one unoccupied array element for every three active elements.

The two versions of **insert** use a modified version of this strategy. Both allocate a new array that is at least 50 per cent larger than the existing array size, wherever possible. This approach yields the same asymptotic time complexity for adding an element, performs somewhat more allocations, and makes better use of storage.

vector<bool> The template partial specialization **vector<bool>** is at least as large as template class **vector**. The two must provide essentially the same services, but **vector<bool>** has additional concerns. It must deal with elements that are individual bits, a feat that does not come naturally to a C or C++ program.

Vbase VBITS The trick here is to implement **vector<bool>** in terms of **vector<Vbase>**, where **Vbase** is an unsigned integer type that the implementation manipulates reasonably efficiently. The type chosen here is **unsigned int**. Assuming at least eight bits per byte (a fairly safe bet, courtesy of the C Standard), the code determines **VBITS**, the minimum number of bits in an object of type **Vbase**. The **vector<bool>** object can thus store **VBITS** Boolean elements per element of the underlying sequence.

reference iterator The real trickery comes in defining the member classes **reference** and **iterator**. A **reference** object must be able to pack and unpack bits from the underlying sequence on demand. An **iterator** object must be able to generate a succession of references. Note that these iterators, and class **vector<bool>** itself, define the added member function **flip**, which flips (inverts the truth value of) one or all of the bits in question. Class **vector<bool>** also overloads **swap** to swap two bits in the controlled sequence.

Testing <vector>

tvector.c Figures 10.17 through 10.19 shows the file **tvector.c**. It is one of three test programs that look very much alike. See the file **tlist.c**, beginning on page 318, and the file **tdeque.c**, beginning on page 350. To ease comparison of these three test programs, we have simply commented out any tests inappropriate for a given container, without removing the unused code.

The test program performs a simple test that each of the member functions and types is present and behaves as intended, for one specialization of template class **vector**. It also tests the member functions peculiar to class **vector<bool>**. If all goes well, the program prints:

```
SUCCESS testing <vector>
```

and takes a normal exit.

Figure 10.17: tvector.c Part 1

```
// test <vector>
#include <assert.h>
#include <iostream>
#include <vector>
using namespace std;

        // TEST <vector>
int main()
        {typedef allocator<char> Myal;

        // TEST vector
        typedef vector<char, Myal> Mycont;
        char ch, carr[] = "abc";
        Mycont::allocator_type *p_alloc = (Myal *)0;
        Mycont::pointer p_ptr = (char *)0;
        Mycont::const_pointer p_cptr = (const char *)0;
        Mycont::reference p_ref = ch;
        Mycont::const_reference p_cref = (const char&)ch;
        Mycont::value_type *p_val = (char *)0;
        Mycont::size_type *p_size = (size_t *)0;
        Mycont::difference_type *p_diff = (ptrdiff_t *)0;

        Mycont v0;
        Myal al = v0.get_allocator();
        Mycont v0a(al);
        assert(v0.empty() && v0.size() == 0);
        assert(v0a.size() == 0 && v0a.get_allocator() == al);
        Mycont v1(5), v1a(6, 'x'), v1b(7, 'y', al);
        assert(v1.size() == 5 && v1.back() == '\0');
        assert(v1a.size() == 6 && v1a.back() == 'x');
        assert(v1b.size() == 7 && v1b.back() == 'y');
        Mycont v2(v1a);
        assert(v2.size() == 6 && v2.front() == 'x');
        Mycont v3(v1a.begin(), v1a.end());
        assert(v3.size() == 6 && v3.front() == 'x');
        const Mycont v4(v1a.begin(), v1a.end(), al);
```

Figure 10.18: tvector.c Part 2

```
    assert(v4.size() == 6 && v4.front() == 'x');
    v0 = v4;
    assert(v0.size() == 6 && v0.front() == 'x');
    assert(v0[0] == 'x' && v0.at(5) == 'x');

    v0.reserve(12);
    assert(12 <= v0.capacity());
    v0.resize(8);
    assert(v0.size() == 8 && v0.back() == '\0');
    v0.resize(10, 'z');
    assert(v0.size() == 10 && v0.back() == 'z');
    assert(v0.size() <= v0.max_size());

    Mycont::iterator p_it(v0.begin());
    Mycont::const_iterator p_cit(v4.begin());
    Mycont::reverse_iterator p_rit(v0.rbegin());
    Mycont::const_reverse_iterator p_crit(v4.rbegin());
    assert(*p_it == 'x' && *--(p_it = v0.end()) == 'z');
    assert(*p_cit == 'x' && *--(p_cit = v4.end()) == 'x');
    assert(*p_rit == 'z'
        && *--(p_rit = v0.rend()) == 'x');
    assert(*p_crit == 'x'
        && *--(p_crit = v4.rend()) == 'x');

    assert(v0.front() == 'x' && v4.front() == 'x');
//  v0.push_front('a');
//  assert(v0.front() == 'a');
//  v0.pop_front();
//  assert(v0.front() == 'x' && v4.front() == 'x');

    v0.push_back('a');
    assert(v0.back() == 'a');
    v0.pop_back();
    assert(v0.back() == 'z' && v4.back() == 'x');

    v0.assign(v4.begin(), v4.end());
    assert(v0.size() == v4.size()
        && v0.front() == v4.front());
    v0.assign(4, 'w');
    assert(v0.size() == 4 && v0.front() == 'w');
    assert(*v0.insert(v0.begin(), 'a') == 'a');
    assert(v0.front() == 'a'
        && *++v0.begin() == 'w');
    v0.insert(v0.begin(), 2, 'b');
    assert(v0.front() == 'b'
        && *++v0.begin() == 'b'
        && *++ ++v0.begin() == 'a');
    v0.insert(v0.end(), v4.begin(), v4.end());
    assert(v0.back() == v4.back());
    v0.insert(v0.end(), carr, carr + 3);
    assert(v0.back() == 'c');
    v0.erase(v0.begin());
    assert(v0.front() == 'b' && *++v0.begin() == 'a');
    v0.erase(v0.begin(), ++v0.begin());
    assert(v0.front() == 'a');
```

Figure 10.19: tvector.c Part 3

```
    v0.clear();
    assert(v0.empty());
    v0.swap(v1);
    assert(!v0.empty() && v1.empty());
    swap(v0, v1);
    assert(v0.empty() && !v1.empty());
    assert(v1 == v1 && v0 < v1);
    assert(v0 != v1 && v1 > v0);
    assert(v0 <= v1 && v1 >= v0);

    // TEST vector<bool>
    typedef vector<bool, allocator<bool> > Bvector;
    Bvector bv(3);
    bv[0] = ~bv[1];
    bv.flip();
    assert(!bv[0] && bv[1] && bv[2]);
    Bvector::swap(bv[0], bv[1]);
    assert(bv[0] && !bv[1]);

    cout << "SUCCESS testing <vector>" << endl;
    return (0); }
```

Exercises

Exercise 10.1 Why can't an integer type serve as an iterator?

Exercise 10.2 How would you "do the right thing" and distinguish integer arguments from iterators on a call to a template function without making use of `Int_iterator_tag`?

Exercise 10.3 One way to grow the storage for a vector (which doesn't conform to the C++ Standard) is to allocate a new array one element larger each time the array has to grow. The existing array is copied over, then destroyed, and the added element is constructed at the end of the new array. Assuming elements are added one at a time, compute the number of allocations, constructor calls, and destructor calls to generate vectors with lengths 1, 10, 100, 1,000, and 1,000,000 elements. What does this tell you about the amortized time complexity of adding a single element to the vector?

Exercise 10.4 Another way to grow the storage for a vector (which does conform to the C++ Standard) is to allocate a new array with twice as many elements each time the array has to grow. Repeat the previous exercise for this strategy, also computing the average unused capacity as the vector grows.

Exercise 10.5 Still another way to grow the storage for a vector (which also conforms to the C++ Standard) is to allocate a new array half again as long (1.5 times larger) each time the array has to grow. Repeat the previous exercise for this strategy.

Exercise 10.6 Generalize what you've learned from the previous exercises to describe the tradeoff between time complexity, performance, and space utilization of different growth strategies.

Exercise 10.7 How much storage would be required for a Boolean vector with 10,000 elements if the partial specialization `vector<bool>` were not provided? Under what circumstances would you prefer the former representation over the latter?

Exercise 10.8 In what way does `vector<bool>` not meet the requirements of an STL container?

Exercise 10.9 **[Harder]** Determine a good rule for shrinking the storage used by template class `vector` to store its controlled sequence.

Exercise 10.10 **[Very hard]** How would you implement template class `vector` using noncontiguous storage for its controlled sequence, without compromising any of its performance requirements?

Chapter 11: <list>

Background

<list> **list** The header **<list>** defines just the template class **list**, which is a container that stores its controlled sequence of length **N** as a bidirectional linked list of **N** nodes, each of which stores a single element. The advantage of a linked list is its flexibility. You can insert and remove elements freely and easily within the list, just by rewriting the forward and backward links in nodes. You can even splice in whole sublists. The list nodes themselves don't move about in memory. As a consequence any iterators you maintain to designate individual nodes remain valid for the life of the node. Similarly, any pointers you maintain to the individual list element itself also remain valid for the life of the node in which the element resides.

The price you pay is sequential access to arbitrary elements in the sequence. To access element number **i**, for example, you have to chain from one node to another **i** times, beginning with a pointer to the head of the list stored in the container object. You can chain in either direction, but chain you must. So the mean time to locate an arbitrary element increases linearly with the total number of elements in the controlled sequence. Using STL terminology, template class **list** supports bidirectional iterators.

Table 11.1, on page 240, shows how template class **list** stacks up against the other STL containers. It is the clear winner for all operations that rearrange list elements (insertions, erasures, and replacements). It is the clear loser for all operations that locate arbitrary elements (searches and random access). It also requires a moderately hefty overhead of two pointers per element, the forward and backward links stored in each node.

splice **sort** **merge** Template class **list** defines several member functions that take advantage of its peculiar properties. For example, you can splice elements from one list into another, sort a list, or merge one ordered list into another. All these operations simply restitch links between list nodes. No copying occurs. The payoff can be significant for a list of elements that are expensive to copy — because they are large or have nontrivial copy semantics.

exception safety Template class **list** has an additional virtue. It alone of the template containers promises to behave predictably in the presence of exceptions thrown by programmer-supplied code. Other containers provide a weaker guarantee. (See Chapter 9: Containers.) For any container, an exception thrown during execution of a member function leaves the container in a consistent state, suitable for destruction; and the container does not lose track of allocated storage. But for many operations, particularly those that affect multiple elements, the exact state of the container is unspecified when the exception is rethrown. `list`, by contrast, guarantees for most member functions that any interrupted member function call leaves the container in its original state when it rethrows the exception.

So in summary, you use template class `list` when you need flexibility in rearranging sequences of elements, and in keeping track of individual elements by storing iterators that remain valid across rearrangements. You also use template class `list` when you need greater determinism in the presence of exceptions. On the other hand, locating arbitrary elements within a `list` object is relatively expensive, even if the list is kept in order, since you have to perform a linear search each time. Consider other containers if more rapid access is important.

Functional Description

```
namespace std {
template<class T, class A>
    class list;

        // TEMPLATE FUNCTIONS
template<class T, class A>
    bool operator==(
        const list<T, A>& lhs,
        const list<T, A>& rhs);
template<class T, class A>
    bool operator!=(
        const list<T, A>& lhs,
        const list<T, A>& rhs);
template<class T, class A>
    bool operator<(
        const list<T, A>& lhs,
        const list<T, A>& rhs);
template<class T, class A>
    bool operator>(
        const list<T, A>& lhs,
        const list<T, A>& rhs);
template<class T, class A>
    bool operator<=(
        const list<T, A>& lhs,
        const list<T, A>& rhs);
template<class T, class A>
    bool operator>=(
        const list<T, A>& lhs,
        const list<T, A>& rhs);
template<class T, class A>
    void swap(
        list<T, A>& lhs,
        list<T, A>& rhs);
    };
```

Include the STL standard header `<list>` to define the container template class `list` and several supporting templates.

▫ list

```
template<class T, class A = allocator<T> >
    class list {
public:
    typedef A allocator_type;
    typedef typename A::pointer pointer;
    typedef typename A::const_pointer
        const_pointer;
    typedef typename A::reference reference;
    typedef typename A::const_reference const_reference;
    typedef typename A::value_type value_type;
    typedef T0 iterator;
    typedef T1 const_iterator;
    typedef T2 size_type;
    typedef T3 difference_type;
    typedef reverse_iterator<const_iterator>
        const_reverse_iterator;
    typedef reverse_iterator<iterator>
        reverse_iterator;
    list();
    explicit list(const A& al);
    explicit list(size_type n);
    list(size_type n, const T& v);
    list(size_type n, const T& v, const A& al);
    list(const list& x);
    template<class InIt>
        list(InIt first, InIt last);
    template<class InIt>
        list(InIt first, InIt last, const A& al);
    iterator begin();
    const_iterator begin() const;
    iterator end();
    const_iterator end() const;
    reverse_iterator rbegin();
    const_reverse_iterator rbegin() const;
    reverse_iterator rend();
    const_reverse_iterator rend() const;
    void resize(size_type n);
    void resize(size_type n, T x);
    size_type size() const;
    size_type max_size() const;
    bool empty() const;
    A get_allocator() const;
    reference front();
    const_reference front() const;
    reference back();
    const_reference back() const;
    void push_front(const T& x);
    void pop_front();
    void push_back(const T& x);
    void pop_back();
    template<class InIt>
        void assign(InIt first, InIt last);
    void assign(size_type n, const T& x);
    iterator insert(iterator it, const T& x);
    void insert(iterator it, size_type n, const T& x);
    template<class InIt>
        void insert(iterator it, InIt first, InIt last);
    iterator erase(iterator it);
    iterator erase(iterator first, iterator last);
    void clear();
```

```
    void swap(list& x);
    void splice(iterator it, list& x);
    void splice(iterator it, list& x, iterator first);
    void splice(iterator it, list& x, iterator first,
        iterator last);
    void remove(const T& x);
    templace<class Pred>
        void remove_if(Pred pr);
    void unique();
    template<class Pred>
        void unique(Pred pr);
    void merge(list& x);
    template<class Pred>
        void merge(list& x, Pred pr);
    void sort();
    template<class Pred>
        void sort(Pred pr);
    void reverse();
    };
```

The template class describes an object that controls a varying-length sequence of elements of type `T`. The sequence is stored as a bidirectional linked list of elements, each containing a member of type `T`.

The object allocates and frees storage for the sequence it controls through a stored allocator object of class `A`. Such an allocator object must have the same external interface as an object of template class `allocator`. Note that the stored allocator object is *not* copied when the container object is assigned.

List reallocation occurs when a member function must insert or erase elements of the controlled sequence. In all such cases, only iterators or references that point at erased portions of the controlled sequence become *invalid*.

All additions to the controlled sequence occur as if by calls to `insert`, which is the only member function that calls the constructor `T(const T&)`. If such an expression throws an exception, the container object inserts no new elements and rethrows the exception. Thus, an object of template class `list` is left in a known state when such exceptions occur.

▫ list::allocator_type

```
typedef A allocator_type;
```

The type is a synonym for the template parameter `A`.

▫ list::assign

```
template<class InIt>
    void assign(InIt first, InIt last);
void assign(size_type n, const T& x);
```

If `InIt` is an integer type, the first member function behaves the same as `assign((size_type)first, (T)last)`. Otherwise, the first member function replaces the sequence controlled by `*this` with the sequence `[first, last)`, which must *not* overlap the initial controlled sequence. The second member function replaces the sequence controlled by `*this` with a repetition of `n` elements of value `x`.

▫ **list::back**

```
reference back();
const_reference back() const;
```

The member function returns a reference to the last element of the controlled sequence, which must be non-empty.

▫ **list::begin**

```
const_iterator begin() const;
iterator begin();
```

The member function returns a bidirectional iterator that points at the first element of the sequence (or just beyond the end of an empty sequence).

▫ **list::clear**

```
void clear();
```

The member function calls `erase( begin(), end())`.

▫ **list::const_iterator**

```
typedef T1 const_iterator;
```

The type describes an object that can serve as a constant bidirectional iterator for the controlled sequence. It is described here as a synonym for the implementation-defined type `T1`.

▫ **list::const_pointer**

```
typedef typename A::const_pointer
    const_pointer;
```

The type describes an object that can serve as a constant pointer to an element of the controlled sequence.

▫ **list::const_reference**

```
typedef typename A::const_reference const_reference;
```

The type describes an object that can serve as a constant reference to an element of the controlled sequence.

▫ **list::const_reverse_iterator**

```
typedef reverse_iterator<const_iterator>
    const_reverse_iterator;
```

The type describes an object that can serve as a constant reverse bidirectional iterator for the controlled sequence.

▫ **list::difference_type**

```
typedef T3 difference_type;
```

The signed integer type describes an object that can represent the difference between the addresses of any two elements in the controlled sequence. It is described here as a synonym for the implementation-defined type `T3`.

▫ **list::empty**

```
bool empty() const;
```

The member function returns true for an empty controlled sequence.

- **list::end**

```
const_iterator end() const;
iterator end();
```

The member function returns a bidirectional iterator that points just beyond the end of the sequence.

- **list::erase**

```
iterator erase(iterator it);
iterator erase(iterator first, iterator last);
```

The first member function removes the element of the controlled sequence pointed to by **it**. The second member function removes the elements of the controlled sequence in the range **[first, last)**. Both return an iterator that designates the first element remaining beyond any elements removed, or **end()** if no such element exists.

Erasing **N** elements causes **N** destructor calls. No reallocation occurs, so iterators and references become invalid only for the erased elements.

The member functions never throw an exception.

- **list::front**

```
reference front();
const_reference front() const;
```

The member function returns a reference to the first element of the controlled sequence, which must be non-empty.

- **list::get_allocator**

```
A get_allocator() const;
```

The member function returns the stored allocator object.

- **list::insert**

```
iterator insert(iterator it, const T& x);
void insert(iterator it, size_type n, const T& x);
template<class InIt>
    void insert(iterator it, InIt first, InIt last);
```

Each of the member functions inserts, before the element pointed to by **it** in the controlled sequence, a sequence specified by the remaining operands. The first member function inserts a single element with value **x** and returns an iterator that points to the newly inserted element. The second member function inserts a repetition of **n** elements of value **x**.

If **InIt** is an integer type, the last member function behaves the same as **insert(it, (size_type)first, (T)last)**. Otherwise, the last member function inserts the sequence **[first, last)**, which must *not* overlap the initial controlled sequence.

Inserting **N** elements causes **N** constructor calls. No reallocation occurs, so no iterators or references become invalid.

If an exception is thrown during the insertion of one or more elements, the container is left unaltered and the exception is rethrown.

▫ **list::iterator**

```
typedef T0 iterator;
```

The type describes an object that can serve as a bidirectional iterator for the controlled sequence. It is described here as a synonym for the implementation-defined type **T0**.

▫ **list::list**

```
list();
explicit list(const A& al);
explicit list(size_type n);
list(size_type n, const T& v);
list(size_type n, const T& v,
    const A& al);
list(const list& x);
template<class InIt>
    list(InIt first, InIt last);
template<class InIt>
    list(InIt first, InIt last, const A& al);
```

All constructors store an allocator object and initialize the controlled sequence. The allocator object is the argument **al**, if present. For the copy constructor, it is **x.get_allocator()**. Otherwise, it is **A()**.

The first two constructors specify an empty initial controlled sequence. The third constructor specifies a repetition of **n** elements of value **T()**. The fourth and fifth constructors specify a repetition of **n** elements of value **x**. The sixth constructor specifies a copy of the sequence controlled by **x**. If **InIt** is an integer type, the last two constructors specify a repetition of **(size_type)first** elements of value **(T)last**. Otherwise, the last two constructors specify the sequence **[first, last)**. None of the constructors perform any interim reallocations.

▫ **list::max_size**

```
size_type max_size() const;
```

The member function returns the length of the longest sequence that the object can control.

▫ **list::merge**

```
void merge(list& x);
template<class Pred>
    void merge(list& x, Pred pr);
```

Both member functions remove all elements from the sequence controlled by **x** and insert them in the controlled sequence. Both sequences must be ordered by the same predicate, described below. The resulting sequence is also ordered by that predicate.

For the iterators **Pi** and **Pj** designating elements at positions **i** and **j**, the first member function imposes the order **!(*Pj < *Pi)** whenever **i < j**.

(The elements are sorted in *ascending* order.) The second member function imposes the order `!pr(*Pj, *Pi)` whenever `i < j`.

No pairs of elements in the original controlled sequence are reversed in the resulting controlled sequence. If a pair of elements in the resulting controlled sequence compares equal (`!(*Pi < *Pj) && !(*Pj < *Pi)`), an element from the original controlled sequence appears before an element from the sequence controlled by `x`.

An exception occurs only if `pr` throws an exception. In that case, the controlled sequence is left in unspecified order and the exception is rethrown.

▫ **list::pointer**

```
typedef typename A::pointer pointer;
```

The type describes an object that can serve as a pointer to an element of the controlled sequence.

▫ **list::pop_back**

```
void pop_back();
```

The member function removes the last element of the controlled sequence, which must be non-empty.

The member function never throws an exception.

▫ **list::pop_front**

```
void pop_front();
```

The member function removes the first element of the controlled sequence, which must be non-empty.

The member function never throws an exception.

▫ **list::push_back**

```
void push_back(const T& x);
```

The member function inserts an element with value `x` at the end of the controlled sequence.

If an exception is thrown, the container is left unaltered and the exception is rethrown.

▫ **list::push_front**

```
void push_front(const T& x);
```

The member function inserts an element with value `x` at the beginning of the controlled sequence.

If an exception is thrown, the container is left unaltered and the exception is rethrown.

▫ **list::rbegin**

```
const_reverse_iterator rbegin() const;
reverse_iterator rbegin();
```

The member function returns a reverse bidirectional iterator that points just beyond the end of the controlled sequence. Hence, it designates the beginning of the reverse sequence.

▫ **list::reference**

```
typedef typename A::reference reference;
```

The type describes an object that can serve as a reference to an element of the controlled sequence.

▫ **list::remove**

```
void remove(const T& x);
```

The member function removes from the controlled sequence all elements, designated by the iterator `P`, for which `*P == x`.

The member function never throws an exception.

▫ **list::remove_if**

```
templace<class Pred>
    void remove_if(Pred pr);
```

The member function removes from the controlled sequence all elements, designated by the iterator `P`, for which `pr(*P)` is true.

An exception occurs only if `pr` throws an exception. In that case, the controlled sequence is left in an unspecified state and the exception is rethrown.

▫ **list::rend**

```
const_reverse_iterator rend() const;
reverse_iterator rend();
```

The member function returns a reverse bidirectional iterator that points at the first element of the sequence (or just beyond the end of an empty sequence). Hence, it designates the end of the reverse sequence.

▫ **list::resize**

```
void resize(size_type n);
void resize(size_type n, T x);
```

The member functions both ensure that `size()` henceforth returns `n`. If it must make the controlled sequence longer, the first member function appends elements with value `T()`, while the second member function appends elements with value `x`. To make the controlled sequence shorter, both member functions call `erase(begin() + n, end())`.

▫ **list::reverse**

```
void reverse();
```

The member function reverses the order in which elements appear in the controlled sequence.

▫ **list::reverse_iterator**

```
typedef reverse_iterator<iterator>
    reverse_iterator;
```

The type describes an object that can serve as a reverse bidirectional iterator for the controlled sequence.

- `list::size`

```
size_type size() const;
```

The member function returns the length of the controlled sequence.

- `list::size_type`

```
typedef T2 size_type;
```

The unsigned integer type describes an object that can represent the length of any controlled sequence. It is described here as a synonym for the implementation-defined type `T2`.

- `list::sort`

```
void sort();
template<class Pred>
    void sort(Pred pr);
```

Both member functions order the elements in the controlled sequence by a predicate, described below.

For the iterators `Pi` and `Pj` designating elements at positions `i` and `j`, the first member function imposes the order `!(*Pj < *Pi)` whenever `i < j`. (The elements are sorted in *ascending* order.) The member template function imposes the order `!pr(*Pj, *Pi)` whenever `i < j`. No ordered pairs of elements in the original controlled sequence are reversed in the resulting controlled sequence. (The sort is stable.)

An exception occurs only if `pr` throws an exception. In that case, the controlled sequence is left in unspecified order and the exception is rethrown.

- `list::splice`

```
void splice(iterator it, list& x);
void splice(iterator it, list& x, iterator first);
void splice(iterator it, list& x, iterator first,
    iterator last);
```

The first member function inserts the sequence controlled by `x` before the element in the controlled sequence pointed to by `it`. It also removes all elements from `x`. (`&x` must not equal `this`.)

The second member function removes the element pointed to by `first` in the sequence controlled by `x` and inserts it before the element in the controlled sequence pointed to by `it`. (If `it == first || it == ++first`, no change occurs.)

The third member function inserts the subrange designated by `[first, last)` from the sequence controlled by `x` before the element in the controlled sequence pointed to by `it`. It also removes the original subrange from the sequence controlled by `x`. (If `&x == this`, the range `[first, last)` must not include the element pointed to by `it`.)

If the third member function inserts `N` elements, and `&x != this`, an object of class `iterator` is incremented `N` times. For all `splice` member functions, If `get_allocator() == str.get_allocator()`, no exception occurs. Otherwise, in this implementation, a copy and a destructor call also occur for each inserted element.

In all cases, only iterators or references that point at spliced elements become *invalid*.

list::swap

```
void swap(list& x);
```

The member function swaps the controlled sequences between `*this` and `x`. If `get_allocator() == x.get_allocator()`, it does so in constant time, it throws no exceptions, and it invalidates no references, pointers, or iterators that designate elements in the two controlled sequences. Otherwise, it performs a number of element assignments and constructor calls proportional to the number of elements in the two controlled sequences.

list::unique

```
void unique();
template<class Pred>
    void unique(Pred pr);
```

The first member function removes from the controlled sequence every element that compares equal to its preceding element. For the iterators `Pi` and `Pj` designating elements at positions `i` and `j`, the second member function removes every element for which `i + 1 == j && pr(*Pi, *Pj)`.

For a controlled sequence of length `N` (> 0), the predicate `pr(*Pi, *Pj)` is evaluated `N - 1` times.

An exception occurs only if `pr` throws an exception. In that case, the controlled sequence is left in an unspecified state and the exception is rethrown.

list::value_type

```
typedef typename A::value_type value_type;
```

The type is a synonym for the template parameter `T`.

operator!=

```
template<class T, class A>
    bool operator!=(
        const list <T, A>& lhs,
        const list <T, A>& rhs);
```

The template function returns `!(lhs == rhs)`.

operator==

```
template<class T, class A>
    bool operator==(
        const list <T, A>& lhs,
        const list <T, A>& rhs);
```

The template function overloads `operator==` to compare two objects of template class `list`. The function returns `lhs.size() == rhs.size() && equal(lhs. begin(), lhs. end(), rhs.begin())`.

- **`operator<`**

```
template<class T, class A>
    bool operator<(
        const list <T, A>& lhs,
        const list <T, A>& rhs);
```

The template function overloads `operator<` to compare two objects of template class `list`. The function returns `lexicographical_compare(lhs. begin(), lhs. end(), rhs.begin(), rhs.end())`.

- **`operator<=`**

```
template<class T, class A>
    bool operator<=(
        const list <T, A>& lhs,
        const list <T, A>& rhs);
```

The template function returns `!(rhs < lhs)`.

- **`operator>`**

```
template<class T, class A>
    bool operator>(
        const list <T, A>& lhs,
        const list <T, A>& rhs);
```

The template function returns `rhs < lhs`.

- **`operator>=`**

```
template<class T, class A>
    bool operator>=(
        const list <T, A>& lhs,
        const list <T, A>& rhs);
```

The template function returns `!(lhs < rhs)`.

- **`swap`**

```
template<class T, class A>
    void swap(
        list <T, A>& lhs,
        list <T, A>& rhs);
```

The template function executes `lhs.swap(rhs)`.

Using `<list>`

`list` Include the header `<list>` to make use of template class `list`. You can specialize `list` to store elements of type `T` by writing a type definition such as:

```
typedef list<T, allocator<T> > Mycont;
```

Using a default template argument, you can omit the second argument.

Template class `list` supports all the common operations on containers, as we described in Chapter 9: Containers. (See the discussion beginning on page 248.) We summarize here only those properties peculiar to template class `list`.

constructors To construct an object of class `list<T, A>`, you can write any of:

- `list()` to declare an empty list.
- `list(al)` as above, also storing the allocator object `al`.
- `list(n)` to declare a list with `n` elements, each constructed with the default constructor `T()`.
- `list(n, val)` to declare a list with `n` elements, each constructed with the copy constructor `T(val)`.
- `list(n, val, al)` as above, also storing the allocator object `al`.
- `list(first, last)` to declare a list with initial elements copied from the sequence designated by `[first, last)`.
- `list(first, last, al)` as above, also storing the allocator object `al`.

If you have specialized the template class for an allocator of type `allocator<T>`, which is the customary (and default) thing to do, there is nothing to be gained by specifying an explicit allocator argument `al`. Such an argument matters only for some allocators that the program defines explicitly. (See the discussion of allocators in Chapter 4: `<memory>`.)

The following descriptions all assume that `cont` is an object of class `list<T, A>`.

`resize` `clear` To change the length of the controlled sequence to `n` elements, call `cont.resize(n)`. Excess elements are erased. If the sequence must be extended, elements with the value `T()` are inserted as needed at the end. You can also call `cont.resize(n, val)` to extend the sequence with elements that store the value `val`. To remove all elements, call `cont.clear()`.

`front` `back` To access the first element of the controlled sequence, call `cont.front()`. To access the last element, call `cont.back()`. If `cont` is not a const object, the expression is an lvalue, so you can alter the value stored in the element by writing an expression such as `cont.front() = T()`. If the sequence is empty, however, these expressions have undefined behavior.

`push_back` `push_front` `pop_back` `pop_front` To append an object with stored value `x`, call `cont.push_back(x)`; to prepend the object, call `cont.push_front(x)`. To remove the last element, call `cont.pop_back()`; to remove the first, call `cont.pop_front()`. In either case, the sequence must, of course, be non-empty or the call has undefined bahavior.

`assign` To replace the controlled sequence with the elements from a sequence designated by `[first, last)`, call `cont.assign(first, last)`. The sequence must not be part of the initial controlled sequence. To replace the controlled sequence with `n` copies of the value `x`, call `cont.assign(n, x)`.

`insert` To insert an element storing the value `x` before the element designated by the iterator `it`, call `cont.insert(it, x)`. The return value is an iterator designating the inserted element. To insert the elements of a sequence designated by `[first, last)` before the element designated by the iterator `it`, call `cont.insert(it, first, last)`. The sequence must not be any part of the initial controlled sequence. To insert `n` copies of the value `x`, call `cont.insert(it, n, x)`.

`erase` To erase the element designated by the iterator `it`, call `cont.erase(it)`. The return value is an iterator designating the element just beyond the erased element. To erase a range of elements designated by `[first, last)`, call `cont.erase(first, last)`.

You can also perform a number of operations on a `list` object that take advantage of its unique representation.

`splice` You can *splice* a sequence of list nodes into a list. The spliced nodes are removed from their existing positions. No elements are copied — a splice simply rewrites links within the nodes as needed.

- To splice the entire contents of the object `cont2` before the element designated by the iterator `it`, call `cont.splice(it, cont2)`. The two list objects must, of course, be distinct.
- To splice the node designated by the iterator `p` in the object `cont2` before the node designated by the iterator `it`, call `cont.splice(it, cont2, p)`. The two list objects need not be distinct. (Splicing a node before itself causes no change
- To splice the sequence of nodes designated by `[first, last)` in the object `cont2` before the element designated by the iterator `it`, call `cont.splice(it, cont2, first, last)`. The two list objects need not be distinct, but `it` must not designate any of the nodes to be spliced.

If a node migrates from one list to another as a result of a splice, it is important that the two lists have allocator objects that compare equal. This requirement is always met by default allocators. Otherwise, the node cannot be safely erased by its new owner.

`remove`
`remove_if` To remove all elements that compare equal (using `operator==`) to the value `v`, call `cont.remove(v)`. To remove each element `x` for which `pr(x)` is true, call `cont.remove_if(pr)`.

`unique` To remove all but the first of each subsequence of elements that compare equal (using `operator==`), call `cont.unique()`. To replace `operator==` with `pr` as the comparison function, call `cont.unique(pr)`. Note that `unique` is generally more effective if you first sort the sequence, so that all groups of equal elements are adjacent.

`sort` To sort the sequence controlled by `cont` call `cont.sort()`. The resulting sequence is ordered by `operator<`. (Elements are left in ascending order.) The sort operation is performed as a succession of splices. To replace `operator<` with `pr` as the ordering function, call `cont.sort(pr)`.

`merge` To merge the ordered sequence controlled by `cont2` into the ordered sequence controlled by `cont`, call `cont.merge(cont2)`. The merge operation is performed as a succession of splices, so `cont2` is left empty (unless it is the same object as `cont`). Both sequences must be ordered by `operator<`

for the merge to work properly. (Sorting them, as above, does the job.) To replace **operator<** with **pr** as the ordering function, call **cont.merge(cont2, pr)**.

reverse Finally, you can reverse the controlled sequence by calling **reverse()**. The operation is performed as a succession of splices.

Implementing <list>

list Figures 11.1 through 11.11 show the file **list**. It defines template class **list**, along with a few template functions that take list operands.

A **list** object stores a pointer and a count to represent the controlled sequence. Besides the allocator objects, described below, a **list** stores two objects:

Head ■ **Head** is a pointer to a dummy "head" node that in turn points forward to the beginning of the controlled sequence and backward to its end.

Size ■ **Size** counts the number of elements in the list.

The dummy head node greatly simplifies many list operations. It eliminates the need for most special handling of the first and last nodes in the list. The price you pay for a head node is unused storage for one list element. This is typically a small price to pay, but for a list of very large elements it can be significant.

That's the easy part, familiar to anyone who has ever managed a linked list. The object also stores three different allocator objects. Here's where the real trickery comes in.

In STL containers, all controlled storage is nominally managed through the allocator object specified when you construct the container object. As we mentioned in the previous chapter, in conjunction with **vector** objects, allocators were originally invented to allocate and free arrays of objects of some element type **T**. They have since been made far more ambitious, and complex. Template class **vector** can get away with the simplest usages, but not so template class **list**, for several subtle reasons.

Node To begin at the beginning, consider how you normally manage a bidirectional linked list. You need to define a class **Node** that stores all the data required of a list node. To store an element of type **T**, you can write:

```
class Node {
    Node *Next, *Prev;
    T Value;
    };
```

The one small trick you must make use of dates back to the earliest days of the C language, from which C++ evolved. The forward link **Next** and the backward link **Prev** are both self-referential pointers — they point at other objects of the same type as the object in which they reside. No sweat. You can declare a pointer to an incomplete type inside a structured type, even if that type is the one you're busy completing.

Figure 11.1: `list` **Part 1**

```
// list standard header
#ifndef LIST_
#define LIST_
#include <functional>
#include <memory>
#include <stdexcept>
namespace std {

          // TEMPLATE CLASS List_nod
template<class Ty, class A>
     class List_nod {
protected:
     typedef typename A::template
          rebind<void>::other::pointer Genptr;
     struct Node;
     friend struct Node;
     struct Node {
          Genptr Next, Prev;
          Ty Value;
          };
     List_nod(A Al)
          : Alnod(Al) {}
     typename A::template rebind<Node>::other Alnod;
     };

          // TEMPLATE CLASS List_ptr
template<class Ty, class A>
     class List_ptr : public List_nod<Ty, A> {
protected:
     typedef typename List_nod<Ty, A>::Node Node;
     typedef typename A::template
          rebind<Node>::other::pointer Nodeptr;
     List_ptr(A Al)
          : List_nod<Ty, A>(Al), Alptr(Al) {}
     typename A::template rebind<Nodeptr>::other Alptr;
     };

          // TEMPLATE CLASS List_val
template<class Ty, class A>
     class List_val : public List_ptr<Ty, A> {
protected:
     List_val(A Al = A())
          : List_ptr<Ty, A>(Al), Alval(Al) {}
     typedef typename A::template
          rebind<Ty>::other Alty;
     Alty Alval;
     };

          // TEMPLATE CLASS list
template<class Ty, class Ax = allocator<Ty> >
     class list : public List_val<Ty, Ax> {
public:
     typedef list<Ty, Ax> Myt;
     typedef List_val<Ty, Ax> Mybase;
     typedef typename Mybase::Alty A;
```

Figure 11.2: list Part 2

```
protected:
     typedef typename List_nod<Ty, A>::Genptr Genptr;
     typedef typename List_nod<Ty, A>::Node Node;
     typedef typename A::template
          rebind::<Node>::other::pointer Nodeptr;
     struct Acc;
     friend struct Acc;
     struct Acc {
          typedef typename A::template
               rebind::<Nodeptr>::other::reference Nodepref;
          typedef typename A::reference Vref;
          static Nodepref Next(Nodeptr P)
               {return ((Nodepref)(*P).Next); }
          static Nodepref Prev(Nodeptr P)
               {return ((Nodepref)(*P).Prev); }
          static Vref Value(Nodeptr P)
               {return ((Vref)(*P).Value); }
          };
public:
     typedef A allocator_type;
     typedef typename A::size_type size_type;
     typedef typename A::difference_type Dift;
     typedef Dift difference_type;
     typedef typename A::pointer Tptr;
     typedef typename A::const_pointer Ctptr;
     typedef Tptr pointer;
     typedef Ctptr const_pointer;
     typedef typename A::reference Reft;
     typedef Reft reference;
     typedef typename A::const_reference const_reference;
     typedef typename A::value_type value_type;

          // CLASS iterator
     class iterator;
     friend class iterator;
     class iterator : public Bidit<Ty, Dift, Tptr, Reft> {
     public:
          typedef Bidit<Ty, Dift, Tptr, Reft> Mybase;
          typedef typename Mybase::iterator_category
               iterator_category;
          typedef typename Mybase::value_type value_type;
          typedef typename Mybase::difference_type
               difference_type;
          typedef typename Mybase::pointer pointer;
          typedef typename Mybase::reference reference;
          iterator()
               : Ptr(0) {}
          iterator(Nodeptr P)
               : Ptr(P) {}
          reference operator*() const
               {return (Acc::Value(Ptr)); }
          Tptr operator->() const
               {return (&**this); }
          iterator& operator++()
```

Figure 11.3: `list` **Part 3**

```
            {Ptr = Acc::Next(Ptr);
            return (*this); }
        iterator operator++(int)
            {iterator Tmp = *this;
            ++*this;
            return (Tmp); }
        iterator& operator--()
            {Ptr = Acc::Prev(Ptr);
            return (*this); }
        iterator operator--(int)
            {iterator Tmp = *this;
            --*this;
            return (Tmp); }
        bool operator==(const iterator& X) const
            {return (Ptr == X.Ptr); }
        bool operator!=(const iterator& X) const
            {return (!(*this == X)); }
        Nodeptr Mynode() const
            {return (Ptr); }
    protected:
        Nodeptr Ptr;
        };

        // CLASS const_iterator
    class const_iterator;
    friend class const_iterator;
    class const_iterator
        : public Bidit<Ty, Dift, Ctptr, const_reference> {
    public:
        typedef Bidit<Ty, Dift, Ctptr, const_reference>
            Mybase;
        typedef typename Mybase::iterator_category
            iterator_category;
        typedef typename Mybase::value_type value_type;
        typedef typename Mybase::difference_type
            difference_type;
        typedef typename Mybase::pointer pointer;
        typedef typename Mybase::reference reference;
        const_iterator()
            : Ptr(0) {}
        const_iterator(Nodeptr P)
            : Ptr(P) {}
        const_iterator(const typename list<Ty, Ax>::iterator& X)
            : Ptr(X.Mynode()) {}
        const_reference operator*() const
            {return (Acc::Value(Ptr)); }
        Ctptr operator->() const
            {return (&**this); }
        const_iterator& operator++()
            {Ptr = Acc::Next(Ptr);
            return (*this); }
        const_iterator operator++(int)
            {const_iterator Tmp = *this;
            ++*this;
            return (Tmp); }
```

Figure 11.4: `list` **Part 4**

```
        const_iterator& operator--()
            {Ptr = Acc::Prev(Ptr);
            return (*this); }
        const_iterator operator--(int)
            {const_iterator Tmp = *this;
            --*this;
            return (Tmp); }
        bool operator==(const const_iterator& X) const
            {return (Ptr == X.Ptr); }
        bool operator!=(const const_iterator& X) const
            {return (!(*this == X)); }
        Nodeptr Mynode() const
            {return (Ptr); }
    protected:
        Nodeptr Ptr;
        };

    typedef std::reverse_iterator<iterator>
        reverse_iterator;
    typedef std::reverse_iterator<const_iterator>
        const_reverse_iterator;

    list()
        : Mybase(), Head(Buynode()), Size(0)
        {}
    explicit list(const A& Al)
        : Mybase(Al), Head(Buynode()), Size(0)
        {}
    explicit list(size_type N)
        : Mybase(), Head(Buynode()), Size(0)
        {insert(begin(), N, Ty()); }
    list(size_type N, const Ty& V)
        : Mybase(), Head(Buynode()), Size(0)
        {insert(begin(), N, V); }
    list(size_type N, const Ty& V, const A& Al)
        : Mybase(Al), Head(Buynode()), Size(0)
        {insert(begin(), N, V); }
    list(const Myt& X)
        : Mybase(X.Alval),
            Head(Buynode()), Size(0)
        {insert(begin(), X.begin(), X.end()); }
    template<class It>
        list(It F, It L)
        : Mybase(), Head(Buynode()), Size(0)
        {Construct(F, L, Iter_cat(F)); }
    template<class It>
        list(It F, It L, const A& Al)
        : Mybase(Al), Head(Buynode()), Size(0)
        {Construct(F, L, Iter_cat(F)); }
    template<class It>
        void Construct(It F, It L, Int_iterator_tag)
        {insert(begin(), (size_type)F, (Ty)L); }
    template<class It>
        void Construct(It F, It L, input_iterator_tag)
        {insert(begin(), F, L); }
```

Figure 11.5: `list` **Part 5**

```
~list()
     {erase(begin(), end());
     Freenode(Head);
     Head = 0, Size = 0; }
Myt& operator=(const Myt& X)
     {if (this != &X)
          assign(X.begin(), X.end());
     return (*this); }
iterator begin()
     {return (iterator(Head == 0 ? 0
          : Acc::Next(Head))); }
const_iterator begin() const
     {return (const_iterator(Head == 0 ? 0
          : Acc::Next(Head))); }
iterator end()
     {return (iterator(Head)); }
const_iterator end() const
     {return (const_iterator(Head)); }
reverse_iterator rbegin()
     {return (reverse_iterator(end())); }
const_reverse_iterator rbegin() const
     {return (const_reverse_iterator(end())); }
reverse_iterator rend()
     {return (reverse_iterator(begin())); }
const_reverse_iterator rend() const
     {return (const_reverse_iterator(begin())); }
void resize(size_type N)
     {resize(N, Ty()); }
void resize(size_type N, Ty X)
     {if (size() < N)
          insert(end(), N - size(), X);
     else
          while (N < size())
               pop_back(); }
size_type size() const
     {return (Size); }
size_type max_size() const
     {return (Mybase::Alval.max_size()); }
bool empty() const
     {return (size() == 0); }
allocator_type get_allocator() const
     {return (Mybase::Alval); }
reference front()
     {return (*begin()); }
const_reference front() const
     {return (*begin()); }
reference back()
     {return (*(--end())); }
const_reference back() const
     {return (*(--end())); }
void push_front(const Ty& X)
     {Insert(begin(), X); }
void pop_front()
     {erase(begin()); }
```

Figure 11.6: `list` **Part 6**

```
void push_back(const Ty& X)
     {Insert(end(), X); }
void pop_back()
     {erase(--end()); }
template<class It>
     void assign(It F, It L)
     {Assign(F, L, Iter_cat(F)); }
template<class It>
     void Assign(It F, It L, Int_iterator_tag)
     {assign((size_type)F, (Ty)L); }
template<class It>
     void Assign(It F, It L, input_iterator_tag)
     {erase(begin(), end());
     insert(begin(), F, L); }
void assign(size_type N, const Ty& X)
     {Ty Tx = X;
     erase(begin(), end());
     insert(begin(), N, Tx); }
iterator insert(iterator P, const Ty& X)
     {Insert(P, X);
     return (--P); }
void Insert(iterator P, const Ty& X)
     {Nodeptr S = P.Mynode();
     Nodeptr Snew = Buynode(S, Acc::Prev(S));
     Incsize(1);
     try {
     Mybase::Alval.construct(&Acc::Value(Snew), X);
     } catch (...) {
     --Size;
     Freenode(Snew);
     throw;
     }
     Acc::Prev(S) = Snew;
     Acc::Next(Acc::Prev(Snew)) = Snew; }
void insert(iterator P, size_type M, const Ty& X)
     {size_type N = M;
     try {
     for (; 0 < M; --M)
          Insert(P, X);
     } catch (...) {
     for (; M < N; ++M)
          {iterator Pm = P;
          erase(--Pm); }
     throw;
     }}
template<class It>
     void insert(iterator P, It F, It L)
     {Insert(P, F, L, Iter_cat(F)); }
template<class It>
     void Insert(iterator P, It F, It L,
          Int_iterator_tag)
     {insert(P, (size_type)F, (Ty)L); }
template<class It>
     void Insert(iterator P, It F, It L,
          input_iterator_tag)
```

Figure 11.7: `list` **Part 7**

```
          {size_type N = 0;
          try {
          for (; F != L; ++F, ++N)
               Insert(P, *F);
          } catch (...) {
          for (; 0 < N; --N)
               {iterator Pm = P;
               erase(--Pm); }
          throw;
          }}
     template<class It>
          void Insert(iterator P, It F, It L,
               forward_iterator_tag)
          {It Fs = F;
          try {
          for (; F != L; ++F)
               Insert(P, *F);
          } catch (...) {
          for (; Fs != F; ++Fs)
               {iterator Pm = P;
               erase(--Pm); }
          throw;
          }}
     iterator erase(iterator P)
          {Nodeptr S = (P++).Mynode();
          Acc::Next(Acc::Prev(S)) = Acc::Next(S);
          Acc::Prev(Acc::Next(S)) = Acc::Prev(S);
          Mybase::Alval.destroy(&Acc::Value(S));
          Freenode(S);
          --Size;
          return (P); }
     iterator erase(iterator F, iterator L)
          {while (F != L)
               erase(F++);
          return (F); }
     void clear()
          {erase(begin(), end()); }
     void swap(Myt& X)
          {if (Mybase::Alval == X.Alval)
               {std::swap(Head, X.Head);
               std::swap(Size, X.Size); }
          else
               {iterator P = begin();
               splice(P, X);
               X.splice(X.begin(), *this, P, end()); }}
     void splice(iterator P, Myt& X)
          {if (this != &X && !X.empty())
               {Splice(P, X, X.begin(), X.end(), X.Size); }}
     void splice(iterator P, Myt& X, iterator F)
          {iterator L = F;
          if (F != X.end() && P != F && P != ++L)
               {Splice(P, X, F, L, 1); }}
     void splice(iterator P, Myt& X, iterator F, iterator L)
          {if (F != L && P != L)
               {size_type N = 0;
```

Figure 11.8: `list` **Part 8**

```
            for (iterator Fs = F; Fs != L; ++Fs, ++N)
                if (Fs == P)
                    return;             // else granny knot
            Splice(P, X, F, L, N); }}
    void remove(const Ty& V)
        {iterator L = end();
        for (iterator F = begin(); F != L; )
            if (*F == V)
                erase(F++);
            else
                ++F; }
    template<class Pr1>
        void remove_if(Pr1 Pr)
        {iterator L = end();
        for (iterator F = begin(); F != L; )
            if (Pr(*F))
                erase(F++);
            else
                ++F; }
    void unique()
        {iterator F = begin(), L = end();
        if (F != L)
            for (iterator M = F; ++M != L; M = F)
                if (*F == *M)
                    erase(M);
                else
                    F = M; }
    template<class Pr2>
        void unique(Pr2 Pr)
        {iterator F = begin(), L = end();
        if (F != L)
            for (iterator M = F; ++M != L; M = F)
                if (Pr(*F, *M))
                    erase(M);
                else
                    F = M; }
    void merge(Myt& X)
        {if (&X != this)
            {iterator F1 = begin(), L1 = end();
            iterator F2 = X.begin(), L2 = X.end();
            while (F1 != L1 && F2 != L2)
                if (*F2 < *F1)
                    {iterator Mid2 = F2;
                    Splice(F1, X, F2, ++Mid2, 1);
                    F2 = Mid2; }
                else
                    ++F1;
            if (F2 != L2)
                Splice(L1, X, F2, L2, X.Size); }}
    template<class Pr3>
        void merge(Myt& X, Pr3 Pr)
        {if (&X != this)
            {iterator F1 = begin(), L1 = end();
            iterator F2 = X.begin(), L2 = X.end();
```

Figure 11.9: `list` **Part 9**

```
            while (F1 != L1 && F2 != L2)
                if (Pr(*F2, *F1))
                    {iterator Mid2 = F2;
                    Splice(F1, X, F2, ++Mid2, 1);
                    F2 = Mid2; }
                else
                    ++F1;
            if (F2 != L2)
                Splice(L1, X, F2, L2, X.Size); }}
    void sort()
        {if (2 <= size())
            {const size_t MAXN = 25;
            Myt X(Mybase::Alval), Arr[MAXN + 1];
            size_t N = 0;
            while (!empty())
                {X.splice(X.begin(), *this, begin());
                size_t I;
                for (I = 0; I < N && !Arr[I].empty(); ++I)
                    {Arr[I].merge(X);
                    Arr[I].swap(X); }
                if (I == MAXN)
                    Arr[I - 1].merge(X);
                else
                    {Arr[I].swap(X);
                    if (I == N)
                        ++N; }}
            for (size_t I = 1; I < N; ++I)
                Arr[I].merge(Arr[I - 1]);
            swap(Arr[N - 1]); }}
    template<class Pr3>
        void sort(Pr3 Pr)
        {if (2 <= size())
            {const size_t MAXN = 25;
            Myt X(Mybase::Alval), Arr[MAXN + 1];
            size_t N = 0;
            while (!empty())
                {X.splice(X.begin(), *this, begin());
                size_t I;
                for (I = 0; I < N && !Arr[I].empty(); ++I)
                    {Arr[I].merge(X, Pr);
                    Arr[I].swap(X); }
                if (I == MAXN)
                    Arr[I - 1].merge(X, Pr);
                else
                    {Arr[I].swap(X);
                    if (I == N)
                        ++N; }}
            for (size_t I = 1; I < N; ++I)
                Arr[i].merge(Arr[I - 1], Pr);
            swap(Arr[N - 1]); }}
    void reverse()
        {if (2 <= size())
            {iterator L = end();
```

Figure 11.10: list **Part 10**

```
                for (iterator F = ++begin(); F != L; )
                     {iterator M = F;
                     Splice(begin(), *this, M, ++F, 1); }}}
protected:
     Nodeptr Buynode(Nodeptr Narg = 0, Nodeptr Parg = 0)
          {Nodeptr S = Alnod.allocate(1, (void *)0);
          Alptr.construct(&Acc::Next(S),
               Narg != 0 ? Narg : S);
          Alptr.construct(&Acc::Prev(S),
               Parg != 0 ? Parg : S);
          return (S); }
     void Freenode(Nodeptr S)
          {Alptr.destroy(&Acc::Next(S));
          Alptr.destroy(&Acc::Prev(S));
          Alnod.deallocate(S, 1); }
     void Splice(iterator P, Myt& X, iterator F, iterator L,
          size_type N)
          {if (Mybase::Alval == X.Alval)
               {if (this != &X)
                    {Incsize(N);
                    X.Size -= N; }
               Acc::Next(Acc::Prev(F.Mynode())) =
                    L.Mynode();
               Acc::Next(Acc::Prev(L.Mynode())) =
                    P.Mynode();
               Acc::Next(Acc::Prev(P.Mynode())) =
                    F.Mynode();
               Nodeptr S = Acc::Prev(P.Mynode());
               Acc::Prev(P.Mynode()) =
                    Acc::Prev(L.Mynode());
               Acc::Prev(L.Mynode()) =
                    Acc::Prev(F.Mynode());
               Acc::Prev(F.Mynode()) = S; }
          else
               {insert(P, F, L);
               X.erase(F, L); }}
     void Incsize(size_type N)
          {if (max_size() - size() < N)
               throw length_error("list<T> too long");
          Size += N; }
     Nodeptr Head;
     size_type Size;
     };

          // list TEMPLATE OPERATORS
template<class Ty, class A> inline
     void swap(list<Ty, A>& X, list<Ty, A>& Y)
     {X.swap(Y); }

template<class Ty, class A> inline
     bool operator==(const list<Ty, A>& X,
          const list<Ty, A>& Y)
     {return (X.size() == Y.size()
          && equal(X.begin(), X.end(), Y.begin())); }
```

Figure 11.11: `list` **Part 11**

```
template<class Ty, class A> inline
     bool operator!=(const list<Ty, A>& X,
          const list<Ty, A>& Y)
     {return (!(X == Y)); }
template<class Ty, class A> inline
     bool operator<(const list<Ty, A>& X,
          const list<Ty, A>& Y)
     {return (lexicographical_compare(X.begin(), X.end(),
          Y.begin(), Y.end())); }
template<class Ty, class A> inline
     bool operator>(const list<Ty, A>& X,
          const list<Ty, A>& Y)
     {return (Y < X); }
template<class Ty, class A> inline
     bool operator<=(const list<Ty, A>& X,
          const list<Ty, A>& Y)
     {return (!(Y < X)); }
template<class Ty, class A> inline
     bool operator>=(const list<Ty, A>& X,
          const list<Ty, A>& Y)
     {return (!(X < Y)); }
} /* namespace std */
#endif /* LIST_ */
```

But allocators cause problems. The first problem is that an object of type `list<T, allocator<T> >` is constructed with an allocator object that doesn't do the whole job. We're not interested in allocating objects of type `T`, which is all that an `allocator<T>` object knows how to allocate. (But it does know how to *construct* and *destroy* such an object, so it is still needed.) Instead, we want to allocate objects of type `Node`. That means we need an allocator object of type `allocator<Node>`. And we want to associate it, in some obvious way, with the `allocator<T>` object supplied to the `list` object when it is constructed. The allocator might be allocating objects from a private storage pool, for example, which we certainly want to use as intended.

`rebind` Two bits of trickery, supplied by all allocator types, give you the power you need. The first is member template class `rebind` — the bizarre formula `A::rebind<Node>::other` is a way of naming the type `allocator<Node>` when all you have is the synonym `A` for the type `allocator<T>`. Once you can name the kind of allocator object you want, you still have to construct one from the original allocator object. So all allocator types supply a template constructor. For the default template class `allocator`, this constructor looks like:

```
template<class U>
    allocator(const allocator<U>&);
```

You can thus construct an `allocator<Node>` object from an `allocator<T>` object. For a more complex allocator than template class `allocator`, the constructor must be smart enough to copy over any pointers to private storage, or what have you.

smart pointers Allocators cause yet another problem. They reserve the right to store the objects they allocate in funny places. More precisely, an allocator type **A** defines the type **A::pointer**, which you are obliged to use to describe any "pointer" to an allocated object. We use quotes here because the type need not be a pointer in the old-fashioned sense inherited from C. (See the discussion of smart pointers on page 99.) If **p** has type **A::pointer**, it promises that ***p** is an lvalue that designates the allocated object. (You can access the value or assign to it via ***p**.) But not much more.

This weaker promise causes a real problem with the declaration of class **Node**. You want to write:

```
class Node {
    A::rebind<Node>::pointer Next, Prev;
    T Value;
    };
```

but you can't. An allocator template can be specialized only for a complete type. Type **Node** is not complete until the closing brace of its definition. You need to describe the pointers it stores before you can complete its definition. What can you do?

void pointers When such dependency loops occur, the usual copout in C is to introduce generic, or "void," pointers, as in:

```
class Node {
    void *Next, *Prev;
    T Value;
    };
```

A void pointer is obliged to store any kind of object pointer you can declare in C. You lose a bit of type checking this way, and you have to write occasional type casts when you use the pointers, but it does solve the problem.

When it comes to pointers supplied by allocators, however, the C++ Standard is less than clear. It *suggests* that an **A::pointer** can be an arbitrary template class type, subject to the restrictions we sketched above. But it imposes no requirement that such a template class type define the equivalent of a void pointer. An implementation has to fill in the blanks.

This implementation assumes that any **A::pointer** is interconvertible with any **A::rebind<void>::pointer**. Put another way, the type **A::<void>::pointer** supplies the generic pointer type for the family of types A<T>::pointer, all of which have the same representation. Whoever writes the allocator template must supply an explicit specialization for type **void** anyway. It shouldn't be all that hard to ensure that the explicit specialization supplies a sufficiently flexible pointer type in the bargain.

null pointers This implementation also assumes that an integer zero still serves as a null pointer, no matter how exotic the pointers defined by the allocator. Specifically, you can assign zero to a generic pointer object; the resulting value will not compare equal to a generic pointer to any allocated object. And you can compare a generic pointer object to zero, using **operator==**; the result is true only if the generic pointer object stores a null pointer. (We quietly made this assumption in the previous chapter, with respect to the member object **First**.)

Smart pointers introduce one last wrinkle. This implementation assumes that they may have a nontrivial constructor and destructor, unlike the scalar pointers inherited from C. To play the game strictly by the rules, you need an allocator object to perform these tasks for you (though it's hard to imagine what special magic might be required). So a **list** object makes use of three allocator objects:

- **Alnod** — **Alnod** for the node type, to allocate and free nodes
- **Alptr** — **Alptr** for the node pointer type, to construct and destroy links stored in nodes
- **Alty** — **Alty** for the element type, to construct and destroy elements stored in nodes

In principle, it is necessary to store only one of these allocator objects. Either of the others can be generated on the fly as needed, as in:

```
A::rebind<Node>::other(Alty).destroy(p);
```

which generates a temporary allocator akin to **Alnod** long enough to destroy the node pointer **p**. Perhaps a compiler will know enough to optimize away the actual generation of a temporary, at least for default allocator objects. On the other hand, we know that the storage for a typical allocator object can be optimized away. (See the discussion of zero-size allocator objects on page 266.) So this implementation takes the safer bet that storing three allocator objects in a **list** object involves no real overheads in space or time.

After that long preamble, we can now study the code with a bit more wisdom. The file **list** reveals that a specializaton **list<T, A>** derives from a succession of three base classes:

- **List_nod** — **List_nod<T, A>** defines the generic pointer type **Genptr** and the node type **Node**. It also stores the allocator object **Alnod**.
- **List_ptr** — **List_ptr<T, A>** defines the node pointer type **Nodeptr**. It also stores the allocator object **Alptr**.
- **List_val** — **List_val<T, A>** stores the allocator object **Alnod**.

A smart enough compiler knows to allocate no storage within a **list<T, A>** object for any of these base objects.

Still more complexity is encapsulated in the member struct **Acc**. It supplies handy functions for accessing the objects stored in a list node. Thus, the expression **Acc::Next(Ptr)** lets you access the forward pointer **Next** in the node designated by **Ptr**. To make the expression an lvalue, the function **Acc::Next** must return a reference to the stored object. Opinions differ considerably on how much latitude an allocator has in defining reference types. Some feel that **Alloc<T>::reference** must always be a synonym for **T&**. But just in case someone supplies an allocator that succeeds in being more clever, these functions make uniform use of the reference types defined by the allocators.

list defines nontrivial member classes **iterator** and **const_iterator**. They are even simpler than template class **Ptrit**, which **vector** uses to define its iterators — **list** supports just bidirectional iterators, not random-access iterators as does **vector**. The iterators for both containers store only a single pointer.

Buynode **Freenode** **Incsize** A handful of protected member functions perform a number of common operations. The call **Buynode(next, prev)** allocates a node and initializes the two pointer member objects appropriately. The call **Freenode(p)** frees a node. Both assume that some other agency will construct and destroy the stored element value as needed. The call **Incsize(n)** increments the stored length of the controlled sequence. It checks for the unlikely event that the list has grown too large.

Splice The call **splice(p, cont2, first, last, n)** splices the sequence of **n** nodes designated by **[first, last)**, in the list object **cont2**, just before **p**. It assumes that the caller has checked for any overlap that could cause problems. But it does check for an attempt to splice between two containers with incompatible allocators, in which case it copies (and erases) the nodes instead. The order in which links are altered here is very delicate, if various special cases are to work properly.

The member functions that **list** shares with other template containers introduce little new. We described most of the machinery in conjunction with template class **vector**. What you will find here is a greater effort to recover gracefully when programmer-supplied code throws an exception. Recall that **list** alone among the containers promises to roll back any operation interrupted by a thrown exception.

splice The three versions of **splice** defer the actual work to **Splice** and **Incsize**, after suitable checking. An attempt to splice a sequence of nodes to a point somewhere inside the sequence is a particular concern. The C++ Standard simply says this operation is undefined. Moreover, it requires a splice of a subrange from the same container to occur in constant time, independent of the number of elements in the subrange. This requirement leaves no room for the kind of checking required to avoid generating a knot in the list.

This implementation deviates from the C++ Standard by checking anyway. If the splice would generate a knot, the controlled sequence is left unaltered.

sort Both forms of **sort** work the same way. They perform a succession of merges to an array of temporary **list** objects. Each element of the array stores a list that can grow twice as long as the one that precedes it, before it is merged into the next larger list. The last element is a special case — it stores an arbitrarily long list. But the array size is (arbitrarily) set at 25 elements, plus the overflow list at the end. So **sort** can sort up to 32 million elements before it has to deviate from the simple doubling algorithm. The final step is to merge the temporary lists back into the (now empty) container.

Testing <list>

tlist.c Figures 11.12 through 11.14 shows the file **tlist.c**. It is one of three test programs that look very much alike. See the file **tvector.c**, beginning on page 285, and the file **tdeque.c**, beginning on page 350. To ease comparison of these three test programs, we have simply commented out any tests inappropriate for a given container, without removing the unused code.

The test program performs a simple test that each of the member functions and types is present and behaves as intended, for one specialization of template class **list**. If all goes well, the program prints:

```
SUCCESS testing <list>
```

and takes a normal exit.

Figure 11.12: tlist.c Part 1

```
// test <list>
#include <assert.h>
#include <iostream>
#include <functional>
#include <list>
using namespace std;

    // TEST <list>
int main()
    {typedef allocator<char> Myal;

    // TEST list
    typedef list<char, Myal> Mycont;
    char ch, carr[] = "abc";
    Mycont::allocator_type *p_alloc = (Myal *)0;
    Mycont::pointer p_ptr = (char *)0;
    Mycont::const_pointer p_cptr = (const char *)0;
    Mycont::reference p_ref = ch;
    Mycont::const_reference p_cref = (const char&)ch;
    Mycont::size_type *p_size = (size_t *)0;
    Mycont::difference_type *p_diff = (ptrdiff_t *)0;
    Mycont::value_type *p_val = (char *)0;

    Mycont v0;
    Myal al = v0.get_allocator();
    Mycont v0a(al);
    assert(v0.empty() && v0.size() == 0);
    assert(v0a.size() == 0 && v0a.get_allocator() == al);
    Mycont v1(5), v1a(6, 'x'), v1b(7, 'y', al);
    assert(v1.size() == 5 && v1.back() == '\0');
    assert(v1a.size() == 6 && v1a.back() == 'x');
    assert(v1b.size() == 7 && v1b.back() == 'y');
    Mycont v2(v1a);
    assert(v2.size() == 6 && v2.front() == 'x');
    Mycont v3(v1a.begin(), v1a.end());
    assert(v3.size() == 6 && v3.front() == 'x');
```

Figure 11.13: tlist.c Part 2

```
    const Mycont v4(v1a.begin(), v1a.end(), al);
    assert(v4.size() == 6 && v4.front() == 'x');
    v0 = v4;
    assert(v0.size() == 6 && v0.front() == 'x');
//  assert(v0[0] == 'x' && v0.at(5) == 'x');

//  v0.reserve(12);
//  assert(12 <= v0.capacity());
    v0.resize(8);
    assert(v0.size() == 8 && v0.back() == '\0');
    v0.resize(10, 'z');
    assert(v0.size() == 10 && v0.back() == 'z');
    assert(v0.size() <= v0.max_size());

    Mycont::iterator p_it(v0.begin());
    Mycont::const_iterator p_cit(v4.begin());
    Mycont::reverse_iterator p_rit(v0.rbegin());
    Mycont::const_reverse_iterator p_crit(v4.rbegin());
    assert(*p_it == 'x' && *--(p_it = v0.end()) == 'z');
    assert(*p_cit == 'x' && *--(p_cit = v4.end()) == 'x');
    assert(*p_rit == 'z'
        && *--(p_rit = v0.rend()) == 'x');
    assert(*p_crit == 'x'
        && *--(p_crit = v4.rend()) == 'x');

    assert(v0.front() == 'x' && v4.front() == 'x');
    v0.push_back('a');
    assert(v0.back() == 'a');
    v0.pop_back();
    assert(v0.back() == 'z' && v4.back() == 'x');

    v0.push_front('b');
    assert(v0.front() == 'b');
    v0.pop_front();
    assert(v0.front() == 'x');

    v0.assign(v4.begin(), v4.end());
    assert(v0.size() == v4.size()
        && v0.front() == v4.front());
    v0.assign(4, 'w');
    assert(v0.size() == 4 && v0.front() == 'w');
    assert(*v0.insert(v0.begin(), 'a') == 'a');
    assert(v0.front() == 'a'
        && *++v0.begin() == 'w');
    v0.insert(v0.begin(), 2, 'b');
    assert(v0.front() == 'b'
        && *++v0.begin() == 'b'
        && *++ ++v0.begin() == 'a');
    v0.insert(v0.end(), v4.begin(), v4.end());
    assert(v0.back() == v4.back());
    v0.insert(v0.end(), carr, carr + 3);
    assert(v0.back() == 'c');
    v0.erase(v0.begin());
    assert(v0.front() == 'b' && *++v0.begin() == 'a');
    v0.erase(v0.begin(), ++v0.begin());
```

Figure 11.14: `tlist.c` **Part 3**

```
assert(v0.front() == 'a');

v0.clear();
assert(v0.empty());
v0.swap(v1);
assert(!v0.empty() && v1.empty());
swap(v0, v1);
assert(v0.empty() && !v1.empty());
assert(v1 == v1 && v0 < v1);
assert(v0 != v1 && v1 > v0);
assert(v0 <= v1 && v1 >= v0);

v0.insert(v0.begin(), carr, carr + 3);
v1.splice(v1.begin(), v0);
assert(v0.empty() && v1.front() == 'a');
v0.splice(v0.end(), v1, v1.begin());
assert(v0.size() == 1 && v0.front() == 'a');
v0.splice(v0.begin(), v1, v1.begin(), v1.end());
assert(v0.front() == 'b' && v1.empty());
v0.remove('b');
assert(v0.front() == 'c');
v0.remove_if(binder2nd<not_equal_to<char> >(
     not_equal_to<char>(), 'c'));
assert(v0.front() == 'c' && v0.size() == 1);

v0.merge(v1, greater<char>());
assert(v0.front() == 'c' && v0.size() == 1);
v0.insert(v0.begin(), carr, carr + 3);
v0.unique();
assert(v0.back() == 'c'&& v0.size() == 3);
v0.unique(not_equal_to<char>());
assert(v0.front() == 'a' && v0.size() == 1);
v1.insert(v1.begin(), carr, carr + 3);
v0.merge(v1);
assert(v0.back() == 'c' && v0.size() == 4);
v0.sort(greater<char>());
assert(v0.back() == 'a' && v0.size() == 4);
v0.sort();
assert(v0.back() == 'c' && v0.size() == 4);
v0.reverse();
assert(v0.back() == 'a' && v0.size() == 4);

cout << "SUCCESS testing <list>" << endl;
return (0); }
```

□

Exercises

Exercise 11.1 This implementation of template class `list` never copies elements between nodes. Elements are constructed and destroyed, but never assigned. Under what circumstances is this behavior most desirable?

Exercise 11.2 Why must an allocator be specialized only for a complete type?

Exercise 11.3 Rewrite template class `list` to eliminate the use of a head node. Under what circumstances is this rewrite a better design?

Exercise 11.4 Write the template class `forward_list`, which stores only a single forward pointer in each node. What operations become more difficult (have less desirable time complexity) compared to template class `list`? What are the relative sizes of nodes for the two containers?

Exercise 11.5 Alter the definition of list iterators so that it is easy to determine if two iterators designate elements in different lists.

Exercise 11.6 One way to implement a *hash table* is as a vector of lists. A *hash function* maps a key value to an index into the vector. All elements of a given list share the same *hash value* even if their keys differ. (With a good hash function, a typical hash table has lists that are uniformly short, so lookup time for a given key is essentially constant.) Write the template class `hash_list` that implements a simple hash table.

Exercise 11.7 Alter the implementation of `hash_list` from the previous list to use a single list and a vector of list iterators. What are the advantages and disadvantages of the two versions?

Exercise 11.8 **[Harder]** How can you implement a bidirectional linked list storing only one pointer object per node?

Exercise 11.9 **[Very hard]** How can you eliminate the need for generic pointers in defining a list node?

Chapter 12: <deque>

Background

<deque> **deque** The header `<deque>` defines just the template class **deque**, which is a container that stores its controlled sequence of length **N** in blocks of uniform length **B**. You reach these blocks through a map array of block pointers **Map**. So in principle, you can access element **N** with the expression:

```
Map[N / B][N % B]
```

Thus, a deque supports access to an arbitrary element in constant time, much like a vector.

Table 12.1, on page 240, shows the payoff for the added complexity in template class **deque**. It is the only container besides **vector** that supports random-access iterators. (You can tell this from the table because accessing an arbitrary element, with the expression **X[N]**, is a constant-time operation.) But it outperforms **vector** in one significant way — you can add or remove elements at the beginning of the controlled sequence in constant time. You can do the same at the end, of course, but this distinction is not so clear cut. There are circumstances under which appending to a vector can be a constant-time operation as well, as we discussed earlier. (See page 251.)

As an aside, there seems to be two schools of thought as to how to pronounce "deque." One school pronounces it as a homophone for "deck." It is indeed a queue that behaves much like a deck of cards — you can add or remove elements at either end with equal ease. But others pronounce it "DEE-queue," for Double Ended QUEUE, with an equally convincing rationale. Take your pick.

To provide for efficient growth at both ends, a deque actually begins the active contents at some offset **Off**. It stores the number of active elements (the length of the sequence) as another integer **Size**. Replace **N** with **N + Off** in the expression above and you'll get a more realistic recipe for finding element **N**.

Reality is still not that simple. An STL deque has an additional promise. An iterator continues to designate the same element even as you push and pop elements at either end, provided you perform no internal inserts or erases within the controlled sequence. This promise constrains how the map can change as the controlled sequence grows and shrinks, as we shall see later in this chapter.

A deque is thus as good as a list for implementing a first-in first-out (FIFO) queue or a last-in first-out (LIFO) queue, also known as a stack. It is not as good as a list if you often need to insert a new item at an arbitrary place — a deque takes linear time versus constant time for a list. If you need random access to the elements of a controlled sequence, however, a deque beats a list any day.

vector The table raises an interesting question. A deque matches or exceeds a vector in the time complexity of all operations, so why should you ever use a vector? There are two answers. One is that a deque has greater storage overhead than a vector, averaging up to one additional pointer per element. That may or may not be important, depending on the amount of useful data stored in each element and the total number of elements simultaneously used by a given application.

A more important issue is the cost of each operation. Accessing an arbitrary element of a deque may be a constant-time operation, on average, but it is still rather more expensive than accessing an arbitrary element of a vector. A given application may not benefit sufficiently from the added flexibility of a deque to justify the added overheads in code space and execution time, compared to analogous operations on vectors.

In summary, you can look at a deque as an interesting compromise between a vector and a list. Choose one of these two simpler containers if it has acceptable time complexity for the most used operations in a given application. Choose a deque when its unique balance of properties justifies the added complexity it introduces.

Functional Description

```
namespace std {
template<class T, class A>
    class deque;

        // TEMPLATE FUNCTIONS
template<class T, class A>
    bool operator==(
        const deque<T, A>& lhs,
        const deque<T, A>& rhs);
template<class T, class A>
    bool operator!=(
        const deque<T, A>& lhs,
        const deque<T, A>& rhs);
template<class T, class A>
    bool operator<(
        const deque<T, A>& lhs,
        const deque<T, A>& rhs);
template<class T, class A>
    bool operator>(
        const deque<T, A>& lhs,
        const deque<T, A>& rhs);
```

```
template<class T, class A>
    bool operator<=(
        const deque<T, A>& lhs,
        const deque<T, A>& rhs);
template<class T, class A>
    bool operator>=(
        const deque<T, A>& lhs,
        const deque<T, A>& rhs);
template<class T, class A>
    void swap(
        deque<T, A>& lhs,
        deque<T, A>& rhs);
    };
```

Include the STL standard header **<deque>** to define the container template class **deque** and several supporting templates.

deque

```
template<class T, class A = allocator<T> >
    class deque {
public:
    typedef A allocator_type;
    typedef typename A::pointer pointer;
    typedef typename A::const_pointer const_pointer;
    typedef typename A::reference reference;
    typedef typename A::const_reference const_reference;
    typedef typename A::value_type value_type;
    typedef T0 iterator;
    typedef T1 const_iterator;
    typedef T2 size_type;
    typedef T3 difference_type;
    typedef reverse_iterator<const_iterator>
        const_reverse_iterator;
    typedef reverse_iterator<iterator>
        reverse_iterator;
    deque();
    explicit deque(const A& al);
    explicit deque(size_type n);
    deque(size_type n, const T& v);
    deque(size_type n, const T& v,
        const A& al);
    deque(const deque& x);
    template<class InIt>
        deque(InIt first, InIt last);
    template<class InIt>
        deque(InIt first, InIt last, const A& al);
    iterator begin();
    const_iterator begin() const;
    iterator end();
    const_iterator end() const;
    reverse_iterator rbegin();
    const_reverse_iterator rbegin() const;
    reverse_iterator rend();
    const_reverse_iterator rend() const;
    void resize(size_type n);
    void resize(size_type n, T x);
    size_type size() const;
    size_type max_size() const;
    bool empty() const;
    A get_allocator() const;
    reference at(size_type pos);
```

```
    const_reference at(size_type pos) const;
    reference operator[](size_type pos);
    const_reference operator[](size_type pos);
    reference front();
    const_reference front() const;
    reference back();
    const_reference back() const;
    void push_front(const T& x);
    void pop_front();
    void push_back(const T& x);
    void pop_back();
    template<class InIt>
        void assign(InIt first, InIt last);
    void assign(size_type n, const T& x);
    iterator insert(iterator it, const T& x);
    void insert(iterator it, size_type n, const T& x);
    template<class InIt>
        void insert(iterator it, InIt first, InIt last);
    iterator erase(iterator it);
    iterator erase(iterator first, iterator last);
    void clear();
    void swap(deque& x);
    };
```

The template class describes an object that controls a varying-length sequence of elements of type **T**. The sequence is represented in a way that permits insertion and removal of an element at either end with a single element copy (constant time). Such operations in the middle of the sequence require element copies and assignments proportional to the number of elements in the sequence (linear time).

The object allocates and frees storage for the sequence it controls through a stored allocator object of class **A**. Such an allocator object must have the same external interface as an object of template class **allocator**. Note that the stored allocator object is *not* copied when the container object is assigned.

Deque reallocation occurs when a member function must insert or erase elements of the controlled sequence:

- If an element is inserted into an empty sequence, or if an element is erased to leave an empty sequence, then iterators earlier returned by **begin()** and **end()** become *invalid*.
- If an element is inserted at **first()**, then all iterators but no references, that designate existing elements become invalid.
- If an element is inserted at **end()**, then **end()** and all iterators, but no references, that designate existing elements become invalid.
- If an element is erased at **first()**, only that iterator and references to the erased element become invalid.
- If an element is erased at **last() - 1**, only that iterator, **last()**, and references to the erased element become invalid.
- Otherwise, inserting or erasing an element invalidates all iterators and references.

- **deque::allocator_type**

```
typedef A allocator_type;
```

The type is a synonym for the template parameter **A**.

- **deque::assign**

```
template<class InIt>
    void assign(InIt first, InIt last);
void assign(size_type n, const T& x);
```

If `InIt` is an integer type, the first member function behaves the same as `assign((size_type)first, (T)last)`. Otherwise, the first member function replaces the sequence controlled by `*this` with the sequence `[first, last)`, which must *not* overlap the initial controlled sequence. The second member function replaces the sequence controlled by `*this` with a repetition of `n` elements of value `x`.

- **deque::at**

```
const_reference at(size_type pos) const;
reference at(size_type pos);
```

The member function returns a reference to the element of the controlled sequence at position `pos`. If that position is invalid, the function throws an object of class `out_of_range`.

- **deque::back**

```
reference back();
const_reference back() const;
```

The member function returns a reference to the last element of the controlled sequence, which must be non-empty.

- **deque::begin**

```
const_iterator begin() const;
iterator begin();
```

The member function returns a random-access iterator that points at the first element of the sequence (or just beyond the end of an empty sequence).

- **deque::clear**

```
void clear();
```

The member function calls `erase( begin(), end())`.

- **deque::const_iterator**

```
typedef T1 const_iterator;
```

The type describes an object that can serve as a constant random-access iterator for the controlled sequence. It is described here as a synonym for the implementation-defined type `T1`.

- **deque::const_pointer**

```
typedef typename A::const_pointer const_pointer;
```

The type describes an object that can serve as a constant pointer to an element of the controlled sequence.

deque::const_reference

```
typedef typename A::const_reference const_reference;
```

The type describes an object that can serve as a constant reference to an element of the controlled sequence.

deque::const_reverse_iterator

```
typedef reverse_iterator<const_iterator>
    const_reverse_iterator;
```

The type describes an object that can serve as a constant reverse random-access iterator for the controlled sequence.

deque::deque

```
deque();
explicit deque(const A& al);
explicit deque(size_type n);
deque(size_type n, const T& v);
deque(size_type n, const T& v,
    const A& al);
deque(const deque& x);
template<class InIt>
    deque(InIt first, InIt last);
template<class InIt>
    deque(InIt first, InIt last, const A& al);
```

All constructors store an allocator object and initialize the controlled sequence. The allocator object is the argument `al`, if present. For the copy constructor, it is `x.get_allocator()`. Otherwise, it is `A()`.

The first two constructors specify an empty initial controlled sequence. The third constructor specifies a repetition of `n` elements of value `T()`. The fourth and fifth constructors specify a repetition of `n` elements of value `x`. The sixth constructor specifies a copy of the sequence controlled by `x`. If `InIt` is an integer type, the last two constructors specify a repetition of `(size_type)first` elements of value `(T)last`. Otherwise, the last two constructors specify the sequence `[first, last)`.

deque::difference_type

```
typedef T3 difference_type;
```

The signed integer type describes an object that can represent the difference between the addresses of any two elements in the controlled sequence. It is described here as a synonym for the implementation-defined type `T3`.

deque::empty

```
bool empty() const;
```

The member function returns true for an empty controlled sequence.

deque::end

```
const_iterator end() const;
iterator end();
```

The member function returns a random-access iterator that points just beyond the end of the sequence.

deque::erase

```
iterator erase(iterator it);
iterator erase(iterator first, iterator last);
```

The first member function removes the element of the controlled sequence pointed to by `it`. The second member function removes the elements of the controlled sequence in the range `[first, last)`. Both return an iterator that designates the first element remaining beyond any elements removed, or `end()` if no such element exists.

Removing `N` elements causes `N` destructor calls and an assignment for each of the elements between the insertion point and the nearer end of the sequence. Removing an element at either end invalidates only iterators and references that designate the erased elements. Otherwise, erasing an element invalidates all iterators and references.

The member functions never throw an exception.

deque::front

```
reference front();
const_reference front() const;
```

The member function returns a reference to the first element of the controlled sequence, which must be non-empty.

deque::get_allocator

```
A get_allocator() const;
```

The member function returns the stored allocator object.

deque::insert

```
iterator insert(iterator it, const T& x);
void insert(iterator it, size_type n, const T& x);
template<class InIt>
    void insert(iterator it, InIt first, InIt last);
```

Each of the member functions inserts, before the element pointed to by `it` in the controlled sequence, a sequence specified by the remaining operands. The first member function inserts a single element with value `x` and returns an iterator that points to the newly inserted element. The second member function inserts a repetition of `n` elements of value `x`.

If `InIt` is an integer type, the last member function behaves the same as `insert(it, (size_type)first, (T)last)`. Otherwise, the last member function inserts the sequence `[first, last)`, which must *not* overlap the initial controlled sequence.

When inserting a single element, the number of element copies is linear in the number of elements between the insertion point and the nearer end of the sequence. When inserting a single element at either end of the sequence, the amortized number of element copies is constant. When inserting `N` elements, the number of element copies is linear in `N` plus the number of elements between the insertion point and the nearer end of the sequence — except when the template member is specialized for `InIt` an input or forward iterator, which behaves like `N` single insertions. Inserting an element at either end invalidates all iterators, but no references, that designate existing elements. Otherwise, inserting an element invalidates all iterators and references.

If an exception is thrown during the insertion of a single element, the container is left unaltered and the exception is rethrown. If an exception is thrown during the insertion of multiple elements, and the exception is not thrown while copying an element, the container is left unaltered and the exception is rethrown.

- **`deque::iterator`**

```
typedef T0 iterator;
```

The type describes an object that can serve as a random-access iterator for the controlled sequence. It is described here as a synonym for the implementation-defined type `T0`.

- **`deque::max_size`**

```
size_type max_size() const;
```

The member function returns the length of the longest sequence that the object can control.

- **`deque::operator[]`**

```
const_reference operator[](size_type pos) const;
reference operator[](size_type pos);
```

The member function returns a reference to the element of the controlled sequence at position `pos`. If that position is invalid, the behavior is undefined.

- **`deque::pointer`**

```
typedef typename A::pointer pointer;
```

The type describes an object that can serve as a pointer to an element of the controlled sequence.

- **`deque::pop_back`**

```
void pop_back();
```

The member function removes the last element of the controlled sequence, which must be non-empty. Removing the element invalidates only iterators and references that designate the erased element.

The member function never throws an exception.

- **`deque::pop_front`**

```
void pop_front();
```

The member function removes the first element of the controlled sequence, which must be non-empty. Removing the element invalidates only iterators and references that designate the erased element.

The member function never throws an exception.

▫ **deque::push_back**

```
void push_back(const T& x);
```

The member function inserts an element with value **x** at the end of the controlled sequence. Inserting the element invalidates all iterators, but no references, to existing elements.

If an exception is thrown, the container is left unaltered and the exception is rethrown.

▫ **deque::push_front**

```
void push_front(const T& x);
```

The member function inserts an element with value **x** at the beginning of the controlled sequence. Inserting the element invalidates all iterators, but no references, to existing elements.

If an exception is thrown, the container is left unaltered and the exception is rethrown.

▫ **deque::rbegin**

```
const_reverse_iterator rbegin() const;
reverse_iterator rbegin();
```

The member function returns a reverse iterator that points just beyond the end of the controlled sequence. Hence, it designates the beginning of the reverse sequence.

▫ **deque::reference**

```
typedef typename A::reference reference;
```

The type describes an object that can serve as a reference to an element of the controlled sequence.

▫ **deque::rend**

```
const_reverse_iterator rend() const;
reverse_iterator rend();
```

The member function returns a reverse iterator that points at the first element of the sequence (or just beyond the end of an empty sequence). Hence, it designates the end of the reverse sequence.

▫ **deque::resize**

```
void resize(size_type n);
void resize(size_type n, T x);
```

The member functions both ensure that **size()** henceforth returns **n**. If it must make the controlled sequence longer, the first member function appends elements with value **T()**, while the second member function appends elements with value **x**. To make the controlled sequence shorter, both member functions call **erase(begin() + n, end())**.

▫ **deque::reverse_iterator**

```
typedef reverse_iterator<iterator>
    reverse_iterator;
```

The type describes an object that can serve as a reverse random-access iterator for the controlled sequence.

- **deque::size**

```
size_type size() const;
```

The member function returns the length of the controlled sequence.

- **deque::size_type**

```
typedef T2 size_type;
```

The unsigned integer type describes an object that can represent the length of any controlled sequence. It is described here as a synonym for the implementation-defined type `T2`.

- **deque::swap**

```
void swap(deque& x);
```

The member function swaps the controlled sequences between `*this` and `x`. If `get_allocator() == x.get_allocator()`, it does so in constant time, it throws no exceptions, and it invalidates no references, pointers, or iterators that designate elements in the two controlled sequences. Otherwise, it performs a number of element assignments and constructor calls proportional to the number of elements in the two controlled sequences.

- **deque::value_type**

```
typedef typename A::value_type value_type;
```

The type is a synonym for the template parameter `T`.

- **operator!=**

```
template<class T, class A>
    bool operator!=(
        const deque <T, A>& lhs,
        const deque <T, A>& rhs);
```

The template function returns `!(lhs == rhs)`.

- **operator==**

```
template<class T, class A>
    bool operator==(
        const deque <T, A>& lhs,
        const deque <T, A>& rhs);
```

The template function overloads `operator==` to compare two objects of template class `deque`. The function returns `lhs.size() == rhs.size() && equal(lhs. begin(), lhs. end(), rhs.begin())`.

- **operator<**

```
template<class T, class A>
    bool operator<(
        const deque <T, A>& lhs,
        const deque <T, A>& rhs);
```

The template function overloads `operator<` to compare two objects of template class `deque`. The function returns `lexicographical_compare(lhs. begin(), lhs. end(), rhs.begin(), rhs.end())`.

▫ operator<=

```
template<class T, class A>
    bool operator<=(
        const deque <T, A>& lhs,
        const deque <T, A>& rhs);
```

The template function returns `!(rhs < lhs)`.

▫ operator>

```
template<class T, class A>
    bool operator>(
        const deque <T, A>& lhs,
        const deque <T, A>& rhs);
```

The template function returns `rhs < lhs`.

▫ operator>=

```
template<class T, class A>
    bool operator>=(
        const deque <T, A>& lhs,
        const deque <T, A>& rhs);
```

The template function returns `!(lhs < rhs)`.

▫ swap

```
template<class T, class A>
    void swap(
        deque <T, A>& lhs,
        deque <T, A>& rhs);
```

The template function executes `lhs.swap(rhs)`.

Using <deque>

deque Include the header `<deque>` to make use of template class `deque`. You can specialize `deque` to store elements of type `T` by writing a type definition such as:

```
typedef deque<T, allocator<T> > Mycont;
```

Using a default template argument, however, you can omit the second argument.

Template class `deque` supports all the common operations on containers, as we described in Chapter 9: Containers. (See the discussion beginning on page 248.) We summarize here only those properties peculiar to template class `deque`.

constructors To construct an object of class `deque<T, A>`, you can write any of:

- `deque()` to declare an empty deque.
- `deque(al)` as above, also storing the allocator object `al`.
- `deque(n)` to declare a deque with `n` elements, each constructed with the default constructor `T()`.
- `deque(n, val)` to declare a deque with `n` elements, each constructed with the copy constructor `T(val)`.

- `deque(n, val, al)` as above, also storing the allocator object `al`.
- `deque(first, last)` to declare a deque with initial elements copied from the sequence designated by `[first, last)`.
- `deque(first, last, al)` as above, also storing the allocator object `al`.

If you have specialized the template class for an allocator of type `allocator<T>`, which is the customary (and default) thing to do, there is nothing to be gained by specifying an explicit allocator argument `al`. Such an argument matters only for some allocators that the program defines explicitly. (See the discussion of allocators in Chapter 4: `<memory>`.)

The following descriptions all assume that `cont` is an object of class `deque<T, A>`.

resize To change the length of the controlled sequence to `n` elements, call `cont.resize(n)`. Excess elements are erased. If the sequence must be extended, elements with the value `T()` are inserted as needed at the end. You can also call `cont.resize(n, val)` to extend the sequence with elements that store the value `val`.

clear To remove all elements, call `cont.clear()`. Note, however, that `clear` does not promise to reduce the amount of reserved storage. (Blocks of elements are allocated and freed as needed, but the map may grow arbitrarily large and never shrink.) This implementation does indeed release all reserved storage if you call `cont.clear()` or if you assign to it a deque with zero size, but that behavior is not required by the C++ Standard. The one sure way to release all reserved storage is with the peculiar idiom:

```
cont.swap(deque<T, A>());
```

This expression statement constructs a temporary empty deque and swaps its contents with `cont`. The temporary is destroyed at the end of the statement, taking any allocated storage obtained from `cont` along with it.

front To access the first element of the controlled sequence, call `cont.front()`.
back To access the last element, call `cont.back()`. If `cont` is not a const object, the expression is an lvalue, so you can alter the value stored in the element by writing an expression such as `cont.front() = T()`. If the sequence is empty, however, these expressions have undefined behavior.

operator[] To access element `i` (counting from zero), write the expression `cont[i]`.
at If `cont` is not a const object, the expression is an lvalue. `cont[i]` has undefined behavior if `i` is not in the half-open interval `[0, cont.size())`. You can also write `cont.at(i)` in place of `cont[i]`. For this call, however, if `i` is not a valid element number, the expression throws an object of class `out_of_range`.

push_back To append an object with stored value `x`, call `cont.push_back(x)`. To
push_front prepend an object with stored value `x`, call `cont.push_front(x)`.

pop_back To remove the last element, call `cont.pop_back()`. To remove the first
pop_front element, call `cont.pop_front()`. For either pop operation, the sequence must, of course, be non-empty or the call has undefined bahavior.

assign To replace the controlled sequence with the elements from a sequence designated by `[first, last)`, call `cont.assign(first, last)`. The sequence must not be any part of the initial controlled sequence. To replace the controlled sequence with `n` copies of the value `x`, call `cont.assign(n, x)`.

insert To insert an element storing the value `x` before the element designated by the iterator `it`, call `cont.insert(it, x)`. The return value is an iterator designating the inserted element. To insert the elements of a sequence designated by `[first, last)` before the element designated by the iterator `it`, call `cont.insert(it, first, last)`. The sequence must not be any part of the initial controlled sequence. To insert `n` copies of the value `x`, call `cont.insert(it, n, x)`.

erase To erase the element designated by the iterator `it`, call `cont.erase(it)`. The return value is an iterator designating the element just beyond the erased element. To erase a range of elements designated by `[first, last)`, call `cont.erase(first, last)`.

Implementing `<deque>`

Figures 12.1 through 12.12 show the file **deque**. It defines template class **deque**, along with a few template functions that take deque operands. Template class **deque** stores a controlled sequence of length **N** as a two-level hierarchy. Two parameters determine the shape of this hierarchy:

DEQUESIZ
- Deque elements are stored in fixed-size blocks, which are contiguous arrays of **DEQUESIZ** elements. (**DEQUESIZ** corresponds to the parameter **B** in descriptions earlier in this chapter.) The definition is contrived to ensure at least one element per block, while endeavoring to pack multiple smaller elements in blocks of a more sensible size.

DEQUEMAPSIZ
- Each block is designated by an element in a map array. The map array consists of a (logically) contiguous sequence of pointers to blocks stored inside a larger containing array. The containing array, once allocated, always has at least **DEQUEMAPSIZ** elements. The size is chosen to minimize map reallocations when a deque first begins to grow, and to justify the typical overhead inherent in any object allocated on the heap.

Needless to say, both **DEQUESIZ** and **DEQUEMAPSIZ** are parameters subject to tradeoffs. The smaller they are, the less storage wasted for short controlled sequences. The larger they are, the less time wasted in growing large controlled sequences. This implementation endeavors to allocate blocks of at least 16 bytes, to justify the overhead of allocating blocks on the heap. It also tries to keep maps as small as possible, but not ridiculously small. Thus the minimum of eight pointers in a map.

Template class **deque** defines allocator objects much the same way as does template class **list**, and for much the same reasons. (See the discussion beginning on page 303.) It stores two kinds of allocator objects:

Figure 12.1: deque Part 1

```
// deque standard header
#ifndef DEQUE_
#define DEQUE_
#include <memory>
#include <stdexcept>
namespace std {

		// TEMPLATE CLASS Deque_map
template<class Ty, class A>
	class Deque_map {
protected:
	Deque_map(A Al)
		: Almap(Al) {}
	typedef typename A::template
		rebind<Ty>::other::pointer Tptr;
	typename A::template rebind<Tptr>::other Almap;
	};

		// TEMPLATE CLASS Deque_val
template<class Ty, class A>
	class Deque_val : public Deque_map<Ty, A> {
protected:
	Deque_val(A Al = A())
		: Deque_map<Ty, A>(Al), Alval(Al) {}
	typedef typename A::template
		rebind<Ty>::other Alty;
	Alty Alval;
	};

		// TEMPLATE CLASS deque
template<class Ty, class Ax = allocator<Ty> >
	class deque
		: public Deque_val<Ty, Ax> {
public:
	enum {DEQUEMAPSIZ = 8};                              /* at least 1 */
	enum {DEQUESIZ = sizeof (Ty) <= 1 ? 16
		: sizeof (Ty) <= 2 ? 8
		: sizeof (Ty) <= 4 ? 4
		: sizeof (Ty) <= 8 ? 2 : 1};

	typedef deque<Ty, Ax> Myt;
	typedef Deque_val<Ty, Ax> Mybase;
	typedef typename Mybase::Alty A;
	typedef A allocator_type;
	typedef typename A::size_type size_type;
	typedef typename A::difference_type Dift;
	typedef Dift difference_type;
	typedef typename A::pointer Tptr;
	typedef typename A::const_pointer Ctptr;
	typedef Tptr pointer;
	typedef Ctptr const_pointer;
	typedef typename A::template
		rebind::<Tptr>::other::pointer Mapptr;
	typedef typename A::reference Reft;
```

Figure 12.2: deque Part 2

```
typedef Tptr pointer;
typedef Ctptr const_pointer;
typedef Reft reference;
typedef typename A::const_reference const_reference;
typedef typename A::value_type value_type;

     // CLASS iterator
class iterator;
friend class iterator;
class iterator : public Ranit<Ty, Dift, Tptr, Reft> {
public:
     typedef Ranit<Ty, Dift, Tptr, Reft> Mybase;
     typedef typename Mybase::iterator_category
          iterator_category;
     typedef typename Mybase::value_type value_type;
     typedef typename Mybase::difference_type
          difference_type;
     typedef typename Mybase::pointer pointer;
     typedef typename Mybase::reference reference;
     iterator()
          : Idx(0), Deque(0)
          {}
     iterator(difference_type I, const deque<Ty, A> *P)
          : Idx(I), Deque(P)
          {}
     reference operator*() const
          {size_type Block = Idx / DEQUESIZ;
          size_type Off = Idx - Block * DEQUESIZ;
          if (Deque->Mapsize <= Block)
               Block -= Deque->Mapsize;
          return ((Deque->Map)[Block][Off]); }
     Tptr operator->() const
          {return (&**this); }
     iterator& operator++()
          {++Idx;
          return (*this); }
     iterator operator++(int)
          {iterator Tmp = *this;
          ++*this;
          return (Tmp); }
     iterator& operator--()
          {--Idx;
          return (*this); }
     iterator operator--(int)
          {iterator Tmp = *this;
          --*this;
          return (Tmp); }
     iterator& operator+=(difference_type N)
          {Idx += N;
          return (*this); }
     iterator& operator-=(difference_type N)
          {return (*this += -N); }
     iterator operator+(difference_type N) const
          {iterator Tmp = *this;
          return (Tmp += N); }
```

Figure 12.3: deque Part 3

```
        iterator operator-(difference_type N) const
            {iterator Tmp = *this;
            return (Tmp -= N); }
        difference_type operator-(const iterator& X) const
            {return (Idx - X.Idx); }
        reference operator[](difference_type N) const
            {return (*(*this + N)); }
        bool operator==(const iterator& X) const
            {return (Deque == X.Deque && Idx == X.Idx); }
        bool operator!=(const iterator& X) const
            {return (!(*this == X)); }
        bool operator<(const iterator& X) const
            {return (Idx < X.Idx); }
        bool operator<=(const iterator& X) const
            {return (!(X < *this)); }
        bool operator>(const iterator& X) const
            {return (X < *this); }
        bool operator>=(const iterator& X) const
            {return (!(*this < X)); }
    protected:
        difference_type Idx;
        const deque<Ty, A> *Deque;
        };

        // CLASS const_iterator
    class const_iterator;
    friend class const_iterator;
    class const_iterator
        : public Ranit<Ty, Dift, Ctptr, const_reference> {
    public:
        typedef Ranit<Ty, Dift, Ctptr, const_reference>
            Mybase;
        typedef typename Mybase::iterator_category
            iterator_category;
        typedef typename Mybase::value_type value_type;
        typedef typename Mybase::difference_type
            difference_type;
        typedef typename Mybase::pointer pointer;
        typedef typename Mybase::reference reference;
        const_iterator()
            : Idx(0), Deque(0)
            {}
        const_iterator(difference_type I,
            const deque<Ty, A> *P)
            : Idx(I), Deque(P)
            {}
        const_iterator(
            const typename deque<Ty, A>::iterator& X)
            : Idx(X.Idx), Deque(X.Deque)
            {}
        const_reference operator*() const
            {size_type Block = Idx / DEQUESIZ;
            size_type Off = Idx - Block * DEQUESIZ;
```

Figure 12.4: deque Part 4

```
            if (Deque->Mapsize <= Block)
                Block -= Deque->Mapsize;
            return ((Deque->Map)[Block][Off]); }
        Ctptr operator->() const
            {return (&**this); }
        const_iterator& operator++()
            {++Idx;
            return (*this); }
        const_iterator operator++(int)
            {const_iterator Tmp = *this;
            ++*this;
            return (Tmp); }
        const_iterator& operator--()
            {--Idx;
            return (*this); }
        const_iterator operator--(int)
            {const_iterator Tmp = *this;
            --*this;
            return (Tmp); }
        const_iterator& operator+=(difference_type N)
            {Idx += N;
            return (*this); }
        const_iterator& operator-=(difference_type N)
            {return (*this += -N); }
        const_iterator operator+(difference_type N) const
            {const_iterator Tmp = *this;
            return (Tmp += N); }
        const_iterator operator-(difference_type N) const
            {const_iterator Tmp = *this;
            return (Tmp -= N); }
        difference_type operator-(
            const const_iterator& X) const
            {return (Idx - X.Idx); }
        const_reference operator[](difference_type N) const
            {return (*(*this + N)); }
        bool operator==(const const_iterator& X) const
            {return (Deque == X.Deque && Idx == X.Idx); }
        bool operator!=(const const_iterator& X) const
            {return (!(*this == X)); }
        bool operator<(const const_iterator& X) const
            {return (Idx < X.Idx); }
        bool operator<=(const const_iterator& X) const
            {return (!(X < *this)); }
        bool operator>(const const_iterator& X) const
            {return (X < *this); }
        bool operator>=(const const_iterator& X) const
            {return (!(*this < X)); }
    protected:
        difference_type Idx;
        const deque<Ty, A> *Deque;
        };

    typedef std::reverse_iterator<iterator>
        reverse_iterator;
```

Figure 12.5: deque Part 5

```
typedef std::reverse_iterator<const_iterator>
     const_reverse_iterator;

deque()
     : Mybase(), Map(0),
          Mapsize(0), Offset(0), Size(0)
     {}
explicit deque(const A& Al)
     : Mybase(Al), Map(0),
          Mapsize(0), Offset(0), Size(0)
     {}
explicit deque(size_type N)
     : Mybase(), Map(0),
          Mapsize(0), Offset(0), Size(0)
     {insert(begin(), N, Ty()); }
deque(size_type N, const Ty& V)
     : Mybase(), Map(0),
          Mapsize(0), Offset(0), Size(0)
     {insert(begin(), N, V); }
deque(size_type N, const Ty& V, const A& Al)
     : Mybase(Al), Map(0),
          Mapsize(0), Offset(0), Size(0)
     {insert(begin(), N, V); }
deque(const Myt& X)
     : Mybase(X.Alval), Map(0),
          Mapsize(0), Offset(0), Size(0)
     {insert(begin(), X.begin(), X.end()); }
template<class It>
     deque(It F, It L)
     : Mybase(), Map(0),
          Mapsize(0), Offset(0), Size(0)
     {Construct(F, L, Iter_cat(F)); }
template<class It>
     deque(It F, It L, const A& Al)
     : Mybase(Al), Map(0),
          Mapsize(0), Offset(0), Size(0)
     {Construct(F, L, Iter_cat(F)); }
template<class It>
     void Construct(It F, It L, Int_iterator_tag)
     {insert(begin(), (size_type)F, (Ty)L); }
template<class It>
     void Construct(It F, It L, input_iterator_tag)
     {insert(begin(), F, L); }

~deque()
     {clear(); }
Myt& operator=(const Myt& X)
     {if (this == &X)
          ;
     else if (X.size() == 0)
          clear();
     else if (X.size() <= size())
          {iterator S = copy(X.begin(), X.end(), begin());
          erase(S, end()); }
```

Figure 12.6: deque Part 6

```
        else
            {const_iterator Sx = X.begin() + size();
            copy(X.begin(), Sx, begin());
            insert(end(), Sx, X.end()); }
        return (*this); }
    iterator begin()
        {return (iterator(Offset, this)); }
    const_iterator begin() const
        {return (const_iterator(Offset, this)); }
    iterator end()
        {return (iterator(Offset + Size, this)); }
    const_iterator end() const
        {return (const_iterator(Offset + Size, this)); }
    reverse_iterator rbegin()
        {return (reverse_iterator(end())); }
    const_reverse_iterator rbegin() const
        {return (const_reverse_iterator(end())); }
    reverse_iterator rend()
        {return (reverse_iterator(begin())); }
    const_reverse_iterator rend() const
        {return (const_reverse_iterator(begin())); }
    void resize(size_type N)
        {resize(N, Ty()); }
    void resize(size_type N, Ty X)
        {if (size() < N)
            insert(end(), N - size(), X);
        else if (N < size())
            erase(begin() + N, end()); }
    size_type size() const
        {return (Size); }
    size_type max_size() const
        {return (Alval.max_size()); }
    bool empty() const
        {return (size() == 0); }
    allocator_type get_allocator() const
        {return (Alval); }
    const_reference at(size_type P) const
        {if (size() <= P)
            Xran();
        return (*(begin() + P)); }
    reference at(size_type P)
        {if (size() <= P)
            Xran();
        return (*(begin() + P)); }
    const_reference operator[](size_type P) const
        {return (*(begin() + P)); }
    reference operator[](size_type P)
        {return (*(begin() + P)); }
    reference front()
        {return (*begin()); }
    const_reference front() const
        {return (*begin()); }
    reference back()
        {return (*(end() - 1)); }
```

Figure 12.7: deque Part 7

```
const_reference back() const
     {return (*(end() - 1)); }
void push_front(const Ty& X)
     {if (Offset % DEQUESIZ == 0
          && Mapsize <= (Size + DEQUESIZ) / DEQUESIZ)
          Growmap(1);
     size_type Newoff = Offset != 0 ? Offset
          : Mapsize * DEQUESIZ;
     size_type Block = --Newoff / DEQUESIZ;
     if (Map[Block] == 0)
          Map[Block] = Alval.allocate(DEQUESIZ, (void *)0);
     try {
     Offset = Newoff;
     ++Size;
     Alval.construct(Map[Block] + Newoff % DEQUESIZ, X);
     } catch (...) {
     pop_front();
     throw;
     }}
void pop_front()
     {if (!empty())
          {size_type Block = Offset / DEQUESIZ;
          Alval.destroy(Map[Block] + Offset % DEQUESIZ);
          if (Mapsize * DEQUESIZ <= ++Offset)
               Offset = 0;
          if (--Size == 0)
               Offset = 0; }}
void push_back(const Ty& X)
     {if ((Offset + Size) % DEQUESIZ == 0
          && Mapsize <= (Size + DEQUESIZ) / DEQUESIZ)
          Growmap(1);
     size_type Newoff = Offset + Size;
     size_type Block = Newoff / DEQUESIZ;
     if (Mapsize <= Block)
          Block -= Mapsize;
     if (Map[Block] == 0)
          Map[Block] = Alval.allocate(DEQUESIZ, (void *)0);
     try {
     ++Size;
     Alval.construct(Map[Block] + Newoff % DEQUESIZ, X);
     } catch (...) {
     pop_back();
     throw;
     }}
void pop_back()
     {if (!empty())
          {size_type Newoff = Size + Offset - 1;
          size_type Block = Newoff / DEQUESIZ;
          if (Mapsize <= Block)
               Block -= Mapsize;
          Alval.destroy(Map[Block] + Newoff % DEQUESIZ);
          if (--Size == 0)
               Offset = 0; }}
```

Figure 12.8: deque Part 8

```
template<class It>
     void assign(It F, It L)
     {Assign(F, L, Iter_cat(F)); }
template<class It>
     void Assign(It F, It L, Int_iterator_tag)
     {assign((size_type)F, (Ty)L); }
template<class It>
     void Assign(It F, It L, input_iterator_tag)
     {erase(begin(), end());
     insert(begin(), F, L); }
void assign(size_type N, const Ty& X)
     {Ty Tx = X;
     erase(begin(), end());
     insert(begin(), N, Tx); }
iterator insert(iterator P, const Ty& X)
     {if (P == begin())
          {push_front(X);
          return (begin()); }
     else if (P == end())
          {push_back(X);
          return (end() - 1); }
     else
          {iterator S;
          size_type Off = P - begin();
          Ty Tx = X;
          if (Off < size() / 2)
               {push_front(front());
               S = begin() + Off;
               copy(begin() + 2, S + 1, begin() + 1); }
          else
               {push_back(back());
               S = begin() + Off;
               copy_backward(S, end() - 2, end() - 1); }
          *S = Tx;
          return (S); }}
void insert(iterator P, size_type M, const Ty& X)
     {iterator S;
     size_type I;
     size_type Off = P - begin();
     size_type Rem = Size - Off;
     if (Off < Rem)
          if (Off < M)
               {for (I = M - Off; 0 < I; --I)
                    push_front(X);
               for (I = Off; 0 < I; --I)
                    push_front(begin()[M - 1]);
               S = begin() + M;
               fill(S, S + Off, X); }
          else
               {for (I = M; 0 < I; --I)
                    push_front(begin()[M - 1]);
               S = begin() + M;
               Ty Tx = X;
               copy(S + M, S + Off, S);
               fill(begin() + Off, S + Off, Tx); }
```

Figure 12.9: deque Part 9

```
            else
                if (Rem < M)
                    {for (I = M - Rem; 0 < I; --I)
                        push_back(X);
                    for (I = 0; I < Rem; ++I)
                        push_back(begin()[Off + I]);
                    S = begin() + Off;
                    fill(S, S + Rem, X); }
                else
                    {for (I = 0; I < M; ++I)
                        push_back(begin()[Off + Rem - M + I]);
                    S = begin() + Off;
                    Ty Tx = X;
                    copy_backward(S, S + Rem - M, S + Rem);
                    fill(S, S + M, Tx); }}
    template<class It>
        void insert(iterator P, It F, It L)
        {Insert(P, F, L, Iter_cat(F)); }
    template<class It>
        void Insert(iterator P, It F, It L,
            Int_iterator_tag)
        {insert(P, (size_type)F, (Ty)L); }
    template<class It>
        void Insert(iterator P, It F, It L,
            input_iterator_tag)
        {size_type Off = P - begin();
        for (; F != L; ++F, ++Off)
            insert(begin() + Off, *F); }
    template<class It>
        void Insert(iterator P, It F, It L,
            bidirectional_iterator_tag)
        {size_type M = 0;
        Distance(F, L, M);
        size_type I;
        size_type Off = P - begin();
        size_type Rem = Size - Off;
        if (Off < Rem)
            if (Off < M)
                {It Qx = F;
                advance(Qx, M - Off);
                for (It Q = Qx; F != Q; )
                    push_front(*--Q);
                for (I = Off; 0 < I; --I)
                    push_front(begin()[M - 1]);
                copy(Qx, L, begin() + M); }
            else
                {for (I = M; 0 < I; --I)
                    push_front(begin()[M - 1]);
                iterator S = begin() + M;
                copy(S + M, S + Off, S);
                copy(F, L, begin() + Off); }
        else
            if (Rem < M)
                {It Qx = F;
                advance(Qx, Rem);
```

Figure 12.10: deque Part 10

```
                    for (It Q = Qx; Q != L; ++Q)
                        push_back(*Q);
                    for (I = 0; I < Rem; ++I)
                        push_back(begin()[Off + I]);
                    copy(F, Qx, begin() + Off); }
                else
                    {for (I = 0; I < M; ++I)
                        push_back(begin()[Off + Rem - M + I]);
                    iterator S = begin() + Off;
                    copy_backward(S, S + Rem - M, S + Rem);
                    copy(F, L, S); }}
    iterator erase(iterator P)
        {return (erase(P, P + 1)); }
    iterator erase(iterator F, iterator L)
        {size_type N = L - F;
        size_type M = F - begin();
        if (M < (size_type)(end() - L))
            {copy_backward(begin(), F, L);
            for (; 0 < N; --N)
                pop_front(); }
        else
            {copy(L, end(), F);
            for (; 0 < N; --N)
                pop_back(); }
        return (M == 0 ? begin() : begin() + M); }
    void clear()
        {while (!empty())
            pop_back();
        Freemap(); }
    void swap(Myt& X)
        {if (Alval == X.Alval)
            {std::swap(Map, X.Map);
            std::swap(Mapsize, X.Mapsize);
            std::swap(Offset, X.Offset);
            std::swap(Size, X.Size); }
        else
            {Myt Ts = *this; *this = X, X = Ts; }}

protected:
    void Xlen() const
        {throw length_error("deque<T> too long"); }
    void Xran() const
        {throw out_of_range("deque<T> subscript"); }

    void Freemap()
        {for (size_type M = Mapsize; 0 < M; )
            {Alval.deallocate(*(Map + --M), DEQUESIZ);
            Almap.destroy(Map + M); }
        Almap.deallocate(Map, Mapsize);
        Mapsize = 0;
        Map = 0; }
    void Growmap(size_type N)
        {if (max_size() / DEQUESIZ - Mapsize < N)
            Xlen();
        size_type I = Mapsize / 2;          // try to grow by 50%
```

Figure 12.11: deque Part 11

```
        if (I < DEQUEMAPSIZ)
            I = DEQUEMAPSIZ;
        if (N < I && Mapsize <= max_size() / DEQUESIZ - I)
            N = I;
        size_type Ib = Offset / DEQUESIZ;
        Mapptr M = Almap.allocate(Mapsize + N, (void *)0);
        Mapptr Mn = M + Ib;
        for (I = Ib; I < Mapsize; ++I, ++Mn)
            {Almap.construct(Mn, Map[I]);
            Almap.destroy(Map + I); }
        if (Ib <= N)
            {for (I = 0; I < Ib; ++I, ++Mn)
                {Almap.construct(Mn, Map[I]);
                Almap.destroy(Map + I);
                Almap.construct(M + I, 0); }
            for (; I < N; ++I, ++Mn)
                Almap.construct(Mn, 0); }
        else
            {for (I = 0; I < N; ++I, ++Mn)
                {Almap.construct(Mn, Map[I]);
                Almap.destroy(Map + I); }
            for (Mn = M; I < Ib; ++I, ++Mn)
                {Almap.construct(Mn, Map[I]);
                Almap.destroy(Map + I); }
            for (I = 0; I < N; ++I, ++Mn)
                Almap.construct(Mn, 0); }
        Map = M;
        Mapsize += N; }

    Mapptr Map;
    size_type Mapsize, Offset, Size;
    };

    // deque TEMPLATE OPERATORS
template<class Ty, class A> inline
    void swap(deque<Ty, A>& X, deque<Ty, A>& Y)
    {X.swap(Y); }

template<class Ty, class A> inline
    bool operator==(const deque<Ty, A>& X,
        const deque<Ty, A>& Y)
    {return (X.size() == Y.size()
        && equal(X.begin(), X.end(), Y.begin())); }
template<class Ty, class A> inline
    bool operator!=(const deque<Ty, A>& X,
        const deque<Ty, A>& Y)
    {return (!(X == Y)); }
template<class Ty, class A> inline
    bool operator<(const deque<Ty, A>& X,
        const deque<Ty, A>& Y)
    {return (lexicographical_compare(X.begin(), X.end(),
        Y.begin(), Y.end())); }
template<class Ty, class A> inline
    bool operator<=(const deque<Ty, A>& X,
        const deque<Ty, A>& Y)
```

Figure 12.12: deque Part 12

```
    {return (!(Y < X)); }
template<class Ty, class A> inline
    bool operator>(const deque<Ty, A>& X,
        const deque<Ty, A>& Y)
    {return (Y < X); }
template<class Ty, class A> inline
    bool operator>=(const deque<Ty, A>& X,
        const deque<Ty, A>& Y)
    {return (!(X < Y)); }
} /* namespace std */
#endif /* DEQUE_ */
```

□

Almap

- **Almap** for the element pointer type, to allocate and free arrays of pointers (maps), and to construct and destroy pointers in those arrays (in case they are other than scalar pointers).

Alty

- **Alty** for the element type, to allocate and free arrays of elements (blocks), and to construct and destroy elements in those arrays.

Deque_map

Also in parallel with the file **list**, the file **deque** defines two template base classes to store these allocators, in the hopes of economizing storage in deque objects. (See the discussion of zero-size allocators beginning on page 266.) The first of these is template class **Deque_map**. The specialization **Deque_map<T, A>** serves as the ultimate base class for **deque<T, A>**. Its sole purpose in life is to store the allocator object **Alval**.

Deque_val

Template class **Deque_val** supplies the second allocator object. The specialization **Deque_val<T, A>** derives publicly from **Deque_map<T, A>** and serves as a public base class for **deque<T, A>**. Its sole purpose in life is to store the allocator object **Alval**.

Besides the allocator objects, a **deque** object stores several objects to represent the controlled sequence. More specifically, a **deque** stores a map pointer and three counts:

Map

- **Map** is a pointer to a map array of pointers. It is initially a null pointer, for a newly constructed empty deque. Unused map array elements also store null pointers.

Mapsize

- **Mapsize** counts the number of pointer elements in the full map array.

Offset

- **Offset** counts the number of free elements before the first active element in the deque. (The first active element is at **Map[Offset / DEQUEMAPSIZ][Offset % DEQUEMAPSIZ]**.)

Size

- **Size** counts the number of active elements in the deque.

The blocks at the beginning and end of a deque can be partially filled. Blocks at the end fill from front to back while those at the beginning fill from back to front. If no room exists to add an element within a block, the deque object allocates another block and extends the active map to point at the new block.

growing the map

A deque object endeavors to leave room to extend the map at either end, so that prepending a new element is as efficient as appending one. Once the map has no further room to grow as needed in its containing array, the deque object must allocate a new containing array and copy over the map. You certainly don't want this to happen any more often than necessary. Otherwise, the time complexity for adding an element will be linear (increasing with the length of the controlled sequence) instead of constant (independent of the length of the controlled sequence).

This raises an interesting issue. To a large extent, a deque simply replaces an array of elements with an array of pointers to (blocks of) those elements. It has to repeatedly reallocate and copy over those pointers as it grows, much as a vector has to repeatedly reallocate and copy over the elements. So it looks like the time complexity for growing a deque is the same as for a vector. What you save is actual copying time if pointers are smaller than the blocks of elements they designate. You also save if pointers have trivial constructors and destructors (as scalar pointers do), and the elements do not. But in any case, a deque must be as careful in growing its map as a vector is in growing its array of elements.

We already mentioned the essential trick in the description of **vector::insert** on page 284. It lowers the amortized time complexity of growing a vector or a deque map. In its simplest form, each newly allocated map array is twice as large as the map it must initially hold. As the controlled sequence grows longer, the rate of reallocation declines. And that bounds the average cost of growing the controlled sequence. This implementation actually tries to grow the map by 50 per cent each time, following the lead of **vector::insert**. The resulting time complexity is the same, but the code trades a greater number of reallocations for more effective storage utilization.

wrapping the map This implementation utilizes still another important technique. It allows the active map to wrap around if it grows off either end of the map array. That way, the active map needs to be reallocated only when elements at the beginning of the controlled sequence threaten to share the same block as elements at the end — when the map is full, in other words. For example, the member function **push_front** begins with the test:

```
if (Offset % DEQUESIZ == 0
    && Mapsize <= (Size + DEQUESIZ) / DEQUESIZ)
    Growmap(1);
```

You will find a similar test at the beginning of **push_back**. By contrast, a common implementation of template class **deque** does not allow the map to wrap. If the active map reaches either end of the map array, one of two things happens. Either the active map is moved away from the end, or it is copied into a newly allocated map that has room for growth.

There are pros and cons to each approach. If the map does not wrap:

- **operator*()** for deque iterators is trivial.
- **operator++()** and other arithmetic can be more ornate.
- Overflow can occur at either end of the map, even if the map array is not completely full.

- Growing the map is much more complex.

If the map does wrap:

- `operator*()` for deque iterators is more ornate.
- `operator++()` and other arithmetic is trivial.
- Overflow occurs only when the map is completely full.
- Growing the map is reasonably simple.

Thus, this implementation gambles that the extra cost of accessing elements through iterators is more than offset by savings in several other areas.

iterator **const_iterator**

Everything you need to know about accessing elements in a deque you can learn by studying the nested classes **iterator** and **const_iterator**. These perform the magic required to walk through a controlled sequence, wrapping around the map and leaping from block to block. Deque iterators are otherwise very similar to template class **Ptrit** (see page 82), which serves as the basis for vector iterators. Both implement random-access iterators.

Each deque iterator stores two objects:

Deque

- **Deque**, a pointer to the deque object

Idx

- **Idx**, the offset of the designated element

Thus, the designated element is:

```
Deque->Map[(Idx / DEQUESIZ) % Deque->Mapsize]
    [Idx % DEQUESIZ]
```

(See the definition of **operator*()** in each of the nested iterator classes.) As the map grows, its active contents are copied in a way that preserves the validity of this expression for all active elements in the controlled sequence.

Nested class **const_iterator** differs from nested class **iterator** in the obvious ways. It also adds a constructor that supports implicit conversion of a **iterator** object to a **const_iterator** object. You will find similar mechanisms in the definitions of all STL container iterators.

push_back **push_front** **Growmap**

Everything you need to know about growing a deque you can learn by studying the member functions **push_back** and **push_front**. These in turn call on the protected member function **Growmap** to grow the map when it has no space to add a new block pointer. **Growmap** is careful to "unwrap" the map as it copies it, in order to preserve the validity of existing iterators as described above.

pop_back **pop_front**

Everything you need to know about shrinking a deque you can learn by studying the member functions **pop_back** and **pop_front**. Note that these member functions do not free blocks as they become empty. Rather, they are left for rapid recycling if the controlled sequence once again grows longer. An implementation more concerned about economizing storage might choose to free blocks more aggressively.

clear **Freemap** **operator=**

The member function **clear** does free all blocks, as well as the map. It empties the container by popping all its elements, then calls the protected member function **Freemap** to free storage and destroy map pointers. Note

Figure 12.13: `tdeque.c` **Part 1**

```
// test <deque>
#include <assert.h>
#include <iostream>
#include <deque>
using namespace std;

     // TEST <deque>
int main()
     {typedef allocator<char> Myal;

     // TEST deque
     typedef deque<char, Myal> Mycont;
     char ch, carr[] = "abc";
     Mycont::allocator_type *p_alloc = (Myal *)0;
     Mycont::pointer p_ptr = (char *)0;
     Mycont::const_pointer p_cptr = (const char *)0;
     Mycont::reference p_ref = ch;
     Mycont::const_reference p_cref = (const char&)ch;
     Mycont::size_type *p_size = (size_t *)0;
     Mycont::difference_type *p_diff = (ptrdiff_t *)0;
     Mycont::value_type *p_val = (char *)0;

     Mycont v0;
     Myal al = v0.get_allocator();
     Mycont v0a(al);
     assert(v0.empty() && v0.size() == 0);
     assert(v0a.size() == 0 && v0a.get_allocator() == al);
     Mycont v1(5), v1a(6, 'x'), v1b(7, 'y', al);
     assert(v1.size() == 5 && v1.back() == '\0');
     assert(v1a.size() == 6 && v1a.back() == 'x');
     assert(v1b.size() == 7 && v1b.back() == 'y');
     Mycont v2(v1a);
     assert(v2.size() == 6 && v2.front() == 'x');
     Mycont v3(v1a.begin(), v1a.end());
     assert(v3.size() == 6 && v3.front() == 'x');
     const Mycont v4(v1a.begin(), v1a.end(), al);
     assert(v4.size() == 6 && v4.front() == 'x');
     v0 = v4;
     assert(v0.size() == 6 && v0.front() == 'x');
     assert(v0[0] == 'x' && v0.at(5) == 'x');

//   v0.reserve(12);
//   assert(12 <= v0.capacity());
     v0.resize(8);
     assert(v0.size() == 8 && v0.back() == '\0');
     v0.resize(10, 'z');
     assert(v0.size() == 10 && v0.back() == 'z');
     assert(v0.size() <= v0.max_size());

     Mycont::iterator p_it(v0.begin());
     Mycont::const_iterator p_cit(v4.begin());
     Mycont::reverse_iterator p_rit(v0.rbegin());
     Mycont::const_reverse_iterator p_crit(v4.rbegin());
     assert(*p_it == 'x' && *--(p_it = v0.end()) == 'z');
     assert(*p_cit == 'x' && *--(p_cit = v4.end()) == 'x');
```

Figure 12.14: `tdeque.c` **Part 2**

```
    assert(*p_rit == 'z'
        && *--(p_rit = v0.rend()) == 'x');
    assert(*p_crit == 'x'
        && *--(p_crit = v4.rend()) == 'x');

    assert(v0.front() == 'x' && v4.front() == 'x');
    v0.push_front('a');
    assert(v0.front() == 'a');
    v0.pop_front();
    assert(v0.front() == 'x' && v4.front() == 'x');

    v0.push_back('a');
    assert(v0.back() == 'a');
    v0.pop_back();
    assert(v0.back() == 'z' && v4.back() == 'x');

    v0.assign(v4.begin(), v4.end());
    assert(v0.size() == v4.size()
        && v0.front() == v4.front());
    v0.assign(4, 'w');
    assert(v0.size() == 4 && v0.front() == 'w');
    assert(*v0.insert(v0.begin(), 'a') == 'a');
    assert(v0.front() == 'a'
        && *++v0.begin() == 'w');
    v0.insert(v0.begin(), 2, 'b');
    assert(v0.front() == 'b'
        && *++v0.begin() == 'b'
        && *++ ++v0.begin() == 'a');
    v0.insert(v0.end(), v4.begin(), v4.end());
    assert(v0.back() == v4.back());
    v0.insert(v0.end(), carr, carr + 3);
    assert(v0.back() == 'c');
    v0.erase(v0.begin());
    assert(v0.front() == 'b' && *++v0.begin() == 'a');
    v0.erase(v0.begin(), ++v0.begin());
    assert(v0.front() == 'a');

    v0.clear();
    assert(v0.empty());
    v0.swap(v1);
    assert(!v0.empty() && v1.empty());
    swap(v0, v1);
    assert(v0.empty() && !v1.empty());
    assert(v1 == v1 && v0 < v1);
    assert(v0 != v1 && v1 > v0);
    assert(v0 <= v1 && v1 >= v0);

    cout << "SUCCESS testing <deque>" << endl;
    return (0); }
```

□

that `clear` is called only when the deque is destroyed or when the assignment operator (`operator=`) assigns an empty deque. The C++ Standard does not address the allocation and freeing of "hidden" storage in an STL container, so this behavior primarily reflects implementation decisions. Once again, an implementation more concerned about economizing storage might choose to free map storage more aggressively.

`vector` The rest of template class `deque` looks remarkably like the innards of template class `vector`, and for good reason. Both implement random-access containers with a uniform external interface. The primary difference is that `deque` reduces all efforts to increase the size of the controlled sequence to a succession of push operations, and all efforts to decrease the size to a succession of pops. But otherwise, we have discussed the remaining features of interest either in conjunction with template class `vector` (see Chapter 10: `<vector>`) or template class `list` (see Chapter 11: `<list>`).

Testing `<deque>`

`tdeque.c` Figures 12.13 through 12.14 show the file `tdeque.c`. It is one of three test programs that look very much alike. See the file `tvector.c`, beginning on page 285, and the file `tlist.c`, beginning on page 318. To ease comparison of these three test programs, we have simply commented out any tests inappropriate for a given container, without removing the unused code.

The test program performs a simple test that each of the member functions and types is present and behaves as intended, for one specialization of template class `deque`. If all goes well, the program prints:

```
SUCCESS testing <deque>
```

and takes a normal exit.

Exercises

Exercise 12.1 When would you favor a deque over a string?

Exercise 12.2 What would be the effect of permitting block sizes to vary within a deque?

Exercise 12.3 Determine a good rule for shrinking the array used by template class `deque` to store its map.

Exercise 12.4 Add a parameter to template class `deque` that lets you specify an alternate block size. Why would you want to do so?

Exercise 12.5 [**Harder**] Alter template class `deque` so that it stores one element per block and never assigns to elements. Why would you want to do so?

Exercise 12.6 [**Very hard**] Alter template class `deque` so that `iterator::operator*` and `iterator::operator++` are both "cheap."

Chapter 13: <set>

Background

`<set>` `set` `multiset`

The header `<set>` defines the template class **set** and the template class **multiset**. Each is a container that stores its controlled sequence of length **N** as an ordered binary tree of **N** nodes. Each node stores a single const element. The sequence is ordered by a function object whose type is one of the template parameters for the class. A multiset permits two (adjacent) elements to have equivalent ordering, while a set does not. More colloquially, all the elements of a set are unique, but a multiset permits duplicates.

`<map>` `map` `multimap`

In the next chapter, we present the companion header **<map>**. It defines the template class **map** and the template class **multimap**. They differ from **set** and **multiset** in one fundamental way — each stores elements of type **pair<const Key, T>**, and only the **const Key** component participates in ordering comparisons. For a set or multiset, by contrast, the entire element value participates in ordering comparisons. More colloquially, a map or multimap stores a "mapped value" along with each key. And as you might guess, all the keys of a map are unique, but a multimap permits duplicates.

associative containers

The template classes **set**, **multiset**, **map**, and **multimap** are all called *associative containers*. They all associate a key value with each element, and can use the key to speed lookup, insertion, and deletion of elements. Table 13.1, on page 240, shows the payoff for the added complexity in the associative containers. (They are labeled "set/map" in the table.) They are clearly superior to all other STL containers when you need to lookup an element by key value. While an ordered vector or deque can match this behavior, neither can do better than linear time for inserts and erases. The underlying tree representation can perform these operations in logarithmic time as well.

A vector or deque can win if you also need to perform indexed lookups as well as associative ones, but this is a rare occurrence. It can also win if you begrudge the extra storage consumed by all those extra pointers per element. Once again, however, this is rarely a major consideration.

So if you need to maintain an ordered sequence to speed associative lookups, insertions, and/or deletions, you can't do better than to use one of the associative containers. But if you don't need the extra performance in these areas, you should probably avoid the considerable extra complexity required to deliver the better time complexity.

All members of this group of four containers typically use both ordering and tree structure to advantage. Consider first just the use of order to speed the lookup of elements. Say you have some value `val` and you want to determine whether a container object stores an element with this value. If the container is not ordered, you have to inspect every element of the container to locate all with matching values. To find just one matching element, you must on average inspect half the elements. In either case, the time complexity is linear, or order `N`, for a container with `N` elements.

ordered containers You can speed up searches if you can impose some order on the values you're comparing, and if you can take advantage of that order to skip comparisons. For example, let's say that `operator<` is defined on pairs of values `X` and `Y` of some common type `T`. You can then use `X < Y` comparisons to order the elements in a container. If you want the smallest values at the beginning of the controlled sequence, and you do not permit duplicate keys, that means `X < Y` is true for any `X` that precedes `Y` in the sequence. If you want to permit duplicates, that means `!(Y < X)` is true for any `X` that precedes `Y` in the sequence. (This is a finicky way of allowing elements with equivalent ordering next to each other in the ordered sequence, without having to define `operator<=` as well.)

`binary_search` Having a neatly ordered bidirectional list doesn't do much good, however. You still have to chain from one element to the next in the linked list to visit all the elements. Put more formally, template class `list` supports access only via bidirectional iterators. You're rather better off with a vector or a deque. They support access via random-access iterators, so you can perform a binary chop to locate a particular value (or its absence) in an ordered sequence. The template function `binary_search`, defined in `<algorithm>`, searches by this method. (See Chapter 6: `<algorithm>`.)

The search time for binary chop increases as the logarithm of `N`. That's a dramatic improvement over a linear search. Consider the payoff for searching a sequence of 1,000 elements. On average, a linear search must make 500 comparisons, while a binary chop must make only 10. And the difference only gets more striking with increasing `N`. For 1,000,000 elements, the relative number of comparisons becomes 500,000 and 20. No contest.

`priority_queue` We could thus define the template classes `ordered_vector` and `ordered_deque`. And we do in fact, at least after a fashion. See the template container adapter `priority_queue` in Chapter 16: `<queue>`. Each ordered container can be implemented in terms of the existing template containers. We might want to add a template parameter `Pred` to specify the ordering rule. An object `pred`, of class `Pred`, can then provide the predicate `pred(X, Y)` as a generalization of the ordering rule `X < Y`.

The payoff for this added machinery is rapid lookup by key value. We can, for example, add the member function `find(Key)`. Give it a key value for an argument and it locates a matching element jiffy quick. Of course, we need to be a bit more precise about what we mean by "matching." Given just an ordering rule such as `X < Y`, we say the two operands match if `!(X < Y) && !(Y < X)`. (Neither operand is less than the other.) This definition of a match is what we have consistently called equivalent ordering. And the ordering rule, based on `operator<` or an equivalent predicate, is what we have consistently called "strict weak ordering."

But there's usually more to administering an ordered sequence than just looking up elements by key value. You have to build the sequence, perhaps in stages over time. You may well have to erase elements from time to time. If the number of insertions and erasures is comparable to the number of lookups, and all these operations are interleaved, then an ordered random-access container is not the best solution. That's where trees come in.

binary trees The basic idea behind a tree data structure is obvious enough. It's good old "divide and conquer" at work. Assume every element you want to store contains a key of type `Key` that defines `operator<(const Key&)`. You can define a tree node, of type `Node` that looks something like:

```
class Node {
    class Node *parent, *left, *right;
    Key key;
    ..... };
```

A `Node` object `x` is the basic building block of a particularly simple kind of tree called a binary tree. Each node has a single parent and up to two children. If every key in the controlled sequence is unique, the tree is ordered by two rules:

- If `left` is any node in the left subtree of `x`, then `left->key < x.key`.
- If `right` is any node in the right subtree of `x`, then `x.key < right->key`.

A tree-based `set` container obeys these rules. (So does a `map` container. It differs only in storing additional data in each node. We suggest that possibility by the ellipsis in the declaration of `Node`, above.)

If not every key in the controlled sequence is unique, the tree is ordered by two slightly different rules:

- If `left` is any node in the left subtree of `x`, then `!(x->key < left.key)`.
- If `right` is any node in the right subtree of `x`, then `!(right.key < x->key)`.

A tree-based `multiset` container obeys these rules. (And so does a `multimap` container. It just carries extra baggage, as does a `map`.)

You can visit the elements of an ordered tree in increasing order, starting at the root of the tree, by recursively visiting the left subtree of each node, followed by the node itself, followed by its right subtree. That's what happens when you increment an iterator designed to walk a binary tree. (Note that it is a bidirectional iterator.) More important, you can find a given search key — or where it belongs in the tree — by climbing down the tree and comparing the search key with the key value stored at each node. Each comparison eliminates a whole subtree from consideration.

If the tree is long and skinny, this doesn't win you much. Say every right subtree consists of a single node. The left subtree always contains all the remaining elements. Then you've simply found a more expensive way to implement a linked list. Searches have linear time complexity — the mean time to lookup an element is directly proportional to N, the number of elements in the controlled sequence. Specifically, it is $N/2$ for a random distribution of keys. And worst-case lookup time is N. Not good.

balanced binary trees

But let's say you can contrive to keep the tree short and bushy. In the case of a perfectly *balanced* tree, the difference in path length from root to any two leaves is never greater than one link. (If the tree holds 2^N-1 nodes, all paths should have the same length.) For such a tree, the longest path is essentially log_2N. Time complexity for lookups is thus logarithmic. That means you can find that one-in-a-million search keys with roughly 20 comparisons. Even better, if the mean number of comparisons is 19, the worst case is 20. Much better.

So the trick is to keep the tree in balance as it grows and shrinks. Otherwise, you lose the payoff in improved time complexity. Every time you hang a new node at the bottom of the tree, you have to rebalance the tree. That means working your way up from the bottom and reconsidering each node on the path to the top. If the longest path lengths of each pair of subtrees now differ by more than one, you have to rearrange a few nearby nodes to restore the balance.

Fortunately, there are multiple ways to represent any given sequence. You have some useful latitude in rewriting trees. It is a nontrivial, but manageable, exercise to implement a balanced binary tree. The interesting part is the two functions that insert and erase single nodes in the tree. The time complexity in both cases is logarithmic, just as for lookups. What's regrettable is that you have to climb to the top of the tree on every insert and erase, just to keep the tree perfectly balanced.

mostly balanced trees

Wouldn't it be nice if you could keep a tree *mostly* in balance, without having to do the job perfectly? You could probably speed up both insertions and erasures if you could cut yourself a little slack. Put proper limits on the permitted slack and you can still avoid sacrificing that nice logarithmic time complexity. It turns out that you have several options in this regard, with the usual tradeoffs between mean cost of operations, code complexity, and guaranteed worst-case behavior. Actually, you have quite a number of options. The literature on ordered trees is incredibly broad and deep. We'll stick with the basics here.

First, you can do nothing. Most trees stay remarkably well balanced however much you neglect them. You can eliminate all the overhead of maintaining a balanced tree and luck out almost all the time. But we have already discussed how bad the worst case can be. Unbalanced trees may be fine for custom code, but they don't make for the kind of reusable tools that STL strives to provide.

AVL trees You can also allow just a little bit of imbalance on a per-subtree basis. An AVL tree, for example, is a balanced binary tree that allows an imbalance of –1 to +1 links, between left and right sub-subtrees, for each subtree. The cumulative cost is to make trees a bit higher, on average, but not all that much. The payoff is that rebalancing is rather faster, on average. You can usually soak up the imbalance caused by an erasure without climbing clear to the top of the tree.

Unfortunately, you need to keep track of path lengths to know how to rebalance at each node. At the very least, you have to store in each node a three-state path difference between the two subtrees. Legitimate values for an AVL subtree are –1, 0, and +1. A two-bit code will do the job, but those two bits usually cost you one to four bytes of storage in each node, given the padding constraints in modern computers.

red-black trees The STL code from Hewlett-Packard uses an even more sophisticated variant, the red-black tree. Essentially all existing implementations of STL do the same, including the one presented in this book. The C++ Standard does not mandate the use of a red-black tree, or any other kind of tree, but such an implementation certainly meets the time-complexity requirements.

A red-black tree is a balanced tree that has three kinds of nodes. The simplest flavor is our old friend, the binary node. It stores one element and designates up to two children. But the tree can also have a node that holds two elements and designates three children. The middle subtree, if present, has elements ordered between the left and right elements in the node. Finally, the tree can have a node that holds three elements and designates four children.

The slack in a red-black tree lies in these larger nodes. Inserting an element is easy if it abuts a node that has room for more. Just change the node to a bigger flavor of node. Only when the insertion point is full do you have to work harder. You make two nodes, each with two elements, and rebalance the tree. Rebalancing involves climbing up the tree and rearranging nodes until you find a node that can absorb the change. Rarely do you have to climb all the way to the top to rebalance the tree. Similarly, erasing an element requires rebalancing only when a one-element node evaporates. Rebalancing after an erasure is also likely to result in just a localized change to the tree.

Implementing this description directly in C++ code is graceless, however. You have to declare three different kinds of node classes, or leave lots of wasted space for unused elements if you try to get by with only one node class. Binary trees are so much more elegant. Of course, you can represent those three different flavors of nodes as little bitty binary trees in their own right. The various flavors have zero, one, or two children. Stitch those little trees into the links between the fatter nodes and you have something that looks for all the world like a single binary tree once again. Certainly, you can search such a tree as though it were just a conventional binary tree. You need to distinguish links inside a node from links between nodes only when you have to insert or erase an element.

And that's where the eponymous red and black colors come in. Paint all the links inside a big node red and all the links between big nodes black. Actually, you paint the binary node itself. Each link points to just one node, and nodes contain all the storage for a tree. Instead of a two-bit balance count for an AVL tree, you need a one-bit color designator. But that's all the extra information you need to store to keep track of the slack offered by red-black trees.

There's yet another way to describe a red-black tree. Let's say the black links represent the proper tree and the red links are a kind of poetic license. You want to allow an imbalance of up to two to one in subtree heights, but no more. So you impose two rules on making links:

- Adding a red link does not change the official height of a subtree.
- You can't have two red links in a row.

The second rule is what keeps the tree from getting too far out of balance. It is equivalent to the size restriction on nodes in the original description of red-black trees above.

The advantage of this description is that it lets you forget about those ghostly multi-element big nodes that aren't really there. Instead, insertions and erasures are all about preserving invariants on subtree heights, just as with AVL trees. Only the rules are changed slightly, to lower the mean cost of insertions and erasures. Note that the time complexity for all operations remains logarithmic. The payoff is that you perform slightly more complex rebalancing operations rather less often, for a net savings of execution time. And you still maintain good bounds on worst-case times for various operations on trees.

set
multiset

We have discussed the mechanics of (almost) balanced binary trees at some length to justify their use in associative containers. But in practice, you don't see the tree structure. Instead, what you see are the template classes `set` and `multiset`:

```
template<class Key, class Pred = less<Key>,
    class A = allocator<K> >
    class set;
template<class Key, class Pred = less<K>,
    class A = allocator<K> >
    class multiset;
```

Both store elements with values of type `Key`. Both are ordered by function objects of type `Pred`, as described above for the fictitious ordered vector and deque classes. And both have the allocator parameter that is common to all STL containers. An object of class `A` allocates and frees storage for the container, as we have discussed at length in earlier chapters. The fundamental difference between the two template classes, as we have emphasized earlier in this chapter, is that a multiset permits elements with equivalent ordering while a set does not.

map **multimap** The other two associative containers that you see are **map** and **multimap**. We discuss them at length in the next chapter.

The associative containers define member functions that take advantage of the order they impose on controlled sequence. They also omit member functions that make little or no sense for an ordered container. You will *not* find member functions such as **push_front**, **pop_back**, or even **front**. You will *not* find constructors or member functions that specify a repetition of some value, such as **assign(3, 'x')**. What you will find instead are member functions such as:

- **insert** — **insert(const Key&)**, which inserts an element with a given key value
- **erase** — **erase(const Key&)**, which erases an element with a matching key value
- **find** — **find(const Key&)**, which locates an element with a matching key value
- **lower_bound** — **lower_bound(const Key&)**, which locates the earliest element with an equivalent or greater key value
- **upper_bound** — **upper_bound(const Key&)**, which locates the latest element with an equivalent or lesser key value
- **equal_range** — **equal_range(const Key&)**, which locates a subsequence of elements with equivalent key values
- **count** — **count(const Key&)**, which counts the number of elements with equivalent key values

We describe these member functions in greater detail later, in the **Using** **<set>** section of this chapter.

Functional Description

```
namespace std {
template<class Key, class Pred, class A>
    class set;
template<class Key, class Pred, class A>
    class multiset;

        // TEMPLATE FUNCTIONS
template<class Key, class Pred, class A>
    bool operator==(
        const set<Key, Pred, A>& lhs,
        const set<Key, Pred, A>& rhs);
template<class Key, class Pred, class A>
    bool operator==(
        const multiset<Key, Pred, A>& lhs,
        const multiset<Key, Pred, A>& rhs);
template<class Key, class Pred, class A>
    bool operator!=(
        const set<Key, Pred, A>& lhs,
        const set<Key, Pred, A>& rhs);
template<class Key, class Pred, class A>
    bool operator!=(
        const multiset<Key, Pred, A>& lhs,
        const multiset<Key, Pred, A>& rhs);
template<class Key, class Pred, class A>
    bool operator<(
```

```
        const set<Key, Pred, A>& lhs,
        const set<Key, Pred, A>& rhs);
template<class Key, class Pred, class A>
    bool operator<(
        const multiset<Key, Pred, A>& lhs,
        const multiset<Key, Pred, A>& rhs);
template<class Key, class Pred, class A>
    bool operator>(
        const set<Key, Pred, A>& lhs,
        const set<Key, Pred, A>& rhs);
template<class Key, class Pred, class A>
    bool operator>(
        const multiset<Key, Pred, A>& lhs,
        const multiset<Key, Pred, A>& rhs);
template<class Key, class Pred, class A>
    bool operator<=(
        const set<Key, Pred, A>& lhs,
        const set<Key, Pred, A>& rhs);
template<class Key, class Pred, class A>
    bool operator<=(
        const multiset<Key, Pred, A>& lhs,
        const multiset<Key, Pred, A>& rhs);
template<class Key, class Pred, class A>
    bool operator>=(
        const set<Key, Pred, A>& lhs,
        const set<Key, Pred, A>& rhs);
template<class Key, class Pred, class A>
    bool operator>=(
        const multiset<Key, Pred, A>& lhs,
        const multiset<Key, Pred, A>& rhs);
template<class Key, class Pred, class A>
    void swap(
        set<Key, Pred, A>& lhs,
        set<Key, Pred, A>& rhs);
template<class Key, class Pred, class A>
    void swap(
        multiset<Key, Pred, A>& lhs,
        multiset<Key, Pred, A>& rhs);
    };
```

Include the STL standard header `<set>` to define the container template classes `set` and `multiset`, and their supporting templates.

▫ **multiset**

```
template<class Key, class Pred = less<Key>,
    class A = allocator<Key> >
    class multiset {
public:
    typedef Key key_type;
    typedef Pred key_compare;
    typedef Key value_type;
    typedef Pred value_compare;
    typedef A allocator_type;
    typedef A::pointer pointer;
    typedef A::const_pointer const_pointer;
    typedef A::reference reference;
    typedef A::const_reference const_reference;
    typedef T0 iterator;
    typedef T1 const_iterator;
    typedef T2 size_type;
    typedef T3 difference_type;
```

```
typedef reverse_iterator<const_iterator>
    const_reverse_iterator;
typedef reverse_iterator<iterator> reverse_iterator;
multiset();
explicit multiset(const Pred& comp);
multiset(const Pred& comp, const A& al);
multiset(const multiset& x);
template<class InIt>
    multiset(InIt first, InIt last);
template<class InIt>
    multiset(InIt first, InIt last,
        const Pred& comp);
template<class InIt>
    multiset(InIt first, InIt last,
        const Pred& comp, const A& al);
const_iterator begin() const;
const_iterator end() const;
const_reverse_iterator rbegin() const;
const_reverse_iterator rend() const;
size_type size() const;
size_type max_size() const;
bool empty() const;
A get_allocator() const;
iterator insert(const value_type& x);
iterator insert(iterator it, const value_type& x);
template<class InIt>
    void insert(InIt first, InIt last);
iterator erase(iterator it);
iterator erase(iterator first, iterator last);
size_type erase(const Key& key);
void clear();
void swap(multiset& x);
key_compare key_comp() const;
value_compare value_comp() const;
const_iterator find(const Key& key) const;
size_type count(const Key& key) const;
const_iterator lower_bound(const Key& key) const;
const_iterator upper_bound(const Key& key) const;
pair<const_iterator, const_iterator>
    equal_range(const Key& key) const;
};
```

The template class describes an object that controls a varying-length sequence of elements of type `const Key`. The sequence is ordered by the predicate `Pred`. Each element serves as both a *sort key* and a *value*. The sequence is represented in a way that permits lookup, insertion, and removal of an arbitrary element with a number of operations proportional to the logarithm of the number of elements in the sequence (logarithmic time). Moreover, inserting an element invalidates no iterators, and removing an element invalidates only those iterators which point at the removed element.

The object orders the sequence it controls by calling a stored *function object* of type `Pred`. You access this stored object by calling the member function `key_comp()`. Such a function object must impose a strict weak ordering on sort keys of type `Key`. For any element `x` that precedes `y` in the sequence, `key_comp()(y, x)` is false. (For the default function object `less<Key>`, sort keys never decrease in value.) Unlike template class `set`, an object of template class **multiset** does not ensure that **key_comp()(x, y)** is true. (Keys need not be unique.)

The object allocates and frees storage for the sequence it controls through a stored allocator object of class **A**. Such an allocator object must have the same external interface as an object of template class **allocator**. Note that the stored allocator object is *not* copied when the container object is assigned.

- **multiset::allocator_type**

```
typedef A allocator_type;
```

The type is a synonym for the template parameter **A**.

- **multiset::begin**

```
const_iterator begin() const;
```

The member function returns a bidirectional iterator that points at the first element of the sequence (or just beyond the end of an empty sequence).

- **multiset::clear**

```
void clear();
```

The member function calls **erase(begin(), end())**.

- **multiset::const_iterator**

```
typedef T1 const_iterator;
```

The type describes an object that can serve as a constant bidirectional iterator for the controlled sequence. It is described here as a synonym for the implementation-defined type **T1**.

- **multiset::const_pointer**

```
typedef A::const_pointer const_pointer;
```

The type describes an object that can serve as a constant pointer to an element of the controlled sequence.

- **multiset::const_reference**

```
typedef A::const_reference const_reference;
```

The type describes an object that can serve as a constant reference to an element of the controlled sequence.

- **multiset::const_reverse_iterator**

```
typedef reverse_iterator<const_iterator>
    const_reverse_iterator;
```

The type describes an object that can serve as a constant reverse bidirectional iterator for the controlled sequence.

- **multiset::count**

```
size_type count(const Key& key) const;
```

The member function returns the number of elements **x** in the range **[lower_bound(key), upper_b3und(key))**.

▫ **multiset::difference_type**

```
typedef T3 difference_type;
```

The signed integer type describes an object that can represent the difference between the addresses of any two elements in the controlled sequence. It is described here as a synonym for the implementation-defined type `T3`.

▫ **multiset::empty**

```
bool empty() const;
```

The member function returns true for an empty controlled sequence.

▫ **multiset::end**

```
const_iterator end() const;
```

The member function returns a bidirectional iterator that points just beyond the end of the sequence.

▫ **multiset::equal_range**

```
pair<const_iterator, const_iterator>
    equal_range(const Key& key) const;
```

The member function returns a pair of iterators `x` such that `x.first == lower_bound(key)` and `x.second == upper_bound(key)`.

▫ **multiset::erase**

```
iterator erase(iterator it);
iterator erase(iterator first, iterator last);
size_type erase(const Key& key);
```

The first member function removes the element of the controlled sequence pointed to by `it`. The second member function removes the elements in the range `[first, last)`. Both return an iterator that designates the first element remaining beyond any elements removed, or `end()` if no such element exists.

The third member removes the elements with sort keys in the range `[lower_bound(key), upper_bound(key))`. It returns the number of elements it removes.

The member functions never throw an exception.

▫ **multiset::find**

```
const_iterator find(const Key& key) const;
```

The member function returns an iterator that designates the earliest element in the controlled sequence whose sort key has equivalent ordering to `key`. If no such element exists, the function returns `end()`.

▫ **multiset::get_allocator**

```
A get_allocator() const;
```

The member function returns the stored allocator object.

- **multiset::insert**

```
iterator insert(const value_type& x);
iterator insert(iterator it, const value_type& x);
template<class InIt>
    void insert(InIt first, InIt last);
```

The first member function inserts the element `x` in the controlled sequence, then returns the iterator that designates the inserted element. The second member function returns `insert(x)`, using `it` as a starting place within the controlled sequence to search for the insertion point. (Insertion can occur in amortized constant time, instead of logarithmic time, if the insertion point immediately follows `it`.) The third member function inserts the sequence of element values, for each `it` in the range `[first, last)`, by calling `insert(*it)`.

If an exception is thrown during the insertion of a single element, the container is left unaltered and the exception is rethrown. If an exception is thrown during the insertion of multiple elements, the container is left in a stable but unspecified state and the exception is rethrown.

- **multiset::iterator**

```
typedef T0 iterator;
```

The type describes an object that can serve as a bidirectional iterator for the controlled sequence. It is described here as a synonym for the implementation-defined type `T0`.

- **multiset::key_comp**

```
key_compare key_comp() const;
```

The member function returns the stored function object that determines the order of elements in the controlled sequence. The stored object defines the member function:

```
bool operator(const Key& x, const Key& y);
```

which returns true if `x` strictly precedes `y` in the sort order.

- **multiset::key_compare**

```
typedef Pred key_compare;
```

The type describes a function object that can compare two sort keys to determine the relative order of two elements in the controlled sequence.

- **multiset::key_type**

```
typedef Key key_type;
```

The type describes the sort key object which constitutes each element of the controlled sequence.

- **multiset::lower_bound**

```
const_iterator lower_bound(const Key& key) const;
```

The member function returns an iterator that designates the earliest element `x` in the controlled sequence for which `key_comp()(x, key)` is false. If no such element exists, the function returns `end()`.

▫ **multiset::multiset**

```
multiset();
explicit multiset(const Pred& comp);
multiset(const Pred& comp, const A& al);
multiset(const multiset& x);
template<class InIt>
    multiset(InIt first, InIt last);
template<class InIt>
    multiset(InIt first, InIt last,
        const Pred& comp);
template<class InIt>
    multiset(InIt first, InIt last,
        const Pred& comp, const A& al);
```

All constructors store an allocator object and initialize the controlled sequence. The allocator object is the argument `al`, if present. For the copy constructor, it is `x.get_allocator()`. Otherwise, it is `A()`.

All constructors also store a function object that can later be returned by calling `key_comp()`. The function object is the argument `comp`, if present. For the copy constructor, it is `x.key_comp()`). Otherwise, it is `Pred()`.

The first three constructors specify an empty initial controlled sequence. The fourth constructor specifies a copy of the sequence controlled by `x`. The last three constructors specify the sequence of element values `[first, last)`.

▫ **multiset::max_size**

```
size_type max_size() const;
```

The member function returns the length of the longest sequence that the object can control.

▫ **multiset::pointer**

```
typedef A::pointer pointer;
```

The type describes an object that can serve as a pointer to an element of the controlled sequence.

▫ **multiset::rbegin**

```
const_reverse_iterator rbegin() const;
```

The member function returns a reverse bidirectional iterator that points just beyond the end of the controlled sequence. Hence, it designates the beginning of the reverse sequence.

▫ **multiset::reference**

```
typedef A::reference reference;
```

The type describes an object that can serve as a reference to an element of the controlled sequence.

▫ **multiset::rend**

```
const_reverse_iterator rend() const;
```

The member function returns a reverse bidirectional iterator that points at the first element of the sequence (or just beyond the end of an empty sequence). Hence, it designates the end of the reverse sequence.

▫ **multiset::reverse_iterator**

```
typedef reverse_iterator<iterator> reverse_iterator;
```

The type describes an object that can serve as a reverse bidirectional iterator for the controlled sequence.

▫ **multiset::size**

```
size_type size() const;
```

The member function returns the length of the controlled sequence.

▫ **multiset::size_type**

```
typedef T2 size_type;
```

The unsigned integer type describes an object that can represent the length of any controlled sequence. It is described here as a synonym for the implementation-defined type `T2`.

▫ **multiset::swap**

```
void swap(multiset& x);
```

The member function swaps the controlled sequences between `*this` and `x`. If `get_allocator() == x.get_allocator()`, it does so in constant time, it throws an exception only as a result of copying the stored function object of type `Pred`, and it invalidates no references, pointers, or iterators that designate elements in the two controlled sequences. Otherwise, it performs a number of element assignments and constructor calls proportional to the number of elements in the two controlled sequences.

▫ **multiset::upper_bound**

```
const_iterator upper_bound(const Key& key) const;
```

The member function returns an iterator that designates the earliest element `x` in the controlled sequence for which `key_comp()(key, x)` is true. If no such element exists, the function returns `end()`.

▫ **multiset::value_comp**

```
value_compare value_comp() const;
```

The member function returns a function object that determines the order of elements in the controlled sequence.

▫ **multiset::value_compare**

```
typedef Pred value_compare;
```

The type describes a function object that can compare two elements as sort keys to determine their relative order in the controlled sequence.

▫ **multiset::value_type**

```
typedef Key value_type;
```

The type describes an element of the controlled sequence.

- `operator!=`

```
template<class Key, class Pred, class A>
    bool operator!=(
        const set <Key, Pred, A>& lhs,
        const set <Key, Pred, A>& rhs);
template<class Key, class Pred, class A>
    bool operator!=(
        const multiset <Key, Pred, A>& lhs,
        const multiset <Key, Pred, A>& rhs);
```

The template function returns `!(lhs == rhs)`.

- `operator==`

```
template<class Key, class Pred, class A>
    bool operator==(
        const set <Key, Pred, A>& lhs,
        const set <Key, Pred, A>& rhs);
template<class Key, class Pred, class A>
    bool operator==(
        const multiset <Key, Pred, A>& lhs,
        const multiset <Key, Pred, A>& rhs);
```

The first template function overloads `operator==` to compare two objects of template class `multiset`. The second template function overloads `operator==` to compare two objects of template class `multiset`. Both functions return `lhs.size() == rhs.size() && equal(lhs. begin(), lhs. end(), rhs.begin())`.

- `operator<`

```
template<class Key, class Pred, class A>
    bool operator<(
        const set <Key, Pred, A>& lhs,
        const set <Key, Pred, A>& rhs);
template<class Key, class Pred, class A>
    bool operator<(
        const multiset <Key, Pred, A>& lhs,
        const multiset <Key, Pred, A>& rhs);
```

The first template function overloads `operator<` to compare two objects of template class `multiset`. The second template function overloads `operator<` to compare two objects of template class `multiset`. Both functions return `lexicographical_compare(lhs. begin(), lhs. end(), rhs.begin(), rhs.end())`.

- `operator<=`

```
template<class Key, class Pred, class A>
    bool operator<=(
        const set <Key, Pred, A>& lhs,
        const set <Key, Pred, A>& rhs);
template<class Key, class Pred, class A>
    bool operator<=(
        const multiset <Key, Pred, A>& lhs,
        const multiset <Key, Pred, A>& rhs);
```

The template function returns `!(rhs < lhs)`.

- **operator>**

```
template<class Key, class Pred, class A>
    bool operator>(
        const set <Key, Pred, A>& lhs,
        const set <Key, Pred, A>& rhs);
template<class Key, class Pred, class A>
    bool operator>(
        const multiset <Key, Pred, A>& lhs,
        const multiset <Key, Pred, A>& rhs);
```

The template function returns `rhs < lhs`.

- **operator>=**

```
template<class Key, class Pred, class A>
    bool operator>=(
        const set <Key, Pred, A>& lhs,
        const set <Key, Pred, A>& rhs);
template<class Key, class Pred, class A>
    bool operator>=(
        const multiset <Key, Pred, A>& lhs,
        const multiset <Key, Pred, A>& rhs);
```

The template function returns `!(lhs < rhs)`.

- **set**

```
template<class Key, class Pred = less<Key>,
    class A = allocator<Key> >
    class set {
public:
    typedef Key key_type;
    typedef Pred key_compare;
    typedef Key value_type;
    typedef Pred value_compare;
    typedef A allocator_type;
    typedef A::pointer pointer;
    typedef A::const_pointer const_pointer;
    typedef A::reference reference;
    typedef A::const_reference const_reference;
    typedef T0 iterator;
    typedef T1 const_iterator;
    typedef T2 size_type;
    typedef T3 difference_type;
    typedef reverse_iterator<const_iterator>
        const_reverse_iterator;
    typedef reverse_iterator<iterator> reverse_iterator;
    set();
    explicit set(const Pred& comp);
    set(const Pred& comp, const A& al);
    set(const set& x);
    template<class InIt>
        set(InIt first, InIt last);
    template<class InIt>
        set(InIt first, InIt last,
            const Pred& comp);
    template<class InIt>
        set(InIt first, InIt last,
            const Pred& comp, const A& al);
    const_iterator begin() const;
    const_iterator end() const;
    const_reverse_iterator rbegin() const;
    const_reverse_iterator rend() const;
```

```
    size_type size() const;
    size_type max_size() const;
    bool empty() const;
    A get_allocator() const;
    pair<iterator, bool> insert(const value_type& x);
    iterator insert(iterator it, const value_type& x);
    template<class InIt>
        void insert(InIt first, InIt last);
    iterator erase(iterator it);
    iterator erase(iterator first, iterator last);
    size_type erase(const Key& key);
    void clear();
    void swap(set& x);
    key_compare key_comp() const;
    value_compare value_comp() const;
    const_iterator find(const Key& key) const;
    size_type count(const Key& key) const;
    const_iterator lower_bound(const Key& key) const;
    const_iterator upper_bound(const Key& key) const;
    pair<const_iterator, const_iterator>
        equal_range(const Key& key) const;
    };
```

The template class describes an object that controls a varying-length sequence of elements of type `const Key`. The sequence is ordered by the predicate `Pred`. Each element serves as both a *sort key* and a *value*. The sequence is represented in a way that permits lookup, insertion, and removal of an arbitrary element with a number of operations proportional to the logarithm of the number of elements in the sequence (logarithmic time). Moreover, inserting an element invalidates no iterators, and removing an element invalidates only those iterators which point at the removed element.

The object orders the sequence it controls by calling a stored *function object* of type `Pred`. You access this stored object by calling the member function `key_comp()`. Such a function object must impose a strict weak ordering on sort keys of type `Key`. For any element `x` that precedes `y` in the sequence, `key_comp()(y, x)` is false. (For the default function object `less<Key>`, sort keys never decrease in value.) Unlike template class `multiset`, an object of template class `set` ensures that `key_comp()(x, y)` is true. (Each key is unique.)

The object allocates and frees storage for the sequence it controls through a stored allocator object of class `A`. Such an allocator object must have the same external interface as an object of template class `allocator`. Note that the stored allocator object is *not* copied when the container object is assigned.

▫ **`set::allocator_type`**

```
typedef A allocator_type;
```

The type is a synonym for the template parameter `A`.

▫ **`set::begin`**

```
const_iterator begin() const;
```

The member function returns a bidirectional iterator that points at the first element of the sequence (or just beyond the end of an empty sequence).

- **set::clear**

```
void clear();
```

The member function calls `erase( begin(), end())`.

- **set::const_iterator**

```
typedef T1 const_iterator;
```

The type describes an object that can serve as a constant bidirectional iterator for the controlled sequence. It is described here as a synonym for the implementation-defined type `T1`.

- **set::const_pointer**

```
typedef A::const_pointer const_pointer;
```

The type describes an object that can serve as a constant pointer to an element of the controlled sequence.

- **set::const_reference**

```
typedef A::const_reference const_reference;
```

The type describes an object that can serve as a constant reference to an element of the controlled sequence.

- **set::const_reverse_iterator**

```
typedef reverse_iterator<const_iterator>
    const_reverse_iterator;
```

The type describes an object that can serve as a constant reverse bidirectional iterator for the controlled sequence.

- **set::count**

```
size_type count(const Key& key) const;
```

The member function returns the number of elements `x` in the range `[lower_bound(key), upper_bound(key))`.

- **set::difference_type**

```
typedef T3 difference_type;
```

The signed integer type describes an object that can represent the difference between the addresses of any two elements in the controlled sequence. It is described here as a synonym for the implementation-defined type `T3`.

- **set::empty**

```
bool empty() const;
```

The member function returns true for an empty controlled sequence.

- **set::end**

```
const_iterator end() const;
```

The member function returns a bidirectional iterator that points just beyond the end of the sequence.

set::equal_range

```
pair<const_iterator, const_iterator>
    equal_range(const Key& key) const;
```

The member function returns a pair of iterators `x` such that `x.first == lower_bound(key)` and `x.second == upper_bound(key)`.

set::erase

```
iterator erase(iterator it);
iterator erase(iterator first, iterator last);
size_type erase(const Key& key);
```

The first member function removes the element of the controlled sequence pointed to by `it`. The second member function removes the elements in the range `[first, last)`. Both return an iterator that designates the first element remaining beyond any elements removed, or `end()` if no such element exists.

The third member removes the elements with sort keys in the range `[lower_bound(key), upper_bound(key))`. It returns the number of elements it removes.

The member functions never throw an exception.

set::find

```
const_iterator find(const Key& key) const;
```

The member function returns an iterator that designates the element in the controlled sequence whose sort key has equivalent ordering to `key`. If no such element exists, the function returns `end()`.

set::get_allocator

```
A get_allocator() const;
```

The member function returns the stored allocator object.

set::insert

```
pair<iterator, bool> insert(const value_type& x);
iterator insert(iterator it, const value_type& x);
template<class InIt>
    void insert(InIt first, InIt last);
```

The first member function determines whether an element `y` exists in the sequence whose key has equivalent ordering to that of `x`. If not, it creates such an element `y` and initializes it with `x`. The function then determines the iterator `it` that designates `y`. If an insertion occurred, the function returns `pair(it, true)`. Otherwise, it returns `pair(it, false)`.

The second member function returns `insert(x)`, using `it` as a starting place within the controlled sequence to search for the insertion point. (Insertion can occur in amortized constant time, instead of logarithmic time, if the insertion point immediately follows `it`.) The third member function inserts the sequence of element values, for each `it` in the range `[first, last)`, by calling `insert(*it)`.

If an exception is thrown during the insertion of a single element, the container is left unaltered and the exception is rethrown. If an exception is thrown during the insertion of multiple elements, the container is left in a stable but unspecified state and the exception is rethrown.

▫ **`set::iterator`**

```
typedef T0 iterator;
```

The type describes an object that can serve as a bidirectional iterator for the controlled sequence. It is described here as a synonym for the implementation-defined type `T0`.

▫ **`set::key_comp`**

```
key_compare key_comp() const;
```

The member function returns the stored function object that determines the order of elements in the controlled sequence. The stored object defines the member function:

```
bool operator(const Key& x, const Key& y);
```

which returns true if `x` strictly precedes `y` in the sort order.

▫ **`set::key_compare`**

```
typedef Pred key_compare;
```

The type describes a function object that can compare two sort keys to determine the relative order of two elements in the controlled sequence.

▫ **`set::key_type`**

```
typedef Key key_type;
```

The type describes the sort key object which constitutes each element of the controlled sequence.

▫ **`set::lower_bound`**

```
const_iterator lower_bound(const Key& key) const;
```

The member function returns an iterator that designates the earliest element `x` in the controlled sequence for which `key_comp()(x, key)` is false. If no such element exists, the function returns `end()`.

▫ **`set::max_size`**

```
size_type max_size() const;
```

The member function returns the length of the longest sequence that the object can control.

▫ **`set::pointer`**

```
typedef A::pointer pointer;
```

The type describes an object that can serve as a pointer to an element of the controlled sequence.

set::rbegin

```
const_reverse_iterator rbegin() const;
```

The member function returns a reverse bidirectional iterator that points just beyond the end of the controlled sequence. Hence, it designates the beginning of the reverse sequence.

set::reference

```
typedef A::reference reference;
```

The type describes an object that can serve as a reference to an element of the controlled sequence.

set::rend

```
const_reverse_iterator rend() const;
```

The member function returns a reverse bidirectional iterator that points at the first element of the sequence (or just beyond the end of an empty sequence). Hence, it designates the end of the reverse sequence.

set::reverse_iterator

```
typedef reverse_iterator<iterator> reverse_iterator;
```

The type describes an object that can serve as a reverse bidirectional iterator for the controlled sequence.

set::set

```
set();
explicit set(const Pred& comp);
set(const Pred& comp, const A& al);
set(const set& x);
template<class InIt>
    set(InIt first, InIt last);
template<class InIt>
    set(InIt first, InIt last,
        const Pred& comp);
template<class InIt>
    set(InIt first, InIt last,
        const Pred& comp, const A& al);
```

All constructors store an allocator object and initialize the controlled sequence. The allocator object is the argument **`al`**, if present. For the copy constructor, it is **`x.get_allocator()`**. Otherwise, it is **`A()`**.

All constructors also store a function object that can later be returned by calling **`key_comp()`**. The function object is the argument **`comp`**, if present. For the copy constructor, it is **`x.key_comp()`**). Otherwise, it is **`Pred()`**.

The first three constructors specify an empty initial controlled sequence. The fourth constructor specifies a copy of the sequence controlled by **`x`**. The last three constructors specify the sequence of element values **`[first, last)`**.

set::size

```
size_type size() const;
```

The member function returns the length of the controlled sequence.

▫ **set::size_type**

```
typedef T2 size_type;
```

The unsigned integer type describes an object that can represent the length of any controlled sequence. It is described here as a synonym for the implementation-defined type `T2`.

▫ **set::swap**

```
void swap(set& x);
```

The member function swaps the controlled sequences between `*this` and `x`. If `get_allocator() == x.get_allocator()`, it does so in constant time, it throws an exception only as a result of copying the stored function object of type `Pred`, and it invalidates no references, pointers, or iterators that designate elements in the two controlled sequences. Otherwise, it performs a number of element assignments and constructor calls proportional to the number of elements in the two controlled sequences.

▫ **set::upper_bound**

```
const_iterator upper_bound(const Key& key) const;
```

The member function returns an iterator that designates the earliest element `x` in the controlled sequence for which `key_comp()(key, x)` is true. If no such element exists, the function returns `end()`.

▫ **set::value_comp**

```
value_compare value_comp() const;
```

The member function returns a function object that determines the order of elements in the controlled sequence.

▫ **set::value_compare**

```
typedef Pred value_compare;
```

The type describes a function object that can compare two elements as sort keys to determine their relative order in the controlled sequence.

▫ **set::value_type**

```
typedef Key value_type;
```

The type describes an element of the controlled sequence.

▫ **swap**

```
template<class Key, class Pred, class A>
    void swap(
        multiset <Key, Pred, A>& lhs,
        multiset <Key, Pred, A>& rhs);
template<class Key, class Pred, class A>
    void swap(
        set <Key, Pred, A>& lhs,
        set <Key, Pred, A>& rhs);
```

The template function executes `lhs.swap(rhs)`.

Using <set>

set **multiset** Include the header `<set>` to make use of template class `set` or template class `multiset`. Use the latter only if you want to permit multiple elements with the same key value — or more precisely, pairs of elements that have equivalent ordering. The two containers are very similar, so we first describe `set` as an example of both. Later on in this section, we highlight the differences between the two.

You can specialize `set` to store elements of type `const Key` and with an ordering rule of type `less<Key>` by writing a type definition such as:

```
typedef set<Key, less<Key>, allocator<Key> > Mycont;
```

Using default template arguments, you can omit the second and/or third arguments.

less If you omit the second argument, the default is given by a function object of type `less<Key>`. The controlled sequence in the stored container is ordered by this rule. Thus, for numeric types at least, the last element in the sequence is the one with the largest stored value.

Template class `set` supports all the common operations on containers, as we described in Chapter 9: Containers. (See the discussion beginning on page 248.) We summarize here only those properties peculiar to template class `set`.

constructors To construct an object of class `set<Key, Pred, A>`, you can write any of:

- `set()` to declare an empty set that is ordered by `Pred()`.
- `set(pr)` to declare an empty set that is ordered by the function object `pr`.
- `set(pr, al)` as above, also storing the allocator object `al`.
- `set(first, last)` to declare a set that is ordered by `Pred()` and whose initial content is copied from the sequence designated by `[first, last)` (and ordered, of course).
- `set(first, last, pr)` to declare a set that is ordered by `pr` and whose initial content is copied from the sequence designated by `[first, last)`, as above, and ordered.
- `set(first, last, pr, al)` as above, also storing the allocator object `al`.

If you have specialized the template class for an allocator of type `allocator<Key>`, which is the customary (and default) thing to do, there is nothing to be gained by specifying an explicit allocator argument `al`. Such an argument matters only for some allocators that the program defines explicitly. (See the discussion of allocators in Chapter 4: `<memory>`.)

The following descriptions all assume that `cont` is an object of class `set<Key, Pred, A>`.

clear To remove all elements, call `cont.clear()`.

erase To erase the element designated by the iterator `it`, call `cont.erase(it)`. The return value is an iterator designating the element just beyond the erased element. To erase a range of elements designated by `[first, last)`, call `cont.erase(first, last)`.

You can also perform a number of operations on a `set` object that take advantage of its unique representation. In particular, you can also erase the element whose key (value) has equivalent ordering to `key` by calling `cont.erase(key)`. Other operations peculiar to **set** (and the other associative containers) are:

insert To insert an element with the key (value) `key`, call `cont.insert(key)`. The return value is an object `ans`, of class `pair<iterator, bool>`. The member object `ans.second` is true only if an element with equivalent ordering was not already present in the controlled sequence. In this case, `ans.first` designates the inserted element. Otherwise the insertion fails and `ans.first` designates the preexisting element.

To insert the elements of a sequence with keys (values) designated by `*it`, for `it` in the range `[first, last)`, call `cont.insert(first, last)`. The sequence must not be any part of the initial controlled sequence.

To insert an element with the key (value) `key` that is likely to immediately follow the element designated by `it`, call `cont.insert(it, key)`. If this "hint" proves to be correct, insertion should occur in constant time instead of logarithmic time. In any event, the call has the same effect as `insert(key)` and returns the same iterator value.

find To locate an element whose key (value) has equivalent ordering to `key`, call `cont.find(key)`.

lower_bound To locate the earliest element in the controlled sequence whose key (value) is not ordered before `key`, call `cont.lower_bound(key)`. Note that this is the beginning of any subsequence of elements with equivalent ordering to `key`.

upper_bound To locate the earliest element in the controlled sequence whose key (value) is ordered after `key`, call `cont.upper_bound(key)`. Note that this is just beyond the end of any subsequence of elements with equivalent ordering to `key`.

equal_range To determine the subsequence of elements in the controlled sequence with equivalent ordering to `key`, call `cont.equal_range(key)`. Note that this is just the pair of iterators `pair<iterator, iterator>(cont.lower_bound(key), cont.upper_bound(key))`. For a `set<Key>` object, the length of the subsequence is either zero or one.

count To determine just the length of the subsequence determined by calling `cont.equal_range(key)`, call `cont.count(key)`. For a `set<Key>` object, the value returned is either zero or one.

key_comp To obtain an object that orders keys by the same rule as `cont`, call `cont.key_comp()`. Specifically, if `key1` is ordered before `key2`, then `cont.key_comp()(key1, key2)` is true.

`value_comp` To obtain an object that can order the values stored in elements of `cont`, call `cont.value_comp()`. For a `set<Key>` object `cont`, the return value is the same as for `cont.key_comp()`.

`multiset` The differences between template class `set` and template class `multiset` all stem from their fundamental difference — a `multiset` can store elements with equivalent ordering while a `set` will not. All constructors and member functions have the same signatures. But for a `multiset` object:

- `insert` The call `cont.insert(key)` always inserts a new element, so the function returns just the iterator designating the new element, not an object of class `pair<iterator, bool>`.
- `find` If multiple elements have equivalent ordering to `key`, the earliest such element is designated by the iterator returned from the call `cont.find(key)`.
- `equal_range` The subsequence determined by the call `cont.equal_range(key)` can have any length in the range `[0, cont.size()]`.
- `count` Similarly, the subsequence length returned by the call `cont.count(key)` can have any value in the range `[0, cont.size()]`.

Implementing <set>

The four template classes `set`, `multiset`, `map`, and `multimap` are more alike than different. Each stores its controlled sequence as a red-black tree. They differ primarily in the outcome of two choices:

- whether the stored element is just a key (`set` and `multiset`) or a {key, value} pair (`map` and `multimap`)
- whether any two stored elements may have keys with equivalent ordering (`multiset` and `multimap`) or not (`set` and `map`)

The natural thing to do, then, is to write a common underlying implementation, suitably parameterized to permit any combination of these choices.

`Tree` This implementation provides a template class `Tree` that implements a container as a red-black tree. It is designed to serve as a base class for the template classes `set`, `multiset`, `map`, and `multimap`. Quite a few parameters must be specified for `Tree`. To keep template parameter lists manageable, we follow the usual practice of introducing a "traits" class, as a vehicle for transporting several type parameters with one handle. A traits object can also smuggle in one or more objects that might change at runtime, such as function objects used to perform comparisons.

Thus, template class `Tree` is declared simply as:

```
template<class Tr>
    class Tree;
```

where `Tr` conveys a bouquet of parameters. Template class `Tree` expects a parameter `Tr` with a number of properties. Here is a representative traits class for `Tree`, which we have arbitrarily named `tree_traits`:

Tree traits

```
struct tree_traits {
    typedef T1 key_type;
    typedef T2 value_type;
    typedef T3 allocator_type;
    enum {Multi = <allow equivalent keys>};
    typedef T4 key_compare;
    typedef T5 value_compare;
    struct Kfn {
        const key_type& operator()(const value_type&) const;
        };
    key_compare comp;
    tree_traits(key_compare);
    };
```

More specifically:

- `key_type` is the type of the key component of the value stored in each element
- `value_type` is the type of the entire value stored in each element
- `allocator_type` is the type of the allocator used to allocate and free storage for the controlled sequence
- `Multi` is a constant value that is nonzero if any two stored elements may have keys with equivalent ordering
- `key_compare` is the type of a function object `prk` that can compare two keys of type `key_type`, as in `prk(key1, key2)`
- `value_compare` is the type of a function object `prv` that can compare two values of type `value_type`, as in `prv(val1, val2)`
- `Kfn` is the type of a function object `prx` that can extract the key component, of type `key_type`, from a value of type `value_type`, as in `prx(val)`
- `comp` is a stored function object of type `key_compare` that is used to perform the actual key comparisons
- `tree_traits(key_compare)` is a constructor that initializes the stored function object `comp` from its argument

Later on in this chapter, you will see versions of this traits class that make `Tree` behave like either a `set` or a `multiset`. In the next chapter, you will see still more versions that make `Tree` behave like either a `map` or a `multimap`.

xtree Figures 13.1 through 13.1 show the file `xtree`. It defines template class `Tree`, along with a few template functions that take tree operands. Much of the basic machinery of `Tree` looks remarkably similar to that for template class `list`. (See Chapter 11: `<list>`.)

Both containers store elements in individual nodes that are linked together. The only difference is that a list has just two links, to the previous and next nodes in the list, while a tree has three, to the left and right subtrees as well as back to the parent node. And both containers use a dummy "head" node to anchor the controlled sequence. But the business of buying and selling nodes, and accessing fields within nodes, looks very much alike between the two containers.

Figure 13.1: `xtree` Part 1

```
// tree internal header
#ifndef XTREE_
#define XTREE_
#include <functional>
#include <memory>
#include <stdexcept>
namespace std {

          // TEMPLATE CLASS Tree_nod
template<class Tr>
     class Tree_nod : public Tr {
protected:
     typedef typename Tr::allocator_type allocator_type;
     typedef typename Tr::key_compare key_compare;
     typedef typename Tr::value_type value_type;
     typedef typename allocator_type::template
          rebind<void>::other::pointer Genptr;
     struct Node;
     friend struct Node;
     struct Node {
          Genptr Left, Parent, Right;
          value_type Value;
          char Color, Isnil;
          };
     Tree_nod(const key_compare& Parg,
          allocator_type Al)
          : Tr(Parg), Alnod(Al) {}
     typename allocator_type::template
          rebind<Node>::other
          Alnod;
     };

          // TEMPLATE CLASS Tree_ptr
template<class Tr>
     class Tree_ptr : public Tree_nod<Tr> {
protected:
     typedef typename Tree_nod<Tr>::Node Node;
     typedef typename Tr::allocator_type allocator_type;
     typedef typename Tr::key_compare key_compare;
     typedef typename allocator_type::template
          rebind<Node>::other::pointer Nodeptr;
     Tree_ptr(const key_compare& Parg,
          allocator_type Al)
          : Tree_nod<Tr>(Parg, Al), Alptr(Al) {}
     typename allocator_type::template
          rebind<Nodeptr>::other
          Alptr;
     };

          // TEMPLATE CLASS Tree_val
template<class Tr>
     class Tree_val : public Tree_ptr<Tr> {
protected:
     typedef typename Tr::allocator_type allocator_type;
     typedef typename Tr::key_compare key_compare;
```

Figure 13.2: `xtree` **Part 2**

```
    Tree_val(const key_compare& Parg,
        allocator_type Al)
        : Tree_ptr<Tr>(Parg, Al), Alval(Al) {}
    allocator_type Alval;
    };

        // TEMPLATE CLASS Tree
template<class Tr>
    class Tree
        : public Tree_val<Tr> {
public:
    typedef Tree<Tr> Myt;
    typedef Tree_val<Tr> Mybase;
    typedef typename Tr::key_type key_type;
    typedef typename Tr::key_compare key_compare;
    typedef typename Tr::value_compare value_compare;
    typedef typename Tr::value_type value_type;
    typedef typename Tr::allocator_type allocator_type;
protected:
    typedef typename Tree_nod<Tr>::Genptr Genptr;
    typedef typename Tree_nod<Tr>::Node Node;
    enum Redbl {Red, Black};
    typedef typename allocator_type::template
        rebind::<Node>::other::pointer Nodeptr;
    typedef typename allocator_type::template
        rebind::<Nodeptr>::other::reference Nodepref;
    typedef typename allocator_type::template
        rebind::<key_type>::other::const_reference Keyref;
    typedef typename allocator_type::template
        rebind::<char>::other::reference Charref;
    typedef typename allocator_type::template
        rebind::<value_type>::other::reference Vref;

    static Charref Color(Nodeptr P)
        {return ((Charref)(*P).Color); }
    static Charref Isnil(Nodeptr P)
        {return ((Charref)(*P).Isnil); }
    static Keyref Key(Nodeptr P)
        {return (Kfn()(Value(P))); }
    static Nodepref Left(Nodeptr P)
        {return ((Nodepref)(*P).Left); }
    static Nodepref Parent(Nodeptr P)
        {return ((Nodepref)(*P).Parent); }
    static Nodepref Right(Nodeptr P)
        {return ((Nodepref)(*P).Right); }
    static Vref Value(Nodeptr P)
        {return ((Vref)(*P).Value); }
public:
    typedef typename allocator_type::size_type size_type;
    typedef typename allocator_type::difference_type Dift;
    typedef Dift difference_type;
    typedef typename allocator_type::template
        rebind::<value_type>::other::pointer Tptr;
    typedef typename allocator_type::template
        rebind::<value_type>::other::const_pointer Ctptr;
```

Figure 13.3: `xtree` **Part 3**

```
    typedef typename allocator_type::template
        rebind::<value_type>::other::reference Reft;
    typedef Tptr pointer;
    typedef Ctptr const_pointer;
    typedef Reft reference;
    typedef typename allocator_type::template
        rebind::<value_type>::other::const_reference
        const_reference;

        // CLASS iterator
    class iterator;
    friend class iterator;
    class iterator : public Bidit<value_type, Dift,
        Tptr, Reft> {
    public:
        typedef Bidit<value_type, Dift,
            Tptr, Reft> Mybase;
        typedef typename Mybase::iterator_category
            iterator_category;
//      typedef typename Mybase::value_type value_type;
        typedef typename Mybase::difference_type
            difference_type;
        typedef typename Mybase::pointer pointer;
        typedef typename Mybase::reference reference;
        iterator()
            : Ptr(0) {}
        iterator(Nodeptr P)
            : Ptr(P) {}
        reference operator*() const
            {return (Value(Ptr)); }
        Tptr operator->() const
            {return (&**this); }
        iterator& operator++()
            {Inc();
            return (*this); }
        iterator operator++(int)
            {iterator Tmp = *this;
            ++*this;
            return (Tmp); }
        iterator& operator--()
            {Dec();
            return (*this); }
        iterator operator--(int)
            {iterator Tmp = *this;
            --*this;
            return (Tmp); }
        bool operator==(const iterator& X) const
            {return (Ptr == X.Ptr); }
        bool operator!=(const iterator& X) const
            {return (!(*this == X)); }
        void Dec()
            {if (Isnil(Ptr))
                Ptr = Right(Ptr);
            else if (!Isnil(Left(Ptr)))
                Ptr = Max(Left(Ptr));
```

Figure 13.4: `xtree` **Part 4**

```
                else
                     {Nodeptr P;
                     while (!Isnil(P = Parent(Ptr))
                          && Ptr == Left(P))
                          Ptr = P;
                     if (!Isnil(P))
                          Ptr = P; }}
          void Inc()
               {if (Isnil(Ptr))
                     ;
               else if (!Isnil(Right(Ptr)))
                     Ptr = Min(Right(Ptr));
               else
                     {Nodeptr P;
                     while (!Isnil(P = Parent(Ptr))
                          && Ptr == Right(P))
                          Ptr = P;
                     Ptr = P; }}
          Nodeptr Mynode() const
               {return (Ptr); }
     protected:
          Nodeptr Ptr;
          };

          // CLASS const_iterator
     class const_iterator;
     friend class const_iterator;
     class const_iterator : public Bidit<value_type, Dift,
          Ctptr, const_reference> {
     public:
          typedef Bidit<value_type, Dift,
               Ctptr, const_reference> Mybase;
          typedef typename Mybase::iterator_category
               iterator_category;
//        typedef typename Mybase::value_type value_type;
          typedef typename Mybase::difference_type
               difference_type;
          typedef typename Mybase::pointer pointer;
          typedef typename Mybase::reference reference;
          const_iterator()
               : Ptr(0) {}
          const_iterator(Nodeptr P)
               : Ptr(P) {}
          const_iterator(const typename Tree<Tr>::iterator& X)
               : Ptr(X.Mynode()) {}
          const_reference operator*() const
               {return (Value(Ptr)); }
          Ctptr operator->() const
               {return (&**this); }
          const_iterator& operator++()
               {Inc();
               return (*this); }
          const_iterator operator++(int)
               {const_iterator Tmp = *this;
               ++*this;
```

Figure 13.5: `xtree` **Part 5**

```
                return (Tmp); }
        const_iterator& operator--()
                {Dec();
                return (*this); }
        const_iterator operator--(int)
                {const_iterator Tmp = *this;
                --*this;
                return (Tmp); }
        bool operator==(const const_iterator& X) const
                {return (Ptr == X.Ptr); }
        bool operator!=(const const_iterator& X) const
                {return (!(*this == X)); }
        void Dec()
                {if (Isnil(Ptr))
                        Ptr = Right(Ptr);
                else if (!Isnil(Left(Ptr)))
                        Ptr = Max(Left(Ptr));
                else
                        {Nodeptr P;
                        while (!Isnil(P = Parent(Ptr))
                                && Ptr == Left(P))
                                Ptr = P;
                        if (!Isnil(P))
                                Ptr = P; }}
        void Inc()
                {if (Isnil(Ptr))
                        ;
                else if (!Isnil(Right(Ptr)))
                        Ptr = Min(Right(Ptr));
                else
                        {Nodeptr P;
                        while (!Isnil(P = Parent(Ptr))
                                && Ptr == Right(P))
                                Ptr = P;
                        Ptr = P; }}
        Nodeptr Mynode() const
                {return (Ptr); }
protected:
        Nodeptr Ptr;
        };

typedef std::reverse_iterator<iterator>
        reverse_iterator;
typedef std::reverse_iterator<const_iterator>
        const_reverse_iterator;
typedef pair<iterator, bool> Pairib;
typedef pair<iterator, iterator> Pairii;
typedef pair<const_iterator, const_iterator> Paircc;

explicit Tree(const key_compare& Parg,
        const allocator_type& Al)
        : Mybase(Parg, Al)
        {Init(); }
Tree(const value_type *F, const value_type *L,
        const key_compare& Parg, const allocator_type& Al)
```

Figure 13.6: `xtree` **Part 6**

```
        : Mybase(Parg, Al)
        {Init();
        insert(F, L); }
    Tree(const Myt& X)
        : Mybase(X.key_comp(), X.get_allocator())
        {Init();
        Copy(X); }
    ~Tree()
        {erase(begin(), end());
        Freenode(Head);
        Head = 0, Size = 0; }
    Myt& operator=(const Myt& X)
        {if (this != &X)
            {erase(begin(), end());
            comp = X.comp;
            Copy(X); }
        return (*this); }
    iterator begin()
        {return (iterator(Lmost())); }
    const_iterator begin() const
        {return (const_iterator(Lmost())); }
    iterator end()
        {return (iterator(Head)); }
    const_iterator end() const
        {return (const_iterator(Head)); }
    reverse_iterator rbegin()
        {return (reverse_iterator(end())); }
    const_reverse_iterator rbegin() const
        {return (const_reverse_iterator(end())); }
    reverse_iterator rend()
        {return (reverse_iterator(begin())); }
    const_reverse_iterator rend() const
        {return (const_reverse_iterator(begin())); }
    size_type size() const
        {return (Size); }
    size_type max_size() const
        {return (Alval.max_size()); }
    bool empty() const
        {return (size() == 0); }
    allocator_type get_allocator() const
        {return (Alval); }
    key_compare key_comp() const
        {return (comp); }
    value_compare value_comp() const
        {return (value_compare(key_comp())); }
    Pairib insert(const value_type& V)
        {Nodeptr X = Root();
        Nodeptr Y = Head;
        bool Addleft = true;
        while (!Isnil(X))
            {Y = X;
            Addleft = comp(Kfn()(V), Key(X));
            X = Addleft ? Left(X) : Right(X); }
        if (Multi)
            return (Pairib(Insert(Addleft, Y, V), true));
```

Figure 13.7: `xtree` **Part 7**

```
            else
                {iterator P = iterator(Y);
                if (!Addleft)
                    ;
                else if (P == begin())
                    return (Pairib(Insert(true, Y, V), true));
                else
                    --P;
                if (comp(Key(P.Mynode()), Kfn()(V)))
                    return (Pairib(Insert(Addleft, Y, V), true));
                else
                    return (Pairib(P, false)); }}
    iterator insert(iterator P, const value_type& V)
        {if (size() == 0)
            return (Insert(true, Head, V));
        else if (P == begin())
            {if (comp(Kfn()(V), Key(P.Mynode())))
                return (Insert(true, P.Mynode(), V)); }
        else if (P == end())
            {if (comp(Key(Rmost()), Kfn()(V)))
                return (Insert(false, Rmost(), V)); }
        else
            {iterator Pb = P;
            if (comp(Key((--Pb).Mynode()), Kfn()(V))
                && comp(Kfn()(V), Key(P.Mynode())))
                if (Isnil(Right(Pb.Mynode())))
                    return (Insert(false, Pb.Mynode(), V));
                else
                    return (Insert(true, P.Mynode(), V)); }
        return (insert(V).first); }
    template<class It>
        void insert(It F, It L)
        {for (; F != L; ++F)
            insert(*F); }
    iterator erase(iterator P)
        {if (Isnil(P.Mynode()))
            throw out_of_range("map/set<T> iterator");
        Nodeptr X, Xpar;
        Nodeptr Y = (P++).Mynode();
        Nodeptr Z = Y;
        if (Isnil(Left(Y)))
            X = Right(Y);
        else if (Isnil(Right(Y)))
            X = Left(Y);
        else
            Y = Min(Right(Y)), X = Right(Y);
        if (Y == Z)
            {Xpar = Parent(Z);
            if (!Isnil(X))
                Parent(X) = Xpar;
            if (Root() == Z)
                Root() = X;
            else if (Left(Xpar) == Z)
                Left(Xpar) = X;
            else
```

Figure 13.8: `xtree` **Part 8**

```
                    Right(Xpar) = X;
               if (Lmost() != Z)
                    ;
               else if (Isnil(Right(Z)))
                    Lmost() = Xpar;
               else
                    Lmost() = Min(X);
               if (Rmost() != Z)
                    ;
               else if (Isnil(Left(Z)))
                    Rmost() = Xpar;
               else
                    Rmost() = Max(X); }
          else
               {Parent(Left(Z)) = Y;
               Left(Y) = Left(Z);
               if (Y == Right(Z))
                    Xpar = Y;
               else
                    {Xpar = Parent(Y);
                    if (!Isnil(X))
                         Parent(X) = Xpar;
                    Left(Xpar) = X;
                    Right(Y) = Right(Z);
                    Parent(Right(Z)) = Y; }
               if (Root() == Z)
                    Root() = Y;
               else if (Left(Parent(Z)) == Z)
                    Left(Parent(Z)) = Y;
               else
                    Right(Parent(Z)) = Y;
               Parent(Y) = Parent(Z);
               std::swap(Color(Y), Color(Z)); }
          if (Color(Z) == Black)
               {for (; X != Root() && Color(X) == Black;
                    Xpar = Parent(X))
                    if (X == Left(Xpar))
                         {Nodeptr W = Right(Xpar);
                         if (Color(W) == Red)
                              {Color(W) = Black;
                              Color(Xpar) = Red;
                              Lrotate(Xpar);
                              W = Right(Xpar); }
                         if (Isnil(W))
                              X = Xpar;          // shouldn't happen
                         else if (Color(Left(W)) == Black
                              && Color(Right(W)) == Black)
                              {Color(W) = Red;
                              X = Xpar; }
                         else
                              {if (Color(Right(W)) == Black)
                                   {Color(Left(W)) = Black;
                                   Color(W) = Red;
                                   Rrotate(W);
                                   W = Right(Xpar); }
```

Figure 13.9: `xtree` Part 9

```
                        Color(W) = Color(Xpar);
                        Color(Xpar) = Black;
                        Color(Right(W)) = Black;
                        Lrotate(Xpar);
                        break; }}
            else
                {Nodeptr W = Left(Xpar);
                if (Color(W) == Red)
                    {Color(W) = Black;
                    Color(Xpar) = Red;
                    Rrotate(Xpar);
                    W = Left(Xpar); }
                if (Isnil(W))
                    X = Xpar;          // shouldn't happen
                else if (Color(Right(W)) == Black
                    && Color(Left(W)) == Black)
                    {Color(W) = Red;
                    X = Xpar; }
                else
                    {if (Color(Left(W)) == Black)
                        {Color(Right(W)) = Black;
                        Color(W) = Red;
                        Lrotate(W);
                        W = Left(Xpar); }
                    Color(W) = Color(Xpar);
                    Color(Xpar) = Black;
                    Color(Left(W)) = Black;
                    Rrotate(Xpar);
                    break; }}
        Color(X) = Black; }
    Destval(&Value(Z));
    Freenode(Z);
    if (0 < Size)
        --Size;
    return (P); }
iterator erase(iterator F, iterator L)
    {if (size() == 0 || F != begin() || L != end())
        {while (F != L)
            erase(F++);
        return (F); }
    else
        {Erase(Root());
        Root() = Head, Size = 0;
        Lmost() = Head, Rmost() = Head;
        return (begin()); }}
size_type erase(const key_type& X)
    {Pairii P = equal_range(X);
    size_type N = 0;
    Distance(P.first, P.second, N);
    erase(P.first, P.second);
    return (N); }
void erase(const key_type *F, const key_type *L)
    {while (F != L)
        erase(*F++); }
void clear()
```

Figure 13.10: xtree Part 10

```
            {erase(begin(), end()); }
        iterator find(const key_type& Kv)
            {iterator P = lower_bound(Kv);
            return (P == end()
                || comp(Kv, Key(P.Mynode()))
                    ? end() : P); }
        const_iterator find(const key_type& Kv) const
            {const_iterator P = lower_bound(Kv);
            return (P == end()
                || comp(Kv, Key(P.Mynode()))
                    ? end() : P); }
        size_type count(const key_type& Kv) const
            {Paircc Ans = equal_range(Kv);
            size_type N = 0;
            Distance(Ans.first, Ans.second, N);
            return (N); }
        iterator lower_bound(const key_type& Kv)
            {return (iterator(Lbound(Kv))); }
        const_iterator lower_bound(const key_type& Kv) const
            {return (const_iterator(Lbound(Kv))); }
        iterator upper_bound(const key_type& Kv)
            {return (iterator(Ubound(Kv))); }
        const_iterator upper_bound(const key_type& Kv) const
            {return (iterator(Ubound(Kv))); }
        Pairii equal_range(const key_type& Kv)
            {return (Pairii(lower_bound(Kv), upper_bound(Kv))); }
        Paircc equal_range(const key_type& Kv) const
            {return (Paircc(lower_bound(Kv), upper_bound(Kv))); }
        void swap(Myt& X)
            {if (get_allocator() == X.get_allocator())
                {std::swap(comp, X.comp);
                std::swap(Head, X.Head);
                std::swap(Size, X.Size); }
            else
                {Myt Ts = *this; *this = X, X = Ts; }}
protected:
        void Copy(const Myt& X)
            {Root() = Copy(X.Root(), Head);
            Size = X.size();
            if (!Isnil(Root()))
                {Lmost() = Min(Root());
                Rmost() = Max(Root()); }
            else
                Lmost() = Head, Rmost() = Head; }
        Nodeptr Copy(Nodeptr X, Nodeptr P)
            {Nodeptr R = Head;
            if (!Isnil(X))
                {Nodeptr Y = Buynode(P, Color(X));
                try {
                Consval(&Value(Y), Value(X));
                } catch (...) {
                Freenode(Y);
                Erase(R);
                throw;
                }
```

Figure 13.11: xtree Part 11

```
                Left(Y) = Head, Right(Y) = Head;
                if (Isnil(R))
                     R = Y;
                try {
                Left(Y) = Copy(Left(X), Y);
                Right(Y) = Copy(Right(X), Y);
                } catch (...) {
                Erase(R);
                throw;
                }}
           return (R); }
      void Erase(Nodeptr X)
           {for (Nodeptr Y = X; !Isnil(Y); X = Y)
                {Erase(Right(Y));
                Y = Left(Y);
                Destval(&Value(X));
                Freenode(X); }}
      void Init()
           {Head = Buynode(0, Black);
           Isnil(Head) = true;
           Root() = Head;
           Lmost() = Head, Rmost() = Head;
           Size = 0; }
      iterator Insert(bool Addleft, Nodeptr Y,
           const value_type& V)
           {if (max_size() - 1 <= Size)
                throw length_error("map/set<T> too long");
           Nodeptr Z = Buynode(Y, Red);
           Left(Z) = Head, Right(Z) = Head;
           try {
           Consval(&Value(Z), V);
           } catch (...) {
           Freenode(Z);
           throw;
           }
           ++Size;
           if (Y == Head)
                {Root() = Z;
                Lmost() = Z, Rmost() = Z; }
           else if (Addleft)
                {Left(Y) = Z;
                if (Y == Lmost())
                     Lmost() = Z; }
           else
                {Right(Y) = Z;
                if (Y == Rmost())
                     Rmost() = Z; }
           for (Nodeptr X = Z; Color(Parent(X)) == Red; )
                if (Parent(X) == Left(Parent(Parent(X))))
                     {Y = Right(Parent(Parent(X)));
                     if (Color(Y) == Red)
                          {Color(Parent(X)) = Black;
                          Color(Y) = Black;
                          Color(Parent(Parent(X))) = Red;
                          X = Parent(Parent(X)); }
```

Figure 13.12: xtree Part 12

```
                else
                        {if (X == Right(Parent(X)))
                                {X = Parent(X);
                                Lrotate(X); }
                        Color(Parent(X)) = Black;
                        Color(Parent(Parent(X))) = Red;
                        Rrotate(Parent(Parent(X))); }}
        else
                {Y = Left(Parent(Parent(X)));
                if (Color(Y) == Red)
                        {Color(Parent(X)) = Black;
                        Color(Y) = Black;
                        Color(Parent(Parent(X))) = Red;
                        X = Parent(Parent(X)); }
                else
                        {if (X == Left(Parent(X)))
                                {X = Parent(X);
                                Rrotate(X); }
                        Color(Parent(X)) = Black;
                        Color(Parent(Parent(X))) = Red;
                        Lrotate(Parent(Parent(X))); }}
    Color(Root()) = Black;
    return (iterator(Z)); }
Nodeptr Lbound(const key_type& Kv) const
    {Nodeptr X = Root();
    Nodeptr Y = Head;
    while (!Isnil(X))
        if (comp(Key(X), Kv))
            X = Right(X);
        else
            Y = X, X = Left(X);
    return (Y); }
Nodeptr& Lmost()
    {return (Left(Head)); }
Nodeptr& Lmost() const
    {return (Left(Head)); }
void Lrotate(Nodeptr X)
    {Nodeptr Y = Right(X);
    Right(X) = Left(Y);
    if (!Isnil(Left(Y)))
        Parent(Left(Y)) = X;
    Parent(Y) = Parent(X);
    if (X == Root())
        Root() = Y;
    else if (X == Left(Parent(X)))
        Left(Parent(X)) = Y;
    else
        Right(Parent(X)) = Y;
    Left(Y) = X;
    Parent(X) = Y; }
static Nodeptr Max(Nodeptr P)
    {while (!Isnil(Right(P)))
        P = Right(P);
    return (P); }
static Nodeptr Min(Nodeptr P)
```

Figure 13.13: xtree Part 13

```
        {while (!Isnil(Left(P)))
            P = Left(P);
        return (P); }
    Nodeptr& Rmost()
        {return (Right(Head)); }
    Nodeptr& Rmost() const
        {return (Right(Head)); }
    Nodeptr& Root()
        {return (Parent(Head)); }
    Nodeptr& Root() const
        {return (Parent(Head)); }
    void Rrotate(Nodeptr X)
        {Nodeptr Y = Left(X);
        Left(X) = Right(Y);
        if (!Isnil(Right(Y)))
            Parent(Right(Y)) = X;
        Parent(Y) = Parent(X);
        if (X == Root())
            Root() = Y;
        else if (X == Right(Parent(X)))
            Right(Parent(X)) = Y;
        else
            Left(Parent(X)) = Y;
        Right(Y) = X;
        Parent(X) = Y; }
    Nodeptr Ubound(const key_type& Kv) const
        {Nodeptr X = Root();
        Nodeptr Y = Head;
        while (!Isnil(X))
            if (comp(Kv, Key(X)))
                Y = X, X = Left(X);
            else
                X = Right(X);
        return (Y); }
    Nodeptr Buynode(Nodeptr Parg, char Carg)
        {Nodeptr S = Alnod.allocate(1, (void *)0);
        Alptr.construct(&Left(S), 0);
        Alptr.construct(&Right(S), 0);
        Alptr.construct(&Parent(S), Parg);
        Color(S) = Carg;
        Isnil(S) = false;
        return (S); }
    void Consval(Tptr P, const value_type& V)
        {Alval.construct(P, V); }
    void Destval(Tptr P)
        {Alval.destroy(P); }
    void Freenode(Nodeptr S)
        {Alptr.destroy(&Parent(S));
        Alptr.destroy(&Right(S));
        Alptr.destroy(&Left(S));
        Alnod.deallocate(S, 1); }
    Nodeptr Head;
    size_type Size;
    };
```

Figure 13.14: **xtree Part 14**

```
        // Tree TEMPLATE OPERATORS
template<class Tr> inline
    void swap(Tree<Tr>& X, Tree<Tr>& Y)
    {X.swap(Y); }

template<class Tr> inline
    bool operator==(const Tree<Tr>& X, const Tree<Tr>& Y)
    {return (X.size() == Y.size()
        && equal(X.begin(), X.end(), Y.begin())); }
template<class Tr> inline
    bool operator!=(const Tree<Tr>& X, const Tree<Tr>& Y)
    {return (!(X == Y)); }
template<class Tr> inline
    bool operator<(const Tree<Tr>& X, const Tree<Tr>& Y)
    {return (lexicographical_compare(X.begin(), X.end(),
        Y.begin(), Y.end(), X.value_comp())); }
template<class Tr> inline
    bool operator>(const Tree<Tr>& X, const Tree<Tr>& Y)
    {return (Y < X); }
template<class Tr> inline
    bool operator<=(const Tree<Tr>& X, const Tree<Tr>& Y)
    {return (!(Y < X)); }
template<class Tr> inline
    bool operator>=(const Tree<Tr>& X, const Tree<Tr>& Y)
    {return (!(X < Y)); }
} /* namespace std */
#endif /* XTREE_ */
```

Just like a `list`, a `Tree` object stores a pointer and a count to represent the controlled sequence. Besides the allocator objects, described below, a `Tree` stores two objects:

`Head`
- `Head` is a pointer to the dummy head node, whose left pointer designates the first element in the controlled sequence, whose right pointer designates the last element in the controlled sequence, and whose parent pointer designates the root of the tree. For an empty tree, all of these pointers point back to the head node itself.

`Size`
- `Size` counts the number of elements in the tree.

The dummy head node serves an additional purpose. A missing subtree has to be indicated somehow. An obvious way is to use a null pointer, but that has its drawbacks. Much of the code in template class `Tree` spends its time crawling up and down trees. Such code, compilcated to begin with, gets even more involved if it has to repeatedly check for a null pointer wherever a subtree might be absent. Nevertheless, at least one popular implementation uses null node pointers to indicate missing subtrees.

nil node A common alternative is to effectively surround the entire frontier of the tree with "nil" nodes. A sidelong glance, as it were, can often treat a nil node just like any other. Special attention is required only when the code threatens to wander onto a nil node and do something nontrivial. Some implementations use a common, static node for all nil nodes. This can cause problems, however, in a multithreaded environment, because some code temporarily alters the color stored in a nil node. A static nil node shared across trees can cause surprising interactions between threads.

This implementation uses a nil node, but with a twist. It recycles the head node as a nil node unique to each list. A bit in the same object that stores the color of a node is set, only in this head node, to mark it as a nil node as well. The resulting code is as simple and efficient as code that uses a distinct nil node, and arguably no less readable.

A specialization `Tree<Tr>` derives from a succession of base classes. The ultimate base class is just the traits class `Tr`. The remaining three serve to store allocator objects, also much like a `list`:

`Tree_nod`
- `Tree_nod<T, A>` defines the generic pointer type `Genptr` and the node type `Node`. It also stores the allocator object `Alnod`.

`Tree_ptr`
- `Tree_ptr<T, A>` defines the node pointer type `Nodeptr`. It also stores the allocator object `Alptr`.

`Tree_val`
- `Tree_val<T, A>` stores the allocator object `Alnod`.

A smart enough compiler knows to allocate no storage within a `Tree<Tr>` object for any of these base objects.

`Tree` defines the usual host of type definitions. Some of these are hoisted up from the traits base class. Others are imported, in the usual fashion from the allocator class, which is in turn a type designated by the traits class. `Tree` also defines static accessor functions, such as `Key` and `left`, for manipulating the objects stored in a node.

`iterator`
`const_iterator`

The member classes `iterator` and `const_iterator` support just bidirectional iterators, as does `list`, not random-access iterators as does `vector`. Each iterator stores just a single pointer to a node. The member functions `Inc` and `Dec` defined in these member classes perform the magic of walking the sequence in proper order. Here, for example, is the code for incrementing an iterator:

```
void Inc()
    {if (Isnil(Ptr))
         ;
    else if (!Isnil(Right(Ptr)))
         Ptr = Min(Right(Ptr));
    else
         {Nodeptr P;
         while (!Isnil(P = Parent(Ptr))
              && Ptr == Right(P))
              Ptr = P;
         Ptr = P; }}
```

An iterator pointing at the nil (head) node is the end-of-sequence value just past the end of the controlled sequence. Incrementing such an iterator value is an invalid operation. Rather than do anything rash, this code does nothing. An iterator pointing at a node with a right subtree advances to the "smallest," or leftmost, element in that subtree. That's what the expression `Min(Right(Ptr))` delivers up. Otherwise, the code climbs the tree until it finds a parent node that lies to its right in the tree. (The child is not the root of the parent's right subtree.) If it reaches the head node while searching, then the successor to the original value is the end-of-sequence value just past the end. (The iterator was pointing at the "largest," or rightmost, element in the controlled sequence.)

You will find similar logic in the **Dec** functions in both iterator classes. If you can understand **Inc** and **Dec**, you can understand a lot about how the tree structure enforces the ordering requirements.

Buynode
Freenode

A handful of protected member functions perform a number of common operations. The call **Buynode(parent, color)**, for example, allocates a node and initializes the parent pointer and color member objects appropriately. The call **Freenode(p)** frees a node. Both assume that some other agency will construct and destroy the stored element value, and the stored left and right pointers, as needed.

Note that none of the constructors, or template arguments for that matter, have defaults. Template class **Tree** is intended for internal use by other STL containers. It does not need all the shorthand conveniences of a user-level template class.

insert

The hard work of inserting an element between two adjacent elements is encapsulated in the member functions **insert** and **Insert**. Basically, **insert** climbs down the tree until it finds the proper node **Y** to attach the new node as a leaf. If the resulting value of **Addleft** is true, the leaf attaches as the left child of **Y**; otherwise it attaches as the right child. Here, **Pairib** is just a type definition for **pair<iterator, bool>**.

Insert

Insert does the actual insertion. The code optimistically adds the new node with a red link. If the link above is black, the job is done. Otherwise, the code works its way up the tree until it finds a place where it can correct for the introduction of an extra black link. Two versions of the same code occur in mirror image. Understanding either half should tell you how the other half lives and works. (It is not easy code to understand.)

All rearrangements are performed by calls to the protected member functions **Lrotate(X)** and **Rrotate(X)**. The former essentially picks up the right subtree of **X** and hangs it in place of **X**, letting **X** dangle as its left subtree. (Note that the ordering of the tree is preserved with such a transformation.) The latter is its mirror image, promoting the left subtree of **X** in its place.

erase

The hard work of erasing an element is encapsulated in the first member function **erase**. If you want to understand how it works, we recommend that you set aside plenty of time and scratch paper. You have to draw a lot of subtrees to convince yourself that all possible cases are handled properly. If it is not lucky enough to be asked to erase a leaf, it replaces the erased element with the next element in sequence — which must itself be a leaf — and erases that instead. If the erased leaf had a red link, the job is done. Otherwise, the code must correct for the removal of a black link. Once again, two versions of the same code occur in mirror image. Neither half is easy to understand.

Figure 13.15: `set` Part 1

```
// set standard header
#ifndef SET_
#define SET_
#include <xtree>
namespace std {
          // TEMPLATE CLASS Tset_traits
template<class K, class Pr, class Ax, bool Mfl>
     class Tset_traits {
public:
     typedef K key_type;
     typedef K value_type;
     typedef Pr key_compare;
     typedef typename Ax::template rebind<value_type>::other
          allocator_type;
     enum {Multi = Mfl};
     Tset_traits()
          : comp()
          {}
     Tset_traits(Pr Parg)
          : comp(Parg)
          {}
     typedef key_compare value_compare;
     struct Kfn {
          const K& operator()(const value_type& X) const
               {return (X); }
          };
     Pr comp;
     };

          // TEMPLATE CLASS set
template<class K,
     class Pr = less<K>,
     class A = allocator<K> >
     class set
          : public Tree<Tset_traits<K, Pr, A, false> > {
public:
     typedef set<K, Pr, A> Myt;
     typedef Tree<Tset_traits<K, Pr, A, false> >
          Mybase;
     typedef K key_type;
     typedef Pr key_compare;
     typedef typename Mybase::value_compare value_compare;
     typedef typename Mybase::allocator_type allocator_type;
     typedef typename Mybase::size_type size_type;
     typedef typename Mybase::difference_type difference_type;
     typedef typename Mybase::pointer pointer;
     typedef typename Mybase::const_pointer const_pointer;
     typedef typename Mybase::reference reference;
     typedef typename Mybase::const_reference const_reference;
     typedef typename Mybase::iterator iterator;
     typedef typename Mybase::const_iterator const_iterator;
     typedef typename Mybase::reverse_iterator reverse_iterator;
     typedef typename Mybase::const_reverse_iterator
          const_reverse_iterator;
     typedef typename Mybase::value_type value_type;
```

Figure 13.16: `set` Part 2

```
    set()
        : Mybase(key_compare(), allocator_type()) {}
    explicit set(const key_compare& Pred)
        : Mybase(Pred, allocator_type()) {}
    set(const key_compare& Pred, const allocator_type& Al)
        : Mybase(Pred, Al) {}
    template<class It>
        set(It F, It L)
        : Mybase(key_compare(), allocator_type())
        {for (; F != L; ++F)
            insert(*F); }
    template<class It>
        set(It F, It L, const key_compare& Pred)
        : Mybase(Pred, allocator_type())
        {for (; F != L; ++F)
            insert(*F); }
    template<class It>
        set(It F, It L, const key_compare& Pred,
        const allocator_type& Al)
        : Mybase(Pred, Al)
        {for (; F != L; ++F)
            insert(*F); }
    };

        // TEMPLATE CLASS multiset
template<class K,
    class Pr = less<K>,
    class A = allocator<K> >
    class multiset
        : public Tree<Tset_traits<K, Pr, A, true> > {
public:
    typedef multiset<K, Pr, A> Myt;
    typedef Tree<Tset_traits<K, Pr, A, true> >
        Mybase;
    typedef K key_type;
    typedef Pr key_compare;
    typedef typename Mybase::value_compare value_compare;
    typedef typename Mybase::allocator_type allocator_type;
    typedef typename Mybase::size_type size_type;
    typedef typename Mybase::difference_type difference_type;
    typedef typename Mybase::pointer pointer;
    typedef typename Mybase::const_pointer const_pointer;
    typedef typename Mybase::reference reference;
    typedef typename Mybase::const_reference const_reference;
    typedef typename Mybase::iterator iterator;
    typedef typename Mybase::const_iterator const_iterator;
    typedef typename Mybase::reverse_iterator reverse_iterator;
    typedef typename Mybase::const_reverse_iterator
        const_reverse_iterator;
    typedef typename Mybase::value_type value_type;
    multiset()
        : Mybase(key_compare(), allocator_type()) {}
    explicit multiset(const key_compare& Pred)
        : Mybase(Pred, allocator_type()) {}
    multiset(const key_compare& Pred, const allocator_type& Al)
```

Figure 13.17: set Part 3

```
            : Mybase(Pred, Al) {}
        template<class It>
            multiset(It F, It L)
            : Mybase(key_compare(), allocator_type())
            {for (; F != L; ++F)
                insert(*F); }
        template<class It>
            multiset(It F, It L, const key_compare& Pred)
            : Mybase(Pred, allocator_type())
            {for (; F != L; ++F)
                insert(*F); }
        template<class It>
            multiset(It F, It L, const key_compare& Pred,
            const allocator_type& Al)
            : Mybase(Pred, Al)
            {for (; F != L; ++F)
                insert(*F); }
        iterator insert(const value_type& X)
            {return (Mybase::insert(X).first); }
        iterator insert(iterator P, const value_type& X)
            {return (Mybase::insert(P, X)); }
        template<class It>
            void insert(It F, It L)
            {for (; F != L; ++F)
                insert(*F); }
        };
} /* namespace std */
#endif /* SET_ */
```

The essential strategy is to look for an opportunity to turn a red link into a black one. Until that can happen, the code has to keep climbing the tree. With each climb, it has to deal with the other subtree it passes by. For example, how do you introduce a black link above a node, to fix up the subtree with the erasure, without messing up the other subtree at that node? The operations you have to perform are really no harder than solving a Rubik's Cube. And no easier to capture in code.

Template class **Tree** has plenty of other mysteries, to be sure. It is a difficult class to design, to write, and to understand. But most of the remaining complexities can also be found in the other STL container classes we have presented here. We resist the urge to repeat earlier sermons, however much they might help explain this complex template class. If you enjoy learning clever algorithms, however, we encourage you to study template class **Tree** with care.

set Figures 13.15 through 13.17 show the file **set**. It defines the template classes **set** and **multiset**. Given template class **Tree**, the rest of the work required to implement these containers is pretty easy.

Tset_traits Template class **Tset_traits** is a version of the **Tree** traits class we showed earlier, suitable for defining a set. As you can see, there's not much to it, but it saves writing a long list of parameters when specializing **Tree**.

Note that `key_type` is a synonym for `value_type` for a set, so the key extractor supplied by `Kfn` simply returns the entire value.

`multiset` Template class `set` has nothing left to do but echo a few type definitions and supply the appropriate constructors. Template class `multiset` does the same, and just a bit more. It wraps calls to `Tree::insert` primarily to simplify the value returned by the member function `insert(const value_type&)`. The other wrappers are not strictly necessary, but they help certain compilers that tend to get confused.

Testing `<set>`

Figures 13.18 through 13.21 shows the file `tset.c`. It provides tests for template class `set` and template class `multiset` that are very much alike. It is, in turn, one of two test programs that look very much alike. See the file `tmap.c`, beginning on page 428. To ease comparison of the four tests spread over these two files, we have simply noted any tests that are particular for a given container.

The test program performs a simple test that each of the member functions and types is present and behaves as intended, for one specialization of template class `set` and for one specialization of template class `multiset`. If all goes well, the program prints:

```
SUCCESS testing <set>
```

and takes a normal exit.

Exercises

Exercise 13.1 This implementation of template class `Tree` never copies elements between nodes. Elements are constructed and destroyed, but never assigned. Under what circumstances is this behavior most desirable?

Exercise 13.2 Rewrite template class `Tree` to eliminate the use of a head node. Under what circumstances is this rewrite a better design?

Exercise 13.3 Alter the definition of `Tree` iterators so that it is easy to determine if two iterators designate elements in different controlled sequences.

Exercise 13.4 Some people believe the C++ Standard permits the value stored in a `set` or `multiset` element to be altered. What are the advantages and disadvantages of permitting this behavior?

Exercise 13.5 **[Harder]** Alter template class `Tree` to remove the tree-balancing logic, then measure the relative performance of balanced and unbalanced trees for a range of applications. Under what circumstances do unbalanced trees offer an advantage over balanced trees?

Exercise 13.6 **[Very hard]** Alter template classes `set` and `multiset` so that they automatically reorder elements as needed if any stored values change.

Figure 13.18: tset.c Part 1

```
// test <set>
#include <assert.h>
#include <iostream>
#include <functional>
#include <set>
using namespace std;

     // TEST set
void test_set()
     {typedef allocator<char> Myal;
     typedef less<char> Mypred;
     typedef set<char, Mypred, Myal> Mycont;
     char ch, carr[] = "abc", carr2[] = "def";

     Mycont::key_type *p_key = (char *)0;
     Mycont::key_compare *p_kcomp = (Mypred *)0;
     Mycont::value_type *p_val = (char *)0;
     Mycont::value_compare *p_vcomp = (Mypred *)0;
     Mycont::allocator_type *p_alloc = (Myal *)0;
     Mycont::pointer p_ptr = (char *)0;
     Mycont::const_pointer p_cptr = (const char *)0;
     Mycont::reference p_ref = ch;
     Mycont::const_reference p_cref = (const char&)ch;
     Mycont::size_type *p_size = (size_t *)0;
     Mycont::difference_type *p_diff = (ptrdiff_t *)0;

     Mycont v0;
     Myal al = v0.get_allocator();
     Mypred pred;
     Mycont v0a(pred), v0b(pred, al);
     assert(v0.empty() && v0.size() == 0);
     assert(v0a.size() == 0 && v0a.get_allocator() == al);
     assert(v0b.size() == 0 && v0b.get_allocator() == al);
     Mycont v1(carr, carr + 3);
     assert(v1.size() == 3 && *v1.begin() == 'a');
     Mycont v2(carr, carr + 3, pred);
     assert(v2.size() == 3 && *v2.begin() == 'a');
     Mycont v3(carr, carr + 3, pred, al);
     assert(v3.size() == 3 && *v3.begin() == 'a');
     const Mycont v4(carr, carr + 3);
     v0 = v4;
     assert(v0.size() == 3 && *v0.begin() == 'a');

     Mycont::iterator p_it(v1.begin());
     Mycont::const_iterator p_cit(v4.begin());
     Mycont::reverse_iterator p_rit(v1.rbegin());
     Mycont::const_reverse_iterator p_crit(v4.rbegin());
     assert(*p_it == 'a' && *--(p_it = v1.end()) == 'c');
     assert(*p_cit == 'a' && *--(p_cit = v4.end()) == 'c');
     assert(*p_rit == 'c' && *--(p_rit = v1.rend()) == 'a');
     assert(*p_crit == 'c' && *--(p_crit = v4.rend()) == 'a');

     v0.clear();                             // DIFFERS FROM multiset
     pair<Mycont::iterator, bool> pib = v0.insert('d');
     assert(*pib.first == 'd' && pib.second);
```

Figure 13.19: `tset.c` **Part 2**

```
    assert(*--v0.end() == 'd');
    pib = v0.insert('d');
    assert(*pib.first == 'd' && !pib.second);
    assert(*v0.insert(v0.begin(), 'e') == 'e');
    v0.insert(carr, carr + 3);
    assert(v0.size() == 5 && *v0.begin() == 'a');
    v0.insert(carr2, carr2 + 3);
    assert(v0.size() == 6 && *--v0.end() == 'f');
    assert(*v0.erase(v0.begin()) == 'b' && v0.size() == 5);
    assert(*v0.erase(v0.begin(), ++v0.begin()) == 'c'
        && v0.size() == 4);
    assert(v0.erase('x') == 0 && v0.erase('e') == 1);

    v0.clear();
    assert(v0.empty());
    v0.swap(v1);
    assert(!v0.empty() && v1.empty());
    swap(v0, v1);
    assert(v0.empty() && !v1.empty());
    assert(v1 == v1 && v0 < v1);
    assert(v0 != v1 && v1 > v0);
    assert(v0 <= v1 && v1 >= v0);

    assert(v0.key_comp()('a', 'c')
        && !v0.key_comp()('a', 'a'));
    assert(v0.value_comp()('a', 'c')
        && !v0.value_comp()('a', 'a'));
    assert(*v4.find('b') == 'b');
    assert(v4.count('x') == 0 && v4.count('b') == 1);
    assert(*v4.lower_bound('a') == 'a');
    assert(*v4.upper_bound('a') == 'b');
    pair<Mycont::const_iterator, Mycont::const_iterator> pcc =
        v4.equal_range('a');
    assert(*pcc.first == 'a' && *pcc.second == 'b'); }

    // TEST multiset
void test_multiset()
    {typedef allocator<char> Myal;
    typedef less<char> Mypred;
    typedef multiset<char, Mypred, Myal> Mycont;
    char ch, carr[] = "abc", carr2[] = "def";

    Mycont::key_type *p_key = (char *)0;
    Mycont::key_compare *p_kcomp = (Mypred *)0;
    Mycont::value_type *p_val = (char *)0;
    Mycont::value_compare *p_vcomp = (Mypred *)0;
    Mycont::allocator_type *p_alloc = (Myal *)0;
    Mycont::pointer p_ptr = (char *)0;
    Mycont::const_pointer p_cptr = (const char *)0;
    Mycont::reference p_ref = ch;
    Mycont::const_reference p_cref = (const char&)ch;
    Mycont::size_type *p_size = (size_t *)0;
    Mycont::difference_type *p_diff = (ptrdiff_t *)0;

    Mycont v0;
```

Figure 13.20: `tset.c` **Part 3**

```
    Myal al = v0.get_allocator();
    Mypred pred;
    Mycont v0a(pred), v0b(pred, al);
    assert(v0.empty() && v0.size() == 0);
    assert(v0a.size() == 0 && v0a.get_allocator() == al);
    assert(v0b.size() == 0 && v0b.get_allocator() == al);
    Mycont v1(carr, carr + 3);
    assert(v1.size() == 3 && *v1.begin() == 'a');
    Mycont v2(carr, carr + 3, pred);
    assert(v2.size() == 3 && *v2.begin() == 'a');
    Mycont v3(carr, carr + 3, pred, al);
    assert(v3.size() == 3 && *v3.begin() == 'a');
    const Mycont v4(carr, carr + 3);
    v0 = v4;
    assert(v0.size() == 3 && *v0.begin() == 'a');

    Mycont::iterator p_it(v1.begin());
    Mycont::const_iterator p_cit(v4.begin());
    Mycont::reverse_iterator p_rit(v1.rbegin());
    Mycont::const_reverse_iterator p_crit(v4.rbegin());
    assert(*p_it == 'a' && *--(p_it = v1.end()) == 'c');
    assert(*p_cit == 'a' && *--(p_cit = v4.end()) == 'c');
    assert(*p_rit == 'c' && *--(p_rit = v1.rend()) == 'a');
    assert(*p_crit == 'c' && *--(p_crit = v4.rend()) == 'a');

    v0.clear();                                        // DIFFERS FROM set
    assert(*v0.insert('d') == 'd');
    assert(*--v0.end() == 'd');
    assert(*v0.insert('d') == 'd');
    assert(v0.size() == 2);
    assert(*v0.insert(v0.begin(), 'e') == 'e');
    v0.insert(carr, carr + 3);
    assert(v0.size() == 6 && *v0.begin() == 'a');
    v0.insert(carr2, carr2 + 3);
    assert(v0.size() == 9 && *--v0.end() == 'f');
    assert(*v0.erase(v0.begin()) == 'b' && v0.size() == 8);
    assert(*v0.erase(v0.begin(), ++v0.begin()) == 'c'
        && v0.size() == 7);
    assert(v0.erase('x') == 0 && v0.erase('e') == 2);

    v0.clear();
    assert(v0.empty());
    v0.swap(v1);
    assert(!v0.empty() && v1.empty());
    swap(v0, v1);
    assert(v0.empty() && !v1.empty());
    assert(v1 == v1 && v0 < v1);
    assert(v0 != v1 && v1 > v0);
    assert(v0 <= v1 && v1 >= v0);

    assert(v0.key_comp()('a', 'c')
        && !v0.key_comp()('a', 'a'));
    assert(v0.value_comp()('a', 'c')
        && !v0.value_comp()('a', 'a'));
    assert(*v4.find('b') == 'b');
```

Figure 13.21: `tset.c` **Part 4**

```
     assert(v4.count('x') == 0 && v4.count('b') == 1);
     assert(*v4.lower_bound('a') == 'a');
     assert(*v4.upper_bound('a') == 'b');
     pair<Mycont::const_iterator, Mycont::const_iterator> pcc =
          v4.equal_range('a');
     assert(*pcc.first == 'a' && *pcc.second == 'b'); }

     // TEST <set>
int main()
     {test_set();
     test_multiset();
     cout << "SUCCESS testing <set>" << endl;
     return (0); }
```
□

Chapter 14: <map>

Background

<map>
map
multimap

The header <map> defines the template class **map** and the template class **multimap**. Each is a container that typically stores its controlled sequence of length **N** as an ordered binary tree of **N** nodes. Each node stores a single element of type **pair<const Key, T>**. The sequence is ordered by a function object whose type is one of the template parameters for the class. Only the **const Key** component participates in ordering comparisons. A multimap permits two (adjacent) elements to have keys with equivalent ordering, while a map does not. More colloquially, a map or multimap stores a "mapped value" along with each key. And as you might guess, all the keys of a map are unique, but a multimap permits duplicates.

<set>
set
multiset

In the previous chapter, we presented the companion header **<set>**. It defines the template class **set** and the template class **multiset**. They differ from **map** and **multimap** in one fundamental way — each stores elements of type **const Key**, so the whole element value participates in ordering comparisons. For a set or multiset, by contrast, the entire element value participates in ordering comparisons. More colloquially, a set or multiset stores just an immutable key for each element. And as you might guess, all the elements of a set are unique, but a multiset permits duplicates.

associative containers

As we discussed at length in the previous chapter, the template classes **set**, **multiset**, **map**, and **multimap** are all called *associative containers*. They all associate a key value with each element, and can use the key to speed lookup, insertion, and deletion of elements. Table 9.1, on page 240, shows the payoff for the added complexity in the associative containers. (They are labeled "set/map" in the table.) They are often superior to all other STL containers when you need to lookup an element by key value. While an ordered vector or deque can match this behavior, neither can do better than linear time for inserts and erases. The underlying tree representation can perform these operations in logarithmic time as well. See the previous chapter for a more detailed discussion of the merits of associative containers and ordered binary trees.

A set is ordered on the values it stores. That can be a handy way to represent many collections — a set in the usual mathematical sense, for example. But sometimes it can be overly restrictive. Sometimes, you'd like to order a sequence on just part of the information stored in each element. Other information should just go along for the ride. Consider, for example, a symbol table. You want it ordered on the names of the symbols, for quick lookup. But you'd rather the order not be sensitive to the value of the symbol, or any attribute flags.

No problem. You can simply define the predicate class as you see fit. It can compare the name components of stored values and ignore the rest. While this is not a big problem, it is a common enough occurrence to be a nuisance. You'd rather not have to write a special predicate class for every container that holds both a key and a separate value component. Thus, STL provides this second pair of template classes implemented in terms of binary trees:

```
template<class Key, class T, class Pred = less<Key>,
    class A = allocator<pair<const Key, T> > >
    class map;
template<class Key, class T, class Pred = less<Key>,
    class A = allocator<pair<const Key, T> > >
    class multimap;
```

Both store elements with a pair of values. One element of the pair is the ordering key, of type `const Key`. The other element has type `T`. The remaining parameters are the same as for `set` and `multiset`. Indeed, the four associative containers are more alike than they are different.

`operator[]` Template class `map` does have one unique feature, however. It defines the member operator `T& operator[const Key& key]`, which maps the key value `key` to its corresponding mapped value. More specifically, it endeavors to lookup an element whose key has equivalent ordering to `key`. If the lookup fails, it inserts an element with that key value and a default mapped value. In either case, the member operator returns a reference to the mapped value of the one and only entry that matches the key argument.

This is a cute notation for locating the element uniquely determined by a given key value, or adding such an element if it is not present. Of course, it makes rather less sense for the other associative containers to define such an operator. For `set` the mapping is trivial — `insert(const Key&)` does the job. And for `multiset` and `multimap` the mapping can be ambiguous. So only `map` defines this member operator.

Functional Description

```
namespace std {
template<class Key, class T, class Pred, class A>
    class map;
template<class Key, class T, class Pred, class A>
    class multimap;

        // TEMPLATE FUNCTIONS
template<class Key, class T, class Pred, class A>
    bool operator==(
        const map<Key, T, Pred, A>& lhs,
        const map<Key, T, Pred, A>& rhs);
```

```
template<class Key, class T, class Pred, class A>
    bool operator==(
        const multimap<Key, T, Pred, A>& lhs,
        const multimap<Key, T, Pred, A>& rhs);
template<class Key, class T, class Pred, class A>
    bool operator!=(
        const map<Key, T, Pred, A>& lhs,
        const map<Key, T, Pred, A>& rhs);
template<class Key, class T, class Pred, class A>
    bool operator!=(
        const multimap<Key, T, Pred, A>& lhs,
        const multimap<Key, T, Pred, A>& rhs);
template<class Key, class T, class Pred, class A>
    bool operator<(
        const map<Key, T, Pred, A>& lhs,
        const map<Key, T, Pred, A>& rhs);
template<class Key, class T, class Pred, class A>
    bool operator<(
        const multimap<Key, T, Pred, A>& lhs,
        const multimap<Key, T, Pred, A>& rhs);
template<class Key, class T, class Pred, class A>
    bool operator>(
        const map<Key, T, Pred, A>& lhs,
        const map<Key, T, Pred, A>& rhs);
template<class Key, class T, class Pred, class A>
    bool operator>(
        const multimap<Key, T, Pred, A>& lhs,
        const multimap<Key, T, Pred, A>& rhs);
template<class Key, class T, class Pred, class A>
    bool operator<=(
        const map<Key, T, Pred, A>& lhs,
        const map<Key, T, Pred, A>& rhs);
template<class Key, class T, class Pred, class A>
    bool operator<=(
        const multimap<Key, T, Pred, A>& lhs,
        const multimap<Key, T, Pred, A>& rhs);
template<class Key, class T, class Pred, class A>
    bool operator>=(
        const map<Key, T, Pred, A>& lhs,
        const map<Key, T, Pred, A>& rhs);
template<class Key, class T, class Pred, class A>
    bool operator>=(
        const multimap<Key, T, Pred, A>& lhs,
        const multimap<Key, T, Pred, A>& rhs);
template<class Key, class T, class Pred, class A>
    void swap(
        map<Key, T, Pred, A>& lhs,
        map<Key, T, Pred, A>& rhs);
template<class Key, class T, class Pred, class A>
    void swap(
        multimap<Key, T, Pred, A>& lhs,
        multimap<Key, T, Pred, A>& rhs);
    };
```

Include the STL standard header **<map>** to define the container template classes **map** and **multimap**, and their supporting templates.

▫ map

```
template<class Key, class T, class Pred = less<Key>,
    class A = allocator<pair<const Key, T> > >
    class map {
```

```
public:
    typedef Key key_type;
    typedef T mapped_type;
    typedef Pred key_compare;
    typedef A allocator_type;
    typedef pair<const Key, T> value_type;
    class value_compare;
    typedef A::pointer pointer;
    typedef A::const_pointer const_pointer;
    typedef A::reference reference;
    typedef A::const_reference const_reference;
    typedef T0 iterator;
    typedef T1 const_iterator;
    typedef T2 size_type;
    typedef T3 difference_type;
    typedef reverse_iterator<const_iterator>
        const_reverse_iterator;
    typedef reverse_iterator<iterator> reverse_iterator;
    map();
    explicit map(const Pred& comp);
    map(const Pred& comp, const A& al);
    map(const map& x);
    template<class InIt>
        map(InIt first, InIt last);
    template<class InIt>
        map(InIt first, InIt last,
            const Pred& comp);
    template<class InIt>
        map(InIt first, InIt last,
            const Pred& comp, const A& al);
    iterator begin();
    const_iterator begin() const;
    iterator end();
    const_iterator end() const;
    reverse_iterator rbegin();
    const_reverse_iterator rbegin() const;
    reverse_iterator rend();
    const_reverse_iterator rend() const;
    size_type size() const;
    size_type max_size() const;
    bool empty() const;
    A get_allocator() const;
    mapped_type operator[](const Key& key);
    pair<iterator, bool> insert(const value_type& x);
    iterator insert(iterator it, const value_type& x);
    template<class InIt>
        void insert(InIt first, InIt last);
    iterator erase(iterator it);
    iterator erase(iterator first, iterator last);
    size_type erase(const Key& key);
    void clear();
    void swap(map& x);
    key_compare key_comp() const;
    value_compare value_comp() const;
    iterator find(const Key& key);
    const_iterator find(const Key& key) const;
    size_type count(const Key& key) const;
    iterator lower_bound(const Key& key);
    const_iterator lower_bound(const Key& key) const;
    iterator upper_bound(const Key& key);
    const_iterator upper_bound(const Key& key) const;
```

```
    pair<iterator, iterator> equal_range(const Key& key);
    pair<const_iterator, const_iterator>
        equal_range(const Key& key) const;
    };
```

The template class describes an object that controls a varying-length sequence of elements of type `pair<const Key, T>`. The sequence is ordered by the predicate `Pred`. The first element of each pair is the *sort key* and the second is its associated *value*. The sequence is represented in a way that permits lookup, insertion, and removal of an arbitrary element with a number of operations proportional to the logarithm of the number of elements in the sequence (logarithmic time). Moreover, inserting an element invalidates no iterators, and removing an element invalidates only those iterators which point at the removed element.

The object orders the sequence it controls by calling a stored *function object* of type `Pred`. You access this stored object by calling the member function `key_comp()`. Such a function object must impose a strict weak ordering on sort keys of type `Key`. For any element `x` that precedes `y` in the sequence, `key_comp()(y.first, x.first)` is false. (For the default function object `less<Key>`, sort keys never decrease in value.) Unlike template class `multimap`, an object of template class `map` ensures that `key_comp()(x.first, y.first)` is true. (Each key is unique.)

The object allocates and frees storage for the sequence it controls through a stored allocator object of class `A`. Such an allocator object must have the same external interface as an object of template class `allocator`. Note that the stored allocator object is *not* copied when the container object is assigned.

▫ **map::allocator_type**

```
typedef A allocator_type;
```

The type is a synonym for the template parameter `A`.

▫ **map::begin**

```
const_iterator begin() const;
iterator begin();
```

The member function returns a bidirectional iterator that points at the first element of the sequence (or just beyond the end of an empty sequence).

▫ **map::clear**

```
void clear();
```

The member function calls `erase( begin(), end())`.

▫ **map::const_iterator**

```
typedef T1 const_iterator;
```

The type describes an object that can serve as a constant bidirectional iterator for the controlled sequence. It is described here as a synonym for the implementation-defined type `T1`.

▫ **map::const_pointer**

```
typedef A::const_pointer const_pointer;
```

The type describes an object that can serve as a constant pointer to an element of the controlled sequence.

▫ **map::const_reference**

```
typedef A::const_reference const_reference;
```

The type describes an object that can serve as a constant reference to an element of the controlled sequence.

▫ **map::const_reverse_iterator**

```
typedef reverse_iterator<const_iterator>
    const_reverse_iterator;
```

The type describes an object that can serve as a constant reverse bidirectional iterator for the controlled sequence.

▫ **map::count**

```
size_type count(const Key& key) const;
```

The member function returns the number of elements `x` in the range `[lower_bound(key), upper_bound(key))`.

▫ **map::difference_type**

```
typedef T3 difference_type;
```

The signed integer type describes an object that can represent the difference between the addresses of any two elements in the controlled sequence. It is described here as a synonym for the implementation-defined type `T3`.

▫ **map::empty**

```
bool empty() const;
```

The member function returns true for an empty controlled sequence.

▫ **map::end**

```
const_iterator end() const;
iterator end();
```

The member function returns a bidirectional iterator that points just beyond the end of the sequence.

▫ **map::equal_range**

```
pair<iterator, iterator> equal_range(const Key& key);
pair<const_iterator, const_iterator>
    equal_range(const Key& key) const;
```

The member function returns a pair of iterators `x` such that `x.first == lower_bound(key)` and `x.second == upper_bound(key)`.

▫ **map::erase**

```
iterator erase(iterator it);
iterator erase(iterator first, iterator last);
size_type erase(const Key& key);
```

The first member function removes the element of the controlled sequence pointed to by `it`. The second member function removes the elements in the interval `[first, last)`. Both return an iterator that designates the first element remaining beyond any elements removed, or `end()` if no such element exists.

The third member function removes the elements with sort keys in the range `[lower_bound(key), upper_bound(key))`. It returns the number of elements it removes.

The member functions never throw an exception.

▫ **map::find**

```
iterator find(const Key& key);
const_iterator find(const Key& key) const;
```

The member function returns an iterator that designates the element in the controlled sequence whose sort key has equivalent ordering to `key`. If no such element exists, the function returns `end()`.

▫ **map::get_allocator**

```
A get_allocator() const;
```

The member function returns the stored allocator object.

▫ **map::insert**

```
pair<iterator, bool> insert(const value_type& x);
iterator insert(iterator it, const value_type& x);
template<class InIt>
    void insert(InIt first, InIt last);
```

The first member function determines whether an element `y` exists in the sequence whose key has equivalent ordering to that of `x`. If not, it creates such an element `y` and initializes it with `x`. The function then determines the iterator `it` that designates `y`. If an insertion occurred, the function returns `pair(it, true)`. Otherwise, it returns `pair(it, false)`.

The second member function returns `insert(x)`, using `it` as a starting place within the controlled sequence to search for the insertion point. (Insertion can occur in amortized constant time, instead of logarithmic time, if the insertion point immediately follows `it`.) The third member function inserts the sequence of element values, for each `it` in the range `[first, last)`, by calling `insert(*it)`.

If an exception is thrown during the insertion of a single element, the container is left unaltered and the exception is rethrown. If an exception is thrown during the insertion of multiple elements, the container is left in a stable but unspecified state and the exception is rethrown.

▫ **map::iterator**

```
typedef T0 iterator;
```

The type describes an object that can serve as a bidirectional iterator for the controlled sequence. It is described here as a synonym for the implementation-defined type `T0`.

- **map::key_comp**

```
key_compare key_comp() const;
```

The member function returns the stored function object that determines the order of elements in the controlled sequence. The stored object defines the member function:

```
bool operator()(const Key& x, const Key& y);
```

which returns true if **x** strictly precedes **y** in the sort order.

- **map::key_compare**

```
typedef Pred key_compare;
```

The type describes a function object that can compare two sort keys to determine the relative order of two elements in the controlled sequence.

- **map::key_type**

```
typedef Key key_type;
```

The type describes the sort key object stored in each element of the controlled sequence.

- **map::lower_bound**

```
iterator lower_bound(const Key& key);
const_iterator lower_bound(const Key& key) const;
```

The member function returns an iterator that designates the earliest element **x** in the controlled sequence for which `key_comp()(x. first, key)` is false. If no such element exists, the function returns `end()`.

- **map::map**

```
map();
explicit map(const Pred& comp);
map(const Pred& comp, const A& al);
map(const map& x);
template<class InIt>
    map(InIt first, InIt last);
template<class InIt>
    map(InIt first, InIt last,
        const Pred& comp);
template<class InIt>
    map(InIt first, InIt last,
        const Pred& comp, const A& al);
```

All constructors store an allocator object and initialize the controlled sequence. The allocator object is the argument `al`, if present. For the copy constructor, it is `x.get_allocator()`. Otherwise, it is `A()`.

All constructors also store a function object that can later be returned by calling `key_comp()`. The function object is the argument `comp`, if present. For the copy constructor, it is `x.key_comp())`. Otherwise, it is `Pred()`.

The first three constructors specify an empty initial controlled sequence. The fourth constructor specifies a copy of the sequence controlled by **x**. The last three constructors specify the sequence of element values `[first, last)`.

- **map::mapped_type**

```
typedef T mapped_type;
```

The type is a synonym for the template parameter `T`.

- **map::max_size**

```
size_type max_size() const;
```

The member function returns the length of the longest sequence that the object can control.

- **map::operator[]**

```
T& operator[](const Key& key);
```

The member function determines the iterator `it` as the return value of `insert( value_type(key, T())`. (It inserts an element with the specified key if no such element exists.) It then returns a reference to `(*it).second`.

- **map::pointer**

```
typedef A::pointer pointer;
```

The type describes an object that can serve as a pointer to an element of the controlled sequence.

- **map::rbegin**

```
const_reverse_iterator rbegin() const;
reverse_iterator rbegin();
```

The member function returns a reverse bidirectional iterator that points just beyond the end of the controlled sequence. Hence, it designates the beginning of the reverse sequence.

- **map::reference**

```
typedef A::reference reference;
```

The type describes an object that can serve as a reference to an element of the controlled sequence.

- **map::rend**

```
const_reverse_iterator rend() const;
reverse_iterator rend();
```

The member function returns a reverse bidirectional iterator that points at the first element of the sequence (or just beyond the end of an empty sequence). Hence, it designates the end of the reverse sequence.

- **map::reverse_iterator**

```
typedef reverse_iterator<iterator> reverse_iterator;
```

The type describes an object that can serve as a reverse bidirectional iterator for the controlled sequence.

- **map::size**

```
size_type size() const;
```

The member function returns the length of the controlled sequence.

- **map::size_type**

```
typedef T2 size_type;
```

The unsigned integer type describes an object that can represent the length of any controlled sequence. It is described here as a synonym for the implementation-defined type `T2`.

- **map::swap**

```
void swap(map& x);
```

The member function swaps the controlled sequences between `*this` and `x`. If `get_allocator() == x.get_allocator()`, it does so in constant time, it throws an exception only as a result of copying the stored function object of type `Pred`, and it invalidates no references, pointers, or iterators that designate elements in the two controlled sequences. Otherwise, it performs a number of element assignments and constructor calls proportional to the number of elements in the two controlled sequences.

- **map::upper_bound**

```
iterator upper_bound(const Key& key);
const_iterator upper_bound(const Key& key) const;
```

The member function returns an iterator that designates the earliest element `x` in the controlled sequence for which `key_comp()(key, x.first)` is true. If no such element exists, the function returns `end()`.

- **map::value_comp**

```
value_compare value_comp() const;
```

The member function returns a function object that determines the order of elements in the controlled sequence.

- **map::value_compare**

```
class value_compare
    : public binary_function<value_type, value_type,
        bool> {
public:
    bool operator()(const value_type& x,
        const value_type& y) const
        {return (comp(x.first, y.first)); }
protected:
    value_compare(key_compare pr)
        : comp(pr) {}
    key_compare comp;
    };
```

The type describes a function object that can compare the sort keys in two elements to determine their relative order in the controlled sequence. The function object stores an object `comp` of type `key_compare`. The member function `operator()` uses this object to compare the sort-key components of two element.

- **map::value_type**

```
typedef pair<const Key, T> value_type;
```

The type describes an element of the controlled sequence.

<map>

▫ multimap

```
template<class Key, class T, class Pred = less<Key>,
    class A = allocator<pair<const Key, T> > >
    class multimap {
public:
    typedef Key key_type;
    typedef T mapped_type;
    typedef Pred key_compare;
    typedef A allocator_type;
    typedef pair<const Key, T> value_type;
    class value_compare;
    typedef A::reference reference;
    typedef A::const_reference const_reference;
    typedef T0 iterator;
    typedef T1 const_iterator;
    typedef T2 size_type;
    typedef T3 difference_type;
    typedef reverse_iterator<const_iterator>
        const_reverse_iterator;
    typedef reverse_iterator<iterator> reverse_iterator;
    multimap();
    explicit multimap(const Pred& comp);
    multimap(const Pred& comp, const A& al);
    multimap(const multimap& x);
    template<class InIt>
        multimap(InIt first, InIt last);
    template<class InIt>
        multimap(InIt first, InIt last,
            const Pred& comp);
    template<class InIt>
        multimap(InIt first, InIt last,
            const Pred& comp, const A& al);
    iterator begin();
    const_iterator begin() const;
    iterator end();
    const_iterator end() const;
    reverse_iterator rbegin();
    const_reverse_iterator rbegin() const;
    reverse_iterator rend();
    const_reverse_iterator rend() const;
    size_type size() const;
    size_type max_size() const;
    bool empty() const;
    A get_allocator() const;
    iterator insert(const value_type& x);
    iterator insert(iterator it, const value_type& x);
    template<class InIt>
        void insert(InIt first, InIt last);
    iterator erase(iterator it);
    iterator erase(iterator first, iterator last);
    size_type erase(const Key& key);
    void clear();
    void swap(multimap& x);
    key_compare key_comp() const;
    value_compare value_comp() const;
    iterator find(const Key& key);
    const_iterator find(const Key& key) const;
    size_type count(const Key& key) const;
    iterator lower_bound(const Key& key);
    const_iterator lower_bound(const Key& key) const;
    iterator upper_bound(const Key& key);
```

```
    const_iterator upper_bound(const Key& key) const;
    pair<iterator, iterator> equal_range(const Key& key);
    pair<const_iterator, const_iterator>
        equal_range(const Key& key) const;
    };
```

The template class describes an object that controls a varying-length sequence of elements of type `pair<const Key, T>`. The sequence is ordered by the predicate `Pred`. The first element of each pair is the *sort key* and the second is its associated *value*. The sequence is represented in a way that permits lookup, insertion, and removal of an arbitrary element with a number of operations proportional to the logarithm of the number of elements in the sequence (logarithmic time). Moreover, inserting an element invalidates no iterators, and removing an element invalidates only those iterators which point at the removed element.

The object orders the sequence it controls by calling a stored *function object* of type `Pred`. You access this stored object by calling the member function `key_comp()`. Such a function object must impose a strict weak ordering on sort keys of type `Key`. For any element `x` that precedes `y` in the sequence, `key_comp()(y.first, x.first)` is false. (For the default function object `less<Key>`, sort keys never decrease in value.) Unlike template class `map`, an object of template class `multimap` does not ensure that `key_comp()(x.first, y.first)` is true. (Keys need not be unique.)

The object allocates and frees storage for the sequence it controls through a stored allocator object of class `A`. Such an allocator object must have the same external interface as an object of template class `allocator`. Note that the stored allocator object is *not* copied when the container object is assigned.

▫ **`multimap::allocator_type`**

```
typedef A allocator_type;
```

The type is a synonym for the template parameter `A`.

▫ **`multimap::begin`**

```
const_iterator begin() const;
iterator begin();
```

The member function returns a bidirectional iterator that points at the first element of the sequence (or just beyond the end of an empty sequence).

▫ **`multimap::clear`**

```
void clear();
```

The member function calls `erase( begin(), end())`.

▫ **`multimap::const_iterator`**

```
typedef T1 const_iterator;
```

The type describes an object that can serve as a constant bidirectional iterator for the controlled sequence. It is described here as a synonym for the implementation-defined type `T1`.

▫ **multimap::const_pointer**

```
typedef A::const_pointer const_pointer;
```

The type describes an object that can serve as a constant pointer to an element of the controlled sequence.

▫ **multimap::const_reference**

```
typedef A::const_reference const_reference;
```

The type describes an object that can serve as a constant reference to an element of the controlled sequence.

▫ **multimap::const_reverse_iterator**

```
typedef reverse_iterator<const_iterator>
    const_reverse_iterator;
```

The type describes an object that can serve as a constant reverse bidirectional iterator for the controlled sequence.

▫ **multimap::count**

```
size_type count(const Key& key) const;
```

The member function returns the number of elements `x` in the range `[lower_bound(key), upper_bound(key))`.

▫ **multimap::difference_type**

```
typedef T3 difference_type;
```

The signed integer type describes an object that can represent the difference between the addresses of any two elements in the controlled sequence. It is described here as a synonym for the implementation-defined type `T3`.

▫ **multimap::empty**

```
bool empty() const;
```

The member function returns true for an empty controlled sequence.

▫ **multimap::end**

```
const_iterator end() const;
iterator end();
```

The member function returns a bidirectional iterator that points just beyond the end of the sequence.

▫ **multimap::equal_range**

```
pair<iterator, iterator> equal_range(const Key& key);
pair<const_iterator, const_iterator>
    equal_range(const Key& key) const;
```

The member function returns a pair of iterators `x` such that `x.first == lower_bound(key)` and `x.second == upper_bound(key)`.

▫ **multimap::erase**

```
iterator erase(iterator it);
iterator erase(iterator first, iterator last);
size_type erase(const Key& key);
```

The first member function removes the element of the controlled sequence pointed to by `it`. The second member function removes the elements in the range `[first, last)`. Both return an iterator that designates the first element remaining beyond any elements removed, or `end()` if no such element exists.

The third member removes the elements with sort keys in the range `[lower_bound(key), upper_bound(key))`. It returns the number of elements it removes.

The member functions never throw an exception.

▫ **`multimap::find`**

```
iterator find(const Key& key);
const_iterator find(const Key& key) const;
```

The member function returns an iterator that designates the earliest element in the controlled sequence whose sort key has equivalent ordering to `key`. If no such element exists, the function returns `end()`.

▫ **`multimap::get_allocator`**

```
A get_allocator() const;
```

The member function returns the stored allocator object.

▫ **`multimap::insert`**

```
iterator insert(const value_type& x);
iterator insert(iterator it, const value_type& x);
template<class InIt>
    void insert(InIt first, InIt last);
```

The first member function inserts the element `x` in the controlled sequence, then returns the iterator that designates the inserted element. The second member function returns `insert(x)`, using `it` as a starting place within the controlled sequence to search for the insertion point. (Insertion can occur in amortized constant time, instead of logarithmic time, if the insertion point immediately follows `it`.) The third member function inserts the sequence of element values, for each `it` in the range `[first, last)`, by calling `insert(*it)`.

If an exception is thrown during the insertion of a single element, the container is left unaltered and the exception is rethrown. If an exception is thrown during the insertion of multiple elements, the container is left in a stable but unspecified state and the exception is rethrown.

▫ **`multimap::iterator`**

```
typedef T0 iterator;
```

The type describes an object that can serve as a bidirectional iterator for the controlled sequence. It is described here as a synonym for the implementation-defined type `T0`.

▫ **`multimap::key_comp`**

```
key_compare key_comp() const;
```

The member function returns the stored function object that determines the order of elements in the controlled sequence. The stored object defines the member function:

```
bool operator()(const Key& x, const Key& y);
```

which returns true if `x` strictly precedes `y` in the sort order.

▫ **multimap::key_compare**

```
typedef Pred key_compare;
```

The type describes a function object that can compare two sort keys to determine the relative order of two elements in the controlled sequence.

▫ **multimap::key_type**

```
typedef Key key_type;
```

The type describes the sort key object stored in each element of the controlled sequence.

▫ **multimap::lower_bound**

```
iterator lower_bound(const Key& key);
const_iterator lower_bound(const Key& key) const;
```

The member function returns an iterator that designates the earliest element `x` in the controlled sequence for which `key_comp()(x. first, key)` is false. If no such element exists, the function returns `end()`.

▫ **multimap::mapped_type**

```
typedef T mapped_type;
```

The type is a synonym for the template parameter `T`.

▫ **multimap::max_size**

```
size_type max_size() const;
```

The member function returns the length of the longest sequence that the object can control.

▫ **multimap::multimap**

```
multimap();
explicit multimap(const Pred& comp);
multimap(const Pred& comp, const A& al);
multimap(const multimap& x);
template<class InIt>
    multimap(InIt first, InIt last);
template<class InIt>
    multimap(InIt first, InIt last,
        const Pred& comp);
template<class InIt>
    multimap(InIt first, InIt last,
        const Pred& comp, const A& al);
```

All constructors store an allocator object and initialize the controlled sequence. The allocator object is the argument `al`, if present. For the copy constructor, it is `x.get_allocator()`. Otherwise, it is `A()`.

All constructors also store a function object that can later be returned by calling `key_comp()`. The function object is the argument `comp`, if present. For the copy constructor, it is `x.key_comp()`). Otherwise, it is `Pred()`.

The first three constructors specify an empty initial controlled sequence. The fourth constructor specifies a copy of the sequence controlled by `x`. The last three constructors specify the sequence of element values `[first, last)`.

▫ **`multimap::pointer`**

```
typedef A::pointer pointer;
```

The type describes an object that can serve as a pointer to an element of the controlled sequence.

▫ **`multimap::rbegin`**

```
const_reverse_iterator rbegin() const;
reverse_iterator rbegin();
```

The member function returns a reverse bidirectional iterator that points just beyond the end of the controlled sequence. Hence, it designates the beginning of the reverse sequence.

▫ **`multimap::reference`**

```
typedef A::reference reference;
```

The type describes an object that can serve as a reference to an element of the controlled sequence.

▫ **`multimap::rend`**

```
const_reverse_iterator rend() const;
reverse_iterator rend();
```

The member function returns a reverse bidirectional iterator that points at the first element of the sequence (or just beyond the end of an empty sequence). Hence, it designates the end of the reverse sequence.

▫ **`multimap::reverse_iterator`**

```
typedef reverse_iterator<iterator> reverse_iterator;
```

The type describes an object that can serve as a reverse bidirectional iterator for the controlled sequence.

▫ **`multimap::size`**

```
size_type size() const;
```

The member function returns the length of the controlled sequence.

▫ **`multimap::size_type`**

```
typedef T2 size_type;
```

The unsigned integer type describes an object that can represent the length of any controlled sequence. It is described here as a synonym for the implementation-defined type `T2`.

▫ **multimap::swap**

```
void swap(multimap& x);
```

The member function swaps the controlled sequences between `*this` and `x`. If `get_allocator() == x.get_allocator()`, it does so in constant time, it throws an exception only as a result of copying the stored function object of type `Pred`, and it invalidates no references, pointers, or iterators that designate elements in the two controlled sequences. Otherwise, it performs a number of element assignments and constructor calls proportional to the number of elements in the two controlled sequences.

▫ **multimap::upper_bound**

```
iterator upper_bound(const Key& key);
const_iterator upper_bound(const Key& key) const;
```

The member function returns an iterator that designates the earliest element `x` in the controlled sequence for which `key_comp()(key, x.first)` is true. If no such element exists, the function returns `end()`.

▫ **multimap::value_comp**

```
value_compare value_comp() const;
```

The member function returns a function object that determines the order of elements in the controlled sequence.

▫ **multimap::value_compare**

```
class value_compare
    : public binary_function<value_type, value_type,
        bool> {
public:
    bool operator()(const value_type& x,
        const value_type& y) const
        {return (comp(x.first, x.second)); }
protected:
    value_compare(key_compare pr)
        : comp(pr) {}
    key_compare comp;
    };
```

The type describes a function object that can compare the sort keys in two elements to determine their relative order in the controlled sequence. The function object stores an object `comp` of type `key_compare`. The member function `operator()` uses this object to compare the sort-key components of two element.

▫ **multimap::value_type**

```
typedef pair<const Key, T> value_type;
```

The type describes an element of the controlled sequence.

▫ **operator!=**

```
template<class Key, class T, class Pred, class A>
    bool operator!=(
        const map <Key, T, Pred, A>& lhs,
        const map <Key, T, Pred, A>& rhs);
template<class Key, class T, class Pred, class A>
```

```
    bool operator!=(
        const multimap <Key, T, Pred, A>& lhs,
        const multimap <Key, T, Pred, A>& rhs);
```

The template function returns `!(lhs == rhs)`.

- **operator==**

```
template<class Key, class T, class Pred, class A>
    bool operator==(
        const map <Key, T, Pred, A>& lhs,
        const map <Key, T, Pred, A>& rhs);
template<class Key, class T, class Pred, class A>
    bool operator==(
        const multimap <Key, T, Pred, A>& lhs,
        const multimap <Key, T, Pred, A>& rhs);
```

The first template function overloads `operator==` to compare two objects of template class `multimap`. The second template function overloads `operator==` to compare two objects of template class `multimap`. Both functions return `lhs.size() == rhs.size() && equal(lhs. begin(), lhs. end(), rhs.begin())`.

- **operator<**

```
template<class Key, class T, class Pred, class A>
    bool operator<(
        const map <Key, T, Pred, A>& lhs,
        const map <Key, T, Pred, A>& rhs);
template<class Key, class T, class Pred, class A>
    bool operator<(
        const multimap <Key, T, Pred, A>& lhs,
        const multimap <Key, T, Pred, A>& rhs);
```

The first template function overloads `operator<` to compare two objects of template class `multimap`. The second template function overloads `operator<` to compare two objects of template class `multimap`. Both functions return `lexicographical_compare(lhs. begin(), lhs. end(), rhs.begin(), rhs.end())`.

- **operator<=**

```
template<class Key, class T, class Pred, class A>
    bool operator<=(
        const map <Key, T, Pred, A>& lhs,
        const map <Key, T, Pred, A>& rhs);
template<class Key, class T, class Pred, class A>
    bool operator<=(
        const multimap <Key, T, Pred, A>& lhs,
        const multimap <Key, T, Pred, A>& rhs);
```

The template function returns `!(rhs < lhs)`.

- **operator>**

```
template<class Key, class T, class Pred, class A>
    bool operator>(
        const map <Key, T, Pred, A>& lhs,
        const map <Key, T, Pred, A>& rhs);
template<class Key, class T, class Pred, class A>
    bool operator>(
        const multimap <Key, T, Pred, A>& lhs,
        const multimap <Key, T, Pred, A>& rhs);
```

The template function returns `rhs < lhs`.

▫ **operator>=**

```
template<class Key, class T, class Pred, class A>
    bool operator>=(
        const map <Key, T, Pred, A>& lhs,
        const map <Key, T, Pred, A>& rhs);
template<class Key, class T, class Pred, class A>
    bool operator!=(
        const multimap <Key, T, Pred, A>& lhs,
        const multimap <Key, T, Pred, A>& rhs);
```

The template function returns `!(lhs < rhs)`.

▫ **swap**

```
template<class Key, class T, class Pred, class A>
    void swap(
        map <Key, T, Pred, A>& lhs,
        map <Key, T, Pred, A>& rhs);
template<class Key, class T, class Pred, class A>
    void swap(
        multimap <Key, T, Pred, A>& lhs,
        multimap <Key, T, Pred, A>& rhs);
```

The template function executes `lhs.swap(rhs)`.

Using <map>

map **multimap** Include the header `<map>` to make use of template class **map** or template class **multimap**. Use the latter only if you want to permit multiple elements with the same key value — or more precisely, pairs of elements that have equivalent ordering. The two containers are very similar, so we first describe **map** as an example of both. Later on in this section, we highlight the differences between the two.

You can specialize **map** to store elements of type `pair<const Key, T>` and with an ordering rule of type `less<Key>` by writing a type definition such as:

```
typedef map<Key, T, less<Key>,
    allocator<pair<const Key, T> > > Mycont;
```

Using default template arguments, you can omit the third and/or fourth arguments.

less If you omit the third argument, the default is given by a function object of type `less<Key>`. The controlled sequence in the stored container is ordered by this rule. Thus, for numeric types at least, the last element in the sequence is the one with the largest stored value.

Template class **map** supports all the common operations on containers, as we described in Chapter 9: Containers. (See the discussion beginning on page 248.) We summarize here only those properties peculiar to template class **map**.

constructors To construct an object of class `map<Key, T, Pred, A>`, you can write any of:

- `map()` to declare an empty map that is ordered by `Pred()`.
- `map(pr)` to declare an empty map that is ordered by the function object `pr`.
- `map(pr, al)` as above, also storing the allocator object `al`.
- `map(first, last)` to declare a map that is ordered by `Pred()` and whose initial content is copied from the sequence designated by `[first, last)` (and ordered, of course).
- `map(first, last, pr)` to declare a map that is ordered by `pr` and whose initial content is copied from the sequence designated by `[first, last)`, as above, and ordered.
- `map(first, last, cont, pr)` as above, also storing the allocator object `al`.

If you have specialized the template class for an allocator of type `allocator<pair<const Key, T> >`, which is the customary (and default) thing to do, there is nothing to be gained by specifying an explicit allocator argument `al`. Such an argument matters only for some allocators that the program defines explicitly. (See the discussion of allocators in Chapter 4: `<memory>`.)

The following descriptions all assume that `cont` is an object of class `map<Key, Pred, A>`.

`clear` To remove all elements, call `cont.clear()`.

`erase` To erase the element designated by the iterator `it`, call `cont.erase(it)`. The return value is an iterator designating the element just beyond the erased element. To erase a range of elements designated by `[first, last)`, call `cont.erase(first, last)`.

You can also perform a number of operations on a `map` object that take advantage of its unique representation. In particular, you can also erase the element whose key has equivalent ordering to `key` by calling `cont.erase(key)`. Other operations peculiar to **map** (and the other associative containers) are:

`insert` To insert an element with the {key, value} pair `val`, call `cont.insert(val)`. The return value is an object `ans`, of class `pair<iterator, bool>`. The member object `ans.second` is true only if an element with equivalent ordering was not already present in the controlled sequence. In this case, `ans.first` designates the inserted element. Otherwise the insertion fails and `ans.first` designates the preexisting element with equivalent ordering.

To insert the elements of a sequence with {key, value} pairs designated by `*it`, for `it` in the range `[first, last)`, call `cont.insert(first, last)`. The sequence must not be any part of the initial controlled sequence.

To insert an element with the {key, value} pair `val` that is likely to immediately follow the element designated by `it`, call `cont.insert(it, key)`. If this "hint" proves to be correct, insertion should occur in constant time instead of logarithmic time. In any event, the call has the same effect as **insert(val)** and returns the same iterator value.

find To localte an element whose key has equivalent ordering to **key**, call **cont.find(key)**.

lower_bound To locate the earliest element in the controlled sequence whose key (value) is not ordered before **key**, call **cont.lower_bound(key)**. Note that this is the beginning of any subsequence of elements with equivalent ordering to **key**.

upper_bound To locate the earliest element in the controlled sequence whose key is ordered after **key**, call **cont.lower_bound(key)**. Note that this is just beyond the end of any subsequence of elements with equivalent ordering to **key**.

equal_range To determine the subsequence of elements in the controlled sequence with equivalent ordering to **key**, call **cont.equal_range(key)**. Note that this is just the pair of iterators **pair<iterator, iterator>(cont.lower_bound(key), cont.upper_bound(key))**. For a **map<Key, T>** object, the length of the subsequence is either zero or one.

- **count** To determine just the length of the subsequence determined by calling **cont.equal_range(key)**, call **cont.count(key)**. For a **map<Key, T>** object, the value returned is either zero or one.

key_comp To obtain an object that orders keys by the same rule as **cont**, call **cont.key_comp()**. Specifically, if **key1** is ordered before **key2**, then **cont.key_comp()(key1, key2)** is true.

value_comp To obtain an object that can order the {key, value} pairs stored in elements of **cont**, call **cont.value_comp()**. For a **map<Key, T>** object **cont**, the return value is the same as for **cont.key_comp()**.

multimap The differences between template class **map** and template class **multimap** all stem from their fundamental difference — a **multimap** can store elements with equivalent ordering while a **map** will not. With one notable exception, all constructors and member functions have the same signatures.

operator[] A **map** adds one operation not found in **multimap**. To locate the stored element whose key value has equivalent ordering to **key**, write the expression **cont[key]**. If no such element is present, the operator adds the element {**key, mapped_type()**}.

Otherwise, for a **multimap** object:

- **insert** The call **cont.insert(val)** always inserts a new element, so the function returns just the iterator designating the new element, not an object of class **pair<iterator, bool>**.
- **find** If multiple elements have equivalent ordering to **key**, it is unspecified which element is designated by the iterator returned from the call **cont.find(key)**.
- **equal_range** The subsequence determined by the call **cont.equal_range(key)** can have any length in the range **[0, cont.size()]**.
- **count** Similarly, the subsequence length returned by the call **cont.count(key)** can have any value in the range **[0, cont.size()]**.

Implementing <map>

map Figures 14.1 through 14.3 show the file **map**. It defines the template classes **map** and **multimap**. You will find that it is very similar to the file **set**, beginning on page 395. Both rely heavily on template class **Tree**, defined in the file **xtree**, beginning on page 379.

Figure 14.1: map Part 1

```
// map standard header
#ifndef MAP_
#define MAP_
#include <xtree>
namespace std {
		// TEMPLATE CLASS Tmap_traits
template<class K, class T, class Pr, class Ax, bool Mfl>
	class Tmap_traits {
public:
	typedef K key_type;
	typedef pair<const K, T> value_type;
	typedef Pr key_compare;
	typedef typename Ax::template rebind<value_type>::other
		allocator_type;
	enum {Multi = Mfl};
	Tmap_traits()
		: comp()
		{}
	Tmap_traits(Pr Parg)
		: comp(Parg)
		{}
	class value_compare
		: public binary_function<value_type, value_type, bool> {
		friend class Tmap_traits<K, T, Pr, Ax, Mfl>;
	public:
		bool operator()(const value_type& X,
			const value_type& Y) const
			{return (comp(X.first, Y.first)); }
		value_compare(key_compare Pred)
			: comp(Pred) {}
	protected:
		key_compare comp;
		};
	struct Kfn {
		const K& operator()(const value_type& X) const
			{return (X.first); }
		};
	Pr comp;
	};

		// TEMPLATE CLASS map
template<class K, class T,
	class Pr = less<K>,
	class A = allocator<pair<const K, T> > >
	class map
		: public Tree<Tmap_traits<K, T, Pr, A, false> > {
public:
```

Figure 14.2: map Part 2

```
    typedef map<K, T, Pr, A> Myt;
    typedef Tree<Tmap_traits<K, T, Pr, A, false> >
        Mybase;
    typedef K key_type;
    typedef T mapped_type;
    typedef T referent_type;
    typedef Pr key_compare;
    typedef typename Mybase::value_compare value_compare;
    typedef typename Mybase::allocator_type allocator_type;
    typedef typename Mybase::size_type size_type;
    typedef typename Mybase::difference_type difference_type;
    typedef typename Mybase::pointer pointer;
    typedef typename Mybase::const_pointer const_pointer;
    typedef typename Mybase::reference reference;
    typedef typename Mybase::const_reference const_reference;
    typedef typename Mybase::iterator iterator;
    typedef typename Mybase::const_iterator const_iterator;
    typedef typename Mybase::reverse_iterator reverse_iterator;
    typedef typename Mybase::const_reverse_iterator
        const_reverse_iterator;
    typedef typename Mybase::value_type value_type;
    map()
        : Mybase(key_compare(), allocator_type()) {}
    explicit map(const key_compare& Pred)
        : Mybase(Pred, allocator_type()) {}
    map(const key_compare& Pred, const allocator_type& Al)
        : Mybase(Pred, Al) {}
    template<class It>
        map(It F, It L)
        : Mybase(key_compare(), allocator_type())
        {for (; F != L; ++F)
            insert(*F); }
    template<class It>
        map(It F, It L, const key_compare& Pred)
        : Mybase(Pred, allocator_type())
        {for (; F != L; ++F)
            insert(*F); }
    template<class It>
        map(It F, It L, const key_compare& Pred,
        const allocator_type& Al)
        : Mybase(Pred, Al)
        {for (; F != L; ++F)
            insert(*F); }
    mapped_type& operator[](const key_type& Kv)
        {iterator P =
            insert(value_type(Kv, mapped_type())).first;
        return ((*P).second); }
    };

        // TEMPLATE CLASS multimap
template<class K, class T,
    class Pr = less<K>,
    class A = allocator<pair<const K, T> > >
    class multimap
        : public Tree<Tmap_traits<K, T, Pr, A, true> > {
```

Figure 14.3: map Part 3

```
public:
    typedef multimap<K, T, Pr, A> Myt;
    typedef Tree<Tmap_traits<K, T, Pr, A, true> >
        Mybase;
    typedef K key_type;
    typedef T mapped_type;
    typedef T referent_type;        // old name, magically gone
    typedef Pr key_compare;
    typedef typename Mybase::value_compare value_compare;
    typedef typename Mybase::allocator_type allocator_type;
    typedef typename Mybase::size_type size_type;
    typedef typename Mybase::difference_type difference_type;
    typedef typename Mybase::pointer pointer;
    typedef typename Mybase::const_pointer const_pointer;
    typedef typename Mybase::reference reference;
    typedef typename Mybase::const_reference const_reference;
    typedef typename Mybase::iterator iterator;
    typedef typename Mybase::const_iterator const_iterator;
    typedef typename Mybase::reverse_iterator reverse_iterator;
    typedef typename Mybase::const_reverse_iterator
        const_reverse_iterator;
    typedef typename Mybase::value_type value_type;
    multimap()
        : Mybase(key_compare(), allocator_type()) {}
    explicit multimap(const key_compare& Pred)
        : Mybase(Pred, allocator_type()) {}
    multimap(const key_compare& Pred, const allocator_type& Al)
        : Mybase(Pred, Al) {}
    template<class It>
        multimap(It F, It L)
        : Mybase(key_compare(), allocator_type())
        {for (; F != L; ++F)
            insert(*F); }
    template<class It>
        multimap(It F, It L, const key_compare& Pred)
        : Mybase(Pred, allocator_type())
        {for (; F != L; ++F)
            insert(*F); }
    template<class It>
        multimap(It F, It L, const key_compare& Pred,
        const allocator_type& Al)
        : Mybase(Pred, Al)
        {for (; F != L; ++F)
            insert(*F); }
    iterator insert(const value_type& X)
        {return (Mybase::insert(X).first); }
    iterator insert(iterator P, const value_type& X)
        {return (Mybase::insert(P, X)); }
    template<class It>
        void insert(It F, It L)
        {for (; F != L; ++F)
            insert(*F); }
    };
} /* namespace std */
#endif /* MAP_ */
```
□

Tmap_traits Template class **Tmap_traits** is a version of the **Tree** traits class we showed in the previous chapter, suitable for defining a map. As you can see, there's not much tô it, but it saves writing a long list of parameters when specializing **Tree**. Note that, unlike for a set, **key_type** is *not* a synonym for **value_type** for a map. The key extractor supplied by **Kfn** has some work to do, howerver slight.

multimap Template class **map** has nothing left to do but echo a few type definitions, supply the appropriate constructors, and define **operator[]**. Template class **multiset** does much the same, with just a few small differences. It omits **operator[]**, of course. It also wraps calls to **Tree::insert** primarily to simplify the value returned by the member function **insert(const value_type&)**. As with similar wrappers in template class **multiset**, the other wrappers are not strictly necessary, but they help certain compilers that tend to get confused.

Testing <map>

Figures 14.4 through 14.7 show the file **tmap.c**. It provides tests for template class **map** and template class **multimap** that are very much alike. It is, in turn, one of two test programs that look very much alike. See the file **tset.c**, beginning on page 399. To ease comparison of the four tests spread over these two files, we have simply noted any tests that are particular for a given container.

The test program performs a simple test that each of the member functions and types is present and behaves as intended, for one specialization of template class **map** and for one specialization of template class **multimap**. If all goes well, the program prints:

```
SUCCESS testing <map>
```

and takes a normal exit.

Exercises

Exercise 14.1 Is it possible to implement a map as a set? Explain why or why not.

Exercise 14.2 Is it possible to implement a set as a map? Explain why or why not.

Exercise 14.3 Define **operator[]** for template class **multimap**. Provide at least three sensible alternatives if the function can return more than one value.

Exercise 14.4 Implement your preferred version of **operator[]** for template class **multimap**.

Exercise 14.5 [**Harder**] Alter template class **map** to permit a change of ordering rule after construction.

Exercise 14.6 [**Very hard**] Alter template class **map** to permit logarithmic-time lookups for two or more ordering rules.

Figure 14.4: `tmap.c` **Part 1**

```
// test <map>
#include <assert.h>
#include <iostream>
#include <functional>
#include <map>
using namespace std;

     // TEST map
void test_map()
     {typedef allocator<int> Myal;
     typedef less<char> Mypred;
     typedef pair<const char, int> Myval;
     typedef map<char, int, Mypred, Myal> Mycont;
     Myval x, xarr[3], xarr2[3];
     for (int i = 0; i < 3; ++i)
          {new (&xarr[i]) Myval('a' + i, 1 + i);
          new (&xarr2[i]) Myval('d' + i, 4 + i); }

     Mycont::key_type *p_key = (char *)0;
     Mycont::mapped_type *p_mapped = (int *)0;
     Mycont::key_compare *p_kcomp = (Mypred *)0;
     Mycont::allocator_type *p_alloc = (Myal *)0;
     Mycont::value_type *p_val = (Myval *)0;
     Mycont::value_compare *p_vcomp = 0;
     Mycont::pointer p_ptr = (Myval *)0;
     Mycont::const_pointer p_cptr = (const Myval *)0;
     Mycont::reference p_ref = x;
     Mycont::const_reference p_cref = (const Myval&)x;
     Mycont::size_type *p_size = (size_t *)0;
     Mycont::difference_type *p_diff = (ptrdiff_t *)0;

     Mycont v0;
     Myal al = v0.get_allocator();
     Mypred pred;
     Mycont v0a(pred), v0b(pred, al);
     assert(v0.empty() && v0.size() == 0);
     assert(v0a.size() == 0 && v0a.get_allocator() == al);
     assert(v0b.size() == 0 && v0b.get_allocator() == al);
     Mycont v1(xarr, xarr + 3);
     assert(v1.size() == 3 && (*v1.begin()).first == 'a');
     Mycont v2(xarr, xarr + 3, pred);
     assert(v2.size() == 3 && (*v2.begin()).first == 'a');
     Mycont v3(xarr, xarr + 3, pred, al);
     assert(v3.size() == 3 && (*v3.begin()).first == 'a');
     const Mycont v4(xarr, xarr + 3);
     assert(v4.size() == 3 && (*v4.begin()).first == 'a');
     v0 = v4;
     assert(v0.size() == 3 && (*v0.begin()).first == 'a');

     assert(v0.size() <= v0.max_size());

     Mycont::iterator p_it(v1.begin());
     Mycont::const_iterator p_cit(v4.begin());
     Mycont::reverse_iterator p_rit(v1.rbegin());
     Mycont::const_reverse_iterator p_crit(v4.rbegin());
```

Figure 14.5: tmap.c Part 2

```
    assert((*p_it).first == 'a' && (*p_it).second == 1
        && (*--(p_it = v1.end())).first == 'c');
    assert((*p_cit).first == 'a'
        && (*--(p_cit = v4.end())).first == 'c');
    assert((*p_rit).first == 'c' && (*p_rit).second == 3
        && (*--(p_rit = v1.rend())).first == 'a');
    assert((*p_crit).first == 'c'
        && (*--(p_crit = v4.rend())).first == 'a');

    v0.clear();                              // DIFFERS FROM multimap
    pair<Mycont::iterator, bool> pib = v0.insert(Myval('d', 4));
    assert((*pib.first).first == 'd' && pib.second);
    assert((*--v0.end()).first == 'd');
    pib = v0.insert(Myval('d', 5));
    assert((*pib.first).first == 'd'
        && (*pib.first).second == 4 && !pib.second);
    assert((*v0.insert(v0.begin(), Myval('e', 5))).first == 'e');
    v0.insert(xarr, xarr + 3);
    assert(v0.size() == 5 && (*v0.begin()).first == 'a');
    v0.insert(xarr2, xarr2 + 3);
    assert(v0.size() == 6 && (*--v0.end()).first == 'f');
    assert(v0['c'] == 3);
    assert((*v0.erase(v0.begin())).first == 'b'
        && v0.size() == 5);
    assert((*v0.erase(v0.begin(), ++v0.begin())).first == 'c'
        && v0.size() == 4);
    assert(v0.erase('x') == 0 && v0.erase('e') == 1);

    v0.clear();
    assert(v0.empty());
    v0.swap(v1);
    assert(!v0.empty() && v1.empty());
    swap(v0, v1);
    assert(v0.empty() && !v1.empty());
    assert(v1 == v1 && v0 < v1);
    assert(v0 != v1 && v1 > v0);
    assert(v0 <= v1 && v1 >= v0);

    assert(v0.key_comp()('a', 'c')
        && !v0.key_comp()('a', 'a'));
    assert(v0.value_comp()(Myval('a', 0), Myval('c', 0))
        && !v0.value_comp()(Myval('a', 0), Myval('a', 1)));
    assert((*v4.find('b')).first == 'b');
    assert(v4.count('x') == 0 && v4.count('b') == 1);
    assert((*v4.lower_bound('a')).first == 'a');
    assert((*v4.upper_bound('a')).first == 'b');
    pair<Mycont::const_iterator, Mycont::const_iterator> pcc =
        v4.equal_range('a');
    assert((*pcc.first).first == 'a'
        && (*pcc.second).first == 'b'); }

    // TEST multimap
void test_multimap()
    {typedef allocator<int> Myal;
    typedef less<char> Mypred;
```

Figure 14.6: `tmap.c` **Part 3**

```
typedef pair<const char, int> Myval;
typedef multimap<char, int, Mypred, Myal> Mycont;
Myval x, xarr[3], xarr2[3];
for (int i = 0; i < 3; ++i)
     {new (&xarr[i]) Myval('a' + i, 1 + i);
     new (&xarr2[i]) Myval('d' + i, 4 + i); }

Mycont::key_type *p_key = (char *)0;
Mycont::mapped_type *p_mapped = (int *)0;
Mycont::key_compare *p_kcomp = (Mypred *)0;
Mycont::allocator_type *p_alloc = (Myal *)0;
Mycont::value_type *p_val = (Myval *)0;
Mycont::value_compare *p_vcomp = 0;
Mycont::pointer p_ptr = (Myval *)0;
Mycont::const_pointer p_cptr = (const Myval *)0;
Mycont::reference p_ref = x;
Mycont::const_reference p_cref = (const Myval&)x;
Mycont::size_type *p_size = (size_t *)0;
Mycont::difference_type *p_diff = (ptrdiff_t *)0;

Mycont v0;
Myal al = v0.get_allocator();
Mypred pred;
Mycont v0a(pred), v0b(pred, al);
assert(v0.empty() && v0.size() == 0);
assert(v0a.size() == 0 && v0a.get_allocator() == al);
assert(v0b.size() == 0 && v0b.get_allocator() == al);
Mycont v1(xarr, xarr + 3);
assert(v1.size() == 3 && (*v1.begin()).first == 'a');
Mycont v2(xarr, xarr + 3, pred);
assert(v2.size() == 3 && (*v2.begin()).first == 'a');
Mycont v3(xarr, xarr + 3, pred, al);
assert(v3.size() == 3 && (*v3.begin()).first == 'a');
const Mycont v4(xarr, xarr + 3);
assert(v4.size() == 3 && (*v4.begin()).first == 'a');
v0 = v4;
assert(v0.size() == 3 && (*v0.begin()).first == 'a');

assert(v0.size() <= v0.max_size());

Mycont::iterator p_it(v1.begin());
Mycont::const_iterator p_cit(v4.begin());
Mycont::reverse_iterator p_rit(v1.rbegin());
Mycont::const_reverse_iterator p_crit(v4.rbegin());
assert((*p_it).first == 'a' && (*p_it).second == 1
     && (*--(p_it = v1.end())).first == 'c');
assert((*p_cit).first == 'a'
     && (*--(p_cit = v4.end())).first == 'c');
assert((*p_rit).first == 'c' && (*p_rit).second == 3
     && (*--(p_rit = v1.rend())).first == 'a');
assert((*p_crit).first == 'c'
     && (*--(p_crit = v4.rend())).first == 'a');

v0.clear();                                  // DIFFERS FROM map
assert((*v0.insert(Myval('d', 4))).first == 'd');
```

Figure 14.7: tmap.c Part 4

```
    assert((*--v0.end()).first == 'd');
    assert((*v0.insert(Myval('d', 5))).first == 'd');
    assert(v0.size() == 2);
    assert((*v0.insert(v0.begin(), Myval('e', 5))).first == 'e');
    v0.insert(xarr, xarr + 3);
    assert(v0.size() == 6 && (*v0.begin()).first == 'a');
    v0.insert(xarr2, xarr2 + 3);
    assert(v0.size() == 9 && (*--v0.end()).first == 'f');
    assert((*v0.erase(v0.begin())).first == 'b'
        && v0.size() == 8);
    assert((*v0.erase(v0.begin(), ++v0.begin())).first == 'c'
        && v0.size() == 7);
    assert(v0.erase('x') == 0 && v0.erase('e') == 2);

    v0.clear();
    assert(v0.empty());
    v0.swap(v1);
    assert(!v0.empty() && v1.empty());
    swap(v0, v1);
    assert(v0.empty() && !v1.empty());
    assert(v1 == v1 && v0 < v1);
    assert(v0 != v1 && v1 > v0);
    assert(v0 <= v1 && v1 >= v0);

    assert(v0.key_comp()('a', 'c')
        && !v0.key_comp()('a', 'a'));
    assert(v0.value_comp()(Myval('a', 0), Myval('c', 0))
        && !v0.value_comp()(Myval('a', 0), Myval('a', 1)));
    assert((*v4.find('b')).first == 'b');
    assert(v4.count('x') == 0 && v4.count('b') == 1);
    assert((*v4.lower_bound('a')).first == 'a');
    assert((*v4.upper_bound('a')).first == 'b');
    pair<Mycont::const_iterator, Mycont::const_iterator> pcc =
        v4.equal_range('a');
    assert((*pcc.first).first == 'a'
        && (*pcc.second).first == 'b'); }

    // TEST <map>
int main()
    {test_map();
    test_multimap();
    cout << "SUCCESS testing <map>" << endl;
    return (0); }
```
□

Chapter 15: <stack>

Background

<stack>

stack

The header `<stack>` defines just the template class **`stack`**. It is a *container adapter* — a template class that does not itself directly maintain controlled sequences. Rather, it stores as a member object a container object that does the job. Template class **`stack`** is arguably the simplest of the container adapters in STL. (The others are the template classes **`queue`** and **`priority_queue`**, which we describe in the next chapter.)

container adapters

So what's to adapt? Well, a typical template container class in STL has lots of member functions. The general idea is to provide all the operations on the controlled sequence that might possibly make sense. Remember, these creatures are designed to be maximally reusable. It's generally easier to supply a member function that's not used in a given application than to require an application to extend a container in some nontrivial fashion. But flexibility of access is not always a virtue.

Say, for example, that what you really need is a stack. Also known as a last-in first-out (LIFO) queue, a stack maintains a rigorous access discipline. All you can see within the controlled sequence is the *top* of the stack — the last element you insert, or *push,* on the stack. And the only element you can erase, or *pop,* from the stack is that top element. All other elements remain buried, like the middle members of a stack of cafeterial trays in one of those spring-loaded dispensers.

vector

You might choose to implement a stack as, say, template class **`vector`**. (See Chapter 10: **`<vector>`**.) If you do, you can then get to all those buried elements a lot quicker and easier than you can in an arbitrary stack. But that doesn't mean you *should* do so. Object-oriented design stresses the importance of information hiding. You declare the member objects of a class private, for example, to prevent programmers from writing code that depends on a particular implementation of the class. That way, you have more flexibility in altering (and presumably improving) the implementation at a later date with no fear of breaking code that uses the class and (improperly) accesses its members directly.

Similarly, you might well want to hide all that extra power of template class **`vector`**. Like those private member objects, the member functions of **`vector`** say too much and do too much to be exposed in the implementation of a stack. For this reason, you want to avoid the "is-a" relationship that comes when you derive a stack from a template, as in:

```
template<class T>
    class stack : public vector<T>; // "is-a" vector
```

`push` `pop` `top`

Such derivation lets you add member functions, such as **push**, **pop**, and **top**; but it doesn't help you hide the member functions you'd like to keep hidden. Yes, you can make the base protected or private, but the stack still "is-a" vector for many purposes, and that relationship is simply inappropriate.

`stack`

STL thus provides a template class **stack** that "has-a" container as a member object. The container object stores the actual controlled sequence that implements the stack. Whatever operations the container may support, however, the stack only lets you push and pop elements. The template class is declared as:

```
template<class T, class C = deque<T> >
    class stack;
```

Template parameter **T** specifies the type of elements stored in the stack. Template parameter **C** specifies the type of container used to control the sequence of elements.

`deque`

Using a default template argument, you can write **stack<int>** and the translator will automatically supply the container type **deque<int>**. A deque makes a pretty good stack. (See Chapter 12: **<deque>**.) Otherwise, you must specify the container type yourself. It is then up to you to ensure that your container **C** can store elements of type **T** properly. We describe the requirements on such containers more precisely below. For now, it is enough to know that the three STL containers **vector**, **deque**, and **list** all satisfy the requirements demanded by template class **stack**.

Functional Description

```
namespace std {
template<class T, class Cont>
    class stack;

        // TEMPLATE FUNCTIONS
template<class T, class Cont>
    bool operator==(const stack<T, Cont>& lhs,
        const stack<T, Cont>&);
template<class T, class Cont>
    bool operator!=(const stack<T, Cont>& lhs,
        const stack<T, Cont>&);
template<class T, class Cont>
    bool operator<(const stack<T, Cont>& lhs,
        const stack<T, Cont>&);
template<class T, class Cont>
    bool operator>(const stack<T, Cont>& lhs,
        const stack<T, Cont>&);
template<class T, class Cont>
    bool operator<=(const stack<T, Cont>& lhs,
        const stack<T, Cont>&);
template<class T, class Cont>
```

```
    bool operator>=(const stack<T, Cont>& lhs,
        const stack<T, Cont>&);
    };
```

Include the STL standard header `<stack>` to define the template class `stack` and two supporting templates.

operator!=

```
template<class T, class Cont>
    bool operator!=(const stack <T, Cont>& lhs,
        const stack <T, Cont>& rhs);
```

The template function returns `!(lhs == rhs)`.

operator==

```
template<class T, class Cont>
    bool operator==(const stack <T, Cont>& lhs,
        const stack <T, Cont>& rhs);
```

The template function overloads `operator==` to compare two objects of template class `stack`. The function returns `lhs.c == rhs.c`.

operator<

```
template<class T, class Cont>
    bool operator<(const stack <T, Cont>& lhs,
        const stack <T, Cont>& rhs);
```

The template function overloads `operator<` to compare two objects of template class `stack`. The function returns `lhs.c < rhs.c`.

operator<=

```
template<class T, class Cont>
    bool operator<=(const stack <T, Cont>& lhs,
        const stack <T, Cont>& rhs);
```

The template function returns `!(rhs < lhs)`.

operator>

```
template<class T, class Cont>
    bool operator>(const stack <T, Cont>& lhs,
        const stack <T, Cont>& rhs);
```

The template function returns `rhs < lhs`.

operator>=

```
template<class T, class Cont>
    bool operator>=(const stack <T, Cont>& lhs,
        const stack <T, Cont>& rhs);
```

The template function returns `!(lhs < rhs)`.

stack

```
template<class T,
    class Cont = deque<T> >
    class stack {
public:
    typedef Cont container_type;
    typedef typename Cont::value_type value_type;
    typedef typename Cont::size_type size_type;
    stack();
```

```
        explicit stack(const container_type& cont);
        bool empty() const;
        size_type size() const;
        value_type& top();
        const value_type& top() const;
        void push(const value_type& x);
        void pop();
    protected:
        Cont c;
        };
```

The template class describes an object that controls a varying-length sequence of elements. The object allocates and frees storage for the sequence it controls through a protected object named `c`, of class `Cont`. The type `T` of elements in the controlled sequence must match `value_type`.

An object of class `Cont` must supply several public members defined the same as for `deque`, `list`, and `vector` (all of which are suitable candidates for class `Cont`). The required members are:

```
typedef T value_type;
typedef T0 size_type;
Cont();
bool empty() const;
size_type size() const;
value_type& back();
const value_type& back() const;
void push_back(const value_type& x);
void pop_back();
bool operator==(const Cont& X) const;
bool operator!=(const Cont& X) const;
bool operator<(const Cont& X) const;
bool operator>(const Cont& X) const;
bool operator<=(const Cont& X) const;
bool operator>=(const Cont& X) const;
```

Here, `T0` is an unspecified type that meets the stated requirements.

stack::container_type

```
typedef Cont container_type;
```

The type is a synonym for the template parameter `Cont`.

stack::empty

```
bool empty() const;
```

The member function returns true for an empty controlled sequence.

stack::pop

```
void pop();
```

The member function removes the last element of the controlled sequence, which must be non-empty.

stack::push

```
void push(const T& x);
```

The member function inserts an element with value `x` at the end of the controlled sequence.

▫ **stack::size**

```
size_type size() const;
```

The member function returns the length of the controlled sequence.

▫ **stack::size_type**

```
typedef typename Cont::size_type size_type;
```

The type is a synonym for `Cont::size_type`.

▫ **stack::stack**

```
stack();
explicit stack(const container_type& cont);
```

The first constructor initializes the stored object with `c()`, to specify an empty initial controlled sequence. The second constructor initializes the stored object with `c(cont)`, to specify an initial controlled sequence that is a copy of the sequence controlled by `cont`.

▫ **stack::top**

```
value_type& top();
const value_type& top() const;
```

The member function returns a reference to the last element of the controlled sequence, which must be non-empty.

▫ **stack::value_type**

```
typedef typename Cont::value_type value_type;
```

The type is a synonym for `Cont::value_type`.

Using `<stack>`

stack Include the header `<stack>` to make use of template class `stack`. You can specialize `stack` to store elements of type `T` in an object of type `deque<T>` by writing a type definition such as:

```
typedef stack<T, deque<T, allocator<T> > > Mycont;
```

Using a default template argument, you can omit the second argument.

Alternatively, you can replace the second argument with `vector<T>` or `list<T>`, A vector can make a small and efficient stack, provided it does not have to reallocate storage too often. Remember that you can preallocate space for a vector `vec` to grow without further reallocation by calling `vec.reserve(n)`, to reserve storage for at least `n` elements.

container requirements You can also specify as the second template argument a container type of your own devising. More specifically, a container `Cont` must have at least the following external interface:

- **value_type size_type** It must define the member types `value_type` (as `T`) and `size_type` (typically as `size_t`).
- **empty size** It must define the const member functions `empty` and `size`, with the usual meanings.

back ■ It must define the member function back, in both const and non-const forms, with the usual meaning.

push_back pop_back ■ It must define the member functions push_back, and pop_back, with the usual meanings.

■ It must define the six comparison operators, such as operator==(const Cont&, const Cont&), in a way that imposes a total ordering on objects of type Cont.

Template class stack does *not* support all the common operations on containers, as we described in Chapter 9: Containers. (See the discussion beginning on page 248.) It intentionally provides only a restricted set of operations. The following descriptions all assume that cont is an object of class stack<T, C>.

constructors To construct an object of class stack<T, C>, you can write:

- stack() to declare an empty stack.
- stack(cont) to declare a stack whose initial content is copied from cont.

push To push a new element with value v on the stack, call cont.push(v).

pop To pop the stack, call cont.pop(). If the stack is empty, the result is undefined. Note that cont.pop() is a void function — it does *not* return the value of the popped element.

top To access the top element on the stack, call cont.top(). If the stack is empty, the result is undefined. Note that cont.top() returns a reference — if the stack is not a const object, you can alter the value stored in the top element by writing an assignment expression such as cont.top() = 0.

empty size To test whether the stack is empty, call cont.empty(). To obtain the number of elements in the stack, call cont.size().

comparisons You can compare the stack cont in its entirety against another stack cont2 by writing any of the usual six comparison operators, such as cont == cont2 or cont >= cont2. The result is the same as comparing the stored container objects, for what that may be worth.

c Finally, if you define a class with stack<T, C> as a public base class, you can access the stored container object. It is a protected member named c.

Implementing <stack>

stack Figures 15.1 through 15.2 show the file stack. As you can see, it performs all its operations by calling corresponding member functions for the stored container object c. It's a pretty simple template class.

Eq Lt The only implementation peculiarity is the use of the two member functions Eq and Lt to perform all comparisons in the template operators that follow the template class definition. These "secret names" supply the minimum access to the protected member c for the six comparison operators to do their work.

Figure 15.1: `stack`, **part 1**

```
// stack standard header
#ifndef STACK_
#define STACK_
#include <deque>
namespace std {
          // TEMPLATE CLASS stack
template<class T, class C = deque<T> >
     class stack {
public:
     typedef C container_type;
     typedef typename C::value_type value_type;
     typedef typename C::size_type size_type;
     explicit stack(const C& Cont)
          : c(Cont) {}
     stack()
          : c() {}
     bool empty() const
          {return (c.empty()); }
     size_type size() const
          {return (c.size()); }
     value_type& top()
          {return (c.back()); }
     const value_type& top() const
          {return (c.back()); }
     void push(const value_type& X)
          {c.push_back(X); }
     void pop()
          {c.pop_back(); }
     bool Eq(const stack<T, C>& X) const
          {return (c == X.c); }
     bool Lt(const stack<T, C>& X) const
          {return (c < X.c); }
protected:
     C c;
     };
          // stack TEMPLATE FUNCTIONS
template<class T, class C> inline
     bool operator==(const stack<T, C>& X,
          const stack<T, C>& Y)
     {return (X.Eq(Y)); }
template<class T, class C> inline
     bool operator!=(const stack<T, C>& X,
          const stack<T, C>& Y)
     {return (!(X == Y)); }
template<class T, class C> inline
     bool operator<(const stack<T, C>& X,
          const stack<T, C>& Y)
     {return (X.Lt(Y)); }
template<class T, class C> inline
     bool operator>(const stack<T, C>& X,
          const stack<T, C>& Y)
     {return (Y < X); }
```

Figure 15.2: `stack`, part 2

```
template<class T, class C> inline
     bool operator<=(const stack<T, C>& X,
          const stack<T, C>& Y)
     {return (!(Y < X)); }
template<class T, class C> inline
     bool operator>=(const stack<T, C>& X,
          const stack<T, C>& Y)
     {return (!(X < Y)); }
} /* namespace std */
#endif /* STACK_ */
```

Testing `<stack>`

`tstack.c` Figure 15.3 shows the file `tstack.c`. It is fairly simple, since the header is rather small and has little to test in the bargain. It checks for the overt presence of all the definitions. It specializes template class `stack` for several STL containers. And it exercises the member functions in the obvious way. If all goes well, the program prints:

```
SUCCESS testing <stack>
```

and takes a normal exit.

Exercises

Exercise 15.1 What are the absolute minimum requirements for a container to serve as the underlying representation of a stack?

Exercise 15.2 Why are the six template comparison operators defined outside template class `stack`, as two-argument functions, instead of inside the class, as one-argument member functions?

Exercise 15.3 Why does template class `stack` define both `Eq` and `Lt`? Can you eliminate one of these member functions and still write the six template comparison operators?

Exercise 15.4 Under what circumstances would you want to use `list<T>` as the underlying container for a stack?

Exercise 15.5 Under what circumstances would you want to derive a class from `stack<T, C>`? Why would you want access to the stored container object `c`?

Exercise 15.6 Alter template class `stack` to throw an exception when `top` or `pop` is called on an empty stack.

Exercise 15.7 [**Harder**] Alter template class `stack` so that it maintains its own controlled sequence instead of relying on another container type to do the work. What data representation do you think is best for a general-purpose stack?

Exercise 15.8 [**Very hard**] Implement a stack that adapts dynamically to the pattern of pushes and pops so that it minimizes unused storage while preserving (amortized) constant time for pushing and popping.

Figure 15.3: `tstack.c`

```
// test <stack>
#include <assert.h>
#include <iostream>
#include <deque>
#include <list>
#include <stack>
#include <vector>
using namespace std;

    // TEST <stack>
int main()
    {typedef allocator<char> Myal;
    typedef deque<char, Myal> Myimpl;
    typedef stack<char, Myimpl> Mycont;
    typedef list<char, Myal> Myimpl2;
    typedef stack<char, Myimpl2> Mycont2;
    typedef vector<char, Myal> Myimpl3;
    typedef stack<char, Myimpl3> Mycont3;
    Mycont::container_type *p_cont = (Myimpl *)0;
    Mycont::value_type *p_val = (char *)0;
    Mycont::size_type *p_size = (size_t *)0;

    Mycont v0(Myimpl(3, 'x')), v0a;
    Mycont2 v1;
    Mycont3 v2;
    assert(v0.size() == 3 && v0.top() == 'x');
    assert(v0a.empty());
    v0 = v0a;
    v0.push('a');
    assert(v0.size() == 1 && v0.top() == 'a');
    v0.push('b');
    assert(v0.size() == 2 && v0.top() == 'b');
    v0.push('c');
    assert(v0.size() == 3 && v0.top() == 'c');
    assert(v0 == v0 && v0a < v0);
    assert(v0 != v0a && v0 > v0a);
    assert(v0a <= v0 && v0 >= v0a);
    v0.pop();
    assert(v0.top() == 'b');
    v0.pop();
    assert(v0.top() == 'a');
    v0.pop();
    assert(v0.empty());

    cout << "SUCCESS testing <stack>" << endl;
    return (0); }
```

□

Chapter 16: <queue>

Background

<queue> The header `<queue>` defines two template classes, `queue` and `priority_queue`. Each is a *container adapter* — a template class that does not itself directly maintain controlled sequences. Rather, it stores as a member object a container object that does the job. We discussed the simplest container adapter, template class `stack`, in the preceding chapter.

queue Template class `queue` imposes a first-in first-out, or FIFO, discipline. By contrast, a stack imposes a last-in first-out, or LIFO, discipline. Queues occur widely in programming; they are at least as prevalent as stacks. They are also highly similar in structure. And they share a reusability problem with stacks — no single data structure is clearly superior to all others for implementing a generic queue. Herein lies the advantage of packaging stacks and queues as container adapters. You can choose the underlying representation you think best for a given application, then specialize the container adapter to create just the kind of queue or stack you need.

priority_queue The last of the container adapters is also the most ornate. Template class `priority_queue`, like the simpler `queue` and `stack`, restricts access to the controlled sequence, but with an added wrinkle. The queue is ordered by a predicate that determines which element has the highest priority. The template class ensures that each element you extract from the controlled sequence by calling `pop` is the remaining element with highest priority. It does so by reordering the sequence, as needed, each time you add an element by calling `push`. More specifically, it maintains the controlled sequence as a heap, using some of the algorithms we described in Chapter 6: `<algorithm>`.

Template class `priority_queue` is, in many ways, the culmination of all the STL machinery we have seen so far. It uses existing containers to manage the details of controlling a sequence, with different tradeoffs in performance and complexity. It uses the heap algorithms to keep the sequence in order. It lets you specify different function objects, to determine the meaning of "highest priority" for a given priority queue.

It is fitting that we end this presentation by describing queues and priority queues, because they demonstrate so much of the power and flexibility, and the extensibility, of STL.

Functional Description

```
namespace std {
template<class T, class Cont>
    class queue;
template<class T, class Cont, class Pred>
    class priority_queue;

        // TEMPLATE FUNCTIONS
template<class T, class Cont>
    bool operator==(const queue<T, Cont>& lhs,
        const queue<T, Cont>&);
template<class T, class Cont>
    bool operator!=(const queue<T, Cont>& lhs,
        const queue<T, Cont>&);
template<class T, class Cont>
    bool operator<(const queue<T, Cont>& lhs,
        const queue<T, Cont>&);
template<class T, class Cont>
    bool operator>(const queue<T, Cont>& lhs,
        const queue<T, Cont>&);
template<class T, class Cont>
    bool operator<=(const queue<T, Cont>& lhs,
        const queue<T, Cont>&);
template<class T, class Cont>
    bool operator>=(const queue<T, Cont>& lhs,
        const queue<T, Cont>&);
    };
```

Include the STL standard header `<queue>` to define the template classes `priority_queue` and `queue`, and several supporting templates.

▫ `operator!=`

```
template<class T, class Cont>
    bool operator!=(const queue <T, Cont>& lhs,
        const queue <T, Cont>& rhs);
```

The template function returns `!(lhs == rhs)`.

▫ `operator==`

```
template<class T, class Cont>
    bool operator==(const queue <T, Cont>& lhs,
        const queue <T, Cont>& rhs);
```

The template function overloads `operator==` to compare two objects of template class `queue`. The function returns `lhs.c == rhs.c`.

▫ `operator<`

```
template<class T, class Cont>
    bool operator<(const queue <T, Cont>& lhs,
        const queue <T, Cont>& rhs);
```

The template function overloads `operator<` to compare two objects of template class `queue`. The function returns `lhs.c < rhs.c`.

▫ `operator<=`

```
template<class T, class Cont>
    bool operator<=(const queue <T, Cont>& lhs,
        const queue <T, Cont>& rhs);
```

The template function returns `!(rhs < lhs)`.

▫ **operator>**

```
template<class T, class Cont>
    bool operator>(const queue <T, Cont>& lhs,
        const queue <T, Cont>& rhs);
```

The template function returns `rhs < lhs`.

▫ **operator>=**

```
template<class T, class Cont>
    bool operator>=(const queue <T, Cont>& lhs,
        const queue <T, Cont>& rhs);
```

The template function returns `!(lhs < rhs)`.

▫ **priority_queue**

```
template<class T,
    class Cont = vector<T>,
    class Pred = less<typename Cont::value_type> >
    class priority_queue {
public:
    typedef Cont container_type;
    typedef typename Cont::value_type value_type;
    typedef typename Cont::size_type size_type;
    priority_queue();
    explicit priority_queue(const Pred& pr);
    priority_queue(const Pred& pr,
        const container_type& cont);
    priority_queue(const priority_queue& x);
    template<class InIt>
        priority_queue(InIt first, InIt last);
    template<class InIt>
        priority_queue(InIt first, InIt last,
            const Pred& pr);
    template<class InIt>
        priority_queue(InIt first, InIt last,
            const Pred& pr, const container_type& cont);
    bool empty() const;
    size_type size() const;
    const value_type& top() const;
    void push(const value_type& x);
    void pop();
protected:
    Cont c;
    Pred comp;
    };
```

The template class describes an object that controls a varying-length sequence of elements. The object allocates and frees storage for the sequence it controls through a protected object named `c`, of class `Cont`. The type `T` of elements in the controlled sequence must match `value_type`.

The sequence is ordered using a protected object named `comp`. After each insertion or removal of the top element (at position zero), for the iterators `P0` and `Pi` designating elements at positions `0` and `i`, `comp(*P0, *Pi)` is false. (For the default template argument `less<typename Cont::value_type>` the top element of the sequence compares largest, or highest priority.)

An object of class `Cont` must supply random-access iterators and several public members defined the same as for `deque` and `vector` (both of which are suitable candidates for class `Cont`). The required members are:

```
typedef T value_type;
typedef T0 size_type;
typedef T1 iterator;
Cont();
template<class InIt>
    Cont(InIt first, InIt last);
template<class InIt>
    void insert(iterator it, InIt first, InIt last);
iterator begin();
iterator end();
bool empty() const;
size_type size() const;
const value_type& front() const;
void push_back(const value_type& x);
void pop_back();
```

Here, `T0` and `T1` are unspecified types that meet the stated requirements.

- **`priority_queue::container_type`**

```
typedef typename Cont::container_type container_type;
```

The type is a synonym for the template parameter `Cont`.

- **`priority_queue::empty`**

```
bool empty() const;
```

The member function returns true for an empty controlled sequence.

- **`priority_queue::pop`**

```
void pop();
```

The member function removes the first element of the controlled sequence, which must be non-empty, then reorders it.

- **`priority_queue::priority_queue`**

```
priority_queue();
explicit priority_queue(const Pred& pr);
priority_queue(const Pred& pr,
    const container_type& cont);
priority_queue(const priority_queue& x);
template<class InIt>
    priority_queue(InIt first, InIt last);
template<class InIt>
    priority_queue(InIt first, InIt last,
        const Pred& pr);
template<class InIt>
    priority_queue(InIt first, InIt last,
        const Pred& pr, const container_type& cont);
```

All constructors with an argument `cont` initialize the stored object with `c(cont)`. The remaining constructors initialize the stored object with `c`, to specify an empty initial controlled sequence. The last three constructors then call `c.insert(c.end(), first, last)`.

All constructors also store a function object in **comp**. The function object **pr** is the argument **pr**, if present. For the copy constructor, it is **x.comp**. Otherwise, it is **Pred()**.

A non-empty initial controlled sequence is then ordered by calling **make_heap(c.begin(), c.end(), comp)**.

▫ **priority_queue::push**

```
void push(const T& x);
```

The member function inserts an element with value **x** at the end of the controlled sequence, then reorders it.

▫ **priority_queue::size**

```
size_type size() const;
```

The member function returns the length of the controlled sequence.

▫ **priority_queue::size_type**

```
typedef typename Cont::size_type size_type;
```

The type is a synonym for **Cont::size_type**.

▫ **priority_queue::top**

```
const value_type& top() const;
```

The member function returns a reference to the first (highest priority) element of the controlled sequence, which must be non-empty.

▫ **priority_queue::value_type**

```
typedef typename Cont::value_type value_type;
```

The type is a synonym for **Cont::value_type**.

▫ **queue**

```
template<class T,
    class Cont = deque<T> >
    class queue {
public:
    typedef Cont container_type;
    typedef typename Cont::value_type value_type;
    typedef typename Cont::size_type size_type;
    queue();
    explicit queue(const container_type& cont);
    bool empty() const;
    size_type size() const;
    value_type& back();
    const value_type& back() const;
    value_type& front();
    const value_type& front() const;
    void push(const value_type& x);
    void pop();
protected:
    Cont c;
    };
```

The template class describes an object that controls a varying-length sequence of elements. The object allocates and frees storage for the sequence it controls through a protected object named `c`, of class `Cont`. The type `T` of elements in the controlled sequence must match `value_type`.

An object of class `Cont` must supply several public members defined the same as for `deque` and `list` (both of which are suitable candidates for class `Cont`). The required members are:

```
typedef T value_type;
typedef T0 size_type;
Cont();
bool empty() const;
size_type size() const;
value_type& front();
const value_type& front() const;
value_type& back();
const value_type& back() const;
void push_back(const value_type& x);
void pop_front();
bool operator==(const Cont& X) const;
bool operator!=(const Cont& X) const;
bool operator<(const Cont& X) const;
bool operator>(const Cont& X) const;
bool operator<=(const Cont& X) const;
bool operator>=(const Cont& X) const;
```

Here, `T0` is an unspecified type that meets the stated requirements.

▫ **queue::back**

```
value_type& back();
const value_type& back() const;
```

The member function returns a reference to the last element of the controlled sequence, which must be non-empty.

▫ **queue::container_type**

```
typedef Cont container_type;
```

The type is a synonym for the template parameter `Cont`.

▫ **queue::empty**

```
bool empty() const;
```

The member function returns true for an empty controlled sequence.

▫ **queue::front**

```
value_type& front();
const value_type& front() const;
```

The member function returns a reference to the first element of the controlled sequence, which must be non-empty.

▫ **queue::pop**

```
void pop();
```

The member function removes the first element of the controlled sequence, which must be non-empty.

▫ **queue::push**

```
void push(const T& x);
```

The member function inserts an element with value `x` at the end of the controlled sequence.

▫ **queue::queue**

```
queue();
explicit queue(const container_type& cont);
```

The first constructor initializes the stored object with `c()`, to specify an empty initial controlled sequence. The second constructor initializes the stored object with `c(cont)`, to specify an initial controlled sequence that is a copy of the sequence controlled by `cont`.

▫ **queue::size**

```
size_type size() const;
```

The member function returns the length of the controlled sequence.

▫ **queue::size_type**

```
typedef typename Cont::size_type size_type;
```

The type is a synonym for `Cont::size_type`.

▫ **queue::value_type**

```
typedef typename Cont::value_type value_type;
```

The type is a synonym for `Cont::value_type`.

Using <queue>

<queue> Include the header `<queue>` to make use of template class `queue` or `priority_queue`.

queue You can specialize template class `queue` to store elements of type `T` in an object of type `deque<T>` by writing a type definition such as:

```
typedef queue<T, deque<T, allocator<T> > > Mycont;
```

Using a default template argument, you can omit the second argument.

container requirements Alternatively, you can replace the second argument with `list<T>`. (You cannot, however, use `vector<T>`.) You can also specify as the second template argument a container type of your own devising. More specifically, a container `Cont` must have at least the following external interface:

- **value_type size_type** It must define the member types `value_type` (as `T`) and `size_type` (typically as `size_t`).
- **empty size** It must define the const member functions `empty` and `size`, with the usual meanings.
- **back front** It must define the member functions `back` and `front`, in both const and non-const forms, with the usual meanings.
- **push_back pop_front** It must define the member functions `push_back`, and `pop_front`,with the usual meanings.
- It must define the six comparison operators (such as `operator==(const Cont&, const Cont&)` in a way that imposes a total ordering on objects of type `Cont`.

Template class `queue` does *not* support all the common operations on containers, as we described in Chapter 9: Containers. (See the discussion beginning on page 248.) It intentionally provides only a restricted set of operations. The following descriptions all assume that `cont` is an object of class `queue<T, C>`.

constructors To construct an object of class `queue<T, C>`, you can write:

- `queue()` to declare an empty queue.
- `queue(cont)` to declare a queue whose initial content is copied from `cont`.

`push` To push a new element with value `v` on the back of the queue, call `cont.push(v)`.

`pop` To pop the front element from the queue, call `cont.pop()`. If the queue is empty, the result is undefined. Note that `cont.pop()` is a void function — it does *not* return the value of the popped element.

`front` `back` To access the front (least recently pushed) element on the queue, call `cont.front()`. To access the back (most recently pushed, next to be popped) element on the queue, call `cont.back()`. In either case, if the queue is empty, the result is undefined. Note that both member functions return a reference — if the queue is not a const object, you can alter the value stored in the front or back element by writing an assignment expression such as `cont.front() = 0`.

`empty` `size` To test whether the queue is empty, call `cont.empty()`. To obtain the number of elements in the queue, call `cont.size()`.

comparisons You can compare the queue `cont` in its entirety against another queue `cont2` by writing any of the usual six comparison operators, such as `cont == cont2` or `cont >= cont2`. The result is the same as comparing the stored container objects, for what that may be worth.

`c` Finally, if you define a class with `queue<T, C>` as a public base class, then you can access the stored container object. It is a protected member named `c`.

`priority_queue` You can specialize template class `priority_queue` to store elements of type `T` in an object of type `vector<T>` and with an ordering rule of type `less<T>` by writing a type definition such as:

```
typedef priority_queue<T, vector<T, allocator<T>,
    less<T> > > Mycont;
```

Using default template arguments, you can omit the second and/or third arguments.

`less` If you omit the third argument, the default is given by a function object of type `less<T>`. The controlled sequence in the stored container is ordered by this rule. Thus, for numeric types at least, the "highest priority" element is the one with the largest stored value.

container requirements You can also replace the second argument with, for example, `deque<T>`. (You cannot, however, use `list<T>`.) Or you can specify as the second template argument a container type of your own devising. More specifically, a container Cont must have at least the following external interface:

value_type size_type
- It must define the member types value_type (as T) and size_type (typically as size_t).

iterator
- It must define the member type iterator (a random-access iterator).
- It must define the defalut constructor Cont() and a template constructor Cont(first, last) that initializes the controlled sequence from the sequence designated by [first, last).

empty size
- It must define the const member functions empty and size, with the usual meanings.

begin end
- It must define the member functions begin and end, with the usual meanings.

front
- It must define the member function front, with the usual meaning.

insert
- It must define a template member function insert(it, first, last) that inserts before it the sequence designated by [first, last).

push_back pop_back
- It must define the member functions push_back, and pop_back, with the usual meanings.

This interface is regrettably ornate. Most of the extra requirements, beyond those for queue and stack, result from additions made to priority_queue during standardization with no consideration for their effect on underlying container requirements.

Template class priority_queue does *not* support all the common operations on containers, as we described in Chapter 9: Containers. (See the discussion beginning on page 248.) It intentionally provides only a restricted set of operations. The following descriptions all assume that cont is an object of class priority_queue<T, C, Pred>.

constructors To construct an object of class priority_queue<T, C>, you can write:

- priority_queue() to declare an empty priority queue that is ordered by Pred().
- priority_queue(pr) to declare an empty priority queue that is ordered by the function object pr.
- priority_queue(pr, cont) to declare a priority queue that is ordered by pr and whose initial content is copied from cont and then ordered.
- priority_queue(first, last) to declare a priority queue that is ordered by Pred() and whose initial content is copied from the sequence designated by [first, last) and then ordered.
- priority_queue(first, last, pr) to declare a priority queue that is ordered by pr and whose initial content is copied from the sequence designated by [first, last), as above, and then ordered.
- priority_queue(first, last, cont, pr) to declare a priority queue that is ordered by pr and whose initial content is copied from cont plus the sequence designated by [first, last), as above, and then ordered.

push To push a new element with value `v` onto the priority queue, call `cont.push(v)`.

pop To pop the top (highest priority) element from the priority queue, call `cont.pop()`. If the priority queue is empty, the result is undefined. Note that `cont.pop()` is a void function — it does *not* return the value of the popped element.

top To access the top (highest priority, next to be popped) element on the priority queue, call `cont.top()`. If the priority queue is empty, the result is undefined. Note that the member functions returns a const reference — you cannot alter the stored value.

empty **size** To test whether the priority queue is empty, call `cont.empty()`. To obtain the number of elements in the priority queue, call `cont.size()`.

comparisons You cannot compare priority queues as you can queues and stacks.

c **comp** Finally, if you define a class with `priority_queue<T, C, Pred>` as a public base class, then you can access the stored container and function objects. The container is a protected member named `c`, while the function object used for ordering the priority queue is called `comp`.

Implementing `<queue>`

Figures 16.1 through 16.2 show the file `queue`. As you can see, both `queue` and `priority_queue` perform practically all their operations by calling corresponding member functions for the stored container object `c`. Indeed, `queue` looks remarkably like `stack` (in the preceding chapter) in this regard.

Figure 16.1: queue Part 1

```
// queue standard header
#ifndef QUEUE_
#define QUEUE_
#include <algorithm>
#include <deque>
#include <functional>
#include <vector>
namespace std {
        // TEMPLATE CLASS queue
template<class T, class C = deque<T> >
    class queue {
public:
    typedef C container_type;
    typedef typename C::value_type value_type;
    typedef typename C::size_type size_type;
    queue()
        : c() {}
    explicit queue(const C& Cont)
        : c(Cont) {}
    bool empty() const
        {return (c.empty()); }
    size_type size() const
        {return (c.size()); }
```

Figure 16.2: queue Part 2

```
    value_type& front()
        {return (c.front()); }
    const value_type& front() const
        {return (c.front()); }
    value_type& back()
        {return (c.back()); }
    const value_type& back() const
        {return (c.back()); }
    void push(const value_type& X)
        {c.push_back(X); }
    void pop()
        {c.pop_front(); }
    bool Eq(const queue<T, C>& X) const
        {return (c == X.c); }
    bool Lt(const queue<T, C>& X) const
        {return (c < X.c); }
protected:
    C c;
    };

        // queue TEMPLATE FUNCTIONS
template<class T, class C> inline
    bool operator==(const queue<T, C>& X,
        const queue<T, C>& Y)
    {return (X.Eq(Y)); }
template<class T, class C> inline
    bool operator!=(const queue<T, C>& X,
        const queue<T, C>& Y)
    {return (!(X == Y)); }
template<class T, class C> inline
    bool operator<(const queue<T, C>& X,
        const queue<T, C>& Y)
    {return (X.Lt(Y)); }
template<class T, class C> inline
    bool operator>(const queue<T, C>& X,
        const queue<T, C>& Y)
    {return (Y < X); }
template<class T, class C> inline
    bool operator<=(const queue<T, C>& X,
        const queue<T, C>& Y)
    {return (!(Y < X)); }
template<class T, class C> inline
    bool operator>=(const queue<T, C>& X,
        const queue<T, C>& Y)
    {return (!(X < Y)); }

        // TEMPLATE CLASS priority_queue
template<class T, class C = vector<T>,
    class Pr = less<typename C::value_type> >
    class priority_queue {
public:
    typedef C container_type;
    typedef typename C::value_type value_type;
    typedef typename C::size_type size_type;
```

Figure 16.3: queue Part 3

```
        priority_queue()
              : c(), comp() {}
        explicit priority_queue(const Pr& X)
              : c(), comp(X) {}
        priority_queue(const Pr& X, const C& Cont)
              : c(Cont), comp(X)
              {make_heap(c.begin(), c.end(), comp); }
        template<class It>
              priority_queue(It F, It L)
              : c(F, L), comp()
              {make_heap(c.begin(), c.end(), comp); }
        template<class It>
              priority_queue(It F, It L, const Pr& X)
              : c(F, L), comp(X)
              {make_heap(c.begin(), c.end(), comp); }
        template<class It>
              priority_queue(It F, It L, const Pr& X,
                    const C& Cont)
              : c(Cont), comp(X)
              {c.insert(c.end(), F, L);
              make_heap(c.begin(), c.end(), comp); }
        bool empty() const
              {return (c.empty()); }
        size_type size() const
              {return (c.size()); }
        const value_type& top() const
              {return (c.front()); }
        void push(const value_type& X)
              {c.push_back(X);
              push_heap(c.begin(), c.end(), comp); }
        void pop()
              {pop_heap(c.begin(), c.end(), comp);
              c.pop_back(); }
protected:
        C c;
        Pr comp;
        };
} /* namespace std */
#endif /* QUEUE_ */
```

Testing <queue>

tqueue.c Figures 16.4 through 16.4 show the file **tqueue.c**. It is fairly simple, since the header is rather small and has little to test in the bargain. In fact, it tests template classes **queue** and **priority_queue** much the same way as **tstack.c** tests **stack** in the preceding chapter. If all goes well, the program prints:

```
SUCCESS testing <queue>
```

and takes a normal exit.

Figure 16.4: `tqueue.c` **Part 1**

```
// test <queue>
#include <assert.h>
#include <iostream>
#include <deque>
#include <functional>
#include <list>
#include <queue>
#include <vector>
using namespace std;

     // TEST queue
void test_queue()
     {typedef allocator<char> Myal;
     typedef deque<char, Myal> Myimpl;
     typedef queue<char, Myimpl> Mycont;
     typedef list<char, Myal> Myimpl2;
     typedef queue<char, Myimpl2> Mycont2;
     Mycont::container_type *p_cont = (Myimpl *)0;
     Mycont::value_type *p_val = (char *)0;
     Mycont::size_type *p_size = (size_t *)0;

     Mycont v0(Myimpl(3, 'x')), v0a;
     Mycont2 v1;
     assert(v0.size() == 3 && v0.front() == 'x');
     assert(v0a.empty());
     v0 = v0a;
     v0.push('a');
     assert(v0.size() == 1 && v0.front() == 'a'
          && v0.back() == 'a');
     v0.push('c');
     assert(v0.size() == 2 && v0.front() == 'a'
          && v0.back() == 'c');
     v0.push('b');
     assert(v0.size() == 3 && v0.front() == 'a'
          && v0.back() == 'b');
     assert(v0 == v0 && v0a < v0);
     assert(v0 != v0a && v0 > v0a);
     assert(v0a <= v0 && v0 >= v0a);
     v0.pop();
     assert(v0.front() == 'c');
     v0.pop();
     assert(v0.front() == 'b');
     v0.pop();
     assert(v0.empty()); }

     // TEST priority_queue
void test_priority_queue()
     {typedef allocator<char> Myal;
     typedef less<char> Mypred;
     typedef vector<char, Myal> Myimpl;
     typedef priority_queue<char, Myimpl, Mypred> Mycont;
     typedef deque<char, Myal> Myimpl2;
     typedef priority_queue<char, Myimpl2, Mypred> Mycont2;
     Mycont::container_type *p_cont = (Myimpl *)0;
     Mycont::value_type *p_val = (char *)0;
```

Figure 16.5: `tqueue.c` **Part 2**

```
    Mycont::size_type *p_size = (size_t *)0;

    Mypred pr;
    char carr[] = "acb";
    Mycont v0(pr, Myimpl(3, 'x')), v0a(pr), v0b;
    Mycont2 v1;
    const Mycont v2(carr, carr + 3), v2a(carr, carr + 3, pr),
        v2b(carr, carr + 3, pr, Myimpl(3, 'x'));
    assert(v0.size() == 3 && v0.top() == 'x');
    assert(v0a.empty());
    v0 = v0a;
    assert(v2.size() == 3 && v2.top() == 'c');
    assert(v2a.size() == 3 && v2a.top() == 'c');
    assert(v2b.size() == 6 && v2b.top() == 'x');
    v0.push('a');
    assert(v0.size() == 1 && v0.top() == 'a');
    v0.push('c');
    assert(v0.size() == 2 && v0.top() == 'c');
    v0.push('b');
    assert(v0.size() == 3 && v0.top() == 'c');
    v0.pop();
    assert(v0.top() == 'b');
    v0.pop();
    assert(v0.top() == 'a');
    v0.pop();
    assert(v0.empty()); }

    // TEST <queue>
int main()
    {test_queue();
    test_priority_queue();
    cout << "SUCCESS testing <queue>" << endl;
    return (0); }
```

□

Exercises

Exercise 16.1 Why can't you use template class **`vector`** with template class **`queue`**? Why can't you use template class **`list`** with template class **`priority_queue`**?

Exercise 16.2 Why can't you use template class **`set`** with template class **`queue`**?

Exercise 16.3 What are the absolute minimum requirements for a container to serve as the underlying representation of a queue? Of a priority queue?

Exercise 16.4 [**Harder**] Alter template class **`queue`** so that it can also work with a **`set`** or **`multiset`** container. Do you still need **`priority_queue`**?

Exercise 16.5 [**Very hard**] Alter template class **`priority_queue`** so that it behaves as either a queue or a priority queue. Specifically, add the member functions **`back`** and **`pop_back`** to provide FIFO behavior in conjunction with **`push`**, while retaining **`top`** and **`pop`** to access and remove the highest-priority element.

Appendix A: Interfaces

The STL headers are remarkably self contained. They require no supporting C++ source files, since all template definitions can be confined to just the headers. They can be written in highly portable Standard C++ code. In fact, the STL headers depend directly on only four other headers from the Standard C++ library;

<cstddef>
- <cstddef>, to obtain the type definitions **ptrdiff_t and size_t**

<iosfwd>
- <iosfwd>, to obtain forward references to several templates

<new>
- <new>, to obtain declarations for **operator delete** and several versions of **operator new**

<stdexcept>
- <stdexcept>, to obtain definitions for two exception classes

Of course, these headers depend in turn on still other headers from the Standard C++ library, but the direct interface to STL is narrow indeed.

cstddef

Figure A.1 shows the relevant portion of the file **cstddef**. The C++ Standard introduced this header to define in namespace **std** the type names previously defined in the Standard C header **<stddef.h>**. STL uses only the type definitions **ptrdiff_t** and **size_t** from **<cstddef>**.

iosfwd

Figure A.2 shows the relevant portion of the file **iosfwd**. The C++ Standard introduced this header to supply forward references (declarations of incomplete types) for templates and classes defined as part of other headers. Of interest to STL are four template declarations referred to by the template iterators **istream_iterator**, **ostream_iterator**, **istreambuf_iterator**, and **ostreambuf_iterator**:

char_traits
- **char_traits** describes the properties of an element (or character, in the general sense) in an input stream or an output stream.

basic_istream
- **basic_istream** describes an object that controls extraction of elements from an input stream. An example is the standard input stream **cin**.

basic_ostream
- **basic_ostream** describes an object that controls insertion of elements into an output stream. An example is the standard output stream **cout**.

Figure A.1: cstddef

```
// cstddef standard header (partial)
namespace std {
      // TYPE DEFINITIONS
typedef int ptrdiff_t;              // or another signed integer type
typedef unsigned int size_t;      // or another unsigned integer type
} /* namespace std */                                                □
```

Figure A.2: `iosfwd`

```
// iosfwd standard header (partial)
namespace std {
     // FORWARD REFERENCES
template<class E>
     class char_traits;
template<class E, class Tr>
     class basic_istream;
template<class E, class Tr>
     class basic_ostream;
template<class E, class Tr>
     class basic_streambuf;
} /* namespace std */
```

`basic_streambuf`

- **basic_streambuf** describes an object that performs the actual buffering for an input stream or an output stream.

`new` Figure A.3 shows the relevant portion of the file **new**. The C++ Standard introduced this header as a successor to the traditional **<new.h>**. You need to include **<new>** to make explicit calls to **operator new** or **operator delete**. (By contrast, if you write just the simplest **new** expressions and **delete** expressions, you do *not* need to include this header.) Template classes **allocator** and **get_temporary_buffer** call these operators directly, to decouple storage allocation and freeing from object construction and destruction.

`nothrow_t` `nothrow` Struct **nothrow_t** is an invention of the Committee. It is used only to distinguish a version of **operator new** that returns a null pointer if it cannot perform the requested storage allocation. By contrast, the traditional version of **operator new** no longer returns a null pointer. Instead, it throws an exception if it cannot perform the requested storage allocations. The constant **nothrow** is a convenience, so you can write **new(nothrow) X**, to make an object of type **X**, instead of **new(nothrow_t()) X**. The latter is wordier and more likely to generated unnecessary additional code.

`new` STL uses three forms of **operator new**:

- **operator new(N)** if the requested storage allocation must succeed or throw an exception
- **operator new(N, nothrow)** if the requested storage allocation may fail and return a null pointer
- **operator new(N, P)** to support *placement* **new** syntax

placement new The last form lets you write a kind of **new** expression that constructs an object in storage you have previously allocated, as in:

```
new(P) T()
```

which calls the default constructor for an object of type **T** using unconstructed storage previously allocated at **P**.

`delete` You call **operator delete(P)** to delete storage earlier allocated by a call to **operator new**. If an object has been constructed in this storage, it must first be explicitly destroyed.

Figure A.3: `new`

```
// new standard header (partial)
namespace std {
     // STRUCT nothrow_t
struct nothrow_t {};
extern const nothrow_t nothrow;                         // = nothrow_t()
} /* namespace std */
     // OPERATOR new
void *operator new(size_t);
void *operator new(size_t, const std::nothrow_t&) throw();
inline void *operator new(size_t, void *P);            // just return P
     // OPERATOR delete
void operator delete(void *);
```
□

`stdexcept` Figure A.4 shows the relevant portion of the file **`stdexcept`**. The C++ Standard introduced this header to define several exception classes. STL classes explicitly throw objects of two exception class types:

`length_error`
- **`length_error`** to report an attempt to make the controlled sequence too long in a container

`out_of_range`
- **`out_of_range`** to report an index value outside the valid range for accessing an element of a random-access container

`logic_error` Both of these classes derive from class **`logic_error`**. You throw an object of this base class to report an error that probably results from incorrrect program logic.

`exception` `string` Class **`logic_error`**, in turn, derives from class **`exception`**, the base class for all exceptions thrown by the Standard C++ library. **`exception`** is defined, naturally enough, in the header **`<exception>`**. Each of these exception classes defines a constructor that obtains an error message from an object of type **`string`**. You include the header **`<string>`** to define the

Figure A.4: `stdexcept`

```
// stdexcept standard header (partial)
#include <exception>
namespace std {
          // CLASS logic_error
class logic_error : public exception {
public:
     explicit logic_error(const string& S);
     };

          // CLASS length_error
class length_error : public logic_error {
public:
     explicit length_error(const string& S);
     };

          // CLASS out_of_range
class out_of_range : public logic_error {
public:
     explicit out_of_range(const string& S);
     };
} /* namespace std */
```
□

template classes `basic_string` and `char_traits`. That header also defines `string` as a synonym for the specialization `basic_string<char, char_traits<char> >`.

And so on, and so on. Were we to try to show *all* the dependencies of the STL headers, we would end up visiting a large portion of the full Standard C++ library. The presentation here has a more limited goal. It shows the narrow top of the pyramid upon which all of STL rests.

Appendix B: Terms

This appendix lists terms that have special meaning within this book. Check here if you suspect that a term means more (or less) than you might ordinarily think.

A

access — to obtain the value stored in an object or to store a new value in the object

allocated storage — objects whose storage is obtained during program execution

allocator — an object that encapsulates strategies for allocating and freeing storage for objects of some type `T`

Amendment 1 — the first amendment to the ISO C Standard

amortized — spread over a large number of operations, as when an operation takes "amortized constant time" (any occasions that take extra time are sufficiently rare that the overall time complexity remains constant)

ANSI — American National Standards Institute, the organization authorized to formulate computer-related standards in the U.S.

argument — an expression that provides the initial value for one of the parameters in a function call

arithmetic type — an integer or floating-point type

array type — an object type consisting of a prespecified repetition of an object element

assign — to store a value in an object

assignment operator — an operator that stores a value in an object, such as `operator=`,

B

base class — a class from which another class is derived by inheriting the properties of the base class

beginning — the first element of a sequence, or the end of an empty sequence

benign redefinition — a macro definition that defines an existing macro to have the same sequence of tokens spelled the same way and with white space between the same pairs of tokens, or a type definition that defines an existing type to be a synonym for its earlier definition

balanced binary tree — a binary tree all of whose terminal nodes (leaves) have essentially the same minimum path length to the root node

bidirectional iterators — a category of iterators that can be incremented or decremented

binary tree — a sequence whose elements are stored as nodes linked to a parent and two child nodes (hence a sequence that also supports bidirectional access to neighboring elements in constant time)

block — a group of statements in a C++ function enclosed in braces

Boolean — an expression (of type `bool` in C++) with two meaningful values, true and false (represented by the keywords `true` and `false` in C++)

buffer — an array object used as a convenient work area or for temporary storage, as between a program and a file

C

C header — one of the headers in the Standard C++ library inherited from the Standard C library, having a name ending in `.h`

C Standard — a description of the C programming language adopted by ANSI and ISO to minimize variations in C implementations and programs

C++ header — one of the headers unique to the Standard C++ library, having a name *not* ending in `.h`

C++ Standard — a description of the C programming language adopted by ANSI and ISO to minimize variations in C implementations and programs

***catch* clause** — a sequence of tokens that specifies how to handle an exception thrown within an associated *try* block

character — an object type in C++ that occupies one byte of storage and that can represent all the codes in the basic C++ character set

character constant — a token in a C++ program, such as `'a'`, whose integer value is the code for a character in the execution character set

class — an object type consisting of a sequence of function, object, and type members of different types

code — colloquial term for programming language text or the executable binary produced from that text

compiler — a translator that produces an executable file

computer architecture — a class of computers that can all execute a common executable-file format

constant type — the type of an object that you cannot store into (it is read-only) once it is initialized because it has the `const` type qualifier

constructor — a member function that constructs an object, typically by constructing its subobjects and storing initial values in its scalar member objects

container — a class that supplies an organizing structure for a sequence of elements of some contained class

conversion, type — altering the representation of a value of one type (as necessary) to make it a valid representation of a value of another type

copy constructor — a constructor that can be called with a single argument that is a const reference to another object of the same class, whose stored value provides the initial value of the object being constructed

D **declaration** — a sequence of tokens in a C++ program that gives meaning to a name, allocates storage for an object, defines the initial content of an object or the behavior of a function, and/or specifies a type

default — the choice made when a choice is required and none is specified

definition — a declaration that, among other things, allocates storage for an object, associates a value with a *const* object, specifies the behavior of a function, or gives a name to a type; also the *define* directive for a macro

***delete* expression** — an expression involving `operator delete`, which destroys the object, then calls the operator function to free storage for the object

deque — a queue that also supports random access to arbitrary elements in constant time

derived class — a class that inherits properties from one or more base classes

destructor — a member function that destroys an object, typically by freeing any storage or other resources associated with the constructed object

destroy — to call the destructor for an object

diagnostic — a message emitted by a C++ translator reporting an invalid program

dynamic storage — objects whose storage is allocated on entry to a block (or function) and freed when the activation of that block terminates, such as function parameters, `auto` declarations, and `register` declarations

E **element** — one of the repeated components of an array object, or one of the components of a sequence designated by a pair of iterators, or one of the components of a sequence controlled by a container object

encapsulation — localizing a design decision so that a change of design results in changes within a small and easily identified region of source text

end — the position just beyond the last element of a sequence (same as the beginning of an empty sequence)

end-of-file — the file position just after the last byte in a file

end-of-sequence — the iterator value that signals the end of a sequence, such as end-of-file or just past the end of an array

equivalence relationship — a transitive and commutative ordering that guarantees that a value is always "ordered before" itself (`operator==` on integers imposes an equivalence relationship)

equivalent ordering — a commutative ordering between two values where neither value is ordered before the other

erase — to remove an element from a sequence

exception — an object specified by a *throw* expression within a *try* block and caught by a *catch* clause that specifies the object type, used to report an abnormal condition

exception handler — the part of a *catch* clause that responds to a thrown exception

exception specification — a qualifier appended to a function declaration that specifies the types of exceptions that can propagate out of the function when it executes

executable file — a file that the operating system can execute without further translation or interpretation

explicitly specialize — to write a template class or template function definition by hand that replaces a particular specialization of the template

expression — a sequence of tokens in a C++ program that specifies how to compute a value and generate side effects

extract — to obtain the value of the next character in a sequence controlled by a stream, and to point past that character position in the stream

extractor — a function that extracts one or more characters from a stream, converts them to the value of some object type, and stores the value in the object

F **field** — a contiguous group of characters that matches a pattern specified by a scan format conversion specification, and hence by an extractor

file — a contiguous sequence of bytes that has a name, maintained by the environment

floating-point type — any of the types *float*, *double*, or *long double*

forward iterators — a category of iterators that can be incremented but not decremented

free — to release storage allocated for an object during earlier program execution

friend — a class or function declaration within a class that makes the name space of the class available within the declared class or function

function — a contiguous group of executable statements that accepts argument values corresponding to its parameters when called from within an expression and (possibly) returns a value for use in that expression

function signature — the name of a function, along with the type information for its parameters, used in overload resolution to determine which function to call in an expression

function type — a type that describes a function, as opposed to an object type

H **has-a relationship** — describes the use of an existing class to declare a member object (which the newly declared class "has" as a member), as opposed to the use of an existing class as a base (which the newly declared class "is" by derivation)

header file — a text file that is made part of a translation unit by being named in an `#include` directive in a C++ source file

heap — a portion of memory that an executable program uses to store objects allocated and freed in arbitrary order, also a weakly ordered sequence whose first element is not ordered before any of the others (the first element is the largest)

I **identifier** — a name

implementation — a working version of a specification, such as a programming language

include file — a text file made part of a translation unit by being named in an `#include` directive in a C++ source file or another include file

incomplete type — a type that describes an object, but supplies incomplete information for determining its content (such as `void`, an array of unknown size, or a struct or union of unknown content)

inheritance — obtaining the member definitions and type equivalence from a base class

input iterators — a category of iterators used only to read elements from a sequence until the input iterator compares equal to an end-of-sequence value (such as end-of-file)

input stream — a stream that can be read from

insert — to add an element to a sequence before a designated point

inserter — a function that converts a value of some object type to a sequence of one or more characters and inserts those characters into a stream

instantiate — when applied to templates, often used as a synonym for "specialize"

integer — a whole number, possibly negative or zero

integer type — an object type that can represent some contiguous range of integers including zero

invalid — not conforming to the C++ Standard

I/O — input and output

ISO — International Organization for Standardization [sic], the organization charged with developing international computer-related standards

is-a relationship — describes the use of an existing class as a base (which the newly declared class "is" by derivation), as opposed to the use of an existing class to declare a member object (which the newly declared class "has" as a member)

iterator — an object used to access elements, of some type `T`, from an ordered collection, behaving much like a pointer to `T`

J

J16 — the ANSI-authorized committee responsible for C++ Standard, formerly X3J16

L

length error — specifying a sequence length that is too large

librarian — a program that maintains libraries of object modules

library — a collection of object modules that a linker can selectively incorporate into an executable program to provide definitions for names with external linkage

linker — a program that combines object modules to form an executable file

list — a sequence whose elements are stored as nodes linked in both the forward and backward direction (hence a sequence that also supports bidirectional access to neighboring elements in constant time)

lvalue — an expression that designates an object

M

machine — colloquial term for a distinct computer architecture

macro — a name defined by the `#define` directive that specifies replacement text for subsequent invocations of the macro in the translation unit

macro definition — the replacement text associated with a macro name

macro guard — a macro name used to ensure that a text sequence is incorporated in a translation unit at most once

macro, masking — a macro definition that masks a declaration of the same name earlier in the translation unit

member — an object declaration that specifies one of the components of a class, struct, or union declaration

modifiable lvalue — an expression that designates an object that you can store a new value into (having neither a constant nor an array type)

multithread — supporting more than one program execution in a given time interval, possibly allowing interactions between the separate program executions

N

name — a token from a large set used to designate a distinct entity — such as a function, macro, type, or member — in a translation unit

name space — a set of names distinguishable by context within a C++ program

namespace — a region of source code qualified by a namespace name

***new* expression** — an expression involving `operator new`, which calls the operator function to allocate storage for an object, then constructs the object

null pointer — the value of a pointer object that compares equal to zero, and hence designates no function or object

O

object — a group of contiguous bytes in memory that can store a value of a given type

object module — the translated form of a translation unit, suitable for linking as part of an executable program

object type — a type that describes an object, as opposed to a function type

offset — the relative address of an element within a sequence

operand — a subexpression in a C++ expression acted on by an operator

operating system — a program that runs other programs, usually masking many variations among computers that share a common architecture

operator — a token in a C++ expression that yields a value of a given type, and possibly produces side effects, given one to three subexpressions as operands

operator function — a function called implicitly by the evaluation of an operator in an expression, such as `operator=`

ordering — satisfying a predicate between two values `x` and `y`, such as `x < y`

ordered binary tree — a binary tree ordered by a predicate such that elements in nodes of each left subtree are ordered before the element in the node, and the element in the node is ordered before the elements in the nodes of each right subtree

ordered sequence — a sequence ordered by a predicate such that elements earlier in the sequence are ordered before each element

output iterators — a category of iterators used only to append elements to a sequence of unspecified length

output stream — a stream that can be written to

overload — to provide more than one definition for a name in a given scope

overload resolution — to determine which of two or more overloaded functions to call within an expression

override — to provide a definition in a derived class that masks a definition in its base class

P

parameter — an object declared in a function that stores the value of its corresponding argument on a function call

parse — to determine the syntactic structure of a sequence of tokens

partially specialize — to write a template class or template function definition that determines some, but not all, of the parameters for another template

pointer — an object that can designate a function or object when used as the (lone) operand of `operator*`

pointer type — an object type that describes a pointer

PODS — an object type that describes a "plain old data structure," essentially a class type whose non-static member objects could equally well be declared as a C struct

portability — cheaper to move to another environment than to rewrite for that environment

predicate — an expression that yields a Boolean result

preprocessor — that portion of a C++ translator that processes text-oriented directives and macro invocations

priority queue — a queue that is ordered after each push back, so that each pop back erases the element that orders highest

program — a collection of functions and objects that a computer can execute to carry out the semantic intent of a corresponding set of C++ source files

program startup — the period in the execution of a program just before `main` is called

program termination — the period in the execution of a program just after `main` returns or `exit` is called

pop back — to erase an element at the end of a sequence

pop front — to erase an element at the beginning of a sequence

push back — to append an element to a sequence

push front — to prepend an element to a sequence

Q

queue — a sequence that supports the operations pop back, pop front, push back, and push front in constant time

R

raise — to throw an exception

random-access iterators — a category of iterators that can be incremented, decremented, or altered by an integer offset in constant time

read-only — containing a stored value that cannot be altered

reachable iterator — an iterator that serves as an end values for a finite sequence (the beginning iterator, incremented a finite number of times, will eventually compare equal to a reachable end iterator)

recursion — calling a function while an invocation of that function is active

red-black tree — an ordered binary tree that permits a bounded degree of imbalance (hence an ordered sequence that supports searches in logarithmic time and also supports bidirectional access to neighboring elements in constant time)

reference — an object that designate a function or another object

reference type — an object type that describes a reference

representation — the number of bits used to represent an object type, along with the meanings ascribed to various bit patterns

reserved names — names available for use only for a restricted purpose

reverse iterators — iterators that, when incremented, walk backwards through a sequence

rvalue — an expression that designates a value of some type (without necessarily designating an object)

S **secret name** — a name from the space of names reserved to the implementor, such as `_Abc`

semantics — the meaning ascribed to valid sequences of tokens in a language

side effect — a change in the value stored in an object or in the state of a file when an expression executes

signed integer — an integer type that can represent negative as well as positive values

source file — a text file that a C++ translator can translate to an object module

space — a character that occupies one print position but displays no graphic

specialize — to write a template class or template function and supply any parameter values to specify a particular instance of the template, as in `vector<float>` (often used improperly to mean "explicitly specialize")

Standard C — that dialect of the C programming language defined by the ANSI/ISO C Standard

Standard C library — the set of functions, objects, and headers defined by the C Standard, usable by any hosted C or C++ program

Standard C++ — that dialect of the C++ programming language defined by the ANSI/ISO C++ Standard

Standard C++ library — the set of functions, objects, templates, and headers defined by the C++ Standard, usable by any hosted C++ program

standard header — one of many headers defined by the C++ Standard

statement — an executable component of a function that specifies an action, such as evaluating an expression or altering flow of control

static storage — objects whose lifetime extends from program startup to program termination, initialized prior to program startup

store — to retain a value, or to replace the value stored in an object with a new value

stream — an object that maintains the state of a sequence of reads, writes, and file-positioning requests for an open file

strict weak ordering — a transitive ordering that guarantees that a value is never ordered before itself and that also defines an equivalent ordering between pairs of values (`operator<` on integers imposes a strict weak ordering, but `operator<=` does not)

string — an object of class `basic_string<E>` that controls a sequence of characters (of type `E`)

structure type — an object type consisting of a sequence of function, object, and type members of different types (usually called a "class" in C++)

synonym — an alternate way of designating a type that is otherwise equivalent to the original type

syntax — the grammatical constraints imposed on valid sequences of tokens in a language

T **template** — a class or function declaration written in terms of one or more type or value parameters for later specialization with specific parameter values

text — a sequence of characters nominally suitable for writing to a display device (to be read by people)

thread of control — the execution of a program by a single agent

throw expression — an expression of the form `throw ex` that throws the object `ex` as an exception

token — a sequence of characters treated as a single element in a higher-level grammar

translation unit — a C++ source file plus all the files included by `#include` directives, excluding any source lines skipped by conditional directives

translator — a program, such as a compiler, that converts a translation unit to executable form

try **block** — a block followed by one or more *catch* clauses prepared to handle exceptions thrown within the block

type — the attribute of a value that determines its representation and what operations can be performed on it, or the attribute of a function that determines what arguments it expects and what it returns

type definition — a declaration that gives a name to a type

U **union type** — an object type consisting of an alternation of object members, only one of which can be represented at a time

unsigned integer — an integer type that can represent values between zero and some positive upper limit

V **variable** — older term for an object

vector — a sequence implemented as an array whose length can vary (hence a sequence that also supports random access to arbitrary elements in constant time)

virtual member — a member function whose overriding definition is called even when accessed as an object of its base class

void type — a type that has no representation and no values

volatile type — a qualified type for objects that may be accessed by more than one thread of control

W **WG21** — the ISO-authorized committee responsible for C++ standardization

white space — a sequence of one or more space characters, possibly mixed with other spacing characters such as horizontal tab

wide character — a code value of type `wchar_t` used to represent a very large character set

width — part of a conversion specification in a format that partially controls the number of characters to be transmitted

writable — can have its value altered, opposite of read-only

X

X3J16 — the older name for J16, the ANSI-authorized committee responsible for C++ Standard

Appendix C: References

What follows is an assortment of books and documents that are either directly related to the material in this book or useful in their own right as tutorial material. This list is *not* intended as an exhaustive list of books on the subject.

ANS89 *ANSI Standard X3.159-1989* (New York NY: American National Standards Institute, 1989). The original C Standard, developed by the ANSI-authorized committee X3J11. The Rationale that accompanies the C Standard explains many of the decisions that went into it, if you can get your hands on it.

Aus99 Matthew H. Austern, *Generic Programming and the STL* (Reading MA: Addison-Wesley, 1999). A recent book by one of the people actively enhancing and extending STL.

ISO90 *ISO/IEC Standard 9899:1990* (Geneva: International Standards Organization, 1990). The official C Standard around the world. Aside from formatting details and section numbering, the ISO C Standard is identical to the ANSI C Standard.

ISO94 *ISO/IEC Amendment 1 to Standard 9899:1990* (Geneva: International Standards Organization, 1994). The first (and only) amendment to the C Standard. It provides substantial support for manipulating large character sets.

ISO98 *ISO/IEC Standard 14882:1998* (Geneva: International Standards Organization, 1998). The official C++ Standard around the world. The ISO C++ Standard is identical to the ANSI C++ Standard.

Jos99 Nicolai M. Josuttis, *The C++ Standard Library, A Tutorial and Reference* (Reading MA: Addison-Wesley, 1999). An overview of the entire Standard C++ Library, including STL.

M&S87 David R. Musser and Alexander Stepanov, "A Library of Generic Algorithms in Ada," *Proceedings of the 1987 SIGAda International Conference* (New York NY: Association for Computing Machinery, 1987).

M&S89 David R. Musser and Alexander Stepanov, *Ada Generic Library* (Berlin: Springer Verlag, 1989).

M&S94 David R. Musser and Alexander Stepanov, "Algorithm-Oriented Generic Libraries," *Software—Practice and Experience,* Vol. 24(7), pp. 623-642 (New York NY: John Wiley & Sons, Ltd., July 1994).

M&S96 David R. Musser and Atul Saini, *STL Tutorial and Reference Guide* (Reading MA: Addison-Wesley, 1996).

Pla92 P.J. Plauger, *The Standard C Library* (Englewood Cliffs NJ: Prentice Hall, 1992). Contains a complete implementation of the Standard C library, as well a text from the library portion of the C Standard and guidance in using the Standard C library. It is one of the predecessor and companion volumes to this book.

Pla95 P.J. Plauger, *The Draft Standard C++ Library* (Englewood Cliffs NJ: Prentice Hall, 1995). Contains a complete implementation of the draft Standard C++ library as of early 1994, just before STL was added. It is one of the predecessor and companion volumes to this book.

Pla98 P.J. Plauger, *The Standard C++ Library* (Concord MA: Dinkumware, Ltd., 1998). A complete reference to the full Standard C++ library, including STL. It is the principal source of the material in the **Functional Description** sections of this book.

S&L95 A.A. Stepanov and M. Lee, "The Standard Template Library," *Technical Report HPL-95-11* (Palo Alto CA: Hewlett-Packard Laboratories, February 1995). The basis for the STL addition to the draft Standard C++ Library.

Str94 Bjarne Stroustrup, *The Design and Evolution of* C++ (Reading MA: Addison Wesley, 1994). Reflections on changes made to C++, including those made as part of the standardization process.

Str97 Bjarne Stroustrup, *The C++ Programming Language, Third Edition* (Reading MA: Addison Wesley, 1997). An excellent overview by the developer of the C++ language.

Index

C

D

E

F

G

H

I

N

O

P

Q

R

V

W

X